D0285950

Michael Asher has been called 'one of the two greatest living British desert explorers – the other being Wilfred Thesiger'. He is one of the few to travel consistently on foot and by traditional transport in preference to motor vehicles.

His early life was dominated by a quest for adventure which led him, at the age of eighteen, into the Parachute Regiment and later into an SAS squadron. Later still he served in the élite Special Patrol Group of the RUC.

His books include *In Search of the Forty Days Road* (1984), *A Desert Dies* (1986) and *Impossible Journey* (1988), an account of a 4,500-mile trek on foot and by camel made with his wife, the photographer Mariantonietta Peru. This journey, the first west–east crossing of the Sahara by such means, was lauded by the Royal Geographical Society as 'the most remarkable of recent explorations'.

Michael Asher has also written *Shoot to Kill*, the highly praised autobiographical account of the élite fighting units of the British Army and his search for the dark side that exists in us all. *Thesiger* (1994), written after three years of intense research, is a biography of the great traveller. Asher befriended Thesiger while based in Nairobi for two years, visiting his home in Kenya on many occasions, and has an evident respect and admiration for the man.

THESIGER

A BIOGRAPHY

Michael Asher

With colour photographs by
Mariantonietta Peru

PENGUIN BOOKS

PENGUIN BOOKS

Published by the Penguin Group
Penguin Books Ltd, 27 Wrights Lane, London W8 5TZ, England
Penguin Books USA Inc., 375 Hudson Street, New York, New York 10014, USA
Penguin Books Australia Ltd, Ringwood, Victoria, Australia
Penguin Books Canada Ltd, 10 Alcorn Avenue, Toronto, Ontario, Canada M4V 3B2
Penguin Books (NZ) Ltd, 182–190 Wairau Road, Auckland 10, New Zealand

Penguin Books Ltd, Registered Offices: Harmondsworth, Middlesex, England

First published by Viking 1994
Published in Penguin Books 1995
1 3 5 7 9 10 8 6 4 2

Printed in England by Clays Ltd, St Ives plc

While I was researching and writing this book, my wife Mariantonietta trekked with me, six months pregnant, along the Awash river in Ethiopia by donkey and, in Dhofar, was involved in a serious car accident. During the same period my son, Burton, was born in Africa, and travelled in Arabia's Empty Quarter by camel, aged only two years. Before the book was completed, my parents, Kathleen and Frederick Asher, died within a few days of each other. My mother asked for her ashes to be scattered in the desert.

This book is dedicated to my wife and son,
and to my parents' memory

CONTENTS

———

LIST OF MAPS

LIST OF ILLUSTRATIONS

COLOUR

ILLUSTRATION ACKNOWLEDGEMENTS

The author and publishers are grateful to the following for permission to reproduce photographs:

Colour

Ian Bailey, 20; Gavin Young, 21–4; all the other colour photographs were taken by Mariantonietta Peru.

Black and White

Wilfred Thesiger, 38; Julian Lush, 5–10, 12, 16–17, 25–7, 32; Sir Gawain Bell, 35; Reginald Dingwall, 20–21; Ronald Codrai, 36–7, 39–52; Gavin Young, 59–61, 68–71, 73; Jimmy Watt, 53–8, 62; Nik Wheeler, 63; Viscount Hambleden, 64–7; Eric Newby, 74; Derek Hill, 72; Mariantonietta Peru, 75; Royal Geographical Society, 1, 4, 13–15, 19, 22–4, 38; Imperial War Museum, 28–31, 33–4; Sudan Archive, Durham University Library, 18; Hulton Deutsch Collection Ltd, 11; P. H. G. Powell-Cotton, *A Sporting Trip Through Abyssinia*, 2–3.

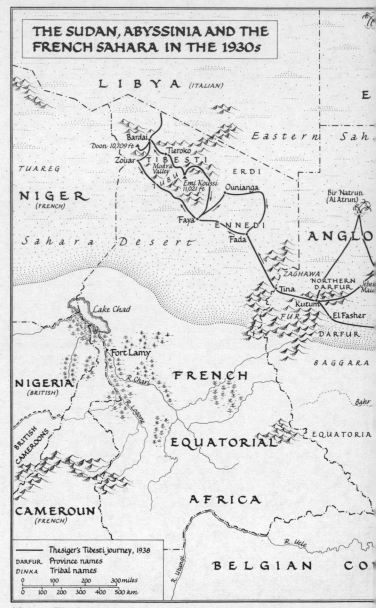

Map 1.   The Sudan, Abyssinia and the French Sahara in the 1930s

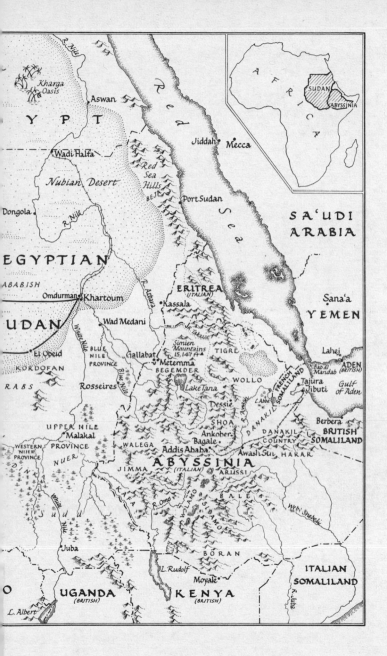

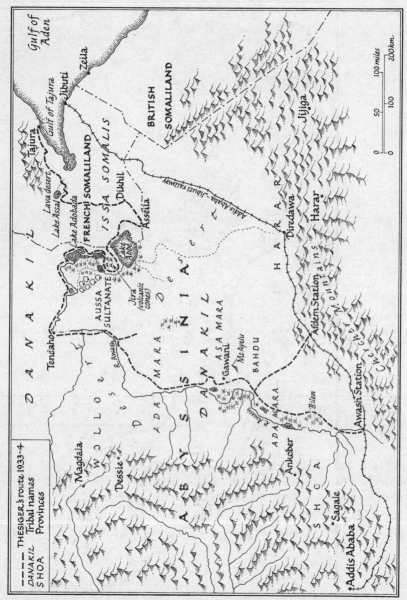

Map 2. Danakil country.

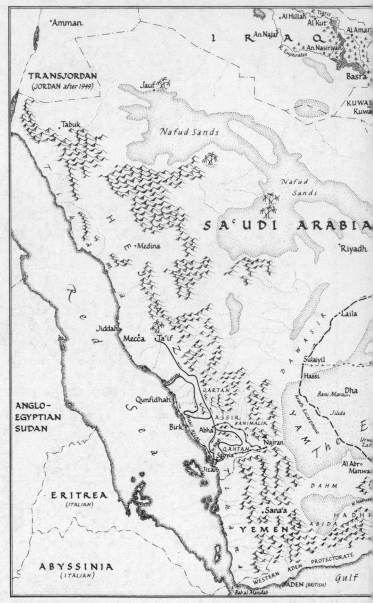

Map 3. Sa'udi Arabia.

PERSIA
(IRAN)

Shiraz

Bushire

Persian Gulf

Strait of Hormuz

SA'UDI ARABIA

THESIGER'S ROUTES
— Dhofar and Hadhramaut, 1945-6
—1946— —1947— Journeys in Southern Hejaz
·········· First traverse of the Empty Quarter, 1946-7
– – – – – Dhofar and Hadhramaut, 1947
— — — Second traverse of the Empty Quarter, 1948
———— Journeys in Trucial Coast and Inner Oman, 1948-50

OTHER JOURNEYS
==============Ⓣ==== Bertram Thomas's route, 1930-31
+ —ᴾ+ — + — H. St John Philby's route, 1932

Dhahran Bahrain

Hufur QATAR Doha

abrin Dhiby

Wadi Jaub

Sabkhat Mutti

DHAFARA

Khaba

Uruq as Shiban

Umm as Samim
Quicksands

Quarter

Khali

ub al

DAKAKA

Khaur bin
Atarit
Bir Halu

Salima

Wabar

Mughshin

Jiddat al Harasis Boi
YAZE
HARASIS

Sanaw

Shisur

DHOFAR

Mughair

Thamud Habarut

Hulaiya

Tarim
ibam

Salalah
Dhofar Mount Simi

MAHRA

Ghaydat al Mahra

EASTERN ADEN PROTECTORATE

Mukalla

den

Gulf of Oman

Sharjah
Dubai
BANI
QITAB
TRUCIAL COAST
ABU DHABI
MANASIR Liwa
GHAMIR
Buraimi
Muwaiih
Jebel al Akhdar
Ibri
Nazwah Birkat
al Maut
DIRUH
WAHIBA
Sharqiya

Muttrah
Muscat
Hajar Mountains
Sur

Wahiba
Sands

Masira

Arabian
Sea

Legend
▒▒▒▒▒ Main areas of the 'Sands'
〰〰〰 Rivers   ·········· Seasonal watercourses
°∘°°∘° Wells   🌴🌴 Main oases
MANAHIL Tribal names
—·—·— International boundaries of the period

0   100   200   300 miles
0   100   200   300   400   500 km

ACKNOWLEDGEMENTS

I am deeply indebted to those who gave me practical help and advice in the making of this book: Dr Rolf Wichmann of the United Nations Commission on Human Settlement (Habitat), Nairobi, and his wife, Viviana; Dr Martin Walsh of Mombasa; Sir Terence Clark, HM Ambassador, Oman; Ian Bailey of HM Embassy, Muscat, and his wife, Teresa; Janet Williamson and Mbarak bin Musallim ash Shahri of Salalah; John Crowther of the British Council, Salalah; Santha and Scott Faiia in Addis Ababa; Hugh Morgan, HM Consul, Addis Ababa, and his wife, Pam; Jean-Claude Luyat of Paris; Steve and Susan Clark in Jibuti. I particularly appreciate the assistance of Al Muhandis Muhammad bin Sa'id al Mashali in Salalah.

I am very grateful for contributions to this book, either by letter or by interview, made by the following: Sir David Attenborough, Salim bin Kabina, Salim bin Ghabaisha, Sheikh Musallim bin Tafl, Sa'id bin Muhammad, Salim bin Muhammad al Atauf, Sa'id bin Musallim al Kamam, Sheikh Sahail bin Musallim Abdallah, 'Amair bin 'Omar, Sulayim bin Salim Tamtaim, Sheikh Nashran bin Sultan, Hugh Carless, Roger Clark, Mark Cocker, Ronald Codrai, Donald Powell-Cole, Johnny Cooper, Reginald Dingwall, Christina Dodwell, Neil Flanagan, Ernest Gellner, Susan Gellner, John Hemming, Edward Henderson, Colin Hepburn, Wally Herbert, Martin and Tanis Jordan, Alexander Maitland, George Popov, Tim Severin and Frank Steele; also to Timothy Green for extracts from his book *The Restless Spirit*.

I would like to add special thanks to Alex Tinson and Douglas Cluer, veterinary surgeons of Al 'Ain in the United Arab Emirates, who generously loaned us camels and made our journey in the Empty Quarter possible, and to Peter Hudson of Arabian Antiquities, Al 'Ain, for the loan of traditional camel equipment.

I am most grateful to Paul D. Gabriel and his team at Al Bustan House Trading, Muscat, for their excellent service in providing us with a four-wheel-drive car and driver to visit remote parts of Oman. I thoroughly recommend their service.

I am equally grateful to Universal Travel of Sana'a, Republic of Yemen, for providing us with a vehicle and a very accomplished driver for our journey in the Hadhramaut and Mahra country.

I much appreciate the patience and encouragement of my agent, Anthony Goff of David Higham Associates, and the faith of my editor, Eleo Gordon, of the Penguin Group. I would like to thank my parents-in-law, General and Mrs Peru, once again for generosity I can never repay. Only my wife, Mariantonietta, knows what writing this book cost me, over a period of almost four years. But for her fortitude and encouragement in the dark times, it would almost certainly not have been written. I am forever in her debt.

MICHAEL ASHER

Stamford, UK and Frazione Agnata, Sardinia

25 November 1993

A NOTE ON NAMES

Thesiger displayed his concern with the past in his idiosyncratic use of proper names. The country of his birth continued, for him, to be *Abyssinia* long after it had officially been named Ethiopia, despite the fact that *Abyssinia* derived from an Arabic root and was generally regarded as pejorative by most Ethiopians. Since the country appears so frequently in the text, however, I have bowed to Thesiger's own usage and preserved *Abyssinia* throughout.

With tribal names, Thesiger himself admitted that 'We usually called them one thing, and they called themselves another.' This is particularly true of the nomads whom Thesiger referred to as *Danakil*, but who call themselves *Afars*. I have preferred the current and more correct usage *Afars*, but have preserved the geographical term *Danakil country* for the region they inhabit. Thesiger used the Arabic word *Bedu* for the nomads of southern Arabia, which is indeed the name they give themselves collectively. However, *Bedu* is a plural form: no Arab could ever really have said (to quote the script of David Lean's legendary *Lawrence of Arabia*) 'I am Bedu', any more than an Englishman might have said 'I am Englishmen'. The English translation of the word *Bedu* is 'Bedouin': I have used the words *Bedu* and Bedouin interchangeably. The singular of *Bedu* is *Bedui* and the singular of 'Bedouin' is, correctly, 'Bedouin'.

Thesiger simplified the names of Bedouin tribes in Arabia. One of the principal tribes whom he refers to as *Rashid* generally call themselves *Rawashid*. I have preferred this usage, and I have also preferred to render *Beit* in the tribal name *Beit Kathir* as *Bayt*, which is closer to the Arabic phonetics. The singular of *Rawashid* is *Rashidi* and the singular of *Bayt Kathir* is *Bayt Kathiri*. Thesiger's tribal name *Umbarak* has been rendered *Mbarak*: there is a semi-vowel before the 'M' which does not exist in English. In phonetics it would properly be rendered *ðmbarak*. The same is true for all other Arabic words in this dialect with this prefix. The camel-name *Umbrausha*, for instance, is rendered Mbrausha.

Bin means 'son of' in southern Arabia, though in northern Arabia this word is pronounced *ibn*. It occurs in the name of the great Sa'udi King Ibn Sa'ud: 'son of Sa'ud'. Naturally the southern tribes with whom Thesiger travelled referred to the King as bin Sa'ud after their own dialect. Incidentally, I have sometimes replaced the word 'sultan' with 'king', though in Arabic it means simply 'he who is in authority'. I have done this mainly to avoid confusion with one of Thesiger's travelling-companions, Sultan bin Ahmad, for whom 'Sultan' was a given name rather than a title. The ruler of the United Arab Emirates is here rendered as Sheikh *Zaayid* rather than the more familiar *Zayid*, which is phonetically confusing.

The ' in my text refers to the consonant *'ain*, very common in Arabic. It occurs in the name *'Ali* and in the word *'Arab* itself.

Where there are alternative spellings of place-names, or where names have been changed since Thesiger's time, these have mostly been included in brackets: thus French Somaliland (now Jibuti), Arussi (Arssi) Mountains, etc. This practice has also been followed where foreign words have been used, rather than obliging the reader to search for them in a glossary, thus *pangas* (machetes), *hadr* (townsmen), etc.

There is inevitably controversy about the spelling of foreign names in English, those familiar with certain ways being convinced that their accustomed spelling is correct. Thesiger himself constantly varied his spellings over different works. Having been trained in phonetics, I have generally tried simply to adopt the spelling which is nearest phonetically to the pronunciation. There is absolutely no reason, for example, why Jibuti should be spelled *Djibouti* in English, except perhaps that it looks more exotic.

PROLOGUE

The Old Man Up There

The cabin stands on a bald hillside above the sleepy town on the edge of Kenya's northern wilderness – a sprawl of dark rooms and cracking walls, without either electricity or running water. From its baked mud verandah, often drumming with the tread of small Samburu children, the hillside falls steeply away into a valley painted with bright primary colours – blood-red soil, sharp shadows of blue-grey and chocolate, swelling purple hills, thick veins of lush green forest. This panorama could only exist in Africa, under a sky of breathtaking immensity, sometimes heavy with orange tones and gilt-edged cumuli, or simply radiating a limpid methylene blue – the sky of Africa, vaster than any sky on earth.

There is nothing especially distinctive about the house: dozens like it are scattered through this bushland. What makes it unique is that it is the home of a distinguished English gentleman. Observed emerging from the verandah each morning, he might be mistaken for a country squire. He wears a tweed jacket with silk handkerchief, twill trousers, broad-brimmed hat, good but much-cobbled shoes, and carries a slender walking-stick. Closer up, however, one observes the ravages of a life of utter hardship – his face is that of a professional hunter, perhaps, an ancient mariner or a grizzled war-veteran. His frame bears not an ounce of spare flesh, yet the long limbs and torso suggest, despite his eighty-two years, uncommon physical strength. He is tall and unbent, and his walking-stick seems almost superfluous. His eyes – slightly dim now from decades in glaring sunlight, are hunter's eyes – concentrated, determined, intense. The head bears the distinctive tribal cast of the English aristocracy – great brow ridges above a hawk-like nose and a granite boxer's jaw, his face a hachuring of lines that seem to have been chiselled out of a mountain. His leanness is marked by an aura of unmistakable dignity, and his gentle voice holds both humour and authority. He is a man of many places and accomplishments – Old Etonian, Oxford boxing blue, big-game hunter, colonial administrator, guerrilla fighter, war hero, one-time trawler fisherman, horseman, photographer, medical amateur, foster-father to Samburu and Turkana children, poetic writer, locust-hunter, Arabist, friend of emperors and sultans, honorary game-warden and traveller extraordinary. To the tribesmen of the Sudan he was 'Lion's Bane', to the Bedu of southern Arabia, Mbarak, 'The Blessed One', to the Marsh Arabs of Iraq, simply 'Friend'. To the people of Maralal, among whom he has made his home for almost thirty years, he is Mzee Juu – 'the old man, up there', but to the outside world he is Wilfred Patrick Thesiger, perhaps the most distinguished explorer of this century.

His achievements alone rank with those of the greatest explorers of the nineteenth century – Burton, Speke, Stanley, Livingstone. Aged only twenty-three he solved one of Africa's last mysteries – the destination of the Awash river in Ethiopia. He traversed the perilous country of the Afars or Danakil, where several previous expeditions had been massacred, and entered the unknown Sultanate of Aussa. He returned over a period of five years to the legendary Empty Quarter of Arabia, and lived among the Marsh Arabs of Iraq over a period of eight years. He trekked to the little-known mountains of Tibesti, visited every corner of the Nuer country in the Equatorial Sudan, and climbed in the yet-unfrequented Atlas Mountains in Morocco. He explored the mountains of western Pakistan as far as the Chinese border, travelled among the Hazaras of Afghanistan, crossed the Dasht-i-Lut in Iran, trekked on migrations with Bakhtiari nomads, rode mules across most of Ethiopia, donkeys in Yemen, horses in Kurdistan and trekked with camels in Kenya. Always travelling by foot, animal transport or open boat, he reached these places while they still remained virtually unchanged by the outside world.

Thesiger's uniqueness as a traveller lies in the manner of his accomplishments. Today, the very idea of travel – the art of the journey – has been generally lost. People do not travel, but commute. They are largely tourists, remaining outsiders and observing the landscape and its peoples from a distance. Travelling on the same level as the local people, sharing their everyday lives and hardships, he was able to enter into a total relationship with the environment and its often exotic peoples, rather than remaining a mere spectator. He lived through the greatest period of change the world has ever known – a period when Western technology was slowly tightening its stranglehold on the earth. While others – even before him, and most certainly after – were gleefully adapting to the possibilities of cars, aircraft and radio, he chose to venture into the wilderness and meet it on its own terms. He spurned motor transport. He deliberately looked for those places where motor cars had not yet penetrated, and where something of the old ways survived. As he grew older, such places grew steadily fewer – many of the regions he knew as unspoiled wilderness have now succumbed to the motorway and the service-station. We shall never see them as he was able to. Yet there is a note of tragedy in all this. Thesiger was aware of and resented the fact that, as a District Commissioner in the Sudan during the 1930s, his job was ultimately to impose the values and customs of an alien civilization. Even as an explorer in the Empty Quarter, he realized that he himself was the harbinger of a different world: 'When I was with the Arabs,' he wrote, 'I wished only to live as they lived, and now that I have left them I would gladly think that nothing in their lives was altered by my coming. Regretfully, however, I realize that the maps I made helped others with more material aims to visit and corrupt a people whose spirit once lit the desert like a flame.'[1] Thesiger was drawn to the traditional ways, to the wild and unspoiled lands, with a rare passion, yet he belonged to a generation and an era that did more than any other to destroy them. Perhaps this is why he prefaced one of his books with Oscar Wilde's famous lines, 'Yet each man kills the thing he loves.'

Thesiger has rightly been called 'old-fashioned' and 'a throwback to the Victorian era', yet in one sense his views were ahead of their time. Even as a boy he foresaw the way in which technology would ride like a juggernaut across the earth, devastating what was priceless in traditional life. All his life he saw technology as an intrusion into the unspoiled world, and as a barrier between man and nature. Traditional peoples were to him the most significant aspect of the environment, and truly to understand them, he believed, one must live as they lived – eating the same food, drinking the same water, enduring the same privations, facing danger shoulder to shoulder, accepting common rules of behaviour. What generated this unique attitude was Thesiger's need to express certain ideals which the technetronic twentieth century was quickly discarding. In a society run by machines, the traditional values that govern the idea of manhood disintegrate. Courage, the warrior-instinct, close loyalty to companions, even hospitality, dignity, stoic endurance and honesty, become irrelevant. Thesiger believed that technological society tended to breed selfish individuals, mostly concerned with amassing material wealth. He stood out all his life against this disintegration of traditional values, living by a personal code of integrity he never lost. Summed up, perhaps, by the concept of 'nobility' – a quality he claimed to find in both kings and illiterate tribesmen alike – he believed that these ideals were developed to their fullest extent among the Bedu of Arabia, whose ethic of *miruwa*, or 'manliness' – courage, loyalty, endurance, hospitality and generosity – matched almost perfectly with his own.

Every man's life must be seen in the context of his time and place in history. Thesiger lived in a world of adventure, yet one which he saw being steadily tamed throughout his life. He never denied that he sought fame as an explorer, but in him this ambition was unconnected with material gain. Nor were his splendid journeys made with the object of dissecting and analysing the earth and its peoples. Though, to be worthwhile, his explorations must be dangerous and challenging, they were never 'stunts', but true adventures. He had no interest in feats of pure physical endurance – crossing the Sahara in a wheelbarrow, for instance, or canoeing down Everest, would have been to him as ludicrous as climbing a mountain with a ball and chain attached to one's leg. He was proud to live in an era – or at the very end of it – when travelling in the traditional way was still, in those places that interested him, the only way to travel. In this sense, coming at the very end of the great era of world exploration, Thesiger saw himself as the 'last explorer in the tradition of the past'.

Thesiger explored one of the last extensive regions of the earth

4

that remained unknown – the Empty Quarter of Arabia. He was the first outsider to enter the Liwa oasis, the first to sight the Umm as Samim quicksands. If exploration is to be defined as 'going where no man has gone before', then he was the last explorer of an era. He knew that those who followed him would be specialists, each with their own small domain of knowledge – ornithologists, anthropologists, geologists, who would travel by car, be supplied by helicopter and keep in touch by radio. 'They will bring back results far more interesting than mine,' he wrote, 'but they will never know the spirit of the land nor the greatness of the Arabs.'[2] This is Thesiger's legacy: he reminded us that there is more to our relationship with the earth than can be understood through a windscreen or analysed in a technical report. It is that elusive quality best understood by poets, writers, artists, and romantics – the spirit.

Though driven by the spirit of adventure, then, Thesiger was no 'stuntman'. He maintained always that people were more important than places, and the vast emptiness of the deserts and mountains he traversed would have proved simply a form of self-punishment, had it not been for the local companions he always travelled with. Thesiger is not to be equated with the single-handed sailor or mountaineer. Though he chose to travel in the remotest areas, enduring hardship and danger, he insisted that his journeys should also bring him into contact with tradi-tional peoples, and provide him with companions from among them. These companions gave him some of the most meaningful relationships of his life. His greatest works, *Arabian Sands* and *The Marsh Arabs*, are tributes, not merely to wild places, but to the unmatchable spirit of the tribes who lived there.

Fame as an explorer was important to him, yet it took second place to the sheer love of travel and particularly the deep bonds of friendship he formed on the way. The true rewards he asked for were intangible and often symbolic ones. Thus, after his first magnificent crossing of the Empty Quarter, he would write: 'To others my journey would have little importance. It would produce nothing but a rather inaccurate map which no one was ever likely to use. It was a personal experience, and the reward had been a drink of clean, nearly tasteless water. I was content with that.'[3]

Thesiger's integrity and his commitment to adventure never

ceased, so much so that at eighty-two, when most men have long since retired to the comforts a long life has provided, Thesiger spends most of his time living with a Samburu family in the most basic of conditions. Few other distinguished men, perhaps, would consider this rambling cabin in Africa much of a recompense for a life of hardship and danger, for attaining the peak of distinction as one of the greatest explorers of all time. Yet Thesiger is content with the companionship of tribal peoples, the simplicity of life unhampered by possessions, the raw beauty of the landscape, and the immensity of the sky. In an age of materialism, such modesty may be unfashionable, yet the ideals that enabled Thesiger to reach such summits of achievement have not yet been replaced by superior values – indeed, in his eyes, by any values at all.

PART ONE

THE PRELUDE

CHAPTER I

The Immense Cultural Baggage He Carried to Arabia

It was almost sunset when we arrived at Salim's house. The drab Dhofar desert had sparked aflame, the sands themselves riding on rivers of floating fire. There were no trees here, no sign of shade or comfort, just the stark concrete cabin with the frayed Bedu tent flapping outside, as lonely as an outpost on the moon. We emerged from our vehicle and the desert soared over us, smelling of chalk and flint, shooshing with the seashell sound of emptiness. I could taste the odour of animals and the faint traces of gasoline. Near the cabin a ravaged Toyota Land-Cruiser pick-up seemed tethered like a riding-beast, its tyres bald, its windscreen split, its wings stoved in. A squad of greasy oil-drums propped up the fractured frame of a child's bike, and discarded milking-bowls of palmetto fibre lay beside it caked with dust. Amid the debris an old Bedouin waited patiently to greet us.

He was a small man, tight with muscle. His sandpaper face was rimmed with snow-white bristle, and his bright eyes lay in a filigree pattern of ancient wrinkles. He wore a spotless *dishdasha* drawn in with a belt full of bullets and a curved silver dagger, a ragged brown headcloth knotted across his temples. His feet were the flat, hard, horny feet of a man who has never worn shoes. His grip was bracing as he shook hands. 'Welcome to my house!' he said. Inside, the cabin was as austere as the desert, but for rugs, coffee-set and transistor radio. A swaddled infant was dozing in a cradle, and four young children squatted on the floor. We sat on a rug while he doled out coffee in cups like great thimbles – each containing a single swallow, strong and bitter. The desert wind swilled a drift of sand through the door: the desert waited at bay for the sunset prayer. It had taken me twelve years to track him down, and I was not disappointed. Despite the battered vehicle and the concrete cell, there was an aura about him: starkness, austerity, human warmth. This place – the open desert, the smell of camels – was after all a fitting place for Salim bin Ghabaisha of the Rawashid, notorious bandit, hunter, traveller, camel-thief extraordinary, friend, protégé and travelling-companion of Wilfred Thesiger.

Arabian Sands – Thesiger's finest work, and arguably the finest book ever written on Arabia and its Bedouin – is dedicated to bin Ghabaisha and his kinsman Salim bin Kabina. Thesiger saw it as a tribute to them and the other Arabs with whom he trekked more than 10,000 miles by camel in and around the legendary Empty Quarter, the *Rub' al Khali*: the requiem to a way of life that has now – in Arabia at any rate – completely disappeared.

Nothing has influenced my life more than *Arabian Sands*. Somebody lent me the book a few weeks after I arrived in the Sudan in 1979, and I was totally carried away by its brilliant pristine vision of the desert and its nomads. I decided there and then that, if possible, I would follow, metaphorically, in Thesiger's footsteps. As fate would have it, I was almost uniquely well placed to do so. Shortly after reading it, I was at a tea-party held by one of my colleagues – a Sudanese teacher – who introduced me to another young schoolmaster from the western Sudan. I was talking about Thesiger and Bedouin, and I remarked that the traditional nomadic life had ended years ago. 'Not in the western Sudan,' the teacher told me, and as I looked at him open-mouthed he went on to describe how, in his province, there were nomadic tribes of Arab ancestry, still riding camels, still living in tents, still carrying out armed raids and blood-feuds, almost completely unaffected by the outside world. He even told me that these tribes still exported camels to Egypt along the ancient 'Forty Days Road', 1,000 miles on the hoof across the desert, and offered to introduce me to some of the Bedouin who occasionally called in to the market of Dongola – the town where I was teaching – on their way to Egypt. That night I lay on my bed, unable to sleep. A tense feeling of excitement throbbed through me that seemed quite out of proportion with what I had learned. I can hardly explain it: looking back, it seemed almost a premonition. My entire future opened before me like a book. The world of Bedouin

and camels and tents might no longer exist in Arabia, but in the
Sudan it was virtually unchanged. Over the next fourteen years I
explored that world to the full. I spent ten years in the Sudan,
three of them with the most famous of the Arab tribes there – the
Kababish – and travelled by camel in other parts of North Africa.
I learned to speak Arabic fluently, and made the first ever west–
east crossing of the Sahara by camel, with my wife, Mariantonietta
Peru. *Arabian Sands* began all that. Now, 15,000 camel-miles later,
I was meeting a character from a book that had profoundly
changed my life: it was like meeting someone glimpsed in a
dream.

I had brought the book with me as a guide, and I was thrilled to
see him thumbing through the pictures, murmuring with pleasure:
'Ah! That camel was called Fatila!' or 'That is Salim bin Hamuda
of the Mahra!' Twelve years, I thought, since I had first held that
dog-eared Penguin paperback in my fist and thumbed through
the pictures as he was doing. Could I ever have imagined sitting
here with one of the book's main characters? Bin Ghabaisha
pondered Thesiger's stunning portrait of himself – the adolescent
bin Ghabaisha – beautiful, brooding, slightly melancholy. 'I was
about fifteen then,' he said. 'By God, I knew nothing!'
  Later, when he introduced his wife, I asked her if she recognized
the handsome lad in the picture. She giggled beneath the purple
burqa. 'I've never seen him before!' she said. 'What!' Ghabaisha
roared in mock anger. 'Don't recognize your own husband!' But I
understood the lady's difficulty. It was hard to visualize this staid
paterfamilias as the young Bedouin tearaway who had once
kidnapped the governor of Ibri's coffee-maker in revenge for an
insult and threatened to sell him as a slave. When I asked him
about this, he guffawed with laughter. Then he looked at me –
slightly embarrassed I thought – and said, 'That was the way we
all lived then.' The old Arabia of raids, blood-feuds and derring-
do had gone and taken his youth with it. Now he didn't like to
talk about the old times much. He thought of those things as
'childish', his eldest son, Sa'id, told me. Long since, he had made
the Haj – the pilgrimage to Mecca incumbent on Muslims – and
his sins had been expiated, the slate wiped clean. In 1975 he had
bought a Land-Cruiser, and when his first wife had died, had

taken on a younger one. The six children crouching around us were all his – including, he told us proudly, the three-month-old in the cradle. All who were old enough went to school at the government centre twelve miles away.

A ghostly figure wafted out of the night in black, shiny velveteen. It was bin Ghabaisha's daughter, carrying an enamel bowl full of frothing goat's milk fresh from the udder. Her father watched with pleasure as we took long draughts in turn: 'You don't get milk like that out of a tin!' he said. 'They haven't invented anything to beat it yet!' Bin Ghabaisha owned a pack of goats, and his camel-herd was over 100 strong, though his camels were mostly the dark-haired *hazmi* breed, once despised as riding-beasts. 'I can't say when I last rode a camel,' he told us. 'Not for years. I go by car now. I'm not much of a driver, but you get used to it. Now I can get to Salalah and back in a day. It used to take us four by camel.'

It hadn't rained for three years, he said, but that was nothing unusual in these parts. 'If there's no grazing we fetch dried sardines for the beasts from Salalah in the pick-up,' he explained, 'and we carry water to the herds in tankers – we can fill them up right here.' Now, after millennia of combing the desert for a dribble of water or a chuff of green bush, the mountain had come to Muhammad: a well had been sunk behind the cabin, and cascades of fresh water would come gurgling up at the push of a button. Bin Ghabaisha had been appointed well-overseer by Sultan Qaboos's government and got a rent-free cabin and a salary for doing much as he had always done – herding his goats and camels in the desert. 'You know,' he told me, almost shame-facedly, 'the camels have more milk now than we can drink or sell. Sometimes we even pour it into the desert.' A far cry, it seemed, from the desperate life celebrated in Thesiger's stirring overture to *Arabian Sands* – the most quoted lines, perhaps, in the whole of Western orientalist literature: 'A cloud gathers, rain falls, men live; the cloud disperses without rain, and men and animals die. In the deserts of Arabia there is no rhythm of the seasons, no rise and fall of sap, but empty wastes where only the changing temperature marks the passing of the year. It is a bitter, desiccated land which knows nothing of gentleness or ease. Yet men have lived there from the earliest times.'[1]

Man, with what Thesiger regarded as his 'terrible technical ingenuity', had changed all that. The Rawashid had been born nomads, but the motor car had dissolved their need for motion. They could bring camel-feed and water from outside the desert. Bin Ghabaisha didn't seem to mourn the old times much. 'Since Sa'id bin Taimur went we've been much better off,' he said, 'and thank God for that!'

For five years, Thesiger led a life of action with these young men and others, constantly on the move, constantly sampling the desert's austere fare – hunger, thirst, sun, wind, cold and weariness. Only those who have lived such a life, he asserted, could appreciate its bitter hardship. The Bedu were acutely observant, missing not a single detail – unrelenting assessors of a man's strengths and weaknesses. The desert was, to Thesiger, the greatest of equalizers, the mother of selection-tests. Knowing nothing of the outside world, the Bedu judged all candidates by their standards, docking points for lack of patience, lack of good humour, generosity, loyalty and courage. Whoever would travel with them must adapt to their ways, and as T.E. Lawrence wrote, their 'ways were hard even for those brought up in them, and for strangers terrible: a death in life'.[2] Thesiger, like so many English gentlemen, saw the Bedu as the embodiment of a heroic code that appealed to his chivalric instincts, a code that had endured among them since the days of the *Jahiliyya* – 'the Time of Ignorance'. French author Maxime Rodinson has shown that the Bedouin tribes of this pre-Islamic era had developed a system of honour that had, like that of the English cult of the 'gentleman', assumed some of the functions of a religion: 'The members of these scattered, wandering tribes – half-starved and extremely anarchic – were in fact striving to conform to a moral ideal of their own ... the ideal man possessed in the highest degree the quality known as *miruwa*, which can literally be translated as "virility". This comprised courage, endurance, loyalty to one's social obligations, generosity and hospitality. The feeling that drove a man to conform to this ideal was one of honour (*'ird*). Infringements of the moral code of the desert rendered him liable to insult and hence loss of honour.'[3]

The Bedu had been reared in these rigid ways from childhood –

Thesiger had to adapt himself to them. They were the product of an unforgiving landscape – he was the product of St Aubyn's, Eton and Oxford. This disparity in origins was not, it seemed to him perhaps, as wide as it first appeared. The Bedu code of 'virility' was the playing-fields of Eton revisited, the stark quest for 'honour' scarcely distinguishable from the code of the 'gentleman' that had carried Britons through 10,000 colonial encounters. Generations of Britons had admired the desert Arabs as impoverished aristocrats, feeling at home in their all-male, public-school world of hardship and 'nobility'. As Jan Morris has commented: 'They continued to claim, until the end of the Empire, a particular kinship between Englishman and desert Arab – "We understand each other, you see, we use the same language, so to speak." '⁴ One notable aspect of this belief is that the individuals who perpetuated it – the Glubbs, the Peakes, the Philbys, the Dicksons, and so many others – were always in a position of superior prestige vis-à-vis the Bedu. They were 'Sheikhs', not rank-and-file tribesmen. The Englishman loved the Bedouin essentially because he treated him with a rough-and-ready frankness that suggested equality, without ever questioning his right to rule – which would have meant true equality.⁵ Admiration for the simple tribesman quickly died when he became the oil-rich Sheikh.

In the Bedu, Thesiger believed he had found a people who combined his love for the primitive with the standards of decency he had learned at Eton. As a misogynist, the segregation of women suited him, and the Bedu's ruthless truculence – the quality that enabled them to 'knife a herdsboy with a jest' – reflected the aggression he had demonstrated amply. Untarnished with the bourgeois vice of materialism, they possessed nothing but their rifles, camels, daggers, saddles, and a few pots, skins and bowls, enjoying a freedom that Thesiger could envy but never quite emulate. Thesiger believed that 'the harder the life the finer the person', and he claimed that it was the Bedu's constant struggle for survival that had moulded them as they were. Scattering widely to scavenge a living in almost sterile desert, they existed for months with no food or drink other than camel's milk. When at last water was found, it would be salty or sulphurous. On freezing winter evenings a Bedouin herdsboy would scrape out a shallow trench in the sand, lying down in it naked with only his shirt to cover him. Always subject to drought, disease and raids by more powerful tribes, they faced the future with stoic determination. Curiously, Thesiger pointed out, such a life did not engender 'barbarism', but behaviour that was distinctly 'civilized'. They had, for example, an almost sacred regard for the travelling companion, whom they would defend with their lives against any comer – even their own families. They would welcome strangers into their tents, offering them the best food and drink they had, even if it meant going hungry themselves. Their magnificent generosity was reflected in the awe with which Thesiger's companions regarded an old Sheikh who had given all his camels away, himself becoming destitute in the process. The Bedu loved liberty, and, according to Thesiger, they lived their 'unendurable' life out of choice. Any of them could have found a job in the villages and towns of Oman or the Hadhramaut had they wanted to, he asserted, but they would have rejected labour as the life of lesser men. 'Lesser men' meant anyone who was not a Bedouin, for although Thesiger represented them as being free from prejudice of class, caste or race – indeed as the most democratic of all peoples – they were, obversely, as obsessed with pedigree as any patrician. Courteous, dignified, unselfish, individualistic, so mindful of the dignity of others that they would have killed a man rather than humiliate him, they were not just content with their lives, but happy. Among them, Thesiger maintained, he never met a depressed or neurotic individual.

Bin Ghabaisha hefted in a tray creaking under the mass of a goat slaughtered in our honour. The meat looked succulent and mouthwatering on its bed of buttered rice. 'Eat! Eat!' he ordered us, but as we crouched round the trencher, I noticed that he hung back. In true Bedu fashion, he waited for his guests to eat before taking his share. We stuffed ourselves until our stomachs seemed to swell, but still he insisted we should take more. Only when we protested with prolonged assurance did he sit down and consume what was left. Sa'id, his son, brought water and we settled down to more cups of bitter coffee and sweet tea.

Sitting back in the flickering lamplight, I remembered another fire trembling like a candle-flame, a fragile island of life in the infinite blackness that hid the Sahara desert. A knot of men and camels huddled round the flame on a bitter night, 200 miles from the nearest settlement. I had been travelling with a Kababish salt-caravan for days – our destination, that of Thesiger's début camel-trek, was the salt-pans of Al 'Atrun (his Bir Natrun) – still lying beyond many horizons. We were hungry, exhausted, and feverish with cold. In the dim orbit of the fire, Balla was talking. He was a gaunt, gristly youth with the aggressively vacant leer of the street-corner hooligan. He owned no shoes, nor even a blanket to cover himself at night. He spoke about the great Fiat lorries that now spanned the desert with their huge loads of salt, robbing the desert Arabs of their age-old monopoly: 'We should shoot them all!' he said, tightening his grip on an old shotgun, 'Ha! What can the government do? This is the government here!' Looking back, I suppose these Bedu must have found me an awkward character. Almost as poor as they were, without even a camel fit enough for the journey, I had done little but tag along with them as an uninvited guest. In compensation, though, I shared their work fully, and what work it was! Heaving 100-kilo sacks of rock-salt on an empty stomach, cutting out salt with a shovel and pick, filling waterskins in freezing mornings, drawing water from deep wells, herding camels, hobbling camels, dodging kicks and gnashing camel-jaws as we roped them in, leading the caravan for hour after monotonous hour on foot. On this journey I learned how incredibly hard the lives of the Bedu could be, and I admired them. They still lived in intimate contact with the earth, a contact that we, with our machines and technology, had lost. There was nothing more in the world I wanted than to become one of them, but that, of course, was a romantic dream. During my three years with these tribesmen, I discovered, with some bitterness, that you can never unlearn what you know, never become what you are not. For all his genuine love and regard for the Bedu, Thesiger was never able to abandon his place in civilization, never really to become one of them. Yet by travelling with them at the pace of the camel, dressing as they did, speaking their language, practising their customs, even sharing their religious rituals, one could, at least for a time, regain some of that sense of unity with nature which thousands of generations of human beings had known, but which ours had lost.

These feelings were, of course, no more unique to me than they were to Thesiger, or to Lawrence before him: a great deal in Thesiger's view of the Bedu as the 'noble savage' is derived from his predecessors: part of a cultural myth created by the West.[6] It was a myth born during the years following the industrial revolution, when the green fields of Europe were steadily being swallowed up in the maw of smoking factories and red-brick streets. The industrial age ripped the old assumptions apart, drawing agricultural workers to the city, undermining a society whose roots lay in feudal times and bringing to the fore a trading class whose *raison d'être* was commerce. As industrial society grew ever more greedy and the focus of life shifted from country to town, so the ancient cord between man and nature was severed. The old ties that had bound lord and tenant disintegrated. The skills the aristocracy had nurtured since feudal times – riding and arms – with their concomitant notions of chivalry and nobility, were increasingly shown to be meaningless. By the beginning of the twentieth century – about the time of Thesiger's birth – it had become evident that Europe had cut itself adrift from its historical roots: a society once regulated by tradition was now on a different tack.

In the midst of all these upheavals, European travellers discovered in the deserts of Arabia a people who had apparently managed to preserve all the noble standards of a chivalric era. Unlike the forests of the Amazon, or the savannahs of Africa, it was not a completely alien land: Europeans had known of Arabia since Biblical times – its Bedu were, after all, easily visualized as characters like Abraham, Isaac, Ismael and others, whose names were known even to the illiterate. They were not savages, but part of an ancient civilization that had once ruled much of the known world. As Peter Brent has written: 'There, it appeared, were a free people, with each individual his own master, living proudly by the skills of hardship, disdainful of cities, his code half chivalric, half that of the freebooter and brigand – it must have seemed like a vision of perfection.'[7] Such was the vision Thesiger went in search of in and around the Empty Quarter: such was the immense cultural baggage he carried with him when he arrived in Arabia in 1945, to begin what he considered the five most memorable years of his life.

In his small cabin at Ghafaʻ I asked Salim bin Ghabaisha why he had travelled with Wilfred Thesiger. 'He was generous,' bin Ghabaisha said, 'and he gave us the things we were interested in: money, rifles, camels. He was canny, he was loyal, he was tireless, and he was afraid of nothing. He was a wonderful man to travel with. We knew nothing about his background: where he was born, where he came from or why he came. We were just Bedu and our heads were empty. We knew nothing then, you see.'[8]

CHAPTER 2

A Clue to the Perverse Necessity
Which Drives Me to the East

The Addis Ababa in which Wilfred Thesiger was born in 1910 was not the lush, verdant city it is today. The forest of mimosas that had attracted the Emperor Menelik there in 1889 had long since been lopped down for firewood and timber, and by 1910 the place was almost treeless, a rambling sprawl of encampments that bore little resemblance to the European idea of an Imperial capital. The eucalyptus – that brash Australian upstart soon to transform the Abyssinian landscape – was as yet only to be seen sprouting aloft from the palace or the compounds of European houses. The capital was sited on uneven ground, 8,000 feet above sea-level and 2,000 below the summit of the Entoto Hills, where the Emperor had made his former capital. The lack of roads and bridges made travel there both difficult and treacherous: muddy tracks wound up and down the precipitous sides of watercourses, and each year a number of people were drowned trying to ford them in the rainy season. There were no streets to speak of, only gaggles of thatched huts, fortress-like stockades, laagers of ragged white tents in slow and painful transition to wattle and stone dwellings, and the military camps of the feudal barons dominating the hilltops. Between these habitations were open spaces on which grazed cattle, sheep and goats. By 1910 the town encompassed an area one quarter the size of Paris, yet contained only one-thirtieth of its population.

The Imperial palace was a village in itself, a kilometre and a half long by two kilometres wide, its walls enclosing scores of buildings in a host of clashing styles. The Emperor's private residence was a distempered colonial-style villa with ornate balustrades, external staircases, piped water and electric light. Near by stood a banqueting hall into which 7,000 guests might be crammed for the notorious *gebbur* feasts, where diners squatted in perspiring rows and gorged themselves on flaps of Ethiopian bread and raw steaks carved from freshly dead oxen, carried round on poles. The palace compound held springs and streams, a forest of eucalyptus, turpentines, juniper and wild olive. There were ranks of stables for the Imperial mules and horses, haystacks like giant bread-loaves for their fodder, flower-beds, vineyards, paddocks where cattle and sheep were fattened for future feasts, and even a menagerie housing two lions, three ostriches, and twelve hornbills. There was a council hall, a treasury, a lawcourt, several churches and chapels, a post and telegraph office, a jeweller's shop, a saddlery, a smith's forge, a joinery shop, an arsenal, a mint, a pharmacy, cellars for *tella* (beer) and *tej* (mead), and secret magazines for silver dollars. In hidden store-rooms were to be found such items as Singer sewing-machines, Parisian furniture and even a full-sized merry-go-round.

The market lay three-quarters of an hour's mule-ride away, beneath the hill on which stood St George's Cathedral and the notorious hanging-tree. Here, pullulating crowds of 40 or 50,000 people might jostle for access to the stalls of Indian, Syrian, Greek and Armenian traders. Almost every conceivable product found its way there at some time: ivory from the south, cotton from the Blue Nile, civet-oil from Socotra, salt, spices, gold and coffee-beans, cane-sugar, wild honey and beeswax, mead and beer in plump jars called *gombos*, silver nose-rings, filigree hairpins, leopard-skins and lion-skins, dyed red leather, curved Galla sabres, buffalo-hide shields, ploughshares, daggers and spearheads, chewing tobacco, rhino-hide whips and lengths of bamboo for tent-poles.[1] Often the crowds would part like the waves of a sea as an Abyssinian chief swept past on his mule with his white shawl flying, clustered round by a group of retainers who jogged on foot beside him through the dust. Occasionally the throng would be split instead by a troop of five or six mounted Sikhs – Siwars of Skinner's Horse – with square-clipped beards, close-bound turbans, and red and white pennons snapping on their lances. Behind them rode the tall, imperturbable figure of Captain the Honourable Wilfred Gilbert Thesiger, His Britannic Majesty's Consul-General and Minister Plenipotentiary at the Imperial court.

The Honourable Wilfred was the youngest son of the 2nd Baron Chelmsford, the notorious Victorian general who had commanded the British forces in South Africa during the Zulu or Kaffir wars. He had incurred the wrath of the British public by allowing a column under his command to be wiped out by Tsetswayo's Zulu impis at Isandhlwana in 1879. All his life, the younger Wilfred Thesiger would claim more sympathy with the Zulus – finally destroyed by Chelmsford at Ulundi – than with his grandfather: 'I never felt it was a ghastly tragedy that they'd overrun half my grandfather's army,' he said. 'I gave them full marks for it – they jolly well deserved it. But then my grandfather broke Zulu power at Ulundi, and I think he was probably justified in doing so because all of Natal was threatened by this vast Zulu army only too anxious to wash its spears. I don't deny one had to get in first, but my sympathies were with the Zulus.'[2]

When Wilfred Gilbert arrived in Addis Ababa in December 1909 he had been married for only five months to Kathleen Mary Vigors, a radiantly attractive girl from a landed Anglo-Irish family whose seat lay at Bagnoldstown in County Carlow. She had never before ventured further than Italy: now, five months pregnant, she had ridden mules for hundreds of miles across plains and mountains to make her home in a country that seemed hardly to have emerged from the dark ages. The British Legation lay to the north-east of the town, and stood, as it still does, in spacious parkland at the foot of the Entoto Hills. Today you can drive there from your hotel in a modest fifteen minutes by taxi, along a smooth macadam road that takes you through dappling tunnels of eucalyptus, past dilapidated wooden cabins with rust-pickled zinc roofs, right up to the cast-iron gates with their royal crest and paramilitary guards. In 1910, though, the Legation stood above a wide, empty plain, and to reach it one had to jog cross-country by mule, negotiating ravines and rivers. It was within this compound that Wilfred Patrick Thesiger was born on 3 June 1910. His birthplace still stands, a complex of thatched wattle and mud-brick huts the shape of giant mushrooms, with connecting passages, now painted an almost supernatural white and subsiding gently down the side of the Entoto Hills. When the Thesigers arrived the site was grassy and unkempt, dominated by the bald humps of the hills. Today, largely through their skilful work as gardeners, there are rose-beds and billiard-table lawns, and the eucalypts stand in lush avenues 100 feet high, cutting out the view of hills and valleys, dwarfing the cactus-like euphorbias draped with scarlet flowers, the pencil-cedars, the wild figs, hibiscus, poinsettias and oleanders of brilliant red. The building is now the British Consulate, and the wide, cool, cylindrical room in which Wilfred Thesiger came into the world, almost impossible, they say, to furnish with suitably shaped tables and pictures, is the office of HM Consul.

1910 was the year Edward VII died.[3] It was also the year in which Henry Ford set up his first European plant at Trafford Park, Manchester – a plant that by 1913 would annually be churning out 6,000 Model 'T's – the world's first mass-produced motor car. These two events may seem unconnected, but they are symbolically of deep significance in the life of Wilfred Thesiger. Edward's passing sounded the death-knell of an era in which the world had danced to an all-British tune – a tune played largely to the beat of steam-pistons and the whistle of locomotives. It had been the age of the steamship and the railway – the technology which had spread the British way of life into the far-flung corners of the globe, creating the greatest empire the world had ever seen. But by 1900 the internal combustion engine had arrived. Britain's economic hegemony had reached its peak in 1870, and in 1900 it had already been surpassed by Germany and America. These two countries would become the masters of the technology that would dominate the twentieth century: it was in Germany, not Britain, that the carburettor was invented, and in the USA, not in Britain, that the first aeroplane flew. A new age was dawning, in which the American way would prove supreme. Britain had had its century at the world's helm: the long-drawn-out twilight of its Empire had begun.

It was Wilfred Thesiger's bane, and his fortune, that he was born on the very cusp of this new age. Bane, because he lived to see the world he had grown up in with all its assumptions shattered, fortune, because it was as a chronicler of the death of traditional ways that he found his fame. Yet all his life the past seemed to lie on him with peculiar weight: 'Personally, I'd like to have gone back to the Edwardian age,' he said years later, 'when a lot of the world was still untouched. When I was born there were almost no cars or aeroplanes. I never had the slightest interest in them and indeed, [don't remember] seeing a car until I was seven or eight in India. I'd have liked to have lived my whole life in an era when there were no cars or aeroplanes – I would have accepted trains and steamships because they didn't have the same disastrous effect. Even at the battle of Waterloo, the fastest you could go anywhere in the world was on a galloping horse – less than 200 years ago. I don't dispute that trains ended that, but when you travel on a train you're confined to the railway, so they don't have the same shattering impact on the environment. There's more horror, more unhappiness, more distress in the world today than there's ever been in history. If there were no cars or aeroplanes the world would be infinitely better. They have brought nothing but destruction and unhappiness and in fact doomed the world. Human beings had gone on living without them for hundreds of years and led contented lives, each in his own slot.'[4]

To Thesiger, his father seemed to epitomize all that was good about the traditional life. The Thesigers were aristocrats of the British Empire and had found their niche in service to the Crown. Not of the old landed gentry, they belonged to the new class of plutocrats raised to the peerage in Victorian times. Indeed, in origin they were not British at all, being descended from a German émigré, John Andrew Thesiger, who had arrived in Britain from the Saxon country around Dresden in the middle of the eighteenth century. John Andrew took up employment as amanuensis to the Duke of Rockingham, and his descendants prospered. His grandson, Frederic, the 1st Baron Chelmsford, was a barrister and later a Member of Parliament, who became Attorney-General under Disraeli. He had, it is said, a fine presence and handsome features, a beautiful voice, a pleasant if too frequent wit, an imperturbable temper, and a gift of natural eloquence. His son, Frederic Augustus, Victoria's commander at Ulundi, did not inherit this gift, being known as a man of stiff and icy reserve, who was nevertheless a perfect gentleman, a model of tact and diplomacy, and a clean-living teetotaller. In the Honourable Wilfred Gilbert's generation alone, the family had produced a general, an admiral, a Lord of Appeal, a High Court judge and a famous actor. His brother, the 3rd Baron Chelmsford, would reach the dizzy heights of Empire as Viceroy of India.

Wilfred Gilbert, like his grandfather, embodied the virtues of the 'perfect gentleman' – still, during Thesiger's childhood, the ideal to which all his class aspired. It was a code of conduct not necessarily describing how men of a certain rank actually behaved, but how they should behave. With its origin in feudal times, it had been trundled out and dusted off by those factories of the British Empire, the public schools. Not the exclusive preserve of the aristocracy, but an aspiration which even the rising middle class might espouse for their children, its standards filtered down from the major public schools into all walks of life. According to writer Philip Mason, by 1900 the ideal had almost become a religion. 'To be a gentleman was a sub-Christian cult,' he has written, 'that is to say, a code of conduct derived from the ethics, not from the theology of Christianity.'[5] Thesiger acknowledged that he had grown up in the Christian tradition and though he never accepted Christ's divinity or the idea of a personal God, he regarded himself as an observer of Christian ethics, and to that extent a Christian. It was principally from his parents that Thesiger derived this gentlemanly code: 'I don't in any way reject proper English values,' he said later, 'honesty, integrity, loyalty to your friends and country, a sense of responsibility. They were the values I acquired from my family and to a large extent were reinforced at Eton. One got them from one's father and mother. It's true my father died when I was nine but all the same he had a very strong influence on me. They were what you might call the values of a gentleman. I could never have become a [Bohemian] when I was at Oxford, for instance . . . I belong to the establishment by nature and everything else.'[6] Until the end of the Great War, English leaders had been gentlemen almost by definition: 'They used power with some restraint,' Mason says, 'and as a rule with courtesy and generosity. They thought of the public good with some degree of detachment. They admired courage and truthfulness.'[7] Yet this ideal was another aspect of the traditional world into which he was born that had already become impotent by the time Thesiger reached manhood: 'The desire to be a gentleman,' Mason has written, 'seems to me to illuminate English history from the time of

Chaucer to the First World War, after which it began to die at least as a social force.'[8] 'I think obviously the standards of behaviour in Western society have gone down since I was a boy,' Thesiger said. 'There's corruption in England, and no feeling for the [old] values of life. Today, if you mentioned patriotism, for example, you'd be laughed at.'[9]

Never an enthusiastic supporter of democracy, especially as disseminated throughout his life among traditional peoples, Thesiger remained true to the Victorian principle of advancement through acceptance rather than talent. He held to the dominance of hereditary aristocracy, and believed that human beings were more contented when each man knew his place and lived out his life within his pre-ordained 'slot'. Liberal assumptions about equality of opportunity and the effect of the social environment on success are the orthodoxies – some might even say the bigotries – of the late twentieth century. To Thesiger and his family there was nothing immoral about the idea of inequality: it was a fact of life which everyone accepted. They believed that certain families – even certain races – were superior because they were bred to excellence like a bloodline of fine racehorses. It is an assumption that would deeply influence Thesiger's view of the world in later life, when his highest compliment to the Arabian Bedouin would be that they were 'the purest race in the world'. 'Being a traditionalist I'm very glad there is still a hereditary aristocracy in Britain,' he commented years afterwards. 'But I don't believe, for instance, that my grandfather became a general merely because his father was a lord. Now if you want to get to the top and make millions, you've got to be a black pop-singer who's had his nose operated on and rubs white paint on his face, and there he is with more money than anybody else. A society that can spend its millions on promoting that – well, you can keep it!'[10] He never forgave the Americans for spreading the mass, materialist, technological culture he would live to see penetrating almost every corner of the world. He saw the Americans as brash, vulgar, Johnny-come-latelys – a mongrel hotch-potch of peoples without breeding, history or tradition. 'What I reject is the material aspect of modern Western civilization which finds its greatest manifestation in America,' he said. 'I wouldn't have rejected the civilization of my father's time, but for me now civilization is identified with machines, pop music played on radios, motorcycles going down the street, aeroplanes taking off – and the Americans are the archetypes of this civilization. I dislike everything I hear about them.'[11] It was almost inconceivable to the English gentlemen of the Edwardian age that these braggart upstarts with their populist ideology and social democracy should usurp the position of power traditionally held by their class. Thesiger's bitterness against them and the century they created is summed up, perhaps unconsciously, in his insistence that 'all change is for the worse'.[12]

Since Thesiger lived much of his life among foreign tribes, it is apposite to examine the nature of the tribe into which he himself was born in 1910. First of all, it *was* a tribe. The British aristocracy was socially exclusive, highly interbred, and despite being imbued with the ideals of duty, loyalty and service, owed allegiance to itself rather than to an abstract idea of 'Britain'. It might be said that for them, 'Britain' *was* the aristocracy, irrespective of the fact that they represented only 2 per cent of its population. In 1910 they were still distinguishable physically from the other classes: they were taller, more robust, and possessed a distinctive similarity of physical cast – jutting chins, oriental cheekbones, kedge-like noses, deep-set eyes. They were set apart, too, by the elegance of their attire, for in a world without dry-cleaning only the toff could afford to have his suit unstitched and the parts washed piecemeal. The social upheavals of the Victorian age had left them fundamentally untouched. True, Victoria's reign had seen the admittance of new recruits from industry, the military and the professions into a class which had traditionally comprised only the great landowners, but these plutocrats were soon absorbed into the old élite by marriage, and quickly became indistinguishable from them. The aristocracy wielded massive power both at home and within the Empire: between 1886 and 1916, over half of Britain's cabinet ministers, over two-thirds of high posts in India and the Dominions, a third of army officers above the rank of colonel, and 42 per cent of all military officers were drawn from a mere 300 families. In 1914 thirty-three of Britain's thirty-seven High Court judges were hereditary noblemen, who also represented eighty-six out of 103 directors of the country's top banks, and more than three-quarters of all directors of British industry. This oligarchy was trained at only five schools: Eton, Winchester, Rugby, Harrow and Marlborough, the most exclusive of all being Eton.

Thesiger's early life in the British Legation, in which he was a small prince among an army of servants and retainers, was a perfect model of the hierarchical empire in the world outside. He formed no close bonds with people of foreign race during his childhood. Social and racial divisions were rigid. People expected to be born, marry, and die within their own group – and were, moreover, proud of it. The classes and races were as fixed in place as the paths of planets in the solar system, with the ruling class of the Empire emanating light from the centre. In the Legation there was the tiny British élite, the Indian Siwars, the Anglo-Indian ayahs, the Abyssinian servants, all separate and distinct in religion, colour and creed. 'I did feel a sense of superiority to the Abyssinians,' Thesiger admitted. 'At that time I hadn't met Haile Selassie – that came later. After all, I was the eldest son of the Minister. The Abyssinians I knew were servants – people like the syce who went with us when we were riding. The servants were there, but there was no sense of close friendship – no intimacy such as a lot of boys had with their servants in India. We had no association with the local people, either – one lived a life apart. That doesn't mean, of course, that I felt superior to people like Ras Tafari and Ras Kassa. When I saw them later, they seemed heroic figures – very impressive. But we didn't really have any contact with them as boys. I didn't identify with them, I identified with my father and the British Legation.'[13] Thesiger was to live, of course, to see all these discrete divisions broken down – to see a world of fixed points explode into a welter of confusion, as tribes, cultures and classes mixed and intermingled like random splashes of paint on an op-art canvas. It must have been almost as if the planets had come adrift from their celestial moorings. Without such divisions, there could no longer be excitement and adventure in breaching them: one can appreciate, even sympathize perhaps, with Thesiger's resentment.

Loyalty to and pride in his family and class were the anchor which later allowed Thesiger to cruise in and out of foreign cultures with ease. Able to share the world of traditional peoples for a time, all his life he migrated between them and civilization.

The personal eqilibrium he was able to maintain between these two opposing extremes was made possible only by the presence of a financially secure world in the background. More than economic security, though, or a sense of home, it was Thesiger's absolute knowledge of who he was and in which 'slot' he belonged – his pronounced sense of identity – which enabled him to maintain this equilibrium. When asked if he thought himself a conventional English gentleman, he replied, 'I wouldn't wish to be thought anything else. At the end I suppose my loyalty is to [England]. But since I left Oxford I've rarely spent more than three months a year in England during the rest of my life. When I've been starving in Arabia I've never longed for England. England as a place means nothing to me. I don't think of how marvellous it would be to be in an English wood in spring with the daffodils – it's the last sort of thought I should have. Whereas when I thought I couldn't get to Arabia, I was frantic.'[14] Thesiger never 'went native' in the sense of adopting the values and traditions of another culture. Throughout his life he respected traditional peoples and argued desperately for their preservation, yet he never became, or even believed he could become, one of them: 'I would never want to be anything but English,' he said. 'When I'm in Africa I live very much as the locals do, but my family is British and I'm very proud to be British. It's one of the reasons I never contemplated becoming a Muslim or anything else just for convenience.'[15] For Thesiger Britain was an idea, an abstract concept represented by his father and mother and the few staff at the Legation, by his uncle the Viceroy, by a class with its own unique culture and traditions, and above all, by the British royal family. In old age, he would insist, 'I feel very, very strongly about the royal family. It's the symbol of the whole of Britain, England, everything. Something for which I'd be prepared to die, perfectly willingly. What do you want, a Bush or a Clinton? The royal family are something better and higher. If it came to riots in England and they were trying to storm the palace or something I'd be there straight away. I regard the royals as an integral part of Britain. If we ever became a republic I'd never set foot in the place again.'[16]

Thesiger's earliest years were marked by periodic family migrations – arduous journeys by mule and camel, then by train and steamship. As a ten-month-old baby, in February 1911, he was carried on a litter slung between two mules along the edge of Danakil country, to Dire Dawa on the border of Abyssinia and French Somaliland (now Jibuti), where the railway had been halted by the resistance of conservative Abyssinian nobles. His ayah, an Anglo-Indian called Susannah, would carefully boil the water for his food and strain it through fine cloth. She would probe every corner of his tent for blood-sucking ticks. Once, as she carried the tiny baby around the camp, she was suddenly confronted by a troop of spear-carrying Afars. She grinned at them nervously and tried to edge back to camp, only realizing later that they had been lured by the almost magical sight of a white infant. A two-week voyage by ship was followed by a year's stay in England, and then the same protracted voyage back to Addis Ababa in 1912. Naturally, Thesiger remembered nothing distinctive about these early moves, yet of his next journey – a similar migration to England in 1914 – he retained vague recollections of riding along with his brother Brian in a mule-palanquin. He recalled diaphanous images of Afar warriors, camels watering at muddy pools, hyenas running round the camp at night. 'The baggage would probably have been carried on camels,' he said, 'but whether we actually rode them on that journey I don't remember. My father only escorted us as far as the railhead at Dire Dawa, because he had to go to Nairobi to see the Governor. The Danakil weren't giving much trouble at that time, though we probably had a troop of zabanias [Abyssinian soldiers] with us. I don't remember clearly, anyway.'[17]

This was a time of some turmoil in Abyssinian politics. In his youth the Emperor Menelik had been a dynamic power in the land. Now, old and ailing, he was a sinister wraith haunting the palace recesses, more dead than alive. His heir-elect was Lij Yasu, his grandson, an adolescent youth given to dark and self-indulgent vices. In June 1912, when Thesiger – known as Billy to distinguish him from his father – was already toddling about the Legation garden in his basin-like sun-helmet, his father invited the Crown Prince to dinner in celebration of the Official Birthday of King George V. Lij Yasu duly arrived in splendour with his retinue of nobles and church dignitaries, escorted by more than 1,000 fighting men, who were fed in the Legation compound.

It was a magnificent occasion when the dignity of two great empires was on display. As the 200 guests, gorgeous in their best lions' manes and scarlet cloaks, took their places around the table in the Legation hall, Wilfred Gilbert arose to wish their country unity and prosperity, and to propose a toast to the young prince. Some time later, obviously overcome by the gravity of the evening, Lij Yasu staggered out – blind drunk. Meanwhile, a more abstemious young guest called Ras Tafari, Lij Yasu's distant cousin and, at only twenty-one, Governor of Harar, observed acutely, and exercised his well-known capacity for patience.

As the Rases manoeuvred for power in the land, however, life within the Legation in these early years went on with surprising tranquillity. Billy and his younger brother Brian were inseparable companions. Indeed, Brian, only a year and a half younger, seems to haunt Thesiger's early life like a shadowy presence, confounding, as Thesiger himself acknowledged, the conclusion that it was his early experience alone which turned him into one of the greatest travellers of his age. Brian grew up with the desire to become an army officer, and having moved to England with the family in 1919 felt no desire ever to visit Abyssinia again. Though they shared most of their childhood experiences, and retained a certain affection for each other into adulthood, they were as different as chalk and cheese, regarding one another later, as one friend commented, almost as 'inhabitants of a different planet'.[18] Even at four, Thesiger was already the dominating character he would remain until old age. Once, he decided that he and Brian should lie up all night to wreak revenge with air-rifles on a porcupine that was insistently making a meal of his parents' precious gladioli bulbs. They took up ambush-positions, but soon after dusk, three-year-old Brian wailed that he could hear a hyena coming. 'I'm frightened, Billy,' he said. 'Let's go in now.' Thesiger eyed him with a look of four-year-old contempt. 'Nonsense,' he replied. 'You will stay here with me.' They lay in silence, waiting for the absent porcupine, until the chill of the mountain night set in. Thesiger, who throughout his life suffered from the cold, quickly changed his mind about the night-long vigil. 'All right, we'll go in now,' he declared. The four-year-old autocrat had spoken.

Thesiger's ayah, Susannah, was extremely indulgent to the little boy, letting him do more or less as he pleased, which must have added to his sense of autonomy. The boys were taught to ride ponies from the age of three. 'At first we were just sitting on them being held on by the syce, Habta Wold,' Thesiger recalled, 'but by the time we were four we were riding on our own inside the Legation compound. By the time we were five, we were riding everywhere.'[19] Everywhere, that was, but into the town itself: Addis Ababa was strictly out of bounds. 'If we were going on a short journey,' he said, 'we'd have a syce with us, jogging along on foot. If we were going on a longer trip – to the Italian Legation, for instance, which was about forty-five minutes away, we'd have a Siwar with us.'[20] It was on one such expedition that Billy got his first sight of blood. The Siwar who was escorting the boys, Seran Singh, dismounted from his horse to show them a bird's nest. 'He had laid his lance against his side,' Thesiger said, 'and then the horse bucked and the lance went in through his chest and I saw it come out through the back of his shoulder. He managed to wrench it loose and then he fell on the ground. I sent Brian racing off back to the Legation to get help and I sat beside him. I was very distressed and concerned for him – he was a particular favourite of ours. Anyway he was all right and got over it. In fact, he recovered quite quickly.'[21]

Often, the boys would canter up the hillside at the back of the Legation, where, on the summit, there was a crude grotto from which they could look down over the horizons to the north and south. Out of sight, beyond the Abyssinian downs, beyond the villages of wattle huts with their donkeys, mules, and placid oxen hauling ploughs, lay the country of the homicidal Afars or Danakil. Perhaps even then Thesiger sensed that his destiny would lie out there in that savage land.

Thesiger's greatest accolade to his father is that he was a man of 'absolute integrity'. Like most of his class Wilfred Gilbert had a predilection for manly, outdoor sports: riding, shooting, cricket and yachting. Yet it is interesting, too, that in a tradition which regarded the sporting 'hearty' as preferable to the artistic intellectual, Thesiger should give prominence to his father's intelligence, sensitivity and artistic bent, even noting his diffidence, a family trait inherited from the 2nd Baron, which Thesiger said added to his charm. His father's greatest passion in Abyssinia was big-game hunting, and his enthusiasm for it rubbed off on young Billy. From the age of three he was trying to bag birds in the Legation grounds with a tennis racket and spent cartridge-cases, an occupation which convinced his father that his hunting instincts were very strongly developed. One of his earliest memories was of his father shooting an oryx – all his life he would remember with vivid accuracy the report of his father's rifle and the maddened animal dashing off to collapse kicking in a cloud of dust. If there is a single image which dominated Thesiger's early years, it is surely this. Throughout his childhood and youth, it was the idea of big-game hunting that inspired him more than anything else. 'Hunting was all important,' he said. 'I was mad-keen on it. Ever since I was a little boy I was determined to hunt.'[22] By the time he had grown to manhood, the idea of hunting in the wilds of Africa had become an obsession. As a young man in his twenties, a colleague in the Sudan would say of him: 'Big-game hunting played an all-important part in Wilfred's life. I think he saw the job mainly as a good opportunity to shoot big-game, especially lion.'[23] Although he did not know it, this ideal was merely the early guise of the passion that would fire his entire life: the quest for adventure.

While the Thesigers were in England during 1914, war was declared, and, despite being on leave, his father managed to get a temporary appointment in the French war-zone as an officer in the intelligence branch. He had previously served with a Yeomanry regiment in the Boer war, winning a DSO for bravery, and this distinction may have helped him to jump the queue of regular officers who were desperately waiting to see action. When his leave expired, however, he took his family, now enlarged by the arrival of a third son, Dermot, back to Addis Ababa. It was there, in the new stone-built Legation which had been completed in 1911, that Thesiger's youngest brother, Roderic, was born in 1915. The two younger boys were cared for by an English nurse whom Thesiger remembered simply as 'Nanny'. He and Brian were looked after by Mary Buckle, a young girl from Oxfordshire whom the boys referred to affectionately as 'Minna'. Thesiger's mother had engaged her after Brian's birth on their previous visit to England in 1911. 'My mother advertised for someone to look after myself and Brian,' Thesiger recalled, 'and about eighteen people turned up to apply. But when they found out it involved going abroad, they all dropped out. The only one who stuck to it was Minna. I suppose she'd been as far as Oxford, but that was the extent of her previous travels. She said [travel] was what she'd always wanted to do.'[24] In contrast to the Abyssinian servants, 'Minna' was to occupy a cherished place in Thesiger's affections for the rest of his life.

Thesiger recalled his childhood in the Legation as a time of freedom. In the mornings they rode, had breakfast, and were then given lessons in the huts of the Old Legation, punctuated by periods of drilling with the Siwars. Afternoons were filled with riding, and as the boys became older they perfected their shooting, snapping off at birds in the Legation compound with air-rifles. Each summer the family would camp for ten days in a secluded spot further up the Entoto Hills, where young Billy would spend fascinated hours watching the antics of birds and baboons with his father's binoculars. These were occasions of family closeness when Wilfred Gilbert, freed from the strains of diplomatic life, would relax. Thesiger would always savour the image of his father, a tall, lean figure in his Wolseley helmet, smoking his pipe or oiling his rifle on the verandah of his tent in the cool evenings. So vivid was this picture of domestic harmony that he would remember even the objects that adorned his father's camp-table, 'a bottle of Rose's Lime-Juice, a tobacco tin, and a copy of *Blackwood's Magazine*'.[25] The most exciting times were those evenings when he would lie up with his father for the chance to shoot a leopard – a chance which, sadly, never arose. The idea of a proper schooling did not loom up in this carefree life. The exigencies of the war meant that he could not be sent back to Britain to school, and most lessons were provided by his mother or his father. 'My father used to read to us,' he remembered. '*Jock of the Bushveld* was my favourite book. It was about hunting, and of course, I was mad-keen on that.'[26] Outside the timeless cell of the Legation, though, Abyssinia was beginning to rumble with the turbulent forces unleashed by the death of the Emperor Menelik – forces that would draw the Thesigers inexorably into the fray.

*

Menelik died in 1913, leaving the empire he had painfully built up to the tender mercies of Lij Yasu. In the following three years the young Emperor systematically massacred, tortured, raped and enslaved his way round the country, bringing it to the verge of chaos. Lij Yasu is, perhaps rightly, the bogey-figure of Thesiger's youth: 'When it came to the point,' he said, 'Lij Yasu was a vicious, bloodthirsty, sadistic, brutal boy.'[27] Yet it is a fact that despite his excesses, Wilfred Gilbert continued to hope that something might be made of him. 'This country can only be ruled by autocratic power resting in the hands of one man,' he wrote in a 1913 dispatch. 'Shall we counteract his youth and inexperience and back him?'[28] The illusion that Lij Yasu might be improved was shattered when in 1916 he began unmistakably to flirt with Islam. In an empire whose central myth was the descent of its leaders from Solomon and Sheba, and where it was axiomatic that the Emperor should be a Coptic Christian, his announcement that he was a descendant of the Prophet Muhammad was met with profound consternation. 'There is no shadow of a doubt that he was on the verge of becoming a Muslim,' Thesiger opined, 'and that he had no sympathy with the established church. He hated Addis Ababa and spent all his time in the Danakil and Somali country.'[29] In September 1916 a council of nobles and churchmen rebelled, excommunicating him and proclaiming Menelik's daughter, Zauditu, Empress. Her regent would be the reserved guest of Wilfred Gilbert's 1912 dinner-party, the eminently competent Ras Tafari, whose burning ambition – achieved fourteen years later – was to rule Abyssinia as the Emperor Haile Selassie.

If Lij Yasu is the villain of Thesiger's childhood, then Ras Tafari is decidedly its hero. A friend and confidant of his father, he later came to symbolize almost all the virtues and qualities that Thesiger held dear, so much so, indeed, that he was to dedicate his autobiography to Ras Tafari's memory. The son of Menelik's cousin, the formidable Ras Makonnen, Tafari had spent part of his childhood in the palace with his kinsman Lij Yasu, where he was mocked for his shyness and abstemiousness, yet secretly respected for his patience, stoicism and implacability in the face of pain and ridicule. He was nicknamed 'the Shy One' by members of the court, and the Emperor Menelik himself was perspicacious enough to realize that 'he had all the qualities of a hawk and sighed at the thought that he would never see him pounce and on whom it would be'.[30] Thesiger never knew Ras Tafari as a young man, yet he was later to assess him as determined, just, compassionate and able. The esteem in which he held Haile Selassie throughout his life stemmed directly from his reverence for tradition, yet it also had a personal basis. Having met Haile Selassie on numerous occasions later, he described the Emperor unhesitatingly as 'one of the noblest men I have ever met'. Haile Selassie was a reformer whose dearest wish was to bring his country into the modern age. It was for this reason, Thesiger himself admitted, that he had originally been passed over as heir to the throne by Menelik, despite his evident qualities. 'The whole country felt that he was full of modern ideas,' Thesiger said, 'and he'd want schools and hospitals and roads and all that sort of thing, and he'd want to centralize the government. The nobles had almost dictatorial powers in their provinces and didn't want any of that.'[31] It is an interesting paradox of Thesiger's life that, as a man who revered tradition and rejected the material aspects of Western civilization, he should hero-worship someone whose most treasured ambition was to introduce such developments to Africa. It is a first indication of the irrationality of the adventurer: Thesiger's pride in his family's association with the Emperor was partisan, and far outweighed any philosophical considerations. In any case, despite being a reformer, Haile Selassie remained an autocrat – albeit a benevolent one – and, as author Mark Cocker has commented, 'Thesiger was in favour of the kind of society of which his own was a microcosm. He wanted a "Top-dog" and worshipped the hero, the individual.'[32] This model, the benevolent autocrat – the paternalist – was an Imperial ideal far more suited to the dominant Thesiger than the populist, egalitarian ideology he would later see envelop the globe. In old age he would argue passionately that democracy and liberalism were totally unsuited to the African character.

In 1916, when Abyssinia was at sea, it was Ras Tafari who was called upon to take the helm. Lij Yasu's father, the powerful Negus Mikael, learned of his son's humiliation through the country's embryonic telephone system, and at once ordered his vast northern army to march on Addis Ababa and retrieve the throne. The stage was set for a showdown which would affect Thesiger's entire life. A pulse of excitement shot through the Legation. 'We knew what was going on,' Thesiger said. 'I was seven years old – old enough to understand. We heard talk when people came to the Legation, and my father did explain a certain amount. I can remember preparations for receiving people into the compound and putting them in the field down by the wood. There were a certain amount of alterations in the house – sandbags being put into place, and on one occasion I saw rifles being brought up from the cellar.'[33] In this moment of crisis Ras Tafari paid Wilfred Gilbert the supreme compliment of entrusting him with his eldest son, later the Crown Prince Asfa Wossen, then still a baby. 'He was on closer terms with my father than any of the other Ministers,' Thesiger said. 'He told me later that my father was someone whose advice he could always rely on.'[34] Nevertheless, it is clear that Wilfred Gilbert was aware of the difficulties of the situation: '[Tafari] has now given me a further and most embarrassing proof of his confidence in me,' he wrote, 'by asking me to take charge of his son and heir ... I felt it impossible to refuse without risking his friendship. It is a grave responsibility and very inconvenient.'[35] The little boy was brought up to the Legation in a cradle with two servants. 'They carried him in and he had a room to himself,' Thesiger remembered. '[If Ras Tafari had been defeated] his presence would have made us a target, of course.'[36]

Bad news was quickly to follow. An advance guard of troops under Ras Lul Seged had been virtually exterminated by Ras Mikael's vast army at Ankober. The Ras was now encamped at Sagale in the Shoan uplands, opposed only by a much smaller force. Addis Ababa seemed doomed. If Negus Mikael had made his move then it almost certainly would have been, but surprisingly, he hesitated. Ras Tafari was given time to rally his army and to receive a consignment of Maxim machine-guns from French Somaliland. As soon as they arrived, he marched north to strengthen the rebel force. Standing at the gates of the Legation, the wide-eyed Billy watched the warriors go. 'The whole day they were pouring past,' he remembered, 'some on foot, some on horses. You saw Gallas mounted on horses with their lances, and then a chief going past with his retainers jogging along behind him at a shuffling trot. Then you'd get camp-followers – women with donkeys and mules loaded with provisions. Then it thinned out and you'd get people hurrying to catch up, and then another mass of soldiers coming past. I was quite aware they were going to fight against Lij Yasu, and yes, I suppose I did know that Lij Yasu was the villain of the piece.'[37]

Thesiger was not, of course, to see the battle that would perhaps decide his family's fate: Negus Mikael's horsemen charging across the plain of Sagale, urged on by bleating shawms and pulsing drums, only to be scattered by withering machine-gun fire. All day the northerners crashed upon a wall of fire and shields, and at one point they almost broke through Ras Tafari's lines only to be repulsed by a headlong rush of his Harar cavalry, pressing through the northern ranks with such force that they were obliged to flee in panic back to their own side. It was the turn of Negus Mikael's men to try to halt the rebels' advance with rifle fire.[38] But the armies of Ras Tafari had seized the initiative, and Mikael's Wollo and Galla warriors wavered as the rebels attacked in wave after wave with renewed ferocity. Just before sunset they had cut off the seventy-year-old Negus himself, still fighting like the very devil. According to an eye-witness, a Shoan noble cried out to the Negus, 'Lay down your arms and I guarantee your life!' Every warrior suddenly stopped in his tracks as, with tears streaking the coagulated blood in his beard, the Negus of the North threw down his sword and shield. Young Thesiger did not see all this, but forty-four years later, when he visited the site of the battle and inspected the hill where Negus Mikael had made his final stand, he found clefts and crannies in the rock still full of the bones of the dead. Sitting on that hill, sipping coffee and eating scrambled eggs, he pondered what might have been if Negus Mikael had won.

While the battle thundered on Sagale plain, however, there was chaos in Addis Ababa. Ras Balcha, the ruthless governor, had restored order by stringing up thieves and looters on makeshift gibbets at every bridge and cross-road. Curious foreigners sneaked into the town to photograph these dreadful exhibits. 'People were being hanged round the town,' Thesiger recalled. 'As children we were told we weren't to go to bridges where there were corpses hanging, but Minna did go past once and she said she couldn't resist the temptation to look.'[39] Some days later, Billy and Brian were out riding as usual when they heard heavy firing coming from the direction of the town. They raced back to the Legation to discover that the rebel forces had won a great victory at Sagale. The reign of Lij Yasu was over. Beneath the imperturbable exterior, Wilfred Gilbert must have heaved a secret sigh of relief. Indeed, many foreign diplomats had been convinced that Negus Mikael's forces would prevail, and had agreed that in this case the Italian Minister, Count Colli, would ride out to beg the Negus to observe the diplomatic immunity of the Legations. It is almost unthinkable that Wilfred Gilbert would willingly have given up Ras Tafari's son, whatever the battle's outcome. Whether the Negus would have had the magnanimity to spare him and his family we shall never know.

Later, there was a great victory parade on the town race-course, the Jan Meda, before the Empress Zauditu. Wilfred Gilbert, with his wife and their two eldest sons, rode down the avenues of troops preceded by their Siwars with pennons flying. The British Minister presented his family to the Empress, then took his place with them to watch the procession. 'Ras Balcha's troops had already formed into two great lines,' Thesiger recalled. 'I can remember the kettle-drums on the mules and the trumpets. Ras Lul Seged's small son brought in the remnants of his army – 300 men out of 8,000. We were sitting at the front near the Empress, and the boy came and sat right beside us with a goatskin over his shoulders! This was really thrilling. The horses were draped in the bloodstained clothing the men had taken off the dead, so we had a good idea of what it was all about.'[40] In his book *Arabian Sands*, written more than forty years afterwards, Thesiger gives a scintillating description of the victory parade: 'The Zulu impis parading before Chaka,' he wrote, 'or the Dervishes drawn up to give battle in front of Omdurman, can have appeared no more barbaric than this frenzied tide of men which surged past the royal pavilion throughout the day . . . This was no ceremonial review. These men had just returned after fighting desperately for their lives, and they were still wild with the excitement of those frantic hours . . . They came past in waves, horsemen half concealed in dust and a great press of footmen. Screaming out their deeds of valour and brandishing their weapons, they came right up to the steps of the throne, whence the Court chamberlains beat them back with long wands. Above them, among glinting spearpoints, countless banners dipped and danced.'[41]

Thesiger must have relived this scene many times through the rest of his youth: it was to become for him a symbol of the 'barbaric splendour' and the 'savagery and colour' which his Abyssinian childhood was to represent during the dark, fatherless schooldays in England. Though he maintained that it was this day alone that changed his life, its significance probably did not become evident until the death of his father sparked off a yearning for the golden days in Abyssinia. The most interesting aspect of his description – as brilliant as anything he ever wrote – is the light it sheds on his romantic view of history. He said later that he had been reading *Tales from the Iliad*, and imagined these Abyssinian warriors as the likes of Achilles, Ajax and Ulysses passing by in triumph before him. This was not the prosaic real world of machine-guns and political connivance, but a glorious, fantastic, heroic world cast in brilliant primary colours out of a primeval epic. It was an illusory dimension which lay just beyond the twilight of reality, yet a world Thesiger would seek for the rest of his life. In the role of the defeated 'Priam' came Negus Mikael, who stalked between the rows of warriors in a shawl and breeches, manacled at the ankles, wrists and neck and led on a chain by a rebel officer. He stared back defiantly at the crowds, walking like a king. Outside the royal pavilion, where the young Thesigers sat, he paused and bowed slightly, expecting to be admitted, but instead the Empress waved him on. Lij Yasu, his son, had taken no part in the battle and had long since escaped to the Danakil country. Wilfred Gilbert himself felt sympathy with the old Negus, who had fought ferociously for a son who had scampered away at the first sign of defeat.

In February 1917, Zauditu was crowned Empress in St George's Cathedral, an event which, in contrast to the great victory parade, made no impression on Thesiger. 'I remember Geoffrey Archer came up from Somaliland,' he recalled, 'a great giant of a man, who was good with children. Hugh Dodds came up from Harar, where he was Consul, but all I remember of the coronation itself is the carriages going off. We were watching from the old Legation and we saw the wheel come off one of the carts. My mother was injured as a piece of the wheel stuck in her leg, and for the rest of the time she was in bed.[42] The coronation was the signal for the many Muslim tribes in the north to revolt. Lij Yasu was still at large in the low country of the Rift Valley, and a new period of instability followed in which, as Wilfred Gilbert wrote, 'Ras Tafari stands alone, shouldering full responsibility, but without real power and uncertain whom he can trust.'[43] Convinced that the Regent was a friend of Britain and supported the British war-effort, Wilfred Gilbert urged the British authorities to supply him with the 30,000 modern rifles he needed for his army, in return for the expulsion of the German and Turkish Legations from Addis Ababa. Tafari, walking a tightrope between the great powers, was unable to comply.

The rebellion must have been emotionally draining for the British Minister, and by December 1917 he was sorely in need of a rest. War was still raging in Europe, so instead of returning to England he decided to take his family to India, where his elder brother Frederic, Baron Chelmsford, had been appointed Viceroy the previous year. By now the railway had been completed from Dire Dawa to Addis Ababa, and the mule-trains and camels that had marked the family's earlier excursions became a thing of the past. Despite his later assertion that he 'hated machines', it is clear that Thesiger was excited when the railway reached Addis Ababa and enjoyed travelling on the train as it slowly descended from the escarpment and into the riffling grassland of the Rift Valley, where the inverted boat-shaped huts of Afars and Itu Gallas were scattered about. Game down here was plentiful, and leaning out of the carriage windows the boys could spot zebra, waterbuck and beisa oryx. Soon the train was rattling across the stony lava-desert of French Somaliland, passing the spare figures of Issa tribesmen leading their camel-caravans across salt-pans that gleamed a blinding white in the high sun.

Jibuti, lodged on the flat, tideless shore of the Red Sea, was already the regular yet squalid Mediterranean-style town it remains, with its white-painted boulevards, shaded cafés and bustling market. There, in a harbour crammed with the lateen-rigged sails of gaudily painted sambuks, they found a steamer to take them to Berbera in British Somaliland further down the coast, where they were to be the guests of the Consul, the gentle giant Geoffrey Archer. They remained there for the best part of a month, while Wilfred Gilbert sailed up to Egypt to report to the High Commissioner, Sir Reginald Wingate, on the situation in Abyssinia. Meanwhile, Archer took the older boys bird-shooting with his .410 shotgun on the salt-packed beach, a pastime Thesiger relished. On Wilfred Gilbert's return in January 1918, the family embarked on HMS *Minto* for Aden. 'It was a very rough journey indeed,' Thesiger remembered, 'and I can recall Minna being violently sick, struggling to get us dressed between bouts of sea-sickness.'[44] In Aden the family stayed with General Stewart, a former Commander of the British army in East Africa. 'He hadn't done very well there, obviously,' Thesiger commented. 'Not well enough for him to be sent to Europe, anyway. But my mother found him very agreeable.'[45] During their stay, Stewart took the Thesigers and their two eldest sons to see the troops defending Aden against the Turks. 'We were put in some sort of trench protected with sand-bags,' Thesiger said, 'and we saw the British troops in blue uniforms and heard the guns firing.'[46] Later, his father was received by the local Arab Sheikhs and presented with a curved Yemeni dagger of fine workmanship. 'It disappeared later,' Thesiger recalled, 'which was a pity, because I'd have liked to have worn it when I travelled with the Bedu in Arabia.'[47]

From Aden the Thesigers sailed by P&O to Bombay, where they stayed with the Governor, before moving to Delhi. Young Billy was deeply impressed, indeed, for once in his life 'overawed', by the superhuman image of his uncle, the Viceroy, in his robes of state. 'India was my first contact with history and civilization,' he said. 'If you were taken, as I was by my father, to the ridge outside Delhi and it was explained to you what had gone on there, when the rebels were attacking the British troops on the ridge and then the Guides arrived having marched at some incredible pace from the Punjab, or you saw an orb that had come off the church spire with bullet-holes in it, or you were told how Nicholson had been killed fighting just down there – well wouldn't you call that contact with history?[48] ... Then there were the buildings – I have no recollection of buildings of any consequence in England as I was too small to remember. In

Addis Ababa there were only the Legations, and there wasn't anything spectacular in Jibuti or Aden – but then you got to India and saw the Red Fort and the big mosques and the Lutyens buildings which were still being erected – well you were suddenly conscious of what history and civilization meant.'[49] Later the boys visited Rajasthan, where they were guests of the Maharaja of Jaipur. 'I remember seeing the Palace of the Winds,' Thesiger said, 'and all the ceremonies that went on, the servants coming in and out with their brilliant red turbans, all the crowds in the street, and hearing the muezzin's cry at dawn.'[50] The high points of the holiday came when Thesiger was taken pig-sticking with his father, riding in a litter on elephant-back, and the day on which, concealed in a *machan* or tree-platform, he lay up for tiger. He would remember with vivid clarity how the tiger came padding towards them out of the jungle, moving its head from side to side, looking magnificent, larger even than he expected, its coat reddish against the pastel setting of the grass. In his autobiography, Thesiger commented that he was too young during the visit to appreciate this privileged glimpse of Indian court life, seeing the gorgeous trappings only as a background to the hunting with which he was obsessed. However, the six weeks he spent in India were certainly seminal. They made him aware suddenly of the power and dignity of the British Empire: the significance – perhaps the superiority – of his race and class. Though later commentators were to see Thesiger as a man who 'rejected civilization', it was clearly not the civilization that existed during his childhood in the British Empire on which he turned his back.[51]

In March the Thesigers put into Jibuti harbour in HMS *Juno*, the flagship of the British East Indies squadron. 'I remember the admiral fired off one of the ship's guns,' Thesiger said. 'We had been told to put cotton-wool in our ears, and I always remember seeing one of the shells hitting the water not very far away.'[52] Like the train journeys, Thesiger seems to have enjoyed plodding about the world in steamships, and although he later found long voyages somewhat tedious, he never resented their presence as he did that of the car and the aeroplane. 'Steamships were a limiting factor,' he commented. 'I mean, if you were going to take a fortnight to get to Mombasa or somewhere by ship, how many people were going to come? You'd only come if you intended to live out there or to visit relations or spend a year hunting. Now you've got this mass invasion of tourism – in every single place.'[53] In the Legation in Addis Ababa life returned to normal, a routine punctuated by the welcome arrival of the Consuls who worked in the distant corners of the land – men like Hugh Dodds, Arthur Lawrence, Robert Cheeseman and above all, Arnold Hodson. To Billy, these men with their tales of lion-hunts and ferocious tribes seemed almost magical. They were heroes out of Buchan: upright, often unmarried English gentlemen, who seemed to live lives of constant adventure. Together with his father, these were the men upon whom the young Thesiger modelled himself.

An earlier traveller in Abyssinia, P.H.G. Powell-Cotton, whose book *A Sporting Trip through Abyssinia* was published in 1903, was another of Billy's heroes. The book must have had a personal appeal to the boy, for Powell-Cotton had been present while Billy's birthplace – the Old Legation – was being built, and there were photographs of the actual construction in his volume. Though it was too difficult for the boy to read himself, he loved the quiet evenings at home when his mother or father would read it to him. It was on one such occasion, in 1918, that Thesiger came down suddenly with Spanish flu, and he would always remember the precise point they had reached in the book when the fever struck: 'We'd just got to the part where he'd gone to shoot a buffalo and the servant came running down hill and disturbed it,' he recalled. 'My brother Dermot was already in bed with fever and my mother looked at me and thought I seemed a bit flushed. She popped me into bed.'[54] The epidemic had already swept across Europe the previous year, leaving thousands dead in its wake. By 1918 it had spread to Africa, and by way of Dar es Salaam and Jibuti had made its way to Addis Ababa. Among thousands affected there was Ras Tafari, who was struck down in September and hovered between life and death, causing a wave of unrest throughout the city. 'People were dying in the town and being shovelled into pits,' Thesiger said. 'They were dug up by dogs and hyenas at night and eaten in the streets.'[55] In the Legation's servants' quarters alone, seventy people died, but neither Billy nor Dermot became dangerously ill and the other two Thesiger brothers were not affected at all. 'I think I survived because I was put in bed and taken care of,' Thesiger commented. 'It was just good luck and decent nursing.'[56] Wilfred Gilbert sent the Legation doctor, one of only four in the city, to treat Ras Tafari, who, much to his relief, managed to pull through. 'I've often wondered what would have happened if he'd died then,' Thesiger said later.[57]

In May 1919 the family left Addis Ababa for the last time. Wilfred Gilbert's period as Minister was over, and he was due for a posting in America, and a very different life. As their steamer passed through the Suez canal, bound for England, Minna called Billy to look at the British troops on the quayside in their khaki uniforms. The Great War had ended, and with it the foundations of a new world order had been laid. Billy was nine years old, and had spent all but two of those years abroad. It is interesting to ask what kind of boy it was who stood on the decks of that ship in May 1919, on the verge of a new life. Already a very distinctive, dominant, wilful character had been formed. He had grown up as the eldest of four brothers, of whom he was the unrivalled leader, deciding what they should do, leading them in everything, practising his boxing mercilessly on anyone who argued. He had never been to school and had thus never been challenged by boys his own age. He had been the Minister's eldest son: a small sultan within the 'empire' of the Legation, where, apart from the adults, there was no authority higher than his own. He was already possessed of the conflicting facets that would become apparent later. Aware of his racial and social superiority, he was physically powerful, assertive and aggressive, yet sensitive, reserved with strangers, and intensely shy. He had been well schooled in the traditional arts of the English ruling class, riding, shooting and hunting, had seen sights which few other boys of his age had witnessed, yet had been brought up largely in an enclave of the British Empire where Edwardian values, elsewhere faded, still ruled supreme. How much had his Abyssinian childhood shaped the boy who was to grow into a world-famous explorer? 'I have often looked back into my childhood for a clue to the perverse necessity which drives me from my own land to the deserts of the east,' Thesiger wrote later, yet the view that his extraordinary life can be put down entirely to the uniqueness of his upbringing is a part of the Thesiger story that is not wholly satisfying, even to himself.[58] First of all, many thousands of English boys were born and grew up in exotic places in the world during this period – in India, in China, in the Pacific Islands – but did not become explorers. Second, most of the greatest explorers of the nineteenth century grew up in the most unexotic of surroundings: Livingstone in the slums of Glasgow, and Stanley in a Welsh workhouse, to name but two. Third, Thesiger's childhood was not entirely unique: three boys who grew up to be perfectly ordinary upper-class citizens shared it with him: his brothers. One must conclude that it was Thesiger's particular genetic make-up – a desire for dominance, a profound inner conflict of qualities, a restlessness – that moulded his future, factors that may have been influenced by his childhood circumstances, but which would perhaps have surfaced in one way or another even in a less exotic environment. Thesiger himself accepted this view: 'One can't really say it came from my childhood,' he admitted years later. 'My childhood was an influence on it, but there must have been something in me that differentiated me from my three brothers. They wouldn't have been the slightest bit interested in the things I did. One has to accept that I inherited something from my father which only appeared in me, but which my upbringing as a child brought to full flower.'[59]

CHAPTER 3

The Emperor's Guest

It was more than a decade before Thesiger saw Addis Ababa again. He arrived there on 28 October 1930 for the coronation of Haile Selassie, a dark star in a galaxy of luminaries that included His Royal Highness the Duke of Gloucester, his equerry the Earl of Airlie, Governor-General of the Sudan Sir John Maffey, Sudan Civil Secretary Harold MacMichael, Aden Resident Sir Stewart Symes, and Sir Harold Kittermaster, Governor of British Somaliland. Though still an Oxford undergraduate and somewhat out of his depth among these dignitaries, Thesiger could comfort himself with the knowledge that while they were official representatives of Britain, he was there as the personal guest of the Emperor of Abyssinia himself. His invitation was Haile Selassie's gesture of affection for Thesiger's dead father, on whose advice he had so often relied. On Thesiger's side this was to be a nodal point, a knot connecting his childhood and his adulthood: an experience which raised high his sense of personal worth and ultimately committed him to a chosen path. Thesiger had dreamed throughout his school years in England of shooting big-game in Africa. Now, aged only twenty, he was in Addis Ababa as the guest of an Emperor, in the company of a royal prince, with a rifle in his baggage: 'When I went to Haile Selassie's coronation,' he said later, 'I was absolutely determined I would go and hunt big-game, which is what I did.'[1]

Thesiger found the town much changed. It now stood in a coarse forest of eucalyptus stretching right up to the neck of the Entoto Hills. There were more European houses, a number of rather flea-ridden hotels, bars, and cafés, and a night-club where foreigners could guzzle sweet champagne, watch a floor show direct from the Munich Winter Gardens, or flirt with European cabaret girls. There were several asphalt roads – joining the palace, the cathedral, the market, and the Foreign Legations and they were already choked with honking motor taxis and private vehicles. But the changes were superficial. Haile Selassie was anxious to show Addis Ababa off in a favourable light, but beyond the façade Abyssinia remained as barbarous as ever. Despite the apparent improvements, Thesiger confessed himself 'drunk with excitement'. He was housed in a tent at his birthplace, the Legation, and watched the same kites skirting the trees in the compound, the same blue pencil-line of smoke rising from the servants' quarters. He met servants he had known as a boy, even the syce Hapta Wold, who had held him on his pony as a three-year-old, now a grizzled old man. It all seemed incredibly familiar: 'It needed a conscious effort to remember Eton, Oxford and my home in Radnorshire,' he wrote. 'I could not believe that I had been away for more than ten years.'[2]

Those years had not been particularly happy ones. At St Aubyn's, his prep school at Rottingdean near Brighton, Thesiger had been unpopular with the other boys. 'I told them stories about the things I'd seen and done,' he said, 'like going on a tiger-shoot, seeing guns firing near Aden, and most of all about the review after the battle of Sagale.'[3] His classmates greeted these tales with derision and branded him a hopeless liar. 'I'd never seen English boys before,' he went on. 'There'd been one Irish boy – Roche – at my mother's home in Ireland – and I've a recollection of some girls in Delhi and there were the daughters of the Consul in Addis Ababa, but no boys of our own age who featured in our lives. Then suddenly we were pitchforked into this crowd of seventy boys – never for a moment on our own – you were either in a dormitory, or on a playing-field or in a classroom, or having meals together and so on . . . We knew none of the conventions that boys do have in behaviour – we'd be constantly saying something [wrong], like I'd call Brian Brian instead of Thesiger Minor – I was probably laughed at for that.'[4]

Thesiger's own recollection is that he arrived at St Aubyn's a naturally responsive, even-tempered boy, but became unsociable and aggressive due to the persecution of his fellows. One day he lost his temper and ended up being dragged off the limp body of a boy called Lucas, whom he had throttled unconscious. 'I fairly soon found myself the odd man out,' Thesiger said, 'and I was called aggressive, and at the same time spurned genuine offers of friendship.'[5] This experience of rejection, he later maintained, gave him a profound mistrust of his contemporaries which was to last into adulthood. In Thesiger's view, the treatment he received from his peers is directly connected with his later lust for remote places and wild people. This is the definitive 'clue to the perverse necessity' that took him from his own land to the deserts, marsh and mountains of the East. Years later he would write in *Arabian Sands*: 'Many who venture into dangerous places have found . . . comradeship among members of their own race; a few find it more easily among people from other lands, the very differences which separate them binding them ever more closely. I found it among the Bedu.'[6] 'To some extent [my attraction to foreign peoples] was a result of my rejection at prep school by some of my contemporaries,' he told the author. 'I think it had some impact. I didn't hate them but I never felt they accepted me. I was the odd man out . . . I'd seen Abyssinia and all the rest of it, though I'd never identified myself with the Abyssinians in any sense.'[7]

There is a touch of the self-styled tragic hero in Thesiger's version, though. How much his peers were actually responsible for the anti-social aspects of his character can only be surmised. At nine his personality must have been fairly well developed, and already included a streak of aggression coupled with a tendency to boastfulness and a need to be 'top dog'. His childhood in Abyssinia had been marked by an unusual degree of freedom and autonomy. It had been an almost paradisal world of games and action in which Thesiger invariably took the leader's role and in which he could do no wrong – he had been pampered and admired. Inevitably, this had helped to develop a self-centred personality. Suddenly, at St Aubyn's, that paradisal life with Thesiger as the centre of the universe was rudely altered. He found his life constrained by the presence of other boys to whose rules and conventions he was systematically forced to conform. The tales of adventure he told in order to raise his standing were thrown back in his face, and his notion of his own importance was severely wounded. He needed to hold on to his self-centred image, since his entire sense of worth and identity was based on it. He interpreted the rejection of his stories by other boys as a personal attack and reacted with a disproportionate intensity of aggressive rage. In contrast there was, as always, the ghostly presence of 'Thesiger Minor' – Brian – who received the same treatment as his elder brother yet who grew up to become an army officer and to lead a relatively ordinary life. That Thesiger's pugnaciously egocentric character was fixed before he moved to St Aubyn's is strongly suggested by the piece his younger brother Dermot wrote about him later in the Oxford University magazine, *Isis*: 'A kindly fortune favoured him with means of practising and ripening his fistic [*sic*] ability. It entrusted him to the care of an Indian ayah, who devotedly assured him that there was no reason why he should do anything other than what he pleased. Further, it produced a self-willed child of six with three brothers smaller than himself, thus mitigating the danger of an embryo boxer being sadly battered in the early stages of his career.'[8] Thesiger was never ascetic: all his life he displayed a craving for company and a hatred of loneliness, to the extent that he disliked spending even a short time alone. He would have seen no value in Francis Chichester's feat of sailing around the world single-handed; Reinholt Messner's solo ascent of Everest would have left him cold. He never had a desire to cross the desert by himself, writing of his first crossing of the Empty Quarter in 1946: 'I knew that if I travelled here alone the weight of this vast solitude would crush me utterly.'[9] He told author Mark Cocker, 'I've always had a kind of entourage,' leading Cocker, like several others, to comment on Thesiger's 'gang-leader' tendencies. 'I think he has always loved that idea of being leader of the gang,' Cocker has said, 'and it was manifest in his relationship with the Bedu, and later with his Samburu in Maralal.'[10] Even as a boy Thesiger was dominant. What he desired from his contemporaries at St Aubyn's was not only acceptance, but acceptance as a leader. It was a need that would later be wholly satisfied in the deserts of Africa and the Middle East.

During their second term at St Aubyn's, in January 1920, Thesigers Major and Minor were called into the study of the headmaster. 'Your mother wants you,' was his peremptory message. Donning their bowler hats – a curious part of the school uniform – the brothers were placed in a cab and sent to their parents' lodgings in Brighton. There, sitting solemnly in the dining-room, their mother told them that Wilfred Gilbert had died. Only forty-eight, he had collapsed from a heart attack while shaving. Though Thesiger never expressed much emotion about his father's death, he must inwardly have been devastated. Here was a fresh assault on the egocentric universe in which his father had been the brightest star. It also altered the course of his life: 'My father was due for a posting to Washington as Minister under the Ambassador,' he said, 'and if he'd done that my life would have been oriented a very different way. I'd have grown up like one of those children whose parents live abroad, like Kipling or somebody.'[11] Mark Cocker has speculated that the effect of his father's early death on Thesiger's future might actually have been far more decisive than his treatment by his peers. 'Many of the great explorers like Philby and Thesiger and others either didn't have fathers or had poor relationships with their fathers,' he has commented, 'and this is a classic aspect of delinquency – using the word in its very broadest terms ... Travel is a kind of delinquency, because it is anti-social, a rejection of the norms that most people live by.'[12] What is the likely effect of his father's early death on the life of a nine-year-old boy? Thesiger's silence on this score seems ominous. He had hero-worshipped his father as a sportsman and a hunter, as the king-pin in the small universe of the British Legation in Abyssinia: the friend and confidant of a Regent ('It's true my father died when I was nine, but all the same he had a very strong influence on me'). Suddenly, inexplicably, his hero was taken away by a remorseless fate. The disillusionment this must surely have engendered was perhaps enough to shatter any belief in a benevolent universe: hence his irreligion, his apparent lack of concern with human life ('I have no belief in the "sanctity" of human life'),[13] his misoneism or, as he termed it, 'traditionalism' – a desperate groping for certainty which in itself, perhaps, conceals a character that is basically insecure. For much of his life he would experience the past as being more real than the present or the future. His life would be ruled largely by institutions, laws, and traditions reflecting what had been rather than what was. Everything new would be worthless, and change an affront to the 'natural order': only the past would be sacred.

There is clearly an anti-authoritarian strain in Thesiger, but it is selective and directed mostly towards his peers: the school prefect, as it were, rather than the headmaster. This strain would evince itself in his declared sympathies for anti-colonial movements, such as the Zulus, the Dervishes and the Druzes, but never mature into open rebellion. Thesiger never could have become an outlaw. He was far too backward-looking ever to have become an iconoclast and was always proud of his place in the establishment. His unruly spirit was tempered by a reverence for figures who symbolized tradition, such as Haile Selassie and the British royal family. This is not to suggest that all the effects of his father's untimely death were necessarily negative; as Winston Churchill wrote, '. . . a boy deprived of a father's care often develops, if he escapes the perils of youth, an independence and vigour of thought which may restore in after life the heavy loss of early days'.[14] It was probably at this point that he began to look to the past – the happiness he had known in Abyssinia during the lifetime of his father – and build in his imagination a romantic, magical, alternative dimension which would never quite match the reality. The loss of his father may explain Thesiger's incurable need to produce romantic models which would inevitably be smashed down by the same pitiless destiny, a need that would evolve into an almost pathological gloom in old age. It might also explain the constant theme of the destruction and decline of a world of child-like innocence which pervades all his writings. For the Thesigers, however, the immediate problem was financial: Wilfred Gilbert had left no large fortune, no house, and no salary. Wisely turning down the offer of a house in London, Kathleen Mary eventually settled the family at a spacious manor in Radnorshire in the Welsh marches, named the Milebrook.

Meanwhile Thesiger and his brother returned to St Aubyn's. It was a cold, bleak winter, with damp sea breezes dragging over the dormitories and the muddy playing-fields. To add to Thesiger's problems, he now discovered that the headmaster, R.C.V. Lang, was a homosexual sadist who derived pleasure from lashing small boys. The Thesigers were favourite victims, and Lang would whip them with a riding crop on the slightest excuse, leaving deep, bloody weals over their backs and buttocks. These savage beatings only ceased three years later, when Thesiger's childhood hero, Arnold Hodson, to whom the brothers had shown their scars, threatened the headmaster with legal action. It was during these damp, depressing winter days that Brian passed on to his brother a book by a writer named John Buchan, entitled *Prester John*. 'I don't know how he got hold of it,' Thesiger commented. 'Brian never read a book, but he had read this and said you must read it. I was absorbed. It made a tremendous impression on me.'[15] Published in 1910, *Prester John* was Buchan's first novel. Ostensibly, its hero is a young Scottish gentleman named David Crawfurd, whose university studies are cut short by the early death of his father, and who is sent to South Africa to work in a remote outpost during the Zulu rebellion. The rebellion is led by the sinister John Laputa, whom Crawfurd has met earlier disguised as a clergyman, and who is, in fact, a direct descendant of the legendary Emperor of Abyssinia, Prester John. Though Crawfurd eventually helps to defeat Laputa, the Zulu chief is evidently a superior character of deep nobility, and it was Laputa whom Thesiger saw as the true hero of the book. 'It was not a period in which blacks were normally made into heroes as opposed to whites,' he said. 'Laputa was the heroic figure to me – take out Crawfurd and it makes no difference: take out Laputa and the story is nothing.'[16]

Since Thesiger considered the book so important in his life, even mentioning it in his autobiography, it is worth dwelling for a moment on the significance of *Prester John*. Laputa, the black hero, is the enemy of white Imperialism, the forces of which Thesiger himself was a product. Certainly, most of his tormentors at St Aubyn's would have chosen Crawfurd, the British gentleman, as the hero of the book. His identification with Laputa at the age of nine seems to express deep contradictions that already lay in his character: the same genus of conflict which appeared later in his enthusiastic support for the Moroccan rebel Abdal Krim, the Druze revolutionary Sultan Pasha, the Dervishes at Omdurman and the Zulus at Isandhlwana. When his partisanship of these 'nationalist' figures was taken by a journalist as indicating that Thesiger had always been anti-establishment, he angrily replied, 'Nonsense – they *were* the establishment!' Like a number of explorers before him, particularly T.E. Lawrence's hero, Wilfrid Scawen Blunt, Thesiger identified the 'unspoiled peoples' of the world with the social order which had produced him – the aristocracy of the British Empire. Just as his own people were becoming social dinosaurs stranded in a flood of modernism led by the parvenu Americans, so the traditional peoples were being eroded and changed by machinations beyond their control. These peoples were part of the same world he himself was born into: a world in which everyone belonged in his 'slot'. Thesiger's requiem for traditional peoples is, in a sense, a requiem for himself. His story is that of the decline of an Empire: the passing of an age. He could never reconcile this desire to identify with the traditional while knowing himself to be a cog in the machine by which that traditional life was ultimately being crushed. Just as he contrasted the 'noble' Laputa against the 'vulgar' Europeans, so he would later contrast the 'crudeness' of the 'Western innovator' with the 'decorum' of the 'uncorrupted African or Arab'.[17] He was unable to extricate himself from the conundrum: he belonged to the dominant Western culture, and no matter how much he might sing the praises of traditional peoples, he was unable to abandon the power, the choice and the privilege that culture offered. He could share their lives over a period of years, even decades, but he could never truly become one of them, for becoming one of them forever would have taken away his choice of migrating from one culture to another and bound him to a far more exacting set of social rules than he had ever been subject to at home.

Thesiger's uncle, Percy, offered to pay for his education at Eton, but first he had to clear the formidable hurdle of the 'Common Entrance' exam. 'We were abominably taught [at St Aubyn's],' he said. 'At least I was. I may have been an unreceptive pupil but when I took the Common Entrance I'd never done any geography or algebra, so both those papers had to be handed in blank. The school wrote to my mother saying it's pointless this boy trying again, so she whipped me away from there and sent me to a crammer's at Chesham. There were ten or fifteen boys and we were given intensive and very good teaching, and after two terms I took the Common Entrance again and passed. I passed not into the bottom form at Eton but the one above it, so it seemed to prove I could be taught.'[18]

In September 1923 Thesiger arrived with his mother at Windsor station and together they rattled up to Eton in a horse-drawn cab. They passed under the towers of Windsor Castle, which would remain for Thesiger a symbol of Britain and his position in life. 'The school lies just the opposite side of the river from the castle,' he said, 'and the castle dominated the scene. In fact, in my last year I had a magnificent view of it from my room.'[19] Founded by Henry VI in 1440–41, Eton had originally been intended as a school for seventy poor scholars and up to twenty others, who lived either in college or in inns and houses outside. Despite its image as the bastion of the rich, Eton scholarships – still seventy in number – are open to any boy between the ages of twelve and fourteen who can pass the stringent entrance exams. By Thesiger's day, though, the number of fee-paying pupils – the 'non-scholars' or 'Oppidans' – had risen to 1,200. 'The scholars lived a separate life from the rest of the school,' Thesiger said. 'It was up to them to work hard and get distinctions. For the rest of us what was important was to get school colours at football or into the cricket eleven.'[20] At Eton College, he and his mother were taken to meet the man who was to be his housemaster, Archie McNeile, an austere, aloof, but intelligent figure. 'He wasn't a man who made friends with the boys like the best of the masters did,' Thesiger said, 'but he did me well.'[21] After tea in McNeile's study he was shown his room, and found the prospect of privacy appealing: 'It was unbelievable to find you had a room of your own, having come from dormitories and schoolrooms in my prep school where you were always in a crowd of other boys. It was quite a small one but it was your own – you had your bed there and your wash stand and an armchair and a fireplace where in the winter evenings you had your fire. It was a sort of privacy and I valued that enormously. You had your own books and I went down with my mother to buy a carpet and some pictures for the walls. In a bookshop were some drawings by Caldwell – the man who did *Jock of the Bushveld* – they were animals, a waterbuck and that sort of thing – they were framed and I put them in my room.'[22]

Thesiger said that he remained distant from his fellows at Eton. 'Lingering suspicions and ingrained wariness of his contemporaries,' author Alexander Maitland has written, 'affected his attitude towards Eton and blighted what otherwise might have been a far more rewarding experience.'[23] In his autobiography Thesiger intimated that he was never popular, though his description of his warmest memories of the school – chattering and arguing with his cronies beside a blazing fire on winter evenings – suggests a cosy gregariousness in the right company. It is clear that he made some very close friendships at Eton, many of which would be long-lasting. Harry Phillimore – later a Lord Justice of Appeal – arrived at McNeile's house on the same day as Thesiger, and the two were to remain friends for much of their lives. Their first days at school were fraught, however, for the place sprawled over a vast area. 'You had to find out which classes you were in, and the classes might be half a mile apart,' Thesiger explained. 'You had to find out which master you were up to, for which lesson and on what particular day. There was "Upper Chapel" – the one Henry VII built – which was going to be an enormous great building, but he was killed before it was finished, and there was "Upper School" and "Lower School" which was in "Lower Chapel", and it was all very confusing to a newly arrived boy with no one to show him round . . .'[24] Eton, like the other major public schools, was designed as a boot-camp for the future leaders of the British Empire. Intellectual achievement counted less than what was referred to as 'character' – a quality that was developed by team-games, shared hardship, and spartan conditions. The houses were cold and damp, and after a frost water would trickle down the walls of the corridors. Food was plain: only one meal a day was provided, and the boy would have to make up the rest from his pocket-money, an exercise good for the character because it taught him the value of money. Washing facilities were of the most basic kind: the water was sometimes cold, and all but the most senior boys were restricted in the number of baths they were allowed. Punishments were savage and involved ritualized birchings or beatings by members of the 'Library' – the house prefects. 'You got beaten for making a noise or any minor mischief,' Thesiger said. 'Anybody in the Library only had to shout "Boy!" at the top of his voice and all the Lower Boys had to come running down to see what he wanted. They formed up outside and when the last one came in he might give him three shillings and tell him to go down town and get him this or that . . . or to get his hat from his room. If you didn't turn up he would ask the others where you were and send them to fetch you. When you got there he'd ask you why you hadn't come when he called. You might say you hadn't heard. Well, then, he'd say, "We'll teach you this evening to listen!" This happened to me frequently, and of course I did hear, I just didn't bother to go down. After supper when you were in your room, the Library fag would come up and tell you you were wanted in the Library. You knew what was going to happen: it'd be six of the best or eight of the best bent over a chair in the Library, and they each gave you two. It was always the Library who beat you – never the housemaster. I didn't resent it, even though I knew, of course, it was going to be unpleasant. By modern standards it would be regarded as far too severe.'[25] The system was intentionally severe and spartan because it had been developed to harden the boy physically and mentally to become part of the Empire's ruling class. The British establishment believed that the great empires of the past had fallen because their ruling élites had become degenerate. The way to prevent this happening in their Empire, they believed – wrongly, as it happened – was to turn out young men who were hard, just, cool in the face of pain or danger, assured of their ability to make decisions, and confident they would be unquestioningly obeyed. Philip Mason has quoted the housemaster, who on hearing that a boy had had two hot baths in a week told him sternly: 'That is the kind of thing that brought down the Roman Empire!'[26] The boys were kept in place by an intricate web of privileges: parting one's hair down the middle, putting one's hands in one's pockets, the right to have a bath at any time, which were first denied then might be earned as the boy progressed up the school. 'You'd automatically be a Lower Boy for a year,' Thesiger explained, 'and some like myself were Lower Boys for two years. When you reached a certain form you were an Upper Boy. The Lower Boys were fags for the Upper Boys.'[27]

The Library or house-prefects were not, as in most other schools, appointed by the masters, but 'elected themselves', choosing a suitable candidate from members of the house. This was paralleled on the grander scale of the school, where the school-prefects, known as 'Pop', were also chosen by the incumbent boys. It is unlikely that Thesiger would have been elected to the Library by his seniors: his delinquent attitude to authority was well known. Once, in his very first year as a Lower Boy, he was walking down the corridor carrying a rolled-up newspaper when the captain of house games walked past him in the opposite direction. Seized by a sudden, suicidal impulse, Thesiger whacked the god-like Upper Boy smartly on the bottom with the newspaper. Unable to believe what had happened, the boy carried on for a moment until it dawned on him that he had actually been assaulted by a despised Lower Boy. His fury knew no bounds: Thesiger accepted the inevitable thrashing stoically. Similarly, his undue aggression may have prevented him from representing the school in team sports. Ironically, though, he later became captain of games in what he called an 'athletically undistinguished house',[28] which gave him an automatic entrée to the Library. 'I never resented fagging,' he said, 'because in turn you were in the Library and had your own fag, who cooked your dinner or tea for you. [As for beating] I think it's a question of discipline, and I mean from what one reads now, in some schools the boys gang up and wait for the teacher to come out and then attack him. And all this because caning is forbidden – if you gave them a good thrashing they wouldn't do it. If you could birch people you'd soon do away with all this hooliganism. Then at Eton, the final punishment – one for which you'd have to do something very severe – would be to get expelled from the school. That would mark you for life. Now in the ordinary state school they are only too pleased if they get expelled.'[29]

In Thesiger's first year at Eton, his self-esteem soared when he and his mother were invited to a private meeting with Ras Tafari, then on an official state visit to Britain. The Regent expressed his sorrow over Wilfred Gilbert's death and told the boy how much he had valued his father's counsel. They spoke in French over tea and cakes, and as they got up to leave, Thesiger, who had seen Ras Tafari in Addis Ababa, but had never spoken to him previously, said: 'My dearest wish, sir, is that one day I should be able to return to your country.' The Regent smiled at him silently for a moment, then replied with unassumed warmth: 'One day you shall come as my guest.'[30]

Set against the background of Thesiger's unpopularity and inadequacy at school, his relationship with Ras Tafari must surely have promoted him into a dimension in which, far from being despised, he felt himself singled out for especial honour. A need for this feeling of uniqueness – a distinction from his peers – is a major theme of Thesiger's life, and recurs continually: he was 'the first English baby born in Abyssinia'; he was 'the only one' who worked on a steamer while at Oxford; he was 'the only one' who got a private invitation to Haile Selassie's coronation; he was 'the only one' who hunted lion systematically in the Sudan; his childhood was 'unique'; he was the 'only one' who travelled in local style in the Sudan: the 'only Englishman' to live on the level of the Africans in Kenya. Variations on the phrase 'which few others had done' crop up with noticeable regularity throughout Thesiger's writings. This is not to say that there is no truth in these assertions, only that their continual repetition indicates Thesiger's need to promote his 'specialness'. Even his pride in being at Eton was not apparent while he was a rather undistinguished Oppidan, but became discernible later when having been there conferred on him some distinction in a wider society. His glowing praise for those instititutions he has been part of and those societies he has lived among is a classic aspect of the egocentric personality. The theme of his uniqueness would eventually find its culmination in his role as 'the last explorer in the tradition of the past': a niche in history that must, by definition, be unique.

The academic tradition in public schools like Eton was anti-scientific, a bias traceable back to the almost legendary headmaster of Rugby, Thomas Arnold, who believed that instruction in the sciences was unsuitable for gentlemen. In the Victorian era, science had been something practised by well-to-do parsons like Darwin, in their spare time. All but the most distinguished scientists were ranked no higher than traders or craftsmen. Nevertheless, by Thesiger's time science was taught at Eton: 'We had a science lesson once a week,' he recalled. 'I have no idea what it was. You had a bunsen burner and you played about with it – you never took it seriously, and I'm none the worse for that. One hears a lot about physics and things, but I haven't a clue what it really means. What advantage would it have been to me if I'd learned physics?' Jeremy Paxman has commented that it was the public school's disregard for science and research, its contempt for industry, its blind respect for authority which was actually accelerating the decline of empire while purporting to be its protector.[31] Thesiger fared little better in a more traditional subject: Latin. 'I hated Latin and saw no good in it,' he commented. 'They say it's good training for the mind, but it didn't train mine.'[32] Indeed, Thesiger himself came very near to sampling the school's ultimate sanction – thus being 'marked for life' – over a brush with his Latin master, C.O. Bevan, in an episode that illustrates well his delinquent attitude to authority. Bevan was a public-school master in the old style – academically distinguished but with no flair for teaching and no sense of humour. Once, in Thesiger's second 'half' at the school, Bevan was dragging the class through an interminably tedious translation when he pounced on the day-dreaming Thesiger and ordered him to continue. As the boy struggled helplessly to find the place, Bevan observed in truculent silence. Already, the previous half, he had had Thesiger birched for idleness and poor marks in Latin. Growing impatient, the master sent him out for another helping. Murderously angry rather than cowed and repentant, Thesiger marched back into class with an armful of pillows, which he impertinently arranged before seating himself – no doubt to the great amusement of his classmates. Bevan promptly expelled him from the class, and only the intervention of his housemaster, McNeile, prevented his expulsion from the school. It must be said that despite Thesiger's advocacy of 'a good thrashing' as a panacea for 'hooliganism' it hardly seems to have been efficacious in his case.

He considered himself 'barely moderate' in his academic work. He got by in French, which he had learned as a child, and could hold his own in history and geography. In all other subjects he judged himself 'below average'. His essays were modelled on the style of John Buchan – his favourite author – although as yet with little success: Bevan commented in one report on his 'unintelligible English'. He considered himself fortunate later not to have been taught English formally. 'By the Grace of God we weren't taught English,' he said. 'We had one lesson a week that was put down as English and the master might read to you, but there were no lessons where we had to know what a preposition was or something like that. One was expected to know English grammar instinctively. If they'd taught us English like they taught us Latin grammar I should never have written anything.'[33]

In history – later to become his subject at Oxford – he was interested in accounts of military campaigns, but loathed rote learning. Once, hearing that the class was to be tested the following day on 'Kings and Queens of Britain', he absented himself. As it happened, the master decided not to hold the test, postponing it until the next week. Fortunately he failed to notice Thesiger's absence. When his lesson came around again, of course, the boy was obliged to play truant a second time. This time he was missed. 'I was sent to the headmaster,' he recalled, 'and he asked me what I was doing. I told him I had been in my room, reading. He asked why I didn't go and I said, "Because I knew I wouldn't pass." "Are you sure you weren't at Ascot?" he asked me. I said, "What's Ascot?" because I knew nothing about racing. He said, "Do you seriously mean to tell me you don't know what Ascot is?" I said, "It's racing or something, isn't it?" Then he laughed and told me to go and apologize to the history master for not having turned up. I thought it was a very civilized way of doing it.'[34] Thesiger's reaction was undoubtedly genuine, though it must be added that it is a detectable trait in Thesiger – perhaps an aspect of his craving for uniqueness – to plead naïveté in things others took for granted. The classic example of this is to be found in his driving. Thesiger acquired a driving licence at the age of eighteen, in an era when licences were less commonplace than they are today, and frequently drove his mother on holiday after the war. He drove a box-car in the Sudan, and a jeep in North Africa, and later, in Kenya, owned at least two cars over a period of thirty years. He must have been a fairly experienced driver, yet he loved to maintain the illusion that he had hardly been near a motor car. Ernest Gellner, who encountered Thesiger in Morocco when he was forty-five, wrote: 'His aversion to modernity went as far as claiming to be unable to drive, and reluctant to soil himself with a modern contraption such as the motor car. We found out later that he made an exception for his mother and did drive *her*.'[35] In 1967 he would tell Johnny Cooper in Yemen, 'Gentlemen do not travel in motor cars.'[36]

Thesiger considered himself only average in team sports, though he excelled at boxing and was selected for the school team while still a Lower Boy. 'They soon found out I had this very heavy punch which used to win me fights,' he said. 'Brian, who was with me at Eton, was a better boxer than me but didn't have my punch. There were no school colours for boxing because it wasn't a school sport. It was one you did almost in your spare time. On the other hand, when we had these boxing competitions almost the whole school would turn up to watch. A number of people I met afterwards, who were my contemporaries at Eton, used to say, "I remember you. You used to box." '[37] Boxing had originally been a lower-class sport, regarded by the nobility as something – rather like cock-fighting – to be watched and bet upon but not taken part in. The fashion for pugilism among the aristocracy was a reaction to the levelling doctrines that were rife after the turn of the nineteenth century. Previously a gentleman had defended his honour by challenging his opponent to duel, but this could not apply to the lower classes, who had no weapons to fight with. Thereafter, many a gentleman learned to use his fists to prove that he did not take shelter behind his rank. Thesiger was taught to box as a very young boy, and as Dermot Thesiger noted in his piece in *Isis*, he had had plenty of practice, using his younger brothers as punch-bags. Thesiger himself traced his initiation in the art back to Arthur Bentinck, a Consul in Abyssinia, who had once turned up at the Legation with a couple of pairs of boxing-gloves and taught Wilfred and Brian to fight. He felt an atavistic pleasure in boxing which perhaps satisfied his deep feeling of aggression, yet he never understood this need. 'I often wondered,' he wrote, 'sitting with the gloves on waiting for the fight before mine to end, why on earth I did it.'[38]

One of his greatest pleasures during his time at Eton was exploring the world of books. He had never lost his obsession with the idea of big-game hunting, and began to build up a library on the subject, collecting anything he could find. He read Selous's book *African Nature Notes and Reminiscences*, which fascinated him, and thereafter, Selous became his beau ideal of the big-game hunter. He soon acquired the rest of Selous's books, followed by the works of Baldwin, Gordon-Cumming and Hope-Newman. He read avidly on the romantic lost causes he felt strongly about – particularly the Zulus, with whom, since they had been destroyed by his own grandfather, he felt a personal sympathy. He also continued to read fiction, especially those writers who reflected his passion for adventure and his view of the world. Among his most contented times were winter evenings when he would sit by a blazing fire with his feet up, engrossed in a story by Buchan, Conrad, Kipling, Rider Haggard, or one of the African big-game hunters: 'There was a civilized comfort about these winter evenings,' he wrote, 'that gained by contrast to the hardships of the daytime.'[39] Thesiger began to live more in the world of his adventure books than in reality, and he had already acquired a resentment of the technologies of transport and communications, sensing that cars and aeroplanes spelled an end to the romantic world of big-game and adventure he thought of as his own. 'When . . . he heard the news that Amy Johnson had flown across the Atlantic, he was furious. "I thought, Oh God damn the bloody woman!"' Alexander Maitland has written. 'And when the Citroën expedition set off to drive across the Sahara, again he felt bitterly resentful at "this intrusion of machines into a world where I didn't want them".'[40] Journalists who met Thesiger in old age often cast him as a tragic figure born down by the weight of his experiences. It was a view at which Thesiger, to some extent, connived. Yet Maitland's statement makes clear the fact that he was already aware of the way his idealized world was being threatened before he had ever experienced it as an adult, and that as a youth he had already formed the 'tragic' framework in which he would set his life's work.

Part of the process of hardening future leaders that went on at Eton was the exclusion of the feminine. It was an all-male society where mothers were spoken of in Latin and sisters not at all. Even to mention a lady's name was considered by some a solecism. As an institution it had inherited some of the prudishness of the Victorian era, when much had been achieved by lonely bachelors in distant outposts, separated for so long from the society of women that they had come to prefer the platonic company of young men or boys. The archetypes of such figures are Gordon and Baden-Powell. As in all such institutions, however, male friendships were formed which, while not overtly homosexual, were more than platonic. Boys would sometimes get into bed and sleep together, but their fondling would fall short of active sex. Older boys would form bonds with younger ones, and offer them protection. All his life Thesiger would be more attracted to men than to women: 'I do prefer men to women physically,' he said. 'In statues and everything, the shape of a man is much more appealing. A woman tends to bulge in the wrong places. I think it's the ancient Greek ideal that the young male is the symbol of human beauty.'[41] He would later admit that he was physically attracted to the string of adolescent youths with whom he was to form close relationships throughout his life, while maintaining that these liaisons were essentially platonic. His brother Dermot wrote of him that, 'as to his normal pleasure, it would appear that women have no part therein' and noted his 'approval of aestheticism as the ultimate goal of mankind'.[42] His attraction to young males throughout his life seems to have been aesthetic rather than sexual: 'I never heard of anyone being sodomized [at Eton],' Thesiger commented, 'which is what homosexuality is. I can conceive of nothing more unpleasant than sodomy. To me it would be absolutely appalling.'[43] Though always denying he was a misogynist, Thesiger would maintain strongly anti-feminist views, which perhaps had their root in his Victorian–Edwardian upbringing. 'I don't dislike women,' he said. 'In fact I have some very close women friends. It's just that I like women in their own place. I don't like the intrusion of women into men's lives, for example, I think it's ridiculous to put women in the fighting units of the army, and the thing about women priests . . .'[44] At other times Thesiger showed his claws more openly: 'In general I think it's a pity you can't have babies in bottles,' he said.[45]

Though Eton does today admit a handful of girls in the sixth form, it still remains essentially an exclusively male society, a situation of which Thesiger would profoundly approve. 'By the Grace of God it hasn't taken girls yet,' he said. 'It's madness to go and mix boys and girls in a school like Eton: it would alter the whole character of the school at once. I knew Eton as it was, and I don't want it to go down, just as women wrecked the colleges at Oxford. I'm not a believer in mixed education, certainly – I wouldn't have wanted to share a passage and bathroom with girls.'[46] However, shortly after leaving Eton, on a fortnight's grouse-shooting at the home of Sir John Maffey, Governor-General of the Sudan, in Scotland, Thesiger found himself violently attracted to one of Sir John's daughters. 'I thought she was very attractive,' he said, 'and I liked being with her, but then

I thought, Good God, no! I must stop this at once or it will wreck the whole of my life!'[47] According to Thesiger, this was the first and last time he felt attracted to a woman. 'There are quite a lot of women whom I have respect for,' he said. 'I like talking to them but I don't want them in bed. I have seen women's faces and thought, "That's a beautiful face," and there have been plenty of women I've liked but never to the extent of wanting to sleep with them. I have no desire to sleep with a woman. Sex has never been of importance to me. It's probably true to say that I have a low sex-drive, and in that I've been very fortunate. My brother Brian certainly wouldn't have managed to do what I've done. All those months – five years in the desert – there was no question of sex and it left me untroubled, just as it did that I couldn't get a drink or a decent meal. It was no more important to me than that.'[48] This asexuality was another vital advantage Thesiger was to have over other, less fortunate, explorers.

In their vacations the Thesiger brothers would return to the Milebrook, where Kathleen Mary provided a stable home environment. Naturally adventurous, she had delighted in the constant riding and trekking in Abyssinia, though after her husband's death she became to Thesiger a symbol of the home. A remarkably tough and resourceful woman, she brought up four assertive sons single-handed on a relatively limited budget. She exerted enormous influence on Thesiger's life. Despite the dreadful loss of her husband she encouraged his ventures in perilous lands, knowing there was always a chance he might never return: she also helped to persuade him to write books about his experiences, and read his manuscripts carefully before publication. Visitors to the Thesiger household in later years remarked on the apparent awe with which the middle-aged Wilfred regarded his mother, and the 'ritual' of paying one's respects to her that was always expected of them. Ernest Gellner, who, with his wife, Susan, dined at the Thesiger flat in Chelsea in the 1950s, remarked that Mrs Astley (as she then was) was 'an impressive imperial *grande dame*': 'I remember we talked about the ascent of Everest,' Gellner recalled, 'and she inquired with a touch of anger why John Hunt had failed to go to the top. She gave the impression that if she had been present, she would have stood no nonsense from Hunt and told him firmly to get right up there to the summit . . .'[49] After the war she was to accompany Wilfred on numerous excursions by motor car, bus and train as far afield as Syria, Turkey, Morocco, and many times to Italy and Portugal. Only a few years before her death, aged ninety-three, they travelled on the Saharan side of the Anti-Atlas in Morocco, and she expressed her readiness to 'sleep outside by the car'. Kathleen Mary was jealously possessive of her sons, and when an impertinent neighbour remarked that she must have been disappointed not to have had a daughter, she rejoined, 'If I had had a girl I should have had her taken away and drowned!'[50] Thesiger rejected any idea that it was his mother's possessiveness that prevented him marrying. 'I'd never have got married,' he said. 'I wasn't prepared to sacrifice my life. I don't think my mother had any effect on that. After all, my brothers all got married. When we were at the Milebrook we were self-sufficient, though. At Eton I did have certain contemporary friends down to stay but there was hardly ever a girl in the house. The last thing I'd have dreamt of was to settle down and have a family and live in England. All I wanted to do was to get off abroad, at that time to Abyssinia. I don't regret not having married. I'd have been appalled.'[51]

The Milebrook stood on the Stanage estate, perched on the slopes of the Teme valley and overlooking the lush green scarp of Stowe Hill, where the Thesigers leased a couple of thousand acres of rough shooting with pheasant, grouse, partridge and woodcock at a nominal rent of £5 a year. The owner of Stanage, Guy Rogers, must have appreciated the family's relatively impoverished circumstances, which, though they did not imply any diminution in status, taught Thesiger to be thrifty, even parsimonious, for the rest of his life. At the Milebrook the Thesigers lived, within their limited means, like country squires. As hardened to the saddle from childhood as Genghis Khan's Mongols, they were already experienced horsemen, and though Wilfred's true penchant was for shooting rather than riding, at fourteen he was coursing foxes with the Teme Valley Hunt. His mother owned a horse, but he and Brian rode a pony whose hard mouth made it almost uncontrollable. After she had finally sold it Wilfred hardly set foot in stirrup again until he began his career in the Sudan, where he quickly saw the advantages of camels. He had inherited an interest in ornithology from his father in Abyssinia, which was to fade in later life, but which as a youth took him on long rambles across the undulating downs, sometimes at the head of a tail of small brethren, sometimes accompanied only by a piebald spaniel for which he had great affection. He would spend long hours stretched out in the heather watching a pair of peregrine falcons gliding around their nest. He thought the sight of a falcon diving, its tail-feathers spread like fingers, a thrilling experience. His fascination with birds of prey would lead him to an interest in Arabian falconry later. He had been raised on airguns and had been handling a .410 shotgun since, as a seven-year-old, he had shot birds with Geoffrey Archer. Not surprisingly, he was a superb shot by the age of eighteen. Patrolling their rough shoot with broken shotguns under their arms in search of pheasant and woodcock, accompanied by a gamekeeper, the boys would carry a flagon of cider which would be gulped down in strict order of precedence. This meant Wilfred first, the gamekeeper second, and the younger brothers having to be content with the dregs. While a pupil at Eton he was invited to shoot at Stanage, which had one of the best shoots and some of the highest-flying pheasants in England. 'They were a syndicate and were very good shots,' Thesiger said, 'but I did find I could hold my own with them. For a boy of my age I was exceptionally good with a shotgun. Then I went off to Abyssinia and used a rifle down in Danakil country and I never hit anything with a shotgun again. I acquired complete confidence with a rifle – I mean, you can't go on hunting lion if you think you're going to miss the damn thing.'[52]

But it was his experience at Eton which did more than anything to stamp Thesiger in the mould of the English gentleman, a mould he would never lose despite all his wanderings and his sojourns with foreign peoples. 'Eton influenced my life because of the standards of behaviour which were expected there,' he said. 'They were very high ones – standards of decency. You weren't expected to lie or to cheat. You were expected to be patriotic and loyal. It was accepted that coming from your family and that school you would be brave if the situation required it. The very fact that in the cloisters were the names of over 1,000 old Etonians who were killed in the First World War – a bigger proportion than any other school – proves that.'[53] The sense of racial and class pride he had acquired from his family was now overlaid with the knowledge that he belonged to the oligarchy of an Empire. What touched the romantic Thesiger most of all about Eton was the sense of continuity: 'You had this feeling that here was a school that had been built in the time of Henry VI,' he said, 'before the American continent was even known to exist. It was a feeling of age, tradition, history – all that. In the Upper School there were wooden walls with thousands of names carved on them of people like Wellington and Pitt and all the famous people who'd been at the school in the past.'[54] In 1929 Thesiger left Eton to go up to Magdalen College, Oxford, taking with him the sense of superiority he had absorbed with his Latin. 'I don't know what it is, but Etonians are different from others,' he said. 'On the whole, while you get conventional Harrovians and Wykehamists, you couldn't say someone was a typical Etonian. On the other hand you'd know at once that he'd been at Eton . . . I think Eton made a profound impression on me and influenced my life: the feeling of history and tradition . . . my pride in being at Eton was associated with a pride in being English.'[55] Thesiger believed that Eton gave him not only a sartorial style – which he would display in old age even when wearing worn-out and travel-stained tweeds, and whose like he would recognize among the Bedouin of Arabia who 'wore their rags with distinction' – but also a particular way of behaviour and thought. His pride in the school was shared by most Etonians, but not all. Contemporary with Thesiger at Eton was a boy whom he instinctively disliked and felt disliked him, and who had evidently not been impressed by the school's standards of decency. The boy's name was Guy Burgess, and he was to become, with Philby and Maclean, one of the three most notorious Communist spies of the century.

It is interesting to note that Thesiger was Burgess's contemporary, for although they were obviously very different, both belonged to the British ruling class and both reacted in an extreme, perhaps 'delinquent' way to the same historical forces. The fact is that, though schoolboys in the late 1920s continued to observe Empire Day, and to believe the Empire would last for at least the rest of their lives, all was not well. The ideals of the British army's officer class lay buried in the mud of Flanders: the myth of the British navy had foundered off the coast of Gallipoli. There was a gap of almost a decade in awareness of what had actually gone on in the filth and squalor of the trenches until, in the 1920s, books such as Remarque's *All Quiet on the Western Front*, and Sassoon's *Memoirs of an Infantry Officer* confronted public consciousness with the true picture of the war's incompetence, arrogance and futility. The poetry of Wilfred Owen interred forever the Victorian assumption of what he called 'the old lie': *Dulce et decorum est pro patria mori*. Many young people felt betrayed by leaders who had grown up in the Edwardian era and who looked back to the past as a golden age of tranquillity and prosperity. Many no longer believed in Buchan's heroes Richard Hannay, Sandy Arbuthnot and David Crawfurd. The English gentleman was still around, but it became fashionable to refer to him with mockery. The tone was set by Evelyn Waugh in his novel *Decline and Fall*, published the year before Thesiger left Eton, 1928. 'There were many demons at large in the 1930s,' Anthony Boyle has written. 'They flourished because the British ruling class had lost some of its self-confidence and, with it, its traditional sureness of touch. Britain had ceased to be the leader of nations; her Empire was beginning to disintegrate.'[56] Worse, many realized that it was the Americans, with their infuriatingly informal ways and their lack of respect for tradition, who had done best out of the war. Though it would take another world war to dismantle the Empire entirely, many realized with resentment that President Woodrow Wilson's policy of 'self-determination' for colonies was the writing on the wall. The anti-Americanism felt among the British ruling class would profoundly affect Thesiger's attitudes later. For now, though, having little interest in current politics, he remained aloof: 'I simply wasn't conscious of any of this,' he said. 'I already disliked America, but I wasn't aware she was taking over as a world power ... The [political turmoils] of the thirties – the hunger marches and general strike and all that – I regarded as being a damned nuisance. My attitude was the conventional attitude of an Englishman of my background.'[57] The Oxford he attended in the 1930s, though still the bastion of ruling-class privilege it had always been, was no less radicalized than Burgess's Cambridge, for it was there, in 1933, that the Union passed a motion which shocked and scandalized the British establishment: 'That this house would under no circumstances fight for king and country.' Thesiger remained disdainful: 'I merely thought it was the kind of thing these people *would* say,' he commented. 'It in no sense influenced my life, I despised it, but I had nothing to do with it. It was a moment of strong political feeling but it made no impression on me. I never set foot in the Union and never would have.'[58]

Though Oxford, like Cambridge, was divided into the rugby-playing, boozing, womanizing 'hearties', and the intellectual 'aesthetes', Thesiger remained aloof from these categories also. His clique was composed almost entirely of his Eton contemporaries who, like him, maintained a regal indifference to party politics: Tories and Socialists might come and go, they believed, but the Empire went on forever. Thesiger was never puritanically teetotal, or even opposed to others drinking. As a young District Officer in the Sudan he had sufficient consideration for the tastes of others to keep whisky for his guests, and on a camel journey in Kenya with Frank Steele in the 1960s was solicitous enough to make provision on the camels for a case of whisky for his companion, and was astonished when Steele turned it down. He detested beer, which he had tasted as a youth on a shooting expedition with his uncle Frederic, when it had been substituted for the sweet cider he was accustomed to. It was part of his conventional side that he would not refuse a sociable glass of wine, vintage port, or sherry at a dinner-party, and at least one visitor to his flat in Chelsea, during his mother's lifetime, noted the family's curious habit of pouring port into the soup. Later in his life he acquired a taste for sticky liqueurs such as Drambuie, though he never drank to excess. At Oxford he objected to drunken rowdiness and people being sick on his floor. He already belonged to the famous Travellers' Club in Pall Mall, and at the age of twenty-one had been its youngest member. At Oxford he became a member of dining clubs such as the Gridiron and Vincent's – the latter a club reserved almost exclusively for blues. 'I was elected to it because I had a boxing blue,' Thesiger said. 'But I didn't even know I'd been elected. I only found out later. Anyway, I don't suppose I went there more than half a dozen times.'[59] He also belonged to the Raleigh Club, a semi-political association for Empire enthusiasts, which engaged interesting and distinguished guest speakers. One of these was Mahatma Gandhi, of whom Thesiger's first impression was poor: 'This little man wandering about in nothing but a shirt!' he said. 'I felt he was a threat to the Empire and I was a supporter of the Empire. I didn't give a damn about politics, but I admired the Empire. It was a tremendous achievement, in contrast with any other – the French, the Dutch, the Belgians, the Italians – give me an instance of something to be ashamed of in the way of repression in the Empire. You've got Amritsar and General Dyer – perhaps 200 people were shot down – but that was the only occasion when an overworked general lost his nerve and ordered his men to open fire. Can you give me any other?'[60] It is highly representative of Thesiger's inherent contradictions that he should declare himself indifferent to politics, while being an almost fanatical supporter of the Empire: and even more so, in view of his sympathies with the Zulus and the Dervishes, that he should have been prejudiced against the Nationalist Gandhi. Probably it was simply a matter of temperament: he worshipped the autocratic, authoritarian, individualistic warrior-hero as a reflection of his own character. The self-deprecating, intellectual Gandhi, with his policy of *ahimsa* or non-violence, did not appeal to Thesiger in the same way. However, in his autobiography he admits that he came away from Gandhi's talk with his prejudices shattered: 'captivated by his personality, amazed by the endearing quality he radiated'.[61] Some of his most treasured memories from this period, however, are of the times he visited John Buchan – still his favourite author – at Elsfield Manor near Oxford. Buchan – Lord Tweedsmuir – was president of the Oxford University Exploration Society, and gave Thesiger encouragement for his early expeditions.

Thesiger spent four years at Oxford and retained happy memories of the place. 'It had a strong influence on me,' he said in old age, 'but it didn't have the same effect as Eton, even though I was more successful there. I was later made an honorary Fellow of Magdalen, which was a rare honour.'[62] In his first long vacation, in summer 1930, Thesiger signed on with a tramp steamer making for Istanbul and the Black Sea. The idea of adventure at sea had perhaps been picked up from reading Conrad, and from his brief spell working with a Breton fisherman in 1929. This was Thesiger's first real taste of adventure, and in many ways it set the pattern he was to continue. He was aware that this was highly unusual, and was proud of it: 'There were a few others who did that sort of thing,' he said, 'but it wasn't typical. Utterly not! Nobody else signed on with a tramp steamer in the long vacation. There was John Buchan's son who went up to visit the Eskimos, and people who were studying classics might go off to Greece. Today, with greater ease of transport, everyone's heading for other countries, but it didn't apply at that time.'[63] The steamer was called the SS *Sorrento* and belonged to the Ellerman-Wilson line.

Thesiger made arrangements through the owners to be taken on as fireman for the nominal pay of one shilling. Although an ordinary crewman, he had a cabin to himself and messed with the ship's officers: he had, he admitted, the best of both worlds. Metaphorically, this was almost exactly the position Thesiger would assume on future journeys in Africa and Arabia. Able to live and work with traditional peoples, doing exactly as they did, he was always ultimately able to return to his privileged position back home: he had the best of both worlds. 'Working on the *Sorrento* was interesting,' Thesiger said, 'because you were getting to see places like Gibraltar and Malta, where there was half the British fleet. The skipper told me I could take the time off to see these places. "But if you're not here we shall leave without you," he told me. In point of fact I spent every night on board and often I would just sit and talk to the seamen.'[64] The steamer put into Piraeus, and for several days Thesiger occupied himself in inspecting the Acropolis. Athens was certainly a tourist destination then, but it was summer and Thesiger found that – apart from a dozing goat-herd and a few sheep – he had the place to himself, giving him the illusion of personal discovery that he would always prize. But if Athens had proved even better than it had promised, Istanbul was a let-down. Wilfred Gilbert had been British Consul at Van in eastern Turkey as a young man, and had fascinated his son with his vivid description of the Turkish capital. But the old Turkish Empire under its Sultan had gone forever in the wake of the First World War, taking with it the ancient pageantry and colour for which Thesiger yearned. For the first time he was affronted by the sight of orientals wearing cast-off Western clothes. As soon as he landed, he was told that his presence was requested at the British Embassy: the Ambassador, Sir George Clerk, had worked under his father. Thesiger, the stickler for sartorial convention, felt embarrassed to present himself to an Ambassador in the clean but worn shirt and flannels he was wearing. There was no choice, however, but to go as he was. At the Embassy, he recounted, he had difficulty getting past an elegantly uniformed doorman, and, after seating himself on a small silken chair in an ornate drawing-room, was confronted by the august person of Sir George, clad in an Ambassador's formal tail-coat. Thesiger muttered his apologies for his poor appearance, but though, when telling the story later, he liked to add, 'I was not asked to stay' – suggesting there had been some awkwardness – he wrote later in his autobiography that in fact there had been none, and that the Ambassador had immediately put him at his ease. Indeed, this was the first of many such meetings with Ambassadors and Consuls whose support he was able to draw on throughout his life. Though never a diplomat himself – Thesiger seems to have lacked the necessary detachment – he was a hereditary member of the British Foreign Office 'mafia', a privilege which would prove of immense importance to his success as an explorer, and a pronounced advantage over less fortunate travellers. In Hagia Sophia he watched Islamic prayers being performed for the first time, and was impressed by the spectacle, yet in general Istanbul remained a disappointment. He journeyed back overland by train, through the great capitals of pre-war Europe: 'Travelling by train is a nice way to travel,' he commented, 'but you don't remember much. There were these great plains which may have been Romania and I stopped in Budapest, which I was very impressed with. Vienna didn't interest me much. I stopped for a few nights in Berlin, which was much as I expected. From there I went to Ostend and straight back to the Milebrook.'[65] It was here that he found waiting for him the invitation to Haile Selassie's coronation – one of the greatest thrills of his life. 'I'd met him four years earlier,' he said, 'and I had mentioned to him that I'd like to return to Abyssinia. What other ruler would remember a fourteen-year-old boy's request to come to his country and send him a personal invitation – the only personal invitation anybody got? In the same post there was a notification that I was to join the royal party. On the strength of that I was away from Oxford

1. Samburu *moran* guarding his cattle near Maralal.

2. Awash Rift Valley – it was here in 1933 that Thesiger made his name as an explorer.

3. A waterbuck in Danakil country – one of Thesiger's abiding memories of his first trip there in 1930.

4. Afar (Danakil) warriors in Danakil country today.

5. Young Afars by Lake Adobad (now Gammarre) – today the lake is almost dry.

6. Landscape of Eastern Chad which Thesiger crossed on his way to Tibesti in 1938.

7. Two boys filling waterskins in the Sudan.

8. Making *asida*, the staple diet of the Western Sudan.

9. Salim bin Kabina in 1991.

10. Salim bin Ghabaisha in 1991.

11. The Empty Quarter, crossed by Thesiger first in 1946.

12. The author's caravan passing through the 'Uruq ash Shiban.

13. Bedu of the Bayt Musann today, whose uncles and fathers met Thesiger in Ramlat al Ghafa in 1946.

14. Wahiba boys practising shooting today, looking much as bin Kabina and bin Ghabaisha did in the 1940s.

for the whole winter term, but I stayed on an extra year to make up and they had no objection to that.'[66]

For ten days Thesiger took part in the coronation ceremonies. On 2 November, Haile Selassie was crowned by the Patriarch of the Coptic Church in a vast canvas pavilion at St George's Cathedral. The rites began in the early morning and from before dawn tribesmen were flocking into the city on foot, pony and mule, dressed in their blindingly white shirts and breeches and carrying swords, daggers and rifles. The crowds slowed down the cars carrying the British delegation and Thesiger watched them gratefully: he was back in his heroic world again, a world of spectacle, pomp and circumstance that stretched back to the time of Solomon and Sheba. He recognized with sadness that this was not only the beginning of Haile Selassie's Imperial reign, but also the end of traditional Abyssinia – the last time its glory would be on display. Already, he noted, it was 'tarnished at the edges', by the presence of motor cars, concrete buildings, hotels and asphalt roads. He saw with distaste that the Emperor's guards now wore khaki uniforms instead of the traditional lions' manes and brilliantly striped shirts, and the Emperor had even introduced a new kind of busby. 'I was hoping to God that he wouldn't have gone all Western,' Thesiger said, 'and I hoped there wouldn't have been any cars. He had invented busbies made out of lionskin, and I thought, well, why didn't they stick to their own traditional clothing?'[67] 'I regretted and resented any changes,' he said on another occasion, 'the cars and everything . . . you can say I've always been a traditionalist. I hate changes. I can't say there have been very many I'm grateful for.'[68] Thesiger rejected all such innovations because they brought him with a jolt back to the real world, shattering the romantic illusion which sustained him. Ras Tafari had planned the coronation partly as a huge publicity stunt: a chance to convince the world that Abyssinia was entering the modern age. What Thesiger wanted to see, however, was not a leader struggling desperately to free the country from barbarous medieval fetters, in which most peasants were the chattels of their emperor lords, but a mythical hero in a land of knights and giants: a country of the mind: he wrote that he ignored what he had no desire to see.[69] It was not the first occasion on which he had retreated into his own heroic landscape: certainly it would not be the last.

The delegations converged on the cathedral at 7 o'clock. The Duke of Gloucester and Lord Airlie in their braided cavalry uniforms were dwarfed by the towering figures of Maffey, Kittermaster, Admiral Fullerton — and indeed Thesiger himself — all well over six feet in height. Evelyn Waugh, himself first cousin of one of the British delegates, Sir Stewart Symes, but attending the coronation as a journalist, watched them assemble. 'The English party ... was undoubtedly the most august ...' he wrote. 'It happened that our delegation was largely composed of men of unusually imposing physique; it was gratifying both to our own national loyalty ... and also to the simpler Abyssinians, who supposed, rightly enough, that this magnificent array was there with the unequivocal purpose of courtesy towards the emperor.'[70] Haile Selassie and his Empress had been meditating all night while the priests chanted and danced ecstatically to the percussion of drums and rattles. Soon they appeared and took up their places on crimson thrones, while a choir sang hymns, and priests recited psalms, prayers and scriptures in the ancient Abyssinian tongue of Ge'ez. Throughout the interminable ceremony, Haile Selassie sat impassive and upright, according to Waugh a 'small, elegant figure, Oriental rather than African, formal, circumspect, inscrutable'.[71] The solemnities continued for hours, according proper gravity to a rite that was supposed to date back to Solomon and Sheba, though Waugh noted that after a while the foreign delegates began to shift uncomfortably in their chairs and to look strained.[72] Thesiger, who later admitted that some of his party had complained about the length of the service, declared that he would not have been uncomfortable had it lasted twice as long. He had a special love of ceremony and ritual — even in later life he would enjoy the ritual of the Catholic Mass despite being agnostic, and when in London would take every opportunity to watch the Trooping the Colour. It was an aspect of his traditionalism: a craving for the unchanging in a world of change, and this was precisely what he had come to see and to be part of. The Emperor was presented with robe, orb, sceptre, ring, and spears, and the singing of the choir reached a crescendo as finally the Patriarch anointed him and placed on his head the cylindrical golden crown with its Coptic cross. A salvo of guns boomed outside the pavilion, and the milling crowds roared back their approval. Shortly, a flight of three aircraft banked and yawed over the tent in deafening salute. Haile Selassie and his wife moved forward under a gold and crimson umbrella to show themselves to the crowd, and the man who had been known in childhood as 'The Shy One' made his first proclamation as King of Kings.

Circling planes do not feature in Thesiger's description of the ceremony, neither do the machine-guns that were mounted on the cathedral steps as a security measure: these were perhaps in that class of things that he wished to ignore. They do appear in Waugh's version, though, and symbolize the intellectual abyss which existed between the two Englishmen. Waugh was the leader of the post-war literary movement challenging the old assumptions of Empire which Thesiger both epitomized and revered. More than this, he represented *in extremis* a different tradition among English travellers, which can be traced back to Alexander Kinglake in the nineteenth century, and which attempted to reconcile prosaic 'English common sense' with the romantic appeal of the East. Thesiger castigated Waugh in his autobiography for having failed to appreciate the historical significance of the coronation and for ridiculing the ceremonies: certainly, Waugh was unable to enter into Thesiger's private world where inconsistencies were simply ignored. Where Thesiger saw the 'last manifestation of Abyssinia's traditional pageantry', Waugh encountered 'something quite new ... a succession of events of startling spectacular character, and a system of life, in a tangle of modernism and barbarity, European, African and American, of definite, individual character'.[73] While Thesiger wrote of the coronation as the 'last time the age-old splendour of Abyssinia was to be on view', admitting at the same time that the splendour was somewhat besmirched by innovations from the West,[74] Waugh found a fascinating Alice-in-Wonderland world of 'galvanized and translated reality, where animals carry watches in their waistcoat pockets, royalty paces the croquet lawn beside the chief executioner, and litigation ends in a flutter of playing-cards'.[75]

Though Thesiger did not meet Waugh at the coronation, he spotted him once at a reception and immediately acquired a dislike for the older man (Waugh was then twenty-seven), whose taste in dress – suede shoes, dicky-bow and wide trousers – did not conform to Thesiger's strictly conventional standards. 'He had collected this sort of entourage about him,' Thesiger recalled. 'He was the sort of man who would. They were standing around him and talking to him and I asked, "Who's that?" and somebody said, "Evelyn Waugh" . . . I thought what an unattractive person he was . . . He had two books out by then: *Vile Bodies* and something else, and he was quite well known as a rising novelist . . . but there is nothing distinguished or noble about his books. They are rather spiteful things, mocking everything, running down the establishment. Well, I belong to the establishment by nature and everything else . . .'[76] Whether Waugh was aware of this rather truculent young undergraduate is not clear: Thesiger is not mentioned in his diaries or letters, and neither is Waugh's desire to accompany him in Danakil country, where he had decided to take his shooting expedition: 'A message came from Chapman-Andrews or one of these people saying that if I was going down to Danakil country, Evelyn Waugh would be very anxious to come,' Thesiger said. 'I sent back a message saying no, and I made a comment in my autobiography saying that I knew if we went down there only one of us would come back – presumably myself.'[77]

Thesiger never forgave Waugh for slighting the British Minister in Addis Ababa, Sir Sidney Barton, and his family. 'He didn't feel he'd been properly treated,' he said, 'because he hadn't been invited to lunch at the Legation and in consequence he was vindictive about the Bartons, whom I liked very much.'[78] A thorough perusal of the material, however, reveals little to justify Thesiger's assertion. True, Waugh mentions that Barton was a Chinese scholar who had spent most of his life in the Far East – implying, perhaps, that his appointment as Minister in Abyssinia was inappropriate – and mocks British organizational shortcomings, but there is no personal attack on the Bartons or any suggestion of pique at not being invited to dinner. The truth is perhaps that Waugh's book *Remote People*, published the following year, presents a view of Abyssinia and its history that is strikingly different from Thesiger's. To Waugh, Haile Selassie was not a figure in the heroic mould, but a man undistinguished either by noble blood or feat of arms, merely one of a clique of Shoan nobles chosen for his ability to continue in the old Abyssinian pastime of playing off the great powers one against the other, and whose prestige outside his own provinces was slight – hence the machine-guns mounted on the cathedral steps. Waugh characterized the coronation itself as a sort of double-bluff through which Haile Selassie planned to show the world that Abyssinia was more than a mere congeries of tribes and petty kingdoms, while at the same time letting the Abyssinians see that the world paid him homage, thus raising his prestige at home. To the romantically inclined Thesiger, who had grown up in Abyssinia and had a personal attachment to Haile Selassie, this view must have been anathema. Many years later, Thesiger was introduced to Waugh at Brooks's Club in London, where he was for a short time a member: 'A friend of mine came over and asked me if I knew Evelyn Waugh,' Thesiger remembered, 'and I said I'd never really met him. He told me he was with Waugh and said why don't you come over for a bit? He asked Waugh what he would have to drink and Waugh said, "My usual." His usual was a mixed half crème de menthe, half brandy. Well again, that's just the sort of affectation he would have had. I suppose I spoke no more than half a dozen words to him and very soon got up and left them.'[79]

Two days after the coronation Thesiger was invited to a private audience with the Emperor, who reaffirmed his debt of gratitude to his young guest's dead father. It was a typical gesture of courtesy on the part of Haile Selassie, who never forgot a friend: years later he would voluntarily become godfather to the son of Orde Wingate, the man who had done most to restore him to his throne, after Wingate was killed in Burma. Thesiger was proud and impressed that His Majesty had singled him out for this honour at a time when the world's eyes were upon him. Thereafter, he became Haile Selassie's advocate for life. Later, he received as gifts from His Majesty a pair of elephant tusks, a gold cigarette-case, a decorated rug and the Star of Ethiopia, Third Class. These excitements did not, however, cause Thesiger to forget the .318 Wrigley-Richards rifle he had brought out from England, nor his intention of hunting big-game. During a moment's lull in the activities, he took the opportunity of speaking to Major Robert Cheeseman, then British Consul in Gondar, in the Abyssinian plateau. Cheeseman was already famous as an Arabian explorer, and the author of a noted book *In Unknown Arabia*. While in Abyssinia, he had made himself an expert on the remote and little-known regions of the Blue Nile. Cheeseman recalled that Thesiger had told him he wanted to 'do some exploring', though Thesiger later said that his interest then had still been mainly in big-game hunting: 'I was talking to Cheeseman, and I said I wanted to do some hunting,' he said, 'and I asked him where the best place would be. He told me that I could start off from Awash Station and trek north to the edge of Danakil country as far as Bilen, where I would find quite a lot of animals ... '[80]' ... I had no intention of exploring then, I just wanted to get down there and hunt. I wanted to get one of everything. I chose the Danakil area because it was the only area near to Addis Ababa where you could find game. The Danakil didn't shoot game and the Abyssinians were afraid to go there because of the Danakil. Everywhere else the game had been shot out. You had to go right the way down to Mega or somewhere, and I simply hadn't got the time.'[81]

There was nothing unconventional in Thesiger's intention to shoot game: almost all the British delegates at the coronation had precisely the same plan. What was unusual was his insistence that he should go it entirely alone. This was not due to unsociability – by now Thesiger could be decidedly gregarious when at home. But here, for the first time, he was entering the mystical landscape of adventure that he would spend the rest of his life pursuing. Intensely romantic, he wanted to be the knight-errant in a King Arthur world of heroes and demons, where a true man relied upon himself and his weapons and accepted responsibility for his band. Here was a chance to experience the timeless dimension of the African bush, the pristine, primeval world he had read about in Powell-Cotton, Gordon-Cumming, Selous, Baldwin and the other hunters he had idolized as a boy. He wanted no one and nothing from his own world with him to remind him of its prosaic existence: 'The last thing I wanted to do was travel with a companion,' Thesiger said. 'I didn't want any European intrusion into [my experience].'[82] When Sir Sidney Barton heard of Thesiger's intention to enter Danakil country alone, he tried to dissuade him. He and Lord Airlie were planning a shooting expedition in another area, and he invited Thesiger to join them. 'He said he'd be much happier if I'd go with them,' Thesiger remembered, 'but I persuaded him that the whole point was that I should go by myself and it should be my own expedition. It would have been pointless doing it otherwise. He said he understood what I meant, but that I should take care not to go beyond Bilen: "It would be a pity if you got yourself cut up just after the coronation," he said. "It would rather spoil the effect of it all!" '[83] Indeed, there was more than Thesiger's neck at stake here, for Barton knew that Danakil country was beyond the effective jurisdiction of the Emperor. Ludovic Nesbitt, who had led an expedition through it only three years earlier, had not even bothered to ask for government permission, knowing it would mean nothing among the wild tribes of the Danakil region. Since – as Barton must have been aware even if Thesiger was not – one major purpose of the coronation was to establish the idea that Abyssinia was not internally divided, the death of the Emperor's young personal guest at the hands of savage nomads would have provided a field-day for a press which, in Evelyn Waugh's words, was 'clamouring for stories of barbaric splendour'.[84]

Bilen, a reed-shrouded hot springs, lay in the Rift Valley, fifty miles north of Awash Station on the Addis Ababa–Jibuti railway, and 2,000 feet below the Abyssinian plateau. It was the only place in the valley where buffalo still existed, and at the turn of the century Powell-Cotton had unsuccessfully stalked them in the reeds there. Thesiger now hoped to improve on his hero's performance. He consulted Dan Sandford, a friend of the Thesiger family, who farmed at Mullu outside Addis Ababa, and who provided him with a Somali called Ali as his head man. At Awash Station, where there existed the famous station 'Buffet', a hotel with a garden exploding with carmine bougainvilleas that still opens almost on to the platform, Thesiger met his string of camels and his squad of Somali camel-men. For a month he hunted in the scrub country to the east of the Awash river, rocky savannah carpeted with grass and layered in places with deep thorn groves, where gazelle, waterbuck and wild boar ranged. He encountered villages belonging to the fierce Danakil or Afar people of the region, who had long possessed a sinister reputation. For centuries they had ravaged the Abyssinian highlands, where the Amhara villagers regarded them with dread. Yet the tribesmen were friendly and Thesiger recalled no sense of apprehension. He experienced a moment of fear only once: when his caravan was challenged by Itu Gallas – who resembled the Afars in all but language – and then it came accompanied by a heady rush of excitement.[85] In 1928 Nesbitt had lost three of his men to Danakil assassins while passing through the country north of Bilen, and prior to this a party of Greeks collecting live zebras for a zoo had been almost wiped out there, resulting in savage punitive measures by the government, which had massacred the entire clan responsible and driven off all their cattle. Yet Thesiger claimed that he had heard of neither Nesbitt nor the Greek party at the time of his trip around Bilen; most probably it would not have deterred him anyway. 'I was doing what I'd always dreamed of,' Thesiger said. 'I was here in a remote part of Africa miles away from anybody, and if anything went wrong I was on my own. Indeed, Barton had said that very thing, and I thought well, that's just what I want.'[86]

It took two days to reach Bilen with the camels. There, about six miles from the Awash river, Thesiger set up the tent and camp furniture he had borrowed from Dan Sandford, and watched hordes of local Afars massing at the pools to bathe and wash their clothes. Like Powell-Cotton he stalked the buffalo through the dense reed-beds, a potentially hazardous occupation, for the buffalo is particularly aggressive and will charge and gore a human being even without provocation. Yet these buffalo were distinctly shy representatives of their race: Thesiger had no more luck with them than his predecessor. He found compensation in the plains around that bristled with game so unaccustomed to being hunted that the noise of a rifle-bolt did not distract it. He shot oryx, greater and lesser kudu, waterbuck and gazelle, carefully selecting his specimens for their heads. The slow exhilaration of tracking down the beasts, the build-up to the ecstatic sensation of the kill, set against this wild, remote backdrop, provided Thesiger with the intensity of sensation he sought. It was adventure: a moment when one seemed to be tapped into a higher plane of existence: to live for an instant in a different, more purposeful dimension from the humdrum world outside. It was this *sensation fort* that Thesiger came to crave like an addict in later years: he wanted to live in a world of adventure: an alternative sphere where the film of history was forever frozen in the frame of the nineteenth century. This month on the edge of Danakil country was decisive: 'If I had not made that trip I suppose I'd have ended up applying for Everest expeditions or something similar,' Thesiger told one interviewer, 'although I'd have been no good as a mountaineer; I get dizzy.'[87]

As the caravan followed the line of the Awash – a ribbon of beef-blood red swilling through a humid cleft in the lava desert below them, its banks forested with a jungle of mimosas, junipers, wild olives and acacias, dripping with green lianas and shadowing the umber stream like giant umbrellas – Thesiger recalled Cheeseman's words: this river never reached the sea: somewhere in the desert between Abyssinia and Jibuti it disappeared, and what happened to it no one had been able to find out. Down there was a mysterious Sultanate called Aussa where there were lakes and forests from which no white man had ever returned: a perilous country where savages ruled. This was Rider Haggard, Buchan and Kipling rolled into one: a challenge even greater than that of facing down dangerous animals. Here was an adventure which would make him truly unique. Thesiger was suddenly overwhelmed with the desire to solve the mystery of the Awash. 'I think one has an inborn desire to explore,' he said. 'Not everybody: my brothers wouldn't in the least have wanted to do it, and they'd had the same upbringing. But there are certain individuals who do want to explore and go into areas where no one else has been.'[88] As his eyes followed the red-brown serpent of the Awash far into the distance, he made his first great resolution: 'I will bloody well go and do it myself,' he said.

CHAPTER 4

One Merely Assumed One Would Be Successful and As It Turned Out One Was

In 1933, Thesiger sat in a clearing in a forest with Muhammad Yayu, the xenophobic Sultan of Aussa. Dappled by rich moonlight, half hidden by the scrub, he could make out the hard bodies of the Sultan's Afar warriors, armed to the teeth with spears, rifles, and the notorious *jile*, the sixteen-inch-long, double-bladed dagger with which they slashed off the scrotums of their victims. The sense of danger here was almost palpable and Thesiger knew that his life hung on a narrow thread. These Afars needed little encouragement to massacre his party: for them, a man's status depended almost entirely on the number of people he had killed. Not for them the rules of chivalry or fair fight: courage was measured by killing in cold blood. Almost unbelievably treacherous, they would cut a man's throat after sharing food with him, shoot an unarmed stranger, or even rip an unborn child from its mother's womb. Records of their kills were displayed proudly: in the brass-bound thongs dangling from their daggers, bracelets, necklaces or split ears. They had wiped out almost every foreign expedition that had come near their country. For Thesiger, the narrow line he walked between survival and bloody death was almost exquisitely thrilling.

The Sultan was a small and finely made man in his thirties, who reminded Thesiger of Haile Selassie. He asked searching questions and between them stroked his beard, regarding the young foreigner with a suspicious silence. His warriors waited soundlessly in the forest, with the bated breath of predators. Which way had the Englishman come? Was he working for the Abyssinian government? Thesiger got the distinct impression that the Sultan already knew the answers to these questions. A glimmer of hope lay in the fact that five years previously Nesbitt, with two

Italian companions, had stood in this spot with this very Sultan, and survived. Yet Nesbitt had been heading north out of the Sultan's territory. Thesiger was heading east through the Sultan's own domain of Aussa, into which, as far as he knew, no European had ever ventured and survived.

After a while Muhammad Yayu called an end to the meeting and ordered Thesiger to return the next morning for an answer. That night, when Thesiger's party of Somali camel-men and Amhara soldiers had retired to the relative safety of their camp, many of them must have lain awake, remembering the Sultan's reputation for cruelty and how his father, the previous Sultan, was rumoured to have had a male and a female slave slaughtered on his deathbed so that their last thrashings of life might give a clue as to how to save him. Yet Thesiger said later that he had few misgivings: 'It was a dramatic meeting,' he recalled, 'in unknown Africa with an autocratic Sultan. Yet I never considered failure. One merely assumed one would be successful and as it turned out one was.'[1]

This journey through Danakil country, achieved when he was only twenty-three, was to make Thesiger's reputation, yet initially he would have preferred to explore in the Abyssinian highlands. 'If there'd been any choice,' he said, 'I'd have gone into the mountains, which were much more Abyssinia to me. But they were all explored, and only this country where the river had never been fully explored offered the challenge of the unknown. Three or four expeditions had been exterminated by the Danakil, and it was a challenge I couldn't resist.'[2] It is among the mountains around Addis Ababa that the Awash rises, curving round in a wide arc along the side of the escarpment until, beneath the still-smoking stump of Fantale crater, it crashes deafeningly down a narrow gorge in a waft of water-vapour. There, hundreds of feet below, the river slows up through jagged shoals and islands between narrow banks of thick-forested jungle, where, even today, silver crocodiles bask shyly on the warm stones, and where the tangled growth of acacias, oleanders and giant tamarisk is vibrant with the calls of saffron-coated bee-catchers and tribes of Colobus monkeys. Beyond the rim of the gorge lies a different landscape: arid scrub merging with riffling acres of golden grass; undulating, unstable volcanic country etched with dry gulches and covered with thorn-brush, and the occasional clump of towering trees. It is a hot, dry land, but it is not a true desert: neither are the Afar or Danakil people who haunt this landscape true desert nomads. They are riverain people, principally cattle-herders, who use camels for moving their ellipsoid booths of palmetto fibre, and who water their stock on the Awash or at wells and waterholes along its sides. Today, an asphalt road traverses Danakil country following almost exactly the route Thesiger took, yet still the people of the Amhara highlands fear to traverse it. In the long stretches between villages drivers wind their windows up and step on the accelerator, speeding past clumps of Afars that cluster round less determined vehicles, still looking lean and dangerous in their white kilts and buttered curls, carrying Kalashnikovs now rather than *fusils gras*, and demanding money with menaces. Still you will see Afars with their ears split, or with thongs dangling from their scabbards as a sign that they have killed and mutilated, and you will hear rumours of recent battles with their ancient enemies the 'Issa Somalis, or the Karayu or Itu Gallas, who also inhabit this country, in which sixteen, twenty or twenty-five men were slaughtered and castrated. Travelling through the scrub with a caravan of donkeys, you are still obliged, as Thesiger was, to take an armed escort of soldiers and forest rangers: all change is for the worse, Thesiger said, but some things hardly change in sixty years. Indeed, looked at from the Buffet at Awash Station – the village from where Thesiger began his first great adventure – the view can have changed very little since his day. Then, it consisted of about thirty thatched huts and a few mud-walled shops belonging to Arab and Indian traders. Today it has acquired a few more shacks, perhaps, but the newer shops and houses are sited along the tarmac road to Assab, largely out of sight, and the station itself is a single fly-blown platform where Somali children sell paper packets of sesame seeds and old men in hennaed beards and chequered loincloths sleep alongside dogs and donkeys, in the dust. On 1 December 1933, Thesiger started off from Awash village with twenty-two camels and thirty-nine men, including Somali cameleers, fifteen government soldiers dressed in khaki uniforms and sun-hats, and an Afar hostage from Awash village to frank them through the territory of his tribe. The expedition very nearly never got under way at all. As Thesiger was marshalling his men and equipment at Awash Station the telephone rang in the tiny hut that still stands opposite the platform. On the end of the line was a nameless government representative who told him bluntly: 'There has been heavy fighting down in Danakil country and I am forbidding the soldiers to go with you.'

'In that case I shall go off without them,' Thesiger replied.

'I forbid you to do that,' came back the voice.

'Do you realize I have the Emperor's personal permission to do this journey?' Thesiger inquired. 'Unless you have authority from higher up, I am going whether you send your men or not.'[3]

At the mention of the Emperor's name the official climbed down, and Thesiger quickly whipped his caravan into shape before heavier guns could be brought into action against him. The packed camels lumbered to their feet spitting and snorting, to be strung into files by the white-clad Somalis. The soldiers cursed, gesticulating as their poorly loaded camels flung off their loads. Finally, after threats and cajoling from the headman, Omar, the great caravan moved out in a trail of dust and flies. Thesiger did not feel at ease until the buildings of Awash village were out of sight behind them.

Three years previously, he had crossed this country on his shooting trip to Bilen, when he had first resolved to trace the course of the Awash to its end. From the hot springs he had returned across the desert scrub to Afdam – a station further down the line from Awash – where he had paid off his caravan and sent his men home. From there he had travelled to Harar, the Islamic holy city first seen by Richard Burton in 1855 after his perilous journey from the Somali coast. Architecturally, the town was a disappointment. It was in a profound state of decay and the clusters of shops, *tej* houses and brothels were interspersed with uninspiring modern buildings such as Government House and the French Hospital. Like other visitors, though, he was stunned by the dazzling colours worn by the women, and their slender, graceful beauty – a feature remarked upon by Burton seventy-five years before. From Harar he returned to Jibuti, where he spent Christmas, and found a passage third class on a French ship carrying Foreign Legion troops back to Europe. At Oxford he was haunted by images of the month he had spent in Danakil country: 'The slow-flowing, muddy river and a crocodile basking on a sandbank,' he wrote, 'a waterbuck stepping out of the tamarisk jungle on its way down to drink; a kudu bull with magnificent, spiral horns silhouetted on a skyline against fast failing light . . . I could feel once more the sun scorching through my shirt; the chill of the early dawn. I could taste the camels' urine in water. I could hear my Somalis singing round the campfire; the roaring of the camels as they were loaded.'[4]

He now had a purpose. For three years this enterprise shone before him like a beacon, and almost every spare minute was devoted to thinking about Danakil country or planning an aspect of his intended journey there. He became a Fellow of the Royal Geographical Society and began to read up all that was known about Danakil. He absorbed Ludovic Nesbitt's three-part paper in the *Geographical Journal*, and discovered that almost all previous expeditions through the region had met with disaster. In 1881, Giulietti and Biglieri had attempted to cross Danakil country north of Aussa to establish a new trade route from the port of Assab to the plateau. The party had been massacred by Afars in the Biru Sultanate. Three years later a squad of fourteen Italian naval ratings led by Gustavo Bianchi had set off from the plateau in the opposite direction, only to be butchered at the well of Tio, a fact established by Nesbitt, who had risked death by erecting a monument to their memory. A third and earlier massacre, which was supposed to have taken place at Lake Assal in French Somaliland, was that of Werner Munzinger, a Swiss in the service of the Khedive of Egypt, who had been heading into the Aussa Sultanate with his wife, children and servants, and a force of Egyptian soldiers armed with cannon. They had been wiped out by the Afars before reaching the frontiers of Aussa. Finally, in the 1920s, there had been the two Greek animal-collectors who were cut down with their party near Bahdu. A third Greek had pretended to be dead and managed to crawl away and raise the alarm. Thesiger learned that although Danakil country belonged nominally to Abyssinia and paid taxes to the Emperor, the Afars were in a constant state of contention with the government for possession of their frontiers, in which sometimes they, and sometimes the government, held sway. Occasionally they had been taught salutary lessons by the Emperor's machine-gun-toting troops, however, and though the rank-and-file tribesmen were bent on killing and looting any human being that moved, the chiefs were wary, knowing the punitive might Haile Selassie could bring down on their heads.

Meanwhile, Thesiger's sense of worth bloomed at Oxford, where he formed a close friendship with Robin Campbell, one of the university's 'blue-eyed boys'. 'He had the looks and the charm of Rupert Brooke,' Thesiger said. 'Everyone was trying to get hold of him and the fact that this most sought-after person actually liked spending time with me brought out my self-confidence. After that I assumed, for the first time really, that people could like me.'[5] Sailing at Port Meadow with Campbell, followed by tea together at the Trout Inn, would be one of Thesiger's dearest memories of Oxford. As his exploits and future plans became well known in the colleges, Thesiger got his first taste of fame: his photograph – in boxing strip – appeared in the weekly magazine *Isis* as 'Isis Idol'. He was made captain of boxing and his team beat Cambridge three years out of four, which raised his standing even further. In his studies, though, he was less successful. He admitted in his autobiography that his conception of history was romantic: closer to the poetry of the tribal bard than to that of Gibbon. Indeed, he was little interested in what is normally termed history at all, seeing the past as a kind of static state existing since time immemorial, which had suddenly been rudely burst by the imprecations of technical man. He was *laudator temporis acti*, looking back to the past as a garden of Eden from which man had been expelled, rather than as a continuum of which the present and future form an integral part. In this his view was not untypical of many British administrators in the Empire, who tended to believe that the traditional peoples they administered had remained unchanged since the beginning of time. A more current view is that even the most primitive-seeming cultures are dynamic and in a gradual state of change and evolution, with or without external influences. The Zulus of whom Thesiger was a lifelong supporter, for example, did not exist as a tribe before the time of Chaka, who personally developed the military techniques which made this small clan rulers of an empire. Thesiger was a born romantic, and in his later life suffered the disillusion of all romantics who discover that the world is not as they imagined it to be.

Yet this was still very far in the future, and at Oxford Thesiger was in the shining summer of his life. To harden his body for the Herculean labour to come, he spent a month in summer 1931 working on a Hull trawler off Iceland, an experience he later judged the hardest ordeal he had ever encountered. By comparison, *Sorrento* had been a pleasure-cruise. This was life at its most raw and unadulterated: working cheek by jowl with hardened, professional fishermen, in threshing, icy seas, gutting haddock, coley and cod, for hour after hour in almost perpetual daylight. No sooner had the great alp of fish been cleaned and laid below decks on ice, than the trawl-net was winched aboard again and hauled in by the panting crew to dislodge yet another pile of flapping, shuddering bodies. On the voyage back to Hull, passing through the Pentland Firth in dense fog, the trawler was almost crushed by a much larger ship. Arriving back in port, Thesiger checked into a resplendent-looking hotel, hoping for an interval of luxury after the exhausting and monotonous work, but to his disappointment found the food there worse than on board. This was perhaps the first and last time he would undergo hardship for its own sake. 'It was an interesting thing to have done,' he said, 'and there was a sense of achievement. It was a challenge, but it wasn't the sort of thing I'd have wanted to do again. Working as a fireman on the *Sorrento* was much more interesting because you got to see all those fascinating places.'[6] In the same year Thesiger's mother, now aged fifty-one, married a widower named Reginald Astley, who owned a villa at Varenna on Lake Como in northern Italy. It was there that Thesiger spent his next long vacation – his last from Oxford – with seven friends, including Robin Campbell and Harry Phillimore. It was an idyllic episode. The young men swam in the warm waters of the lake, sunbathed by the magnolias on the lawn, walked on the forested hills, and enjoyed wine and good food, living for a brief interval like a bevy of Greek gods.

In his last year at Oxford, Thesiger was further heartened by the presence of his uncle Frederic, who had been made Viscount Chelmsford on his retirement as Viceroy of India in 1921.

Chelmsford was a Fellow of All Souls College, and Thesiger had responded to his invitations to dine there partly in the unfulfilled hope that he would meet T.E. Lawrence, himself a Fellow of the college. Thesiger had read *Revolt in the Desert* while he was at school, and already idolized Lawrence. In his last two terms, Chelmsford was given the sinecure post of Warden of All Souls, and Thesiger frequently visited him and Lady Chelmsford, a first cousin of Winston Churchill, at the Warden's Lodge. Wilfred and his brother Brian had spent holidays fishing at their uncle's estate in Northumberland, where they had begun to see through the notorious Chelmsford frigidity, which had so overawed them as a children in India, and to warm to the diffident humour and inherent kindness that lay beneath. It was said of Chelmsford, whose career as Viceroy was adjudged by some an utter failure and by others as simply inconsequential, that he did not lack in human sympathy, but in the ability to communicate that sympathy to others. Chelmsford became something of a surrogate father to Thesiger in his last years, and decided to contribute some money to the cost of his Danakil expedition. He died in the spring of 1933, and Lady Chelmsford insisted on Thesiger receiving the promised sum.

As his final year passed, Thesiger became increasingly absorbed with plans for his Danakil expedition. Sir Sidney Barton, still British Minister in Abyssinia, supported him and obtained permission for the trip from Haile Selassie himself. The Royal Geographical Society sponsored him, and both Magdalen College and the Linnean Society gave him grants. He received an unexpected bonus from Haile Selassie in the form of some gold rings on a chain, brought to England by Crown Prince Asfa Wossen, whom Thesiger met at the Dorchester Hotel in London. He accepted the gift gratefully without remarking on the fact that the precious items were wrapped up crudely in somebody's discarded shirt: he later sold them for the considerable sum of £400. Kathleen Mary, now Mrs Astley, encouraged Thesiger's plans but insisted that he took a companion. 'Somebody said why don't you take Peter Scott,' Thesiger recalled. 'He's an ornithologist and it will help you get money. I wrote to Peter and said could he come and said I was doing this expedition and I didn't get a reply. Eventually I got a letter from his mother saying I understand you've invited my son to go on this Danakil journey with you and I can't begin to consent – it sounds too dangerous – unless I know more about it. Would you come and have tea. So I went along and had tea and told her yes the thing is dangerous, otherwise there wouldn't be much point bothering. She said I can only say I'm not prepared to let my son go with you. Well, I'd have been absolutely furious if Peter Scott had invited me on an expedition and I'd had to show the letter to my mother!'⁷ Eventually Thesiger found a companion in David Haig-Thomas, an amateur ornithologist he had known at Eton, whose father his parents had met while in Addis Ababa. Applying to various companies, he obtained his camping equipment free or at a large discount, and in June 1933 he came down from Oxford with a third class degree in history, and his plans for the Danakil complete.

The two young men arrived in Addis Ababa in September 1933 and were met by Dan Sandford, who had been Sudan representative at the British Legation in the time of Thesiger's father, and was a veteran of the First World War. 'The Sandfords went out to live in Abyssinia in 1921,' Thesiger recalled, 'and they have been there ever since. Some of Dan's children are still there. When I did my first trip to the edge of Danakil in 1930 he was very kind, and then he helped me enormously over the second trip.'⁸ It was Sandford who dissuaded the two young explorers from starting out into Danakil territory right away. 'He said to me that I'd be ill-advised to go down there at the moment because it was riddled with malaria,' Thesiger said. 'He advised me to wait until it had dried up a bit.'⁹ Instead, Sandford suggested a preliminary trip in the Arussi (Arssi) Mountains where they could hunt mountain nyala, a species of antelope endemic to that region, which few Europeans had shot. Since Thesiger remembered his father bringing home a fine nyala trophy from Arussi in his childhood, this was an opportunity he could not let pass. Sandford also lent them Omar, a plump, even-tempered Somali who had worked for him for years, as their headman, and an Amhara called Habta Miriam as cook. On 1 October 1933 they took the train to the small station of Mojjo, where they met up with their string of servants, ponies and two dozen mules for riding and carrying baggage.

For two months Thesiger and Haig-Thomas trekked through the hills and glades of Arussi, crossing the Shebelle river and exploring the Bale mountains on the opposite side. They hunted nyala on Chelalo and Thesiger bagged a record head. They captured a bandit who had clubbed one of their men and made off with his rifle, shot a specimen of the Abyssinian wolf for the Natural History Museum, lost half their mules to some mysterious disease, and were halted temporarily by drunken officials. They descended from the escarpment with the camels they exchanged for mules, enduring seething downpours of tropical rain, clearing and widening the track themselves to allow the animals to pass. After all his years of planning, Thesiger was back in his timeless, heroic country of adventure, travelling among a people who were barely affected by the outside world. Encountering parties of mounted Arussi tribesmen and naked cattle-boys, Thesiger wrote, 'I was impressed by these untamed people ... the Abyssinian imprint was as yet barely discernible, for which I was thankful. I have always resented the imposition of an alien culture, whether European or otherwise, on the indigenous inhabitants.'[10] Once again Thesiger wanted nothing to remind him that beyond this land lay a larger world of tarmac roads, motor cars and aeroplanes, wireless, electricity, schools and hospitals. Despite his claim to have 'rejected' that world, for the rest of his life he would always be happy to return to it at intervals. He merely did not want its intrusion here: 'Once we passed a single telephone line,' he wrote, 'dangling on rickety poles, connecting Addis Ababa to some government post; I remember resenting even this slender evidence of outside interference.'[11] The major problem was that the presence of another Westerner, even such an easy-going one as Haig-Thomas, inevitably became an intrusion into Thesiger's private domain. Thesiger wanted no one from the 'civilized' urban world he had left behind to remind him of it. This was in no sense asceticism, as Frank Steele, one of a handful of Westerners who later travelled with Thesiger, commented: 'Wilfred hates being alone. He loves Western company and is very gregarious. It's just that on his journeys he prefers to be alone with the locals.'[12] There was another element, however. Thesiger was fully aware of the importance of this journey. He wished to establish himself as an explorer, and knew that, if successful, the Danakil trek would make his name. Understandably, he wanted no one to intrude upon this. In later years, after he had become famous and his position unassailable, he would be content to travel occasionally with other Englishmen: Frank Steele, Colin Pennycuick, Gavin Young, John Newbould, and a few others. In these early days, though, to have had a partner would have made his achievement into a team effort. He was actually relieved when Haig-Thomas developed a throat infection and tropical ulcers, and had to return to Addis Ababa for medical treatment. He was back some days later though, apparently cured, but by the time Thesiger had found him at the Buffet at Awash village, the infection had flared up again and he could hardly speak. Haig-Thomas took the next train to the capital, and when, the following day, Thesiger received a telegram reading 'Cannot come', he was content.

On the first day the caravan marched until midnight. Five days later, they reached the onyx-blue lake of Hertale standing beneath stark black volcanic walls. All the way along the river the words *Asa Mara* were on the lips of villagers and travellers. Thesiger knew that *Asa Mara*, or 'red men', was the name given to one of the two great branches of the Afars, the other being *Ada Mara* or 'white men'. The *Asa Mara* were the people of Bahdu and Aussa, the dominant and more ferocious of the two branches. The news was that the Asa Mara were on the warpath. Thesiger's informants told him that he and his men would certainly not get through Bahdu alive. At Hertale they had more dramatic evidence of Asa Mara activity: a village here had been pillaged only two nights previously and several people killed. Thesiger's party was just in time to share the funeral feast. The villagers were uneasy and warned him that another attack might come at any moment. As a precaution he ordered a barricade of provision sacks and camel-saddles constructed around his camp, and doubled the guard at night. 'There was continuous killing going on all round the place,' he recalled, 'but it was getting into Bahdu that presented the biggest problem. It was where Nesbitt had been chased out and had been lucky to get away with his life.'[13]

The following day they loaded up and moved the camels cautiously through the swamp of Mataka, along a track threading between reed-filled marshes and a rocky escarpment. Today, the asphalt road passes along the same line, and at Mataka there is a weekly market of palm-fibre stalls where Afars in chequered kilts and 'Issa Somalis bring in laden camels and trade under armed truce. In Thesiger's day, however, this narrow neck of dry land was notorious for ambushes, and dozens of rock graves were scattered across the escarpment near by as a testimony to the desperate battles that had been fought. Deploying armed soldiers along the ridges above them, Thesiger ordered the caravan through the pass at first light, led by the headman of a local village, who nervously exhorted the men to keep together. An hour later they emerged on to a wide plain where they saw an encampment of Afar huts and pickets of long-horned cattle, sheep and the ponies they used in raiding. Under a wild fig tree on the riverbank an assembly of warriors was gathered.

The warriors carried rifles and *jiles*, and watched them like hawks. When Thesiger and Omar marched up to greet them, they turned their backs on the strangers abruptly. Though not outwardly aggressive, there was an aura of danger about these leopard-like warriors. Here in Bahdu, Nesbitt had lost his first man: shot dead with his own rifle while bathing in the river. Thesiger ordered his camp constructed in the open with a clear field of fire, and as the battlements of sacks, saddles and boxes were thrown up, the Afars began to gather curiously around it, trickling out of the village in ones and twos as the news was passed about. Thesiger watched them coming with involuntary fascination, noting the ostrich-feather plumes that proclaimed a recent kill, the split ears, the bracelets and brass-bound thongs that portrayed a hierarchy based on spilt blood. Soon, the Afars began to murmur that Thesiger's Somali camel-men were 'Issas – their deadly foes – in order to provoke a fight. Someone whispered to Thesiger that he had heard them planning to attack after dark. Deciding to bluff, he had it put about that his rifle case contained a machine-gun – a weapon some Afars had cause to fear after encounters with government troops. Later, the local chiefs brought the party a gift of live sheep: '[This] did not reassure us,' Thesiger wrote, 'since these people are notoriously treacherous.'[14] Though sentries were stood to all night, and his men waited in trepidation, the next day dawned without incident. Thesiger moved the caravan down to a village in the swamps, presided over by an old man, 'a very ancient and autocratic savage', called Afleodham, who evidently had some authority in the region. After much discussion through Thesiger's interpreter, and his headman, Omar, Afleodham agreed to give them safe passage to Aussa. It was almost at that moment that disaster struck. 'All was going well,' Thesiger remembered, 'and then there was a noise outside and this message from the government arrived which had been passed from chief to chief. It wasn't for me, but for the chief of the military escort, saying that the guards were to return at once. If I refused to go with them they were to tell the local people that the government had no further responsibility for me. You obviously couldn't go on under those conditions and I had to go back.'[15] Furiously, he turned round and stumped across the plains to Afdem Station, following almost exactly the route he had pioneered three years earlier. On the way the caravan passed the burned-out shards of a village destroyed by the Asa Mara a few months before, in which sixty-one people had been killed.

In Addis Ababa, Thesiger found Sir Sidney Barton, recently returned from leave. Together they confronted Dr Martin, Governor of Chercher Province, of which the Danakil country nominally formed a part. Martin, an Abyssinian who had been adopted by a British officer and had practised medicine in India, stressed the hazards of the Danakil country and the predatory instincts of the Asa Mara. 'Barton thumped the table, more or less,' Thesiger recalled, 'and said if Martin didn't allow me to go, then he would be responsible for all the expenses I'd incurred – the journey out there, my return, and all the people I'd employed and so on. Martin then said I should take more troops, but I said no I don't want that, that would be a stupid thing to do because as we were we didn't look threatening to anybody, but if he went and gave us another forty soldiers or something, we'd almost certainly be attacked because of [the Afars'] resentment at seeing troops and things in their area.'[16] It took six weeks of discussion before Martin agreed to let Thesiger return, on condition that he signed a letter accepting full responsibility. By 11 February 1934, he was back in Bahdu.

This time his passage had been made easier by the presence of Miriam Muhammad, Sheikh or spiritual leader of Bahdu, who had been under detention at Afdem, and whose release Thesiger had negotiated. He learned that it had been the Sheikh's refusal to guarantee his safety that had led to his men's recall two months previously. The Asa Mara of Bahdu were delighted to see their Sheikh again, and performed a number of ceremonial dances in his honour. One night, though, near the chief's own village of Gewani, the old man walked out of his tent and plummeted off the steep bank into the river. Fortunately the sentries hauled him out before the crocodiles could move in: his disappearance would have been disastrous for Thesiger. The party remained at Gewani for four days. Today, Gewani is mainly noted for its Agip Service Station, stinking of spilled petrol, its forecourt black and greasy with motor-oil. Behind the petrol pumps there is a snack-bar with cracked formica tables and broken window-panes repaired with sticky-tape, where bored Ethiopians sit sipping Sprite and chewing *qat*. There is also a squalid hotel, designed for passengers on the weekly bus from the port of Assab, which halts for the night here. Just before sunset, when the bus grinds to a halt, the passengers, mostly in Western dress, come cascading out, racing through the greasy forecourt to reach the cramped room that serves as a lobby, in fear that the last will be obliged to spend the night outside. In 1934, however, no car had ever penetrated Bahdu. Thesiger was tickled to meet a young chief called Hamdo Ouga, who had just returned from a raid on the 'Issas, having killed and castrated four men. 'He struck me,' Thesiger wrote, 'as the Danakil equivalent of a nice, rather self-conscious Etonian who had just won his school colours for cricket.'[17] The youth was killed in a skirmish only a few days later, much to the regret of Thesiger, who had found him 'a most attractive boy'.[18] This whimsical portrait of the 'Afar boy as Etonian' expresses Thesiger's approval of the Afars, despite the fact that by Etonian standards they would surely have been considered 'caddish' for their readiness to murder unarmed men. 'I was prepared to accept the fact that they would kill a man or boy with as little compunction as I would shoot a buck,' he wrote. 'Their motive would be much the same as that of an English sportsman who visited Africa to shoot a lion, and, like him, they preferred to take their quarry unawares.'[19] Yet this does not square completely with Thesiger's own ideals about lion-shooting, in which, he was later to say, he always gave the lion a 'sporting chance' – and in any case, human beings are not game-animals. Thesiger's real reason for approving the Afars was simply that without them and their bloodthirsty name, his trek through Danakil country would have been no more than a 400-mile jaunt. It was the murderous Afars whose notoriety had both preserved the game here for Thesiger to shoot, and protected the mystery of the Awash's destination for him to solve. Precisely as he had told Mrs Scott: 'The thing is dangerous, otherwise there wouldn't be much point bothering' – without the Afars the spice of adventure would have been missing. When Thesiger was asked if it was true that the reputation of the Afars provided a romantic background for his journey, he answered, 'Yes, it did. [Aussa] was nominally French, and . . . I didn't want to see it taken over, and then District Commissioners going in and getting schools and all the rest of it. I wanted them as they were.'[20] Whatever his motive, Thesiger's tolerance for Afar traditions does appear to lack the ethnocentric arrogance of previous travellers: 'The Afars had no sense of what we would call honour,' he said. 'What they wanted was another trophy, another decoration. None of that worried me. I'm not a missionary and I don't consider it's my duty to go round finding fault with other people's morals and behaviour. If they were living in Chelsea, I would say it was. I do have my preferences but it's not my business to enforce these preferences on other people.'[21] Thesiger was ahead of his time in expressing such sentiments, even if he was not invariably able to live up to them.

Thesiger deliberately sought danger in Danakil country as a true test of his manhood, and he would court danger in one guise or another much of his life. 'Fancy offering any self-respecting person security from the cradle to the grave,' he remarked to Timothy Green. 'In society today most men do not experience enough challenge and hardship . . . How can people work off their frustrations by kicking a ball in a tiny park?'[22] There is no doubt a great deal of truth in this concept, yet it is also true that security is, in one sense, precisely what Thesiger always had: the security of a sound economic base and an unquestioned place in society from which to launch his expeditions. At Oxford he already had a private income that was affluent by the standards of most Englishmen: 'I have never done a day's work in my life,' was his proud boast in old age. Certainly from his late thirties he would never work for a living at all. Sociologists recognize that there is among humans a 'hierarchy of needs', with hunger and thirst at the base, and 'leisure activities' at the top. Those who are struggling to provide food and shelter for their families have no time for exploration: 'Exploration is an advanced intellectual concept,' wrote Byron Farwell, one of Burton's biographers. 'The primitive or half-civilized man may move to new lands for food, protection or trade, but he is always driven there by necessity or greed and rarely troubles to record what he has seen. The true explorer goes only to see and to tell others what he has seen.'[23] There is an obvious paradox here: economically satisfied modern man slakes his restlessness by seeking out the hardships that 'primitive' men suffer as a matter of course. 'The explorer pursues a course of activity that seems, logically, at variance with man's basic strivings for the good life,' Farwell wrote, 'the best obtainable in food, shelter, and all those physical, mental and spiritual comforts that characterize civilised life . . .'[24] People who are living on the edge of starvation are not bored, of course, because they are too busy trying to stay alive. 'Among the Bedu nobody is bored,' Thesiger said, 'not even on the longest journey . . . They are calculating all the time where there is water, where you'll find grazing, how the camels will stand up to a journey . . .'[25] The explorer shares such priorities for a time, yet the distinction between him and the 'primitive' is denoted by Farwell's phrase, 'to tell others what he has seen': he does not endure the hardship and deprivation of the journey forever, but always returns sooner or later to civilization to report his activities.

For nine days the caravan marched north, following the Awash. Miriam Muhammad had elected to remain at Gewani, and this caused a problem with Thesiger's soldiers, who refused to go on without him. Thesiger nipped their mutiny in the bud by threatening to send them back to the railway alone. In the Sheikh's stead he had Ali Wali, his nephew, in whom Thesiger placed much confidence, and a dour chief called Ahamado to whom he took an immediate dislike. He was now passing through entirely unexplored country, for here Nesbitt had been forced to turn

west to the base of the Abyssinian plateau, rejoining the Awash
further on. Though the Afars north of Bahdu generally gave the
expedition a wide berth, a small group of reprobates succeeded in
stealing a pair of camels, one of which was retrieved when the
camel-men blitzed them with bullets. They made ponderous
progress – in short marches followed by long days in camp, when
Thesiger would collect birds in the riverain jungle and shoot
sandgrouse and guinea-fowl to vary the diet. After a detour into
the desert, they regained the Awash at Abakaborso. They pitched
camp under umbrella-like thorn-trees on the bank, near some
fortifications where, four years earlier, the formidable Wagerat
Gallas – more notorious even than the Asa Mara – had established
themselves and sallied forth to harass the countryside around.
Half Muslim, half Christian, the Wagerat were an oddly
heterogeneous people who spoke Amharic and normally lived on
the plateau. Here at Abakaborso they had wiped out a force of
Afar warriors sent against them: 'Of them alone,' Thesiger wrote,
'the Dankalis [Afars] stand in awe.'[26] In the distance, Thesiger
sighted the purple ring of hills called the Magenta Mountains,
beyond which lay the mysterious Sultanate of Aussa, and immediately sent Ali Wali and two other Afars to warn its Sultan,
Muhammad Yayu, of his approach. Meanwhile he shot some
unfamiliar antelopes with oddly inflatable noses, and hoped they
might prove a species unknown to science. Later, however, he
identified them from Lydaker as Speke's gazelle. He went off to
glimpse some rare wild asses at a nearby waterhole and learned
on his return that a party of Afars had been in camp asking
questions. They had been especially intent on knowing whether
Thesiger had a machine-gun with him, and Omar said he believed
they were the Sultan's spies. Ali Wali returned eight days after
setting out, bringing the Sultan's permission to cross the frontiers
of Aussa.

At his next camp, Thesiger was visited by two of the Sultan's
guards bearing the 'Silver Baton of Command'. 'The baton is a
stout bamboo,' Thesiger wrote, 'bound round with engraved
silver bands, and gives the bearer the authority of the Sultan
himself.'[27] It was a safe-conduct pass across the borders of Aussa.
Only Nesbitt, of all the Westerners who had attempted to enter
the region, had been granted this honour previously. The quickest

route into Aussa lay through a pass in the Magenta Mountains, but Thesiger was determined to see the unexplored country along the river as far as Tendaho: 'We passed through a country of overwhelming desolation,' he wrote in *The Times*. 'The black precipices of Magenta fell sheer to the river's edge, while to the westward the unending lava quivered in the heat.'[28] At Tendaho, where today the Afars sit idly outside makeshift huts and vacant shops, chewing *qat* and eyeing passing cars aggressively, the river runs through a deep, narrow cleft filled with the creeping fingers of wait-a-bit thorn. Here, Thesiger's caravan turned east across a sandy desert, inhabited by gangs of red and black ostrich. Soon, the forest of Aussa sprang up out of the emptiness like a wall. At Gallifage they were received by Yayu, the Sultan's Dejazmatch or Vizier, who brought them a present of five oxen and some sheep from the Sultan himself. On 29 March Thesiger reached Gurumudlie after moving his caravan through a deep forest of mimosas, slung with creepers and set in a thick carpet of grasses and succulent clover, on which the camels grazed hungrily. News arrived that the Sultan was on his way with a force of warriors too large to be accommodated in Thesiger's camp. That evening, just before sunset, Thesiger left camp to meet him in a clearing in the forest, with all his men armed and dressed in their best clothes. 'The jungle on either side of the path was alive with men and a constant stream of runners came and went,' Thesiger wrote in *The Times*. 'We arrived in a large clearing, where 400 picked Danakils were formed up around the Sultan. They were dressed in clean white loin cloths and *shammas* [shawls]. They carried rifles and all wore the curved [Danakil] knife. Behind the Sultan were grouped his chosen guard, their rifles in red silk covers. The Sultan was dressed in white and wore a very old silver mounted knife, probably his father's.'[29]

Muhammad Yayu was, according to Thesiger, 'small in stature . . . his bearded face . . . oval and rather dark. His features are sensitive and proud and give a striking impression of breeding and power.'[30] The Sultan dismissed his guard to some distance, leaving only his interpreter, Talahun, beside him. 'The full moonlight lit up the long ranks of squatting [Danakil] and the solitary little group of my men,' Thesiger wrote, 'surrounded on all sides by the thick and silent jungle.'[31] Six years previously the

Sultan had quizzed Nesbitt in detail on the character of aeroplanes and compasses, and asked for descriptions of Khartoum, Istanbul and America. He had inquired if it was true that Nesbitt was 'putting all the country on a piece of paper', to which the canny Englishman had replied that 'all the world was in a few books'.[32] For Thesiger, however, he had no such inquiries. 'He asked questions about who I'd met and where I'd been,' Thesiger recounted, 'and he obviously had a very good intelligence service in Danakil country. His Vizier, Dejazmatch Yayu, whom I'd met a few days earlier, said that the Sultan knew all about me and who I'd seen long before I arrived.'[33]

The following morning Thesiger met him again in the same place. In the stark light of day, the sense of peril and foreboding that had lurked in the forest shadows was dispelled. Muhammad Yayu inquired if he knew about the death of a German called Beitz, slain a few days previously by 'Issas while working on the Abyssinian boundary commission. Thesiger realized that the autocrat might suspect him of being engaged in the same work. Seemingly satisfied with Thesiger's replies, the Sultan asked exactly where the Englishman wanted to go. Thesiger mentioned Lake Abbé or Abhebad, standing between Aussa and French Somaliland, which was the putative end of the Awash. The Sultan countered that he had never heard of such a lake; nor had his advisers, who went off supposedly to make inquiries but returned none the wiser.[34] After an entire morning of discussion, however, Muhammad Yayu finally granted Thesiger the right to traverse Aussa, the first time he had ever given such permission: Thesiger believed he had succeeded in persuading him because he was young and appeared 'innocuous'.

From the hills above, Aussa stands out like a green stain of tangled thorn forest and arid grassland against the pastel-coloured deserts that surround it. In Thesiger's time it was alive with warthog, leopard and hyena. About thirty miles square, it forms an inland delta on the meandering Awash, and is one of only two places in Danakil country – the other being Bahdu – where sorghum cultivation is possible. In the wet season, when the river is in flood, the Aussa people tramp out of the jungles into rock shelters pitched above the waterline, on the stark shelves of the hills. The fields hold the water as the flood subsides, by a system of embankments first introduced by Arab immigrants, and Nesbitt reported that among the Aussa people there were 'distinct signs of order and civilization' which he viewed as foundations on which a 'superstructure of progress' might be laid. He asserted that the Sultanate remained deliberately backward so as not to invite the cupidity of European nations which were already settled in Somaliland and Eritrea, and it was suspicion of their encroachment which made the Sultan so circumspect. Even Thesiger himself remarked that the normal Afar pastime of testicle-hunting was unknown in Aussa, and that there prevailed astonishingly orderly conditions of peace and security. Today, Aussa is once again ruled over by a Sultan, who was for many years in exile during Communist rule. Where Muhammad Yayu's palace stood at Furzi, there now stands the small frontier settlement of Aseita, which, resembling rather a Saharan town than an Ethiopian one, consists of old stone buildings with worm-eaten verandahs, and a whitewashed mosque, clustered around a square rough with desert stones, in which rumbling camels are constantly being loaded and unloaded. Its uneven streets are choked with the movement of long-horned cattle, laden camels and Afars with buttered hair, carrying their Kalashnikovs across their shoulders in time-honoured fashion.

From the green oasis of Aussa, the Awash flows out into a series of shallow lakes: Gammarre (Adobad), Affambo, and some smaller meres, into the great sodium lake of Abbé (Abhebad) on the borders of Jibuti. Though Abbé had been reached by French officers – it was only a few days' march from their post at Dikhil – long before Thesiger's arrival, it had not yet been proved conclusively that the lake was the ultimate destination of the Awash. Thesiger was perhaps the first European to see this chain of lakes, with their hordes of crocodiles and hippos. Today the lakes are almost empty, thanks to the state rice farms built by the former Communist government along the headwaters of the Awash near far-off Addis Ababa. Their beds, now broken into a palette of greens, soft browns and veins of yellow, stand almost dry beneath the weathered bronze of their towering walls, to be grazed upon by flocks of sheep and herds of cattle. The hippopotamuses and crocodiles are gone. Thesiger found the crocodiles

– up to twelve feet long – particularly voracious, and was once caught near the water's edge by a huge specimen that came at him at incredible speed with yawning, fang-lined jaws: he was lucky to escape with his life. He slaughtered crocodiles in vast numbers, simply out of distaste for them, slitting open their stomachs to discover what kind of food they ate. The column marched along Adobad under the charge of Dejazmatch Yayu, the Sultan's Vizier, who nursed the precious silver baton and assured Thesiger continually that this was where the river ended: there was no outlet. Thesiger noted that the lake water was fresh, however, and set out with a handful of men to scour its southern shores. Sure enough, he came across a concealed mouth from which the river debouched. He scrambled up a spur near by and saw the Awash trickling west, a gracefully undulating silver serpent that bisected two small lakes, blazing like mirrors amid the dull ochres and greens of marshland.[35] In camp that night he confronted the Dejazmatch with his observations. This was not the end of the Awash: he intended to move the caravan to the other lakes he had seen. Yayu met Thesiger's assertions with exasperation. He had been convinced that he could palm Lake Adobad off as Lake Abbé, and that the inquisitive foreigner would be satisfied enough to take his camels and Abyssinian soldiers straight across country to Tajura on the coast. He told Thesiger that the Afars of Aussa were getting restless at his presence in their land and suspected their Sultan of selling out. No matter what the Dejazmatch came up with, though, Thesiger remained adamant. He had defied fate by getting this far: he had no intention of giving up now. There was a delay of two days while Yayu dispatched a runner to consult the Sultan at Furzi.

Thesiger filled the anxious hours by collecting more birds, and shooting and skinning a sixteen-foot python. The messenger returned bringing news that the Sultan offered him two choices: either to follow the river to its end, or to set his course directly across the stony desert to Tajura. Yayu and the other Afars tried to persuade him to march to Tajura, saying that the other road would take him through the country of the man-killing Uluetto Afars, and equally truculent 'Issas. Only in Aussa was he relatively safe. Thesiger was alarmed at their description, and inquired if he could not return from the river's end by the way he had come.

Yayu demurred: there was no third choice. Reluctantly, therefore, Thesiger decided that, whatever the risk, he must march to the end of the river, and then to the French fortress at Dikhil, which lay beyond.

The Afars went into a huddle, and came back to inform him that since he insisted on going that way, they would escort him. They admitted at last that the Awash did flow into an evil-smelling bitter lake they called Abhebad. Yayu rode back to brief the Sultan, while Thesiger led his caravan along the serpentine shore of Adobad, meeting up with the Dejazmatch two days later. Yayu had brought yet another gift of five oxen and a dozen skins of milk from the Sultan, and Thesiger was overwhelmed by the hospitality: 'They might be a murderously inclined race,' he wrote, 'but no one could call them inhospitable.'[36] It took a further three days to reach the first of the two small mirror-like lakes he had observed from the spur, dragging the footsore camels over a steep plateau so stony that his men had to clear the boulders away before the animals could be couched and unloaded. From here, much nearer than expected, he made out the isinglass sheen of Lake Abbé, the final resting place of the Awash. 'This was where the Awash ended,' he wrote. 'I had come far and risked much to see this desolate scene.'[37]

In the morning they manoeuvred the caravan down to the first lake, its pellucid lapis-lazuli waters shrouded by spiky *phragmites* reeds and echoing with the calls of many varieties of duck. They rested here for two days, roasting succulent tree-duck which Thesiger shot, and feasting on the oxen given to them by the Sultan. Attracted by the savoury scents of offal, Nubian vultures and demonic-looking marabout storks yawed malevolently around the camp and settled expectantly on the water's edge. Here, Thesiger's party was joined by three chiefs and thirteen Afars sent by the Sultan to escort them to the French post at Dikhil. The Sultan had also sent instructions that Yayu should return to his court and hand the silver baton over to one of the chiefs. Thesiger had warmed to the Dejazmatch despite his dissembling, and was sorry to see him go. He gave him a rifle as a present and assured him once more that he intended no harm to the Sultan or to the Afars of Aussa. The goal of the long and dangerous trek was in sight, but beyond it lay the baking lava-deserts of French Somaliland, which Thesiger was determined to traverse. He now decided to split his party, sending the camels with Omar to rendezvous with him on the shores of Lake Abbé, and taking three of his own men, and some Afars, to follow the Awash to its end. For an entire day they marched with mules across a gloomy landscape of jagged and fractured lava blocks which covered the landscape between the extinct volcanic craters on Jira mountain. The sun stewed them, its heat throbbing back from the volcanic slabs underfoot. Thesiger's rifle barrel became too hot to touch, and the mercury in both his thermometers boiled. After an exhausting march, stumbling around craters and avoiding deep fissures, they finally came down to the river, where they encountered some savage-looking Afars of the Uluetto tribe, armed to the teeth, and sporting killing-ornaments. The Afars were paddling across the river in a makeshift boat of reeds that reminded Thesiger of a dabchick's nest. That night, as they lay apprehensively on the ground, they were tortured by the stings of sandflies and mosquitoes, but the following day they set off determinedly to force a path along the Awash, staggering once more over sharp basalt chunks in a sun so blindingly ferocious that at midday they tried desperately to shelter under some overhanging rocks. Before evening, though, they had alighted triumphantly on the sodium beaches of Lake Abbé, where the river bubbled across mud-flats punctuated by salt-caked reefs and the grotesquely distorted remains of trees. The lake water was so saturated with sodium chloride that it was soapy to the touch. This was where the Awash petered out, in this foul-smelling inland lagoon, where the intense heat vaporized the fluid at a fantastic rate, jettisoning its deposit of salt, among the surreal dorsal-fin aggregations of limestone called *sinter* formations.

The following day Thesiger and his men marched fifteen miles around the edge of the lake, to rejoin Omar and the others, who had set up camp near a freshwater spring. The base-camp had been well chosen. Not only was there fresh water, but there were also a few trees, and rich grazing for the mules and camels. Carmine-coloured flamingos waded in the cheesy water of the lake, trawling among the algae, and there were waterbirds of many species, including Egyptian geese, duck, heron, storks and waders. Thesiger also spotted stunted crocodiles. By day, though, the men were plagued by midges, and at night terrible sand-storms blew up, knocking the tents flat. In the week that Thesiger remained on the lake's periphery, he walked around three sides of it, balked only by the Ouraali Mountains, a stronghold of the 'Issas. It would have been foolish for him to enter 'Issa territory with a small party of Afars, their natural foes. However, he inspected the range from several angles and was convinced there was no possible outlet. He had solved the mystery of the Awash. He investigated some of the thirty-foot *sinter* formations and discovered their fine surface tracery, and was also shown the spot where a European expedition had been massacred by the Afars, presuming it must have been here rather than at Lake Assal, as previously supposed, that Munzinger had met his fate. This provided him with the opportunity to reflect on how fortunate he himself had been. His task now was to reach Dikhil safely. Asseila, the first military outpost of French Somaliland, lay three days' march away, though Thesiger was misled by his Afar guide into the belief that it was nearer.

On striking camp, he made the elementary mistake of neglecting to order the goatskins filled with water. Unfortunately, the first day proved pitilessly hot, and camels and men stumbled thirstily uphill over angular boulders and lava blocks. By nightfall, when they pitched camp, the men's throats were as dry as cardboard. Though the guide swore that they would find water the following morning, Thesiger threatened to return to the lake unless the Afars backed up their words by bringing him a skinful of water before sunrise. The Afars hurried off and returned after a few hours with the promised liquid. The following day the caravan came to a water-pool standing in a grove of thorn-trees, but the water did not prevent two of the camels from collapsing with exhaustion, obliging Thesiger to dispatch them with a bullet apiece.

Moving off in broad moonlight, the caravan straddled another range of crooked hills. Soon a veil of night cloud blotted out the moon, and, groping in darkness, they descended painfully from the escarpment on to the Gobad plain, the richest grazing grounds in French Somaliland. The plain had been squabbled over by the Asa Mara, Ada Mara and their common enemies, the 'Issas, since time immemorial, and had been the scene of many a bloody skirmish. The French government in Jibuti had consequently posted a detachment of Somali soldiers to Asseila, under the command of a French sergeant, a Corsican named Antonioli. Two days after reaching Gobad, Thesiger's caravan limped into Asseila, where he was given a hearty welcome by Antonioli.

There is no military post at Asseila today, only broken-down wooden shacks in dust-laden streets, and clutches of the familiar upturned boat-shaped Afar huts, constructed from lengths of dom-palm fibre. The Afars there are sorry shadows of their grandfathers: pale ghosts, unemployed and undernourished, who squat endlessly on the floors of empty shops surrounded by discarded stalks of *qat* and empty Coca Cola bottles. There is no school here, no hospital: technology for them means a battered Toyota and a fridge for cooling Coke. As you walk around the scattered tents, Afar women hold up the greyish, half-starved bodies of tiny children: 'They have no food!' they wail in fractured Arabic. One might easily be tempted to agree with Thesiger that the Afars of his day were better off despite the incessant killing and maiming, unaffected as they were by the boredom and purposelessness that afflict their pathetic descendants in Asseila. Yet, reduced to this pitiful state because they are victims of a government dominated by their ancient enemies, the 'Issas, what the Afars today desire is not less development, but more.

After a three-day rest, Thesiger moved the caravan to the fort at Dikhil, which now stands at the end of the tarmac road from Jibuti. There was no asphalt in the 1930s, but Dikhil was on the main railway line, along which Thesiger was able to pack off his Abyssinian soldiers together with the Afars who had accompanied him from Bahdu, suitably rewarded. Thesiger himself intended to continue across French Somaliland until he reached the Red Sea at Tajura, and the Commandant at Dikhil, Captain Bernard, managed to obtain permission for his journey, which had previously been refused. He provided Thesiger with a new guard of Somali soldiers and a machine-gun, under the command of his adjutant, another Corsican named Dongradi. Characteristically, Thesiger's first thought at having another European along with him was whether the man would try to take over, but fortunately Dongradi remained aloof, feeding with his men and leaving the decisions to him. The long-expected rains at last broke, slashing down on the steaming lava and filling the corries and waterholes. For five days the camels stumped on across lava-fields which, despite the rains, were almost devoid of vegetation. They climbed the pass through the Aluli valley, along a saddle where sheer 1,000-foot drops gaped on both sides, a few dozen feet apart. The animals were already on their last legs, and the camel-men hunted desperately for grass or stunted bush that would save them from starvation. One by one they began to die, sitting down suddenly, laying their great heads on the hot rock and resisting all attempts to spur them on. Thesiger felt heartbroken. Always attached to animals, he had come to know the character of each camel on the long journey from Afdam, and already they were old friends. The unbridled sun hammered on the caravaneers and soldiers mercilessly, sending them crawling into the sparse protection of overhangs in the hottest hours of the day. Often, a salty, scorching wind blasted their faces with needles of stinging sand. From Aluli, the caravan dropped down into the basin of Lake Assal, set like a turquoise jewel in a snow-white circlet of salt. At more than 500 feet below sea-level, Assal is the lowest point on the African continent and the third lowest point on earth. The Assal depression is a furnace heat-trap, where daytime temperatures soar to 50°C, and where the salt encrustations fracture the light into brilliant rainbow colours, smoking with the quiver of heat-haze. Here in the silent shell of a torpid, dead world, Thesiger's ailing caravan tramped for three more days, the sweating Somalis head-hauling the camels from one shattering escarpment to the next. Four more of the beasts died, dropping dead on the bleak, salty earth. Thesiger was greatly relieved when they unexpectedly encountered an Afar camp and managed to persuade the tribesmen to hire out their camels. The following day the going became suddenly easier, and Thesiger spied in the distance the shimmering aquarium blue of the sea. It was the Gulf of Tajura. The sighting came too late for most of the camels, however. Of the animals Thesiger had brought from Abyssinia, fourteen had died of starvation by the time the remnants of his caravan arrived in Tajura two days later. It was 20 May 1934, and he had started out from Awash Station for the first time six months before.

For three years Thesiger had been planning this journey. It was nine months since he had left England to make it: he was only twenty-three, yet his determination had not wavered. He had done the seemingly impossible, surmounted daunting obstacles: encountered homicidal savages, held council with Sultans and tribal chiefs in an unexplored region, solved one of Africa's last geographical mysteries and had not lost a single man. Inevitably, the end of the journey was an anti-climax. For Thesiger, as for every adventurer, it is the almost superhuman intensity of the adventure that counts, the daily proximity of death that throws life into such spectacularly brilliant form. This is what Thesiger meant when he wrote years later: 'It is not the goal but the way there that matters, and the harder the way there, the more worthwhile the journey.'[38] He was impressed with Tajura, which seemed to be part of the semi-magical world that he had crossed. 'It belonged to that authentic Eastern world of which Conrad wrote,' he recalled, 'a world remote, beautiful, untamed.'[39] This is significant, for it has been remarked that Conrad's fiction, particularly *Heart of Darkness*, takes the reader into a mystical landscape, beyond the humdrum world of men, which provides the proper setting for heroic action which is, for him, the ultimate expression of human experience. It does not detract from Thesiger's achievement to note that on a more 'magical' level of his being, he had already cast himself in the role of adventure-hero. Ineluctably, he saw the Europeans in Tajura as intruders in a sense he had not seen the 'heroic' French soldiers in the wilderness. The Commandant, who talked about refrigerators and waved his arms gracelessly, is contrasted starkly in Thesiger's autobiography with the young, handsome, stately Sultan of Tajura with his quietly-spoken dignity. This was the first time, perhaps, that Thesiger had consciously compared the 'nobility' of the native with the 'vulgarity' of Western man: it was a theme he would take up with much greater emphasis later. Tajura was the gateway to the heroic world, but across the water stood Jibuti; a European 'intrusion', it was an outpost of the real world – squalid, fly-blown, unromantic, uninviting, modern. Thesiger hired an Arab dhow to take him and his men across, and on the boat they shared a kind of 'last supper', dining together on grilled fish, unleavened bread and tea spiced with ginger. Thesiger had never fed with his men previously, and it must have occurred to him then, as perhaps it had before, that dramatic though the experience had been, there had been something missing: his distance from the men spoiled his own heroic-romantic image and only served to remind him that it was to the squalid, modern, unromantic world out there that he must return: '[I had] no feeling of close association with them,' he said. 'The differences were clear cut . . . I was an Englishman in charge of an expedition. But I was glad to eat with my companions when we got on the boat which crossed to Jibuti, we all fed together and I couldn't see any reason why we shouldn't. Prior to that I was a European, and Omar would have been shocked if I'd gone over and joined the camel-men.'[40]

The Frenchman Henri de Monfreid carries much of the blame for Thesiger's awareness of the gap between himself and his men. In Addis Ababa he had bought two of de Monfreid's books, and had read them on the journey. For the rest of his life, his Danakil trek would be inextricably linked with images of de Monfreid, a smuggler and gun-runner, who had rebelled against the conventional norms of expatriate life in Jibuti, where he had originally been employed as a clerk. A gang-leader and romantic in the classic style, he had bought a sambuk, recruited an Afar crew and become a Muslim. When he applied to M.Pascal, Jibuti's Governor, for permission to go to Tajura, his Excellency had inquired, 'Are you not ashamed to have the lowest coolies call you by a native name?'

'Not a bit,' de Monfreid replied. 'What does hurt me is the opinion the said natives hold of Europeans, so I do my best not to be included in their number.'

'So the opinion of these savages interests you more than ours?' Pascal continued . . . 'I don't care for revolutionaries like you . . .'[41]

Poring over these books in the shelter of his tent, Thesiger must have become steadily aware of the contrast between himself and the French adventurer. While he travelled as an 'Englishman in Africa', the Imperial 'Bwana' with his hierarchy of servants, sleeping in a tent while they slept on the ground outside, speaking to them through an interpreter, eating separately, maintaining his distance in order to preserve his standing, de Monfreid had become a Muslim, learned Afar, and sweated side by side with his savage crew. In the league-table of adventure, de Monfreid had gone one better, and Thesiger envied him. Later, he found de Monfreid's sambuk in Jibuti harbour, up for sale, and was 'half-tempted' to buy it and emulate his French hero, pearling and smuggling in the Red Sea. Before leaving Oxford, Thesiger had applied for a post as a colonial officer in the Sudan Political Service. 'If I failed that,' he said, 'my plan was to come back and live as de Monfried did.'⁴² Yet the word 'half-tempted' is apposite, for this can never have been a realistic option for Thesiger. Unlike the 'revolutionary' de Monfreid, who had cast his religion and heritage aside like an old coat, Thesiger's sense of revolt against authority was balanced by a reverence for the British establishment, the major anchor of his life. His romantic notion of living like de Monfreid is more likely an expression of rebellious fantasy of the same order as his support for the Dervishes and the Zulus: one which would not practically affect him. Nevertheless this inner conflict between the conventional and unconventional, which is a feature of Thesiger's life, would later be partly resolved by his sojourns in the marshes and desert, whereby he could share the lives of a traditional people for a time without ever losing caste at home. Incidentally, it is worth noting that the very fact that de Monfreid had returned to France and written best-selling books about his exploits indicates that he too had a foot in both camps.

When Thesiger was summoned for an interview with the Governor, M. Baisac, the next day, however, his rebellious instincts came to the fore and he must have recalled de Monfreid's confrontation with the authorities vividly. Baisac, who castigated him in no uncertain terms for entering French territory with an armed escort, is paid back in Thesiger's account by the epithet 'pompous' – one of his most dismissive adjectives. The following day he accompanied his headman Omar and the Somali camel-men to the railway station, where they caught the train to Addis Ababa. Parting with them only increased his sense of anti-climax. Though he admitted feeling no real friendship for Omar, whom he was never to meet again, he confessed, 'I wouldn't have got anywhere if it hadn't been for him. When the soldiers were called back at Bahdu, he brought the Somalis round, and they volunteered to go on anyway, which needed considerable influence.'[43] Yet it is clear that, crucial though Omar was, the real success of the journey was due to the sheer determination of its driving-spirit: Thesiger himself.

CHAPTER 5

Blacks Ruled by Blues

In the summer of 1934 Thesiger arrived at the Sudan Agency in
Buckingham Gate, armed with a sheaf of references, for an interview with the Sudan Political Service. It was a board interview
with six veteran Governors from various corners of this vast
African country, and it promised to be demanding. The Sudan
administration was an élite organization, rated just below the
Indian Civil Service and above the Colonial Service, and entry
was highly competitive: only four to ten applicants were accepted
each year from an average of about sixty, almost exclusively
Oxbridge graduates. But even at twenty-four, Thesiger's reputation had preceded him: a series of four articles on his Danakil
journey had been published in *The Times* a strategic two weeks
before the interview. Thesiger had arranged their publication
date carefully with Geoffrey Dawson, the editor, knowing that his
interviewers were certain to read them and to be impressed.

Looking across the table at the board, Thesiger recognized at
least one friendly face: this was a man called Campbell whom he
had met and got on well with recently while grouse-shooting at
the home of Sir John Maffey – formerly the Sudan's Governor-
General – in Scotland. As it transpired, the interview was neither
grilling nor in the least unfriendly. 'There was only one of them –
Hall, I think his name was – who gave me the impression of being
pompous,' Thesiger commented. 'He asked me "Why do you
want to join the Sudan Political Service?" and I almost answered,
"Because I want to shoot a lion!" Luckily, I managed to choke
that back. With three or four of them that answer would probably
have got me full marks, but I'm sure Hall would have blackballed
me at once. Anyway, I gave some sort of conventional answer
which seemed to please him.'[1]

Only three-quarters of an hour later, Thesiger strode out of the

interview room feeling buoyant: 'I'd have been a bit surprised if I
hadn't got in,' he said. 'They were interested in your athletic
qualifications – well, I'd had a blue for boxing for four years and
that helped. But I'd just carried out a rather remarkable journey
which I'd pulled off and nobody else had managed to do –
finding the end of the Awash river and surviving for eight months
[*sic*] in Danakil country. I felt pretty confident.'² His buoyant
mood was a little punctured, therefore, when he received a
message asking him to present himself for a second interview the
following day. 'I thought, well, what on earth is this?' he said.
'But when I turned up the next day they said there'd been some
sort of error, and they had selected me anyway.'³ Successful
candidates were normally sent to Oxford for a further year to
study Arabic, administration, and surveying, but since Thesiger
had already had four years there he opted for the shorter course
at the School of Oriental and African Studies at the University of
London: 'The trouble there,' he said, 'and this has been a handi-
cap for me ever since – was that while doing my course in
London, I'd also got to give a talk to the Royal Geographical
Society on my journey in Danakil country. I had to write a
paper, and as the whole thing was almost unmapped I had to get
along there and supervise the mapping. Consequently when I
wasn't in the School I was in the RGS or working on this paper.
I did tend to neglect my Arabic studies, and as a result I've never
had classical Arabic firmly behind me.'⁴

The Colonial Service rated lowest on the career scale because
its officers never knew where they would be sent, and were not
assigned to a single place. Sudan officers, on the other hand, were
generally lifers who dedicated their entire career to just this one
country. Consequently they acquired a sense of territorial loyalty
that balanced the breadth of experience they lacked. However,
Thesiger's personal motivation did not fit in with that of the
average Sudan District Commissioner. His ultimate destination
was not the Sudan at all, but Abyssinia. 'I'd wanted to join the
Sudan Political Service since I was about fourteen,' he said,
'possibly even younger than that, because my ambition was to get
back to Abyssinia. As a child I'd talked to Consuls and officials
on the frontiers who had come up to see my father in Addis
Ababa and I'd heard a good deal from them about what was

going on – armed raids and lion-hunts – from people like Arnold Hodson, who had done a lot of lion-hunting. I thought this was the life for me, and the best way to do it would be to join the Sudan Political Service and then get transferred to a post in Abyssinia.'[5]

The Sudan had been reconquered by British and Egyptian forces in 1898 at the battle of Omdurman, when 10,000 Dervishes had been cut down by British Maxim guns and Lee-Metford breech-loading rifles. In theory, at least, it was governed as a 'condominium', and both Egyptian and British flags flew over government offices. Originally most DCs had had an Egyptian aide or *mamur*, but in 1924 the Egyptian army had mutinied and by 1935 administrative officers tended to employ educated Sudanese as their assistants. It was Herbert Kitchener – commander of British forces at Omdurman – who had opened the Sudan's first modern educational facility, Gordon College, later to become the University of Khartoum, to train Sudanese up to play a role in government. By the 1930s, British DCs were being instructed that their objective was to prepare the Sudanese for independence: a process that might reach fulfilment in the distant future. 'I don't think we thought enough about teaching the Sudanese to follow us,' said Reginald Dingwall, one of Thesiger's contemporaries in the Sudan, 'but in the end we only had about two years to decide that it was going to be in our lifetime. We were still looking at 1990 or even 2000.'[6]

Founded by Lord Cromer – British Agent in Egypt – who resolved to recruit 'active young men endowed with good health, high character, and fair abilities . . . the flower of . . . our schools and colleges',[7] the Sudan Political Service developed an ethos derived from that of the public schools. In the inter-war years almost two-thirds of its officers had attended Oxford or Cambridge, and the prevailing witticism was that the Sudan was 'a country of blacks ruled by blues'. In fact, the Service's reputation for athleticism was exaggerated: less than one quarter of its officers recruited between 1918 and 1939 were 'blues'. 'What they were looking for was a good all-rounder,' Reggie Dingwall declared. 'One certainly didn't have to be a "blue".'[8] A redeeming feature of the Service, in Thesiger's eyes, was that, like the Library at Eton, it was totally 'self-selecting': 'We always thought that the Sudan Political Service was the best Service,' he said, 'and I think one of the reasons for this was due to the way it selected its candidates. Unlike the Colonial Service you didn't have to pass an examination to get in.'[9]

If Thesiger had been sanguine about his interview for the Sudan Political Service, though, he was much more daunted by the idea of addressing the Royal Geographical Society: 'That was a frightening experience,' he admitted. 'I mean now the RGS isn't anything like what it used to be. In those days you put on a white tie and the President and Director wore a white tie and there were three or four of us wearing white ties and tail-coats and everybody else wore evening dress. Before the lecture you were guest of honour at a dinner, and I sat next to Sir Percy Cox, the President, who had a reputation that he could be silent in twelve languages. He was a great Arabist and a very interesting man, but it was awe-inspiring for someone like myself, who was frightened enough anyway, to be sitting next to him. He asked me half a dozen questions about what my father had done in Abyssinia and then lapsed into silence. I ate a whole plate of mushrooms without even realizing it and the last two times I'd eaten mushrooms, I'd been violently sick. I thought "Now I shall be sick in the middle of the lecture." It was alarming, but it went all right. I wasn't sick, and afterwards the President was very complimentary.'[10] Indeed, at the conclusion of the evening, Sir Percy stood up in his tail-coat and said to the audience, 'I think you must have realized, in spite of the modest way in which Mr Thesiger has recounted his travels, what a very great accomplishment it has been, without a companion and travelling under the most difficult conditions. It is, to my mind, a splendid piece of determined exploration . . . I will ask you to express your appreciation of a fine piece of work, and your good wishes to Mr Thesiger for his future in the Sudan. I am sure we shall hear more of him as an explorer.'[11]

Thesiger landed in Alexandria in December 1934, and experienced the usual exasperating queues at the Egyptian Customs house, where corrupt officials painstakingly examined the baggage of anyone unwise enough not to offer a bribe. He was in Cairo for Christmas and found sanctuary from the frenzy of the streets with John Hamilton, the Sudan Agent in Egypt, who had a sumptuous flat on the island of Zamalek. Hamilton saw to it that his young guest made a thorough tour of the city's sights: the Pyramids, the Tutankhamun exhibition at the National Museum, the mosques, and Muhammad Ali Pasha's Citadel, patrolled by British guardsmen whose officers Thesiger had known at Eton. A week later he found himself in the chaos of the railway station, heading south to Luxor and fighting off the hordes of porters who bellowed in coarse Arabic as they jostled each other for his suitcases. As the train pulled out of the great city, he sank back into his seat and stared with fascination at the mud-brick villages perched on the water's edge under the shade of palm-groves, at women in luminous flowing dresses of orange, scarlet and yellow washing the family's clothes in the Nile, at men watering camels and cattle and scrubbing indolent water-buffaloes, shinning up palm trees with curved cropping-knives, ploughing rich fields with oxen, or pulling the ploughs themselves as they had done for millennia.

He holed up for a few days in Luxor, already for many years the fashionable watering-place of the European rich, and, like millions of tourists since, was stunned by the scale of the temple at Karnak, whose massive columns seemed to have been built by giants and abandoned due to some great catastrophe. At Shellal, the river port south of Aswan, he embarked on a Nile steamer bound for the Sudan. Even today such ships ply the waters between Aswan and Wadi Halfa, but the few cabins are humid and fly-blown, the food squalid, and the majority of passengers sleep like sardines on the sweltering decks. In Thesiger's time, however, accommodation on the steamer was a byword in luxury: spacious, light, airy cabins with comfortable beds and running water, opening on to a cool covered deck across which streamed the evening breeze. The banks of the Nile slipped by: mile upon mile of sterile sand, broken by the feathery crests of palms which shadowed box-like mud houses, the homes of black Nubians with their goats and donkeys. It was a historic journey which can no longer be fully experienced by travellers to the Sudan: just twenty years later, in 1955, the Russians completed work on the High Dam at Aswan which caused the whole of Egyptian Nubia to be flooded under Lake Nasser. The monumental temple of Abu

Simbel with its colossal statues of Rameses II, where Thesiger's steamer tied up for the night, was one of the few relics of the past rescued from the flood, being moved stone by stone higher up the banks to the place it occupies today.

After two days on the boat Thesiger alighted at the Sudanese port of Wadi Halfa, a neat, white-walled town of hotels and mosques, now drowned under the deep waters of the lake. There he boarded a train for Khartoum. Soon, all traces of vegetation fell away and Thesiger found himself in the bleak, timeless plains of the Nubian desert, where the setting sun transformed the rippling dunes into a moonscape of pastel pink and apricot – a kaleidoscope of primeval stillness and beauty. Despite his lifelong sympathy with the Dervishes, it thrilled him to recall that this railway had originally been built by Kitchener's engineers to advance his Anglo-Egyptian army to Abu Hamid on the Nile bend, from where it had marched out and smashed the Dervish forces on the river Atbara, ultimately shattering the Mahdi's rebellion at Omdurman. The journey was punctuated only by stops at numbered watering-stations – clusters of huts with conical roofs – where the passengers were able to climb out and stretch their legs in the desert.

After the long and interesting journey, Thesiger found Khartoum a disappointment. Built on the confluence of the Blue and White Niles, it had been razed to the ground by the Dervishes in 1885. After the battle of Omdurman Kitchener had reconstructed it on the pattern of a series of interlocking Union Jacks, each one with a gun-post at the centre for defence. The Union Jack pattern had long since been obscured by indiscriminate building, but still Khartoum had the characterless air of a pioneer town: a shoddy African approximation of British suburbia, complete with traffic-lights, spruce villas and public lavatories. There were some impressive buildings along the waterfront: the Governor-General's palace, the Secretariat, the Grand Hotel and, set back slightly, the Anglican Cathedral – all of which still stand today – but in general the modernity of the capital compared unfavourably with Thesiger's experiences in Addis Ababa in 1930 and earlier memories of the chaotic bazaars of India. More than the ambience of the place, though, Thesiger abhorred the pedantic protocol which required every visiting officer to sign the visitors' book at the palace, drop cards in the boxes of the three senior Secretaries, and call on the Commander-in-Chief. Though such rituals were designed to enable any newcomer to be introduced into society, Thesiger was by no means the first adventure-seeker to be appalled at this 'little England' in wildest Africa. 'Before the war,' Rosemary Kenrick has written, 'less gregarious types would not be pleased to be confronted with the social rules and conventions from which they had just escaped at home.'[12]

Yet Thesiger need not have felt 'cheated', as he put it, for Khartoum was an anomaly: a pinprick of civilization on the vast empty canvas of a million square miles of savage wilderness where life had changed but little for millennia. Perhaps the most fascinating country in Africa, the Sudan's vastness and diversity of cultures qualify it almost for the status of a miniature continent. It encompasses a complete cross-section of Africa's landscapes, from the ultimate sterile desert in the north, grading down through desert scrub and savannah of every describable degree, to tropical forest on its southern borders. There are the fertile lands of the Nile valley, the placid beaches and arid mountains of the Red Sea Coast, the volcanic Marra range in the west, and isolated fastnesses like the enclave of the Nuba Mountains in the middle. It is home for hundreds of different tribes, speaking more than 100 different languages: in the north there are Arab Bedouin herding camels, goats and sheep as far as the Libyan borders: in the southern grasslands and forests stalk naked cattle-herding Nilotic tribesmen like the Dinka and Nuer, standing tall and thin as thorn-trees. In the east roam the wild Beja nomads of the Red Sea Hills, who rear the best camels in Africa and wear their hair in uncut plumes as a sign of manhood, and in the west the shy, hill-farming Fur and Tunjur, the black Saharan camel-men known as Zaghawa and Bedayat, and the Africanized Arab tribes which have been called 'the frontier tribes of Arabdom' – the ferocious cattle- and horse-riding Baggara nomads who formed the backbone of the Dervish army. In the 1930s, the country teemed with every kind of game: elephant, lion, buffalo, leopard, and any number of gazelles, antelopes, small mammals and birds.

The day after his arrival, Thesiger met Sir Angus Gillan, the

Civil Secretary, Number Two in the hierarchy under the Governor-General, Sir Stewart Symes, but the *de facto* power in the land. Thesiger had not met Gillan previously, but had once been invited to the theatre in London by John Hamilton, and afterwards to a nightclub, where he had danced, somewhat reluctantly, with Lady Gillan. Thesiger had found her at first 'formidable' but later 'unexpectedly easy to talk to'.[13] He found Gillan equally amiable: 'He was a very friendly man,' Thesiger recalled. 'He had been a rowing blue and he looked every inch a famous oar.'[14] He had good reason to remember Gillan's helpfulness, for he walked out of the Secretary's office beaming with the knowledge that he, an untried Probationer, had been posted to Kutum in Darfur Province, one of the three most coveted Districts in the Sudan. How Thesiger had managed to wangle such a privileged posting had much to do, in his own account, with his social connections. While at home at the Milebrook with his mother, he had been invited to lunch by some friends to meet Charles Dupuis,[15] Governor of Darfur. Dupuis had been impressed by Thesiger's trek through Aussa, and the two had talked for hours. 'When [Dupuis] went back to the Sudan, he asked the [government] where I was going to be posted,' Thesiger commented. 'They said it would be Wad Medani, a big city, where they would break me in to conventional administration. Dupuis said, "I know what's going to happen if you do that: he'll leave. You'd much better let me have him in Darfur and I make sure he sees the appeal of the Sudan. Then at a later date you can put him in a town to get the administration side. But if you do it at once you'll just lose him." '[16] In Kutum, Thesiger would be the Assistant District Commissioner under the almost legendary Guy Moore, still referred to today in Sudanese poetry and folklore as 'the Sultan'.

Thesiger's appointment was not greeted favourably in every quarter, particularly with the young Reginald Dingwall, who was then incumbent ADC in Kutum and who was to be moved out much against his will to make way for Thesiger. Dingwall had been in Kutum only two years and was just beginning to settle in there: 'I was pushed out to make way for him,' Dingwall said, 'and I was really pretty angry about it.' He remained convinced that Thesiger owed his posting to someone other than Dupuis. 'I don't know what strings Thesiger was able to pull in Khartoum,' Dingwall said, 'but it was certainly not with Charles Dupuis, because when I objected to being moved I was told off the record that Dupuis had opposed his being sent to Kutum. As Governor it was Dupuis's prerogative to allocate Districts and he had been overruled by someone in the Civil Secretary's office. Of course, Thesiger had a reputation already, and in a sense they were right to do it, but they shouldn't have broken the custom that the Governor sent people where he liked.'[17]

In Khartoum Thesiger's colleagues goaded him with mock commiseration on being posted into the domain of the notorious Moore: 'They said you'll have an extraordinary life,' he remembered, 'always on the move with camels, not cars, and you'll never know when you're going to get a meal. I thought, well, this is the man I want to be with.'[18] After purchasing his immediate requirements at the glass-fronted shops in Khartoum, Thesiger lingered only a few days in the capital before taking train to El Obeid in the sprawling Sahel country of Kordofan. From there he bounced about in the cab of a lorry for three tedious days as far as El Fasher, capital of Darfur. In this part of Africa, time has virtually stood still since Thesiger's day: though lorries are more numerous now, there is still no proper road across the sea of sand-hills that guards Darfur's eastern borders, and drivers pick their own way across the emptiness, frequently becoming bogged down in the soft sand. To the outsider it seems a world that exists in a different dimension from the bustle of Khartoum. These sand-hills, known collectively as *goz*, are almost certainly relics of an ancient sand-sea remaining from a time when the Sahara desert extended further south than it does today. Dotted with grass-hut villages that blend in harmoniously with the colour and texture of their setting, the works of man seem dwarfed here by the sheer size and power of the land. The low dunes are stabilized by rich veins of thorn-bush and golden-yellow swaths of waving grass. The scrub is dominated in places by the unearthly columns of the baobab – the strangest tree in Africa – which, pollinated nocturnally by bats, produces a fruit valuable as medicine, and whose hollowed-out trunk is used by the local bush people as a water-tank. But, cut off from the landscape by the confining body of a motor vehicle and subjected to the ignominy of its lurching, buffeting progress, Thesiger felt himself out of kilter with his surroundings and took little interest in them. He was very glad when the lorry arrived in El Fasher.

Signifying 'the Palace' in the local dialect of Arabic, El Fasher had been founded upon the banks of a small seasonal lake which in the rainy season still expands up to the rambling grass and timber alleys of the town market. The lake, known simply as the *fula* or 'pool', is encircled by groves of fully grown acacia trees that in fat times echo with the screeching of water-birds. El Fasher had for some time been the capital of the Keira Sultans of Darfur, whose ascendancy was founded on trade along the legendary 'Forty Days Road' – the 1,000-mile caravan route which traversed the formidable eastern Sahara and reached the Nile at Asyut in Middle Egypt. In its heyday, wealth had flowed out of Darfur in the form of slaves, gold, ivory, ostrich-feathers and animal furs, and back again in the form of firearms, cloth and manufactured goods. An independent Sultanate long after the rest of the Sudan had fallen to the British, Darfur had been ruled by Sultan Ali Dinar until 1916, when his courtship of the fanatical Senussi brotherhood in Libya had made him an uncomfortable neighbour. In February that year, Darfur was invaded by a British field force supported by two aircraft of the Royal Flying Corps. Ali Dinar, last Sultan of Darfur, was chased off his throne, to be hunted down in the Darfur mountains later and shot dead in an exchange of fire with British-led forces; Angus Gillan, now Civil Secretary, had witnessed the final event. 'A few shots were exchanged from ridge to ridge,' he wrote, 'and after about the third rise we came on a thick-built form, with a strong and dignified face marred only by cruel, sensuous lips, with a bullet hole drilled through the centre of his forehead. It was Ali Dinar.'[19]

Thesiger stayed in the provincial capital long enough to pay his respects to his colleagues and superiors, and commandeered a lorry for the fifty-mile journey to Kutum in the hills to the north-west. He was looking forward to meeting the unconventional Moore, about whom he had heard so much, but when he arrived the DC was out on trek. Instead, he was confronted by the placid Reggie Dingwall, trying desperately to appear civil but fuming inwardly at his treatment. 'Thesiger stayed with me, and of course I was expected to train him,' Dingwall said. 'He obviously came to me at a very unfortunate time, and I was fairly guarded because I was annoyed at being moved out of this place, which I was really enjoying. I had been there before Moore arrived, and that balanced his wider experience and greater age. We met on pretty equal terms and I'd just established a relationship with him that I thought was very good. Then I found myself having to pack up when I thought I'd got nicely dug in, and hand over to this rather brash young man.'[20] Dingwall, a serious-minded career-ist who had taken Greats and a diploma in anthropology at Oxford, could not have been more different from his unwelcome guest. Though perfectly prepared to shoot lion, or even crazed camels, as an aspect of the job, Dingwall never enjoyed big-game hunting. It seemed to him that Thesiger perceived the job as little more than the chance to hunt. 'Big-game hunting was an all-important part of his life and work,' Dingwall commented. 'He even said to me what a marvellous opportunity this was to shoot game, particularly lion ... I thought it was perfectly all right if you took a week's leave off and went hunting: for many people that was part of the attraction of the job: but to spend all your time doing it and thinking about it ... well, I wasn't terribly impressed.'[21] If Dingwall's judgement seems harsh, Thesiger's choked-back remark at his interview may be borne in mind here. Author Timothy Green has written in his study of Thesiger's life: 'Hunting and travel kept him so enthralled that he had little time for – nor took much interest in – the affairs of the Province. He was always planning his next hunt or his next expedition.'[22] Thesiger also said frequently that it was the British Consuls he had met in Abyssinia as a child, with their stories of 'lion-hunting and savage tribes', who inspired him to take a job with the Sudan Political Service as his avenue back to the country of his birth. Though Dingwall laboured hard not to reveal his resentment, Thesiger did perceive and understand his reluctance to leave. 'They could move you whenever they wanted to,' he commented, 'and Dingwall had been there for a couple of years, so he was just moved.'[23] Indeed, in fairness it must be added that Thesiger himself was abruptly moved on when he had completed two years in the District.

While the two young ADCs trod warily around each other, though, Thesiger was immediately excited by Kutum itself. 'It was unlike any place I'd been in before,' he said, 'and I took a liking to it at once.'[24] Sited on the banks of a deep wadi which coils out of the shadowy mountains beyond, the warren of cone-shaped grass huts remains scarcely changed since the 1930s. Stalls and one-room shops of fermented mud nestle beneath bristling *heraz* trees and oddly tilted date-palms, and on market day the wadi bed is full of couched camels, piles of saddlery and men from half a dozen tribes in their shimmering white *ragis*, breeches and turbans. The government buildings stand above the wadi bed on its steep southern bank: offices, police post and prison cluster around an open square, and across a sandy defile stand two wattle DCs' houses under mops of thatch on a knoll littered with granite boulders. From his house, Thesiger had a clear view across rolling bushland as far as the ghostly outline of Jabal Si.

Thesiger had expected Moore to be an ascetic type – tall, silent, lean and leathery – a misogynist who had rejected the world's pleasures and shunned his fellow men. But the DC whom he met a few days after arriving in Kutum was very different from the preconceived image. Short, red-faced, bearded and tubby, Moore had brilliant blue eyes, a loquacious manner and a short fuse – he looked anything but athletic, and Thesiger found himself doubting his DC's stamina. Moore was a contract officer and belonged to that stratum of Sudan Political Service officers recruited from the forces rather than from Oxbridge. He had served as a pilot with the Flying Corps in the First World War and won the MC for gallantry, but had 'become so interested in Arabs', as his colleague John Bagot Glubb wrote of him, 'that he had given up flying'.[25] While an RAF Flight Lieutenant in the post-war 1920s he had worked with Glubb as Intelligence Special Service officer in the desert of southern Iraq, running a flight of three spotter aircraft charged with protecting the country against bandit incursions by the Ikhwan. In 1928, after a spell back in England, he had turned up again as adviser to Sir Gilbert Clayton, and, with Glubb, had helped negotiate a treaty with Abdal Azziz Ibn Sa'ud, King of Sa'udi Arabia. 'Moore was a nice, simple Christian, really,' Reginald Dingwall commented, 'who had very definite ideas on things. He didn't entirely agree with the administration, and I don't think he really thought the Sudanese could ever look after their own affairs, though I don't think he would have denied them their independence as a long-term trend. He was a product of the Victorian era, and didn't approve of progress in the Sudan or in the world at all. He liked the old-fashioned ways and believed in old-fashioned values.'[26] It is easy to see why Moore should have appealed so perfectly to Thesiger, already since childhood an arch-conservative and traditionalist. He came to consider Moore one of his life's most important influences, characterizing him as a man of great humanity and understanding who was devoted to the people he served. 'Moore not only put up with me,' he wrote in his autobiography, 'he also gave me his confidence and won mine.'[27] Yet it is not entirely clear how Moore reacted to him initially. Certainly, Dingwall believed that Moore was angry that he had been pushed out to make way for Thesiger. 'He told me he was dreadfully sorry that it had happened,' he commented. 'He said that we had just got to know each other and now he'd have to get to know Thesiger from scratch. I don't know how they did get on, but Moore was sufficiently broad-minded to be able to get on with him. And after all, Thesiger had an attractive side and the things he did were quite fun. Moore was unconventional: he liked his wild country in Iraq, and he liked the wildness of Kutum.'[28]

Once Dingwall had left for his new posting, Thesiger and Moore were the only Europeans in the District, a vast region of 50,000 square miles, bounded by sheer desert in the north, the border of French Sahara (now Chad) to the west, and the rolling *goz* of Kordofan to the east. There was no telephone and no telegraph communication, and except for the weekly mail runners, the town was practically cut off from the outside world. Indeed, Kutum kept its own time: 'Our clocks were always set an hour earlier than the rest of the Sudan,' Dingwall said. 'Since we had no electronic communications there was no need to be synchronized with the outside, and it was jolly cold there in the winter. At six in the morning the temperature would be only three or four degrees, and it was too cold to get up. During the day it was a nice, warm climate, so we always set our clocks back an hour. We went out at seven o'clock, but it was actually eight o'clock in the rest of the Sudan.'[29] Within this huge territory and its plethora of tribes – nomads and sedentaries – the two Englishmen were the ultimate arbiters of the law. It was a quasi-feudal society and, like thousands of their colleagues scattered across the red-painted portions of the world map, the District Officers in Kutum were the squires. They administered justice, dispensed mercy, and kept the peace. They identified with their subjects, standing up for them against higher authority, lending their ear to every petitioner, punishing and rewarding like stern but benevolent patriarchs.

Scarcely had Thesiger got the feel of his new home when Moore sent him off by camel to the Tegabo hills. It was low granite scrub country inhabited by the Berti, a black tribe of Saharan origin, which had now become settled and virtually lost its Saharan language. The Berti were farmers and camel-breeders who lived in stockade-like villages of grass and timber. Thesiger had purchased Dingwall's string of camels, including a lightly-built Bishari she-camel from the eastern Sudan which had been his predecessor's favourite: 'She was a lovely ride,' Dingwall recalled fondly, 'awfully comfortable, and so small I could almost put my leg over her back.'[30] Thesiger, who despite his journeys in Danakil country had never ridden a camel before, woke up on the second day aching from head to foot. After a further day's trek, though, the soreness evaporated, and he never experienced it again. On trek, Dingwall had travelled with a caravan of six camels, lugging a very heavy tent for himself, a cookbox, food, spare clothes and rations for his servants, camel-men, and two or three police troopers. This was the way a British DC generally travelled, and at first Thesiger imitated it. He said he found Dingwall's she-camel 'slow and ponderous', though Dingwall recalled that she was actually faster than the camels of any of the police troopers or Sheikhs who would ride with him; her only fault was that she lacked the size and strength to cover the long distances Thesiger rode. Thesiger soon gave her in part exchange for a small bull-camel which he named Habib. 'She wouldn't have been what Thesiger wanted,' Dingwall agreed. 'I would ride thirty miles a day, but he would ride 100.'[31]

In Kutum, Thesiger attended a meeting between the Maidob, a black Darfur tribe, and the Kababish, a large tribe of Bedouin nomads from across the Kordofan border. He was thrilled to see these Bedouin dashing across the desert on their camels, dressed in gleaming white: 'This was my first encounter with an authentic Bedu tribe,' he wrote, 'the first time I heard the inimitable speech of the Arabian desert.'[32] He was even more thrilled when the Kababish leader, the legendary Ali Taum, presented him with a superb Bishari camel named Faraj Allah, the finest riding beast in Darfur. Soon after, he rode through the bush country as far as the Maidob mountains: a volcanic labyrinth of fluted granite seamed by plunging gorges and rocky wadis, teeming with baboons, hyenas and Barbary sheep. At Malha he descended into the deep crater of an extinct volcano, where troops of Maidob camels were being watered around a pool of blood-coloured water, soupy with mineral-salt. The Maidob were a mystery race: speaking a Nubian language whose homeland was in the Nile valley, they were thought by some to be descendants of the refugee royal family of ancient Meroë, the Nile-based civilization conquered by the Axumites in the fourth century AD. Thesiger tracked and shot a Barbary sheep in the gorges of Maidob, and on his return the Maidob chief, Malik Sayyah, suggested riding back to Kutum across the desert plains, watering at the wells at Anka. Retaining only his personal camel-man, Thesiger dispensed with his tent and unnecessary camp furniture and slung across his saddle only blankets and waterskins, in the style of the Maidob. It was a decisive step. Pacing his camel with that of the Maidob chief and four of his tribesmen, he acquired his first taste of open desert. He learned the thrill of riding fast and light, the liberation that comes from abandoning posessions; he learned the tarry taste of water from goatskins: the naturalness of eating from a communal dish. He learned the warmth of companionship born around the hearth of a flickering fire: how differences of race and religion are mocked by the infinity of the desert sky. Suddenly, he was no longer the stranger sleeping on a camp-bed, sheltered by a tent, and waited on by servants, but a man among men who were unashamed of their poverty and looked their superiors straight in the eye, while never questioning their right to rule. They ate the grilled meat of an oryx that Thesiger shot, or fed on the staple diet of the western Sudan: a half football-sized pudding called 'asida, made palatable by a gravy of powdered okra, tomatoes and chilis cooked in oil, and eaten while it was so hot that it burned the fingers. Ever since he had travelled in Danakil country, aloof from his companions, Thesiger had hungered for this closeness and informality. 'I came back and told Guy Moore what a marvellous feeling it had given me,' Thesiger recalled, 'and he said: "When I get back from leave you can go off on a proper desert expedition, and really see what it's like to travel with camels. I'd love you to do that." Well, no other DC would have said that to a newly joined Probationer – one wouldn't think of giving him a month's holiday in the desert for experience.'[33]

There were two motor vehicles available in Kutum, and Moore told Thesiger that theoretically all their work could have been done in cars: 'He said that he went by camel because he could be with the people,' Thesiger said, 'and they could ride alongside him and talk to him, and that you would be depriving yourself of all this if you were travelling by car. If there was a crisis, though, and they were fighting as they did on one or two occasions, we'd jump into a car and rush off to settle it. The very fact that you could do that in Kutum robbed it of something.'[34] In the 'herostory' of Wilfred Thesiger, Moore corresponds to the 'tutelary spirit' who sets the hero on the right road. Thesiger wrote of Moore that he 'taught me to appreciate the desert, its people and their ways',[35] and in 1970 he told Timothy Green: 'He [Moore] explained the life of the desert and the Arab to me. On trek he always lived on native food and didn't care if he didn't eat for twenty-four hours. When he travelled he took only two camelmen and one policeman and fed with the local chiefs, sitting with them on the floor – not aloof in a chair like most DCs. Like this one had a common sense of humanity with them.'[36] This is confirmed by the Sudanese author Hassan Najila, who has described Moore's visit to the Kababish chief Ali Taum in his book *Zikriyaat Fil Baadiya*, and recorded how he sat on the floor among them, ate with his hands from a communal dish, and recited long passages from the Quran. Najila also adds Ali Taum's incisive comment about Moore: 'I am afraid of men like that – they get too close to us': a tantalizing insight into the other side of the colonial experience. Thesiger went further in his autobiography, however, adding that Moore 'taught me to feel affection for tribesmen' – a somewhat curious statement, since affection does not seem to fall into the category of things which can be taught. He traced from Moore's influence the relationships he made over the years with various young tribesmen, though it seems more likely that Thesiger's predisposition to form bonds with young adolescent males had much more to do with his own psyche than with Moore's coaching. During their first weeks together at Kutum, Thesiger and Moore went on trek together and Thesiger, regarding Moore's endurance in the saddle as a challenge, was secretly determined that he would outride the older man.[37]

At home, he eventually got rid of the two professional servants who had been hired for him, and recruited an adolescent youth from the Zaghawa tribe, called Idris, whom he rescued from the town jail. 'I suppose I got hold of him about six months after I arrived in Kutum,' Thesiger remembered. 'I'd come back from a trip, and I was inspecting the prison, and I found this boy of fourteen or fifteen. I asked what he was doing there, and they told me he'd killed another boy in some sort of dispute over a horse. It was obviously a case that would be settled with blood money, so I told them to get two men to guarantee that he wouldn't run away, and send him down to my house. That was the sort of thing you could do in the Sudan. You couldn't have done it in the other Colonies.'[38] Idris became Thesiger's personal valet and constant companion, the first member of his 'gang'. In true feudal style, he wanted retainers who owed him personal loyalty and who could ride and hunt with him in the bush, rather than a retinue of trained servants for whom he would always be the pampered Englishman in Africa. Being surrounded by loyal tribesmen appealed to his taste for the romantic. He took on another local boy from Kutum as his new cook: 'I don't think he'd ever cooked for anybody before,' he commented, 'but he was the cook and Idris was a sort of butler, and when the Governor came to stay this was the service he got, but they did it quite proficiently.'[39]

For much of the time he was in the Sudan, Idris provided Thesiger with the emotional – though platonic – outlet which many other DCs found in their black mistresses. The Crewe Circular of 1909 had banned the practice of concubinage in the

British Empire, but in the rural areas of the Sudan, where most administrators were unmarried, the practice of sleeping with a local girl was fairly common, if discreetly managed so that the woman never appeared in public. 'It was different to what went on in other places in Africa,' Thesiger said. 'In Kenya, for instance, some DCs did have black mistresses, but the feeling would have been very strongly against it. In the Sudan we associated ourselves very much with the locals. We weren't "white people" in the same sense they were in Kenya. We were Sudanese.'[40] In the Sudan Political Service early marriages were frowned upon, requiring the consent of the government. Some hardy Englishwomen did brave the wildest of conditions, as had the wife of Thesiger's predecessor in Kutum, Ewen Campbell. Long before Thesiger had ever heard of Kutum, Campbell had carried his wife over the threshold of the thatched house Moore later inhabited – her first married home.[41] 'A lot of people retired from the Sudan as bachelors,' Thesiger maintained. 'After all, the whole way of life was utterly unsuitable for women. You were better off without a wife if you were living in Kutum, because you could associate with people in a way you wouldn't if you had a family, and then you'd have children and the place decorated with nappies and things. If Guy Moore had had a wife our relationship would to a large extent have been cramped.'[42] Thesiger's contempt for female 'interference' is clearly manifest, here, however: Campbell's marriage had certainly not hampered his success as a DC, for he went on to become Governor of Kordofan. Far from ruining his relationship with the local people, the presence of women and children was the one universal symbol which was likely to have enhanced it. Thesiger was later regarded as peculiar among the Bedouin of Arabia simply because he was not married and had no children. Reggie Dingwall strongly opposed Thesiger's view: 'I think Thesiger is wrong when he says, "The whole way of life was unsuitable for women,"' he commented. 'My wife greatly enjoyed her time when I was DC Beja, based on Sinkat, and she seldom saw other white women . . . the children joined me for eight or nine months every year.'[43] Uninterested in women, it was to Idris that Thesiger looked for a personal relationship: the first of many he was to form with teen-age boys throughout his life. 'There was no intimate relationship with people when I went on my Danakil journey,' Thesiger said, '... but it did exist to some extent when I was in the Sudan because it was the sort of relationship I had with Idris. There was nothing physical in it – Idris was surprisingly negroid for a Zaghawa – but I was very fond of him because we were shoulder to shoulder and side by side in many dangerous situations, and he was loyal to me. There was nothing like it during the war, when I had no personal relationship with anybody – there was nobody like him, really, until I went to Arabia.'[44]

Although Thesiger occasionally bumped around in the District's motor vehicles, he preferred always to ride camels, and never went back to travelling with a formal entourage in the prescribed fashion: 'I associated entirely with the people who went with me,' he said. 'I don't know how many people knew I was doing it. Guy Moore did, of course, and I suspect Newbold did.'[45] According to Reggie Dingwall, though, his reputation as an unconventional officer was well known and not entirely approved of. 'He was never mentioned straightforwardly,' Dingwall said. 'It was always "Well, of course, that's Wilfred Thesiger." He had a good reputation as a camel-rider, but I personally didn't think it was really what he was employed to be doing.'[46] Neither could Dingwall see the advantage in travelling fast and light as Thesiger did: 'One's object in going on trek was to see and be seen,' he commented. 'Thesiger travelled so fast that he could only talk to the people he was with, but couldn't get to know the local people. I didn't approve of that because I didn't think it was doing any good.'[47] That Thesiger did acquire a great number of friends from the local tribes, though, is manifest in Moore's warm letter to Mrs Astley-Thesiger, written after Thesiger left Kutum in 1937. '[He] quickly found his contact with the people,' Moore wrote, 'and having done so, only wanted to be with them and help them.'[48] The hidden agenda of such criticisms was that by travelling in the style of local tribesmen and associating with them, Thesiger was felt to be in danger of diminishing the prestige of the ruling élite. Indeed, one of his colleagues openly frowned upon him for making close social relationships with tribesmen, and reciprocating their hospitality by receiving them in his house. 'A contemporary of mine said I was letting down the respect of the government,' Thesiger recalled. 'I said, "nonsense, one can be friends with them without losing respect." He said, "One is not here to be friends with these people, one is here to administer them." [49]

Thesiger often stated in later life that he 'never really wanted to be the *Bwana*', and this, like his earlier identification with de Monfreid, has frequently been taken to mean that he was essentially an egalitarian who became a rebel against the colonial establishment, and a champion of the underdog. Nothing could be further from the truth. Never 'colour-prejudiced' in the normal sense (though like most Imperial Englishmen he preferred physically attractive races), Thesiger was an authoritarian who respected traditional hierarchies and detested democracy. No matter how unconventional his views and behaviour might seem, he always remained a staunch pillar of the Imperial status quo: 'The Empire was absolutely outstanding,' he said, 'and I was proud to have something to do with it. It was out of this world compared with any other Empire except possibly the French. My sympathies were with the Dervishes at Omdurman, but I recognized that if they hadn't been mown down by the British, they would have been mown down by the Italians or somebody, and they'd have been infinitely worse off.' [50] The difference between Thesiger and many of his colleagues in the Sudan Political Service was a difference of style rather than principle: 'I was the only one there who fed with his servants and the Sheikhs and so on,' he commented, 'and I can see that over certain things I departed from convention ... but I was [still] the District Officer, and people had to obey my orders ... I insisted on having their respect, and wouldn't let them take liberties.' [51] British rule in the Sudan was based on techniques of colonial government perfected in India, and the tiny ruling élite believed it depended for its survival on preserving a certain social distance. There was, however, a different tradition in the Middle East, where Europeans had long ago learned that to show friendship to the Arab and to treat him as an equal was the best method of preserving his loyalty. John Glubb – one of the greatest Arabists of the post-Lawrence era – and his officers in the Bedouin Legion regularly slept on the ground with their men and ate out of the same dish, maintaining discipline by appealing to a man's honour, or by the threat of being expelled from the unit. Thesiger knew about this tradition from his reading of the Arabian explorers and of T.E.Lawrence, but Moore, who had learned it beside Glubb in the Arabian desert, showed him that it was possible to practise it here. The Maidob, Zaghawa and most other Darfur tribes were not Bedouin, but they shared the same cultural affinities: Thesiger's style was only unconventional in the Sudan, and even there was generally tolerated by his colleagues and superiors. 'The Sudan Political Service was strong enough to take eccentrics like Wilfred Thesiger,' Reginald Dingwall admitted. 'It's not a bad thing to have an eccentric or two, but if everyone had behaved like him the whole thing would have broken down.'[52]

The new Probationer quickly settled in to the routine of life in Kutum. Rising at six, Thesiger would bathe in his canvas bath and dress in his quasi-military uniform – shorts, a khaki shirt and tie, a bush-jacket, field-boots and a heavy Wolseley helmet. Official office hours were nine to two, but he would spend the early mornings riding his horse or camel, on the way perhaps inspecting the prisoners who were labouring on cultivation or building projects, or call in at the clinic of the 'native dresser' or medical orderly to watch his treatment and operations. Following Sudanese custom, breakfast would be served between ten and eleven, after which he would man the office until the evening. On his arrival there the police guard would fall in under the British and Egyptian flags, and if Moore was away Thesiger would take the salute to the sound of a bugle. Though they were the only two Englishmen for miles, Moore and Thesiger would always exchange salutes formally: 'It was good for discipline,' Thesiger explained, 'for the police to see me saluting Moore. It emphasized the fact that he was the District Commissioner and I was his ADC.'[53] Far from finding these para-military traditions pretentious, Thesiger actually relished them. Paperwork was rarely heavy unless the fortnightly camel had arrived with the mail pouch from El Fasher, though one major concern was tax collection, which was done through trusted tribal Sheikhs. It was a rough and ready levy on goats, cattle, camels and people, which ensured not only a flow of much-needed revenue, but also recognition of British sovereignty. Most trade in the town was done by barter, cash being of value only for paying taxes and purchasing cloth. Though there were no direct communications and all messages were carried by hand, Kutum did have a sort of 'express courier' for emergencies: an eccentric and dipsomaniac camel-man. 'If you gave him a letter by four in the afternoon he'd start off at seven and deliver it to the Province HQ in Fasher by nine the next morning,' Dingwall remembered. 'He needed the time between four and seven to stoke himself up on *merissa* [sorghum beer], and he used to set off with a leather pouch on each shoulder. He used to say one was food and the other drink, but in fact they were both *merissa*. That would get him through the night.'[54]

Legal cases took up a considerable part of the time. As a second-class magistrate, Thesiger could try cases punishable by up to six months in prison, and award sentences of flogging. Though fifteen lashes was the maximum punishment, offenders due to be flogged were generally given eight to ten, and the sentence would be carried out in the square by a burly policeman, in the presence of the District Officer. The ritual was completed in a few minutes, and there was rarely any rancour. Often the victim of the thrashing would thank the officer sincerely for not sending him to prison. British authority was backed up in Kutum by a squad of two dozen native policemen, armed with Lee Enfield .303 rifles and uniformed in khaki, with slouch hats and shorts. Four of the squad kept their own camels, for which they were paid an allowance. They were the responsibility of the provincial police chief in El Fasher, who came to inspect them at intervals. Further security was provided by the Sudan Defence Force, one battalion of which – the Western Arab Corps – was stationed in the border town of Zalingei. 'They never came up to Kutum,' Thesiger said. 'We never saw them; we didn't want to see them either. The commander, Renouf, was disliked by every-one.'[55]

If both Moore and Thesiger were in town at the same time, which was fairly rare, they would stroll back from the office together, and, drawing close to a roaring log fire on winter evenings, would talk until the early hours, breaking only for dinner at midnight. Thesiger must have found these convivial talks reminiscent of those civilized winter evenings in his room at Eton. Moore was a fascinating conversationalist, with views that both reflected and moulded his own, and Thesiger would listen spellbound to his tales, just as he had listened to the lion-hunting stories of Arnold Hodson and others in his youth. 'He was very easy to talk to,' Thesiger recalled. 'The last word you would use about him was pompous. We talked on a perfectly level basis even though I was only twenty-four at the time.'[56] Moore had been deeply influenced by his experiences among the Bedouin, and had all the affection for them that Thesiger himself would later acquire. 'He had a sympathy and understanding for the Bedu,' Thesiger said, 'and his whole attitude was influenced by an attachment to them, and a belief they were superior to anybody else. He brought the [Arabian] desert to life and filled me with a desire to travel there.'[57] Slowly, almost imperceptibly, the seeds of Thesiger's future were being sown. He had come to Kutum only as a means of reaching Abyssinia, yet already the country of his birth was fading into the background. During the long, quiet hours of the evening, the Englishmen would discuss the great Arabian explorers and the peculiar connection between the English and Arabia. 'Both Moore and I admired T.E. Lawrence,' Thesiger said. 'He is certainly the person I would most like to have met. When you read what his friends wrote about him, you have the feeling that everyone who met him had a tremendous amount of respect for him.' Thesiger considered Charles Doughty the greatest Arabian explorer, but felt that he had set himself up as an Aunt Sally by carrying his Christianity like a banner before him: 'It was as if a fascist had gone round England at the outbreak of the last war and announced constantly that he was a fascist,' Thesiger said. 'I'm not saying I can't conceive of his not joining the Arabs in their prayers – I wouldn't have wanted to do that either – but he was assertively Christian – something I never was.'[58] Author Frank McLynn has noted that T.E. Lawrence himself admired Doughty's integrity in refusing to compromise with Islam, contrasting him with those Arabian travellers, exemplified by Richard Burton, who tried to remain inconspicuous.[59] Though Thesiger was later to employ disguise in Arabia, he had little interest in Burton, writing him off as 'a sort of academic'. McLynn has underlined Burton's academic bent: '[His] fascination with the Arab world was primarily that of a great scholar,' he has written, 'a detached observer, a linguist and anthropologist of genius.'[60] Moore's hero was General Gordon, and Thesiger recorded that he 'raised more than an eyebrow' when the younger man mentioned his partiality for Abdal Rahman Wad an Nijumi, the Dervish general. Always tempted to shock, Thesiger may have been trying to test his new-found friendship with unorthodox opinions. If so, then Moore was perceptive enough to recognize them for what they were, an assertion of independence. In another sense, perhaps, Moore filled for Thesiger a paternal role which had largely been absent from the age of nine: from here on Thesiger's views strike a less overtly rebellious pose. 'He never snubbed me,' Thesiger reported, 'however extreme, unconventional or irrational the views I expressed.'[61]

Thesiger's irrationality seems manifest partly in the incompatibility of his pride in being a colonial officer, and therefore by definition an intruder, with his resentment of Western intrusions in traditional societies. 'I couldn't see the justification for imposing an alien civilization in Darfur, any more than I can anywhere else,' he said. 'I disliked the idea of them being taken over, though it's true [I was one of those who took them over]. But when I read about the battle of Omdurman I didn't know there were people like Moore and Newbold . . . who were giving their lives and everything they had to these people with no thought of personal advantage. They weren't trying to make money out of it, they were just doing it for the people who were subject to them, and I had immense admiration for them.'[62] At its base, this, the fundamental contradiction of Thesiger's life, is but an old and still very present dilemma for Westerners: how to observe and even be part of the strange and the exotic without changing it. The colonialist, like the traveller, has no choice but ultimately to kill the thing he loves. Both Thesiger and Moore – like many of their colleagues in the Sudan – were fierce partisans of the locals and their traditional ways. The paradox is that by their very presence they inevitably changed the consciousness of the natives. However much Thesiger inclined towards them and their traditions – and there is no doubt his feelings for them were genuine – he still remained, and would always remain, an example of the power of a sophisticated, educated, materially advanced society. Inevitably some ambitious Sudanese would aspire to be like him: to acquire the power that had accrued to him, in the end, because his grandfather's generation owned Maxim guns, when the Sudanese did not. A superb example of the unconscious effects of colonialism is given by Carl Jung, who as a young man studied a tribe of hunter-gatherers in East Africa. The tribesmen had been accustomed to take their guidance from the dreams of their chiefs and medicine-men. They told Jung, however, that since the coming of the British they had ceased to have meaningful dreams. The District Commissioner had taken over the function of 'great dreams' that had hitherto guided the tribe's behaviour.[63] All cultural contacts, however small, inevitably result in change, and in Thesiger's eyes 'all change was for the worse': 'I was happy in Kutum because I could find a life there among a people who were still very little affected by the outside world,' he said. 'We gave them justice and virtually stopped tribal fighting. If you take it to the extreme, that was interference, but I didn't reject that.'[64]

This view was not particularly unconventional among members of the Sudan Political Service. Reggie Dingwall's favourite story concerned a trek he once made by camel from Kutum to Kebkabiyya, a small town to the south, during which he encountered a lone woman from the Fur tribe. As soon as she saw the Englishman she fell to her knees and began patting the ground with her hands. When Dingwall inquired what she wanted, she told him, 'You are the first Englishman I have ever seen and I want to thank you. I am on my way to Kutum, which takes several days. Before the English came I couldn't have gone even a short walk from my village.' Dingwall took this as a good example of how Pax Britannica had changed things in Darfur in the few years it had been in operation there. 'I reckoned that's what our job was,' he said, 'and I was proud of it.'[65] The fundamental conviction – one might also, with justification, say 'illusion' – of those who administered the Empire was that it existed for the benefit of its subjects, and few Sudan DCs would have disagreed: the great debate lay in how those subjects could best be served. Moore and Thesiger and many others were 'paternalists'. Theirs was the benevolent face of colonialism: they liked and often admired their subjects, yet they still felt that they knew what was best for them. They believed that their role was to provide justice and security, and to slow down as much as possible the effects of change. They saw themselves as the guardians of a traditional culture against a tide of development which would inevitably engulf the old ways and carry themselves off in the process. Indeed, they were trapped in this paradox – riding the crest of a wave that would ultimately destroy them. Harking back to the Victorian era, opposing almost all material progress, voluntarily or reluctantly they became the protectors of an Old World Order with the British at its summit.

At one end of the spectrum, then, were those who felt it was enough to provide security and justice alone. The other end was occupied by those who believed that they existed to raise the standard of living of the Sudanese by improving agriculture, health facilities and education: a process which would inevitably result in Sudanese independence and the redundancy of British colonialism. For Thesiger, such 'conventional' views were epitomized by Colonel Hugh Boustead, who was DC in another small town in Darfur, Zalingei. 'Boustead found contentment, working to improve the lot of the Fur cultivators in his District,' Thesiger wrote. 'Being convinced that their happiness depended on a raised standard of living, he never questioned the repercussions of Western education and technology. For all his versatility he was by nature conventional, holding firmly to English ways.'[66] Although undoubtedly one of those Englishmen who might have 'dressed for dinner in the jungle', Boustead was a man of high calibre whose name is still honoured by the people of Zalingei. He was a hero of the Richard Hannay stamp, an Olympic pentathlete and a Himalayan mountaineer, who had actually deserted from the British navy during the First World War to serve as a private in an infantry regiment on the Somme, where he had won an MC and a royal pardon. Yet though Thesiger professed a personal liking for Boustead, he admitted that they were incompatible: 'Had I been sent to Zalingei instead of Kutum, I should probably have resigned and left,' he said. 'Boustead wouldn't have given me the freedom to do as I wanted as Guy Moore did. I think he disapproved of my unconventional ways. He was very much liked and respected, but he hadn't got a personal relationship with the locals. He was looking after his people as a duty which he was sent there to perform. Guy Moore was looking after his people because they were his.'[67] It is unlikely that Thesiger would have concurred with Boustead's sentiment that 'there can be no deeper satisfaction than to have played a part in helping a country or a people forward to a life of peace, with agriculture and commerce prospering under an honest government, with justice administered under the rule of law, with education for the young and medical care for the sick . . . our works live after us and by these works we should be judged in days to come. If we have worked well and forthrightly, then it is well.'[68] Dingwall, like many of his colleagues, considered Boustead a man of tremendous stature: 'He was trying to raise the standard of living of the Sudanese,' he said, 'and that was, after all, the job we were sent there to do.'[69]

There is no doubt that Moore's affection for 'his' people was profound and his commitment to them complete. 'If the British had tried to do something in Kutum District which Guy Moore disapproved of, he'd have chucked in his career and resigned,' Thesiger explained. 'On occasions they did come along with something that he thought would be utterly wrong and he would take a very strong line in Khartoum and get away with it. I think as it turned out the Empire was a good thing . . . because the whole of the world was moving that way and you can say thank God the Sudanese had the British ruling them and not anyone else. The British had a kind of basic decency, I think – a value for people's lives. It probably came from the public schools and was passed down by the leaders to all the others. Of course, the Sudanese didn't want us to invade their country, and they defended it at the battle of Omdurman, but then they had no idea that the British were going to bring peace, security and justice. If you went back to Kutum and places like it they'd probably say they'd rather have Guy Moore back than what they've got today.'[70]

Education for Sudanese was the great issue of the 1930s, and for many of the District Officers its upward growth was disturbing. Sir Stewart Symes, who had replaced Sir John Maffey as Governor-General in 1935, had found his advocacy of education decidedly unpopular with his field officers, few of whom believed it would be of use to tribal people. Thesiger and his peers saw education as an alien intrusion that would inevitably lead to a drift from country to city, an abandonment of traditional skills, and destruction of family and tribal life. Yet, despite their reservations, Thesiger and Moore did found a school in Kutum, designed to educate the sons of chiefs and prevent them from being cheated by rascally scribes from the Nile valley. 'We talked it over and we thought it would be a good idea to start a school,' Thesiger recalled. 'If the chiefs could have a son who could read or write, he could supervise the clerks. We started this small school which had about seventeen boys in it, and it was the only school in the District when I left there in 1936. The boys weren't made to go to school by force, but Guy Moore persuaded the chiefs to let their sons come, and in the end we got a lot more applications than we could accept.'[71]

In a world that is becoming increasingly homogenized, one can sympathize with those like Thesiger and Moore who wanted to preserve the identity and traditions of African cultures. Few Westerners who have worked with traditional peoples have denied that the quality of social relationships among them remains far superior to those in materially advanced societies. There is no doubt that Africa today is devastatingly afflicted with the very problems Thesiger and Moore sought to prevent: 'Is [Thesiger] so misguided in his desire to preserve their basis for religious observance and identity?' Alexander Maitland has asked. 'The whole splendour of the animal world, conservation of which now rightly commands worldwide support, is rooted in its diversity, the distinctive character and interdependence of species, each of which contributes to the whole from its own, separate resources. Is it right that mankind should be accorded less and that the splendid panoply of the world's races should be robbed (in the cause of material progress) of their traditional inheritance and their right to live as contributing, independent communities? Thesiger thinks not.'[72] However, though Thesiger believed that traditional people were happier than those in advanced societies, the question of social relations was not the mainspring of his aspiration. He was an adventurer, and the presence of 'unspoiled peoples' was crucial to his sense of adventure. This motive later became obscured as he sought justification for his journeys in a world which came increasingly to demand it, but his fundamental commitment to adventure never changed. Where, he felt, could one born at the end of the Edwardian era find challenge among educated, sophisticated peoples, in an urbanized, mechanized world? Exploration of the ocean bed or outer space was meaningless to him: there were no 'unadministered peoples' to be found there. As he saw the earth turn inexorably into a vast technological village, there was expunged all scope for the lifelong craving for adventure among untamed tribes in unknown lands which inspired Thesiger and many another like him.

The quest for adventure has a distinguished pedigree: it is at least as old as civilization itself. The most ancient fragment of literature we know of, *The Epic of Gilgamesh* – a Sumerian text dating from about 2500 BC – concerns a god-king who, bored with life in the city, goes out into the wilderness to seek adventure. The theme sounds strikingly familiar. Homer's Odysseus is another adventurer in the classic tradition. Today, we expect explorers and adventurers to express some altruistic motive: we find it difficult to accept that some individuals need to take on challenges 'because they are there'. The need for adventure is part of the collective human psyche, and requires no justification: 'For those who believe, no explanation is necessary: for those who do not believe, no explanation is possible.' It would be quite false to apply a late twentieth-century urban morality to a theme so ancient.

Yet, since Thesiger defined adventure almost exclusively in terms of 'untamed tribes', it is necessary to look, for a moment, at the world from their point of view. The people of Darfur had no need or desire for education when the British arrived. Indeed, DCs like Moore and Boustead had a difficult task in persuading the local chiefs to send their sons to school. But since the British had begun to educate the Sudanese in other places from the very moment they had taken control of the country – Gordon College had been founded by Kitchener himself – to have failed to educate the Darfuris would have been ultimately to condemn them to eternal subjection by the more educated, more sophisticated, more materially advanced sections of the Sudanese state, who, naturally, took power when the British left. This very argument was used by the DCs to encourage Darfuri headmen to educate their sons. Once the precedent was set, there was no turning back. Ordinary tribesmen began to see education as a road to greater economic power: it became, in other words, the fashion. Once the British invaded the Sudan sweeping changes were inescapable, whether the rulers willed it or no. It must be noted that, while Thesiger regretted the death of 10,000 Sudanese warriors at Omdurman, and questioned the right of the British to impose their culture on an alien people, he never doubted that, given the inevitability of colonialism, the British variety was ultimately to the good. If Thesiger and Moore – and all the other DCs – had been prepared to become Muslims, marry Sudanese women, adopt Sudanese customs and merge into the population as previous invaders had done, there would have been no such problem. Even though Thesiger might befriend the natives, and adopt their dress and customs on occasions, he still remained 'condescending' (his own word). The far-sighted Douglas Newbold – acknowledged as the most outstanding administrator in the history of the Sudan Service – himself told Thesiger that the Sudan government could not retain 'human game reserves' forever. The problem with the classic paternalist argument is that it ignores the voice of the traditional community itself. It assumes that the 'primitive' only wishes to be left alone and has no desire to see his children grow up healthy, to emerge from poverty, and to be able to read and write – a theory called into question by the number of applications Moore and Thesiger received for places in their new school in the 1930s. The great Amazonian conservationist Claudio Villas Boas ran into trouble with his perfectly well-intentioned policy of isolating the Yanomami Indians from outside influences for a period of twenty years: the policy was condemned as paternalist by many of the Indians themselves.[73] Article One of the Universal Declaration of Human Rights, the charter on which the United Nations is based, looks superficially similar to Thesiger's beliefs: 'All peoples have a right to self-determination. By virtue of that right they fully determine their political status and fully pursue their economic, social and cultural development.' However, while Thesiger is saying, 'Leave ancient cultures alone' a paternalistic argument – the United Nations declaration says, 'Leave traditional cultures alone *if they so wish it*,' thus allowing some play for the ambitions of the people themselves. The Declaration goes on to assert that the individual has the right (though not the compulsion) to education, and to freedom of thought and religion – 'life, health and the pursuit of happiness' – an aspiration Thesiger dismissed in his later years. 'The thing that maddens me is all this fuss about human rights,' he said. 'Who the hell gave us the right to go round interfering and asserting human rights all over the place? I don't believe in the Universal Declaration of Human Rights – it's impractical nonsense.'[74] The British actually resisted development among the primitive peoples of the southern Sudan – the Dinka, the Nuer and others – and the savage civil war that has been fought sporadically there since independence illustrates with terrible clarity the perils of deliberate under-development. Thesiger told Alexander Maitland in 1980 that the Sudanese government was wrong to replace the Dinka's cattle-based economy with cotton, which would mean the destruction of their spiritual identity: yet, as Jung noted, a people's spiritual identity was bound to be eroded by the very presence of a foreign ruling élite. Anyhow, the Dinka never got a chance to practise as cotton-farmers: instead they were subject to the blitzkrieg of tanks, bombers and machine-guns belonging to a more materially advanced government, their villages burned and their precious herds destroyed. Cultures remaining materially backward are precisely those which are most likely to be ravaged by more advanced ones – the British conquest of the Sudan being a classic case in point. It is to Thesiger's credit that, despite his nostalgia for the past, he accepted that once an alien culture, no matter how benevolent, has been introduced into a traditional society, profound change is only a matter of time: '[I questioned] our right to impose our culture, standards, and morals on them,' he said. 'I'd rather it hadn't been necessary, but it was inevitably going to happen, and it was better that it happened under us.'[75]

CHAPTER 6

Lion's Bane

For four hours Thesiger and the three Bani Hussain brothers had been tracking the lion across the wadis and scrubland of Darfur, under a merciless oyster-white sky that throbbed with heat. In the distance a pair of Nubian vultures with obscenely bald heads banked slowly and expectantly over the beast's path. The grass was still shiny with the night's rain, and on the wet sand of a wadi Thesiger came across a trail of great pug-marks which told him that this was no ordinary animal. The Bani Hussain, small, string-muscled men in coarse cotton breeches and skullcaps, held their great lion-spears at the ready, sensing that their quarry was near. Winded after the long, hot run, Thesiger pushed himself towards the high grass beyond the wadi-banks, halting to listen attentively. A tortured panting reached his ears, and for a moment he thought it was a dog he had been hunting with the previous day. An instant later one of the tribesmen hissed 'That's him! That's him!' and Thesiger realized it was the lion. Peering into the thick, shadowless bush, he drew a bead on what he believed to be the lion's head, and squeezed the trigger. The next second a monstrous body hurtled out of the bush with claws out and fangs bared, straight at him. Thesiger reeled over under a glancing blow, his finger contracting instinctively on the trigger. At that instant, one of the tribesmen rammed home his spear into the lion's jaw and then the full weight of the great beast was upon him. As his brothers ran up to help, the lion flailed out at them with razor-sharp claws, bringing one down and mauling the other. Jumping to his feet, Thesiger rushed over and put a round through the lion's ear. There was an instant of pure silence, while the four men recovered from the shock. Crimson blood soaked into the sandy soil, and flies gathered around the dead monster's nostrils. Then Thesiger realized with a jolt that the others were badly injured: 'I suddenly thought, well, here I am in the middle of Africa with three wounded men on my hands,' he recalled. 'What shall I do?'[1] Fortunately some mounted Bani Hussain had followed behind and were able to pick up the wounded men.

Throughout his childhood and youth, Thesiger had dreamed of hunting lion, and only two days earlier his lion-killing career had begun with a bang. Travelling to a meeting with another DC, in the maze of wadis south of Kutum, he heard lion roaring at night. Next morning, with a squad of Bani Hussain spearmen, he flushed a five-strong pride out of a thicket of trees. Without pausing he fired at one crouching under a bush and killed it. The crack and thump seemed to bring lion snarling out from behind every shrub and stand of grass. Yet Thesiger's nerve held. He winged another beast with his second shot, and dropped it with his third as it charged. His fourth shot felled another before it could attack. Thesiger let out a long sigh of intense satisfaction: after all those years of poring over Selous and Gordon-Cumming, wondering what it would be like, he had killed three lion within a few minutes, and he was gripped by the intense exultation of the kill. Like an addict he thirsted for more. When a tribesman came to his camp the following day to report a lion near his village preying on the flocks, he was only too pleased to answer the call. He and his tribesmen pursued the lion for hours until they had it at bay. 'It turned round,' he remembered, 'and I watched its tail. It went straight up, and I'd read that if it did that it meant the lion would charge. Just at that moment I killed it with two shots.'[2]

Thesiger continued to stalk lion on foot even after his close shave. Reared on the great white hunters, it never occurred to him to ride lion down on horses as the Darfur tribes did, until much later. On many of these hunts he took with him Idris, whom he found to his delight an exceptionally good tracker. 'He was very good in the bush,' Thesiger remembered. 'He was staunch and fearless, and an excellent shot with a rifle – perhaps the best shot of anyone I've ever had with me.'[3] He saw Idris as a romantic after his own heart, who 'fretted at security and craved at heart for [the] wild, lawless days . . . [when] young men could prove their manhood and win the approval of the girls'.[4] In his last year in Darfur, though, Thesiger adopted the local practice of galloping down lion on horseback. If a cattle-killer was rumoured to be in the area of a village, he would gather with about two dozen horsemen at sunrise in a piece of likely terrain. Lion was not a difficult beast to track, he discovered, since it preferred to follow a path or stream-bed. The riders would fan out across the scrubland, manhandling the eight-foot-long, leaf-bladed spears called *shalagais*, still carried in Darfur, their ponies snorting and raising dust, until one of them spotted the lion and let fly the *kororak* or 'view halloo'. As the lion made off, the tribesmen would thunder after it at the gallop, the sun flashing on the blades of their spears. Generally winded within a mile, the lion would slow to a lope and the horsemen would slow with him, drawing into line abreast like drilled cavalry. Thesiger would thrill as they broke into their hunting songs, one man roaring out a verse while the rest answered in full-throated chorus. At the first available cover the lion would turn and face his pursuers, who, still roaring out their song in challenge, would encircle him slowly. Finally, a party would dismount and approach the lion in tight phalanx. Unlike the much-admired Masai of East Africa, these tribesmen had no shields to cover themselves with, the man charged merely dropping to one knee, driving the butt of his spear into the ground, and gripping it with both hands. Thesiger wrote that the Darfur tribes expected to lose at least one man – killed or badly mauled – in each encounter. In one case a lion wounded twelve men before it was finally dispatched. If Thesiger was present, however, the kill would end differently: 'When with them I have always spoilt the sport by shooting the lion,' he wrote.[5]

There are no lion left in northern Darfur today. 'It wasn't hunters such as me who wiped out the game,' Thesiger said, 'it was the army and the police and the local people, who all had rifles of their own . . . once you put rifles into the hands of people like that they will shoot at everything.'[6] Reggie Dingwall has pointed out that the peace and security introduced by the British in Darfur itself played a major role: 'Pax Britannica was not good for game,' he said. 'When I was [in Kutum] there were oryx, giraffe, gazelles of all sorts as well as lion and leopard. The reason for this was because before we got there the country wasn't safe for people. We made it safe: we tried to stop people having rifles but we weren't successful, and it meant that anybody could go out and kill the game off.'[7] Thesiger soon became famous for lion-killing in Darfur, and tales about his kills are told by tribesmen there today, who know him still as Sajjar (Thesiger): Samm al 'Usuud, meaning 'Lion's Bane' (literally, Lion's Poison). He killed thirty lion in Kutum District alone and seventy in the Sudan as a whole, considering his hunting the most beneficial service he performed there. 'This was necessary control work,' he said. 'Lions were considered vermin in those days, and the vets were always receiving requests to poison them because they were killing cattle. The lion I killed always had a sporting chance, and I never sat over a bait for them. I reckoned once that I've been charged sixteen times hunting lion.'[8] In Darfur lion preyed mainly on the herds and flocks of the nomads and villagers, some of whom would resolutely track them down and spear them, incurring almost certain death or disfigurement on one of their tribe. Once, while hunting a cattle-killing lion near Jabal Si with Idris, Thesiger identified the animal's head clearly about fifty yards away: 'I shot and missed,' he said, 'and it got away. Two days later the lion killed another cow, and the tribesmen went after it. As a result there were seven casualties – three dead and four mauled. I felt that it was my fault.'[9] Thesiger reckoned that he had saved fifteen or twenty lives in the region by shooting lion, and while this is undeniable, it does not altogether explain his compulsive need to slaughter animals: there is a suggestion of *escusatio non petita* in his insistence that 'lion were vermin'. Lion-hunting was undoubtedly high on his mental agenda when considering the Sudan Political Service as a career. In any case, the 'vermin' argument does not account for thousands of other animals he killed, both before and after his time in Kutum. His motive for gunning down scores of crocodiles in Danakil country, for instance, was simply that he 'disliked these malevolent-looking reptiles and used them as targets, to impress the Danakil with [his] marksmanship'.[10] Similarly, of picking off crocodiles at leisure from the deck of a paddle-steamer later in the southern Sudan, he would write, 'I disliked crocodiles and when I got a chance shot them.'[11] While Thesiger is surely correct in his assumption that most humans have the will and capacity to kill when necessary, his annihilation of almost 2,000 wild boar over a period of seven years in the Iraq marshes seems excessive, a veritable orgy of blood: 'We just shot them [the boar] to kill them,' he explained. '. . . I don't know what I shot . . . I mean I shot seventy-four one day and seventy-seven another . . .'[12]

It would, of course, be quite wrong to judge Thesiger by current standards, and to assert that there was something morally objectionable in his hunting in an era when hunting was commonplace. It would be equally wrong to accept that his killing of animals was motivated altogether by altruism – even though this may have played a part. As author Frank McLynn has argued convincingly, hunters like Thesiger must have been perfectly well aware that any systematic slaughter of a particular species was certain to lead ultimately to its demise.[13] There is no doubt that Thesiger hunted compulsively: he records in his autobiography that although each time he hunted lion he half-expected to be killed, he was unable to resist the urge to continue. Elsewhere he claimed that hunting was more than a desire to kill animals.[14] For almost half of his life, it was, for him, the quintessential expression of manhood. The slow build-up – ideally (though not always in practice) requiring days of hard trekking to get into the area of the game – followed by the exhilarating hours of careful tracking, and the final, orgasmic drama of the kill, had the intensity of the sexual act. At its best it was a gladiatorial competition: a single combat with nature, requiring strength, tenacity and nerve, for which the prize was the kill. 'I thrived on the remote setting and hardship,' Thesiger said. 'For me, hunting meant going into a remote area where you earned your trophy by hard work. Then, when you pulled the trigger after all that, you could see at once whether you'd hit the target or not – the kill was the climax.'[15] After his almost single-handed campaign against the wild boar in Iraq in his mid forties – during which he was once gored in the hand – Thesiger's compulsion to kill big-game burned out. In Kenya in the 1960s he shot only for the pot: 'I shot the odd gazelle for meat,' he said, 'but I wouldn't have wanted to shoot another lion or buffalo, or a rhino – which I never have shot – I just didn't want to do it: I'd done all the hunting I wanted to do, but I don't for a moment regret that I did it.'[16] Almost certainly this was because his nerve had gone. After being charged sixteen times by lion, gored once by a boar, and several near-misses, the odds were against him. Had he kept up his lion-shooting into old age he would sooner or later have been mauled or killed, and like a judicious gambler, he knew when to quit: 'I was quite certain that [a lion] would get me in the end,' he said. 'It was always dangerous and that's why I enjoyed it. If it hadn't been dangerous, I would have shot kudu instead!'[17]

Thesiger was immensely thankful that in his time in the Sudan, as today, there were no professional hunting-parties led by white hunters: 'When I went to the southern Sudan there weren't any hunters,' he said, 'and so by the Grace of God I never encountered them when I was hunting myself. But they were beginning to arrive there, then of course there was independence and the civil war in the south stopped it all.'[18] Having learned his hunting-skills the hard way – by trial and error – Thesiger despised the 'big business' Ernest Hemingway style of big-game shooting, in which the hunter is delivered to the killing-area by car and dropped off, supported by a white hunter who will be there to cover if he misses. 'One of the things these white hunters did in Kenya was that they'd guarantee you'd shoot a lion on the day you arrived,' Thesiger said. 'They'd already laid it on – they'd shot a zebra and dragged it cross-country for a quarter of a mile and left it so that you'd have an easy approach from behind an ant-heap. Then the people arrived in Nairobi and were brought by aeroplane to whatever camp it was. Then they'd get out of the aeroplane, have some lunch and go off in a car to shoot a lion. And they'd say we actually shot a lion the day we arrived in Kenya – and boast about it!'[19] In his Kenya years, much later, Thesiger would be severely critical of Joy and George Adamson, of *Born Free* fame, for bringing up lions in captivity then returning them half-tame to the wild: 'It was the best way of turning them into man-killers I know of,' he commented. 'George Adamson claimed that this lion had an affection for human beings, and then it proved it by killing his cook. I wrote to the [Nairobi] *Standard* about it.'[20]

After Moore had returned from leave, in December 1935, Thesiger made his first journey in the desert proper. Bir Natrun (now Al 'Atrun) is one of a chain of watering-places stretching across the Libyan desert (eastern Sahara), by which the ancient caravans of the Forty Days Road once traversed this most arid of all the world's deserts. Visited by W.G. Browne, the first European known to have crossed the Sahara, in 1794, it was famous as a source of rock-salt and was – and still is – visited by camel caravans from as far away as the Nile and Chad. Little has changed since Thesiger's time, save that Fiat lorries now visit the tiny oasis as well as camel-caravans. Bir Natrun had already been explored by motor vehicle in Thesiger's day, however. Moore himself had undertaken motor expeditions in the Sahara during the thirties and discovered a new oasis, not recognized or named until 1974, and the areas to the north had been extensively investigated by Ralph Bagnold, using Model 'T' Fords, in the early 1930s. In 1928, Douglas Newbold, Governor of Kordofan Province, had made the last great camel-trek of discovery in the region, with William Kennedy-Shaw, a forestry official. Travelling in a diagonal across the south Libyan desert with forty tribesmen from the Hawawir tribe, Newbold and Shaw had as their objective the goal of all explorers in the eastern Sahara at that time: the 'lost' oasis of Zerzura, held in medieval manuscripts to contain a mummified Pharaoh and a hoard of treasure.

As Thesiger was preparing for the journey, however, he heard that he and Moore were invited to a Christmas fancy-dress party in El Fasher at the Governor's residence: an invitation that could not be refused. This tedious social duty meant that he would have to set a good pace to Bir Natrun and back. Travelling with two camel-men, two Maidob guides and four policemen, Thesiger set off on 1 December 1935 for his first voyage into what Moore called 'The High Altar of God'. The party's camels carried water slung in goatskins from the pommels of their saddles, and provisions of flour, dates, tea, powdered vegetables and spices. Stores of grain and bundles of hay were carried for camel-feed, and during the first days, while it was still abundant, they collected firewood. For the first time, Thesiger wore Arab dress: a white headcloth, three or four yards long, layered around the head: baggy trousers loose at the waist and ankles, and a calf-length shirt of coarse cotton. He felt a little self-conscious in this rig, though he conceded that the clothes were more comfortable than anything devised by Westerners for riding camels in the desert. To dress like his companions was itself to enter a different persona, to merge more perfectly into the illusion that demanded the exclusion of everything that reminded Thesiger of the twentieth century. Here, in the plains of the eastern Sahara, time had little meaning: 10,000-year-old arrowheads lay on the surface where they had been dropped by their makers, next to brass cartridge-cases only months old. But for a few insignificant details, one might be back in the Middle Ages. Thesiger was distinct from his companions: a man of a foreign race, colour and creed, but here in the desert such distinctions lost their sharp focus. Yet though he might squat with them on the ground and eat with his right hand from the communal bowl, he was unable to forget his superiority completely.

There has been a long tradition of European travellers in Arab countries adopting native dress: an indication, perhaps, of the interchangeability of the two cultures, and their essential complementarity: based on two sides of the same sea, both centred on monotheistic religions, both descended from ancient, literate civilizations. A stickler for convention where dress was concerned, however, Thesiger claimed that he would not have dreamed of wearing these clothes anywhere but the desert.[21] He despised Harold Ingrams, the British Arabist who pacified the Hadhramaut, for wearing Arab dress in his office: 'Ingrams was a man I had no respect for,' he said, 'because he always dressed up like an Arab. Well, for the Consul to dress up with a tarbush on his head because it felt it got him closer to the people he was administering was poppycock. He'd sit in Mukalla, a European port, and you'd go and see the Consul and there he is dressed in Arab clothes: well, it's undignified.'[22] Similarly, the celebrated traveller Freya Stark evoked Thesiger's displeasure over her choice of dress: 'You see a picture of Freya Stark in Arab dress, and there she is dressed as a man with a dagger and a cartridge-belt and a rifle and all the rest of it – well, why? If she'd wanted to dress like an Arab she should have worn woman's clothes instead of this ridiculous thing of dressing up like a man or a boy – that condemns her from start to finish.'[23] In the marshes of Iraq, his companion Gavin Maxwell received a sharp dose of vitriol for wanting to dress like the natives: 'He wanted to wear Arab dress because it was more romantic,' Thesiger said. 'What was the point in Gavin Maxwell wearing Arab clothes? I mean, if he was going to put them on, he should have behaved like an Arab and talked like an Arab. When I went to the Marshes I was British and I dressed in British clothes – I wasn't going to pretend I was an Arab. After two years there, though, one of the Sheikhs suggested that I might like to wear their dress, and I accepted. But Maxwell looked ridiculous, and my canoe-boys said they wouldn't take him dressed like that.'[24]

This is Thesiger at his most obscure, for none was more romantic than he in his adoption of Arab clothes: wearing them first simply because they were more comfortable – an obvious reason – and secondly because they helped him to fit more perfectly into his role in the adventure. Later, in Arabia, he would claim that he had no choice but to wear Arab dress, since otherwise he would not have been accepted. Even if this is entirely true,[25] it can hardly apply to his earlier journeys in the Sudan. Later he would even adopt Arab dress while serving among British soldiers in North Africa – a practice very similar to that he condemned Ingrams for. Though asking no man's leave to adopt his robes on his trek to Bir Natrun, he came to believe that others, like Maxwell, had somehow to 'earn the right' to them. If too many outsiders were able to adopt foreign dress, Thesiger's belief in his exclusive ability to shift from culture to culture was shattered. For another generation, his insistence on wearing the uniform of the British squirearchy – tweed jacket, twill trousers and hat – in the Iraqi marshes or the wilds of Afghanistan would seem far more eccentric and inappropriate than wearing Arab clothes. At its most basic level this attitude is part of Thesiger's sense of exclusivity – the feeling that no other Westerner but himself had the right to enter into the dream. But there is also his 'conventional' persona to consider. 'I dislike being in the wrong clothes,' he said. 'It embarrasses me if I turn up to a dinner-party in a white tie and they are all wearing black ties. It also bothers me, though less, to turn up in a black tie and they're all wearing tail-coats.'[26]

Previously, Thesiger had ridden his camels at a trot. On the way to Bir Natrun, though, for the first time he learned desert discipline. Camels are never trotted on long desert journeys, even when they are hand-fed on grain. In the desert, a man's life depends on his camel, and the animal's reserves of energy must be preserved at all costs. On this journey Thesiger's party rode from dawn till sunset – the standard practice for winter, when the days are cool and the nights cold, and the camels are able to keep going right through the day. Gradually, almost imperceptibly, the Sahelian scrubland merged into the legendary pasturelands that spread right across the southern Sahara. Known as the *jizzu* in the Sudan, and as *'ushub* in the western Sahara, these rich grasses attract nomad clans from far afield, and here, in a good year, they will remain for months, living only on camel's milk as both food and water. The party spotted a herd of 300 camels belonging to a Kababish family, but as they rode towards him the Arab herdsman bolted, probably suspecting them of being Maidob raiders. On the morning of the third day, the carpet of *jizzu* grasses fell suddenly behind them, and Thesiger saw in front of him the open desert. It was breathtakingly beautiful: folds and counterfolds of mallow pink, cream and chrome orange, littered in places with smooth blue boulders like polished dinosaur eggs – a landscape of naked power from which time had long since flayed all superfluities. The desert seemed alive with a brooding presence of its own: lights sparkled there in will-o'-the-wisp colours and a rainbow haze of heat gave the sands an insubstantial look: '[It was] my first sight of the desert,' Thesiger recalled. 'It was absolutely empty, stretching to infinity ahead of us – the vastness, the emptiness, the cleanness, the feeling of space. That was what I had come to see.'[27]

The following day they arrived in the Wadi Howar, a thick swath of green cutting a gash through the waterless sands of the desert. Draining water from the Ennedi Mountains, Wadi Howar was in prehistoric times the centre of a flourishing community of hunters and cattle-nomads, the remains of whose huts and fires are still to be seen there, and whose culture was destroyed as the Sahara slowly became a desert after 2000 BC. Today, with its vegetation of long-rooted *arak* trees (*Salvadora persica*), Wadi Howar is the home for a handful of Kababish nomads who pitch their camel's-hair tents on the dunes and water their camels at hand-dug wells in the wadi. Thesiger was amazed to find such a haven of green in the midst of sterility.

Three days later his party arrived at Bir Natrun, a salt-pan sparkling brilliant crystal white under the single fang-like hill of Jabal Toli'a (Kashafa), where nomads from Kordofan, Darfur and the Nile valley quarried lumps of pinkish rock-salt using the horns of dead oryx as tools. This rock-salt had been in use since Pharaonic times, when it was a vital ingredient of the mummification process. The salt-plains were the legacy of a lake that existed here millennia ago – probably the centre of a flourishing oasis – and which had slowly shrunk and died, leaving the precious salt deposits for the use of unborn generations. Slightly brackish water was still to be found near the surface, in the vicinity of a few stunted date-palms. Since there were no sources of salt in the sub-Saharan fringe-lands, the natron was crucial to the nomads both for sale in the towns and as a necessary mineral for their livestock. In short, the salt was valuable, and a number of skirmishes had been fought over the place, particularly between the fierce Kababish Bedouin and the black Gur'an nomads from the central Sahara. The possibility of these raids gave Thesiger the excuse for his journey there.

On his way back to Darfur Thesiger reflected for the first time on the desert's unexpected spiritual dimension: how it reduced one to utter insignificance, yet at the same time, paradoxically, seeming to magnify everything – rocks, grass, trees, insects, water – giving each its full significance as if one were seeing it for the first time. On the return journey Thesiger came across the spoor of an astonishing variety of wildlife: seven or eight lion, wild dog, Dorcas gazelle, addra, oryx and addax, scores of ostrich, and even a giraffe. None of these species save the Dorcas gazelle thrives around Wadi Howar today.

Thesiger arrived in Musbat on Christmas Eve, 1935, and was rushed by car to Kutum and then to El Fasher for the Governor's fancy-dress party. Neither Thesiger nor Moore could be persuaded to wear fancy-dress, however, claiming that in their dinner jackets they were parodying Englishmen who dressed for dinner in the jungle. There is an interesting contrast here. The Thesiger who had so recently been able to fling off his ADC's togs in favour of the flowing robes of a tribesman was unable to 'dress up' among his own people. Then, it had been part of the adventure. Here it was the unheroic English drawing-room in the wilds of Africa.

Had it been a tribal people, one feels, who had dressed in exotic and bizarre costumes and proceeded to drink, feast and dance all night, Thesiger would almost certainly have approved. He was prepared to accept the most outlandish of customs among the 'primitive'. In his own race, though, he saw it as 'idiotic' and was ashamed of what the servants might think – never imagining that they might have been absolutely fascinated, just as he would have been had the masqueraders been Sudanese: 'I felt embarrassed,' he recorded. '. . . They saw the Governor dressed as a prisoner, his middle-aged wife as a schoolgirl, other wives dressed as men, their husbands as Sheikhs, troubadours, bull-fighters and God knows what else, and all of them drinking and dancing and getting noisier.'[28] It was a long way from the primeval silence of the desert. It was here, for the first time, though, that Thesiger met Hugh Boustead, with whom he would later serve in the Sudan Defence Force, and Clifford 'Pansy' Drew, the medical officer who would be his colleague at Gojjam. Later, at a dinner-party held by the Commander of the Western Arab Corps, Renouf, he found conversation buzzing with the news that Italian forces from Libya had occupied Bir Natrun. An Italian army had invaded Abyssinia the previous year, much to Thesiger's chagrin, and at the same time had occupied the oasis of 'Uwaynat on the Libyan –Sudanese frontier. Now it began to look as if they planned a slow push into the Sudan, seizing Sudanese oases piecemeal. An RAF squadron at Dongola had been put on red alert. Hearing the news, Thesiger chimed in from the bottom of the dinner-table: 'I've just come back from Bir Natrun, and I didn't see any Italians.' There was a pregnant pause as the facts sank in. Then Renouf thundered, 'What! You've been to Bir Natrun! Then *you* must have been the Italians!'

In February, having completed a marathon camel-ride from Jabal Maidob to Omdurman – a distance of 450 miles in nine days – Thesiger was firmly reprimanded by Gillan for the disturbance he had caused: 'We realized when we selected you that you were rather odd,' the Civil Secretary told him. '. . . It is up to you to fit in. Dupuis spoke well of you, but remember that you don't travel in another District without its DC's permission, and most certainly not in another Province without mine.'[29] The incident did not leave a permanent black mark against him, but gave him 'a reputation': 'I mean, Guy Moore let me do it and gave me a month's leave,' he said, 'but then he was fairly odd himself. Of course, it was outside the District, outside the Province – a forbidden area really.'[30]

In April Thesiger enjoyed his first leave in England and decided to travel back to the Sudan overland. He took the Orient Express through the Balkans and Turkey, changed trains at Aleppo, and visited Beirut and Damascus. He obtained special permission from Robin Buxton to visit the Druzes, whose revolt against the French had been one of his *causes célèbres* while at school. Later he stayed in Amman for a few days with Moore's former colleague, John Bagot Glubb, and was delighted when Glubb took him to visit the Sheikhs of the Bani Sakhr. Thesiger had met the Kababish – an authentic Bedu tribe of the Sudan; now, for the first time, he encountered the Bedu of north Arabia, in the company of Britain's most distinguished Arabist, Glubb Pasha. He travelled on to Cairo, where he met Dan Sandford and his wife, who had escaped from Abyssinia during the Italian invasion the previous October. Sandford assured him that Britain and Italy would inevitably clash before long: 'When that happens,' he predicted, 'there will be a place for both of us in the campaign of liberation.' Finally Thesiger dashed by train, steamer, and lorry back to Kutum, arriving there in July. In September, Moore sent him to another tribal conference between the Maidob and the Kababish, where, to his delight, he met the Governor of Kordofan, Douglas Newbold.

Thesiger had met Newbold only once previously, in London, and had a special admiration for him. Archaeologist, classical scholar, explorer, administrator, diplomat, Newbold was blessed with a particular charm which Thesiger called 'the gift of friendship'. Though not an original thinker, Newbold – who was to become Civil Secretary two years later – was the most outstanding figure of the Anglo-Egyptian Sudan. In the 1920s he had made two camel journeys into the unknown blank of the eastern Sahara, discovering the massif of Tagaru and bringing back some of the first conclusive evidence in rock-drawings and stone implements that the desert had once been more fertile than it is today. Later he had made more remarkable journeys with the famous desert motorist Ralph Bagnold, in the deserts to the north. 'I spent a fascinating three days with him there in the middle of the desert,' Thesiger recalled. 'Mostly we talked about desert travel, and he agreed with me that cars were an unpardonable intrusion into the desert, but in the modern world there they were and you'd got to use them if you were doing it seriously.'[31] Newbold told Thesiger that he had always wanted to trek by camel to Tibesti, the Sahara's highest and least known mountain range. It was an idea that Thesiger never forgot. Some months later, while travelling once again in Wadi Howar, he encountered a tribesman from the Bedayat – one of the cluster of black tribes speaking central Saharan languages – who told him about a great massif of moutains called Tu that he had visited as a boy, inhabited by a people called the Teda. Thesiger realized that Tu was Tibesti, the place Newbold had mentioned, and resolved at once that he would go and explore it.

Meanwhile, however, he had some unpleasant business to attend to. His probationary period was drawing to an end and he was expected to pass examinations in Arabic and Law. He had enjoyed his time in Kutum, but in the excitement of hunting and travelling had neglected his studies. As a result he failed both subjects. Depressed by the lectures on education and development that followed the examinations, and by the notion that very soon his fun in Kutum must end to be replaced by more constructive administration in a big city, Thesiger asked for an interview with Angus Gillan. 'I asked if it was true that I would soon be sent to somewhere like Wad Medani,' Thesiger remembered, 'and Gillan said yes, it's about time you got a bit of that kind of experience. I said look here, what I want you to do is to let me resign here and now from the Service – which was something nobody had ever done before – and then re-employ me on a contract basis, on the understanding that I'll only be sent to the remotest and wildest areas. He said he couldn't contemplate it: it would wreck my entire career and I'd lose my pension and everything, and prospects of promotion.'[32] None of this deterred Thesiger, who already knew that he did not have the kind of commitment to development that was the ultimate justification for the job. In Kutum he had found a tiny enclave, which, under Moore, had attempted as far as possible to resist change. There, for the time being, he wanted to remain. 'He argued away at me,' Thesiger went on, 'and finally he said, well, if you insist, I'll do it. I left the room a contract DC, and lost my pension.'[33] Shortly afterwards he wrote home: 'As a contract DC I shall always be given the wild, exciting, and in my eyes, interesting, jobs. I know it's financial suicide and mad to the last degree if you judge it from ordinary standards; unfortunately my standards are not ordinary and I would always rather live in the present than sacrifice the present to the future.'[34] Thesiger was, of course, already in the happy position of having a private income: the £400 a year which he had inherited from his grandmother and which had taken him through Oxford. 'I was hardly spending anything,' he said, 'a few shillings a day. All my pay was accumulating. I paid my cook a shilling a day and he had to buy the meat and milk and we got the vegetables out of the garden. So if you'd got £400 a year it was more than adequate – it was affluent.'[35]

In El Fasher, Governor Phil Ingleson reiterated Gillan's concern, but the sympathetic Moore, himself a contract DC, told him, 'I think you're probably right.'[36] If Thesiger had been expecting that his transfer to contract status would mean a few more years in Kutum, though, he was disappointed. In June 1937 he learned that he was to be transferred to the Western Nuer District in Upper Nile Province, a very different environment indeed from the arid Darfur.

In November 1937 Thesiger returned to England on leave, and took his mother for a tour of Morocco: the first of many journeys they would make together. 'I'd always wanted to see Morocco,' Thesiger said. 'I thought it was a dramatic and exciting country. I'd read a certain amount about it when they were fighting the French and my feeling was entirely for the Rifs who fought against them. You couldn't fly to Morocco in those days: it was still quite primitive then. It took us seven days to get to Marrakesh: you got on a ferry boat and you went across to France, then you went by train to Marseilles, then you got a steamer which took two days to get to Gibraltar, then from Gibraltar a day across to Tangier, and then from Tangier by train down to Marrakesh. When we got to Marrakesh and saw the mountains and the buildings and everything, we felt we'd achieved something getting there. That's a perfectly good example of what has been destroyed in the world today: now you can leave London and four hours later you'll be in Marrakesh.'³⁷ Though Morocco was then, like Egypt, already a tourist destination, and comfortable hotels existed, it was very much the preserve of the rich. The Thesigers stayed at the Hotel Tarzi in Marrakesh, strolling through the thronging bazaars and drinking in the sights of the Jama al Fna at sunset, when the smell of roasted meat and grilled fish drifts across the square, and when the storytellers, magicians and troupes of tumblers appear, collecting dense circles of clamouring spectators: 'It was this great open space with musicians and acrobats,' Thesiger remembered, 'and the French presence was very little noticeable.'³⁸ He hired a car and drove his mother through the spectacular Sous valley to Taroudant, on a day trip. At Telouet, 8,000 feet up in the High Atlas, they feasted at the notorious 'Eagle's Nest' − the fortress of Tihami al Glawi, the sophisticated yet autocratic Pasha of Marrakesh − to whom Thesiger had acquired a letter of introduction through friends of his brother Roderic. 'We went to all sorts of places, travelling by car,' Thesiger recalled, 'and we'd stay in reasonably priced hotels − there was something in most places, and we didn't need a big hotel, just a place to stay.' From Marrakesh they drove to Fez, which Thesiger thought a fascinating city. He spent all his time in the bazaar delighting at the Arabian Nights atmosphere of the dark, winding alleys with their donkeys and mule-trains, each section assigned to one particular trade, and each distinguished by its own particular odour: the tang of raw leather in the shoemaker's souk, chili and black pepper in the spice souk, sandalwood among the carpenters: 'Fez was one of the more memorable cities I've seen,' he recalled. 'But it was an exclusive city, and one felt a little excluded by religious feeling.' They also visited nearby Meknes, of which he remembered only the spectacular gateways.³⁹ They travelled back through the Rif mountains and crossed the border into Algeria. From there they took the ferry back to Marseilles, where Thesiger said farewell to his mother and embarked on a ship bound for Port Sa'id in Egypt. It was their first journey together since Thesiger's child-hood, and their last until 1954. Geoffrey Dawson, of *The Times*, had commissioned Thesiger to write a piece on the situation in

Morocco, which was published the following December under the title 'The Mind of the Moor'. The piece is largely a pronouncement on French policy in Morocco, which Dawson ascribed to 'A Special Correspondent': 'I didn't put my name to it,' Thesiger said, 'I thought it would be better not – a young Probationer of the Sudan Political Service writing on Moors and things.'[40] The article centres around an argument then pertinent to the Sudan, and one which would become Thesiger's most familiar theme in old age: the spread of education among traditional peoples, the destruction of traditional ways of life and the drift to the cities. Under the sub-title 'Educated but Workless', he wrote: 'French domination in Morocco has resulted in a considerable and yearly increasing spread of . . . education among the native population. There is now a large number of not only literate but educated and able young men in the towns. Yet, while conscious of their fitness for employment, few are able to find it . . .'[41] 'One of the far-reaching effects of the French conquest was the steady drift off the land to the towns . . . now they live . . . in the wretched squalor of settled villages, in hovels of beaten-out petrol tins, crowded in the outskirts of the towns. The consequence of drought, locusts or cattle-plague they had understood and fatalistically accepted. The inscrutable workings of the economic crisis are beyond their grasp . . .'[42] There are some typically Thesigerian touches here, which foreshadow his future writing – the hint, for example, that 'drought, locusts and cattle-plague' were somehow 'preferable' because they were traditional sufferings – but generally the tone is remarkably restrained compared with his later assertions '. . .The benefits Morocco has received from France are incontestable . . . [but] . . . Nationalism is a rising tide among the Eastern peoples and Morocco will continue to claim her right to what others have received . . . it would be difficult to deny there is justice in their demand.'[43] The tone contrasts markedly with his later verdict on Sudanese independence: 'They [the Sudanese] didn't want independence. No one was thinking about independence when we were there, but by the time you'd instituted British-run universities and schools and you'd gone on insisting on the idea of independence . . . we put it into the minds of these people, and it's caused chaos all over Africa.'[44]

Thesiger found Idris waiting for him in Khartoum with all his baggage from Kutum. A few days later they arrived in Kosti, where they boarded the paddle-steamer *Kereri* – the floating headquarters of the Western Nuer District. Lashed alongside the steamer was a barge which served as stable for the officers' horses, a post for the local police, a prison, accommodation for porters, and a general menagerie of sheep, goats, cattle and chickens. A smaller barge, housing the medical orderly and his men, was attached to the bows. Soon the steamer was chugging through Nuer country, a vast area of flat, grassy plains, cut by a web of tributaries debouching into the White Nile like silver threads across a great carpet. In the rainy season much of the lowland lies under water, and in the hollows and along the riverbanks great stands of reeds and papyrus flourish. When the floods subside, the clay soil beneath bursts into rich grassland, and the Nuer migrate back to the plains with the cattle-herds that are their life. The Nuer possess little but their cattle, and their thoughts, customs and conversations revolve around the herds. Tall, lank and spare, the Nuer herdsman wears nothing but simple bead decorations, carries only spears, a pouch for grain, a skin as a mattress and a tiny stool as a pillow. The great anthropologist E.E. Evans-Pritchard has written: 'From a European's point of view, Nuerland has no favourable qualities. It is everywhere hard on man and beast, being for the most part of the year either parched or swamp. But the Nuer think that they live in the finest country on earth and, it must be admitted, for herdsmen their country has many good features. A few Nuer have been taken to Khartoum, which they consider to be the home of all white men, and, having seen the desert vegetation of those parts, have been confirmed in their opinion that their land is superior to ours. All who have lived with the Nuer would agree that though they are poor in goods they are very proud in spirit. Reliant on one another, they are loyal and generous to their kinsmen, but they despise all that lies outside them.'[45] 'I was glad to see it,' Thesiger said, 'because at that time the Nuer had only been taken over about eight years before after a certain amount of fighting and it was an area teeming with animals. I think hardly anybody had been down there hunting and shooting, and I don't suppose any visitors. We lived on the boat and it was a lovely way to live because you could get off in one branch of the river, and meet it again in a different place in a month's time.'[46]

The country had been thoroughly explored by its first DC, Vere Fergusson, who had fought a number of skirmishes with the xenophobic Nuer and had finally been murdered by them. Since his day the region had been pacified and administered by Romilly, a man who had earned the respect of the tribes. Thesiger's DC was Romilly's replacement, the pipe-smoking Wedderburn-Maxwell, who took up his post only a fortnight before Thesiger. Though they were equally strangers in the district, Maxwell had served in another Nuer District and spoke their language. 'Our main object was to get round and see as much of the District as possible,' Thesiger said. 'We weren't doing much in the way of administrative work at all. I think I had thirty porters, but I could have managed with five. Each porter carried food for the man in front of him and we gave them a shilling a day. They weren't under any compulsion and could do as they liked. There was nothing for them to buy with their shilling anyway – what they wanted was cows. The chiefs could inflict fines in cattle, and later we'd auction them, and that was how the porters got more cows.'[47]

Though Thesiger accounted for another forty lion in Nuer country, his prime objective was to bag elephant: 'They spent their time in the papyrus,' he said, 'which was as high as a house, and the result was that if you followed them there you couldn't see them, you could only hear them rumbling just ahead of you. You were allowed to shoot only two elephants a year, and so you wanted to get animals with good tusks so that you could sell them and make a bit of money. Under those circumstances – in the papyrus – you were afraid you'd have to shoot a small, bad elephant that was coming for you or something. I did spend a lot of time following them up in the papyrus, but I never fired a shot at one under those circumstances. The curious thing was that they cleared straight out when it started raining – I don't know why but they went straight out to the open plains. That's when you could get up to them and select the one you wanted. I shot four while I was there.'[48]

During the wet season the bush was waterlogged, and Thesiger's trail of porters tramped through thigh-deep water. In the hot summers, though, when the floods subsided, the landscape became arid: 'You were either walking through water or looking for somewhere to get a drink,' Thesiger said.[49] In the baking summers the small stable of horses the DC kept on the *Kereri* came into its own, for most of the District could be covered by horse. Thesiger and Idris continued their lion-hunting excursions, and Thesiger experienced another providential escape: 'There was a lion and we chased it by horse until it came to bay,' he said. 'I got off my horse to shoot it and gave the reins to Idris. I was using a double-barrelled rifle, and was still shaking a bit from the gallop. Anyway I missed the lion, then like a fool I fired the other barrel instead of reloading the first one, and the lion came at me promptly as I was fumbling to get another cartridge in. I looked up thinking it should have been on me by now, and Idris was still sitting there – for some funny reason the horses hadn't bolted – and I said, "Where is it?" and he said, "It came as far as that grass and turned away." I don't know why that happened, but obviously I'd missed both times or it would certainly have pressed home the attack. Lion are unpredictable. The funny thing was that Idris sat there completely unmoved: he had got my other rifle, but sitting on the horse he couldn't have used it.'[50]

In the Western Nuer, Thesiger had entered the dreamscape of his childhood. Here were lion aplenty, herds of elephant 1,000 strong, buffalo, white rhino, hippo, giraffe in swarming hundreds. Here were naked tribesmen, a fierce warrior race who scarified themselves as a sign of manhood and dyed their hair gold with cow's urine – a people totally unaffected by an outside world they knew nothing of, still at the centre of their own universe, governed by magic and witchcraft. It was an almost untouched world beyond roads, airfields, schools or hospitals, where few outsiders had ever been. It is interesting, then, that Thesiger was not content. Here was everything he had dreamed of as a boy, yet, as on the Danakil journey, there was something missing. There was too great a cultural gap between the British and the Nuer. Unlike the Islamic peoples of northern Sudan, with their comprehensible and compatible notions of courage, loyalty and hospitality, these Nilotic peoples belonged to a tradition difficult to comprehend and impossible to emulate. With the northern, desert people,

Thesiger could dress as they did and behave as they did: he could hardly, he felt, have retained his dignity while dressing as a naked Nuer, dyeing his hair with urine. If he remained among the Nuer he would remain the 'white man in Africa', always surrounded by the excess baggage of the West – the tent, the camp-equipment, the Wolseley helmet – that constantly pricked him with images of the industrial world beyond the dreamscape. In one sense his journeys among the Arabized peoples were the ultimate make-believe, in which he could, for a time, immerse himself in a new role, a new character. This – he believed – was not possible among the Nuer.

They may have named him Kwechuor, after one of their oxen, but inwardly Thesiger knew that with them he could never be more than Wilfred Thesiger, the foreign ADC. 'I liked them but I didn't want to spend the rest of my life among them, which Wedderburn did,' was the way he put it, 'but I'd have been happy and spent the rest of my life at Kutum. The Nuer were too primitive. In the north you could live like the people and stay with them, but I remember seeing this Nuer coming over and putting his hand into the pot where the grain was, and then he turned round and started to pee while he was eating it. Well, you couldn't live on the same level as people like that. I wanted to live to some extent on terms of equality with the people I was administering. I was still the boss, of course, but then you could be administering people in England, as a magistrate or a police-man, and still live under the same conditions as the people you were administering. Among the Nuer you couldn't.'[51] The cultural preferences which Thesiger was later to admit are manifest in his attitude to the Nuer, and although he would never have countenanced trying to change these tribesmen, there remains an implied criticism in the words 'too primitive' and his picture of the tribesman urinating while eating: the Nuer was not, as it were, 'a gentleman'. As in much else, Thesiger was to reverse his opinion of such 'uncouth' peoples later, yet this attitude must stand as a caution to those who have been quick to label Thesiger a 'modernist' in his view of traditional cultures. Though without the overbearing ethnocentrism of many previous travellers, he was essentially a man of his time in most respects. The cultures he identified with during his most active period were almost exclusively Muslim and generally relatively advanced – in the material sense of using money, imported cloth, firearms and riding technology. Even the Afars were nominally Muslim and well accustomed to firearms – those in Aussa had been considered quite 'civilized'. Thesiger never took great interest in hunter-gatherers. He remained remote from cultures such as the Indians of the Amazon, the Bushmen, the Pygmies, the mountaineers of Papua New Guinea and other *causes célèbres* of the late twentieth century. The cultures which interested him sprang out of 'the authentic eastern world' of Kipling and Conrad: the experience of Empire. The model for the way he wished to relate to his people at this stage was provided by John Glubb: 'After all,' he said, 'Glubb with his Arabs was completely one of them, and yet he had tremendous respect, which wouldn't have been any greater had he sat in an office or a tent.'[52] With the Nuer, in other words, you could never be 'one of them'. He expressed this view later with typically ironic humour to a woman anthropologist studying the Nuer: 'I said that in Arabia if you put on Arab clothes you could at least be assimilated to some extent into the crowd, but you couldn't with the Nuer. She said she had done it, and I said she must have looked an extraordinary sight – all pink and peeling!'[53]

Though Thesiger enjoyed his eighteen months among the Nuer, his thoughts turned constantly to the desert. Only a few years earlier he had come to the Sudan looking for a way to get back to Abyssinia, and an environment not unlike the one he was experiencing, yet now – the Italian occupation not withstanding – all thoughts of a career in the country of his birth were expunged from his mind. 'It wasn't just the desert,' Thesiger explained. 'It isn't places but the people who live there . . . I felt these people [the Nuer] would never substitute me for the Darfur people. It would be interesting to be with them for a year or two years, but if you were a contract DC you were likely to be there for seven years and I couldn't see myself living there as long as that.'[54] This was in no sense due to the presence of his DC, Wedderburn-Maxwell, who was as understanding as Moore, and let Thesiger do much as he liked. 'I was very lucky in that I got on well with him,' he said, 'because living on a boat like that with someone you disliked would have been very irritating. I realized that on the occasion when this young vet came aboard: he wanted to go round with me and see some of the country, and I disliked him. We had very little in common and I thought he was assertive – he just exasperated me, I don't know why, but you just dislike some people instinctively. I was very glad when he got off the boat and was gone.'[55]

In August 1938, Thesiger took three months' leave and spent it making his long-planned journey to Tibesti. Straddling northern Chad and southern Libya, Tibesti is the Sahara's greatest mountain range, its highest point, Emi Koussi, reaching more than 11,000 feet. Known since Roman times, the mountains were a refuge for another of the Sahara's mystery races, the Teda or Tubu, distant relatives of Thesiger's Zaghawa, Bedayat and Berti in Darfur. Though dark and negroid with fuzzy hair, the Teda show blood-group patterns totally different from sub-Saharan negroes, while their central Saharan tongue has affinities with no known language. Noted for their hardiness, they had been among the most feared Saharan raiders of the nineteenth century, operating over a vast region from the Nile to the Niger, and covering distances between watering-places that look impossible except for a motor car. Later, however, they had been suppressed by the Turks, operating through the Senussi brotherhood in Libya, and had put up little resistance to the French. Tibesti had been reached by Gustav Nachtigal, who had barely escaped with his life, and extensively explored by the French officer, Colonel Tilho, in the 1920s. By 1938, though, Tibesti still remained largely unknown to the world outside: 'It wasn't unexplored,' Thesiger said, 'because the French administered it and surveyed it all, but apart from Nachtigal no one had been there but French army officers. No aeroplane had ever landed there, and no car had been within 1,000 miles. It was as remote as anywhere you could find, and the Teda interested me as a people. It was a long, hard journey in desert country and a sort of obvious extension from Kutum District.'[56]

Before leaving Nuer Thesiger had written to Guy Moore, requesting him to find Kathir, the old Bedayi who had first interested him in Tibesti: 'I asked him to have Kathir waiting for me at Tini [now Tina] with perhaps four other people,' Thesiger

said, 'and camels to take us as far as Faya. From there we'd have
to hire Teda camels that were used to travelling in the hills.'[57]
The party, including Idris, Kathir, and four Zaghawa camel-
men, left Tini on 3 August 1938, heading across the frontier of
French Sahara. They carried three months' supply of flour in
their saddle-bags, onions, powdered okra, the sun-jerked meat
called *sharmut*, and bags of tea and sugar. They carried goatskins
for water, sheepskins, blankets and a small tent. Thesiger had his
.275 hunting rifle, but none of the others was armed. 'We had the
minimum of stuff with us,' Thesiger recalled, 'no European food –
we ate the local food and carried the same stuff. We were in
inhabited country and you could easily buy a sheep or a goat. I
shot the odd gazelle. Unlike later journeys – in Arabia for
instance – we were never really hungry. We always had enough
water to drink. But then we did far, far longer marches such as
we'd never have contemplated in the desert.'[58] They rode fast
across the stony scrub-country, the camels lurching forwards,
forming and breaking as the sun coalesced from the bulbous globe
of sunrise to the white-hot fireball of midday, shrinking the
shadows to elliptical pools beneath their camels' bellies. They
halted at Zaghawa villages constructed on the hilltops, where
Idris's relatives received them with great hospitality. Soon they
were marching in the lee of the Ennedi Mountains, towering
5,000 feet above them. Unlike the vast sterile plains of the desert
outside, this spine of rocky hills was relatively fertile. Great *heraz*
trees shaded the wadis, and in places there were permanent rock
pools inhabited by small crocodiles and shoals of fish. In a series
of grottos in the Wadi Tuku, Thesiger was fascinated to find some
beautifully executed rock-pictures of hunting scenes, horsemen,
and long-horned cattle.

In Ennedi, Thesiger arrived at the outpost of Fada where he
was entertained by French officers of the Groupe Nomade. He
was evidently impressed by this fine body of men, two sections of
which passed through Fada the day he arrived: 'They live continuously under active service conditions,' he wrote, 'and are in
consequence extraordinarily fit and hard . . . Despite its hardness
or perhaps because of it, all the officers I met were enthusiastically
in love with the life they led.'[59] Thesiger was touched by a sense
of envy: here were men who ranged continuously across the

largest area of desert in the world, living a hard life as a matter of course: a life which among his British colleagues would have been branded 'positively eccentric'.[60] From Fada, Thesiger's party crossed the desert to Faya (now Faya-Largeau) in Bourkou, the French headquarters in Tibesti. His earlier journey to Bir Natrun had been made in midwinter: it was now high summer and the rocky plains were lambent with reflected heat. Thesiger adopted summer marching style, travelling by moonlight and resting in a tent or under thorn-trees in the heat of midday. They made Herculean forced marches of eighteen or twenty-two hours a day – a pace no nomad would adopt in uninhabited desert – only possible, as Thesiger admitted, because of relatively abundant food and water for the camels, and the possibility of exchanging them when they faltered. These forced marches seem out of character for Thesiger: quite unlike his previous journey on the Awash, for instance, when it had taken him some six months to cover a few hundred miles. On most of his travels, past and future, he would always display a tendency to linger, shooting game, collecting botanical specimens, jawing with the locals, yet in Tibesti, as he himself confessed, '. . . At the cost of continuous travelling . . . my observations were superficial . . .'[61] For once on a major journey, Thesiger was pressed: 'I was very short of time,' he said. 'I'd got three months to cover an enormous distance and I wanted to see as much of Tibesti as possible.'[62]

Near the small oasis of Moussou, they were caught at night in a dust-storm that came tumbling out of the bowels of the earth, thrashing them with needles of dust and stifling blasts of heat. Thesiger and his men huddled close to their camels until the storm blew itself out, but as the air cleared he noticed that the hot wind had sucked their goatskins almost dry. For two hours they rode hesitatingly forward, into a sky glowering with a gunmetal-grey cloud-mass that cloaked the stars. At last, Thesiger asked the guide to point north, and, checking against his compass, found that he was pointing south-south-east. The man then confessed, 'My head's going round. I can't tell where I am!'[63] and Thesiger realized the caravan had been off course from the start. Their water was almost finished, the camels already exhausted from the heat, and their firewood gone. Thesiger took over the navigation with his compass, but fortunately just after sunrise the guide noticed some rocks in the distance, and exclaimed, 'Yes, I know those hills over there. We are all right!'[64] From there they rode for twenty hours until they reached the plain of Faya, coming into the sandy shelf at dawn as a knife-blade of chilling rain swept across the mountains. Without firewood they could make no tea, and Thesiger rode on, silent and ill-tempered, until the party reached the first of Faya's palm-groves. The following day they entered the town.

Once again Thesiger was received kindly by the French officers, who helped him exchange his Sudanese camels for Teda mountain camels – small, lightly built animals with hooves calloused by constant tracking in rocky country. The Sudanese camels could then be conserved for the journey back. Once again, Thesiger felt nothing but envy for the lives of these men. In Kutum, he and Moore could have done all their work in motor vehicles. In Faya, the equivalent of a provincial HQ, there were no cars, and the administrators had to trek by camel from Fort Lamy, enduring a three- or four-week journey to get there. For once, Thesiger broke his rule about dressing appropriately: he had brought no Western clothes with him on this journey, and the French had to put up with him in his desert garb. This was not as strange for them as it would have been for their British counterparts, Thesiger maintained, since the French Méhariste officers wore Arab dress as their uniform.[65] Indeed, it must have caught Thesiger's attention once again that those very practices that among the British in the Sudan were branded 'unconventional' – such as feeding with one's men – raised not an eyebrow among the French Méharistes. Founded by General Laperrine, with the very successful objective of beating the Saharan nomads at their own game, a Méhariste patrol under Lieutenant Cottenest had broken the centuries-old power of the aristocratic Ihaggaren Tuareg at Tit in 1902. It was almost certainly this experience of French colonialism in Tibesti that gave Thesiger a rather grudging exception when waxing enthusiastic about the superiority of the British Empire: 'No other Empire had the same sense of responsibility as the British,' he said. 'It never really existed in the French Empire – except to some extent in the Sahara – but certainly not among the Germans, Dutch, Portuguese and Italians.'[66] In his autobiography, however, he contrasted the French sense of

1. The Emperor Menelik II's palace in Addis Ababa at the turn of the century. It was almost an entire village in itself.

2. The huts of the old Legation under construction, Addis Ababa, *c.* 1900.

3. (*Above*) The old Legation against the bare hillside, Addis Ababa, *c.* 1902.

4. (*Left*) Street scene, Addis Ababa, *c.* 1918.

5. The new British Legation, Addis Ababa, completed in 1911.

6. Loading mules at the Legation, Addis Ababa, 1921.

7. The staff and the Indian escort at the British Legation, c. 1920. Thesiger's childhood idol, Arnold Hodson, is on the extreme left.

8. The *tukls* in the Legation compound, 1919. The eucalyptus trees have begun to cover the landscape.

9. (*Above*) Crowds coming to church to celebrate the Feast of the Epiphany, Addis Ababa, c. 1921.

10. (*Right*) Philip Zaphiro, Ras Tafari and Dejazmatch Getatcho on the steps of the British Legation, 1921.

11. Haile Selassie and his Empress after their coronation, 1930. From under the golden umbrella Haile Selassic made his first public address as Emperor.

12. Dan and Christine Sandford, Monogasha. They were close friends of Thesiger and supported him on his Danakil expeditions.

13, 14. Thesiger's caravan crossed the Awash river during his trek in Danakil country, 1933/4.

15. (*Above*) Afar (Danakil) tribesmen in the Awash valley.

16. (*Right*) The Emperor Haile Selassie, whom Thesiger described as 'the noblest man I have ever met'.

17. Dust storm over the Governor-General's Palace, Khartoum, 1932.

18. Douglas Newbold at a gathering of Nuba tribesmen, 1934. Much admired by Thesiger, Newbold was Governor of Kordofan and later Civil Secretary of the Sudan.

19. View of the Wadi at Kutum, taken from the Government offices. Jabal Si is in the distance on the extreme left.

20. Reggie Dingwall's pet oryx outside the house in Kutum, later occupied by Wilfred Thesiger.

21. Kutum market in 1933. Guy Moore's predecessor Ewen Campbell and his wife, Evelyn, are in the background.

22. The first rest house on the El Obeid–El Fasher Road, Kordofan.

23. A herd of oryx. They were common in Darfur in the 1930s but are now unknown in the area.

24. (*Above*) The *fula* at El Fasher, Darfur. The town of El Fasher was built around this seasonal lake.

25. (*Right*) Philip Ingleson, Governor of Darfur Province during Thesiger's time in Kutum.

26. A steamer on the White Nile, 1937. Like Thesiger's steamer, the *Kereri*, this also has a barge attached alongside.

27. The fort at Gallabat, eastern Sudan, showing the hills of Abyssinia.

28. A detachment of the Camel Corps which came to relieve Thesiger's unit at Gallabat after Italian troops had captured the fort, 1940.

29. Aircraft flying over Gojjam, 1941.

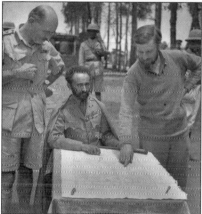

30. (*Above*) Haile Selassie with officers of the British Mission crossing the border between Sudan and Abyssinia at Umm Idla, 20 January 1941. To the Emperor's right is Orde Wingate and opposite him, next to his personal priest, is Sir Edwin Chapman Andrews, holding a letter of congratulation from General Platt.

31. (*Left*) Brig. Sandford, Haile Selassie and Orde Wingate, Dembecha, March 1941.

32. (*Below*) Abyssinian patriots with Brig. Sandford at Debra Markos, March 1941. Wingate's Gideon Force had just liberated the town from the Italians.

33. Lt.-Col. David Stirling, the founder of the SAS, resting against a truck, Western Desert, 1941/2.

34. Thesiger and Col. Gigantes (centre), commander of the Greek Sacred Squadron of the SAS. Thesiger was appointed Liaison Officer to this unit after Stirling's capture.

35. Thesiger at Sahwat el Khudr, Syria, July 1941, while serving with the Druze Legion.

colour-discrimination in the Sahara unfavourably against British attitudes in the Sudan, noting that the Groupe Nomade officers were devoted to their Senegalese troops rather than to the locals, whose language they never bothered to learn.[67]

After two days, equipped with their new camels and provided with two Teda guides, Thesiger's caravan set off into a broken waste-land of volcanic slag, moving so fast that one of the Teda guides complained of the strain on the camels. They camped near the wells of Kada, and at first light next morning Thesiger saw in the distance a smudge of zinc-grey on the distant horizon: his first glimpse of Emi Koussi, the highest mountain in the Sahara. As they pushed on, taking with them a guide who knew the paths into Emi Koussi's crater, the mountain grew into a mulberry-coloured mass, dominating the landscape. Sending part of the caravan to the Teda village of Miski, Thesiger set off with Idris, Kathir, the new guide and the two best camels, to scale the extinct volcano. They picked their way up and down precipitous tracks to the sheer-sided gorge of Mashakezey, where descent seemed impossible. The guide showed them a winding path, and they drove the camels perilously down, hauling back on their headropes and tails to prevent them overbalancing, while loosened boulders rolled away and crashed down into the valley below. By sunset they had crossed the gorge and the camels were trembling with exhaustion. They made camp by some ancient stone circles – probably the tent-rings of the cattle-herding folk who had lived in these valleys when they were still haunted by elephant and rhino, in Neolithic times. Here Thesiger found some temporary rainwater pools in the sand and was, like many Saharan travellers, astonished to find them inhabited by fish. How did the fish get there, Thesiger must have wondered. The answer, we now know, is that fish-eggs are transported huge distances in the mud on birds' feet and deposited even in the most temporary of pools, as the bird alights to drink.

In the morning they came across a Teda camp, where a woman lived with two small children. She agreed to lend Thesiger two camels, and brought the party a bowl of milk. Thesiger marvelled at the hardship of these mountain Teda, who fed their camels on dates during times of drought, and their goats on crushed date-stones. The saying goes that a Teda can himself survive for three days on a single date – the first day eating the skin, the second the fruit, and the third the stone – a tale which, while apocryphal, indicates the legendary toughness of this desert-mountain race. The following day they clambered into the crater of Emi Koussi, and Thesiger and Idris left the camels and scrambled up to the summit, where they lingered for a few moments to drink in the magnificent view: the interlocking saw-edges of rank upon rank of mountains, each varying subtly in shade from the next, deep gorges filled with gold and aniline shadows under a sky weighted with tumescent cloud. A few days later they rejoined the rest of the caravan at Miski. From there, with fresh camels, Thesiger continued his circuit through the gorges and valleys, passing through Modra, Aouzou, Bardai and Zouar. Today, this region has been devastated by Libyan, Chadian and French troops, during their struggle for possession of the Aouzou strip, discovered to hold large supplies of uranium. 'The first sight of Emi Koussi was the thing that stands out most,' Thesiger recalled, 'but after that there isn't one particular thing that sticks in your mind. It was the way one travelled, the scenery, the pattern of the mountains. A whole succession of things. It was this sort of feeling that here was an untouched bit of Africa, which it was then. What it missed of course, was that in Tibesti the tribes were completely administered: tribal fighting had been put down and there was a feeling of justice and peace. Still it did have a lot.'[68]

Thesiger admired the Teda: they considered themselves a noble people, and would not stoop to tending their palm-groves and vegetable gardens, which had originally been worked by slaves. 'I liked them,' Thesiger commented. 'When they did these raids, they were notorious for the distances they covered, though because they were split by blood-feuds they were never able to put up a unified resistance to the Turks or the French. They were individualists. Dadi, one of the Teda boys I travelled with, had a blood-feud. He'd got long hair and said he wouldn't cut his hair until he'd killed the other man, who at that time was a guide with one of the French Groupes Nomades. He intended to kill him sooner or later.'[69] Blood revenge was a hereditary obligation among the Teda, demanding not only the death of the murderer but also the murder of one of his relatives: a case of 'two eyes for an eye' rather than the Biblical 'eye for a eye'.

The origin of the Teda is obscure. The Greek historian Herodotus reported a people called the Garamantes who lived in the Fezzan and hunted black-skinned aborigines[70] in four-horse chariots. The aborigines were swift runners and spoke a language 'like the twittering of bats'. Though Thesiger thought the Teda descendants of the Garamantes, the current trend of thought is that they are descendants of the swift-running aborigines: the Garamantes being ancestors of the Tuareg. Small in stature, they are generally dark, with distinct non-negroid features. Wearing a loose-sleeved *gandourah*, they generally lap their turbans about their mouths to give them the appearance of being veiled like the Tuareg. Inhabiting rocky overhangs, or boat-shaped tents of dom fibre not unlike those of the Afars, the Teda live scattered over a vast area and this geographical dispersion has bred in them a philosophy so resolutely anarchic that many refuse to accept anyone as their chief, even their own family headman. Chapelle, the French Méhariste who became the world's greatest authority on the Teda, wrote of them that 'they are incapable not only of uniting to carry out a joint policy but even of imagining such a policy'.[71]

Using the French HQ at Bardai as a base, Thesiger left the exhausted Kathir and took Idris and the long-haired Dadi to visit Aouzou, where they found a tranquil, lush garden of date-palms, green grass and gushing, crystal-clear water that seemed to have appeared out of a story-book. From Bardai they also climbed up the steep escarpment to the rim of the crater of Doon, camping that night in a gorge. As Idris was cooking the nightly '*asida*, he suddenly pointed to the cliff above them, where Thesiger saw a large Barbary sheep: 'It was there looking down on us,' Thesiger recalled, 'and I just raised my rifle and shot it and it almost fell into the fire. To me it was almost uneatable, it was tough and smelt rather nasty – as you'd expect it to – but the others were able to bear it.'[72] On 22 September they left Bardai and headed their camels towards the hot springs at Soubouron. They found the springs in a valley whose walls were smeared with vivid scarlet, carnelian, sulphur yellow, violet and alabaster, where salt water fizzed and simmered in beds of molten mud, and the air was hazed in hot, sulphurous steam, which Thesiger thought 'pestilential'. The ailing Kathir bathed in one of the hot springs, famous for their medicinal effect. The next day, Thesiger recorded wryly, his leg festered with boils.

Glad to escape the sulphurous atmosphere, the caravan set off again through the wildest country Thesiger had yet seen, riding between the perpendicular sides of the Forchi gorge along a babbling mountain stream dappled with the shade of thorn-bush and reeds. They reached the lone fort at Zouar on 27 September, where the great outside world impinged upon them: Thesiger heard from French officers the news of the crisis at Munich. War with Hitler seemed unavoidable. That night he toasted Anglo-French relations with the French, and next morning he hurried off for Faya with his men, fearing the war would start without him. Again they travelled at tremendous speed: 'There was no average day, really,' he remembered. 'Sometimes we rode for eighteen hours a day, starting off half-way through the night, and would go on right until sunset the next day. We might stop if we found grazing and let the camels have a bit of a meal.'[73] Alternately riding and walking, they arrived in Faya a week later, having clocked up an average of thirteen and a half hours' march a day. At Faya, Thesiger met the famous Méhariste Colonel D'Ornano, who informed him that the war had been averted. D'Ornano suggested that he should see the mysterious lakes at Ounianga before returning to the Sudan. Despite the fact that his time was short, this was a challenge which Thesiger could not refuse in the presence of such a distinguished cameleer. The Ounianga pools were remnants of a vast Neolithic lake system which had once been the home of hippopotamus and crocodile, its shores inhabited by pottery-using hunters and cattle-herders whose artefacts have been found all over the Sahara. Travelling at the same breakneck rate, taking Idris, Kathir and a guide, Thesiger made Ounianga in four days. The sight was worth the hard ride: 'The lakes lie in a deep depression,' he wrote later, 'and our first view of Yoa, the largest of the four lakes, was lovely. The sands were golden in the early light and the dense palm groves along the water's edge threw heavy shadows. The water was a deep sparkling Mediterranean blue, and the cliffs rose-coloured rock . . .'[74] From the lakes he rode directly back to Faya, where he picked up the rest of his caravan on 19 October. A week later they were back at Tini in the Anglo-Egyptian Sudan.

Thesiger was somewhat irritated to discover that he had missed Guy Moore, who had been there with his car only two days earlier. Moore had not received his letter confirming his arrival date. He had no alternative but to ride direct to El Fasher, spending seventy hours in the saddle out of the ninety-six he took to get there.

Thesiger wrote later in his autobiography that during this three months in Tibesti he had lived on 'equal terms' with his companions. Dressing like them, speaking their language, behaving as they did, he had been able to assimilate himself to their culture in a sense impossible among the Nuer. This does not, of course, imply 'equality' in a democratic sense, only that in the desert there had been no material difference in circumstances between himself and his entourage. Where they had slept on the ground, he had slept on the ground, where they had walked, he had walked, where they had saddled their camels, he had done so too. He had not been compromised as their leader, but it was a different style of leadership from the one familiar in most parts of the British Empire, where the Pasha commanded from across a chasm of material privilege. To the men he led he cannot have appeared an equal, being one of the foreign ruling élite and, most of all, an unbeliever, who was received royally by his French counterparts on the frequent occasions during when he met them. This is not to say, of course, that his men did not like and admire him. He experienced with them, especially with Idris, a bond forged by the suffering of shared hardship, and an intimacy created by living shoulder to shoulder. 'Equality', in other words, meant something similar to what the French Méhariste officers had with their troops. This had been possible – as it had not been among the Nuer – largely thanks to the complementarity of European and Islamic cultures and a long tradition of contacts, which made it far easier and more acceptable for a Westerner to wear Arab dress and 'become assimilated'.

Thesiger has often been presented – and indeed has sometimes tended to present himself – as someone for whom the normal pleasures of life had no meaning. Yet no matter how long he might endure self-deprivation among foreign cultures, there was always a point at which he was able to return to his more privileged world. There is no doubt that he revelled in the luxuries of his homecomings after abstinence. His writings drip with the ecstasy of such contrasts. After his nine-day marathon camel-jaunt across much of northern Sudan, for example, he arrived in the Khartoum whose civilized ambience and tedious social demands had so irritated him on his first visit and wrote: 'It was pleasant to relax in the civilized comfort of their house: to eat delicious food and dawdle in a bath that smelt of bath-salts . . . This time I enjoyed the social life, the dinner-parties and watching polo-matches . . .'[75] Though, of course, only the knowledge that he could escape once more into the heroic-adventurous country permitted him to enjoy playing the civilized gentleman: 'I knew,' he added, 'I would do anything rather than be stationed in Khartoum.'[76] There are many such parallel incidents. Arriving in Salalah in 1946 after four solid months in the desert, for instance, he stayed at the RAF camp whose confines had seemed so irksome previously. 'It was a pleasant change talking English instead of the constant effort of talking Arabic, to have a hot bath and eat well-cooked food; even to sit at ease in a chair with my legs stretched out, instead of sitting on the ground with them tucked under me . . . but the pleasure of doing these things was enormously enhanced by the knowledge that I was going back to the desert.'[77]

The periods during which Thesiger lived with a foreign people were always necessarily punctuated by periods back in his own culture, like oases in the desert: the abstinence of one being essential to highlight the pleasure of the other. His annual returns to England throughout his life, sometimes lasting three or four months, fall neatly into this pattern. It was inevitable, of course. Since no man is an island, each one of us – no matter how outrageous or delinquent our behaviour – is gyrating to the inaudible tune of his own society. Even the ascetic is reacting to society by negating it, for without society there would be no such thing as asceticism. Just as the desert and the oasis are two sides of the same coin, so for Thesiger the 'savage' and the 'civilized' were separate yet inseparable facets of the same world. The abstinence-indulgence motif is paralleled, too, in his daily life. Of the Tibesti journey itself he wrote: 'In the desert, life's pleasures are very simple but very real: a long drink of clean water; meat to eat after weeks of flour paste; a few hours sleep when the effort to remain awake has become a torture; or a short linger over a small fire in the cold of the early dawn . . .'[78] In his later work these feelings would reach greater intensity as 'the ecstasy of a single cup of water in the desert, the deliciousness of sleep when half-dead from exhaustion . . .'[79] Author Roger Clark has described Thesiger as an 'inverted sensualist': [He] denies pleasure, not to negate it,' Clark has written, 'but to increase its power when he finally gives in to it.'[80]

During the Tibesti expedition, Thesiger had found to his satisfaction the closeness with his companions and the sense of freedom he sought. Now, faced with the prospect of returning to the Nuer, he decided finally that he was a 'misfit' in the Sudan Political Service. He resolved to hand in his resignation when he arrived in Khartoum. In Darfur, the Gur'an – a tribe closely related to the Teda, and speaking the same language – had been causing trouble by raiding across the frontier and lifting camels from the Kababish. Thesiger proposed to Angus Gillan that he should be given the job of leading a permanent border-patrol to prevent these incursions. There, he could live a life similar to that of the French Méharistes, continually on trek with his men. Knowing that he could live easily on his private income, he volunteered to do the job without pay, asking only his expenses. Gillan refused, saying that this would be taking unfair advantage of him – it would, anyway, have been highly irregular, putting Thesiger effectively beyond the pale of official government control. When he met Gillan again in October 1938, therefore, he offered his resignation. It is not clear what his alternative plan was, though he had already dismissed Idris from his service and sent him on the pilgrimage to Mecca – the youth's major ambition – after which he would return to his family in Tini. Gillan, who had been impressed by Thesiger's recent report on Tibesti, was loath to accept the proffered resignation. War was still looming irrepressibly on the horizon, and in wartime the likes of Thesiger would be invaluable. But in peacetime, there were only three Districts in the Sudan that would suit Thesiger's craving for the desert life: the Kababish, the arid Red Sea Hills, or his old stamping-ground at Kutum. All these vacancies were filled. Nevertheless, he advised

Thesiger to return to the swamps of Nuer and told him conspiratorially: 'I'll see what I can do.' A few months later Thesiger was overjoyed to learn from the new Civil Secretary, Douglas Newbold, that he was to be posted back with Guy Moore at Kutum after his next leave. He had obtained his dearest wish: as a contract officer he might be able to stay in Kutum for six or seven years. He never dreamed then that he was not destined ever to see Moore or Kutum again: on 3 September 1939, while Thesiger was on leave looking forward excitedly to his coming transfer, war with Germany was declared.

CHAPTER 7

The One Great Emotional Cause of My Life

If Captain Dick Whalley had had his way, Thesiger might have become an 'Abyssinian Lawrence'. Whalley had been British Consul in Majji on the Sudan–Abyssinian border before the Italian invasion, and as early as February 1939 had proposed to Governor-General Symes that with the exiled Haile Selassie at their head, 1,000 Sudanese troops should be unleashed on southern Abyssinia to restore the Emperor to his throne. At the same time a second force should invade the country from the north, led by Crown Prince Asfa Wossen with Wilfred Thesiger as his right-hand man. Symes's reaction was immediate. He made disparaging remarks about the idea of 'second Lawrences' and condemned the entire scheme as 'utterly fantastic'. His view was supported by General Platt, commander of the Sudan Defence Force, who reported to the Foreign Office: 'I do not consider it a reasonable proposition to launch a mere one thousand soldiers armed with rifles and one or two machine-guns into the mountains of Ethiopia against a European-led army vastly superior in the air, in ground numbers and in armament, on nebulous information.'[1]

At the moment war with Germany was declared on 3 September 1939, Thesiger was on the SS *Montcalm* in the Clyde, waiting to return to the Sudan with a naval convoy. 'I was staying at the Milebrook,' he remembered, 'when I got a telegram telling me to report to Glasgow in two days' time. I went up there and found that half the Sudan was there. We were just preparing to start off at about eleven o'clock on the Sunday, when we heard Chamberlain declare war. I have never heard anything so unimpressive in my life. It was almost dispiriting – after all, he had tried so hard to avoid it ... I felt that if Churchill had announced the war there'd have been threat and thunder in his voice.'[2] Escorted by a battleship and two cruisers, the convoy swung out into the Atlantic before turning back into the Mediterranean, which they cruised completely undisturbed. Thesiger smiled triumphantly to himself as he remembered Mussolini's claim that this was *mare nostrum*. 'I felt the war was inevitable,' he said. 'It had to come, and I thought we ought to have gone into it really at Munich. I welcomed it because I thought with any luck Italy would come into it and I should have a chance to repay them for what they'd done in Abyssinia. The Italian invasion of Abyssinia was one of the greatest upsets of my life.'[3] Thesiger's attitude to Abyssinia is somewhat ambiguous in retrospect. As a child he had not identified with the Abyssinians, regarding those he had contact with as social inferiors, and though the war in Abyssinia became later a 'personal crusade', he told the author, 'I didn't see [Abyssinia] as my home, I'm not an Abyssinian, I'm British. Yet I felt really upset about the invasion.'[4] On another occasion he declared, 'Abyssinia didn't really mean all that much to me, despite everything, until the Italians invaded it.'[5]

Thesiger's feeling of affection for his country of birth and its people diminished as he grew older, and the abolition of the monarchy in 1975 was the final blow to his faith in the Abyssinians. People always meant more to him than places, and his real commitment was to Haile Selassie and the royal family rather than to Abyssinia itself. When the Emperor arrived in exile at Waterloo Station on 3 June 1936, Thesiger – on leave at the time – was among the small group gathered to meet him. He and his mother visited Haile Selassie two days later at his Legation in Queen's Gate, and Thesiger was conscious of the 'unutterable sadness' that could be glimpsed through the Emperor's outward calm. He felt then an overpowering urge to charge off and join one of the Abyssinian armies fighting the Italians. It is significant that when Thesiger spoke to Timothy Green in 1970 – while Haile Selassie still sat on the throne – the recollection of his attitude to the invasion was distinctly more emotional than it would later be: 'This was my home – the country of my childhood being raped – and England did nothing.'[6] After the Italian invasion, which had begun on 3 October 1935, he had written to a friend, 'It does not look as if any of my generation are going to have a future. We certainly don't deserve it after Abyssinia.'[7] In moral terms, the Italian invasion of Abyssinia was no different from the British conquest of the Sudan: a Western power armed with sophisticated weapons had invaded a more 'primitive' African state for strategic and expansionist motives. Thesiger had 'sympathized' with the Dervishes of the Sudan, yet had reasoned that there was a huge qualitative distinction between the British and the Italian brands of colonialism. Since the British government was theoretically opposed to the invasion of Abyssinia, Thesiger was for the first time in the happy position of finding his commitment to the British establishment and his emotional conviction – in this case his loyalty to Haile Selassie – coinciding. It was this congruence of loyalties which led him to christen the war in Abyssinia as 'the one great emotional cause of my life'.[8]

The Italian army in Abyssinia had been mobilized in August 1939, looming darkly upon the Sudan's south-eastern borders. Thesiger's old friend Dan Sandford had already been summoned from exile in England – where he had been living quietly in Guildford and working as a warden of the cathedral – much as he had predicted to Thesiger in Cairo in 1936. Lieutenant-General Sir Archibald Wavell, Commander-in-Chief of Middle East Forces, required Sandford's expertise to engineer a popular rising against the Italians among Abyssinian rebels. Not all Sudan Political Officers felt the same animosity towards the Italians as Thesiger did, however. They recognized, as the personally involved and romantic Thesiger did not, that there was in practice little difference in the basis of their authority in the Sudan and that of the Italians in Abyssinia. Indeed, many were concerned that a resounding Abyssinian victory over their European aggressors might spark off a sympathetic uprising against the British by the Sudanese. The Sudan government generally had no love for the Abyssinians; 'The fonder a British official was of his charges in the Sudan,' Leonard Mosley has written, 'the less likely he would be to be enthusiastic about the liberation of his [Abyssinian] neighbours to the east.'[9] Sir Stewart Symes, the Governor-General, was a personal friend of the civilized and aristocratic Duke of Aosta, the Italian Viceroy, and even Thesiger's much-admired friend Douglas Newbold, the Sudan's Civil Secretary, tended to shrug his shoulders at the Italian threat. As a young man he had fought with the Italians against the Senussi brotherhood in Libya and helped General Graziani capture the rebel Omar Mukhtar. In any case, British military defences were laughable compared with the force their counterparts in Abyssinia could muster. The Italians had a quarter of a million troops supported by guns, tanks, and modern aircraft. The British had two regular army battalions and the British-led Sudan Defence Force with a total of 9,000 men, and no artillery. 'Who cared about Ethiopia in such circumstances?' Leonard Mosley inquired. 'Only Dan Sandford and Robert Cheeseman, and they were a couple of old white [Ethiopians] themselves, anyway.'[10]

Thesiger arrived in Khartoum to find that all transfers had been cancelled due to the war, and was sent back to Nuer. In October he returned from transporting stores by steamer to Baro, a trading-post inside Italian-occupied territory, to receive a letter from Newbold inviting him to join an officer-cadets' course in Khartoum, as training for the Sudan Defence Force. Frustrated that the Italians had not yet declared war, but still hoping desperately for a crack at them, he accepted immediately: 'I went and spent a month with the Cheshire Regiment, who were very good indeed,' he commented. 'There were about a dozen of us on the course – mostly ex-District Officers and Gezira cotton-project managers – but inevitably it had no relevance to what later happened, because it was mainly based on First World War trench warfare. Anyhow, it was valuable, and we learned quite a lot about weapons. I'd been in the cadets at Eton, but that was a joke. I got a month's fairly intensive training with the Cheshires – tactics and things – then I went back to Nuer.'[11] After a trip to the Nuba Mountains to watch the traditional Nuba wrestling, Thesiger returned to the Province HQ at Malakal, but never went back to his District. A few weeks later he was assigned to a second course, with the Essex Regiment, which had replaced the Cheshires in Khartoum: 'In contrast with the Cheshires, they took absolutely no trouble over us at all,' Thesiger said. 'We were just left to lounge about.'[12] Not long afterwards he received a Governor-General's Commission, with the rank of Bimbashi, and was posted to the Eastern Arab Corps of the Sudan Defence Force at Gedaref in the eastern Sudan.

The Sudan Defence Force was an exotic flower in the annals of

British arms. Composed of four units, the Eastern and Western Arab Corps, the Equatorial Corps and the Camel Corps, each unit was commanded by a British officer with the old Mameluke title of Miralai or 'commander of a thousand'. 'Companies' were commanded by the lesser rank of Bimbashi, commanding more men than a regular army captain, but rating less substantively than a second lieutenant. In 1939 the entire operational strength of the Force was only 5,000. In April 1940, No.3 Company of the Eastern Arab Corps was posted to the fort at Gallabat on the Abyssinian frontier, where it faced the Italian-occupied fort of Metemma across an arid wadi-bed. The company, commanded by Bimbashi Arthur Hanks, set about strengthening the hilltop fort and planning defence works of trenches and barbed wire, though without much genuine enthusiasm. There had always been good relations between the British officers in Gedaref and their opposite numbers in the Italian garrison at Metemma, commanded by Colonel Castagnola, a small, fat, swarthy but genial individual, very astute, and quite a good game shot. However, as war lurked nearer, the mutual lunches ceased and relations cooled. Such was the situation when Bimbashi Thesiger arrived at Gallabat in May with his man Idris, to become second-in-command of No.3 Company. The official diarist noted: 'Bimbashi W.P. Thesiger, a former Assistant DC, came to No.3 accompanied by his personal servant who was a reprieved murderer and quite a charming chap if a shade wilful. Thesiger had accounted for over seventy lion during his Sudan career, was a boxing blue, and altogether a useful man to have about the place.'[13]

In Cairo, Dan Sandford had drawn up his plan. He proposed to collect Abyssinian refugees from both the Sudan and Kenya to form a Refugee Battalion, at the same time taking a company from each of the existing SDF units to form a Frontier Battalion under the command of Colonel Hugh Boustead – Thesiger's fellow DC at Zalingei. The objective of Boustead's force would be to pass arms and supplies to Abyssinian rebels and foment guerrilla warfare inside the country. Wavell and Churchill both approved the plan, and another old friend of Thesiger's, Robert Cheeseman, was installed in Khartoum as Intelligence officer. It was crucial to

Sandford's scheme that the Emperor Haile Selassie should be brought back from exile in London as a figurehead for the troops. Meanwhile Hanks, Thesiger and their Sudanese soldiers waited impatiently at Gallabat for the declaration of war. Thesiger was frustrated at the inertia of developments, but was in his element officering Sudanese troops: 'We were the only two whites in the company,' he said, 'and everybody else – the junior officers, the sergeants and everybody – were all Sudanese. Well, if you'd been in Kenya with the King's African Rifles, even your sergeants would have been white. It was one of the things Slim criticized, saying there was no necessity to have European NCOs. I was under Slim for a brief time at the end of the fighting at Gallabat and he found the Sudanese troops very good indeed.'[14]

Soon after his arrival, a consignment of 300 breech-loading Martini-Henri rifles was dispatched to Gallabat, followed by 400 more, to be distributed to the Abyssinian rebels. On 2 June, the frontier was officially closed, and on the 4th a mob of 200 rebels stalked out of the bush under their one-eyed chief, Fitaurari Worku, to receive the rifles. They were disappointed to discover that Thesiger and Hanks had been given explicit instructions not to issue weapons to the Abyssinians until the official declaration of war. Four days later, with still no word from headquarters, the disgruntled Worku decided to take his men back off into the hills. Thesiger persuaded him to wait another day. Meanwhile, getting wind of the British intentions, Colonel Castagnola sent an official protest to Hanks and requested a parley with his British counterparts. The meeting took place the next morning in the Sudanese Customs shed by the wadi. Castagnola's representative arrived with his interpreter, the Prince de Bourbon-Siciles, to be confronted by the towering and pugnacious Bimbashi Thesiger. 'The Italian government would like to complain about the British government's support for rebel activities in Abyssinia,' said the Italian officer, 'as no state of war as yet exists between our two countries.' Thesiger rejected the complaint flatly: 'Not a single rifle has yet been issued to [Abyssinians],' he said truthfully, 'but we are ready, if Mussolini declares war on us, to pour weapons into Abyssinia. In that case the [Patriots] will exact a bitter vengeance.'[15] He then added, with a rather sinister touch, 'I apologize for not being able to invite you two gentlemen for lunch, because of the manoeuvres planned for this afternoon.'[16]

On 10 June, Hanks and Thesiger heard on the BBC that war with Italy had been declared: 'The exuberance of Wilf Thesiger expressed itself in a savage war-dance,' the official diarist noted.[17] According to Thesiger, he then promptly opened up with a machine-gun on the Italian lines, firing the opening shots in the Abyssinian campaign. The official record, though, indicates that Hanks's men fired the first shots on 14 June, four days later. Thesiger's account is that a coded cable arrived at the fort on the 10th, making the declaration of war official, but forbidding any offensive action, including the issuing of rifles to the rebels, until further notice. The former instruction – according to Thesiger's version – had come too late anyway. The latter he merely ignored, and began to dole out the Martinis to the impatient Worku and his men, who, after their irritating wait, were furious to find themselves fobbed off with rifles that pre-dated the battle of Omdurman.

A couple of hours later, however, a further cable arrived announcing that the Italians planned to attack Gallabat fort an hour before dawn the following morning. The cable also included the intelligence that three native battalions and thirty-one tanks had reinforced the Metemma garrison. At four o'clock Hanks and Thesiger awoke and sipped a solemn cup of tea before taking up positions with their troops around the fort. They lay there expectantly, wondering how their rifles and machine-guns would fare against a squadron of tanks. Hussey de Burgh, commanding troops at Gedaref, had instructed Hanks not to hold Gallabat to the last man in the event of an Italian offensive, but had added ominously, 'Blood must be spilt!'[18] To their relief, however, no tanks grated out of the bush as the dawn broke. Instead, they watched the mauve night shadows slowly take the concrete forms of jutting buttes and rocky bights, and soon the tranquil scene was filled with lowing cattle plodding out to graze and women filling pots of water in the wadi. That day Robert Cheeseman, who had now been moved to Gedaref, sent out six Abyssinian messengers bearing letters written on parchment, destined for prominent rebel chiefs. The letters, signed by the Commander of the SDF, or *qaid*, General Platt, promised rifles, ammunition, food and money, and incited the chiefs to attack the Italians. A few days later a further six letters went out. At sunset on 14 June, the official record goes, Hanks's company, growing weary of the tension, opened up on the Metemma fort, loosing off 8,000 rounds of ammunition before the order to cease fire came. After ten minutes' stunned silence the Italian garrison began to shoot back. The firefight continued for two noisy hours, the only casualty being a Greek merchant in Metemma. De Burgh, furious at this waste of ammunition, cabled Hanks not to repeat the action. The following day, however, Italian marksmen shot down the Union Jack flying over Gallabat fort – an outrage that could not be forgiven.

In late June Colonel Dan Sandford arrived in Khartoum with his '101 Mission', a tiny insurgency force organized by the Special Operations Executive (SOE), of five British and five Abyssinian officers, intended to penetrate Abyssinia and stir up a revolt behind enemy lines. On 28 June he was flown to Wadi Halfa on the Sudanese–Egyptian frontier to rendezvous with a certain 'Mr Strong' – in fact the Emperor Haile Selassie – who had arrived expecting to lead an expeditionary force that would recapture his throne. Sandford was obliged to explain to His Majesty that there was no expeditionary force, and that the British could not start a major offensive at least until the rainy season was over. The Emperor was bitterly disappointed, but Sandford tried to revive his spirits by the news that a combined British–Abyssinian attack on Metemma was in progress as they talked. Hundreds of miles south, at Gallabat, Thesiger, with Idris and his Sudanese warriors, had slipped across the frontier under the cover of darkness to meet a rebel force led by three chiefs who had received Cheeseman's letters, on a hill beyond Metemma. The plan was to lay an ambush and draw the Italian troops into it by sniper fire at the garrison.

Unfortunately, things went wrong. Two of the rebel leaders laid their ambush on the wrong side of the hill, and the third refused to take part in the battle at all. The sun rose to reveal the entire strength of the Italian 27th Colonial Battalion – hardy Eritrean troops – advancing towards Thesiger's single platoon of Sudanese soldiers, with their handful of poorly armed rebels in support. As the Italian-led troops came on they lobbed blue- and red-coloured 'money-box' grenades, which exploded on impact.

Thesiger ordered his men to pull out quickly, and his soldiers were amused by the sight of Idris dashing downhill and firing his rifle backwards over his shoulder without even turning his head: 'He did not,' the official diarist noted, 'claim any hits.'[19] Five men were dead, four missing, and the attack had been a fiasco. The Italian Colonial troops had proved tough, the Italian officers efficient: the Abyssinian rebels had shown themselves inept. Much more care was evidently required before such an operation was launched again.

It was time for air power to take a hand. A week later five RAF Wellesley bombers soared majestically over Hanks's position and blitzed the fort at Metemma. The Italians blasted back with anti-aircraft fire and one of the aircraft fishtailed over Gallabat and dumped in the wadi. Thesiger and his men sprinted down to the smouldering hulk to find the pilot dead and the gunner, Davidson, hanging on by a thread. They hauled him back to the safety of their lines and laid him on a stretcher. 'We did a good job, didn't we, sir?' the young aircraftsman rambled to Thesiger. 'I could do with a nice cold pint of beer right now. How I'd love to be lying in one of those cool Yorkshire streams.'[20] The next morning he was dead. He and the bomber pilot were the first two British casualties of the Abyssinian campaign.

The following day it was the Italian turn. A squadron of Caproni bombers came drumming in over Gallabat and released their payloads, ravaging the fort. In their wake came the 27th Colonial Battalion in all its ferocious glory, charging with bayonets fixed from both flanks. Thesiger and Hanks, dug in some distance away at the pass of Khor al Otrub, were woken abruptly by the sound of shots and explosions. The Sudanese platoon defending the fort had lost one man in the bombing, and had strafed the attackers with a covering fusillade before scrambling back to their emergency rendezvous at the pass. On the way another trooper had been killed and four wounded. The Sudanese officer commanding the unit, Yusbashi Abdallah, reported to Hanks that his men had accounted for twenty-seven of the Italian Colonial troops. Hanks and Thesiger then tried to marshal their men and to contact the Abyssinian rebels, who had inconveniently disappeared. Expecting the 27th to come pouring across the skyline at any moment, they ripped off a desperate message to Khartoum and then burned their telegraph code-books. However, no attack came. Colonel Castagnola's men remained content with the capture of Gallabat fort. When a detachment of the Camel Corps arrived to reinforce Hanks's company a few days later, the crisis was already over.

On the same day, the Italians also captured the British border town of Kassala, and the smaller frontier post at Garura, sending ever-expanding ripples of alarm through Khartoum, Cairo and London. Wavell, in Cairo, feared that this was the start of an Italian pincer movement from Italian-occupied Libya and from Abyssinia at the same moment. In London there was little Churchill could do to aid the SDF in terms of equipment: almost everything the British army possessed had been lost on the beaches of Dunkirk, and an invasion of England itself looked imminent. Anthony Eden, the British War Minister, dashed off a message to Wavell: 'An insurrection in Ethiopia would greatly assist your task.'[21] This was hardly a revelation to Dan Sandford, who had been urging just such a project for more than a year. He put his head together with Haile Selassie, now installed in the 'Pink Palace', a Nile-side villa in Khartoum, to decide how such an insurrection should be approached. They agreed that any 'liberation' of Abyssinia should be seen as an Abyssinian rather than a British operation. The Emperor would lead an army of Abyssinian refugees, trained and led by British officers, into his country, where his forces would be swelled by rebel bands raised by British insurgents. Finally, the army of liberation would encroach upon Addis Ababa and drive out the Italians. On 25 July the Middle East committee approved the plan, granting arms, money and men to Sandford, and incidentally sacking the Sudan's Governor-General, Sir Stewart Symes.

In early August, Sandford's 101 Mission crossed the Abyssinian border south of Thesiger's position near Gallabat with a mule-train laden with rifles, five English soldiers, five Abyssinian officers and fifty muleteers. Thesiger wished desperately he could have been with them. Sandford's ultimate objective was the wild, remote mountain region of Gojjam. As a response to Cheeseman's letters sent out in June, the notorious rebel leader, Dejazmatch Mangasha – who controlled most of Gojjam – had replied that the Italians in his area were scattered and vulnerable, and asked for arms and artillery to strike at them. He also asked for 'someone important' from the British government to meet him at his base at Belaya in Gojjam. That someone was to be Dan Sandford. On 21 August a second mule-train left Gedaref under the command of Major Bentinck, with twenty-four muleteers, an engineer-officer, Captain Tim Foley, and five Sudanese. Ten days later the third section of the 101 Mission, under Lieutenant Arnold 'Rocky' Wienholt, arrived at Thesiger's post near Gallabat with a few bony donkeys and only half a dozen men. Thesiger invited him to stay in the stockade his men had constructed, but Wienholt insisted on sleeping in his own tent. At sixty-three, the lieutenant did not seem likely material for a dangerous mission of deep infiltration, yet the DSO and MC and bar he had won in previous campaigns attested to his courage. Wienholt was an Australian educated at Eton, and Thesiger warmed to the older man, not least because he had been mauled shooting lion in the Kalahari. He had previously been in Abyssinia, working as a transport officer for the Red Cross. He lingered for two weeks at Gallabat until he obtained the transport he needed to continue his mission to Gojjam. He never made it. Only thirty miles south of Metemma he was attacked by an armed band. One of his servants later arrived in Gedaref with the story that he had seen Wienholt, badly wounded, crawling into the bush. The Australian had apparently been sentenced to death despite being in full uniform, and had faced the firing-squad calmly, draped in a Union Jack.

Sandford's wireless began buzzing from Gojjam in mid September, with the message that Abyssinian rebels were starting to rally to the call. Meanwhile more than 4,000 rifles and half a million cartridges had been distributed to rebels through Gallabat and the other gateway to Abyssinia, Rosseires. Thesiger, still in his position near Gallabat, sometimes penetrated across the border on skirmishing raids, but more often spent his time sheltering in slit-trenches against the Caproni bombers which bombarded them almost daily. Pushed by Anthony Eden, Wavell at last decided on an offensive operation to recapture Gallabat fort. To this end the 10th Indian Infantry Brigade was moved to Thesiger's and

Hanks's position in November, under its commander, the redoubt-able Brigadier Slim. Hanks's company received no prior warning because of the need for secrecy, and the first Thesiger knew of the offensive was when the woods around them were suddenly crawl-ing with Indian troops. 'We could scarcely believe our eyes,' Thesiger wrote. 'We had hung on here throughout the rains, conscious that there was nothing behind us and the Italians opposite us were being heavily reinforced. While I was on leave they had tentatively attacked our position, which left Hanks wondering if it was the prelude to an advance on Gedaref . . .'[22]

In the intervening period Castagnola had not been idle. The captured Gallabat fort had been ringed with a wall and barbed-wire entanglements, and the scrub around it cut down to provide a clear field of fire. Across the wadi the Metemma fort had also been turned into a formidable redoubt, with double coils of barbed wire that encircled the buildings and lined the road linking it with Gallabat. It was to break through these fortifica-tions that Slim's secret weapons – six 'invincible' Matilda tanks and six light tanks, brought from Britain at vast expense, and a regiment of field artillery – had been insinuated into position under conditions of the utmost stealth. The tank crews had even removed their distinctive black berets in camp so that the presence of the tanks should not be guessed at by a spy in Italian pay. Dumps of artillery shells were moved by night and stockpiled in Khor al Otrub. The Brigade under Slim comprised three infantry battalions, one British, two Indian. The Indian units were the 3rd/18th Garwhal Rifles, and a Baluch battalion. The British unit was the Essex Regiment, with which Thesiger had trained briefly before receiving his commission as Bimbashi. Hank's No.3 Coy of the SDF, together with another company of six-foot Nuba tribesmen that had been sent to reinforce them, were to go into action with the Indian battalion. Slim himself inspected the SDF companies, conferred with Hanks and raised morale generally. 'There was a massive imperturbable quality about Slim,' Thesiger wrote, 'that was highly reassuring . . . we were all profoundly impressed.'[23]

The attack on Gallabat had been planned down to the smallest detail. It would be the first major offensive launched against the Italians and its success would not only be a propaganda victory –

sorely needed by the much-pressed British – but would also open up the road to Gojjam, where Sandford was even now gathering his irregular troops, henceforth to be officially designated 'Patriots' instead of 'rebels' on the request of Haile Selassie himself. At dawn on 6 November, as the hills beyond Gallabat took form out of the darkness in great stalagmite shapes full of lemon and purple shadows, an ominous hum was heard in the west. The RAF bombers and fighters appeared on the edge of the night, sailplaning over the Italian positions and letting rip with stick upon stick of bombs. At the same moment Colonel Welcher, commanding the artillery regiment, grasping a six-foot spear in one hand and a great telescope in the other, ordered the camouflage-nets that had concealed the British batteries to be flung off. The guns belched fire, battering the walls of the fort. The bombers scored a direct hit on the Italian communications centre at Metemma, and as the squadrons sheered off in a drone of engines the tanks rumbled out of cover towards Gallabat. After them, as if by magic, there sprang out of concealed foxholes and trenches lines of infantry – the Garwhal Rifles and the Sudanese platoons led by Hanks and Thesiger.

The fort was enveloped in a nebula of smoke and dust. As it cleared, it seemed to Thesiger that the position had been devastated, and that no one could possibly be left alive there. He was mistaken, however. A handful of Eritrean troops with their Italian officers fought back obstinately, their machine-guns barking on ceaselessly until the tanks were on top of them. Soon a green and scarlet Very flare burst out of the smoke above Gallabat – a signal that the fort had been retaken by the British. As Slim and Welcher drove forward in a staff car through the gaps in the barbed wire torn by the British tanks, the Italians counter-attacked with their two other Colonial battalions, supported by a company of Savoy machine-gunners. The Garwhalis and the Sudanese drove them off ferociously, inflicting heavy casualties. Slim drove on, coming face to face with a young Italian officer who turned out to be a company commander in the 27th Colonial battalion – the Eritrean troops who had been defending the fort. Slim was disappointed to learn from him that the main force of the 27th had withdrawn according to plan as soon as the bombardment had begun, leaving only a skeleton unit to slow down the British attack and cover their retreat. The artillery pounded the fort at Metemma, but though some of the native huts surrounding it caught fire, most of the fortified buildings remained intact. Crouching behind a sangar in the wall of Gallabat fort, Slim received the distressing news from the Squadron Commander of the Royal Tank Regiment that five of his six 'invincible' Matildas were out of action, as well as four of the six light tanks. Invincible to Italian bullets they might have been, but the tanks' caterpillar treads had been shredded and sloughed off by the sharp rocks of the hills. When the tank crews had clambered out to inspect the damage, having replaced their black berets, the Indian troops had mistaken them for Italians in the confusion and had shot them dead. This was a terrible blow to Slim, because without the tanks it would be virtually impossible to break through the impregnable barbed-wire obstacles that protected Metemma. Reluctantly, Slim decided that the artillery would have to punch holes in the entanglements. He postponed the attack until the afternoon.

Meanwhile the Essex Regiment moved in to occupy the ruins of the fort at Gallabat, and Slim retired to his Command Post at Khor al Otrub pass. At three o'clock he heard the drone of aircraft engines coming from the east. The Italian air force was striking back with ten bombers and twenty fighters. As the aircraft began their assault on the soldiers of the Essex Regiment, two RAF Gloucester Gladiators from Gedaref poled up valiantly to take them on. Both were quickly shot down by the Italian pilots. As more British aircraft appeared in dribs and drabs, the Italian fighters picked them off. It was a triumph for the Italian air force, and air-superiority won them the day.

As the bombing and air combats petered out, Slim sallied forth once more to see how his infantry was faring. When the Brigadier neared the fort an Indian officer in charge of the traffic-control post stopped him, waving frantically. 'The Essex battalion are retreating, Sahib!' he shouted. Slim looked up in disbelief to see lorry-loads of British troops rattling towards him screaming, 'The enemy are coming!' as they jolted past. Marching furiously down the road to the fort, he encountered ragged groups of stragglers who informed him that the Italians had retaken Gallabat. The Essex battalion's colonel had been killed, they said, and under terrible pounding they had withdrawn. The information turned out to be nonsense. The Italians had not even attempted to retake the fort, and despite the pounding, casualties had not been high – only three killed and two wounded. The tough British soldiers – the officers and men who had built an Empire – had simply panicked in the face of the despised 'Wops', and run away. It was a dark day for the men of Essex. Slim moved up his third, reserve battalion of Baluch troops to replace them, planning a counter-attack for the following morning, but he had lost the initiative. That night the Italian bombers returned and decimated the Garwhalis, the SDF and the dispirited Essex, who once again panicked and retreated when the Italians fired smoke shells from Metemma, believing they were gas. The next day, Slim admitted defeat and withdrew his brigade.

In Gojjam, the Patriots' morale was dashed by the British defeat. The disgrace of the Essex Regiment was hushed up as much as possible, but after all the Imperial sabre-rattling it looked as if British troops could not even match the Italians for courage and resolution. No Italian unit in Abyssinia had run away merely because of a bombing. Moreover, the much-vaunted British technical superiority had failed. RAF pilots had been outgunned by Italians, RAF tactics had proved inadequate, British tanks had been defeated by the terrain, and their crews shot by their own side. Slim and the Essex Regiment were pulled out of the Sudan before the end of the year. A few days later, Bimbashi Thesiger was ordered back to Khartoum.

On 6 November, as the guns opened their barrage on Gallabat, an unusual man had arrived in the Sudanese capital. His name was Orde Wingate: he was a major in the Royal Artillery, and he was thirty-seven years old. Wingate seemed to be a man born to trouble. Ever since he had been a cadet at Woolwich he had had a knack of rubbing his pompous superiors up the wrong way. He was reputed to be a distant relative of T.E. Lawrence, and like Lawrence was a small man with penetrating blue eyes and a head that appeared slightly oversized for his body. Wingate had an insatiable lust for battle, a total disregard for personal comfort, the drive of a fanatic, and a brilliant grasp of guerrilla warfare. In Palestine he had formed Israeli night-squads which had operated with devastating effect against the Arabs, and thereby laid the foundations of the modern Israeli army. Yet he was a man who needed a Mission. He had found it in Israel, where he had taken Zionism to heart and become so dangerous politically that Wavell had forbidden him to set foot there again. The son of fanatically religious parents, Wingate had been bullied by his schoolmates in a way that made Thesiger's treatment look positively mild. As a result he had grown up with a manner that was so aggressive towards authority that he alienated almost everyone he came into contact with. Yet he was one of the most remarkable men Thesiger ever met. From the moment he arrived in the Sudan – his path lubricated by a budget of a million pounds – the Abyssinian campaign took a turn for the better. He was to be the 'Lawrence' of Abyssinia that Dick Whalley had once looked for in Wilfred Thesiger. When Thesiger arrived in Khartoum in November 1940 after the débâcle at Gallabat, it was to Orde Wingate that he was instructed to report.

Even Thesiger, hardly renowned for his diplomacy, was staggered by Wingate's uncouthness and deliberate rudeness. 'He didn't behave like a gentleman,' Thesiger said, 'and he fell foul of everybody – actually completely the opposite of Lawrence in the First War. I was one of the few people he would talk to, and I asked him why he was a Zionist when he wasn't a Jew. He said it all stemmed from his school, where he'd been unpopular with the other boys – and I could perfectly understand why – they'd had Wingate-hunts and bullied him and he'd found in the Bible a "people against whom every man's hand was turned, yet they remained bloody and unbowed" and he said – and this was interesting – he said, "I identified them with myself" not "I identified myself with them." So he became a passionate Zionist.'[24]

Thesiger met Wingate in his office at the Grand Hotel on Khartoum's tree-shaded waterfront and, pacing up and down impatiently, the major expounded his plans and explained why Thesiger had been requisitioned. On 20 November, despite the fact that he hated flying (he was later to die in an air crash), Wingate had flown out to a specially prepared airstrip at Faguta in Gojjam to meet Dan Sandford. The flight – in an obsolete Vincent biplane – did not endear Wingate to air travel: neither did the landing and take-off, which proved to be at the edge of a perilously steep precipice.[25] Sandford technically outranked Wingate, though the two got on well together initially. Wingate planned to carry out Sandford's original project, leading a liberating force into Abyssinia that would be the signal for the Abyssinian rebels to rise and throw off their Italian shackles. Both men agreed that any liberation campaign in Abyssinia must be led by Haile Selassie, though Wingate thought Sandford woolly-minded for his promise of air support to the Abyssinian Patriots, which would eventually be perceived as worthless. Sandford had been warned even before he left Cairo that aircraft would, by and large, not be available. However, for his part, Sandford recognized in Wingate the natural leader the campaign needed and bowed to the younger and more vigorous man. He reported that the scrubland between Gojjam and the Sudan was passable for camel-transport, and when Wingate eventually entered the country with Haile Selassie promised to meet him at Mount Belaya with 5,000 mules to cross the escarpment. Wingate told him that the name of the expedition would be Gideon Force. He remained in the field for forty-eight hours and before he left agreed to send a replacement for Sandford's second-in-command, Critchley, who was suffering from a serious eye infection. The replacement was to be Wilfred Thesiger.

Wingate told Thesiger that the Italians had 40,000 troops in their forts in Gojjam. His Gideon Force would include only Boustead's Frontier Battalion of the SDF, an Abyssinian refugee battalion, and six 'Operational Centres', made up of British officers and sergeants and fifty Abyssinian Patriots each. Thesiger noted that although both Sandford and Boustead outranked him, Wingate seemed to have no doubt that he was going to be given the job of leading Gideon Force. Before the end of the interview he asked Thesiger: 'Are you happy?'

'Well yes, I suppose I am, reasonably,' Thesiger answered.

'I am not happy,' Wingate said, 'but then, I have been thinking, no great man was ever really happy.'[26]

At least Thesiger was fortunate in that Wingate received him fully clothed. Another acquaintance reported to Thesiger that when he had been called to Wingate's room, the major had received him reclining stark-naked on the bed, scrubbing himself with somebody else's toothbrush. 'How do you know it was somebody else's toothbrush?' Thesiger inquired. 'Well,' his friend said, 'can you imagine Wingate having one of his own?' In Khartoum, Wingate was considered a madman and a megalomaniac. Always dirty and dishevelled, he wore an out-of-date Wolseley helmet, carried a huge alarm clock instead of a wristwatch – to encourage punctuality – and a fly-whisk instead of a cane. Yet when he was called to Cairo to expound on the feasibility of the Gideon project, General Wavell was profoundly impressed. Wingate assured the Commander-in-Chief that with the right supplies and air support he could raise a revolt in Abyssinia that would end Italian rule there, entirely without the aid of regular troops: 'Give me a small fighting force of first-class men,' he said, 'and from the core of Ethiopia I will eat into the Italian apple and turn it so rotten it will drop into our hands.'[27] Wavell gave him the green light, and Wingate flew back to Khartoum to organize his Gideon Force.

Thesiger spent six frustrating weeks waiting to be sent to Gojjam, his boredom only alleviated by his meetings with Douglas Newbold and, on one occasion, lunch with Haile Selassie. He watched the Abyssinian refugee battalions being trained and listened to Wingate's pep-talks, impressed by his passion which reflected Thesiger's own romantic sense that he was fighting a crusade. At first it was proposed that Thesiger should be dropped by parachute on Gojjam, a suggestion he received with trepidation. Finally, it was agreed that he should ride in by camel from Rosseires and meet Sandford's men at Belaya. Days passed in agonizing inertia, as Thesiger waited for Robert Cheeseman to organize his infiltration, relieved only by the astounding news of Wavell's great victory over the Italians in North Africa, in which 38,000 prisoners had been taken. The tide of the war had turned, and Gallabat had been avenged. At last Thesiger decided to take the matter in hand. He organized his own camels and guide, and three days before Christmas 1940 he crossed the border near Rosseires. Idris had gone back to his family from Khartoum at a request from his father, and Thesiger had with him a Sudanese batman from the SDF, named Muhammad. Arriving at Belaya on Christmas Day, he and Muhammad climbed the escarpment to find a company of Boustead's Frontier Battalion, commanded by Bimbashi Peter Acland, already in position. The company had been sent ahead by Wingate to prepare the ground for his Gideon Force, which was expected to cross the frontier during the third week of January. The following day, Acland packed him off by mule to meet Dan Sandford at Sakalle. On the way his party was nose-dived by an Italian fighter, which made off when Thesiger fired five very accurate, lion-killing shots at it. He found Sandford sitting on a canvas chair at his HQ, wearing khaki shorts and a bush-shirt and beaming through his spectacles. 'Hello, Wilfred,' he said. 'What took you so long?' Somewhat taken aback at this rather brusque reception after his virtually non-stop trek over desert, scrub and mountain, Thesiger replied, 'Actually I have done one of my more energetic rides. I've ridden night and day and hardly slept. I defy anyone to have got here faster.'[28] Only then did it dawn on Thesiger that Sandford had been expecting him for six weeks. With Sandford were Pansy Drew, the old friend who had been medical officer in Darfur, and two British signallers, CSM Grey and Corporal Whitmore. Meanwhile Boustead and Wingate, who had established an uneasy truce after some initial personality clashes, had been collecting camels for their advance to Belaya. By 18 January, when Haile Selassie arrived at the border, they had managed to assemble 25,000 camels and 5,000 men.

Two days later, at forty minutes past midday, the Abyssinian flag was raised on Haile Selassie's native soil. There was a simple ceremony, which, according to journalist Leonard Mosley, who was present on the occasion, was subject to a number of mishaps: 'The troops were ragged in their drill,' he wrote, 'the smell of camel-dung was heavy in the air, the bugler collapsed half-way through, and someone had forgotten to bring the champagne from Khartoum. The toast to Ethiopia was drunk in some bottles of beer rescued from an officer's kitbag.'[29] On 21 January Wingate led the motley convoy of lorries and camels towards Belaya, riding on a horse. It was Wingate's policy never to trust a guide or to travel on a road, and as a result no one with his column knew precisely how to reach Belaya, for the maps Wingate had – made by Robert Cheeseman – were inaccurate. Whereas it had taken Thesiger four days to cover the same distance with a guide, it was only after sixteen days of scrambling over lava chunks, and through bamboo thickets and thorn-scrub that Gideon Force forgathered at Belaya. Reuter's correspondent Kenneth Anderson, following Wingate in a truck which was eventually shaken to pieces on the rough going, wrote of him: 'He was certainly one of the most ruthless chaps I have ever met. Absolutely fearless, tireless and at times uncouth. He never bothered to wash or shave. On the rare occasions when we came to a waterhole, he would lower his trousers and squat with his bottom cooling in the water. But that was as far as he went with his ablutions.'[30]

From his secure base at Belaya, a great block of granite rising out of the plain of Shankalla, Wingate planned to cut the road that linked the Abyssinian capital of Addis Ababa to the ancient city of Gondar, which was guarded by four towns – Bahr Dar at the southern end of Lake Tana, Dangila, Ingebara and Burie – each one garrisoned by Italian troops. While Sandford left to meet Haile Selassie and Wingate at Belaya, Thesiger was sent with Major Simonds, one of Wingate's 'Operation Centre' commanders, to attack the garrison at Dangila with Dejazmatch Mangasha, the local Patriot leader. In fact, the Italian troops there had been ordered to withdraw, and he arrived just as they were pulling out under their commander, Colonel Torelli, leaving the town in flames and moving north towards Bahr Dar. Though Mangasha had 4,000 men under his command, he refused to take part in the fighting. His real object was Dangila itself, and as soon as he had installed himself there in Torelli's place he took no further part in the campaign. Thesiger rode down to Belaya with the news of Torelli's retreat, encountering the Frontier Battalion of the SDF under his old colleague Hugh Boustead. 'Wilfred Thesiger turned up ... with important news,' Boustead wrote. 'Torelli had been so alarmed by the apparent concentration against him that he had started to withdraw part of his forces to the north into the friendly country of the pro-Italian chief Gizzar ... Thesiger ... had come straight from ... Sakalle, after living on the country for two months; he could not understand why people travelled with rations. He took a bathe in the icy waters of the stream and then with enormous appetite demolished the last of Bill Harris's stores while we watched in amusement and sympathy for Bill.'[31] Harris, another Bimbashi in the SDF, himself recalled that Thesiger polished off his last tin of grapefruit, half his supply of sugar, and most of his one and only pot of marmalade.[32] 'It was a memorable meal for Wilfred,' Boustead wrote, 'and in later years he would be reminded of it by his hosts: "It's no good offering you anything, is it, Wilfred? You live off the country," while the marmalade pot was ostentatiously hidden.'[33]

Later, Thesiger went with Simonds to mortar Ingebara. Two days afterwards the Italians withdrew, pulling back to the garrison at Burie, where a system of impregnable fortifications had been prepared. Burie's commander, Colonel Natale, had been ordered to hold it at all costs, for behind it lay Debra Markos, the capital of Gojjam. Wingate decided to concentrate his forces there, to encircle the garrison and, if possible, to force Natale and his troops to withdraw. He began to move his vast armada of camels across the escarpment with enormous difficulty. The mules Sandford had promised him had not been available, and this steep, jagged country was hard going for heavily-laden camels, which were strafed constantly by Italian fighters as they moved. Moreover, many of the camel-men were town Arabs rather than nomads, and knew little of the art of camel-management. Thesiger rejoined Wingate as his force forgathered within striking distance of Burie, preparing for a night march to bypass the town. The camels were carefully camouflaged with mud, and Wingate himself led a party of Abyssinians with the task of lighting signal-fires *en route*, to guide the cameleers. Almost everything went wrong: the caravans straggled, got lost in the darkness, bumped into each other and became entangled. Inevitably, one of the signal-fires spread to the surrounding bush and soon the whole landscape was ablaze, illuminating the strings of camels like a giant spotlight. Nerves frayed. Wingate cursed in English; Boustead swore in Arabic. By morning, however, seemingly against all odds, Gideon Force was in position.

From here, Wingate and Boustead harried the fortresses of Burie piecemeal, aided, for the only time on the campaign, by three Wellesley bombers. Thesiger stood beside him as he watched the onslaught: 'I was struck,' Thesiger wrote, 'by the merciless, almost savage, expression on his face.'[34] Later he sent Thesiger off to contact a Patriot chief called Haile Yusuf in the Chokey mountains and persuade him to attack Dembecha, another fort on the road between Burie and Debra Markos. Haile Yusuf agreed, but as his men moved into position they were spotted by the Italian-led troops, who raked them with machine-guns and then attacked. After some skirmishing Thesiger and the Patriots drove them back to their fort. For two days they sat on a hill overlooking the fort, being buzzed by fighter aircraft, though by sheltering under rocks on the side of the hill they avoided casualties. Thesiger requested a machine-gun from Major Boyle, whose Patriot Battalion Wingate had instructed to cut the road between Burie and Debra Markos. Boyle was encamped only two miles from Thesiger's position, and sent a machine-gun under the charge of one of his officers, Lieutenant Rowe. That evening Thesiger saw a great mass of men, animals and vehicles moving down the road from Burie, and realized that Wingate's strategy had succeeded: the Italians had abandoned Burie and were moving to Dembecha. On the way, they bumped straight into Boyle's battalion, who were just preparing their evening meal. The retreating Italians were 8,000 strong, and had with them lorries, armoured cars, machine-guns, and cavalry squadrons, with three Caproni bombers riding shotgun above. Boyle's unit comprised 500 men, seven British officers, and a mob of camels. They could almost see the whites of their enemies' eyes when they opened up. Set back for a few moments by the shock, the Italians rallied and swamped the tiny opposition. From where Thesiger sat on the nearby hilltop the fray looked like a scene from Napoleonic times. He and his Patriots kept up constant fire on the fort to prevent the garrison charging out and attacking Boyle from the rear. By noon a quarter of Boyle's battalion lay dead or wounded and the rest had been captured or had disappeared. However, his Abyssinians had fought back bravely, killing 250 men, putting two armoured cars out of action and even bringing down a bomber. The Italian column entered Dembecha, but Boustead's force was only a few hours behind them. There was a fierce firefight during the night, in which Bill Harris – whose marmalade Thesiger had so recently polished off – was seriously wounded. The next day, however, the Italian rearguard retreated down the road to their last stronghold – Debra Markos. Thesiger hurried down to the abandoned fort of Dembecha, and found

Wingate already there trying to salvage food from the stores which the Italians had set ablaze. He helped Wingate lay out a landing-ground for aircraft – which never materialized – and while the work was in progress Wingate lost his temper with his interpreter and slashed him across the face with a stick.

The following day, after Wingate had left, the same man was caught in an explosion while smoking in a petrol dump with three Sudanese soldiers from the Frontier Battalion. Thesiger rushed out to find four living fireballs hurtling about the yard. Though he and his men managed to extinguish the flames, it was too late: their skin had been virtually torched off, and the nubs of charred bones showed through their hands. There was no medical orderly present, for Pansy Drew had taken the wounded Bill Harris and the other casualties back to Burie. The men were in agony, and one screamed, 'Shoot me! Shoot me!' Wingate's interpreter cried out for his chief. Thesiger came to a solemn decision, and, explaining his action clearly to their gathered companions, gave each a lethal dose of morphine.

Debra Markos was the final nut to crack. When it fell, Addis Ababa would be ripe for the plucking. In his assault on the capital, Wingate planned to employ the same combination of bluff and guerrilla tactics he had used at Burie. In order to cut off the enemy's retreat if and when they abandoned the town, he ordered Thesiger and Captain Tim Foley, with a small group of Abyssinians, to bypass it and seize the strategic bridge on the Blue Nile at Safertak, with the assistance of a Patriot chief called Belai Zelleka. They would lay an ambush on the bridge and Foley, a demolitions man, would mine it. Content that the trap was laid, Wingate returned to force the enemy out of Debra Markos. He took another daring gamble and dispatched half of the remnants of Boustead's Sudanese, under Bimbashi Johnson, and 140 Abyssinians, towards Safartak. On 3 April Johnson's force ambushed and destroyed a convoy of Italian reinforcements moving up from Addis Ababa, including twenty-eight enemy lorries and two armoured cars, killing eleven Italian officers and scores of Abyssinian troops. The following day, alarmed by Johnson's action in his rear and by Boustead's relentless pounding from the west, the commandant of Debra Markos, Colonel Maravento, ordered his men to withdraw. He handed over the defence of the town to some irregular troops and authority to Ras Hailu, an Italian collaborator and an inveterate enemy of Haile Selassie. The Emperor himself was already in position outside, and Wingate was confident that the Abyssinian irregulars would not dare to fire on him. Wingate was installed in one of the captured forts to the west of Debra Markos, when the telephone rang. An Italian officer stationed at Safartak, unaware that the fort had fallen, asked what was happening in Gojjam's capital. By a stroke of luck Wingate had with him Edmund Stevens of the *Christian Science Monitor*, who spoke fluent Italian. Under Wingate's prompting, Stevens informed the Italian that 10,000 British soldiers were closing in on them. 'What is to be done?' the officer inquired. 'Clear out at once!' came the bogus order. The Italian needed no further encouragement. The Italian-led battalions from Debra Markos were retreating in confusion to the Blue Nile bridge, and Wingate was confident that Thesiger and Foley – and by now Johnson too – would be there to meet them. On 6 April, Haile Selassie took possession of Gojjam's capital, receiving the apparently sincere homage of Ras Hailu. The next morning, Hugh Boustead set off to find out how things had fared at Safartak. He came across Bimbashi Johnson at a village two miles west of a fort called Usata, which commanded the approach to the Nile and was in enemy hands. With him was Wilfred Thesiger. In his autobiography, Boustead wrote: 'Johnson, looking extremely disturbed, asked to see me alone. "You sent me to cut off the Italians' crossing the river gorge and I am afraid I have been badly let down. Wilfred Thesiger, in all good faith, was prevailed upon by Bellai Zelleka to ask me to hold hard, as the Italians were still in forts where we could not attack them successfully with our small force. But he said that he would give us word as soon as they started to move. Only now have I heard that most of their forces have got across." Johnson was terribly upset. I said, "Well, never mind, you have been let down by Wilfred Thesiger's belief in Belai Zelleka and his Patriots. The only thing is to catch the rearguard at first light before they get across." I was furious, but felt this was no time to say any more.'[35]

Boustead then interviewed Thesiger, who was deeply mortified about what had happened. 'He had put his faith utterly in Belai

Zelleka, who had fought with great skill and bravery for years against the Italians,' Boustead wrote. 'We learned afterwards that [Zelleka] had been paid some enormous sum to let the Italian forces through. Thesiger had a very worried expression and I was almost too furious to say much. I felt that Johnson on his own would have been so effective that I could almost have cried at the opportunity that had been missed.'[36]

Thesiger explained that he had pushed Zelleka continually to get his army down to the bridge, but that each time he spoke, the 'Patriot' gave another reason for not moving – that he was waiting for more men, more supplies or information. Finally, he had told Thesiger emphatically that it was his army and that he would move when he was ready. Thesiger had felt that it would be unwise to alienate the chief by moving on ahead, and since his men were carrying no rations they were dependent on the Patriot force. Boustead thought that Thesiger should have suspected something amiss from the man's prevarications and gone on ahead anyway, laying the ambush himself. After his meeting with Boustead, Thesiger went straight back to Debra Markos and reported to Wingate, who was surprisingly sanguine: 'On the one occasion on which he could justifiably have said I'd let him down,' Thesiger remembered, 'he didn't. He backed me and gave me another chance which led on to success. He could have said with the force I had at my disposal – I suppose it was about twenty people – I should have got down the road and done it myself. It probably wouldn't have achieved very much. Boustead was very critical of me, though.'[37] It transpired eventually that Belai Zelleka had been made an offer he could not refuse: the hand of Ras Hailu's daughter in marriage. Ras Hailu, the former Italian puppet, was still ruler of Gojjam, and the peasant-born bandit Zelleka could not resist this unprecedented chance of social advancement. Wingate's carefully prepared climax to the capture of Debra Markos had failed, and he could do nothing but rage. Yet at least Haile Selassie's flag flew once more over Gojjam.

Realizing full well what his trust in Zelleka had cost, Thesiger emerged from his interviews with Boustead and Wingate determined to do something to redeem his reputation, and the chance soon presented itself. With Wingate firmly established in the capital of Gojjam, Bimbashi Johnson, with Thesiger and Lieutenant Rowe, was sent out with a puny force of less than 100 Sudanese and Abyssinians, with one Vickers machine-gun and four bren-guns, to pursue Maravento's fleeing column, which was 12,000 strong. Johnson's orders were to harry the enemy as they retreated towards Amba Alagi, intending to meet up with the Duke of Aosta's forces. The tiny British unit – known as 'Safforce', presumably after 'Safartak' – waded across the Blue Nile under heavy Italian shelling, without any casualties, and for a month pursued the great column like a pack of jackals following a wounded but still ferocious buffalo. Expecting a counter-attack at any moment, they went into action only at night, lying up and sniping at the Italians, or raking their camp with machine-gun fire. Soon, however, the Maravento column reached more broken country, where the pursuers could pick them off even during the day. Only once did the Italians try to attack their pursuers, and then when Safforce were dug in on a spur connected to the main table-land only by a narrow isthmus. As the Italians advanced along the perilous neck of rock, Johnson's men mowed them down. The following day they resumed their pursuit. On 14 May Wingate suddenly turned up with a force of 400 men. He had disobeyed orders by installing Haile Selassie in his capital on 5 May, to the jubilation of the populace but the disapproval of General Cunningham, who had arrived there first after invading Abyssinia from the south. Wingate called for Thesiger and told him that he intended to make Maravento surrender before he could join up with the Duke of Aosta at Amba Alagi. Thesiger was to take Lieutenant Rowe, three Patriot leaders and all their men, and to get in front of the fleeing Italians, cutting them off while Wingate harried them from the rear. 'I want at least 200 dead,' Wingate told him.

The Italians were making for a fort called Agibar, where there was already a large Italian garrison. On the way they intended to halt at the small fort of Wagidi. Rushing ahead on a remarkable march of over fifty miles in twenty-four hours, Thesiger found the fort occupied by local levies, whom he persuaded to leave, saying that Haile Selassie had already retrieved his throne and that his small force was the advance guard of a much larger one. When the irregulars withdrew, Thesiger and his men occupied the position, as the Italian column came up and made camp on the plateau. The next morning, 19 May, Thesiger saw the Italians moving in close formation towards the fort and feared he would be trapped there. He moved his men out to make a stand on a nearby ridge from which they could withdraw more easily. Suddenly the Italian artillery opened up with a deafening crash and Thesiger was sent sprawling to the ground with blood welling from his knee. Assuming he had been grazed by a splinter, he did not discover until twenty-five years later, during a cartilage operation, that he had a piece of shrapnel embedded there. However, the Italians were advancing in battalion strength and there was no time to think about superficial wounds. Thesiger's men opened up with an ancient Hotchkiss machine-gun and, ripping off salvoes with their rifles, brought the attack to a standstill. Thesiger then heard the thunder of hoofbeats and saw coming towards him out of the furls of dust a squadron of native cavalry, which his men fought off with hand-grenades and rifle fire. As the cavalry retreated and the dust cleared, Thesiger ordered his troops to withdraw across another narrow panhandle on to an impregnable plateau. The withdrawal was disorganized, Thesiger himself hobbling with the help of his batman, Muhammad, and in the confusion Lieutenant Rowe was hit and seriously injured. He was captured by the Italians and later died. Thirty Patriots were killed or missing, but Thesiger had notched up his 200 enemy dead.

While this action was going on, Wingate had been harassing the Italians from the rear. Finally he had informed Maravento that he was surrounded by Patriots, who were itching to fall upon his men, and if the Italians refused to surrender, he had orders to pull all British officers out within twenty-four hours and leave the column to the mercies of the Abyssinians (who in fact had had enough of the fighting). Maravento fell for the bluff, and at last the column surrendered. Wingate then sent Thesiger orders to force the garrison at Agibar to surrender using the same trick: 'There were over 2,000 troops in Agibar,' Thesiger said, 'and it would have been fatal if they had realized how few we were. I told them that unless they surrendered I would leave them to the thousands of Abyssinians who were moving up. They surrendered.'[38] Thesiger's main task was then to prevent his

Abyssinian Patriots from looting or massacring the prisoners. He had two looters thrashed at the fort gateway as an example to the rest. It took him four hazardous days to march his prisoners to Wingate's position at Fiche, continually troubled that they would be attacked by Patriots with old scores to settle. He arrived triumphantly at Fiche to hand the prisoners over to Wingate, feeling that he had finally redeemed himself for his failure at Safartak. For his action at Wagidi and the capture of Agibar, Wingate recommended him for the DSO. 'I only had a Governor-General's Commission, not a King's Commission,' Thesiger said, 'so I don't really know how I got away with the DSO, which I thought you could only get with a King's Commission! . . . An MC would have sufficed, anyway.'[39]

Maravento's surrender was Wingate's last action in Abyssinia. He was shortly ordered out of the country and sent back to Cairo, where he was reduced to major. He was never to receive any recognition for the remarkable success he had achieved. 'Wingate was a very remarkable man,' Thesiger said, 'though a very unlikeable man. He had no gift for friendship. I was the only person who got on well with him in the whole thing – everybody else disliked him. We both had the same feeling over Abyssinia. He was determined to restore the Emperor to his throne, just as I was. He had the same sort of crusading feeling. Many people criticized Wingate – one man who'd been on his staff but hadn't taken any part in the fighting, Brian Parker, said why they appointed Wingate I don't know – if they'd given the job to Boustead he'd have got the same results with none of the friction and hostility. Wingate fought with everyone, unlike T.E. Lawrence who could go dressed up as an Arab and have Wavell and everybody cooperating with him and giving him all assistance. Wingate would go in and be bloody rude to one or two generals and leave everybody thinking well, I'm damned if I'll do anything for that bastard! Anyway, when Parker said this to me I thought well, there you are, and I said – and this is my final verdict on Wingate – that no other officer in Platt's or Cunningham's armies could conceivably have achieved what Wingate had achieved in Gojjam with the forces at his disposal. He had one newly raised and virtually untrained Abyssinian battalion and one battalion of the Sudan Defence Force, which doesn't amount to much in the way of men, and he was taking on 40,000 [Italian-led troops] dug in position all over Gojjam and in the end he drove the whole lot out. I said there was nobody else who could have done this but Wingate.'[40]

In Cairo, racked by malaria, reduced in rank, virtually accused of insubordination for his report to Wavell, and physically exhausted, Wingate retired to his hotel room one day and cut his own throat. However, another officer had noticed him looking rather strange, and entered the room to find him still alive, lying in a pool of blood on the floor. Later, as he lay in hospital, Hugh Boustead, who had never forgiven Wingate for accusing him of cowardice during the Abyssinian campaign, visited him and roared, 'You bloody fool, why didn't you use a revolver!'[41] Some time later, Thesiger met him: 'His throat was all scarred, of course,' Thesiger recalled, 'and he said if ever you want to cut your throat, never put your head back and cut horizontally, because you won't get through it, put your chin down and cut vertically, then you'll succeed.'[42]

After the action at Agibar, Thesiger returned to Addis Ababa, where he received a message ordering him to report to Cairo immediately. 'The next day Boustead and I chartered a car from an Italian and told him to drive us up to Massawa to catch a ship,' Thesiger remembered, 'and at that moment General Platt was moving south with his army. It was the first time I'd seen regular troops moving and it was fascinating, but I didn't want to remain in Abyssinia. For me, the war was over there.'[43] Actually, he could hardly contain his excitement: he was to be second-in-command of the Arab Legion in Palestine, under his hero, John Bagot Glubb.

CHAPTER 8

A Most Peculiar Major

Thesiger reached Middle East Headquarters in Cairo in June 1941, and was bitterly disappointed to learn that someone else had been given the job with Glubb's Arab Legion.

'What am I to do then?' he asked the staff major in charge.

'You'll have to rejoin your unit,' the major said.

Thesiger reeled at the prospect. His unit was the Sudan Defence Force, now stationed in Eritrea, where the fighting was over. The real war was in North Africa and the Middle East. Besides, the idea of fighting among the Arabs, with its Lawrentian images of camels and deserts, had fired his imagination. The last thing he wanted was to go back to Eritrea.

'Now I'm here, can't you find me something suitable?' he asked. 'I mean, there's fighting in Syria isn't there? I know Syria.'

'Really? And what do you know about Syria?'

Actually, he had only passed through the country once, on his way back to the Sudan in 1936. 'Well,' he said, 'I know Jabal ad Druze.'

The major looked at him in surprise, and Thesiger realized suddenly that he had pressed the right button. 'What! You know Jabal ad Druze?' he said. 'It so happens we are just in the process of forming a Druze Legion. How would you like to be second-in-command of that?'

Thesiger repressed a triumphant smile. 'That would suit me very well,' he said.

Indeed, it could hardly have suited him better. He had been fascinated by the Druzes ever since he had followed the revolt of Sultan Pasha against the French while at school. Famous warriors named after their first missionary, al Darazi, they followed a religion neither Muslim nor Christian, whose rites were shrouded in secrecy. Richard Burton had admired them tremendously during his time as Consul in Damascus, describing them as proud fighting men who were plain-spoken and honest, and knew neither cheating, stealing or intrigue. Another plum had fallen fortuitously into Thesiger's lap, and his only task was to rid himself of his anachronistic rank of Bimbashi and acquire a proper King's Commission. The following day he sauntered into the HQ wearing his crown and two stars, and told the staff-officer in charge: 'I've come for a proper commission.'

'I see,' said the officer, 'and what rank would you like to be?'

'I should think a major,' Thesiger said.

'Good God!' the other replied. 'That's opening your mouth a bit wide, isn't it?'

'Don't you believe it,' Thesiger said. 'If I'm to be second-in-command of a new battalion I should certainly expect to be a major.'

The officer frowned but finally agreed, and Thesiger marched out of the office as a regular army major without ever having passed so much as an interview. 'I simply chose my own rank!' he said.

Through the Gojjam campaign he had fought on foot in the medieval, feudal style that suited him. 'What mattered to us was where the water was and getting more food,' he said. 'We were in harmony with our surroundings and the traditions and everything else.'[1] With the Druze, he found himself equally fortunate, for the Druze Legion was to be a cavalry unit. Raised by Colonel Gerald de Gaury, a diplomat and prolific traveller and writer on the Middle East, its formation had been ordered by Field Marshal Wilson, and its strength would eventually reach more than 1,000 men, operating on the right flank of Wilson's push against the Vichy French in Syria. Each tribesman was supposed to provide his own horse and weapons in true feudal style, and though never involved in a full-scale charge, de Gaury believed it to have been the last cavalry unit ever formed in war.[2]

When Thesiger arrived at Mafraq in Trans-Jordan some days later, he found the cultured, impeccably dressed de Gaury already recruiting Druzes, a few of whom were deserters from the Vichy French. They handed out some of the Italian rifles captured in

North Africa, but had no more sophisticated equipment for them. 'We had no machine-guns or many spare rifles,' Thesiger said, 'but it didn't bother them. They were natural horsemen, and I liked them immediately.'³ As No.2, Thesiger should properly have been concerned with the administration of the battalion, but this had never been his forte. Instead, he asked the colonel to give him a squadron of his own, and de Gaury agreed. Thesiger was a field-man, and he wanted to get as far away from authority and his countrymen as possible, not out of unsociability, but because he was essentially a feudal leader who wished to run his own small show. Within a few days he was thundering across a lava plain at the head of a mass of horsemen whose flowing black capes, headcloths and striped shirts could not have changed much in hundreds of years. It must have seemed that he was living a romantic daydream from his school years, that he was actually a Sheikh from Sultan Pasha's war on the French, rather than the agent of an Imperial power sent to run partisans. He thrilled as they bellowed out their martial songs, the same ones they must have sung, he thought, as they rode against the French army, and the fires blazed from their rooftops like beacons.

After an hour's going, he ordered a halt. 'I said, now look here, get under those trees over there,' he recalled, 'and what I want you to do is to select two officers, four sergeants and so on – which they did.'⁴ In his own small army, he must have officers: there was already the example of the SDF, where NCOs and junior officers were Sudanese. 'I barred all saluting, though,' he said. 'I didn't want to think of myself as a regular soldier. I wanted the respect they'd have given to a Sheikh.'⁵ De Gaury did not approve of this gratuitous distribution of commissions, however, and told Thesiger he had no right to appoint officers. 'I said, dammit, I've got to have some officers!' Thesiger recalled. 'And anyway, they were a great success. We never had any trouble and I don't think I ever took any disciplinary action. I regarded them as tribesmen who were following me'⁶: a manifestation of Thesiger's gang-leader tendency at its most graphic.

The only problem was that there was no fighting: 'It was an extraordinary war,' he said, 'because they'd say oh, the people of such-and-such a village want you to go there tomorrow to lunch and somewhere else for dinner. I suppose it made the French feel uncomfortable and put the wind up them. They'd had a very nasty time of it with the Druze in the past. If the Druze had ridden against them as a whole their lines of communication would have been cut.'[7] Thesiger installed himself at the village of Malha, a conglomeration of austerely furnished stone-built houses, some of which were of Roman origin. The Druzes were not nomadic Bedouin, but because of their distinct religion formed a cohesive tribal whole, a tightly-knit web of families whose young men tended to remain at home in the Jabal rather than leaving to seek jobs in Damascus. Thesiger's orderly was a sixteen-year-old called Faris. 'He looked after me,' Thesiger said. 'In some ways I had the same relationship with him as I did with Idris.'[8]

The French occupied a fort in the hills on a peak called Salkhad, not far from Malha, where they had guns and a battalion of infantry. They watched Thesiger's to-ing and fro-ing like hawks but never ventured out of their sanctuary. 'Only on one occasion did we get too close,' Thesiger said. 'We had just stopped for lunch and they shelled us. We hopped on our horses and bolted off. That was the only time we ever got fired on.'[9] Thesiger, living the romantic tribesman's life in his fertile imagination, did not wish to be brought down to earth by notions of orderly offices, parade grounds and saluting, but this was still an army, and he exercised here his tendency to 'ignore what he had no desire to see'. In fact, when Lieutenant Edward Henderson arrived with a new major who was to take over a squadron, Thesiger had the whole unit on parade. 'We were a bit late because the road had been damaged by shell-fire,' Henderson recalled, 'and Thesiger was a bit cross. His men had been on parade once and had fallen out, now he had to get them on parade again. You'd have thought we were going on an operation or something rather than just going through a formality, because he introduced us personally to every single tribesman – about 200 men. When it was over he said crossly, "Well, we're going!" The new major inquired where the orderly office was. He was rather small and did not look the outdoor type. Thesiger looked him up and down and said, "Office! There's a war on!" There *was* an office, of course, and Thesiger eventually muttered it was over there in a tent. He had a tendency to be a little impatient with people.'[10]

Thesiger and his men would pound through local villages, feasting with the Druzes and receiving ritual pledges of fealty from the local Sheikhs. Thesiger would be obliged to reply in Arabic, which, though he spoke it fairly competently, was the Sudanese dialect of his SDF troops – quite different from the Arabic spoken here. Other delegations swept into Malha to announce their support for the British or merely to make a social call. Among one such party he was delighted to meet his boyhood hero, Sultan Pasha al 'Atrash, whom he found suitably impressive, though, ironically, the famous leader would make no gesture of allegiance to the British, having promised his good behaviour to the French. After de Gaury had moved the Legion's HQ to Basra Eski Sham, in a great Saracen fort superimposed on the shell of an ancient Roman amphitheatre, he was transferred, and Thesiger heard that he was to be replaced by a Colonel Buller – a regular soldier. 'I realized that being his second-in-command was going to be absolutely bloody,' Thesiger commented. 'I mean, his whole attitude was sort of drilling and discipline and things, and he kept on saying now we can get down to some proper soldiering – he would have had us on parade and all that nonsense.'[11] This was exactly equivalent to Thesiger's impending transfer to Wad Medani from Kutum in 1937: Buller's arrival threatened to pull the plug on Thesiger's game and take away his freedom. 'I said now look here, I want to be left with my squadron,' Thesiger recalled, 'and he said no you can't – you're second-in-command and as such you are supposed to stay here with me. So I said well, you can get someone else to be your second-in-command. I'm going back to my squadron, which I did.'[12]

In December 1941, though, an armistice with the Vichy French brought the campaign to a halt. Jabal ad Druze became French again, and as many of the Druze Legion were deserters from the French army, the Legion was transferred to Palestine, out of French jurisdiction. Thesiger was itching for action: the Druze had been fascinating, but it had not been war. He hungered for North Africa, where the fate of nations was being decided. The Druze Legion, like Sandford's 101 Mission, was a child of the SOE – the Special Operations Executive – an Intelligence unit knocked together in 1936 to coordinate resistance movements against the Axis powers. Thesiger requested a transfer: 'I went down to SOE HQ in Damascus,' he remembered, 'and I asked to be sent to the desert to do an SOE type job behind enemy lines. It was the moment when the Germans were advancing on Stalingrad and it looked as if they might come down through Syria. They said would I stay behind in Syria and conduct operations behind enemy lines, and I said yes, that's just in my line.'[13]

First, though, Thesiger asked for a couple of weeks' leave. 'I expect you'll be wanting to get down to Cairo?' the staff officer inquired.

'Not at all,' Thesiger said. 'I want to get hold of a car and see what I haven't seen of Syria.'

'There's an officer in the next room who's planning to do just that,' the officer said. 'Why not go and see him?'

Thesiger did, and the officer turned out to be a young South African half-colonel who had played a part in the Abyssinian campaign, called Laurens van der Post, later famous for his books about the Bushmen of the Kalahari. Together they rumbled through Syria in a staff-car, and visited the rose-red rock citadel of Petra, built by the Nabataeans in the fourth century BC. There were no other tourists, and the two officers climbed up to the monuments and slept in the caves. Thesiger recalled getting on with van der Post well: 'I've seldom liked anybody more,' he said, 'but there seem to be two contradictory people in him – the one who writes his books and the one I met on that occasion.'[14]

After his leave Thesiger joined twenty other officers on a demolitions course at Natrun in Palestine. Among the officers was Edward Henderson, who had become an instructor on the course. It was held in a deserted monastery where the monks had evacuated a guest-house. 'The thing I remember best is the time Thesiger set off this enormous mine,' Henderson recalled. 'It was to demonstrate cutting charges and they brought up this half-ton sea-mine which they thought was empty. Thesiger was told to put a charge on it and get out of the way. He laid the charge and told the rest of us to get down, and then there was this volcanic explosion as the whole thing went up. It was very lucky no one was hurt. Of course, the demonstration-mine had been live after all!'[15]

Having survived the course, Henderson and Thesiger were assigned to work together, and briefed by SOE. Their main objective was to find lying-up places from which they could launch raids, lead resistance-fighters and blow up bridges in classic SOE style, should the Germans capture Syria. They covered deserts, villages and towns, sleeping in Bedouin tents or deserted cabins. Henderson found Thesiger an unusually quiet character: 'He'd won a DSO in Abyssinia, but he never said how he'd got it,' he recalled, 'apart from that he wasn't in any way a famous person. He was just a young major in the army and wasn't at all well known. He might have been well known in London, but he didn't talk much about what he'd done – genuinely modest I think.'[16]

Henderson recalled that they visited the tents of the famous Bedouin tribe of the Rwalla together on occasions, and remembered how fascinated Thesiger had been with them. 'My Arabic was still basic,' Henderson said, 'and I spent much of the time just listening. The Bedu sounded quite abrupt, but they had their own forms of politeness, and Wilfred fitted in with them very quickly. He spoke Arabic much better than I did: it was Sudanese style, but it was quite good.'[17] Thesiger remembered this period in Syria as his 'introduction to Bedu life'. 'The other places I'd been in were blanks in history,' he said, 'but in Syria you got this patina of peoples left all round the desert, though the Bedu remained isolated and unchanged. I met Nuri ibn Shaalan, the Sheikh of the Rwalla, who was mentioned by Lawrence as an old man. This was twenty years later, and he was still the Sheikh, and far from being senile. This was the first time I'd really come across the customary courtesy of Arab tribes. True, I'd met the Kababish in the Sudan, but though I'd ridden through their country, I'd actually had little to do with them.'[18] On one occasion he visited the tents of another famous Bedouin tribe, the Anaza. Years later, he wrote in the *Listener*: 'Everywhere there were marks of poverty, for that winter had been one of awful severity, and two-thirds of their flocks and herds had perished. Their tents were in tatters and they themselves in rags, but we were guests, and they feasted us on a sheep and a great bowl of rice, sufficient for their frugal needs for a month. Their manners were those of a "great people", and I felt myself an uncouth, impatient representative of a materialistic age. They and their way of life are an anachronism and are bound to disappear.'[19] Although this piece was not written until after Thesiger had met the Bedu of southern Arabia, if it is a true record of his feelings at the time (in 1942) then it is clear that all the motifs that would become familiar in his work – Bedu superiority, Western material-ism, and the 'doom' of traditional Bedouin life – were firmly implanted in his mind several years before he crossed the Empty Quarter, and a decade and a half before putting his pen to work on *Arabian Sands*.

One irritation Thesiger experienced during his reconnaissances with Henderson was the driver. 'He was disappointed that the driver, who was a British soldier, wouldn't adapt to the local conditions,' Henderson recalled, 'and after all, the man had come straight out of the ranks and you couldn't expect it. It was all a bit mystifying to him. Wilfred was never rude but he was a bit impatient. In the end the driver complained, and they changed him for a Ghurka.'[20] After some weeks together, the two officers dispensed with the Humber and decided to go their separate ways, meeting up again on occasions. They travelled by horse, donkey, on foot or even by bus. 'It was fascinating,' Thesiger said. 'Sometimes I'd be with the Bedu, sometimes with villagers, especi-ally in a place called Pan's Garden, which I really liked. I climbed Mount Hermon. I could have worn civilian clothes, but I wore military uniform because there was no reason not to. I established bases among people I could rely on, and I actually spent quite a lot of time in Damascus getting to know the leaders.'[21] Finally, he and Henderson decided that the lava-fields of Laja in the Hauran would be the most suitable base for clandestine operations. Riddled with caves, the area had long served as a hideout for fugitives, yet was near enough to the Damascus road to allow SOE agents to monitor traffic movements. It was also adjacent to Jabal ad Druze, where Thesiger was known. He was looking forward to operating behind enemy lines, but to his disappointment the German threat evapor-ated, as their army was balked by the Russian winter on the outskirts of Moscow. It had been a year since he had left Abyssinia with his DSO, hoping for action. He had had an interesting time, but had scarcely heard a shot fired in anger. He was an adventurer, a man of deeds, and he craved to be where the fighting was.

Unfortunately, to get there was more difficult than he had anticipated. He had had no experience with a regular army unit. He was basically a colonial officer accustomed to native troops. He returned to Cairo and contacted SOE headquarters at Grey Pillars, where an 'unconvincing' RAF wing-commander named Domville assured him continually that there would be something for him soon. At that time the most successful guerilla-style unit operating in North Africa was the Long Range Desert Group, founded by the veteran desert explorer, Ralph Bagnold. Bagnold, a Signals officer, had spent much of his time before the war with a group of like-minded enthusiasts making astounding journeys in Egypt's Western Desert – the most arid stretch of land on earth. Brought back from retirement, Bagnold had woven his exploring amateurs into an astoundingly successful motor unit, which had actually managed to cross Egypt's Great Sand Sea and capture the oasis of Kufra from the Italians. Though Thesiger had always despised motor transport, he would now have given almost anything to be with the LRDG. However, the time was inopportune: hard pressed by the German Afrika Korps under Rommel, it looked as if the British 8th Army might be pushed back and Cairo itself lost to the enemy: 'There was heavy fighting in the Cauldron and Alamein,' Thesiger recalled, 'and it looked as if we might lose Egypt. So SOE asked me if I would stay behind in Cairo and operate as an SOE agent with a safe-house and that sort of thing. I told them I knew nothing about Cairo, and in fact I didn't know a single Cairene. They said well, I'd been here a lot. So I said well, if they couldn't find anyone else I'd try it. They said there were these three very reliable Egyptians who would support me. I saw no reason why they should risk their lives looking after me at all: it seemed wildly improbable. Then it more or less came to a halt, and I went to see Domville and said now look here, it would be much more in my line if you *did* lose Cairo to let me go down to the Red Sea Hills and use the tribes there to cut off the railway line.'[22] Thesiger got his wish, and spent some weeks in the hills with Captain Tim Foley – his old colleague from the Gojjam campaign – who was mining wolfram there. Thesiger made contact with the local nomads of the Ababda tribe, and began to stockpile rifles and explosives. Again, the enemy never came. In October 1942, Rommel's forces were turned back by the British under General Montgomery at the now famous battle of El Alamein – the turning-point of the war. Not waiting for orders, Thesiger commandeered a car and drove furiously to Cairo. He had seen no action since June 1941, and the war was passing him by.

He strode into Grey Pillars and confronted the brigadier in charge. Thesiger was accustomed to getting his way, and this time he was determined to get to the front. 'The SOE were totally incapable of doing anything,' he recalled. 'They were the most incompetent administration I've ever come across. I told the brigadier, "Now look here, let me get off to the desert." I wanted to get into the LRDG. I'd met some of Bagnold's people when they came through Kutum before the war, though I hadn't been interested in their cars then. But to get away from SOE I'd have been happy to join them. The brigadier said they wouldn't take me as a major, and I said, "I don't give a damn if they take me as a second-lieutenant as long as I can get out of this lot!" '[23] The brigadier responded by reprimanding Thesiger for deserting his post in the Red Sea Hills. The next day there were rumours that he was to be court-martialled for insubordination. 'Then I was lucky,' Thesiger remembered, 'because that night I was grumbling about it, and somebody said why don't you go and see David Stirling? I said "Who's David Stirling?" and they told me he'd got a brother called Peter who was on the Embassy staff. They suggested I went to see Peter and got in touch with David – that's what I did.'[24]

Thesiger had never heard, either, of the Special Air Service Brigade, but he marched in double-quick time round to Peter Stirling's flat and by a stroke of luck found both brothers at home. David Stirling, tall, dark, powerful, with a manner that could be disconcertingly vague or incisively alert, had formed the SAS Brigade while only a subaltern in the Scots Guards, at the age of twenty-five. Within two years – still five years Thesiger's junior – he had become a lieutenant-colonel. Of course, the SAS was not a brigade in reality, but a couple of squadrons – the brigade status being a propaganda ruse for the sake of the enemy. Stirling and Thesiger talked for an hour. The tall, dark Scotsman took in Thesiger's DSO ribbon, and his talk of Abyssinia and the

Druzes. He noted, above all, that Thesiger seemed to know he was about to launch a raid: this was extremely sensitive information, and it worried him that it should be public knowledge. Thesiger was impressed with him, however. 'He made exactly the opposite impression to Wingate,' he commented. 'He was a gentleman and treated his troops well. He got what he wanted like that.'[25] Finally, Stirling told Thesiger he would accept him as a recruit for the new squadron he was forming, and told him to get down to the SAS base at Kabrit immediately. Thesiger then broached the sensitive issue of the brigadier, who was threatening him with insubordination: 'Stirling rang up Middle East HQ,' he recalled, 'and told the brigadier, "I'm taking Major Thesiger on my next operation. Will you kindly release him at once." And Stirling was only a lieutenant-colonel then!'[26]

The unit to which Thesiger found himself attached at Kabrit was certainly unlike any with which he had previously served. Stirling had happened across a simple yet heretical idea in terms of military formation: that small groups of high-quality and highly-trained men could, armed with the element of surprise, wreak devastation among the enemy far out of proportion to their numbers. It was, in a sense, a break away from the traditional idea of massed armies, back to that of the individual warrior. Stirling had originally envisaged the SAS as a parachute unit, but the first parachute operations had proved so unsuccessful that he had switched to the idea of delivering his warriors by jeep, at first with the ultra-successful Long Range Desert Group. The collaboration had proved a happy one. By August 1942, the SAS – reduced to only about twenty – had destroyed more Luftwaffe planes on the ground than the RAF had done in the air. By the end of 1942 the SAS had its own special jeeps, armed with Vickers 'K' aircraft-type machine-guns, and would go on to put paid to more than 300 enemy planes before the end of the war. The veteran core of the SAS, 'A' Squadron, under the hard-drinking, brawling rugby international Ulsterman Major Blair 'Paddy' Mayne, was already out in the desert when Thesiger arrived at Kabrit. Rommel's Afrika Korps had retreated down the coast of North Africa from its nemesis at Alamein, and was preparing to make a stand at Aghayla on the Gulf of Sirte. On

8 November, an Anglo-American army had landed in Algeria ready to crush the Germans and Italians in a pincer movement. Mayne's squadron lay at Bir Zoltan, about sixty miles south of Aghayla, poised like vultures to harass enemy traffic along the 400-mile stretch of road between there and Tripoli, to coincide with Montgomery's next push against Rommel which was to start on 13 February. Stirling had been authorized to raise the SAS to regimental status, and Thesiger was attached to the new recruits now being trained at Kabrit, to fill the ranks of 'B' Squadron under Lt.-Colonel Vivian Street.

One peculiarity of the SAS was its multi-national composition. There was a Free French Squadron being primed as a nucleus for the eventual liberation of France, and a proud corpus of Greek volunteers, known as 'the Sacred Squadron', whose battle-traditions were based on the ancient Theban wives' farewell to their husbands: 'Come back with your shield or upon it!' These were to form 'C' and 'D' Squadrons of the new SAS Regiment, while a contingent of the Special Boat Squadron was to form a fifth squadron. 'B' Squadron had not completed its training – Stirling reckoned on five weeks to train an SAS trooper or officer in its special tactics. Thesiger received no training at all, and, like Vivian Street himself, was never officially on the Squadron strength. Yet time was running out. Stirling had returned from the desert via Cairo to lead the new unit – strengthened by a peppering of veterans – to rendezvous with Mayne's 'A' Squadron at Bir Zoltan. From there it would divide with Mayne's squadron the task of harassing enemy columns along the coastal road: this was the operation which Thesiger had been lucky enough to hear about at that crucial moment in Cairo.

Colonel 'Shan' Hackett, coordinating the SAS operations, had, in fact, forbidden Stirling to accompany any more operations, since the detailed information he was party to would prove too valuable to the enemy were he captured. But Stirling insisted, and on 20 November a convoy of forty-five jeeps and three-ton lorries carried ninety-six men out of Kabrit under his command. Among the men was Wilfred Thesiger. They drove along the desert road as far as Agedabia, passing through the battlefield at Alamein, where Thesiger was able to observe burned-out tanks, guns and trucks and the skeletons of shot-down aircraft – the debris of the great battle that had been the turning-point of the war. He was exhilarated by the sight, even though he had not played a part in this historic confrontation. He knew that most of the men around him had served through the entire three years of this campaign and he understood, perhaps with regret, how peripheral his part had been to the focus of the action. This experience of serving with his countrymen was a new one for him: he was accustomed to colonial and native troops, attended by a batman or a personal servant. Here, he was just another officer – indeed, as far as the SAS was concerned, an untrained one – attached to a unit which had a special philosophy. Stirling's concept of operating in small units of three or four men necessarily meant that each man would be capable of taking the decisions that in other units would be taken by officers or NCOs. Whereas the traditional British idea of a 'crack' regiment was simply one that was officered by aristocrats, Stirling's concept followed the ancient Greek idea of aristocracy in which any man with the right attitude and qualities, no matter what his background, should be able to achieve aristocratic status within his lifetime. In other words, the SAS was a meritocracy with no class distinction between officers and men, and Stirling emphasized this by commissioning his most promising NCOs in the field. How well the élitist Thesiger, with his lifelong aversion to the idea of meritocracy, accepted Stirling's ideals is difficult to say: much was rationalized afterwards that could not have been apparent in the heat of war. When asked years later what he thought of the special SAS philosophy, Thesiger replied, 'I don't know anything about the philosophy. [They] didn't have a philosophy when I was with [them].'[27] Nevertheless, he and Stirling had enough mutual respect to remain in contact after the war, though they were never intimate friends. The SAS rank-and-file view of Thesiger is reflected by Johnny Cooper, one of the regiment's 'Originals', and a perfect example of the practice of Stirling's ideals. He had lied about his age and joined the Scots Guards while only seventeen. Commissioned in the field by Stirling, he was to retire from the army almost forty years later as a lieutenant-colonel. Cooper, a sergeant at the time Thesiger was recruited, evidently felt him something of an odd fish. Thesiger was a 'most peculiar major', he wrote. 'On my first contact with Major Thesiger he was attired in a black, flowing galabiyya with full Arab head-dress and sandals. He was a large man with a much-punched boxing nose and quite a high-pitched voice. And he was to accompany us on patrol.'[28]

From Agedabia the convoy turned south into the desert to make contact with Mayne's squadron, arriving at Bir Zoltan on 29 November. Surveying the map of the coast road, Stirling divided up the battle-zone between the two squadrons: Mayne was to have the road between Aghayla and Bouerat to the east, while Street's 'B' Squadron would take the more populated area between Bouerat and Tripoli to the west. Stirling's plan was that the SAS should stay in the field for up to two months, mounting four to six raids every night, while the LRDG fed them intelligence from their secret hides along the road. 'B' Squadron was to move to a new base at Bir Fascia, about 400 miles west. Stirling divided them into eight patrols of two or three jeeps each, and gave them instructions to keep relentless pressure on. His object was to make travel at night so painful along the road that enemy traffic would move by daylight and provide plum targets for the RAF. Thesiger was placed in a jeep with Lt. Gordon Alston, who had been with the SAS on earlier operations, and two signallers. Stirling saw the squadron to Bir Fascia before returning to 8th Army Headquarters in Cairo. In order to avoid being spotted, they made a wide arc through the desert south of the road, lying up by day and travelling through the night, over soft dunes and hard wedges of rock. The going was execrable and Thesiger, who drove alternately with Alston, found the drives exhausting and suffered from the cold. It was then that he reflected bitterly on the ignominy of motor transport and this 'unnatural' way of fighting a war. 'We had to go right round the German lines and we went a long way into the desert,' he recalled. 'One owed nothing to the country or to the people who were there. We carried our water and our food and it was simply good or bad going. I felt utterly and completely dissociated from the whole thing. It meant nothing to you. Whereas when I was fighting in Abyssinia it had meant living with the people and I was dependent on them for food and had to persuade them to fight and everything else.'[29] Thesiger kept his opinions to himself, however, according to Johnny Cooper, who travelled with him later: '[He didn't make any disparaging comments about the jeeps.] If he had he would have received a barrage of abuse from everybody because [our] success in destroying over 300 Axis aircraft behind enemy lines derived from the use of that little motor-car.'[30]

The squadron arrived at Bir Fascia on 13 February, as Montgomery's offensive began. *Bir* signifies 'well' in Arabic, and at Fascia there was a rainwater cistern dating back to Roman times, and a number of wadis lined with thorn-scrub which could be gathered to camouflage the jeeps. The following day the squadron, which had by now separated into its patrols, went into action. Stirling, with a sergeant as his driver, remained at Fascia with Alston and Thesiger. After dark two jeeps set off from Fascia – Stirling and his driver in one, Thesiger and Alston in the other. As they reached the road the jeeps separated, Stirling going off to attack a camp, Thesiger waiting for a convoy. He did not have to wait long. 'There was a big column with all its lights on coming along,' Thesiger recalled. 'They were Germans. We drove down the side of the road till we got in a good position then raked them with our Vickers K.'[31] He squeezed the trigger, not releasing until the drum was empty, then Alston hit the accelerator and the jeep raced exhilaratingly into the cover of the night whence it had come. Further on they dynamited some telegraph poles, severed the phone lines and laid some mines, before coming across a large camp where vehicles were coming and going with their headlamps on. The two officers drove coolly into the camp with their own lights on and machine-gunned a row of tents. No one even fired back, but racing out of the camp they had a flat and had to bale out to change the tyre while still within easy reach of the enemy. Unable to shift the nuts, they drove back to Fascia on a flat tyre, only to have it pointed out by Stirling's amused sergeant that they had been turning them the wrong way. Thesiger had never changed a tyre before.

The following day Stirling left for Cairo. Thesiger, Alston and their men began ten days of lying up during daylight and striking at night: 'There'd be tents on either side of these camps,' he remembered, 'and we'd motor into the camp, look round for a bit and say, "Let's go down there," and we'd just rake them until we came out the other side. Then the next day we'd find another target – on one occasion a [recreation] tent with four lorries drawn up outside – and we could hear them all laughing and singing and we suddenly opened up. Then we just motored out and luckily there were no sentries with the lorries so we just put a drum into each of their engines. We never once got fired at in all this time. I felt that it couldn't go on and that sooner or later we should inevitably be in trouble. I haven't any idea how many people I killed, I mean if you're shooting into a tent which is full of people, providing you aren't shooting high, you'd probably kill the lot. It was interesting, but I can't say exciting because we were never fired at once. It's difficult to say whether or not I felt afraid. I've felt afraid when I've been machine-gunned from the air or going over land which was mined, or when I've been charged as I have sixteen times by lion, but in those circumstances, with the SAS, I didn't feel afraid because I was too preoccupied with what I was doing.'[32] These two weeks saw the only real action Thesiger was to experience with the SAS. 'It was a fascinating thing to do attacking enemy supply columns and camps at night,' Thesiger commented, 'and the jeeps were wonderfully adapted to it – we had four machine-guns on each jeep which were very effective military weapons, but it was entirely different from being with the Patriots where you were dependent on them for their knowledge of the country and everything else. That made all the difference. Apart from Alston and the two signallers, I hardly saw another person till the end. I think we certainly made a considerable effect on the battle and Monty's advance because we stopped them moving any transport at night – they were sitting targets and we just got down to the road and shot them to pieces.'[33]

Though Thesiger, Alston and their patrol were undoubtedly successful in their own individual operations, the other patrols were not. The verdict of the historians is that though Mayne's 'A' Squadron to the east – composed of the hard-core regulars of the SAS – was remarkably successful until outflanked by the encroaching British army, 'B' Squadron was largely ineffective: 'The story of 'B' Squadron is a sad one,' historian Anthony Kemp has written. '. . . Within a few days most of their patrols had either been killed or captured and the enemy occupied their rendezvous at Bir Fascia.'[34] Indeed, Thesiger and his patrol were present when they did so. One morning he was resting by the radio-jeep, which had been carefully camouflaged, when he heard the engine of a spotter plane. Alston and the two signallers had gone to fetch water and he was alone. Waiting tensely, he then heard the grating gears of ground vehicles. At once he grabbed his knapsack and a blanket and ran out into the desert, lying in a hollow with the blanket over him, covered with bits of earth and twigs. Peering from beneath it, he saw armoured cars rumbling up the valley. One of them passed only 200 yards from Thesiger's hiding-place. Suddenly he heard its engine cut. He waited, helpless, for a burst of fire to crack out of the desert. Then the motor grumbled up again. The cars were in no hurry to leave, though: they crawled about the camp manoeuvring their bulks this way and that, but failed to observe the hidden wireless jeep. Just after they drove off, Thesiger heard a crackle of machine-gun fire and assumed the Germans had discovered Alston and the others. In fact they had been firing at one of 'B' Squadron's few surviving patrols, under the Free French officer Lieutenant Martin, which had been on its way back to the RV at Bir Fascia just as the armoured cars were leaving. The Germans had shot them up, but they had escaped into the desert and arrived a few hours later. By that time Thesiger and Alston, who had also been in hiding with the two signallers, had found each other again. Many years later, Thesiger read that Field Marshal Rommel had himself been out in an armoured car around Bir Fascia on that day, and liked to imagine that the 'Desert Fox' had actually been in one of the vehicles that had nosed around his hiding-place.

The squadron commander, Lt.-Colonel Vivian Street, had been captured, and of the men who had driven out from Bir Fascia on 14 December, nine days previously, only four officers had survived or avoided capture, and a handful of other ranks, mostly veterans of the original SAS squadron who had been attached to the new unit. However, the ill-fated squadron had not been without effect: 'Their very presence . . . unsettled the enemy,' Kemp has written, '. . . and forced their commanders to detach valuable troops to round up the raiding parties.'[35] When the signallers got the radio humming once again, Stirling ordered the remnants of the decimated squadron to remain in the area, as he himself was on his way back. In Cairo, Stirling had been planning the SAS's last major operation in North Africa: Montgomery's final push against Tripoli was to start on 15 January, and the SAS would leapfrog forward into Tunisia, where the German supply-bases had been established at the ports of Sfax and Gabes. Before the war the colonial French had constructed a fortified belt known as the Mareth Line between Gabes and Tripoli. To make a reconnaissance of this line was one of Stirling's priorities, but he also intended to put a small party right up through the German lines to make contact with the British 1st Army, which had recently landed in Algeria, and which included Stirling's brother Bill, who had been instructed to form a second SAS regiment there.

Stirling intended to make his forward base at Bir Soltan (not to be confused with the earlier base at Bir Zoltan), which involved another protracted drive of hundreds of miles across open desert in an arc around Tripoli. Meeting up with Thesiger, Alston, Martin, and an advance party under Lieutenant Jordan at Bir Guedaffia, Stirling's plans were finalized. From there, the SAS drove in two groups to Bir Soltan, one navigated by Sergeant Johnny Cooper. For the first fifty miles the going was firm, but after that they entered the Grand Erg Occidental or Great Western Sand-Sea, a vast region of deep sand-dunes, which played havoc with the vehicles. Once again, Thesiger was exasperated by the heavy going and the interminable stops to dig the wheels out of the sand: 'The only thing that was important to us then was whether the going was good or bad,' he said. '. . . I had no interest in the country at all, even when we got into the Great Erg and saw these great dunes, all I thought was "Hell, these bloody obstacles!" – which you didn't when you were trying to get camels over them.'[36] Cooper was a skilled navigator, and before the patrol Stirling had instructed him to give Thesiger a short course in astro-navigation, using a theodolite and sun compass. Cooper patiently gave him lessons, setting up a piece of equipment called a planisphere which showed the planets and stars of the first magnitude which he used to make sightings. He imparted to Thesiger the basics of the art, and the problems of using nautical almanacs and sun charts: 'He seemed to be quite interested,' Cooper remembered, 'but he didn't visit me as I took my night-shots as the patrol progressed across the desert.'[37] One evening, south of the Gulf of Sirte, after taking his readings as usual, Cooper rolled himself in his blankets and drifted off to sleep. He was suddenly woken up by someone's voice saying: 'Sarn't Cooper, I've seen it! I've seen it!' and opened his eyes to take in an obviously excited Wilfred Thesiger. 'What have you seen?' Cooper inquired drowsily, but Thesiger retained an air of mystery, only saying, 'You must come with me!' and pointing to a very steep sand-dune. He shambled up through the cold sand, with Cooper following bemusedly behind, until, sixty feet up on its summit, he pointed breathlessly at the southern sky. 'There it is, Sarn't Cooper,' he announced with Thesigerian assurance. 'The Southern Cross!' Cooper almost gagged to suppress an explosion of laughter, and explained that the Southern Cross could not possibly be sighted from this latitude: 'I'm sorry, sir,' he said, 'but that is the constellation of Capella!' Feeling both foolish and embarrassed, Thesiger mumbled a profuse apology. The two men slithered down the sand-slope in silence and Cooper went gratefully back to his bed. Cooper, who had been with the SAS from the beginning, added that he had not been particularly impressed with Thesiger's military knowledge: 'I put him in the same category as other officers invited, but not trained, by the SAS to take part as "observers",' Cooper said. 'Most of my men seemed to give him quite a wide berth, but he never derided us as Other Ranks as I don't think he considered himself to be a regular officer. He was never aloof, and he didn't seem a lone player. He fitted well into the team, but I would have called him a "passenger" rather than an "operator".'[38]

Once out of the Erg the going proved better, and the convoys soon converged on their forward base at Bir Soltan. Here, on 23 January, Stirling learned that Tripoli had fallen and decided to send his squadron into action at once. Accounts differ as to what happened next. Cooper has said that Stirling decided to set up a base-camp under Thesiger with food, water and ammunition,[39] while his co-biographer, Kemp, adds that Thesiger and Alston were left with the wireless truck to observe any activity along the Mareth line.[40] Thesiger, however, maintained that Stirling had always intended to take him on his foray through the notorious 'Gabes Gap' – a bottleneck between the sea and the Shott al Jerid salt-marsh. 'Stirling said he wanted me to go with them because I spoke Arabic,' he recalled, 'but the day before we were due to start the navigator's car packed up, so David said, "I'm sorry Wilfred, I'll have to take your car and leave this one here." The others were coming along behind so it wasn't as if I was stranded in the desert. He went off with my car and had it not been for that I'd have been rounded up and captured and my whole life would have been different. I'd have been in a POW camp and never got the chance to go to south Arabia. This is the sort of fortuitous way things happen.'[41] Cooper has pointed out, however, that Stirling already had with him a fluent speaker of North African Arabic – Lt. Freddie Taxis from the Free French SAS, and that far from being 'left' in the desert, Thesiger was set up in a proper base: 'It may be true that Stirling used the excuse that Mike Sadler's jeep had packed up,' he said, 'but Thesiger was certainly left behind with a wireless operator, food, petrol, and a proper base. His wireless operator was in contact with Kabrit until long afterwards.'[42]

Thesiger liked to see his life as a series of perfectly fortuitous incidents, and his story of the Gabes Gap patrol falls within this framework. Whether he would indeed have been taken prisoner is a matter of pure conjecture. All that is certain is that when Stirling left Thesiger's base on 22 January, with five jeeps, it was the last Thesiger would see of him until after the war. What happened is already the stuff of legend. Despite the fact that the enemy were already on the alert for raiders, Stirling, with the ubiquitous Cooper navigating, actually managed to drive through a German armoured battalion without being challenged. They then drove off the road and lay up in some rocky hills prickly with bushes, camouflaged the vehicles and erased their tracks. Cooper and Mike Sadler, his fellow navigator, climbed up to the high ground to take their star-fixes and to keep an eye out, though no official sentry was posted, and the men were exhausted after forty-eight hours without sleep. In the night Cooper awoke to a sharp kick, to find a German paratrooper standing over him. Instead of shooting him there and then, though, the German made off to alert the rest of the unit. Cooper raced down to wake Stirling, who bellowed that it was 'every man for himself!' Stirling, the SAS's founding genius, was captured; Cooper and Sadler escaped and after a number of adventures made it to the French Foreign Legion post at Tozeur.

*

Much of the spirit left the SAS after its founder was captured. Thesiger and Alston went to Tripoli and reported to the 8th Army HQ there. Alston returned to Cairo, and Thesiger was posted to the Greek Sacred Squadron under Colonel Gigantes. 'They wanted somebody as liaison officer for it, so I was told to go along and liaise,' Thesiger said. 'B Squadron no longer existed – they'd all been killed or captured.'[43] The squadron made contact with Leclerc's Free French force, which had driven across the Sahara from Fort Lamy in Chad, by way of Tibesti, and was put under the command of Major Bill Fraser, with instructions to operate on the southern flank of the 8th Army. On 17 February they raided German positions along the Mareth line. 'We were driving about,' Thesiger recalled, 'but we didn't really see much action after Stirling was captured. We weren't really behind enemy lines any more. We were only attacked once.'[44] On 10 March the combined force was dive-bombed by Luftwaffe aircraft near Qasr Ghilana (also spelt Rhilana), then attacked by German infantry in battalion strength. For a moment the situation looked exceedingly dangerous, but a squadron of RAF Spitfires quickly sent the bombers packing, and when the German infantry withdrew at sunset, the SAS saw to their amazement that they had knocked out fifty vehicles. The Free French, indeed, had accounted for four enemy aircraft. Thesiger's main memory of the day is that two German bombs landed within a few yards of him, but fortunately did not explode. Later, the Sacred Squadron joined General Freyberg's New Zealand Corps, which forced its way through the Gabes Gap at the battle of Akarit. The SAS squadron took no part in the battle, but afterwards attached itself to the light tanks of the New Zealand cavalry: 'We were pushing on ahead of everyone else,' Thesiger said, 'and we came under heavy fire so we pulled up by some rocks and took refuge, and remained in sheltered ground for the rest of the battle.'[45] Afterwards thousands of Italians and Germans surrendered, and as Thesiger sat idly in his jeep, he watched Italian prisoners being brought up to the New Zealand Intelligence officer, who appeared to be busily at work writing on the turret of his tank. 'Suddenly they brought an Italian officer who'd got a lot of medals and decorations and they said you'd better have a look at this one, sir. He said, "Oh, tell the bastard to fuck off down the road. I'm writing a letter to my mum!" The Italian officer said look here, for half an hour I've been trying to surrender and everybody tells me to fuck off down the road. After all, I am an Italian general. And it turned out he was Commander of the Saharan Corps! The humiliation he suffered on that occasion wiped out all my hatred for the Italians.'[46] The SAS was in the advance-guard of the final Allied push on Enfidaville, and Thesiger drove with them across the Tunisian plains, where the whole of the desert was one vast flower garden: 'I've never seen this mentioned in anybody's account of the battle,' Thesiger said. 'To me it was astounding – poppies and all sorts of flowers – there'd been some heavy rain and as a result these flowers had come up and you felt a sense of desecration when you stopped to brew up and the flowers all round your fire were destroyed. For almost a day we'd been travelling through this vast flower garden and nobody else apparently thought it worth mentioning.'[47]

Long before his capture, Stirling had been planning for the next phase of the war. Soon after Rommel's defeat the Greek Squadron was moved to the new SAS base at Athlit in Palestine to begin training for the invasion of Europe. A great reorganization was under way, and Paddy Mayne – perhaps the most remarkable of a galaxy of remarkable men – was commanding the SAS in Stirling's place. While in Palestine Thesiger encountered Mayne on a number of occasions. 'He was a curious sort of character,' he recalled. 'He liked having fights with everyone – although I never had occasion to fight him. He was notorious for drinking and fighting.'[48] A vast hulk of a man, Mayne was a superb field soldier but unlike Stirling was rude, blunt and awkward in company. He had once been arrested on the steps of Shepheard's Hotel in Cairo, where he had been hunting down the war-correspondent Richard Dimbleby with the intention of 'duffing him up'. Instead, he 'duffed up' no less than seven military policemen sent to arrest him before being thrown in clink. Thesiger was too preoccupied with the idea of parachuting to concern himself with Paddy Mayne. Fearless in the face of homicidal Afars and charging lion, the thought of throwing himself out of an aircraft at 1,000 feet terrified him. 'I hated it,' he said. 'I was simply determined that under no circumstances would I become a

parachutist, then I found myself in the SAS and I had to do it.'[49]
The course consisted of dummy jumps out of the fuselage of an
old Halifax to perfect exit-techniques and jumping off the back of
a moving truck to practise parachute-rolls. There had been a
number of serious accidents in the early days, when men like
Stirling and Jock Lewes had virtually taught themselves to
parachute. Indeed, Stirling had drawn up his ideas for the SAS
while recovering from a drop during which his canopy had
snagged on the tailplane. Then, as now, British parachutists were
required to complete eight jumps to obtain their wings, two of
them at night. The night before Thesiger's first jump he dreaded
it, and thought he would never get out of the aircraft. 'Then, that
night, I had a vivid dream that I was being taken out and shot,
and when I woke up to find I only had to jump out of an
aeroplane, it didn't seem so bad.'[50] Thesiger completed his jump
without mishap. 'I never looked down,' he said. 'I knew if I
looked down I'd never jump so I kept my eyes firmly in the air
and when they shouted go, I went – then you couldn't come
back. I did my eight jumps anyway.'[51] The dangers of parachuting
quickly became clear when one of Thesiger's course was killed.
'He was a member of the Greek Squadron,' Thesiger remembered,
'and he hated it all. He had refused to jump previously, and the
RAF officer in charge said it's futile to take this man on an
operation – better send him back to his unit. But his major said
no, give him another chance. So they went up again and he was
the last man out and they said don't push him – if he goes, he
goes and if he doesn't, he doesn't. I was watching the plane come
over and waiting to see them come out and one, two, three came
out, then there was a long gap and then he came. The lot who
were going to do the next course were all sitting there watching,
being told it was safe as houses and this chap came down slap in
the middle of them – dead! He'd detached his static-line and the
canopy hadn't even developed.'[52] During a military parachute-
jump, each parachutist clips his static-line – a long coil of tough
webbing – to a bar in the aircraft before jumping. As he falls, so
the pressure on the static-line automatically pulls the chute open.
Naturally, if the parachutist forgets to hook up his static-line to
the bar, his parachute will not open at all. 'Obviously you don't
go and commit suicide in the way you most dread dying,' Thesiger

said, 'so I think what had happened was that after they'd checked that he was hooked up, he decided not to jump and unhooked himself. Then, at the last moment he thought dammit, I will go after all, and forgot he wasn't attached. Anyway, it shook the next lot of people who were sitting there being told it was as safe as stepping off a bus!'[53]

While at Athlit Thesiger visited some of his Druze friends, who had been converted to an infantry unit. Delighted to see him, they feasted him and his Greek colleagues royally. He took a week's leave and motored along the Turkish frontier in northern Syria as far as the Tigris valley, passing through the shanty settlement of Qamashlia with its assortment of Kurds, Arabs, Circassians, Armenians, Turks and Turkomans. From the Tigris gorge at Ain Diyar he looked across at the misted outlines of the Kurdistan mountains. He crossed the river and drove south past the black tents of the Shammar Bedouin, reaching Jabal Singhar, inhabited by the Yazidi sect. Though short, the trip had been a fascinating glimpse of Kurdistan, and he decided to return one day when the war was over. Meanwhile, back with his SAS squadron at Athlit, Abyssinia once again loomed up in his life. The Emperor Haile Selassie had asked the British government for political advisers in his provinces, and had naturally thought of Wilfred Thesiger, whose father had been his close confidant. Thesiger was now requested to leave the army and become political adviser at Dessie in the Amhara mountains, under the Crown Prince, Asfa Wossen.

Surprisingly, perhaps, the prospect did not thrill him. The Abyssinian campaign had been a 'personal crusade' for Thesiger, and he had fought like a lion and won his DSO, yet somehow his passion for Abyssinia had burned itself out. Perhaps it was the continual duplicity of the rebel and Patriot leaders – particularly the treachery of Belai Zelleka at Safartak – which had disillusioned him. The battle for Europe was about to begin and the war in the Far East had hardly started and he was loath to leave the SAS for a political post with prospects of action ahead of him. Yet Haile Selassie was calling on a deep strain of loyalty embedded in his character: he could not refuse. In November 1943 he left his squadron at Athlit and flew to Addis Ababa to confer with the

Emperor. While there he motored up to meet Asfa Wossen at Dessie. The idea of being an office-man there for two years was uninspiring, but relieved by the thought of trekking in the Abyssinian plateau. Thesiger was not an administrator by nature. In the Sudan Political Service he had continually shifted ground to secure jobs which involved virtually no administrative duties, beyond the odd court-case. As a youth, his overwhelming ambition had been to return to Abyssinia in just the kind of capacity which the Emperor now offered him, yet Thesiger had viewed such a post almost purely in terms of lion-shooting and trekking. Abyssinia had been eclipsed by the Sudan, the desert, the Arabs, and finally by the war. However, the Emperor had asked for him personally, and he was the Emperor's man. He accepted the two-year assignment and flew back to Cairo, where he obtained permission to spend two months' leave in England before taking up the appointment.

At home there had been many changes. His stepfather, Reg Astley, had died. His brother Dermot, who had served as a Flight-Sergeant Pilot with the RAF, had been shot down on an operational flight. Like his great-grandfather, the 1st Baron Chelmsford, Dermot had been a barrister, hoping to follow his ancestor's footsteps into Parliament and eventually to become prime minister. He had no wish ever to see Abyssinia again, and indeed hardly went abroad at all. Sociable and unassuming, easily adapting into the ranks, he had also inherited his great-grandfather's wit and charm, and was his mother's favourite. Heartbroken after his death, Kathleen Mary left the Milebrook, where she had provided a home for Thesiger in his youth, and moved to a spacious top-storey flat in Shelley Court, off Tite Street, in London's exclusive borough of Chelsea. Due to the incessant blitzing by the Luftwaffe such perilous high-storey flats were hardly in demand, and she was able to pick it up fairly cheaply. Later, as eldest son, Thesiger was to inherit the well-appointed flat, which remained his London home into old age. His youngest brother, Roderic, whose passion in life was art, had joined the Parachute Regiment and dropped at Enfidaville with the 1st Army's Parachute Brigade, though Thesiger, there with his Greek SAS squadron, had not known it. Roddy was later dropped at the Primasole Bridge in Sicily, and was captured during the Parachute Regiment's finest hour at Arnhem in Holland, where, after being ordered to hold the bridge for two days, they held it for ten against a German Panzer Division. Brian, the 'Thesiger Minor' of St Aubyn's days, was a professional soldier who served in the Royal Welch Fusiliers as a result of pressure from his self-appointed 'godmother', a Mrs Doughty-Wylie. As a young man Brian had done something almost inconceivable to his elder brother Wilfred, whose family pride was the great guiding beacon of his life: he had changed his name by deed-poll to Doughty-Wylie. His godfather, Doughty-Wylie – Consul in Addis Ababa when Thesiger's father was Minister – was killed at Gallipoli, where he had won the VC. 'His wife was a rather dominating woman,' Thesiger said, 'and she said if Brian joined the Welch Fusiliers and took the name of Doughty-Wylie, almost as a sort of successor to her husband, he'd get a lot of money, and she'd sort of look after him and make him comfortable. I was dead against it and thought it was a great mistake, but my mother said we must leave it to him to make up his mind. In the end he decided to do it and since then he said it was the biggest mistake of his life, which it certainly was. He didn't get on with her – it was his own fault to a large extent, because he tended to ignore her. In the end she left the money to his two daughters, not to him. I think it was very silly, and certainly not something I should ever have contemplated myself.'[54] Brian, like Dermot, had no desire ever to see Abyssinia again, but fought in the Italian campaign, winning an MC at Anzio.

Thesiger travelled to Abyssinia through the Sudan, where he met his friend Douglas Newbold for the last time. He motored by bus to Addis Ababa, discovering another old friend, Dan Sandford, now working for the Minister of the Interior. A few weeks later he was in Dessie, an attractive town 8,000 feet up on the escarpment that towers over Danakil country, quartered in a modern villa built by the Italians, where he settled down to what turned out to be the most frustrating year of his life. No one sought his advice on anything, and though he was meant to be counselling the Crown Prince Asfa Wossen, who was well aware of the debt of gratitude he and his father owed Thesiger's family, he was allowed to meet him only once a week for a social visit: 'I did nothing memorable at all in Dessie,' he remembered. 'I saw the Crown Prince at intervals, but only when there was a sort of lunch party, and on odd occasions outside that. I think he was warned off having anything to do with me – the local officials were jealous and wanted to control him.'[55]

Denied any real influence, Thesiger turned to the idea of making excursions into the hills. 'I'd hoped when I got there to be given permission to travel extensively over Wollo,' he said, 'which was actually quite interesting because it was largely Galla and to an extent Muslim. I made one or two efforts to get a caravan together, and asked for permission on two or three occasions. I was told I'd have to apply to Addis Ababa and this and that – there'd always be some reason given why I couldn't do it.'[56] He had to content himself with daily rides into the mountains to shoot snipe. On one occasion he drove the truck assigned to him as part of his job down to the port of Assab along the main road, which took him to Tendaho on the borders of Aussa. Memories of his 1933 trek there came flooding back: the mysterious, magical land he had known then seemed tame and ordinary now. Still, at Tendaho he was amazed and delighted to meet the same Dejazmatch Yayu – the Sultan's vizier – who had accompanied him on part of his journey around the lakes. There was little to interest him at Assab, but on his return to Dessie, word had got round that he had been talking with the Afars: 'It caused a certain amount of trouble,' he recalled. 'They wanted to know why I'd gone down there and been talking to the Danakil, and I realized I was being more and more restricted over what I could do. I felt well, God Almighty, if I can't even do this, why am I here!' [57] Moreover, having lived with the Sudanese, the Druzes and the Arabs in Syria, who had overwhelmed him with their invitations, Thesiger began to notice for the first time the Abyssinians' lack of hospitality. Not only was he prevented from making expeditions, which would have been some recompense for this inactivity, he was also unable to get to know the local people. The situation was exacerbated by the news of great events going on in the rest of the world. Orde Wingate was leading his famous Chindits in Burmese rainforests, proving once and for all that the British could outfight the Japanese in the jungle. Paddy Mayne's SAS were raiding in the Mediterranean with astounding success, and Allied armies were fighting in Italy. In February 1945 he consoled himself by driving his truck down to the Arussi mountains and visited Sidamo, Wolamo and Boran – his first experience of the southern Abyssinia of men like Arnold Hodson. Even this did not soothe his temper. He felt that his appointment – whatever the good intentions of the Emperor himself – had been a political one. He was a pawn in the game of international aid of which Waugh had warned ten years previously, in which the Abyssinians were adept at playing the great powers off against each other to their own benefit. At last, Thesiger's long-term affection for the Abyssinians – the romantic edifice built on childhood dreams and memories – began to totter: 'They are a curious race,' he wrote home, 'and in their present mood no one can help them. When you combine arrogance with suspicion to the extent they do, it is difficult to help at the best of times.'[58]

In March 1945, he resigned.

In Addis Ababa, waiting for a plane to take him back to England in three days' time, he ran into Robin Buxton, an old acquaintance from his first trip to Jabal ad Druze in 1936. Buxton apologized for not being able to invite Thesiger to dinner: 'Only I have this very interesting man coming along,' he said. 'He's an entomologist called Lean who's looking for someone to go off into Arabia to get information on locusts.'

Thesiger was immediately interested. 'I'll come,' he said, with characteristically Etonian cheek, 'even if I have to sit on the floor.'[59] O.B. Lean had pioneered research into the origin of the African migratory locust – which had been devastating African crops for millennia – and had finally traced its outbreak-centres to the Niger delta. Until recently he had been employed by ICI, but had been released to take charge of the Middle East Anti-Locust Unit, an organization sponsored by Britain and other colonial powers, in combating a new plague.[60] Lean had abundant funds at his disposal and was looking for someone to investigate the occurrence of locusts in the Arabian desert. At dinner Thesiger took in the information, his thoughts accompanied by the vivid images of Bedouin, camels, black tents, and rolling sands that had haunted him since he had read *Revolt in the Desert*. When Lean had explained, Thesiger sighed. 'How maddening I'm not an entomologist,' he said.

'Oh, but I'm not looking for an entomologist,' Lean said. 'I'm looking for someone who knows about deserts.'

Thesiger was suddenly overwhelmed with excitement. After all the years of waiting, after the frustrating time at Dessie, the chance of a lifetime had come. 'Well,' he said, 'here I am.'

He had been offered the job and accepted it before they had finished the soup.

PART TWO

———

THE GREAT ADVENTURE

CHAPTER 9

The Harder the Life the Finer the Person

The Empty Quarter of Arabia is the world's largest sand desert. Almost quarter of a million square miles in area, containing 4,000 cubic miles of sand, much of its interior was, in 1945, as mysterious as the dark side of the moon. Indeed, to travel there was almost like walking on another planet. Its great dunes – in places giant jelly-mould mountains of sand 1,000 feet high, sculpted into frills and flutings and flourishes by ancient winds – seemed not to belong to this earth at all. Known by the local Bedu as *'urug*, they were arranged in chains sometimes hundreds of miles long, rising sheer out of crusty silver salt-flats called *sebkhas*. The dunes had the subtle life of a sea-anemone, changing shape and colour slowly throughout the day: soft flame red at sunrise, hazy amorphous white at noon, velveteen burgundy at sundown. The Empty Quarter was a clean slate: it had almost no history. Some talked of great cities buried under the sands, and of ancient camel-routes that had once traversed it, carrying incense from the hills of Dhofar to the lost Gulf port of Dilmun. Of these only the legend itself remained. And always there was the presence of the land: brooding, sinister, silent, a dormant dragon from a lost age of giants. To the Arab villagers and townsmen who lived around the desert, it was a place of evil, inhabited by *Jinns* or demons. No human being could live there throughout the year: in summer its temperature in the shade reached 50° C, yet the sand surface underfoot was burnished up to an incredible 80° – too hot for almost any living thing to move. The Bedu nomads who retired to its fringes in the hot months, in the dry-washes and the rock and sand plains, wore coarse black socks as stiff as boots to protect their feet against the roasting sand.

No one is certain where the Rub' al Khali – literally, the Empty

Quarter – acquired its name. Some believe the medieval Arab geographers saw Arabia as a great ball floating in the ocean, half submerged, half exposed. Of the exposed portion, one quarter was inhabitable, and the other 'scorched' or 'empty'. Actually, it was Charles Doughty who first introduced the term to the West. On earlier Western maps, it is referred to as 'The Great Space' or 'The Great Sandy Desert'. It covered almost the entire region of southern Arabia from the foothills of Yemen to the Arabian Gulf, and to cross it had been the dream of every Arabian explorer since Richard Burton, who, after his pilgrimage to Mecca disguised as a Muslim, in 1832, proposed to traverse eastwards from Mecca across it: 'By God, Effendi,' his Arab friends told him, 'thou art surely mad.' Later he observed that he had heard enough of the Empty Quarter to 'conclude that its horrid depths swarm with a large and half-starving population'.[1] His successor, the intrepid Doughty, commented: 'I never found any Arabian who had aught to tell, even by hearsay, of that dreadful country.'[2] Colonel S.B. Miles, author of a definitive early work on the tribes of the Persian Gulf, wrote, 'As regards the physical features of this immense tract we are almost entirely in ignorance.'[3] Early explorers claimed that the Bedu never used the name Empty Quarter, but the Al Murrah – the Bedu tribe living north of the great desert – certainly knew it, 'Empty' signifying to them a place without permanent settlements. To the Rawashid and Bayt Musann and 'Awamir, the three Bedu tribes who lived in the southern and eastern parts, it was simply called ar Raml – the Sands.

The Sands were far from being lifeless. Incredibly, for instance, a kind of sand-shrimp lived there. Triops – a relative of the horseshoe crab – was a species 100 million years old, whose eggs could remain in the furnace of the sands for fifteen years, awaiting a single downpour of rain. Hatching into a shallow pool, the shrimps reached full maturity within a few days, in time to lay the next generation of eggs before the pool dried up. Triops was a seminar in the process of survival in one of the world's most extreme environments, and its lessons in adaptation were paralleled on every level. The language of the Empty Quarter was the language of thirst, and to survive there, man, plant and animal must learn the vocabulary of moisture-conservation. In some places it might not rain for thirty years, but almost always it rained somewhere, and only a few hours of rain were needed to provide vegetation for three or four years. Motorized explorers who traversed it in the 1950s noted that not a single day passed without coming across green vegetation of some kind. The sand-grains absorbed the raindrops like blotting paper and were perfect storage-tanks, losing not a drop in evaporation. Some plants upon the surface were fed by rain that had fallen 1,000 years ago. In much of the Empty Quarter, only six different species of plants grew. Chief among these was calligonum, the dogged, brush-like *abal* of the Bedu, whose white and waxy bark prevented water-loss, and whose roots were designed to suck up rainwater from the sand surface as soon as it fell. The seeds of such plants, like those of the *zahra* or tribulus, lay dormant in the sand for years, bursting forth in an explosion of brilliant yellow flowers when touched by the magic fingers of the rain. The tribulus, also highly valued by the camel-herding Bedu, was said to give a frothy texture to the camels' milk. These plants grew far apart, their great roots worming ninety feet into the sand, or spreading along the surface in testing tentacles, ready for the next shower of rain. Insects and animals hid from the day in niches and tunnels, emerging only in the night and the early morning to sip drops of dew from the hardy plants. Here there were scorpions, skinks, spiders, darkling beetles, sand-vipers and toad-headed lizards. At first light the Bedouin hunter might observe the tracery of tracks of a Cheeseman's gerbil, a Ruppell's sand-fox, or the succulent Cape hare, none of which ever needed to drink water in their entire lives. He might find the distinct hoof-prints of the Arabian oryx, the great antelope with its forked horns, able to locate desert vegetation by its acute sense of smell and migrate sixty miles in a night. The Bedouin made use of the canny oryx's senses and followed its tracks to find pasture, but they also savoured it as a source of liquid, hunting it and drinking the gastric juices from its stomach with relish. Gazelle also abounded here in great herds of 150 individuals.

While for the stranger, then, the Empty Quarter was a savage and inhospitable country, for the nomadic Bedu who lived there during the cool months it was a far more inviting land. The four tribes which ventured into the Sands – the Al Murrah, the Rawashid (also called Rashid), the 'Awamir and the Bayt Musann – themselves often regarded by townsmen as half-bewitched descendants of *Jinns* – thought of the desert as a haven of milk and honey – a refuge from enemies, a place of green plants and good hunting, where the fine-milking black camels, the *hazmiyyin*, with their big bodies and wide hooves, could be raised. The herds were their survival-machines, for as long as they found good grazing – which was always present somewhere in the Empty Quarter – the camels could convert it to the milk that was for them both food and drink. Neither was the Empty Quarter solely a land of men: the Bedu loaded their black tents on to camel-back and broke up into tiny, independent units of three or four families: men, women and children with their camels. Because rain fell only locally, these groups were obliged to be mobile. Everything they had must be light and manageable enough to hoist on to a camel's back. Like triops, they were perfectly adapted to the landscape, but unlike him they had adapted by using technology – the simple technology of camel-saddles, ropes, waterskins and woven tents. To move in larger groups would have meant over-grazing and destroying their own livelihood. To remain static would have been equally fatal. If rain did not fall in one area, they simply packed up their camels and moved to a place near by where it had rained, either then or in previous years. To traverse the great dunes and *sebkhas* alone was, they said, to court death, but to travel there with the herds and families was to travel amidst relative abundance. Life within the Sands was not easy by any normal standards, but by those of the Bedu it was by no means the 'death in life' of which T.E. Lawrence wrote. The Bedu had survived in the Empty Quarter for millennia because they existed in harmony with the environment; indeed, when the tribes migrated into the Sands during the winter months, it was for them a time of joy and celebration. The explorers used Bedu guides and companions but they did not stay with the local Bedu in the course of their normal activities, so they did not see this face of the Empty Quarter. For them the desert was an obstacle to cross, a primeval dragon to be slain.[4]

'Old Arabia' was already condemned to demolition when Thesiger arrived there in in 1945. Sa'udi Arabia's oil had been in moderate production for at least seven years. The British had always believed they knew and understood the Arabs best – that there was a 'special relationship' between them – but now Britain was a ruined nation. As far back as 1931, when an American geologist called Karl S. Twitchell had begun an oil-survey in the eastern Nejd, the green-eyed British Legation staff in Jiddah, the administrative capital, were derisive: 'It seems fairly clear,' one of them wrote, 'that nothing of much importance will result from Mr Twitchell's investigations.'[5] It was surely the misjudgement of the century. Twitchell discovered what was eventually to be revealed as the Ghawar field, the largest oil reservoir on earth. In 1933 King Ibn Sa'ud signed a concession treaty with Standard Oil of California (Socal) in return for £50,000 in gold. Oil was struck near Dammam the same year, and in 1943 at nearby Dhahran the Americans began work on their largest air-base between Germany and Japan. The British could do little but watch from the sidelines. In the 1940s much of the interior of Arabia was closed to foreigners. In Sa'udi Arabia foreign missions were confined to Jiddah, and even diplomatic staff were not permitted to venture further than twenty miles from the city. The King's British adviser – the man who, incidentally, had fixed up the deal with Socal – was Harry St John 'Abdallah' Philby, a Muslim of fifteen years standing, who had not, however, given up his membership of the Athenaeum Club in London. He was allowed to come and go as he pleased, and had the country pretty much to himself – until 1943, when the Anti-Locust Unit arrived. With their motley collection of Humbers, jeeps, Dodge pick-ups and other war-relics, they were given *carte blanche* to travel anywhere – much to the irritation of the prima-donna Philby, and to the umbrage of the Americans, who suspected a covert British oil-exploration plot. Thesiger realized at once how fortunate Lean's offer had been: the humble locust was his key to the heart of Arabia – the fabled Empty Quarter. 'I thought the Empty Quarter was completely out of reach,' he said. 'I'd always wanted to go there, but I never thought I'd get permission. It had always been the sort of "desert of deserts", and the most exciting challenge, because it was unexplored and the tribes there were completely unadministered. It was almost the last corner of the earth that was unexplored – I mean, there might have been something up in Asia or somewhere, but nowhere I was likely to go.'[6]

That his job did not actually require him to cross the Empty Quarter, but rather to investigate places where locust breeding-grounds or 'outbreak-centres' might occur, provided no qualms for Thesiger, whose own priorities, like those of all born adventurers, were highest in his list of needs.

In the late 1920s and early 1940s, there had been a devastating plague of a species called 'the desert locust', spread across a vast area from Baluchistan to North Africa, which threatened to decimate crops badly needed in time of war. O.B. Lean had set up an office in Cairo under the aegis of the Colonial Office to deal with the locust threat in the Middle East. He conceived his campaign as a military operation against an insectile enemy, using the troops of Glubb Pasha's Trans-Jordan Frontier Force as footsoldiers. By the end of the war the military component had largely vanished, though, and in April 1945, when Thesiger landed in Jiddah to meet Vesey-Fitzgerald, the Locust Unit's chief scientist, military personnel were limited to logistics and communications staff. Thesiger made use of his time with Vesey-Fitzgerald, not only to learn about locusts, but also, naturally, to travel. As a Locust Research officer he was entirely unrestricted, and he drove by truck right across the Arabian peninsula from west to east, lingering in the Nejd, where he met the dour Ikhwan. He also took the opportunity to motor down the mud-flats of the Red Sea Coast or Tihama, and was attracted by the friendly and graceful people he met there, comparing them favourably with the puritanical Arabs of the Nejd. He decided to return and visit the place more thoroughly after his mission to the south, and may even have considered on his secret agenda that knowledge of this border region might be of immense value should he cross the Sands.

Boris Uvarov, the mastermind of the Locust Project, was based at the Locust Research Centre at the Natural History Museum in London. A White Russian who had escaped from the USSR in 1920, he was the brilliant founder of the science of 'acridology' –

the study of locusts and grasshoppers. Fascinated by the sinister and unexplained appearances and disappearances of vast locust swarms at the beginning of the century, Uvarov had worked along the rivers in Central Asia, where he had made the discovery that the locust was a very peculiar creature indeed. In fact, it was a kind of 'Jekyll and Hyde' insect: a harmless solitary grasshopper one minute, that could turn suddenly into the savage migratory locust the next, and take wing to terrorize the world. When environmental conditions were favourable, the numbers of solitary locusts swelled until they reached a certain critical threshold. Then the grasshopper eggs hatched into a creature much smaller and different in colour from its parents: the locust-nymph. Being wingless, they would bounce around in great mobs, devouring any greenery within a radius of miles. They grew through five stages, moulting between each stage. When they finally matured they took to the air, chafing thigh against wing-case in an eerie battle-signal that raised swarms millions strong, capable of wiping out the harvests of entire countries. The desert locust was smart, Uvarov discovered, because it kept on shifting its breeding-grounds. Like the Bedu, it was nomadic, but somewhat more mobile – it had the range of a vast spread of more than fifty countries. Where were its sources and breeding-grounds? To answer that question Uvarov had already tapped into every conceivable source of information: consular offices, ships' captains, DCs, missionaries, tribal chiefs and explorers, all of whom had been issued with a simple book giving instructions on how to collect locusts and what information was of use. The problem was that some of the possible breeding-grounds were around sparsely inhabited and unexplored tracts like the Empty Quarter. This was where Wilfred Thesiger came in. In Dhofar, the southernmost region of the area claimed by the Sultan of Muscat and Oman, there lay a crescent of mountains called the Dhofar Range, one part of which, Jabal Qarra, received regular rainfall in the form of the south-west monsoon. The rain drained off from the mountains through great wadi-systems, converging on the 'oasis' of Wadi Mughshin, discovered by explorer Bertram Thomas in 1930, on the very edges of the great desert. Further west, in British Protected territory, there was a knobbly spine of mountains in the little-known Mahra country from which deep wadis drained off to soak the rim of the Sands or debouched into the great valley of the Hadramaut. This entire sweep of wadis seemed a likely place for locusts to breed.

Thesiger revealed to no one the real purpose of his journey. He intended to travel with camels and a small group of Bedu, preferably from the Rawashid tribe, one of the few, he learned, who actually lived in the Sands. He would travel up to Mughshin to look for locusts, then trek west across the rocky steppes of Mahra country into the Hadramaut. From there he would dash north across the Sands. With his hidden agenda close to his heart, he flew to Aden in September 1945 and visited the mountains on the Yemen frontier. He was in Salalah in the Omani province of Dhofar on 13 October.

While Thesiger had been studying bands of hopping locust-nymphs with Vesey-Fitzgerald in the Nejd, a Bedouin tribesman who had cause to know the insects well had made his way to Salalah. His name was Sultan bin Ahmad, and he was Sheikh of one section of the Bayt Kathir, the largest Bedouin tribe in Dhofar. He was small and physically powerful, with a beardless face – unusual among the hirsute Bedu – and his feet and hands were calloused and horny. He wore a ragged shirt, originally white but stained reddish by the juice of a desert herb, drawn in with the ritual cartridge belt and hooked dagger. A weathered rag was his only head-covering. With him was his son, Nashran, a big, bulky man, taller than his father, and then aged about sixteen. As they made their way barefoot into the palace at Salalah, passing through the gateways of the outer courtyard, and the inner courtyard, from which they could see the glittering turquoise swell of the ocean, they presented an image of determination and simple, ragged dignity. The two Bayt Kathir lived in the gravel plains north of the Dhofar mountains that dominated the town of Salalah, and Sultan's family had originally made a living collecting the resin from the frankincense trees that grew there, a substance that would have a profitable market in India until the 1960s. First described by the Greek historian Herodotus, the trees had in classical times been a source of vast wealth and the foundation of a civilization – perhaps the legendary 'Ophir' of the Bible. Even then, they had customarily been infested with locusts, which Herodotus had described as 'small serpents'. The incense civilization had long ago shrivelled to nothing more than piles of rubble along the shores of the Arabian sea, and a legend of lost cities. Sultan had found the incense trade lucrative enough to obtain what he really valued: a flock of goats and a few camels, yet his reputation as Sheikh did not relate to his material possessions. Known as a fearless fighter, in 1929 he had taken part in raids against the Se'ar and Kurub – two of the predatory Ma'areb or western tribes who constantly troubled this region. His party had caught the raiders at Difin, and in the gun-battle that followed seven Bedu had been killed.

In the great hall of the royal palace, Sultan, with ten other elders of the Bayt Kathir, strode forward to meet His Majesty Sa'id bin Taimur, the Sultan, or King, of Muscat and Oman. Bin Taimur was thirty-five years old, a courteous, reserved, devoutly religious man, who had been educated in India and spoke fluent Urdu and English as well as Arabic. He wore a brown, gilt-bordered cloak over his *dishdasha* and a colourful headcloth, knotted and tasselled in a way permitted only to the royal line. With him was his Wali in Dhofar, a much older man called Hamud bin Hamid, who had been a trusted retainer of the King's family for years and had even accompanied him to India during his schooldays. When the Bedu had assembled and the greetings and nose-kisses had been exchanged, they sat down on the floor in the formal style they were accustomed to – not cross-legged, but in a curiously prayer-like pose, on their knees with their feet tucked up beneath them. According to Sultan's son, Nashran, who was present on the occasion, the King then asked his father the extent of the Bayt Kathir tribal territory. Bin Taimur had little knowledge of the desert beyond the mountains – the empire he had 'inherited' (actually he had deposed his father in 1931) was essentially a maritime one, which had at one time included Zanzibar. Though nominally King of the interior, bin Taimur's real authority did not extend beyond the coastal plain. Nevertheless, the Bayt Kathir owed him allegiance, and each tribe had a well-defined territory. 'My father said our borders are from the Dhofar mountains as far west as Wadi Shu'ait and in the north as far as Mughshin and Ramlat al Ghafa,' Nashran said, 'and then the King said, "A Christian is coming to search for locusts. I want you to collect men from your people to accompany him anywhere he wants to go, but do not take him beyond the limits of your tribe." [7]

As they left the King's presence, Sultan and his fellow tribesmen discussed the matter excitedly. Here was a chance to make a tidy profit for all the tribe, for Christians paid well for the hire of men and camels, and always carried abundant rice and flour. Sultan knew this because he had travelled with a Christian previously – a man by the name of Bertram Thomas.

Thomas was the first European to cross the Empty Quarter. In the winter of 1931–2, while Thesiger had been at Oxford preparing for his journey into Danakil, Thomas had set out from this very palace at Salalah, with an escort of Bedu from the Rawashid tribe, and crossed through Dakaka – the central region of the Sands. Two months later he had reached Qatar on the Arabian Gulf, 900 miles away. It was to Thomas's initial advantage that he had been financial adviser to the King, though beyond the coastal plain this gave him little leverage. He had, as Thesiger was later to admit, won the respect of the Bedu with his frankness, generosity and good nature. Thomas was the first Englishman to travel with these Bedu and Thesiger later realized that he owed him a great debt. The Bedouin were to welcome Thesiger simply because he belonged to the same tribe as Thomas, their proven travelling-companion. Thesiger noted later that the Bedu had smirked at Thomas's use of an Indian saddle – much heavier than their local saddles – and his habit of sleeping apart. They had probably been mystified, too, by his cine-camera. Yet these idiosyncrasies had evidently not lowered their respect for him. At Oxford, Thesiger had read Thomas's account of his journey, *Arabia Felix*, and while the subject fascinated him at the time, he said later that he thought Thomas a poor writer. 'I mean, his book could hardly be worse,' he commented. 'It has no feel about it. Having read it I had no knowledge of the Bedu: they just don't emerge as characters.' [8] Part of Thesiger's dissatisfaction, though, may have been raised by the book's foreword, written by his hero T.E. Lawrence, which clearly cites Thomas as 'the last explorer in the tradition of the past' – a title Thesiger would later claim for himself: 'We cannot know the first man who walked the inviolate earth for newness sake but Thomas is the last; and he did his journey in the antique way, by pain of his camel's legs, single-handed and at his own time and cost. He might have flown over it in an aeroplane, sat in a car or rolled over in a tank. Instead, he snatched, in the twenty-third hour, feet's last victory . . ."[9]

It must have been very unwelcome to the aspiring Thesiger to read that Thomas had won 'feet's last victory', but then Lawrence was in the habit of speaking too soon. He himself had predicted in 1929 that the Empty Quarter could only be crossed by an airship, and his image of Thomas's unexpectedly 'snatching' a last-minute victory over technology was surely influenced by this faulty prediction.

Thomas's rival in the race to cross the Sands had been the distinguished Harry St John Philby, King Ibn Sa'ud's adviser. Philby had had some advantages over Thomas in that he was a Muslim, and had the support of the formidable Governor of Al Hasa oasis, ibn Jiluwi. Yet the King made Philby sweat for permission, and the delay cost him the race. He heard of Thomas's arrival in Qatar just as he was about to set off and was bitterly disappointed: he had been planning the expedition for fourteen years. Nevertheless, he continued, striking out from the Al Hasa oasis in the east and making a perilous loop through the unknown Sands, turning round and coming back to Sulayil in the west, covering an astonishing 400 miles between wells. It is another irony of Thesiger's life that Philby, the man who opened up Sa'udi Arabia to the American oil companies, and indeed, who himself had the concession on the sale of Ford cars there, should have become his close friend. Thesiger found Philby's book *The Empty Quarter* stodgy, but admired him as a man who had devoted his life to Ibn Sa'ud. 'Philby was a Muslim and became an Arab and lived with the Arabs,' he said. 'He was quite different to Thomas. Of the two, Philby was outstanding. Thomas's journey was an easy crossing, but then after all if you come to a mountain that's never been climbed and people say it's unclimbable, you're obviously going to find the easiest way – this would have been true of Everest. Thomas did this, but Philby made a much more difficult journey. Thomas wasn't faced with these giant dunes and he did have quite a lot of water because he went right across the middle. Philby was a real Arabist. I don't think Thomas was. He wrote a couple of books, neither of them of great interest. In his book *Arabia Felix* there's nothing to make me think, well, must remember that, but you can get it from Philby's book. Philby is a very bad writer, a deadly dull writer. It's hard labour to read Philby, as it is to read Burton, but anything he says in his books you can take seriously – apart from the politics – but if he mentions anything about birds and animals he was meticulous. Philby was a much more remarkable man than Thomas . . . very much a personality. I don't think Thomas was in any way remarkable and his motive for crossing the Empty Quarter was contemptible.'[10]

The final remark is the key to the complete *volte face* Thesiger made with respect to Thomas in later years. During the war he had encountered him briefly in Cairo, and afterwards wished he could have had an opportunity to express how much he felt he owed him. Later, though, he asserted that Thomas had 'taken the officers' mess with him' – criticizing his use of a foreign saddle and of sleeping apart, despite having admitted in his book that the Bedu merely smiled at these as the habits of a foreigner. 'Here was somebody with a sort of Indian Colonial attitude,' he later remarked on Thomas. 'He'd been in the Indian Civil Service and his attitude to the Arabs grew out of that. He kept himself apart, in the way they did in the Sudan. I don't think in any sense he had an affinity with the Arabs, or modelled himself on them, or accepted the fact that they were in many ways superior to him.'[11] Yet despite his 'Indian Civil Service' ways, Thomas had, evidently, won the respect of the Bedouin. Or had he? In later years Thesiger took even this away from him, in a statement more revealing about himself than Thomas: 'My whole object was to become like the Bedu and to rival them,' he said, 'and there was Thomas sitting on his absurd saddle and sleeping all by himself. I can't imagine anyone less like a Bedu than Thomas. They just bundled him across the Empty Quarter like a [package].'[12] The blame for this change of attitude may lie partly with Harold Dickson, the British Agent in Kuwait, now working for the Kuwait Oil Company. An authority on the Bedu, Dickson had written an influential book, *The Arab of the Desert*, which was an attempt to catalogue the main characteristics of the Arabian Bedouin. Dickson later told Thesiger that Thomas had visited

him in Kuwait a few weeks before beginning his journey across
the Sands. In playful mood perhaps, Dickson swore Thomas to
secrecy and intimated that he himself intended to cross the Empty
Quarter: 'Thomas was absolutely horrified and almost dropped
his pen,' Thesiger recounted. 'He said, "I should consider that a
most unfriendly action. I intend to become the first man ever to
cross the Empty Quarter and live the rest of my life on the
proceeds!" Well . . . that personified Thomas for me.'[13] However,
Thomas's name is still well remembered in Dhofar today and old
Bedouin who travelled with him speak highly of him as a
travelling-companion. Thesiger often insisted that he himself could
not have crossed the Sands had he not won the support of the
Bedu: if so, the same must be true of Thomas, and the remark
about his having been 'bundled' across the Empty Quarter,
unfair. Thomas later became head of the British Middle East
Centre for Arabic Studies in the Lebanon, ran a Rolls-Royce and
dined out on the Empty Quarter. Many of his colleagues regarded
him as being pompous and comical, 'a joke', as one of them said.
Yet Thomas's objectives and his failings do not lessen his achievement, any more than John Speke's duplicity to Burton lessens his
discovery of the Nile's source.

In 1945 the RAF had a base in Salalah, and their aircraft had
flown across the Dhofar mountains and sighted the Sands of the
Empty Quarter, though their limited range prevented them from
going farther without fuel-dumps. There were numerous cars in
Sa'udi Arabia and a few in Oman, but though a large-scale
motor operation would have been theoretically possible, Thesiger
considered the idea impractical: 'In Sa'udi Arabia everything was
by car then,' he said, 'but if the Anti-Locust people had launched
an expedition across the Empty Quarter by car it would probably
have been shot up. It would have been inconceivable because
there was no [infrastructure], no previous contact with the Bedu
who lived there, and in Oman the King wouldn't have agreed to
it anyway. It wouldn't have made any sort of sense going to the
expense of doing it by car – the petrol dumps and everything –
when they could send one man down there and get the information they wanted.'[14] In Salalah the RAF had trucks and jeeps,
and were allowed to drive around the coastal plain, but British

personnel were not permitted to speak to any local tribesmen, or to travel without a guard. Thesiger approved of this regulation, because he detested any kind of cultural interference, though it was obviously ludicrous to apply it to himself when he had come to travel with the natives. The day after his arrival, however, he duly called for his guard at the gate and drove down to the palace to meet Hamud bin Hamid, the Wali. Salalah then was a congeries of half-ruined stone houses set in the thick coconut groves along a pearl-white beach, where, in the fishing season, battalions of glittering sardines were laid out to dry in the sun. There was a dog's leg of frail market-stalls and a quarter of straw-huts or *burastis* inhabited by fisher-folk and Bedouin staying temporarily in the town. The Sultan's palace – occupied by the Wali when bin Taimur was at his main capital in Muscat – was a whitewashed, blocky building standing on the beach itself. Today, a new palace of burnished marble and decorative Indian ceramic work stands in precisely the same place, but apart from the coconut groves, the white sands and the sardine-fishers, the old Salalah is largely lost in a labyrinth of modern flat blocks, supermarkets and Coca Cola bars.

In the Wali's office – the Burza – Thesiger was received by Hamud, who treated him royally and explained the instructions the Sultan had left: 'He had agreed to let me go up as far as Mughshin,' Thesiger said, 'which was the limit of his area.'[15] The Wali then told Thesiger he had arranged for some Bayt Kathir to go with him: 'He did have some authority over the Bayt Kathir,' Thesiger said, 'in fact the Kathir were the King's Arabs, like the Qarra and the Shahra. Anyway, he came out with some preposter-ous number of men – something like fifty – and I said I couldn't possibly go with all those – six or eight would be enough. We eventually compromised at about thirty.'[16] Hamud then called in two or three of the Bedu who were to go with Thesiger: 'One of them was introduced to me as a good hunter, and the Wali said he'd be useful,' Thesiger remembered. 'That was Musallim bin Tafl.'[17]

Bin Tafl, a stocky, muscular man, with a slightly bow-legged stride, was a Bayt Kathiri who had attached himself to the Wali's guard as a retainer. Born to a poor Bedu family in the Wadi Mughsayl, north-west of Salalah, he had lost his mother at three.

Like many Bayt Kathir, his father had owned goats and no camels, but had bequeathed to his son his skill with the rifle. 'I grew up hunting,' bin Tafl recalled. 'My father showed me how to hold the rifle when I was small. I started shooting game when I was still a boy – mostly ibex, gazelle and oryx. In those days you could see herds of forty oryx together. Occasionally I shot a rim antelope.'[18] Nervous energy, long practice, and an unusually keen eye had made him one of the outstanding shots in Dhofar. 'The Bedu didn't do very much hunting,' Thesiger said, 'because they didn't have the enthusiasm for it. One of the few who did was bin Tafl.'[19] When bin Tafl was ten, his father died. The uncle who brought him up after that had been killed in a raid by the Mahra, and later he had put his marksmanship and nerve to good use. He had ridden into Mahra looking for a relation of his uncle's murderer, lain in wait for him, and drilled him neatly through the skull. As a result he had a long-lasting blood-feud with the Mahra.

Bin Tafl recalled his meeting with Thesiger years later. 'I saw him first in the Wali's office – the Burza,' he said. 'He was a tall man, much taller than a Bedouin, and he looked like any other Christian looks. The Wali asked us to find some good men from the Bayt Kathir to go with him, so naturally we thought we should get a few of the best men from each section of the tribe – that way it would be fair. We didn't expect any foreigner to be able to do what we did, but we respected him because the Wali had sent him to us, and because he was a foreigner among the Bedu. We regarded him as being connected with the government. It was also a good opportunity to make money, because we were very poor then.'[20] When Thesiger had gone, bin Tafl sent word to Sultan and the other Bayt Kathir Sheikhs to assemble in Salalah in a fortnight's time.

Meanwhile, Thesiger arranged to travel in the Dhofar mountains with a party of guards lent him by the Wali. As his small party set off, Hamud warned him to be alert with the mountain people – the Jabalis – who, unlike the Bedu from the desert beyond, had no sense of honour. Locking in the coastal plain – the Jerbib – like a protective wall, the Dhofar range is one of the most unexpected landscapes of south-eastern Arabia. The shape of the mountains acts as a windtrap, catching the Indian monsoon. In the rainy season – from July to October – the central part, Jabal Qarra, is continually obscured under a dense nebula of water vapour. Here, deep clefts and sheer valleys bristle with dense green shrubbery as thick as maquis, and water foams down ancient cascades that have chiselled deep passages in the soft rock. Concealed among these valleys are pools shrouded and dappled by reeds and ferns, forested in sycamore, acacia, jasmine and myrtle. Herds of small cattle constantly trickle across rolling downs dominated by the tangled trunks of wild fig trees, limes and tamarinds. The mountains are an ethnologist's paradise. Standing in the midst of unrelieved deserts, they have formed an enclave that reveals the skeleton of local history. The people of the mountains – the Jabalis – are of a different stock from the Arab Bedouin and speak a different language – probably sharing ancestry with the Abyssinians. The dominant tribe are the Qarra, the largest of the Dhofar tribes, from whom the Sultan had himself taken a wife. A thrilling drama of rise and fall had taken place in these hills, for when the Portuguese arrived in the sixteenth century and tried to gain a foothold here they were ferociously resisted by a mountain tribe called the Shahra. Decimated by the invaders, these Shahra recruited Arabs from the Hadhramaut to assist them in the struggle. The mercenaries – the Qarra – eventually acquired control of the Shahra hills through intermarriage, inheriting the Shahra culture and language, while the Shahra themselves, numerically weak, were reduced to the menial status of 'non-tribesmen' – meaning they had no right to bear arms.

Thesiger found the hills fascinating. The mountain people inhabited caves or thatched stone dwellings with tiny entrances. Riddled with blood-feuds, in times of hardship they habitually raided one another for cattle and camels, carrying spears, swords and small leather shields. The Jabalis were cattle-nomads, and because cattle must drink every three days their movements were short-range, though often arduous. The hyena, the wolf and the panther-like wildcat were their particular enemies. They were also farmers, practising monsoon agriculture with the primitive digging-stick, and raising millet, beans, cucumbers, tobacco, maize, and chili peppers. Many sections owned frankincense trees, and they supplemented their crops by collecting wild figs, limes, tamarinds, wild honey and a truffle-like root called *janbet*. In the monsoon season their women made butter-fat, as they still do, by shaking goatskins of milk on a tripod. The mountain tribes were extremely powerful in Dhofar, comprising more than 70 per cent of the entire population. In contrast to the Bedu, Thesiger claimed later, the mountain folk were known for treachery, murder, theft and violating the sanctuary customs of Islam.

He trekked across the clefts and plateaux of these downs until he reached the northern side, where he was startled by the abrupt transformation of the landscape. It was almost as if a magical line had been drawn across the earth here. Behind him lay the rolling, forested hills of Qarra with their mud-and-straw huts and cattle-herds. Before him lay the skeleton of a land which had been gnawed and knapped down to the very bones. It was a landscape of bleakness: smoke-grey stone, sliced through with deep grooves where water had run in the past, its surface ruptured into pimples of limestone like battalions of tiny pyramids stretching far into the distance. This arid shelf of land, looking to Thesiger almost lifeless in comparison with the fertile mountains, was known as the Najd (tableland) or the Sieh (land of wadis). It was the home of the Bedu tribe he was to travel with on his first journey: the Bayt Kathir. Beyond the rose-pink haze that glimmered like mist over that leathery desert skin, invisible to the naked eye, lay the great dunes and salt-plains of ar Raml: the Sands. It was perhaps as early as this, when Thesiger stood at the watershed of these mountains, seeing the green downs on one side and arid desert on the other, that he began to formulate an idea that would come, fifteen years later, to dominate his book *Arabian Sands* – and indeed his entire life. The Wali had talked about the mountain people 'having no honour' – in contrast to the Bedu who inhabited the seemingly empty landscape below him. How could this be, Thesiger must have wondered, when the mountain folk lived in this lush and well-watered 'paradise', unless the harsher environment produced 'finer' people? This theory – summed up by Thesiger's later assertion *the harder the life, the finer the person* – is consciously or unconsciously one of the most satisfying aspects of the book *Arabian Sands*. It seems to offer what amounts to a complete environmental theory of man that appears absolutely watertight at first view. From the lofty vantage-point of the

Dhofar hills, Thesiger could observe a scale of 'nobility' which rarefied as one got further north and more remote from civilization. At the base of the scale were the *Hadr* – the townsmen, and the despised *Bahhara* or fishermen. They represented all that was materialistic, ignoble and inhospitable about man. Further up the scale were the cultivating peasants and the mountain-dwellers – better than townsmen, but without the honour of the Bedu. Further up still were the Bedu of the Sieh – an honourable people touched with avarice – and beyond them, in the Sands themselves, at the very apex of the scale, the people Thesiger had read about in Thomas, but had yet to meet in practice, the sand-dwelling Bedu, the epitome of all things noble.

When Thesiger returned to Salalah he found a great assembly of Bayt Kathir waiting for him, and perceived the true extent of the advantage the Bedu hoped to gain from his visit. Among them were bin Tafl (wearing, Thesiger noted with disapproval, a clean *dishdasha*, and looking like a townsman), Sultan, who reminded Thesiger of a 'Red Indian', and an old man called Tamtaim, chief of the Bayt Ghuwas section of the tribe. These Sheikhs counselled that in the desert there would be danger from large raiding parties and a considerable escort of Bedu would be essential. Thesiger, already a seasoned traveller, suspected exploitation, and in this he was correct. 'It wasn't so much that there was danger from raiders,' bin Tafl admitted. 'After all, we used to travel on our own sometimes: it was just that we wanted as many people as possible to share in the profit. A man has a responsibility to his people, and those left out were likely to cause a lot of arguments.'[21] When the number was finally settled, Thesiger arranged for them to pick him up at the RAF camp the following day.

The British aircraftmen awoke to see what appeared to be a horde of savages bearing down on the camp, armed with old rifles and curved daggers. These Bedu looked nothing like the tribes Thesiger had encountered in Syria. They wore their hair in wild, unkempt masses, or streaming across their shoulders in oiled braids, often naked but for a loincloth that reached to the knees, or an indigo shawl that stained their skin blue, making them look like woad-painted primitives. Their faces were keen and angular, their bodies small, hard, muscular, flayed of every ounce of fat, and they moved with a loping, irregular gait, constantly cursing and squabbling in what sounded to the airmen like savagely threatening tones. As they couched their camels outside, Thesiger and his RAF friends brought out the loads of rice, flour, dates, sugar, tea, coffee and ghee he had prepared: 'I don't know if he had been used to going on camels before,' bin Tafl commented, 'but he had packed it all in baggage that was much too heavy for our camels. We had to untie it all and put it into our saddle-bags.'[22] All this was done with much arguing and the raising of voices, the rearing and spitting and roaring of camels. Thesiger had been accustomed to the hardier carrying camels of the Sudan, and the more efficient double-poled saddles of North Africa and Arabia. Here the tribes merely slung the weight across the beast's back and let it ride by its own balance. While the animals were being loaded, Thesiger changed into Arab dress, and appeared feeling self-conscious in his gleaming white, brand new *dishdasha*. No one paid much attention to him, though. 'It wouldn't have mattered to us if he wore Christian clothes or Arab clothes,' bin Tafl said, 'because after all, he was a Christian. But it was better that he wore Arab dress, because it was more comfortable in the desert. He was far too tall to be a Bedu anyway. When we first went into the mountains you could see him from far away in those new clothes, but I told him, "Don't worry, we've got the medicine for that," and we dyed it for him with the juice of a tree. When he got used to wearing the clothes, he really did look like a Bedu Sheikh.'[23]

The party left Salalah on 5 November, riding across the stony Jerbib coastal plain and climbing up through the Wadi Garzaz whose vegetation, green during the monsoon, had already faded to brown. At each camping place the Bedu were pursued by hill-men of the Qarra, anxious to sell them goats or butter at inflated prices. They watered their camels and filled their skins at the muddy pool at Halluf, then descended slowly into the arid plains of the Sieh, the dreary limestone flats punctuated by dry-washes which outlie the great Sands. There had been abundant rain in the Qarra mountains and the whole of the southern side had been green in the monsoon season. As they descended the northern slopes into the flats and wadis, they came across patches of lush grazing where the Bedu would insist on halting for the entire day. Thesiger began to appreciate how deceptive his first view of the Sieh had been. There was life here, but most of the plants grew no higher than a man's calf, hugging the surface in dense, spiky tufts, lying low, turning their tight surfaces away from the moisture-gobbling rays of the sun. The camels fell on these succulents with hungry abandon. There were already far more men than Thesiger needed, and as soon as they camped on the grazing, knots of Bedouin would bob up like Jack-in-the-boxes out of the desert, licking their lips at the prospect of a free meal, or several. Some lingered on indefinitely, and were never made to feel unwelcome. Thesiger was irritated, knowing that the food would not hold out and that this might cut short his journey. His Sheikhs seemed unable or unwilling to turn anyone away, and he felt as if his journey was becoming a circus – a mobile feeding-programme for the starving nomads. And not very mobile at that, for despite Bedu assurances that each halt would be the last, they continued to make progress at a snail's pace, halting, grazing, and cooking up more vast and well-attended feasts. 'We were dawdling along,' Thesiger said, 'and then after an hour and a half they'd come to some grazing and say we'll stop here. I had a feeling that it was nonsense and they were doing it because they were being paid so much a day.'[24] The Bedu explained defensively that their lives depended on their camels and that there would be no chance of exchanging them if they foundered. There was a modicum of truth in this, but Thesiger's initial suspicions were essentially well-founded: 'We used to travel very slowly because the tribes wanted to increase the number of days,' said Sa'id bin Muhammad, a Bayt Kathiri who accompanied Thesiger later. 'We wanted to make more money, and the longer it lasted the more we would make. Of course, not all going is the same for camels, but our own custom was to travel all day and sometimes all night too. We didn't do that with the Christian Mbarak. He was giving us four riyals a day, so it was a good amount.'[25] Unlike Thomas, Thesiger was determined to master the primitive Omani saddle – little more than a pad perched over the camel's rump. 'He said he had ridden a lot of camels,' bin Tafl remembered, 'but at first you would have said he had never ridden one before. He looked a bit unsteady. We Bedu used to kneel in the saddle, sometimes, because we'd been doing it since we were children, but he didn't do that. After a few days, though, he got accustomed to the saddle and he was all right.'[26] Thesiger was riding a camel belonging to Sultan, a fine animal called Mbrausha (the Speckled One). Unlike the Sudanese tribes, who rode males, these Bedu rode only she-camels, and slaughtered most bull-calves at birth: they could not afford to keep animals which did not supply milk. At first, he admitted, the unaccustomed way of riding was difficult. 'I never knelt in the saddle as they did,' he said. 'I should have fallen off. The amazing thing was that they would ride kneeling even when the camels were going flat out. I rode with my legs dangling down each side, which is how a lot of them used to ride too.'[27] In fact, Thesiger came to dread the moment he would have to ride. The Omani saddle is actually very uncomfortable for those unused to it, and as he was unable to kneel, he could not vary the position of his legs as one could on a Sudanese saddle. As the hours passed, the edge of the saddle-pad would rub viciously into his flesh.

Another problem was communication. The Bayt Kathir spoke a dialect as different from that of the Arabs of Syria as it was from those of the Sudan. Thomas – though an Arabic speaker – had brought an interpreter to solve this problem, but Thesiger wanted to communicate directly. 'I did have a problem with their Arabic,' he recalled. 'When I first started I found it difficult to make them understand what I was saying. In the Sudan I'd never learned proper Arabic because for people like Idriss it was a second language, and I didn't mix that much with the Arabs in Darfur.'[28] Bin Tafl said that he often acted as an 'interpreter' at first. 'The others couldn't understand what he was saying,' he explained, 'but I'd been living in Salalah and had heard different kinds of Arabic, so I could understand.'[29]

Each day followed a similar pattern. Thesiger would wake to the sound of camels shifting as the Bedu released them from their knee-hobbles and sent them off to sniff out grazing. He would lie under his blankets, savouring the extra moments while the Bayt Kathir performed their morning prayers, until the ring of the coffee mortar called him to the fire. These winter mornings were crisply cold and Thesiger would gasp as he splashed a little icy water on his face and hands. As he approached the coffee-hearth, his companions would stand up formally and answer his ritual 'Peace be upon you!' with the formula 'On you be peace!' They would then crouch down around the flickering fire, as tea and then bitter coffee were served. The coffee was poured from a heavy pewter pot into a cup which was passed to each drinker in turn, who shook it from side to side to signify he had drunk his fill. Afterwards, the Bedu would bring up the camels and load them amid tremendous bleating and roaring – a characteristic of she-camels. Thesiger, who all his life had the introvert's sensitivity to loud noises, and was accustomed to the more silent males in the Sudan, was appalled. He asked Sultan how on earth they managed on raids, and the Sheikh replied that they would tie their mouths up with cloth. Since Thesiger was riding Sultan's camel and had not yet mastered the unaccustomed rig, Sultan would saddle for him. On the plains they would start the day walking, tying up the camels' head-ropes and letting them drift along ahead, browsing wherever they could. Thesiger set his men to look for locusts, plants and insects. As the day grew hotter, the Bedu would ride as the fancy took them, bringing the camel's head down and using its neck as a step. If the party stopped at midday they would unload the camels and turn them loose into any nearby grazing. They made a fire and cooked polenta similar to the *'asida* Thesiger had eaten in the Sudan, or baked bread in the sand under the ashes of the fire. Dinner in the evening would be the same fare, and afterwards the Bedu would sit around the fire close together and talk in loud, excited voices so that everyone could hear and join in. Often they would recite poetry, sitting on their knees in the formal, gymnastic pose they had been accustomed to since birth – torture to anyone unused to it. Thesiger would be glad to get away from the talk just in order to be able to stretch out his legs.

He need not have emulated the customs of these men. He was and would remain a Christian and a foreigner, yet an innate self-pride imbued him fiercely with the idea of rivalling them. He did not want to be merely tolerated, but, as always, to be accepted as a leader on their own terms. This had been true in the Sudan and in Syria, but then he had ultimately had an official rank to fall back on. Here, he saw himself as being no longer an official member of the government. The fantasy that had begun imperfectly on his first trek in Danakil country was here expanded to its fullest possible range. With the Bedu, he felt, he could be a Lawrence-like figure, almost, if not quite, one of them. He could assume another identity, become another person. He soon realized that as far as rivalry went, he had picked on the most competitive people on earth. One of the factors which had moulded the Bedouin character was their small number in comparison to the vast area over which they were spread. Scattered yet mobile blotches of life on the immense panorama of wilderness, they were actually incredibly few. The entire six sections of the Bayt Kathir – Dhofar's largest Bedouin tribe – would easily have fitted into a large hotel. The Rawashid numbered perhaps 250 rifles. Even in 1977, the entire Bedouin population of Dhofar, of which the Bayt Kathir was but one tribe, was estimated at only 1,487 families – about 7,700 men, women and children, in an area of more than 25,000 square miles. In such a small yet dispersed society, the cult of the reputation flourished. A man or woman might be known by reputation far better than he or she was known corporeally. In a world where no detail was missed, a Bedui would do almost anything to enhance his prestige. Every event, no matter how insignificant, would sooner or later be reported around the entire community, be it hundreds of miles apart. As soon as a party returned from a raid or journey, every nuance, good or bad, would soon be reverberating through the desert grapevine – who had fallen short in bravery, courage, patience, endurance; who had shirked feeding the camels, collecting firewood, making the fire; who had excelled. This fact made everyone ferociously concerned to outdo the others. To his amazement, Thesiger found that they would compete like boy scouts to perform the most menial tasks, just so it would one day be repeated that 'so-and-so didn't fall short . . .' They would squabble over who should drink last, and on the rare occasions when they were blessed with meat, each would each argue that his share was too large. It was essentially a convoluted egotism, but the paradoxical result was a kind of institutionalized selflessness: 'We call it '*ethar* [lit. altruism],' bin Tafl explained. 'By the custom of the Bedu each one would try to surpass the other in something so that he would become famous and get a good reputation. They would talk about him saying he was very active and not lazy, for example. This is the habit of the Bedu when they travel together – everybody wants to impress the others. Even Sultan, though he was an important Sheikh, used to collect the firewood. Everyone was in competition, even the Sheikhs. We have a saying, "The servant of the group is its master." Sometimes it gets ridiculous, though. Once I was with a party of Arabs and we were very thirsty, and we came to a well and I was inside digging it out, and passing the water up to them. I said "Drink! Drink!" but they wouldn't drink until I climbed up out of the well to drink with them, and of course even though I was in the well with the water, it would have been wrong to drink before passing it up to them.'[30]

While Thesiger could equal and surpass the Bedu physically, outwalking, outshooting, and outriding them, displaying equal courage and endurance – things highly esteemed in his own culture – this exaggerated self-deprecation was difficult to match, especially when taken to such extremes. However, he tried desperately to do so: 'In the beginning we felt that he wouldn't be able to bear the difficulty of the march,' bin Tafl said. 'At night he used to go off and collect firewood and I would say, "No, leave it – you sit down." He wouldn't accept it. We used to feel he would get tired and couch his camel, but he would refuse to ride until after everyone else had mounted. We would offer him a drink and he'd say, no, not until you drink. He drank the same dirty water as us – and we didn't expect that from a foreigner – water so bad sometimes we had to put sugar in it. I gave him a she-camel to ride later in the Sands, and after three months I rode her myself for only a day and I thought she was terrible. I don't know how he managed it. His one fault was that he used to get angry and impatient. Mostly he discussed things calmly, but sometimes he'd get very cross. Like once he said I had left the maps behind and he was very angry indeed. Still, we wouldn't have expected him to be as patient as us – we were natives of the place, and we knew everything about it. He was only one person, and we were so many, yet he was still in charge. We admired him because we felt he did more than he needed to. In the end I think he was better than us in two ways – in the way he organized things, and in the fact that he had money. We were better than him in one way – in that we were Muslims.'[31] 'I was determined to make no concessions,' Thesiger commented, 'and when they all started saying you must be getting tired, get on your camel, I'd snap back at them angrily. They'd just ride when they wanted and they had no sense of deference.'[32]

The men divided themselves up into groups for eating, and besides bin Tafl – who did the cooking – Thesiger found himself sharing meals with Tamtaim – the elder Sheikh of the Bayt Kathir. Thesiger stressed the informality of such titles, however: 'The Wali may have introduced him as Sheikh Tamtaim,' he commented, 'but when we talked among ourselves we just called him Tamtaim. This wasn't like the Rwalla and the northern Bedu who were more formal. A Sheikh was a man whom the tribe followed. The title belonged automatically to one family but if the Sheikh lost the respect of the tribe he wouldn't be dismissed as a Sheikh, it would simply mean that his tents would be empty and they'd go off and sit in his brother's tent.'[33] His other messmates were Sultan and an unusually quiet man called Mabkhaut. 'Mabkhaut was a good man,' bin Tafl said. 'He was married to a woman from the Rawashid so he was friendly with both them and the Bayt Kathir. He wasn't a famous man or anything, and it's true he hardly spoke at all, but he was brave and well respected.'[34] Thesiger never liked bin Tafl, despite the fact that this man was to play a key part in his success. His romantic prejudice caused him to feel that bin Tafl's connection with the town had somehow 'tarnished' him and made him excessively avaricious. 'He also tended to be ingratiating,' Thesiger said, 'which the others weren't. Sultan was definitely the dominant character – he was quite impressive. Tamtaim was the most respected Sheikh, but he was an old man, though still very active and a very pleasant character. He had travelled with Thomas, as Sultan had. He once went to sleep on his camel and fell off, and was terribly ashamed of himself.'[35] Bin Tafl was to prove himself as brave, tough, and ruthless as any of the Bedu who had not been near a town: an anomaly, apparently, in Thesiger's all-embracing theory of the hard life producing the 'finer' person. Bin Tafl may have been ingratiating, but the truth behind Thesiger's dislike for him surely lies in his 'awareness'. Of all

Thesiger's companions, bin Tafl alone had glimpsed the economic realities of the world outside: guessed at the unequal relationship between Christians and Arabs, of which the others – especially the youths whom Thesiger was to hold so dear later – had no inkling. Bin Tafl was, in other words, 'spoiled'. As Thesiger was to tell Timothy Green many years afterwards, speaking of the Turkana tribe: 'I much prefer to be with them than a more sophisticated tribe. You can establish a relationship with them that is quite impossible once a group has been exposed to the outside world.'[36] This issue lies at the very core of Western contacts with the Bedu. Because they knew little of the outside world, and had no sense of outward 'deference', the Western stranger was able to forget the true nature of the relationship between them. He could be their leader without exposing them to any humiliation. They were not deferential, they believed themselves superior because they did not understand the realities of technological power, yet they did not question his right to lead, his right to be there. Despite their ignorance of the world outside, or perhaps because of it, the Bedu did have their reservations about Thesiger's purpose. Bin Tafl respected the Englishman but never trusted his motives: 'He told us he came to look for locusts and destroy them,' bin Tafl said, 'but we never believed that. I still don't believe it. I think he was sent to map out the borders or something like that.'[37] Salim bin Kabina, probably Thesiger's closest Bedouin companion over the five years he spent in Arabia, agreed: 'He said he came to destroy the locusts. Well, the locusts came before him, and they came after him. We were just Bedu and we knew nothing. But I think he had some reason for coming that he didn't tell us.'[38] According to bin Tafl, the Bedu even made up a verse about Thesiger's secret objective:

> 'The Sheikh of the Christians has a dangerous motive,
> But nobody knows what it is!'

'I asked him once,' bin Tafl said. 'I recited this verse to him, and told him that the Bedu suspected his motives. He answered, "Yes, you have hit the nail on the head. I have a secret purpose which nobody knows."'[39] 'Of course,' Thesiger commented years later, 'they *would* suspect I had an ulterior motive.'[40]

Thesiger himself admitted that to the Bedu he was a townsman, a non-Arab, and most of all an unbeliever. Though by no means the fanatic Muslims he would later come across in Sa'udi Arabia, the Bedouin of Dhofar were profoundly religious. Bin Tafl recalled how he once tried to convert the Englishman to Islam: 'Near Mughshin I found a gazelle fawn,' he remembered, 'and I took it to the Christian as a gift. He said we ought to return it to its mother as it was so young, and he spent ages looking for her. In the end he couldn't find her, so he just let the fawn go. I understood that he had a good heart, so I said I had a suggestion for him. He asked me what it was, and I said, "Testify that there is no God but Allah, and Muhammad is his Prophet, may peace and honour be upon Him, because you have a good heart and otherwise you will go to Hell." He told me that there was only a small difference between his religion and ours, and that one day he thought they would come to an understanding. I was disappointed. I thought he might become a Muslim.'[41] Another thing which the Bedu found surprising about Thesiger was his celibacy. He was already thirty-five and still unmarried, while for them marriage was *de rigueur* from an early age – occasionally even before puberty. It was considered 'half the religion' in Islam. 'He said he would get married when all his work with the Arabs was finished,' bin Tafl remembered. 'When he was about forty years old.'[42]

They crossed the Wadi Ghudun, a sheer-sided gorge carved out by water rushing down from the Dhofar hills over generations, which graded the bullet-blue boulders of its bed into complementary sizes and burnished them smooth. The walls of the wadi had been eaten away into natural caves, where the Bayt Kathir kept their goats or even slept themselves in the winter, and its bed was littered with small oases of dwarf palms – fans of close-knit green blades growing no more than a metre high, from which the Bedu made their valuable fibre for ropes and mats. The wadi was also blessed with brakes of shady thorn-trees. Here, Thesiger was in the heartland of the Bayt Kathir, Bedu of the Sieh or steppes. Only a single section of them – the Bayt Musann – ever ventured into the Sands. They raised goats and a few camels and tended the frankincense trees on the lower slopes of the Dhofar range. Wadis like Ghudun and several others, which traversed the steppes like roadways running roughly south to north, shifting the flood-waters of the monsoon to the edge of the Sands, were their lifelines. The Bayt Kathir had no black tents in classic Bedouin style. They made their homes in the open, under thorn-trees or in caves, spreading palmetto fibre mats on the sand for their beds. In summer they would move their flocks of goats and few camels near to one of the six permanent water-sources that existed in their region. In the cool months they would begin to migrate north along the wadis, shifting camp twenty or twenty-five miles a day until they came to their limit: the rim of the Sands. The flocks would graze in a radius around the camp until the next move, but if the Bedu sighted lightning and rain-clouds in the distance, they would break the cycle and move post-haste to wherever the rain had fallen.

This year the area had been fortunate. Rain had fallen in deluges in July and the gravel flats to the west were burgeoning with green. Thesiger's guides suggested that the caravan should swing west to make use of the grazing, before cutting back towards Mughshin in the north-east. They watered the camels at Ma Shadid, where the water stood at forty-five feet in a fissure in the limestone and could be reached only by scrambling perilously down seven successive ledges of rock, each one the home of scorpions and snakes, and hoisting the water back up from ledge to ledge by rope. Not long afterwards they reached Mudhay, where Thesiger found a trickling natural spring in a great lacuna between the flaking silver bosses of limestone hills. Today Mudhay is an area of Bedu settlement, with a mosque and rows of huts containing Indian-style stores and mechanics' shops. The Bedu – Bayt Kathir mainly – live in lines of gleaming white bungalows where camels forever nuzzle the hot walls, or scratch their necks against the ubiquitous Land-Cruisers which have replaced them for transport. The spring is now obscured by a mass of date-palms which did not exist in Thesiger's time. All he found here were some cracked and broken Islamic tombs with dome roofs and some interesting lines of knee-high trilithons – stone monuments like dinosaur vertebrae arranged in threes, probably dating from pre-Islamic times. From Mudhay, they pressed on along the steep-sided Wadi 'Aydam, moving unhurriedly, the camels stopping to browse on the green shoots of the acacias, stalking on to

36. Thesiger photographed by Ronald Codrai in Dubai, 1948/9.

37. A locust attack in Dubai. Thesiger's early journeys in Arabia were undertaken under the aegis of the Locust Research Organization.

38. Thesiger and his final 'assault party' in the Empty Quarter in 1946/7. Left to right: Mabkhaut, bin Tafl, Thesiger, al 'Auf, bin Kabina.

39. Musallim bin al Kamam of the Rawashid. He was Thesiger's beau ideal of the noble Bedouin.

40. Bin Kabina (left) and bin Ghabaisha on a trip to Ras el Khaima with Thesiger and Ronald Codrai, 1950.

41. Bin Ghabaisha with a pet gazelle.

42. Bin Ghabaisha as a young man, 1948/9.

43. Sheikh Salih bin Kalut. He was the most respected sheikh of the Rawashid.

44. Driving the camels back to camp in the Empty Quarter.

45. Thesiger was the first Westerner to explore the Liwa oasis, here photographed in the early 1950s.

46. Bin Ghabaisha and bin Kabina milking a camel, 1948/9.

47. Abu Dhabi in the early 1950s. Thesiger ended his second crossing of the Empty Quarter at the fort (centre).

48. Sheikh Shakhbut, *c.* 1949. He was the ruler of Abu Dhabi when Thesiger first arrived there.

49. Oil Company House, Dubai (centre, with arched façade), which Thesiger made his base over a two-year period.

50. A falconer with his hooded bird and shoulder bag of game. Thesiger enjoyed his hawking trips with Sheikh Zaayid in 1949.

51. Camels crossing to Abu Dhabi island, 1949.

52. Bedu women at a desert well on the edge of the Empty Quarter, *c.* 1949.

the next tempting stand of shrubs and halting again there. Thesiger saw, eighteen feet up in the wadi sides, the knobbled trunks of palms and other woody debris that the Bedu told him had been hurled there by tremendous floods that had ripped through the Sieh two generations before.

They watered at a shallow pool at Ghafa', on the spot where bin Ghabaisha's cabin stands today. The Bedu stood ankle-deep in the water, ladling the stuff – camel-urine, goat-droppings and all – into their upended waterskins. This rainwater was precious: a Gift from God. It was here that Thesiger first met men of the Rawashid, the tribe which was to play such an important role in his life in the future. The Rawashid were 'cousins' of the Bayt Kathir, but unlike them herded camels in the Empty Quarter itself. More mobile than their steppe-dwelling relatives, they might be found as far north as Abu Dhabi and Dubai. Thesiger knew of the Rawashid already, of course: they had been the tribesmen who had successfully guided Bertram Thomas across the Sands. Among them was one outstanding individual, a lean, handsome, charming young man who had already acquired a reputation as a truce-maker and traveller. His name was Musallim bin al Kamam, and he was to become Thesiger's beau ideal of the 'noble Arab'. 'If I had to choose one person to represent the Bedu at their best, it certainly wouldn't be bin Tafl,' he said later. 'It would undoubtedly be Musallim bin al Kamam.'[43] Thesiger knew, having read Thomas's *Arabia Felix*, that if he was to cross the Empty Quarter he must obtain Rawashid guides: they were the only tribe in Dhofar who knew the Sands intimately. 'I had read Thomas's book before making the first journey,' Thesiger commented, 'and that's why I was determined to get hold of the Rashid after my first reconnaissance with the Bayt Kathir.'[44]

The 'Id al Fitr – the greatest feast of the Islamic year, taking place at the end of the month of Ramadan – came upon them while at Ghafa', and Thesiger left the greater part of his men to celebrate it there. He rode off with bin Tafl, another Bayt Kathiri called Jinazil, and a hunter from the Rawashid called bin Shuwas, to spy out the steppes as far west as the Wadi Mitan and, if possible, to shoot an Arabian oryx. As they rode, bin Shuwas pointed to the north, where, beyond the horizon, the Bedu believed there was an ancient city lost under the sand. They came across numerous fresh tracks of oryx and even caught a glimpse of ten of the creatures far away across the plains, but were unable to approach them. 'The Christian had lent this very good rifle to Jinazil,' bin Tafl recalled, 'and the man fired it into the air. The Christian got very angry and told him to give it to me instead of my old rifle. Jinazil refused, and the Christian said, "Look, it is my rifle. You do what I say!" He brought Jinazil a stick and said, "Either you take bin Tafl's old rifle, or you take this stick." That was in the Wadi Mitan.'[45] They returned to Ghafaʿ empty-handed. Before leaving, however, Thesiger asked if bin al Kamam would meet him later at Salalah with a party of his Rawashid to accompany him on his planned trek to the Hadhramaut.

They watered again at Shisur, where the debris that had once been a fort and a more modern block-house stood over a water-source that in ancient times had been vital to the incense-road joining Dhofar to the Hadhramaut and the Yemen. Here the water was almost as inaccessible as at Ma Shadid, for it was to be found in a crack under a rocky overhang in which blown sand had piled up. To water their camels, the Bedu had to scramble about thirty feet down the narrow aperture between rock and sand, then lug the sweating skins back up. Today, the sand has been cleared out and the water is pumped up by electric motor. The old fort, it is now claimed, was part of the legendary city of Ubar, and Shisur itself is the site of lines of air-conditioned bungalows inhabited by the Bayt Musann – the one sand-dwelling section of the Bayt Kathir. Possession of Shisur was of vital importance, since it was the last source of water before entering the Sands. In Thomas's time – about seventeen years previously – some Maʿarab raiders had been caught by a combined patrol of Bayt Kathir and Mahra in the nearby grove of Haylat ash Shisur. The raiding party had comprised twenty-five men of the Seʿar and Karab who had watered at Shisur and fallen on a Mahra encampment at Andhur, shooting dead seven tribesmen but losing their own leader. They had rustled forty camels, but the surviving Mahra had joined with the Bayt Kathir and chased them here, creeping up on them under the cloak of darkness. They had killed four before charging in with their daggers and seizing all the camels raided and five of the raiders' own stock. They had so surprised the Ma'arab that the raiders had abandoned their booty and bolted two to a camel.

Raids from more powerful tribes from the steppes to the west were a traditional hazard to the Bedouin of Dhofar. Due to the sparse fertility of the land, the Dhofar Bedu wandered in scattered groups and were thus vulnerable to the large raiding-parties (*giman*, sing. *gom*) which the western tribes could field. They knew the westerners collectively by the ancient Arabic word *Ma'arab*, simply meaning 'west', whereas they themselves were classed as *Mishqas*, meaning 'east'. These two terms were geographical rather than tribal, for the very tribes which raided Dhofar were themselves known as Mishqas by the tribes on the skirts of the Yemen, still farther west. There was a complex structure of alliances between the Dhofar tribes by which they would forget their individual differences and present a united front to resist the western raiders. The Mahra, a Himyaritic-speaking tribe, for instance, were traditional enemies of the Rawashid and Bayt Kathir, but would unite with them to fight the Ma'arab. These raids were not 'wars', but were prosecuted with the sole object of acquiring livestock or possibly occupying a water-source. They were conducted with as little loss of human life as possible, and ideally non-combatants such as women and small children were inviolate. Modern anthropologists – notably Louise E. Sweet – have seen the reciprocal raiding between tribes as a method of redistributing livestock to areas hit sporadically by drought and famine, and thus as a major factor in the survival of the Bedu as a whole over two or three millennia.[46] Bertram Thomas expressed it thus: 'Raiding to them is the spice of life, and there was never a man in any of my escorts who had not raided into the Hadhramaut, nor one who had not been raided in his own grazing-grounds, and some bore honourable scars of bullet or dagger wounds. Arms and ammunition and the health of the camel are thus the primary necessities of life.'[47]

It took Thesiger's men hours of back-breaking toil to water all their camels and fill all the skins – vital because a waterless week's march lay ahead of them. From Shisur the caravan passed along the great wadi known as Umm al Hayt – 'the Mother of Life' – and Thesiger caught his first thrilling glimpse of the Empty

Quarter: 'It was a stirring moment,' he wrote, 'when the long, rose-coloured wall of the sand first appeared along our front.'[48] From Mersaudid, where today the desert is stained green with fields of wheat, and great irrigation pumps spray water in jets across the landscape, he took eight of his party on his first foray into the Sands.

The dunes here – Ramlat Ghanim – were isolated, rising 2–300 feet from the desert floor, their lower slopes richly green with grazing. The Bedu ran up to the dunes as the camels moved beneath them, collecting bunches of tribulus to handfeed them. It was almost a week since they had watered at Shisur, and the water in their skins was finished. Thesiger suggested they push on to the well of Bir Halu, which was only a few miles distant. They rode on a little way, then discovered another rich patch of grazing. 'They decided to stop there and go on in the evening down to the well,' Thesiger remembered. 'We'd had no water all that morning and I was getting irritated, and I said for Heaven's sake let's get down to the well and you can graze your camels there. They said they didn't think there'd be any grazing there, but Tamtaim said we'll take the Christian on down to the well, so he and I and Sultan and bin Tafl went down to the well. They watered the camels and came and sat down, and I thought why didn't they bring any water? Why the hell can't we have a drink? I said to Tamtaim can't we have some water? So he said to bin Tafl, "Go and get the Christian a drink." He came back with a bowl of water and Tamtaim offered it to me, and I said no, after you, Uncle. He said, "It wouldn't be seemly for me to drink before the others arrive." So then we had to sit there for two hours until they arrived, and the price we paid was that our camels missed out on the grazing. That was my first lesson in Bedouin manners!'[49] To cap it all, the water, after the long wait, was brackish and only just drinkable. 'Bir Halu means the "sweet well" in Arabic,' bin Tafl said, 'but sweet it certainly wasn't!'[50]

Skirting around the sands at Bir Halu, the Bayt Kathir discovered the tracks of a raiding party, which they identified as belonging to a sixteen-man *gom* of the 'Awamir, one of the tribes which lived on both sides of the Sands. This party had come from the north, and they heard later that the 'Awamir had raided the Janaba, a tribe living near the shores of the Arabian Sea, killing three of them and taking fifteen camels. Thesiger was astonished at the distance the raiding party had covered – virtually from the Gulf to the southern coast. The Bayt Kathir with him reckoned that the tracks were a month old, but despite this, the passing of raiders bothered them. That night they were awakened by a startling cry, and lay till the first red smudge of dawn with their rifles at the ready, only to find in daylight the prints of a wolf. Thesiger was impressed by the legendary Bedouin ability to read tracks. Almost all Bedu knew the tracks of their own camels and those of their neighbours, and some could remember the tracks of every camel they had ever seen. Any Bedouin child could distinguish the track of any wild animal living in the desert, and most could tell with amazing accuracy how long ago the tracks were made. Other information was extrapolated from a knowledge of the environment, directions, winds and other geographical data. Not all Bedu were equally good trackers, though certain tribes, especially those of the Sands, were particularly renowned for their skills. The most famous of all Bedu trackers were the Al Murrah of the northern Sands.

From Ghanim the party rode to Mughshin, a belt of green in the emptiness, where groves of date-palms were customarily harvested in season by the Bayt Kathir. Thesiger discovered from his Bedu that the country around here had suffered from drought for twenty-five years, and was thus satisfied that there was no locust outbreak-centre at Mughshin. From here he had been hoping to reach the legendary Umm as Samim – the vast quicksands reported to exist in this area by Bertram Thomas, and reputed by the Bedu to cover about 400 square miles. No Westerner had ever seen Umm as Samim, and Thesiger was keen to stake his claim to it. But the quicksands lay within the territory of the ferocious Duru', the blood enemies of the Bayt Kathir: 'Sultan and the others said we might have trouble if we went into Duru' territory,' Thesiger said, 'and they may have persuaded me not to go any further.'[51] Instead, his caravan turned round within forty miles of Umm as Samim, and trekked through the sands of Sahma. When the Duru' heard about his approach they announced that they would kill any Christian who tried to pass through their land. Thesiger had decided, anyway, to go no further: 'I was intending to go right across the Sands eventually,' he said, 'but I didn't want to give the show away. We played around Mughshin really. I didn't want to get into territory that didn't belong to the Sultan of Muscat, or to enter the country of the Duru', where we might have trouble. This was just a preliminary recce.'[52] They rode back towards Salalah across the polar plains of the Jiddat al Harasis. The nights and days were bitterly cold, but Thesiger was relieved not to be thirsty enough to drink the foul water of the Sands, scarcely taking anything but tea or coffee, occasionally relieved by milk from one of the riding-camels. He craved meat after a diet of tasteless bread and polenta, and on the return journey bin Tafl shot two oryx which they ate ravenously.

Thesiger was both exhausted and excited by this first camel-trek in Arabia through almost unknown country: his first sight of the Empty Quarter, his first real journey with the Bedu. Yet there was an inevitable sense of disillusionment. He felt isolated and lonely, knowing that the Arabs regarded him as an infidel and a foreigner and suspecting, rightly, that they were exploiting him. He was exasperated by their avarice and their constant begging, by their obvious assumption of superiority, their absolute belief that their ways and no others were right. After all the talk of the noble Arab, the reading of T.E. Lawrence, the endless discussions with Moore, the romantic Thesiger felt let down, and like all romantics he would blame the world for not attaining his high standard of expectations, rather than re-analysing his picture of it. He never forgave the Bayt Kathir for spoiling his image of the 'noble' Arab, and claimed later that they were 'corroded by avarice'. It is an interesting parallel of his disillusionment with Bertram Thomas for revealing what he considered an 'ignoble' motive for crossing the Sands. Yet the desert and the Bedu had bitten him like a bug. He could not wait to get back to the Sands again. The party followed the Wadi Qitbit and on the lower slopes of the Dhofar range they came across a tangle of frankincense trees. At the pool of Hanun, they encountered some Bayt Kathir – the first people they had seen since leaving Qafa', forty-four days previously. They crossed the Dhofar mountains by the pass of Arbot, arriving at the RAF camp at Salalah on 9 January, 1946.

True to his word, bin al Kamam was waiting for him at Salalah with about thirty Rawashid tribesmen. Thesiger was impressed with their appearance. He was tired of the Bayt Kathir, admiring them for their good qualities but irritated by their avarice. He was to find the Rawashid less grasping, he wrote. His early description of these tribesmen who would come to represent for him the quintessential Bedu is, however, restrained. In 1946, he wrote simply: 'Small and lightly-built, these Arabs are very hardy, for here none but the fittest can survive.'[53] As years separated him from his experiences in Arabia, though, the picture became distinctly more idealized, as he stirred into its colours all his personal affections and favourite images. 'They were small, deft men, alert and watchful,' he wrote in 1979. 'Their bodies were lean and hard, tempered in the furnace of the desert and trained to unbelievable endurance. Looking at them I realized they were very much alive, tense with nervous energy, vigorously controlled. They had been bred from the purest race in the world and lived in conditions where only the hardiest and the best could survive. They were as fine-drawn and highly-strung as thoroughbreds. Beside them the Beit Kathir lacked the polish of the inner desert.'[54]

There is a core of truth beneath Thesiger's idealized image. Bedu who lived in the remotest places tended to be highly regarded by other Arabs. In the north the Al Murrah, sand-people known as 'the Nomads of the Nomads', were held in awe by the sheep- and goat-herding tribes for their keen senses and almost supernatural tracking skills. However, Thesiger's references to 'thoroughbreds' and 'the purest race in the world' seem less apposite, since the Bayt Kathir and the Rawashid were closely related, probably only a few generations back, and belonged to the same wave of Kathir immigrants who had moved into the region from the Yemen in historical times. The bare fact is that the two tribes occupied different ecological niches. The Bayt Kathir herded their goat-flocks from the slopes of the Dhofar mountains in summer to the edge of the Empty Quarter in winter. The Rawashid overlapped with this cycle, moving from the edges of the Sands in summer to the Sands themselves in winter, their territory stretching right across the Empty Quarter until it touched that of the Al Murrah on the northern side. They bred only camels, and, unlike the Bayt Kathir, used black tents, and litters for their womenfolk in the Sands. Thesiger himself was slightly vague about their normal cycle of migrations, never having accompanied them, and believed that Rawashid women did not join their menfolk in the Empty Quarter, though in Arabia tents are always the property of women, and men on their own never use them. An anthropological survey made by Jorg Janzen, published in 1980, shows that the Rawashid traditionally travelled in the Sands in small groups of two or three households, which included women and children.[55]

In the Empty Quarter grazing for the camels was generally abundant, if limited in kind. The major problem was water. Though the water-table was high and the Bedu sank hand-dug wells, the water was always thick with salt. In the Sieh the water was sweet, but, as Thesiger discovered on this first journey, wells were few and far between and the water very difficult to get at. By normal standards the lives of both tribes were extraordinarily hard. It is undoubtedly true that the Rawashid, with their colonies at Dakaka in the central Sands and right across the desert in Dhafara, were more mobile than the Bayt Kathir – a fact Janzen has underlined: 'The great mobility of this Beduin type [i.e. the Rawashid] is . . . exemplified by the use of a riding saddle for women (*tomah*) which does not exist among the Nejd [i.e. Bayt Kathir] . . . Beduins.'[56] 'The Bayt Kathir lived on the fringes of the desert,' Thesiger said, 'and they never made the journeys the Rashid made. There was no question the Rashid were different and this was due to the harder life – the harder the life the finer the person. There's no question that I was completely justified in distinguishing between the Bayt Kathir and the Rashid. If I wrote my book again I'd write word for word what I've written there . . . The two tribes that used the Sands were the Rashid and the 'Awamir – the Murrah not to any extent – I mean the Rashid could have gone anywhere – right up to Abu Dhabi and Dubai. I mean, bin Kabina and bin Ghabaisha could have been found anywhere in southern Arabia.'[57] The picture is more complicated than it appears, though, for, as Nashran bin Sultan pointed out, most of Thesiger's closest Rawashid friends – including bin Kabina and bin Ghabaisha – came from the Bayt Imani, a section of the Rawashid which occupied the wadis around the wells of Sanaw in what is now the Yemen: 'The Rawashid lived in the Sands,' he explained, 'some as far away as Sa'udi Arabia. But the Bayt Imani didn't live in the Sands, they lived around Sanaw, in the Sieh. There were Rawashid at Dakaka, yes, but not Bayt Imani. Bin Kabina and bin Ghabaisha were Bayt Imani, of course, and their lives were the same as those of the Bayt Kathir.'[58]

According to Nashran, bin Kabina was watering goats in the Wadi Khawat (in the Sieh) during the cool season when Thesiger first met him, and even in Thesiger's own account, bin Kabina was clearly a goat-herder, owning a single house-camel for carrying water: the Rawashid of the Sands did not raise goats, and herded their camels in the Empty Quarter during the winter months. In sum, Thesiger's view is personal and aesthetic rather than objective. The American anthropologist Professor Donald Powell-Cole is perhaps the only Westerner to have shared the ordinary life of a Bedu tribe in the Empty Quarter. He lived with the Al Murrah of the northern Sands in the 1960s, and expressed his view of Thesiger's experience thus: 'Thesiger didn't know much about nomadism, because he never lived with the Bedu during the course of their normal activities. He was travelling with these young men all the time on journeys they would not normally have done alone. His book is brilliantly written and moving, but I regard it as being about the character of his young Bedu friends rather than an objective study of the nomads.'[59]

There is, however, another layer to Thesiger's superlative image of the Rawashid as 'the purest race in the world'. Ever since the first Western travellers came to Arabia, they had been looking for the most remote, most empirical landscape, certain that they would find there Bedouin who retained their 'original purity', uncorrupted by any outside influence. They wanted to believe, as apparently Thesiger did, that each 'nation' had its own collective identity which should remain untainted by contact with others. Of the celebrated Swiss traveller Burckhart, born in 1784, Kathryn Tidrick has written: 'He believed that the Bedouin of the remotest desert ... had kept their national characteristics over millennia, giving them a special claim on the admiration of Europe. He seems to have supposed, like Niebuhr and with as little evidence, that the remoter Bedouin of the peninsula, the ones, so to speak, over the next sand dune, were paragons of bravery, patriotism and honour ... The true Bedouin was a mirage which danced tantalizingly before his eyes and those of many travellers after him.'[60]

One such traveller was surely Wilfred Thesiger, who, comparing the Rawashid with the great and famous Bedouin tribes of the north, such as the Anaza and Rwalla, wrote that 'his Rashid' had had far less contact with towns and therefore were 'more authentic Bedu'. This is another facet of the illusion – for the Rawashid were frequently to be found in Salalah, and the towns along the Mahra coast, and had close contacts with the Hadhramaut. The Bedu of Dhofar, including the Rawashid, bought dried sardines in Salalah during the summer to feed their livestock, and indeed were so dependent on this practice that the King was able to exert some control over them by threat of a 'sardine blockade'.[61] Although technically unadministered as Thesiger claimed, they did pay taxes to the King.

Certainly there was jealousy between the tribes. Sultan was furious that Thesiger had brought the Rawashid to Salalah, since the first part of his planned route to the Hadhramaut lay through Bayt Kathir territory. He and the other Kathir Sheikhs felt that the Englishman should have arranged for the Rawashid to meet him at the border of their tribal land, which was the Wadi Shu'ait. While the Bayt Kathir owed allegiance to bin Taimur, King of Muscat and Oman, the Rawashid acknowledged the Sa'udi King, Ibn Sa'ud, as their overlord. However, when Sultan consulted the King, who happened to be in Salalah at the time, bin Taimur counselled patience: 'There is nothing to stop the Rawashid escorting the Christian,' he said, 'but you will be the guide in your own country, Sheikh Sultan.'[62] Accordingly, Thesiger's caravan set out on 19 January up through the Wadi Garzaz, with Sultan as guide, about twenty-two Rawashid including bin al Kamam, and some *rabi'as* from the Mahra and Manahil tribes which they would meet farther to the west in the British East Aden Protectorate.

Rabi'a literally means 'companion' in Arabic, but in this case refers to the custom in southern Arabia then of taking a kind of 'voluntary hostage' from the local tribe to frank a travelling party through its borders. The local tribe were honour bound not to

attack a party including one of their own, and the *rabi'a* himself
had to swear an oath to protect his companions. To attack them
after this was the most abject disgrace, leading to ostracism by the
tribe. The energetic bin Tafl was also with him, as well as
Sultan's son, Nashran. 'We three Bayt Kathir ate with the Christian,' Nashran recalled, 'and the fires of the Rawashid were all
around us. We stayed with him because the King told us he was
in our special protection.'[63]

The caravan slowly descended from the Qarra mountains into the
broken plains of the Sieh, climbing in and out of wadis where the
sheer cliffs had been smashed and shattered by the passage of
water over aeons into giant blocks, eaten out like slices of Gruyère
cheese, frozen perpetually in the process of crashing to the wadi
floor. The wadis were remarkably green, with their islands of
palmetto and flat-topped thorn-trees thrusting out of the seams of
sand and stones. The daily rhythm of the march varied little from
the earlier journey. In the evenings the camels would be sent out
to graze, then brought into the camp and hobbled near by before
the Bedu retired. In the mornings, after tea with sugar and bitter
coffee, Thesiger would set off to outwalk the Bedu: 'He could ride
a camel well,' Nashran remembered, 'but he preferred to walk
until sun was high, by which time everyone else would be riding,
except my father, Sultan. There was a rivalry between them to
see who would ride first. My father used to say to the others:
"This Christian is worth ten of you!" The Christian was a brave
man and a generous one. His only fault was that he used to get
angry very often, but then he would quickly forget it again. He
would be hospitable to guests, and on that journey we had quite a
lot of food. We had butter, oil, sugar, flour, dates – we lacked
nothing. Also he would buy goats for us and every two days he
would slaughter two – just between the four of us, my father
Sultan, bin Tafl, the Christian and myself – so there was always
plenty of meat.'[64] Moving slowly, the caravan passed beneath
mushroom-topped plinths of limestone with sweeping skirts, and
watered at Mudhay and then at the palm-oasis of Habarut,
where they came into contact with men of the Mahra – the large
Bedu tribe which dominated the region between the Dhofar
mountains and the Wadi Hadhramaut. The Mahra were hostile

to Thesiger's men. In this part of southern Arabia, every tribe belonged to one of two factions – the Hinawis or the Ghafaris. The Kathir tribes, to which the Bayt Kathir and the Rawashid belonged, were Hinawis, while the Mahra, like the Qarra, were Ghafaris. These terms were but a recent version of the ancient antipathy between the so-called 'true Arabs' and 'adopted Arabs' which had riven the peninsula since the earliest times. At Habarut some young braves of the Mahra talked darkly of preventing the Christian from crossing their territory, but at sunrise Thesiger sent his tribesmen to occupy the well and the surrounding hills. There was no trouble.

Shortly afterwards, the caravan reached the Wadi Khawat. It was there that Thesiger met the boy who, for the rest of his time in Arabia, would fill the emotional role which in the Sudan had been occupied by Idris: Salim bin Kabina. 'We spent the night there in Khawat,' Nashran recalled, 'and watered from a pool. Bin Kabina came down with his goats and he had a camel with him to take water back to his family. He was about fifteen years old – younger than me, anyway. Mbarak, the Christian, went to talk to him and bin Kabina said he would come back in the morning, which he did. Mbarak said to my father, "I want this boy, Salim, to travel with me as my assistant." My father said, "All right." Bin Kabina got a camel and came with us. It was a good camel, an Omani camel. We took our water and went.'65 Bin Kabina was the half-brother of a Bedouin already riding with Thesiger, Muhammad bin Salih, known as 'bin Kalut', whose father, Salih bin Kalut, had been Thomas's guide. 'We were watering camels in a wadi,' Thesiger said, 'and I remember he came up wearing this red loincloth and he had this long hair. He asked if he could come with me, and I asked the Sheikhs and they said he would be useful to me, so I said yes, if he could get a rifle and a camel.'66

Bin Kabina's account differs slightly from Thesiger's. 'I met the Christian, Mbarak, first in the Wadi Khawat,' he recalled, 'and he asked me if I would go with him for two riyals a day. I was a bit afraid at first, because I'd never met an Englishman before. I didn't want to go with him. I asked the others what they thought and they said yes, why don't you go, it is a good chance for you. My family and bin al Kamam persuaded me. So I bought a big, fat she-camel with no teeth, for sixty riyals. When we got to Habarut I sold her for forty-six riyals. I lost fourteen riyals on it, but I made up the loss later by buying other camels. I went off with the Christian the next day.'[67] According to Thesiger, he had arrived at an opportune time in bin Kabina's life. The youth had recently ridden to Salalah to fetch a load of dried sardines to feed to his goats, and on the way back his only camel had died. Without a camel he would have been unable to bring water to his flock in the cool season, when they pastured up to ten days away from the wells.

Bin Kabina provided the personal note that Thesiger's first months with the Bedouin had lacked. Though always in a noisy crowd, he had been intensely lonely. In later years Thesiger would admit that after all, it was not 'the Bedu' or even the Rawashid who attracted him, but individuals such as bin Kabina, a yearning for whose company brought him back constantly to a particular country: 'It's not the people as a whole that draw me back,' he said. 'I don't feel that I must be back with the Turkana or the Rashid. It's individuals who draw me back – there might be four or five of them or there might be more – with whom I want to spend my life. I don't know why I feel attached to certain people. Why does anybody feel attracted to anyone else? Why does a man choose his wife? I'm not saying there is anything sexual in it, but certainly you have this feeling of love for them and there you are.'[68]

Like Thesiger's relationship with Idris, his association with bin Kabina was platonic. Homosexuality is widespread among Arab townsmen, but among the Bedu it is unknown: the very subject is taboo, and the mere mention of it would be enough to bring daggers out. To Thesiger, bin Kabina was simply a personal companion. The question is how, in such a tightly-knit community as the Bedu, the other Bedouin interpreted the relationship between this Englishman and a boy twenty years his junior? Bin Kabina was not taken on as a fighting man, for although, of course, all Bedouin youths were considered 'rifles' from the age of puberty, Thesiger already had a large contingent of troops. To most, then, it seemed obvious that bin Kabina was taken on as a personal assistant: bin Tafl, Nashran, and another Kathiri, Sa'id bin Muhammad, all used the word *farrash* to describe bin Kabina's role, a word meaning literally 'one who spreads a rug, an errand boy or assistant'.[69] 'Mbarak told bin Kabina he wanted him to be his *farrash*,' Nashran said. 'Like a companion, an assistant. That didn't mean he had to do all the work. I used to saddle the Christian's camel myself, and bin Tafl did the cooking.'[70] 'Bin Kabina used to help Mbarak in everything,' Sa'id said. 'His family were very poor and so the Christian took him on as *farrash*.'[71] 'Bin Kabina was Mbarak's *farrash*,' bin Tafl commented, 'and as far as I know he was paid two riyals instead of four because he was only a boy.'[72]

Thesiger rejected any suggestion of a master-servant relationship with bin Kabina, however: 'It's nonsense,' he said. 'I don't even know what a *farrash* is. I've never even heard the word. They might have thought this the first time bin Kabina was with me, yes, but there was no question of bin Kabina being a servant or being paid. He wouldn't have risked his life for me under those circumstances. The last thing in the world I wanted was a master-servant relationship with the Bedu. I am horrified to know that they even thought of it.'[73]

Soon they crossed the Wadi Shu'ait into the territory of the Rawashid, and Sultan fell behind to let a Rawashid guide, Awadh bin Khazai, take his place. According to Nashran, bin Khazai and the rest of the Rawashid wanted to halt for the night in their own tents and leave in the morning: 'The Christian said, "I didn't come all the way from London to stay here – I want to get going,"' he recalled. 'So we went off alone, just him and us three Bayt Kathir. None of the Rawashid went with him. We halted further on and Mbarak asked if anyone knew the way to Sanaw, and I told him, yes, I know the way, because I have watered the camels there. He said, "Good, tomorrow we will go to Sanaw, then we'll find someone and offer him a rifle to take us on." Anyway, in the morning my father rode back to persuade the Rawashid to go with us, and they did.'[74]

From here they entered the country which is today part of Yemen and is simply called Mahra. Rich grazing land, almost semi-desert scrub in some places, stands in patches among ochre-brown buttes and blocks that seem to have been hacked out with a giant axe. Between them numerous dry-washes wander, coils of green standing out like veins on the pale parchment of the sand

and the chocolate of the hills. Few Rawashid live in this region today: most migrated to Sa'udi Arabia or Oman under the former Communist government. Their place has been taken by the Mahra, a tribe including both nomadic and settled elements. Despite their Land-Cruisers, the Mahra still range across this desolate landscape, some living in tents like Red Indian wigwams woven from palm fibre. In 1946, though, rain had fallen on the Mahra pastures, and Thesiger's party found them alive with Bedu, mostly from the Manahil, a friendly tribe occupying the same niche in Yemen as the Bayt Kathir occupied in Oman. From them, Thesiger's men heard rumours of a large raiding-party of the Daham – Arabs from the Jauf desert far beyond the Hadhramaut. From here on Thesiger posted scouts, and his men were constantly on the alert. They watered at Sanaw, and the following morning picked up the tracks of a raiding-party. Thesiger's scouts followed the tracks a little way, but found nothing. Two days later, as they lay up in the Wadi Hanq, a party of Manahil approached them and protested that if anyone was to guide the Christian through their territory it should be Manahil. The Rawashid resisted: 'They argued and argued and argued,' Nashran recalled. 'They were shouting with rage. My father sided with them, saying the Rawashid were in the wrong and that this was Manahil country.'[75] Thesiger finally agreed to take four of the Manahil along.

They watered again among low gypsum hills at Mughair, where there had been fighting between the tribes a year previously. For some reason the dead had not been buried, and Thesiger picked up a sun-polished skull and concealed it as an anthropological specimen. Nashran noticed his interest in the object: 'He looked at it, considered it, I thought he was looking for writing on it. I don't know if he took it because I was too busy looking after the camels, but if they'd seen him take it the Manahil might have been angry.'[76] It was here that the Rawashid found the tracks of the Daham raiders, whose rumour had caused alarm in the steppes. The trackers reckoned the raiding-party forty-five strong, and later Thesiger's party followed the trail of destruction it had left in its wake. In one place the Daham had shot down two Manahil herdsmen and lifted fifteen camels. Almost every available man had grabbed his rifle, jumped on his camel and gone off in pursuit. 'In another place they'd taken all the camels except three that were mangy,' Nashran recalled. 'They had slaughtered eight goats to eat, and milked others straight into their mouths: they had even raped some of the women, who were crying when we arrived. That was a disgrace! Their men had been following the Daham for a couple of days, and when the women saw us they thought we were more Daham raiders, because some of the Rawashid dressed in long-sleeved *gandourahs* like they did. Our *rabi'a* from the Manahil rode forward and threw sand in the air, a sign that we were peaceful.'[77] They watered again in Thamud from a stone-lined well sunk fifty feet into the bedrock, today lost in a desert shanty-town of the type that would have disgusted Thesiger: broken-down Communist-built blocks, and a graveyard of rusted machinery. They pressed on through green country of riffling grasses and tall acacia trees to Halayya, the last important well before the Hadhramaut, where Thesiger intended to buy some goats.

At Halayya, the well lay near a few palms by a ruined fort between thick thornscrub and an open plain dotted with white hills of gypsum. At the well today smiling Manahil boys screech to a halt in Land-Cruisers they are too small to drive, and water tumbles up refreshingly from the barrel of a rusted electric pump.

From two old crones of the Manahil, Thesiger purchased a brace of goats. At sunset, when the camels were grazing peacefully in the scrub, he watched the Rawashid making the prostrations of the sunset prayer, enjoying a moment of perfect tranquillity. Suddenly somebody screamed, 'There's a raiding-party behind that hill!' and the Rawashid broke off from their prayers and began to run for cover. Pandemonium ensued. 'I saw some Arabs rushing towards us out of the plain,' Nashran remembered. 'There were fifteen of them on camels. "There they are! There they are!" somebody shouted, and Mbarak and my father and bin Khazai all grabbed their rifles, while I ran to get our camels. They fired at us once or twice and we fired back.'[78]

The first bin Tafl knew of the attack was when the camels roared, and he looked up in astonishment to see a party of Arabs pounding flat out towards him. Having no doubt they were after his party's own camels, he flung himself down and drew a deadly accurate bead on the leading rider. Thesiger saw bin Kabina leaping off to guard the camels with bin Tafl, and called him back. As the mounted men raced towards them, he plumped down next to bin al Kamam. 'Fire in front of them!' the Sheikh shouted. 'We don't know who they are!' Thesiger whanged off five rounds which kicked up spouts of dust in front of the raiders. Bin Kabina's rifle bolt clicked vacantly three times and Thesiger registered the look of frustration on the boy's face. The raiders quickly took cover under a low ridge and more shots rang out, then the firing ceased: 'They realized we were Mishqas from Dhofar,' Nashran said. 'Anyway, one of the Manahil with us got up and walked forwards, and one of them stood up and there were suddenly shouts of Health! Health! Health upon you! They were Manahil who'd been chasing the Daham, and thought we were Daham. We brought them over and the Christian slaughtered the goats for them.'[79]

From Halayya they traversed the shattered, rocky country and tramped down into a tributary of great Wadi Hadhramaut, where suddenly they were in civilization. Here, enclosed by sheer cliffs sometimes forty miles apart, were great cities whose origins lay back in the mists of history. Vast fortresses and block-houses stood on the cliffs, 400 feet above them; shy women wearing sweeping black robes and odd-looking witches'-hats of straw tended goats. Muscular brown boys – looking more Indonesian than Arab, with their jet black hair and smooth cocoa-coloured skin – ploughed rocky fields with their ploughs yoked to camels. Men with faces white like clowns pounded gypsum into lime. Soon the Bedu came to the ancient town of Tarim, with its great mud-built mansions and galleries of tiny windows, locking in shady, dust-laden streets. Despite the vast distance from here to Dhofar, there had always been close cultural contacts between the two regions, and many of the tribes were related, though Thesiger emphasized the distinction between the 'soft' townsmen, and the virile 'wild men' of the desert. In Tarim they were shown rich hospitality by some rich Sayids – descendants of the Prophet Muhammad – a fact that belied the supposed miserliness of settled Arabs. 'We were staying with these Sayids, mostly in Tarim,' Thesiger said. 'I found it very interesting, with these huge houses and narrow streets, but I was sorry I hadn't been there a few years earlier before Ingrams had got there and imposed a degree of peace. The people didn't compare with the Bedu, of course.'[80] Thesiger had not intended Tarim to be the end of the journey. He had already agreed secretly with three of the Rawashid – including bin Kabina – to cross the Sands to Sulayil in Sa'udi Arabia. He had collected detailed information about the wells in the steppes which could be used as a kicking-off point, and chosen one called al 'Abr from which to begin the great adventure. The wells were in the country of the Se'ar – a tribe hostile to his Rawashid – but this did not deter Thesiger. He learned that these Se'ar were in the habit of crossing the Sands to raid the Dawaasir, a Bedu tribe living on the opposite side, and made the waterless journey in sixteen days. However, there was a snag: Ibn Sa'ud. In Tarim Thesiger learned that the Sa'udi King had emphatically refused him permission to enter his country by this route. Thesiger swallowed his disappointment and decided to regard this first year as a training-run. He was secretly determined to come back for another attempt on the Sands. If he had not found locust outbreak-centres, he had at least gathered a great bagful of the insects for Vesey-Fitzgerald, though his specimens were rather the worse for wear after their jolting across the steppes. He was unsure whether the Anti-Locust Unit would sponsor further exploration. If he should cross the Sands, he decided, it would be in the company of the 'noble' Rawashid, who had taken Thomas – both a practical and a romantic decision, for the Rawashid guide, Salih bin Kalut, had got Thomas across when the year previously the Bayt Kathir had failed him.

He paid his men off at Tarim and watched them leading their camels back towards the rocky gorges of the Mahra country, feeling suddenly very alone. His loneliness was alleviated by the knowledge that now he had got to know the Bedu, the way across the Sands would, by hook or by crook, be smoothed for him. It had taken two months to reach the Hadhramaut from Salalah but the Bedu rode back in a month, showing how fast they were able to move when not being paid by the day. Bin Kabina rode with them but Musallim bin Tafl did not. He cadged a ride from an RAF plane returning to Salalah, and so became the first airborne Bedouin in the history of his tribe.

CHAPTER 10

Conditions Where Only the Best Could Survive

One evening in Qunfidhah, on the Tihama or Red Sea Coast of Sa'udi Arabia, Thesiger sat by a blazing fire with George Popov, a young officer of the Anti-Locust Unit, in charge of the detachment there. Popov was listening with riveted attention as Thesiger described how the Bayt Kathir had consumed most of his stores before even starting the journey, leaving him to live on 'a sack of flour and a few bundles of dates' and how the Duru' had threatened they would allow no Christian through their land, when to Popov's amazement Thesiger jumped up, screaming, 'Kill it! Kill it! I hate it!' 'I almost thought the Duru' were about to massacre him!' Popov recalled. 'In fact it was one of those great camel-spiders, and Wilfred hated them. I was very much in awe of him and this made him more human to me, because I'd already been bitten by one – they do have a nasty bite, though it's not poisonous – and I wasn't afraid.'[1]

After bin Tafl had taken off for Salalah, Thesiger had hitched a lift to Aden and flown to Jiddah, hefting his bag of locust specimens. The information he had collected on locusts was largely negative, though it could scarcely have been said that he had put all his time and energy into studying them – he was not, he admitted, much interested in locusts. How accurate was Thesiger's information? George Popov – like Uvarov a Russian expatriate – recalled: 'He came back with quite a lot of specimens, but they were rather crushed and damaged. He did have his Bedu jumping around catching locusts, which he brought back in a bag and dumped on Boris Uvarov's desk.'[2] Popov commented, though, that Thesiger had actually discovered something of immense importance: namely that the Empty Quarter was not the barren monster it was once believed to be. On his preliminary journey in 1929, Bertram Thomas had written of the Empty Quarter: 'Its

sterility is of a peculiarly prohibitive kind.'³ If this were entirely
true, of course, no one would have been able to live there. While
places such as Mughshin might suffer from years of drought, in
Ghanim near by the vegetation might at the same time be
astoundingly rich. The rain was sporadic and showers scattered.
Rain would fall somewhere almost every year, though it would be
unlikely for the same place to get rain two years running. The
Bedu were nomads precisely because they had learned to adapt to
this unpredictable pattern of rainfall.

Thesiger spent only a few days in the Anti-Locust HQ in Jiddah,
where he asked permission from King Ibn Sa'ud to visit the
mountains of the Hejaz and the baking mud-flats of the Tihama as
far as the Assir – the fertile corner of Sa'udi Arabia. Popov was
asked to help provide him with camels. 'We had a few tents,'
Popov remembered, 'but often we slept out round the fire. I was
very much a "chick" then and quite impressed with Thesiger.'⁴
Born in Tehran, Popov was a fluent Persian-speaker and noticed
Thesiger's approval of the effort he was making to learn Arabic:
'His own Arabic was very good,' Popov recalled, 'except that he
did have this very strong English accent that you could hear
clearly. His vocabulary and things were excellent, but – as far as I
could judge anyway – he didn't speak it like a native.'⁵ Another
memory Popov had of Thesiger's stay was that he would take his
guest for spins along the coastal mud-flats in his jeep: 'He would
spend the whole journey complaining about the jeep and its
smell, saying how it was hostile to the Arab way of life and the
thin end of the wedge,' Popov remembered. 'I got a bit fed up
with it, and I stopped the jeep and asked him, "Would you rather
walk?" '⁶ Thesiger declined. 'He was seeing things collapsing and
he was running after the last vestiges of a way of life that was
disappearing,' Popov commented. 'He couldn't forgive technology
for invading the traditional ways of the Bedu. My own view was
that you can't turn back the clock. I didn't feel bad about it in
any way because it wasn't that the Bedu were fighting desperately
to the end to hang on to their old way of life. They welcomed all
this. I think he admired the Bedu and seemed to prefer their
company but I didn't feel he was a man of great human warmth.
I had the impression of a man who was determined to have his

way and didn't particularly care about other people or what they thought of him.'[7]

Starting from the Wadi Ahsaba, north of Qunfidhah, with the statutory guard from the King's levies, a Sharifi servant and two camel-men, Thesiger set out with four hired camels to trek south as far as the Yemen border, back via the Assir capital, Abha, and the mountain fortress-town of Taif. Here was a way of camel-trekking vastly different from that of the southern Bedu. The camels were ponderous animals fitted with large pack-saddles, and capable of shifting astounding weights. They padded along strung head to tail in caravan formation, muzzled with masks of netting and constantly hand-fed on sorghum stalks. Unlike the hardy camels of the desert they were watered at least once a day, and in the sticky heat of the coast the Arabs preferred to travel at night, curled up atop their baggage asleep, while the beasts followed the paths automatically. Thesiger quickly put a stop to this, for travelling at night was of no use for his observations.

If the going contrasted distinctly with his experience in the desert, so did the environment. His party wandered through the Hejazi foothills, through boulder-strewn valleys where they encountered hordes of donkey-borne villagers on their way to one weekly souk or another. They passed through dense palmeries and fields of rich soil sown with sorghum, sesame and bull-rush millet. They rode through villages of flat-topped stone houses, where the crops were watered by streams gushing down from the hills. The people appeared very different from the Bedu of the south – clad in decorated *dishdashas*, some wearing scented herbs in their hair or high-crowned straw sombreros as large as umbrellas. In the broken granite country between the mountains and the coastal plains he encountered the local Bedu, who seemed a sorry contrast to their namesakes in Dhofar. They tilled postage-stamp patches of wheat and sorghum and herded cattle, sheep, goats and a few camels, skulking in mat shelters with string beds as furniture. John Glubb had asserted that 'Bedu' signified only the noble, camel-breeding nomads of Arabia, yet his encounters with these semi-sedentary, cattle-breeding Bedouin led Thesiger to disagree. No one could dispute their claim to 'nobility', at least in genealogical terms, for among them were remnants of the most famous of all Arab tribes – the Bani Hilal, whose forefathers had swept out of Egypt in 1052 and conquered most of North Africa, and the Bani Qahtan, whose ancestor is tabled in the Old Testament as Joktan or Qahtan, the sire of all true Arabs. Once noted for banditry, these tribes had been cowed by the authority of the indomitable Ibn Sa'ud.

From the plateau Thesiger pitched down into the Tihama, through date and dom-palm groves concealing villages of cone-shaped grass almost like those in the Sudan. The Tihama people were very different in behaviour from the reserved and dignified Bedu of the south. 'They seemed totally un-Arabian,' Thesiger said. 'They lived in these houses that seemed African, walked about with flowers in their hair and were always singing and dancing and were very easy to get on with. They lacked the Bedu reserve.'[8] He found them inhospitable and uncouth by the more severe standards of the Bedouin, and despite his preference for the formal and the ceremonial, he was attracted by the delicate, effeminate beauty of the youths and children, and admitted that his earlier tantalizing glimpses of these smiling people in 1945 had lured him back. This counterpoint between the formal and informal, the gay and carefree and the rigidly disciplined, is another aspect of the essentially contradictory nature of Thesiger's response to foreign peoples. Here, he contrasted the 'laughing' people of the Tihama against the 'stern, dour puritans' of the Nejd with apparent approval. Later he would contrast the 'laughing' yet uncouth Turkana against the grim Arabs of the Yemen hills. He would tell Timothy Green: 'The Bedu when I first knew them were a laughing, happy community. Elspeth Huxley has pointed out that the thing we have driven out of Africa is laughter. I agree with her. I doubt if you get the kind of laughter in the slums of Johannesburg or Nairobi that you can still get among the Samburu of northern Kenya.'[9] Ten years later he rejected the idea of the Arab sense of humour, saying he believed in reality that they had no more sense of humour than himself. 'And I always think that I've got none,' he commented.[10]

His camels bowled with easy grace along the old Turkish road up to Abha – the capital of the Assir – winding through fields of wheat and barley and orchards of apricots, peaches, plums and figs. Above them watchtowers reared like eyes on stalks, fluted with projecting ridges of tiles like pylons from some eerie science-fiction scene. In Abha itself Thesiger was thrilled by the mix of peoples, the faces, the matrix of colours in the women's dresses. There were the slender, coffee-coloured men of the Tihama, Bedu from the Nejd in their camel's-hair cloaks, mountain Arabs with their garlands of herbs and straw hats, Yemenis with their tight-bound headcloths and great curved daggers. The yammering crowds ebbed and flowed around stalls stocked with coffee, grain, butter and wild honey, spices, henna, whitewash, baskets, ropes, cloth and goatskins. He was quartered as a guest in the 'Amir's palace overlooking the market, a labyrinth of ancient passages and staircases. 'I was staying with the 'Amir,' he recounted, 'and said I'd been living in the Empty Quarter and the 'Amir asked me why on earth I wanted to go there, with people who were no better than savages, who don't pray and don't fast. His people were running down the Bedu and then they shifted a bit and started talking about generosity and in no time they were praising Bedu hospitality, and by the end of the evening there they were holding up as paragons the very people they'd been running down. They started quoting poetry and the heroes they were talking about were all Bedu!'[11]

The Arabs, like Thesiger himself, were riddled with contradictions, one of the most important being the contrast between the ancient Arab tradition of literary civilization, exalting a knowledge of Islam and classical Arabic literature, and that of the Bedouin code, representing the ideals of austerity, endurance, justice and hospitality. Many Arabian royal families sent their literate sons to spend some time with Bedouin tribes in the desert, so that they might be schooled in both traditions. Foreigners such as Glubb had tried to make rigid lines of demarcation between 'Bedu', 'Arabs' and 'Hadr' (townsmen), building out of Arab society a class-system which reflected their own. In fact one tradition flowed into the other in an unceasing impulse. Lawrence's famous passage about the cyclical nature of nomadism emphasizes this: 'The border people were flung out of the furthest crazy oasis into the untrodden wilderness as nomads ... we see them wandering every year a little further north or a little further east as chance has sent them down one or other of the well-roads of the wilderness, till finally this pressure drives them from the desert again into the sown, with the like unwillingness of their first shrinking experiment in nomad life. This was the circulation which kept the vigour in the Semitic body. There were few, if indeed there was a single northern Semite, whose ancestors had not at some dark age passed through the desert. The mark of nomadism, that most deep and biting social discipline, was on each of them in his degree.'[12]

From Abha, halting each night in the villages of great block-houses whose projecting tiles presented the same unworldly images as the eerie watchtowers, Thesiger visited Sabiya, near the Yemen border. Once the capital of an autonomous state, it had been destroyed by Ibn Sa'ud's Bedouin armies in 1933. He then rode back to Abha and exchanged his camels for donkeys, for a hard slog across the Hejaz mountains to Taif. The going was rough, and Thesiger was forced to walk on bare feet when his sandals disintegrated on the way. Parts of the mountains were barren; in others ice-cold rivulets ribbled down hillsides wooded with olive and juniper, decked with pink and white blossoms, and tumbled into fields of barley and golden wheat in the valleys below. Near the summit of the Hejaz range, 9,000 feet above the plains, Thesiger halted for a moment, taking in the breathtaking panorama. His gaze drifted involuntarily over to the east. There, beyond the heat-haze that concealed the desert, lived the Bedu of the Sands, with whom, for a few months, he had lived an exciting, tense, challenging life. He would have given all the beauty and ease of the lush fields and forests to have been with them at this moment.

He arrived in Taif on 24 June, having covered the 300 miles from Abha in only sixteen days, mostly on foot. Since leaving Qunfidhah in April, he had trekked 1,000 miles: 'And that was a holiday for Thesiger!' Popov commented.[13] His party rode into the city at sunset – a government guard, Thesiger's Sharifi servant, and three Yemenis they had encountered on the way. They hired a room in an inn for pilgrims on their way to Mecca, a spartan cell which opened on to a small courtyard. He and his men set to sweeping it out, unrolled their mats and rugs, and lit an oil-lamp. Someone went out to the souk and came back with meat grilled on charcoal, ovals of fresh bread, sour milk, water-melons and grapes. After they had eaten, pilgrims from the neighbouring cells invaded the room and filled the dickering shadows with talk. It was a scene from Richard Burton which Thesiger relished. He felt utterly contented after his long and arduous half-barefoot journey from Abha. But his contentment was not to last much longer. In the morning he called on the Governor of Taif, a nephew of the grandson of Ibn Sa'ud. 'I'd hoped to stay in some comfort with him in his home,' Thesiger said, 'instead of which I was put in a sort of modern hotel, and left it the next day. There were waiters and tomato sauce on the table – that disappointed me.'[14] Waiters, tomato sauce and tinned food broke the magical spell that had allowed him to imagine he was back in Burton's day. Cars, jeeps and Dodge pick-ups were criss-crossing the old camel-trails in the desert. Out there, oil was pouring out of the Ghawar field, and already there were 'Pioneer camps' of Yankee roustabouts in the desert who cared nothing for the 'old ways'.

From Jiddah Thesiger flew to London, and rushed round to talk to Uvarov at the Natural History Museum as soon as he arrived: 'I told him that though the stuff I'd got was negative, the place I thought the locusts might breed was where the quicksands of Umm as Samim were reported to be,' he said. 'There, you got these high Omani mountains and there must have been far more water going down off them than you got to Mughshin from the Dhofar mountains. I said if you get any outbreak-centres it will be where Wadi Al 'Ain and the rest of the wadis come off the Omani mountains. I said why don't you send me down and I'll find out.'[15] Despite his apparent confidence, Thesiger knew that the region in question was even more inaccessible than the Empty Quarter itself. In northern Oman the edge of the Arabian peninsula warps and buckles into a spectacular mass of interlocking plateaux, with gnarled and fluted sides, rising up to the majestic trunk of Jabal al Akhdar, at almost 10,000 feet. Among the humps and corries of these mountains nestle mud-built hamlets in palm-clumps, watered by narrow feeder-canals called *falaj(es)* centuries old. Wadis with permanent trickles of silver water thread through palm-groves as vast and verdant as tropical jungles, dominated in some places by great fairy-tale castles, the same bullet-blue as the hills themselves. In the rainy season torrents surge down from the mountains, frothing across great parallel bars of wadis and feeding into the sump quicksand of Umm as Samim. The presence of an unknown quicksand in south Arabia had been rumoured ever since the Bavarian soldier, von Wrede, had wandered through the Hadhramaut disguised as an Arab in 1843. He claimed to have discovered a quicksand called the Bahr as Safi in the desert to the north, and recounted that he had sunk a plumb-line there which had immediately been sucked in and swallowed up by the mud. Von Wrede's story was certainly a fabrication, for the Umm as Samim is the only quicksand in the whole of Arabia, and it is hundreds of miles away from the Hadhramaut. Thomas had been the first European to report its existence, having heard of it from many Bedu on his crossing of the Sands in 1930: 'In appearance a sheet of salt plain,' he wrote, 'it gives no indication to the unwary traveller of its treacherous bogs. Many have perished here and only certain Duru' Badus who come to collect salt on its borders are said to brave its secret passages.'[16] The Duru' were the problem. They owed allegiance not to bin Taimur, Sultan of Muscat, but to the real ruler of Inner Oman. 'Nominally Sultan bin Taimur, in Muscat, was in control of the country,' Thesiger explained, 'but in practice he had no control of that area at all. The whole of the northern interior was ruled by Imam Muhammad al Khalili, in Nezwa.'[17] It was precisely for this reason, Uvarov explained, that the Sultan had already refused the Anti-Locust Unit permission to pass through Duru' territory: 'Uvarov had tried to get me permission,' Thesiger said, 'not to go into the Sands but into Duru' country – the steppes to the east – which had governors and things in places like Ibri. They weren't the Sultan's governors, of course, but the Imam's. The Sultan absolutely refused me permission because that would have started trouble with the Imam, who would have been furious that he had allowed a European in his country. The Sultan had authority in Mughshin which was accepted as being his. Uvarov's idea was not that I should go through the Sands, but that I should go through the plains and see where these big wadis ended. I knew from my first journey that it was doubtful I'd be able to get in that way, because the Duru' were already saying after I'd got near their country the previous year that they'd kill any Christian who came into their land.'[18] Thesiger considered the problem for a moment: 'Will you ask the Sultan for permission for me to go back to Mughshin?' he inquired. 'If you do that, I'll cross the Sands there and come down through Duru' country. You can leave it to me: but don't for goodness' sake mention anywhere but Mughshin.'

Uvarov hesitated, deep in thought. Thesiger knew that his entire future lay in the balance of those few moments. There was silence for what seemed an eternity. Then Uvarov said quietly, 'All right. I'll ask if you can go back and do some more investigation at Mughshin and the Sands around it.'

Thesiger almost literally heard the key go 'snick' in the ancient, rusted lock. The Empty Quarter was his.

On his flight back to Salalah, though, he was preoccupied with the problem of explaining to the Bayt Kathir that he intended to cross the Sands. They were the Sultan's Arabs, and if bin Taimur learned of Thesiger's secret plan through them, his steel glove would come crashing down on the venture. Thesiger wanted to take only the sand-wandering Rawashid, as he had planned earlier, but since he was the guest of the Sultan it would have been impossible to exclude the Bayt Kathir. He did not know that, before his previous journey, the Sultan himself had ordered them not to take him beyond their tribal frontier. He landed in Salalah on 16 October and found that the Wali had provided an escort of twenty-four Bayt Kathir, including his old friends Sultan, bin Tafl, Mabkhaut, and a youth called Sa'id, who was to be his guide to the limits of Bayt Kathir territory, Ramlat al Ghafa. Sa'id was the son of the Sheikh of the Bayt Musann, the only section of the Bayt Kathir who grazed camels in the Sands. Thesiger laid in stores that would last the party three months: 2,000 pounds of flour, 500 of rice, liquid butter, dates, sugar, coffee and tea. Having learned his lesson about Bedu improvidence the previous season, he prudently held some in reserve when he distributed the rations. Then he turned his attention to finding bin Kabina and the Rawashid. He ruled out asking Sultan or bin Tafl to help him because there had been friction the previous year over the idea of Rawashid escorting him through Bayt Kathir land. Yet he must have the Rawashid if he was to cross the Sands. He was wandering in the small market one day, at his wits' end, when he happened across a small, almost fragile-looking youth with a permanent scowl, called 'Amair bin 'Omar. Thesiger disliked 'Amair, who had been with him on the journey to the Hadhramaut, yet he was a Rashidi of the same section as bin Kabina, the Bayt Imani. Here was his solution. 'The Christian found me in the market,' 'Amair recalled, 'and asked me if I knew where bin Kabina and bin al Kamam were. I told him bin Kabina was somewhere in Mahra country, and that bin al Kamam was still in the Yemen making peace between the tribes. He asked me to take a message to bin Kabina to meet him at Shisur, and I agreed to do it as long as he promised to take me wherever he was going.'[19]

Thesiger's party of Bayt Kathir rode out of Salalah on 25 October, their camels' feet crunching on the gravelly plain of the Jerbib, with the mountains, cloaked in mist, looming before them. At last, Thesiger felt, he was off to cross the Empty Quarter by a route no other European had dared. He was filled with excitement, but troubled too, knowing that his success would depend on a number of variable factors, not least of them the presence of the Rawashid. His immediate objective was Ramlat al Ghafa, an area within the belly of the great Sands known both to the Rawashid and the Bayt Musann – a waterless area, but one which provided abundant grazing if there had been rain. His guide was young Sa'id of the Bayt Musann. 'I was the guide as far as the borders of Bayt Kathir territory,' Sa'id recalled, 'despite the fact that I was so young. I'd often been up to Ramlat al Ghafa to visit my people there. The Musann are camel-people and generally we used to herd between Mughshin and Ramlat al Ghafa. Anyway, we went with this Englishman – they called him Sheikh Mbarak later, but his real name was Thesiger, and of course, we just called him "the Christian". He gave us each a rifle – a "Mother of Ten Shots". We travelled very slowly because the tribes wanted to make more money – we'd start quite late in the morning and make camp early. We knew the longer it lasted the more money there would be. It was a tour rather than a fast journey – on our own we used to ride to Ibri from Salalah in eight or nine days. The Englishman was a tough man – in the morning he wouldn't ride at all until the sun was high. His fault was that he didn't really like the Bayt Kathir and wanted to go with the Rawashid. Anyway it was winter, and at midday we'd just stop and make tea for a short time or drink water, without bothering to barrack the camels. In summer we had to barrack the camels at midday because it was too hot to ride through the afternoon. It was as well that we went slowly, because the Bayt Kathir camels were quite weak that year. We thought we could probably get some better camels from the Bayt Musann in Ramlat al Ghafa.'[20] Watering at the pool at 'Ayun and again at Ma Shadid, they passed along the Wadi Ghudun, arriving at Shisur on 6 November.

A couple of weeks earlier, Salim bin Kabina had been at Jabal Bigurdab in Mahra country, helping the Mahra cultivators to harvest sorghum. He was a gaunt, string-muscled youth, with a glittering smile and a long, unkempt shag of hair. Lively, energetic, garrulous, with a penetrating wit, he could be truculent when he so desired. He wore a knee-length loincloth, and owned neither a rifle nor a dagger. Despite his journey with Thesiger earlier in the year, he still had no camel to his name. When a Bayt Kathir tribesman called bin Khiteila arrived from Habarut, therefore, and announced that 'the Christian' had arrived in Salalah and was expecting him, he was filled with excitement. Together, they trekked on foot to the palm-oasis of Habarut, halting for the night with Mahra tribesmen in their wigwam-like tents of palmetto fibre. The Mahra and the Rawashid lived under an armed truce, but the Mahra were Bedu. The travellers could count on their hospitality: a bowl of goat's milk still fresh from the udder, perhaps a plate of sticky dates from the palms at Habarut, a porridge of polenta served with liquid butter, or even fresh goat's meat; a mat or a skin to sleep on, and an evening of entertaining talk over coffee and tea around the hearth. Even had one of the travellers had a blood-feud with his hosts, his sanctity as a guest would have been inviolable. His host would have been obliged to defend him, even against his own family. Entertainment was the host's reward for his hospitality, and though the Mahra would sometimes mutter together in their ancient Himyaritic tongue with its lisping consonants, they spoke Arabic too. Before the Bedu retired, every detail of local news would have been exchanged: whom they had seen, where, which way he was going, for what reason – down to the very tracks of men and animals they had encountered on the road. After four unhurried days of this hospitality, they arrived in Habarut, where bin Kabina found 'Amair waiting for him with Thesiger's message: 'I told him the Christian wanted to meet him at Shisur and the day,' 'Amair recalled, 'and he said "I haven't got a camel." Eventually he hired a she-camel from the Bayt Kathir for forty riyals.'[21]

On 7 November, bin Kabina and six other Rawashid slowly materialized like iridescent smears out of the featureless landscape that surrounds Shisur. Thesiger and his Bayt Kathir stood up, and Sultan, bin Tafl, and the others identified the Rawashid one by one before they had come within several hundred yards. Bin Tafl put a couple of rounds over their heads as a sign of welcome. Bin Kabina couched his hired camel, shouting, 'Peace be on you!' and the Bayt Kathir lined up to greet them formally, exchanging handshakes and the triple nose-kiss. Afterwards, old Salim Tamtaim, the eldest of the Bayt Kathir, inquired: 'Have you any news?' It was a formal question always asked on such an occasion, and was invariably answered 'The news is good, thank God!' by the elder Sheikh of the visitors, in this case a grizzled Rashidi called Mahsin. Then the Bedu knelt down to talk, while a boy poured out coffee for the newcomers and offered dates. 'Later the Christian called me aside,' bin Kabina said, 'and showed me a new dagger he had brought for me. He told me he would lend me a rifle – a "Mother of Ten Shots". I said, "What is your plan?" and he answered, "We are going to Mughshin, across the Sands to Dhafara, and then to Oman, but don't reveal it to the others who don't yet know." Then a word came upon my tongue. I said, "The Bayt Kathir cannot go so far, only the Rawashid can go as far as that."'[22]

Actually, Thesiger did not have a definite plan other than his determination to cross the Empty Quarter. His party, now thirty-one, was far too unwieldy for the expedition he had in mind; the Bayt Kathir camels were weak and the food already spread thin. As he had anticipated, more Rawashid than he had asked for had turned up at Shisur, all hoping for a share in the bounty. Among them were Muhammad, nicknamed al 'Auf ('the Bad') Mahsin, 'Amair, bin Shuwas – the noted hunter who had tracked oryx with him the previous year – and two others. Al 'Auf had not been with Thesiger before. Belonging to the Bayt Mbarik section of the Rawashid rather than the Bayt Imani of bin Kabina, he and his three brothers were famous fighters: one of them had recently been killed battling the Se'ar. 'Al 'Auf was the bravest of men,' Sa'id said. 'He had killed people with his dagger, which takes more courage than shooting them . . . He was from the very best family of his people, all renowned for their bravery.'[23] Mahsin, a middle-aged Bedouin, was an even more celebrated warrior, who had accounted for eight or nine enemies and was enmeshed in a web of blood-feuds. His leg was still badly mauled from a recent clash with the Se'ar and he was constrained to sit with it stretched out in front of him. Thesiger accepted him because of his formidable reputation. He had, as always, wanted a small, compact party, but he was reassured by the presence of the Rawashid. His prejudice against the Bayt Kathir, not missed by the acute Sa'id, was confirmed by bin Kabina's words, and he constantly bore in mind how, when Thomas had passed this way in 1930, the Bayt Kathir had let him down and turned back. As observant as a hawk, Sa'id divined bin Kabina's 'treachery': 'It was bin Kabina who changed his opinion of the Bayt Kathir,' he commented. 'I saw them talking at Shisur, and knew very well what was going on: bin Kabina was saying that the Bayt Kathir could not match the endurance of the Rawashid. He spread bad stories about us to show the Rawashid up in a good light. Thesiger was only concerned with bin Kabina and didn't want to listen to anybody else. I don't know why. The Bayt Imani grew up with us, and they weren't any different.'[24]

Bin Kabina told Thesiger that he was very lucky to have al 'Auf because he was a seasoned guide and knew the eastern Sands. 'I would have been happy to let al 'Auf guide from Shisur,' Thesiger recalled, 'but he said, "Well, I'm a Rashidi, and you know these Bayt Kathir distrust the Rashid." He said let Sa'id go on being the guide as far as he knows, and I'll stay in the background. This wasn't anybody's territory really. In so far as the Bedu had territories, I suppose this was barely Bayt Kathir territory: Al 'Auf was just being tactful.'[25]

From Shisur it took the party eight days to reach Mughshin. On the way, Thesiger slowly tried to accustom his men to the idea that they would be going beyond, either to Umm as Samim, or across the Sands to the north. Just how many of the details he disclosed is not clear. He maintained that Sultan had been party to his plan even before they reached Shisur. 'He did tell me he would take me across the Sands,' Thesiger said. 'It was probably on the way before we reached Shisur, but I couldn't swear to it.'[26] One night, he wrote, he was awoken by an eerie howl and sat up to find Sa'id, his young guide, sitting by the fire with a cloth over his head, thrashing madly from side to side as the others chanted around him. The Bedu said that Sa'id was possessed by a *zaar* or evil spirit, a belief in which is spread all over Arabia and North Africa. Thesiger wrote that Sa'id threw himself about dementedly, chanted in a curiously high-pitched voice, and answered questions like a man in a trance. He eventually calmed down, but sobbed bitterly and groaned throughout the night. In the morning he was back to normal. Years later Sa'id denied emphatically that this had happened. 'There was never any *zaar*,' he said. 'I don't remember anything like that, and if I'd been ill like that I would surely have remembered it. I can't say the Christian exaggerated, I just don't remember anything of the kind happening.'[27]

Mughshin had always possessed an evil reputation among the Bedu. The only truly fertile place in a vast tract of desert, its water and grazing were a magnet for every raiding party which passed through the region. Yet more than this, it was a place bristling with evil spirits, a *hauta* or sacred grove where trees could not be cut down nor game shot. The site of countless battles with the Ma'arab, Thomas's companions had called it 'the Tomb of the Muslims'.[28] It was from Mughshin that Thomas's Bayt Kathir had been attacked by nerves and turned back to Salalah on his first attempt to cross the Empty Quarter. Among them had been Sultan. It seems appropriate that it should have been at Mughshin that disaster almost struck Thesiger's party. 'It was a silly thing really,' bin Tafl remembered. 'One of the camels was carrying the cooking equipment and a pot fell down with a bang, and the camel shied. Then Mahsin's camel next to it bolted, and Mahsin, whose leg was weak, couldn't hold on, and fell. I think his leg was broken. The Christian shouted to me to bring the big box of medicines he carried, and then we dragged Mahsin under a tree – the tree is still there today – and the Christian gave him an injection to lighten his pain.'[29] When Mahsin was more peaceful, the Bedu squatted down for a council to consider what was to be done. It was clear that the accident had changed the situation dramatically. 'It wasn't possible to leave Mahsin alone,' bin Kabina explained. 'He had killed a lot of people – nine or ten people – and it didn't matter that he was wounded. Even if half his body was dead, they'd have come to kill the other half. And it wasn't just blood-feuds: any passing Bedouin might have finished him off just to steal his dagger. We were his cousins and it was our duty to look after him.'[30] Thesiger was perturbed. If the Rawashid remained with Mahsin, he was thrown back on the mercies of the Bayt Kathir, in whom he had less confidence. However, accident or no accident, the party was still too large. He had originally planned to send off some of the Bayt Kathir. 'The plan would have been to have a Rashid party with a few trusted Bayt Kathir there,' he said. 'The Rashid were sand-people and the Bayt Kathir had no knowledge of that part of the country. It was obvious that the Rashid were far superior to the Bayt Kathir, the way you instinctively feel it. They lived in the Sands whereas the Bayt Kathir didn't.'[31] A party mostly made up of Rawashid was now out of the question. After some discussion it was decided that five of the Rawashid should stay with Mahsin. A detachment of Bayt Kathir, with the weaker camels, and led by Sheikh Tamtaim, would separate from the main party here and ride south across the arid Jiddat al Harasis to the Yazer – a region of rich grazing near the southern coast in the country of the Janaba. It seems likely that by this stage Thesiger had revealed to all the Bedu his plan to cross the Sands. 'When the Rashid stayed behind at Mughshin I felt this wrecked everything,' he said, 'because they were the people I relied on to take me across the Sands. They talked among themselves and decided – and Sultan must have known this – that they'd come with me; they understood that my intention was to get as far as Dhafara.'[32] Bin Kabina and al 'Auf declared that they would accompany Thesiger across the Sands. Of the Bayt Kathir, Sultan, bin Tafl, Mabkhaut, Sa'id, and four others were to come, making the 'assault party' – including Thesiger himself – up to eleven. Still, Thesiger fretted about the food he must leave for the party staying with Mahsin, and with the rest of the Bayt Kathir. The Bedu set Mahsin's leg by cutting lengths of wood, and remained with him for a week. Thesiger gave him repeated shots of morphine. Finally, when the old veteran seemed to be recovering, the stores were divided, and Thesiger arranged with Tamtaim and the rest of the Bayt Kathir to meet him at Boi, near the coast, in about two and a half months' time. On 23 November the rations were divided and the following morning Thesiger and his Bedu led their frail camels into the dunes of Ghanim. Glad to be out of the large crowd, Thesiger was now optimistically expecting to find the lush grazing that Ghanim had yielded the previous year on the way to Bir Halu. To his great disappointment the sands were now sterile, meaning that the camels would begin their great journey hungry. At the well of Khor bin Atarit, the Bedu filled their skins to bursting point 'with water already bitter with magnesium salts. It would, they knew, slowly ferment into a foul soup after a few days mixing with the tar with which the skins were cured. This was the last watering-place before Dhafara, which lay fourteen days ahead. That evening Thesiger noticed with annoyance that one of the Bayt Kathir was using the water for his ritual ablutions, unnecessary by Islamic custom if water is scarce, when it may be replaced symbolically by sand. He tried to give the tribesmen an idea of the waterless distance that lay before them by telling them that the wells of Dhafara − their destination − were twice as far away as Salalah. Sultan grumbled dejectedly that, if this was true, neither they nor the camels would ever get there. Dhafara lay fourteen days away, yet the desert was not uninhabited. At Ramlat al Ghafa there were the herds of the Bayt Musann and the Bayt Imani. There was no water at Ramlat al Ghafa; but there would be milk and the chance of exchanging the weaker camels. They rode across crystalline salt-flats sparkling silver in the sun. It was lush going for the camels and even a novice could soon have picked up the tracks of the migrating Bedu herds. Thesiger noticed, though, that Sultan began to look increasingly nervous. He felt that his old friend was lost and unnerved by the unfamiliar dune-country, disoriented, worried about the shortage of water, the weakness of the camels and the lack of grazing. One night, Thesiger wrote, he awoke to see Sultan staring into the fire: 'He was on his own, brooding,' he recalled, 'and he'd been brooding for days at the prospect of crossing the Empty Quarter.'[33]

*

On 2 December they reached Ramlat al Ghafa's green havens and camped with some Bayt Musann on the flat, grassy plains between the fantastically carved and twisted confections of isolated dunes. Today there is an Elf plant on this site, an ugly silver spider of steel scaffolding, bloated tanks and wire compounds, where Frenchmen in plastic hardhats live in air-conditioned Portakabins. The oil-flares which rage constantly near by with an unnatural orange glow and acrid black fumes light up the sands for miles. In Thesiger's time such a possibility was not even dreamed of by the Bedu of the Sands. The Musann welcomed the travellers with customary hospitality, and brought them camel's milk: 'They asked us where we were going,' bin Kabina recalled, 'and we said we were going to Dhafara. They said that soldiers of bin Jiluwi [Governor of al Hasa in Sa'udi Arabia] were collecting taxes in the north and they were arresting a lot of people. Especially as we were travelling with a Christian they would certainly capture us and put us in jail. The Bayt Kathir with us were frightened of bin Jiluwi, as everybody was then. The Bayt Kathir were already afraid of the Sands, but what really frightened them was the situation in Sa'udi Arabia, which added fear upon fear. When they heard about bin Jiluwi they said, "Let's go back!" Sultan and some of the others went to look at the Bayt Musann camels, and found them weak. The Bayt Musann told them that the camels of the Rawashid near by were in the same poor condition.'[34] Thesiger recalled that he and bin Kabina watched Sultan and the others walking back from their inspection of the local camels. 'Bin Kabina said, "Sultan won't go with you,"' Thesiger recalled. 'I don't say he used the word "afraid" but he at least implied that Sultan was afraid of the Sands and was going to cause trouble. I told him that in that case the whole thing had collapsed. He said as long as I'd got the Rashid with me I'd be all right. We joined the Bayt Kathir council and as soon as we sat down, Sultan announced, "I've discussed it with the others and we agree that our camels are too weak and we are too short of water." He said the journey was too dangerous and difficult. He didn't mention any other reason for not going.'[35] Thesiger proposed a compromise. The four of them whose camels were weak should return to Mughshin with a Bayt Musann guide, leaving seven to cross the Sands. Sultan objected. 'We are already a small party,' he said. 'There are bin Jiluwi's men ahead of us, and fighting between the ruling families on the coast. Either we must all go on or all go back.' Thesiger then saw with devastating clarity that Sultan and his Bayt Kathir had no intention of crossing the Sands.

He was vexed by the realization that Sultan, the renowned fighter whom he had always relied on as his right-hand man, had lost his nerve. He believed that Sultan was simply afraid of the Sands and the talk of the other dangers was just an excuse. 'The moment he got into the Sands he was bewildered,' Thesiger commented. 'He was afraid of doing that journey and was determined not to do it. He had said to me yes, we'll take you anywhere you want to go, but I had a feeling that when it came to it he didn't mean it. At first I felt furious and let down by the man I liked and had always respected.'[36] His illusions about Bedu courage were also at stake here. It looked as though all the months of preparation and planning were to be wasted by the cowardice of this Bedu Sheikh. Sa'id presented a different light on Sultan's decision, however. 'Sultan was a brave man, who was never known to be afraid of anything,' he said. 'He had fought against the Ma'arab and he was a Sheikh known for his counsel. Sultan certainly wasn't afraid of the Sands. No one was frightened of the Sands. It wasn't a thing for a Bedouin to be frightened of. He and Thesiger had a difference at Ramlat al Ghafa. When the Christian asked me, I said this is the border of the King's authority. Sultan said that the King had forbidden him to cross the borders of his authority, and that was the reason he wouldn't go ahead. The Christian said, "You have done wrong to leave me like this when you were sent by the Wali to escort me," and Sultan said, "We were sent to take you within our tribal territory, no further. That's it. Now we go back." It was just that the talk got out of proportion. The Christian relied too much on his Rawashid and believed everything they said.'[37] Nashran, Sultan's son, although he was not present on the occasion, supported Sa'id's argument: 'My father had orders from the King not to take the Christian beyond the borders of his territory. I know that because I was there in the palace when he told him. He said to me later that to cross the border into Sa'udi Arabia would mean trouble for us and for the King. My father was never afraid of fighting, but he was the Sheikh and the responsibility lay on his shoulders. Mbarak was angry with him, but my father wasn't afraid of the Sands. Plenty of the Bayt Kathir knew the Sands – perhaps only the Bayt Musann grazed there, but a lot of us knew them as individuals more than Mbarak's Bayt Imani boys, who were goat-herds and never went near the Sands in their lives. What Mbarak said was an exaggeration.'[38]

Bin Tafl guessed that Thesiger had, in fact, tricked the King. 'He had asked for permission to go to "Mughshin and the Sands",' he said. 'The Wali of course thought that meant the Sands of Ghanim, Ghafla, and Sahma, where the King had authority. But what Mbarak really meant was the Empty Quarter. I don't think Sultan was really afraid of the Sands – he was a brave man and everyone knows that. It was just that we had no permission to cross the borders.'[39]

Bin Kabina recalled that Sultan had tried to persuade Thesiger to take a different route: 'He said he would lead him to Ghanim or Jiddat al Harasis where he could shoot oryx,' he recounted, 'but the Christian said, "I don't want to go there, I went there last year. I'm going to Dhafara, and I shall go even if I go on my own. Then the Wali will blame you, Sultan, for abandoning your travelling companion." Then he said, "You Rawashid, will you come with me?" and al 'Auf said, "We're your men, we'll go where you go." And I said I would go too. The Christian said, "Thank God, we are three people and need no one else! It's enough."'[40]

Thesiger was riding one of bin Tafl's camels, and bin Tafl at present was standing with his people, the Bayt Kathir. This made his situation look awkward, for there was a shortage of good riding-camels. 'I had two good, fat camels,' bin Tafl remembered, 'and Mbarak was riding one of them, called Rahayib. He was paying me six riyals a day for it, and he complained that it was a lot. I said, "Not when you consider the thirst and fatigue." He said, "Believe me, Musallim, one day soon no one will be interested in hiring a camel even for one riyal a day!" Anyway, the Christian asked me if I'd go with him and I thought that on one hand Sultan was right in not crossing the King's borders. On the other hand it was wrong to abandon a travelling-companion and it was against our custom. I thought we should either take him where he wanted to go, or take him back with us by force. Sultan said no, we can't force him to go back and we cannot take him beyond our borders. So when the Christian asked, I said yes, I will go.'[41]

Thesiger's men spent the night with the Bayt Musann in Ramlat al Ghafa. 'They brought us milk and slaughtered a camel for us and gave us fat and meat,' bin Kabina remembered, 'but they tried to make us afraid, of the Arabs, of bin Jiluwi and of thirst. They said that nine or ten men had ridden across the Sands the previous year and died of thirst. They talked and talked until we really were afraid, but we said, "We will do it, anyway." All the Bayt Kathir were terrified, but then bin Tafl said he would go with us. I think it was because he was jealous of al 'Auf, and wanted to show that he was as brave as him. In the morning Mabkhaut told bin Tafl he wanted to go as well. The Christian didn't really like Mabkhaut, but he was related to al 'Auf by marriage so he was a friend of ours as well as bin Tafl. Bin Turkia, Mabkhaut's cousin, also wanted to go but al 'Auf looked at his camel and said it was too weak. So there were five of us after all, and the rest under Sultan went back to Mughshin and returned to Boi in the Yazer. The Christian was paying us all four riyals a day, and he told them by the Grace of God he would not cut their pay, but that they wouldn't get any bakshish, whereas those who went with him would get clothes, rifles and extra money. Sultan objected to that, but Mbarak said, "Why have you taken me under the orders of the King and then abandoned me? That is not right!" '[42]

Thesiger commented later: 'There was no question of borders and things in those days. Sultan simply lost his nerve. There's no doubt that he was originally going to come, and he was somebody who had never been in the Sands before, and he was trying to turn the whole thing back so that we'd just go off and shoot oryx. It may well be that the King told them not to take me further than Mughshin – I don't dispute that – but Sultan never raised this at the time as a reason for going back that I can remember. At some stage he did know we were going to Dhafara, and he could have said to me at Mughshin, look here, I haven't got permission. He said that the camels weren't fit and the journey was too dangerous, the water low and there was this other party that had died in the Sands – all of which would have been true. I'd always planned to let some of the Bayt Kathir go off from Mughshin, but I thought Sultan would certainly not have refused to have come further. It was a refusal on his part, and he decided to take the Bayt Kathir back from Ramlat al Ghafa. Only bin Tafl and Mabkhaut defied him. But any question of refusing to cross borders is abject nonsense. Sultan was afraid of the Sands!'[43]

Is Thesiger's final verdict on Sultan quite fair? Courage was the first of the virtues of the Bedu code of *miruwa*, and today Sultan's sons, grandsons and great-grandsons are aware of the slur upon the name of their ancestor. Though there were no administrative borders, there were putative frontiers within which the King at least theoretically held sway. When Thesiger had first arrived in Dhofar in 1945, the Sultan had given him permission to go as far as Mughshin, which Thesiger himself commented 'was the limit of his area'.[44] Of his reluctance to push as far as Umm as Samim the previous year, Thesiger listed among his reasons the fact that he 'didn't want to get into territory that didn't belong to the Sultan of Muscat'.[45] Mughshin and its surrounds, Ghanim, Sahma and Ghafa, must have been at least nominally under bin Taimur's authority, otherwise Thesiger would not have sought permission to go there. There is also the eye-witness account of Nashran that the King had forbidden Sultan to cross his tribal frontiers.

Yet although theoretical frontiers did exist, it is equally true that the Bedu took scant notice of them, and would have laughed at any suggestion that the Sultan held real authority there. In practice, as Thesiger said, they were meaningless. It seems apparent that Sultan did, at some stage, accept, tacitly or otherwise, that he would accompany Thesiger across the Sands, and changed his mind later. Thesiger was adamant that he had not used the 'frontiers' argument as an excuse. Young bin Kabina evidently did influence Thesiger, and naturally, those who turn back from a mission, whatever the culture, are likely to be dismissed as 'afraid' by those who continue. Perhaps Sultan, who was quite able to understand why anyone should want to hunt oryx, was equally unable to appreciate why any sane person should see a value in crossing these dunes, into the territory of a hostile tribe. The Rawashid had relatives north of the Sands: the Bayt Kathir did not. The testimony of bin Tafl is interesting, since there was no intertribal jealousy between himself and Sultan, although he continued in defiance of the Bayt Kathir Sheikh. We shall never know precisely why Sultan turned back, perhaps, though it seems unlikely that a man so noted for courage should have balked at riding through the Sands, when his 'town-raised' kinsman bin Tafl persisted. 'I suppose I felt he'd let me down to some extent,' Thesiger said, 'but I was quite content to go without him. In the end, instead of feeling angry, I was relieved and glad to get rid of him rather than having him as a nuisance continuously nagging that it was impossible, and with al 'Auf I had absolute confidence that here was somebody who'd get us across in any way possible.'[46] Thesiger used the instance of Sultan's desertion to underline the distinction between the Bayt Kathir and the 'sand-dwelling' Rawashid. Nevertheless, two of his final party were Bayt Kathir, and it is surely one of the greatest ironies of the crisis that bin Tafl, whom Thesiger regarded as 'a coarser breed' than the others, due to his association with town life, should have proved himself braver than a desert-bred Bedu like Sultan: evidently the hard life did not necessarily breed the 'finer' person in this particular case. 'Bin Tafl said I couldn't have done it without him and his camel,' Thesiger commented, 'and I suppose that's fair, but if he had refused we could still have gone off and bought another camel and I'd have been happy to have gone just the three of us.'[47]

The actual state of the camels being grazed in Ramlat al Ghafa is a mystery. Had Sultan reported on their weakness as an excuse to turn back? Thesiger later wrote that there had been very good grazing there that year, and this is confirmed by one of the Bayt Musann who was present when his party arrived, Muhammad bin Salih: 'The Christian came with some Arabs and spent two nights with us,' he recalled. 'In the afternoon he went off on his own to climb a dune and walk around it, then he came back at sunset. He decided to buy a camel from us – it was a fat male, and I think he paid about 250 riyals for it. It was a riding-camel, not for food. The camels were in quite good condition that year, because the grazing at Ramlat al Ghafa was good.'[48] Thesiger reckoned that the Bayt Musann charged him about four times as much as the camel was worth, but he was glad to have it. His men took only the barest essentials: four skins of water, fifty pounds of flour, sugar, tea, coffee and a pint of liquid butter. The water would have to last them at least another six days, and the food would have to be made to suffice until they came to Liwa. Al 'Auf, who had crossed these Sands before, was Thesiger's ultimate security, and from al Ghafa would take over as his guide. A few days previously, near Mughshin, Thesiger had found a pretext for speaking to him out of earshot of the others, and asked if it was true he knew the eastern Sands, which few Bedu had crossed. Al 'Auf said he had ridden across them only the previous year with a scouting party, and found some vegetation among them. He also astonished Thesiger by saying he had ridden back across the Sands alone. At first Thesiger thought he had misunderstood. It seemed astounding to him that anyone could cross this vast empty space without a companion. Craving company like a drug, he had never in his entire life made a solo journey, nor would he have considered such a journey worthwhile. To travel in this utter desolation by himself would have been to him an unimaginable penance. This was one of the many moments when Arab and Westerner were looking at the world through quite different eyes. Thesiger saw the terrifying spectre of emptiness: al 'Auf saw a place where men, women and children could survive reasonably well as long as they observed its rules. 'We all used to travel alone,' Sa'id commented. 'If you had a companion it was good and if you didn't you didn't, but it wasn't a big thing. It was nothing to make a fuss about.'[49] In fact, bin Kabina maintained years later that al 'Auf had not been completely alone on that journey: 'He crossed the Sands first with a scouting party,' bin Kabina said, 'but he came back with two small children – his nephews – who hung on to his saddle. Only a Rashidi could have done that!'[50] Thesiger afterwards dismissed bin Kabina's addition to the story as a tall tale.

Al 'Auf had a photographic memory and knew precisely what dangers lay ahead. Their main obstacle would be a single chain of giant dunes – the highest in the Empty Quarter – named the 'Urug ash Shiban (or Shaiba) – Himalayas of sand that could be crossed only in certain places. Some of the other dune-chains could be encircled, but the Shiban stretched for several hundred miles and sloped down in the south-east to the treacherous sink of Umm as Samim. There would be more high dunes on the way, interspersed with flat salt-plains where the going would be easier, but al 'Auf was worried that the Bayt Kathir camels would founder on the 'Urug ash Shiban. Beyond the great 'Urug, the sands were lower, and there lay a strange oasis called Liwa, where palmeries and settlements burst like mirages out of hollows in the dunes for two days' march. Thesiger had never heard of Liwa, and indeed, no Westerner had ever seen it then.[51] Despite the obstacles, the weakness of the camels, the unavoidable 'Urug, the paucity of food and water, he was now fairly confident, and the mention of this unknown oasis only whetted his curiosity further. He had the compact party he required: a guide who had been through the area before, five good camels plus a spare, and if water was short, at least it was winter – the coolest time of the year. Finally, according to bin Tafl, he asked his companions: 'If we are in the Sands and ibn Jiluwi's men find us, what will you say about me?'

'We'll say you are a Sheikh from al Yemen – because you look like a Yemeni with your dagger and *dishdasha* and beard,' bin Tafl said.

'I shall have to have a name,' Thesiger went on.

'We'll call you Mbarak,' bin Tafl said, 'because it means "blessing", and you have brought us some good.'

'It is a good name,' Thesiger replied. 'My mother's name is Mary – Mariam in Arabic – so you can call me Mbarak bin Mariam.'

The next day, Sheikh Mbarak led his tiny force further into the Sands.

Looking at the slightly out-of-focus group photograph, the only one taken of the five members of his first crossing of the Sands, one can see almost at a glance the personal dynamics that must have throbbed beneath the smooth pounding of the camels' pace: here is the Christian, Mbarak, in the centre, a head taller than the rest, as hirsute and dishevelled as his companions, quite authentic in his Arab dress, if a touch too self-conscious. Wish as he might, Thesiger will never be more than 'the Christian' – honoured, united with them in the sacred bond of the travelling-companion, yes, but never one of them. On the right of the group is bin Kabina, a boy – little more than a child – a good twenty years younger than Thesiger, and not yet a major player. On the left is the silent Mabkhaut – dependable but not an outstanding character. On Thesiger's right is bin Tafl, his *dishdasha* a shade cleaner than the others, his eyes slightly hooded, his face lean, powerful and hawkish. On the Christian's left is al 'Auf, less powerful physically than bin Tafl, but with a strangely inscrutable expression which combines dignity and power. Bin Tafl is the most famous hunter in Dhofar, al 'Auf one of its most celebrated warriors. The Christian favours one over the other, resorting unconsciously to his own tribe's expertise in the technique of 'divide and rule': given that al 'Auf and bin Tafl are from different tribes, and given the Bedouin cult of competition, there is almost inevitably going to be friction between these two powerful men.

The tiny caravan was a string of ants on the silver salt-flats beneath the scarlet mountains of sand. The configuration of the eastern Empty Quarter is unexpected to those who imagine an endless ocean of frozen sand-waves rolling on and on to eternity: sand-seas like this do exist in the Sahara, but their dunes are nowhere near as high as those in the Rub' al Khali. An aerial photo soon shows what anyone who has visited the eastern Sands realizes at once: that its mountainous dunes are spaced out, some isolated, some in endless chains, but separated by damp, black and silver salt-flats, where the going provides some respite for the camels from the occasional stupendous climb. Were this not so, Thesiger's small party would have been doomed.

Apart from the black bull-camel bought from the Musann, their camels were of the Omani race, steppe-bred camels famous for fast riding, but less efficient on the slip-slopes of the great dunes. Here was the obverse of Thesiger's pronouncement on the distinction between the steppe and sand-dwelling Bedu: while the steppe camels were small, lean, fast and muscular, the sand camels were bulky, slow, big-footed and ugly. On one steep descent, bin Tafl, riding the big Hazmi bull bought from the Musann, was leading his own camel laden with the company's two largest waterskins by a rope tied to his saddle. The she-camel behind staggered, kicking up sand, digging her pads in and slithering to a determined halt. Bin Tafl continued without noticing, and slowly the lead-rope drew taut. Thesiger looked up and realized that within an instant she would be pulled over and the precious skins would burst under her weight. He bellowed out a warning too late, as he watched the camel roll on to her side as if in slow motion. Al 'Auf raced up to slash the rope free, and, praying that there would at least be enough water to return to Khor bin Atarit, Thesiger pelted after him. The she-camel kicked wildly and rumbled plaintively as al 'Auf pulled her up. All eyes sought the skins and the tell-tale stain of water on the sand. Miraculously, they were untouched. 'Praise be to God!' they chanted, and even Thesiger joined in. Bin Tafl's camels were the healthiest animals they had, but al 'Auf declared that it would better in future to load the water on the *hazmi*, whose big hoof-pads were better equipped for these slippery descents: his broad back bore the vital skins from then on. They rode past honey-coloured dunes on the silver flats, circling a vast alp of vermilion sand which blocked the way behind them. Looking back, Thesiger imagined it as a great door swinging heavily shut, as the separate dunes coalesced into a continuous barrier of sand. They were in the heart of the Empty Quarter – there could now be no turning back. Thesiger admitted that this was one of the most frightening experiences of his life: when facing a snarling lion or the enemy in battle, one didn't have time to be afraid, but here he experienced that sudden, momentary, agoraphobic chill that can affect even the most seasoned of desert travellers when all landmarks, all signs of human existence, disappear. 'It comes swiftly and unexpectedly,' wrote the desert veteran Ralph Bagnold. 'Anyone, however well balanced . . . may be seized by a temporary madness, a feverish urge to start moving.'[52] Thesiger fought back this feeling, and placed his faith in al 'Auf and his Bedu companions. At night the terrible emptiness lay cloaked by darkness and the party could stalk along the *sebkhas* under a young moon, the Bedu roaring out their camel-songs to hold off the phantoms of the dark. As the voices faltered with weariness, though, and the weight of the desert descended, there was silence but for the crunch of the camels' feet on the salt-flats and the slap of water in the skins, and the occasional drip of moisture from them, like life-blood into the sand.

At sunrise the first of the monstrous swells of sand reared like a

great tidal wave out of the miserable grey shards of the morning.
It was freezing, and gusts of cold, grit-bearing wind swept into
their faces, forcing them to shroud themselves with their
headcloths. Thesiger's eyes, bleary with cold, grit and hunger,
cast wildly about for an opening in the unfractured wall of sand.
The dunes were the outward and visible expression of the unseen
forces of time and wind. South Arabia has probably never lain
under the great glaciers which once covered Europe, but the
discovery of the skeletons of hippopotamus and crocodiles here
shows that the Empty Quarter may have been a region of
extensive lakes and rivers at some time in the past. When these
waters dried up, their sandy beds were sculpted by the winds into
the surreal shapes Thesiger now saw before him. They were vast
cathedrals designed as if by some brilliant but tortured mind, an
incredible architecture of buttresses, flares and arches, dips and
saddles and flutings like giant organ-pipes. Yet there appeared no
easy way across. They marched into the morning chill in silence
as the great barrier took shape before them across the flat *sebkha*.
They rode on wretchedly in the biting cold until, within a few
hundred yards of the dune-wall, al 'Auf jumped down from his
mount. He strode across the silver salt-flat with his rifle thrown
across his shoulder in its leather case, his head up, scanning the
line of the dunes, a confident David surveying the immense
Goliath that confronted him. Looking on, Thesiger found himself
doubting that the camels would ever climb this dune. 'When we
came to this first big dune, I thought it was the 'Urug ash
Shaiba,' he said, 'and al 'Auf went off to look at it, and bin Tafl
started saying we'll never, never get the camels up that. He said
it's al 'Auf's fault for bringing us the wrong way: he ought to
have taken us further to the west where Thomas crossed. And I
said to him sarcastically, "We should have been far better off if
you'd been our guide, shouldn't we?"'[53] Bin Tafl snapped back
bitterly about Thesiger's unfair preference for the Rawashid,
extolling the fact that he, bin Tafl, had defied Sultan and his
tribe to help the Christian. Thesiger repressed the harsher words
which were forming in his mind, knowing that it would have
been only too easy to make this brash young man a scapegoat. Bin
Tafl himself looked back on the situation philosophically: 'On
long journeys like this, there are often arguments, of course,' he

admitted later. 'Everybody knew that Mbarak had this preference for the Rawashid and disliked the Bayt Kathir, which wasn't right because some of the Bayt Kathir were as accustomed to the Sands as the Rawashid, and not all the Rawashid knew the Sands well. The thing was that Mbarak was supposed to be the leader, not al 'Auf, but al 'Auf acted as if he was the leader, and was always giving orders and the Christian just accepted anything he said.'[54] Thesiger said later that in his opinion they could never have crossed the Sands without the guidance of al 'Auf: 'There's no question about it,' he commented. 'Without al 'Auf it was just conceivable that one of the other Rashid who'd stayed behind at Mughshin might have been able to do it, but I didn't know them well enough. I doubt if anyone could have done it but him.'[55]

Thesiger stifled his scathing answer to bin Tafl, and stalked off to brood alone on a sandbank, watching al 'Auf climbing the dune like a tiny black beetle, leaving a stitch-pattern of tracks behind him as he battled with the deep sand. 'The great problem in crossing the Empty Quarter wasn't really grazing for the camels,' he confessed later, 'it was getting your camels across these dunes. Now they say they are up to 1,000 feet high, I estimated between 5 and 700. Well, in England something 1,000 feet would be called a mountain. You always had two different colours, the light grains and the dark grains, perhaps yellow and pale ochre, and that's what made the whole beauty of the Sands.'[56]

He worried about what they would do if al 'Auf did not find a way across. They could not go round. Their water was short and their camels thirsty. He thought of unloading the camels and ferrying up the equipment by hand, but beyond this range of dunes there were at least two others, and once the camels had scaled one, he felt, they would be too exhausted to get back to Ramlat al Ghafa. Bin Kabina came and sat beside him, and Thesiger asked his opinion. He replied that al 'Auf would find a way, because he 'was a Rashid and not one of these Bayt Kathir', then he began to clean his rifle with evident unconcern. Thesiger watched as al 'Auf slithered down the dune face and walked across the *sebkha* to where the camels waited. Exhausted, they had not bothered to wander off in search of grazing, but stood huddled together. Mabkhaut's camel had sat down, which was a bad sign.

'Al 'Auf walked back, and nobody spoke or asked him anything,' Thesiger recalled. 'Then he just picked up my stick and gave it to me, and said "Come on!"'[57]

On his reconnaissance, al 'Auf had mapped out a rough series of slopes which he thought manageable for the camels. On the leeward side of the dune, the sand-grains appeared dark and the sand was soft, because the grains tended to lie upon each other like a pile of microscopic cannon-balls with air-spaces between them. As soon as they were trodden on, the structure compacted and collapsed, and a camel's or human's foot would sink deep into the sand. Another problem was that the glare thrown back from the silicon particles of the sand often made it impossible to judge the angle of ascent: anyone accustomed to dunes knows that sand-slopes can look impossibly steep, yet turn out to be quite low, for in fact sand cannot assume an angle of more than 33° before it avalanches: a sand-slope more acute than this cannot exist. The skirts of this great dune were perched at the maximum angle, so that the slightest tremor would set off a sandslide. Fortunately, the experienced al 'Auf had ferreted out 'pathways' where the sand-grains were smaller and therefore more compact, and the surface would bear the weight of a camel: 'The grains on the leeward side tended to be soft,' Thesiger recalled, 'and as soon as you were walking up it you loosened it and it started to slip down under your feet. You'd never get a camel up that way, but always there was a sort of way up it at an angle – that was the only hope you had of getting up. But going up put a tremendous strain on the camels.'[58]

Foot by foot, halting for breath, they hauled the great beasts up the impossible slope. Each time they halted Thesiger peered upwards, seeing sandsmoke spinning drifts off the peaks high above them, catching his breath, and then pushing on again. Suddenly, almost unbelievably, they were on top. Thesiger threw himself down into the sand, letting his muscles relax. 'Thank God!' he thought. 'We are across the 'Urug ash Shiban.' That afternoon, however, as they halted to bake bread on the *sebkha* beneath, Thesiger's illusion was shattered. 'That was not the 'Urug ash Shiban,' al 'Auf told him, 'that was another dune. If we go well we shall see the 'Urug ash Shiban tomorrow!'

In the morning bin Kabina made coffee before the sun was up.

They gulped it down in bitter mouthfuls. The camels were loaded and dragged themselves to their feet. The salt-flats beneath Thesiger's bare soles were as cold as snow, and it needed twenty minutes of tramping to get the circulation flowing and throw off the chills of the desert night. Slowly, as the sun rose, the 'Urug ash Shiban took form: 'A rose-red, mountainous range of sand, very lovely in the light of dawn,' Thesiger wrote, 'as it rose in jagged peaks and spurs ... above the ice-coloured sabkhas.'[59] Even to those who have seen sand-dunes, the 'Urug ash Shiban are staggering: it seems impossible that such colossi can be entirely composed of wind-blown silicon particles. The sand-skirts of this range were even softer than those of the previous day, and the Bedu had to drive the camels on once more, heaving on the headropes, pushing from behind, lifting their loads to make the going easier as the beasts staggered on in fright and exhaustion. It was grim work on an empty stomach, and Thesiger felt nauseous and light-headed, his throat thick with thirst, his breath coming in gasps. Often he sat down to rest, only to be urged on by the others shouting 'Mbarak! Mbarak!' They crossed the summit and slithered down three smaller saddles of sand on the windward side, tramped across a salt-flat and, in an incredible last surge of effort, dragged the camels up the slope on the opposite side, on the peak of which they collapsed into the sand and drank a little water in celebration. Three hours after setting off that morning they had conquered the formidable 'Urug ash Shiban. 'These dunes were running across our line of march,' Thesiger recalled, 'and when we climbed the first big dune, we got to the top and saw many more beyond that. We had to climb the second one, which somehow the camels managed to do, and then I saw more, and al 'Auf said no, don't worry, I can find my way round those ones. If he hadn't, I wouldn't be here.'[60]

The great obstacles lay behind them now. For two days they rode across salt-flats, between sheer-sided dunes, travelling late into the night. There were no further climbs, but the camels were thirsty and famished, browsing without satisfaction among the occasional *abal* bushes they found along the skirts of the sands. Once, as they rode through the night, the moon was blotted out by a total eclipse. This did not trouble Thesiger's pragmatic Bedu companions, who merely bellowed out a song about the short life of man and the omnipotence of God, which was appropriate for the vastness of the setting. They crossed the low downs of Ramlat Kharfiya, where the sand glittered in rainbow colours: buff, green, bronze and gold. To their delight, they came upon a great patch of *gassis* – a drought-resistant sedge – resulting from a shower earlier in the year. The camels fell on it hungrily, and Thesiger and his Bedu ran around filling their cloaks with the green and succulent stems, which quickly assuaged the camels' thirst. Not long afterwards al 'Auf spotted a hare and killed it with a deft blow from his stick. Tonight, at last, they would eat meat. They could scarcely wait to halt and cook it, and spent hours debating about how it should be prepared. After they had made camp, bin Tafl baked twice the normal quantity of bread, and bin Kabina boiled the hare in precious water to make soup. When it was ready, he divided the meat into lots, as was the custom. Strangely, bin Tafl was unable to touch it. 'I couldn't eat it,' he said, 'and Mbarak said to me, "Of course, Musallim, if you have a camel it is better than a goat, and a goat is better than a hare, but we only have this hare." He ate it, and the others did, but where I was brought up there were no hares, so I wasn't accustomed to eating it.'[61] After the others had taken their share, bin Kabina realized he had forgotten to divide the liver. The Bedu insisted that it should be given to Thesiger, who protested that it should be divided. They insisted again, and Thesiger eventually accepted. 'I knew I oughtn't to have done it,' he said, 'but I was too hungry to mind. None of them would have done it. So I got a little piece of meat about the size of the end of my thumb!'[62]

It was only five days since they had left the Bayt Musann at Ramlat al Ghafa, though it seemed a lifetime. In those five days the party had been its own tiny world, seeing no one and nothing. Then the unexpected happened. 'It was just after the noon prayer,' bin Kabina recalled, 'and we'd just started riding our camels, when someone shouted at us from behind a dune, "Throw down your weapons, you raiders, or I'll let you have it!" We looked up and we could see this rifle pointing at us, but for all we knew there could have been a hundred of them. The Englishman

said, "Let your camel go down before you open fire!" He wanted
us to hide behind the camels and fight like soldiers, but of course
we were Bedu and we don't know such ways. I ignored him and
drew my rifle. Then al 'Auf recognized the man's voice: it was his
cousin. "Hamad?" he shouted. "Yes!" the other one replied. "It's
Muhammad al 'Auf!" "Ah! Welcome! Welcome!" We understood
it was a friend. It was Hamad bin Saadna, a Rashidi of the Bayt
Hanna, and you know, the funny thing was that he didn't have a
rifle at all. He just had a bit of stick which he pushed over the
edge of the dune to make us think it was a rifle! He had lost a
camel and was tracking it into the 'Urug ash Shiban.'[63]

Bin Saadna agreed to guide the party to Liwa oasis, where they
would need to obtain food. He also confirmed that many of the
Bedu tribes of Sa'udi Arabia were assembled in Dhafara for the
annual assessment of taxes. Thesiger knew that if they ran into
any tax-collectors they would certainly be taken to al Hasa to be
interrogated by the awe-inspiring bin Jiluwi. They decided to
avoid contact with all Bedu except the Rawashid, and that bin
Saadna should go into Liwa to buy provisions for them. The
problem here was that no honest traveller would avoid Bedu
encampments, since Bedu are always avid for news. A *gom* of the
Kurub, from the far-off fringes of the Yemen, had raided Liwa
the previous year, and with their suspicious behaviour they might
well be mistaken for such raiders. The formidable Bedu trackers
would quickly divine that the party had come from the south,
and would recognize Thesiger's gargantuan footprints as belonging to a non-Bedu. For this reason Thesiger was often obliged to
ride, together with bin Tafl – the effect of whose shoe-wearing
years in Salalah would probably be apparent to the keen observers. They were in Dhafara – the destination of their journey – the
ultima Thule of the tribes in Dhofar. Bin Saadna led them aside to
a brackish well named Khor Sabkha, where the water was so
bitter that not even the thirsty camels would drink until their
nostrils were bound. The Bedu filled their skins with the water,
which, salty as it was, was infinitely preferable to the tarry
magnesium-saturated filth they had carried across the dunes. On
13 December they moved to the well at Khaba, where there was
water that was almost untainted. As it was drawn up and the
bowl filled, Thesiger took it and drank, savouring its almost

tasteless flavour. Drinking water in Dhafara was a sacrament for which he had risked everything: he had crossed the Great Space of Arabia. But almost before he had drained this cool and welcome draught, the realities of his situation dawned on him with deep intensity. He had entered a foreign country without permission: his men had no food, and he must ride back through a region where the local tribesmen had been told that to kill a Christian was a sacred duty: the country of the Duru'.

A few days later Thesiger lay starving on a sand-dune at Bir Balagh, only a day's trek south of Liwa, while bin Kabina and bin Saadna went off to the oasis to buy food. That the other three Bedu with him – Mabkhaut, al 'Auf and bin Tafl – could, if not for his presence, have simply ridden off to enjoy the hospitality of the local tribes, weighed heavily upon his conscience. There was no game to shoot, not a hare to be tracked, and even looking at the camels depressed him, since he could see them only in terms of food. There was nothing for it but to wait. He slung his cloak between some thorn-bushes for shade and lay there most of the day. No matter how he tried to divert his thoughts away from food they always returned. He even dreamed of the charred crusts of bread he had thrown away or refused at the beginning of the journey. He rolled over on to his belly, hoping to make the hunger-pains go away. He bloated himself with water from the nearby well to rid it of the hollow feeling. Days passed, nights passed in sleepless hunger. He thought longingly of the food the others would bring back, of the goat he had instructed them to buy. He imagined, detail by detail, how they would slit its throat, butcher it, broil and roast its meat, and eat with the grease running down their chins. Time stood still: there was nothing but the ever more intense ache of hunger. Had he travelled by jeep, like Popov and the other Locust Control officers, such privations would have been unnecessary, he knew. In a jeep you were self-sufficient in food and water. Yet though the vision of jeep-borne comfort became more vivid as the hunger gripped him, he held on to his convictions. He would rather be here starving with his Bedu companions than separated from them and their desert home by motor transport.

No Westerner had ever seen the oasis that lay only a few hours' march away, and he would have been fascinated to get a glimpse of it. But he dared not run the risk of meeting bin Jiluwi's men. Meanwhile, irritated by this unnecessary starvation, bin Tafl and al 'Auf were feuding again. 'If the Sa'udis do find us,' al 'Auf had advised Thesiger, 'don't put up any resistance – just lay your rifle down.'

'All right,' Thesiger said. 'You'd better tell bin Tafl, too.'

'I can't tell him,' al 'Auf said. 'You will have to tell him.'

'Mbarak told me to lay my rifle down if we encountered any Sa'udis,' bin Tafl recalled, 'and I knew that this was something that came from al 'Auf not from the Christian. So I refused. I said, "I have brought this rifle from Salalah and I will hand it back to you in Salalah." "It is my rifle," the Christian said, "and I am ordering you to put it down if any Sa'udis approach us." "Not even if I die!" I said. It was all al 'Auf's doing, because he wanted to be the leader always.'[64]

On the 19th, bin Kabina and bin Saadna returned. 'I'd hoped they would bring a goat with them,' Thesiger said, 'but I looked up and saw they hadn't, and said Oh my God, have they brought nothing! They had brought some flour, and the women had refused to help them grind it and they'd had to grind it themselves, which was a woman's job. Then they had a poor lot of dates with sand in them.'[65] Though their foray had not proved very successful, bin Kabina said later that the women had not refused to grind the grain. 'We arrived in Liwa at noon,' he reported, 'and we tried three different villages. A few people asked where we had come from, but they weren't suspicious because they knew bin Saadna, and they knew he was herding camels near by. If they'd seen the Englishman they would have been suspicious of course. They wouldn't take our money, because they wanted rupees and we only had riyals. In the end they accepted it, but all we could buy was a bit of grain and some dates. But we didn't have any problem with the women grinding the grain. We spent the night there and left in the morning, and we reached the others the same evening.'[66] Possibly bin Kabina had used the 'resistance of the women' as an *escusatio non petita* for his guilt over the fact that he and bin Saadna had lingered in Liwa and, no doubt, eaten there – technically an affront to the Bedu ideal – while their companions out in the desert went hungry. Thesiger's visions of goat stew rapidly vanished, and that night they made a miserable meal. 'There was so little food that we had to use the dates as flavouring for the grain,' bin Tafl remembered. Then, as the Christian put the stuff in his mouth, I started laughing, I couldn't help it. His expression was so odd, and we had looked forward for so long to having a good meal. "Are you laughing at me?" Mbarak asked. "No, I'm just laughing," I said. "Musallim," he said, "you remember that feast that they made for us in the Hadhramaut – the one the rich Sayyid gave us last year?" I said, "Yes." He said, "I have all that and more at my house in England. But I prefer to live like this." Now I understand that he wanted to try something different from that comfortable life. That was his choice.'[67]

From Bir Balagh they moved through the great dunes of Rabadh, almost as tall as those of the 'Urug ash Shiban, riding along the salt-flats, avoiding the distant herds of Manasir and 'Awamir tribesmen, who were certain to raise the alarm if they spotted a Christian. They were searching for tents of sympathetic Rawashid, a few of whom lived in this region, and who would be duty bound to help their kinsmen. While Thesiger remained out of view, al 'Auf and bin Saadna would ride over to ask for news of Rawashid herds.

In Rabadh, bin Tafl spotted a hare peering from its burrow and brained it with a stick. It was the first game they had caught since the last hare in the Sands. They stopped to feast on it at once, Thesiger licking his lips at the thought of meat after long abstinence. They sat round the fire waiting impatiently for the meat to cook. No sooner was it ready than bin Kabina looked up and said, 'Guests!' With sinking heart, Thesiger saw three Arabs approaching. They were Rawashid, and Thesiger's party stood up to greet them and exchange news. Later bin Tafl served them the roasted hare, and though the guests insisted that their hosts should join them, Thesiger's men refused with the appearance of utter sincerity, as if they had gorged on meat every day for a month. Bin Kabina set before the others a mess of sticky dates. This was too much for Thesiger. He retired, feeling murderous at being robbed of his much-deserved meat at the last minute, and at the same time envious, knowing that he could never match the generosity and hospitality of these men. Observing their excitement in meeting each other – the unexpected alien intrusion into the small heroic band his imagination had built up over the previous week – he suddenly became aware, perhaps, with greater intensity, that he could never really be one of them. Crossing the Sands, with all hands and efforts directed to a single objective, the bond between them had seemed very real. Now, suddenly, back in a larger society, it seemed somehow weakened. He was dimly aware of their voices until first light.

Thesiger wrote that the Bedu suggested – against his own reservations – that he should describe himself as a Syrian if anyone inquired as to his identity, saying that no one here would know what a Syrian looked like. Another version is that Thesiger himself came up with the idea, and when bin Kabina asked, 'What's a Syrian?' answered, 'If you don't know I don't suppose anyone here will either.' Neither bin Tafl nor bin Kabina recalled any talk of Syrians, however: 'We were always afraid when we were hiding the Christian,' bin Kabina remembered, 'because if someone saw him they might try to rob us or kill us, thinking we were bandits, or had some kind of secret reason for being there. The Bedu then didn't know anything about Christians or army or police: they only knew Bedu. Once, in Rabadh, Mbarak, Mabkhaut, and I were on our own with the camels – I think the others had gone off to stay the night with some Bedu, saying they were alone – and we were cooking our meal, when the camels bolted. It happened twice. We thought someone had come to kill us, and we searched the place twice with our rifles in our hands, but we found no one.'[68]

The day after cooking the hare they came to a Rawashid camp, where they were treated to bowls of frothing camel's milk, and that evening their hosts slaughtered a young camel for them. For once they went to sleep replete. They remained in the camp for two days and fed well, but it was clear that they would have to get more food very soon. The grain and dates they had obtained in Liwa would last no more than ten days. 'From the Rawashid, we continued to the wadis of Duru' country,' bin Kabina remembered. 'It was not sandy country, but Sieh with a lot of trees and bushes and grass and wadis. We were afraid there would be trouble from the Duru', who were Ghafaris and our enemies. We arrived at the wells of Khaweir in Wadi al 'Ain, one of the big wadis in Duru' country, and there were four or five Duru' there. The Christian sent al 'Auf and another Rashidi who had joined us, Mbarak bin Mayya, to tell them we were friendly. The Duru' were suspicious, though, and they wanted to know why we had come here from so far away. They thought we were raiders, and one even wanted to shoot at us. There was no problem in the end, though. One of the Duru' called Staiyun invited us to his camp, and slaughtered a goat for us.'[69]

That night they discussed the possibility of travelling to Ibri, a large town under the aegis of the Imam, governed by the most feared of all the Imam's governors, al Riqaishi. Only there would they find the provisions they needed. 'We said we needed camel-harness,' bin Kabina said, 'because what we had was worn out. We also needed a lot of food, of course. Then bin Tafl said, "I don't think we should go near Ibri. We should get through Duru' country as fast as possible. The Riqaishi is the worst of all the Imam's governors – he hates Christians. If he finds we have a Christian with us God knows what will happen!" Then, of course, al 'Auf had to oppose bin Tafl's idea. "I think we should go to Ibri!" he said, and then they got really angry and a lot of poison came out between them that had been hidden in their hearts since the beginning. Their hearts were set against each other, because both of them were brave, strong men, and both wanted to be the best.'[70]

Bin Tafl recalled that there had been a dispute between himself and al 'Auf, but explained that it was not because he opposed the idea of going to Ibri. 'We had to get food,' he said, 'but al 'Auf wanted all of us to go there, including the Englishman, which I said was stupid, and if we did that the Riqaishi would kill us. I wanted to send only a small party. In the end that was what we agreed on, and we sent two camels to Ibri – my camels they were too; al 'Auf went, with our host's son, 'Ali bin Staiyun, and Mabkhaut.'[71] Thesiger stayed with the old man, Staiyun, while the others went off: 'He accepted me as an Arab and a Syrian, who was lax about my religion,' Thesiger said. 'Anyway, we expected them back in five days and they didn't turn up, and the old man looked a bit worried. He said they must have had trouble and that we should have to go to Ibri and try to get them released. I thought, well, I can hardly refuse to go after all he's done for us. But it really would have put me in a spot. We were just preparing to go off there and they did turn up – they'd obviously sort of taken it easy.'[72]

Bin Kabina remembered that the foraging party returned from Ibri after six days. 'They brought with them flour and dates,' he said, 'and the things we needed. He who needed a new saddle got a saddle, and he who needed a head-rope got a head-rope, and he who needed a saddle-belt got a saddle-belt. Then 'Ali bin Staiyun said we would need a *rabi'a* in Duru' country, and he would go with us as *rabi'a* as far as Wadi al 'Amairi. When we set off, there was another dispute between al 'Auf and bin Tafl over the camels.'[73] 'It was because they wanted to use my camels to carry all the supplies,' bin Tafl admitted. 'You see, my camels were strong ones, and the Christian was paying six riyals a day for them, but he was paying only four riyals a day for the camels of the others. So they said if any camels should carry the supplies it should be mine, while their camels rested. It wasn't right that only my camels should be tired out. Later, Mbarak apologized and said it was only because my camels were fat and in good health, and later we transferred some of the load to the other camels. These disputes were only caused by fatigue and hunger.'[74]

On their way to Wadi al 'Amairi, one of the great watercourses that drained the Oman mountains, bin Tafl invested money in a black she-camel which he bought from some Rawashid. 'The she-camel was called Sakhayya,' bin Kabina recalled with a grin. 'She was a poor animal, a *hazmiyya* bred in the Sands, so she couldn't walk well in this rocky country as her feet were too soft. He wanted to take her to Salalah, but we could see she wouldn't make it. Of course, while she was alive, bin Tafl thought Mbarak would be paying four riyals a day for her, so he kept shouting at her, "Sakhayya! Sakhayya! Just hang on for another ten days and you will collect forty riyals! If you stop, all you will get is a bullet!" But she was no good, and he decided that we would slaughter her when we reached the Haushi.'[75] From Wadi al 'Amairi, they parted with 'Ali bin Staiyun and took a guide called Rai from the tiny 'Ifaar tribe, accepted as *rabi'as* by the Duru'. This occasioned another round of acrimony between bin Tafl and al 'Auf. 'None of us knew the way,' bin Tafl said, 'and al 'Auf wanted to bring a guide from the Duru', and I wanted to bring this Rai from the 'Ifaar. We went to Mbarak to decide and he agreed it would be better to take Rai who would be accepted as *rabi'a* by all the tribes, whereas one from the Duru' wouldn't. He made us shake hands on it. Rai guided us as far as the Haushi, where I shot a gazelle. We ate all of it but the two hind legs. When Rai left us the next day I gave him the rest of the meat. "What about us?" the Christian asked. "Why did you give him everything?" I told him, "God is bountiful. God will provide." "If God had promised us anything he would provide it," he said, "but God has promised us nothing!" '[16]

Thesiger's caravan moved fast now, determined to make the rendezvous with the Bayt Kathir at Boi. Thesiger had little time to spare for locusts in this dangerous country, nor did he have the opportunity to investigate the mysterious quicksands of Umm as Samim, though he collected as much information about them as he could. He learned that, as Thomas had written, only the hostile Duru' knew the secret paths through it, and that a number of raiders, including a large band of 'Awamir, had been lost in it. It would regularly swallow up flocks of goats which had wandered into it unawares. The Duru' described a gleaming white island lying in the middle of the quicksands and believed that a store of fabulous wealth was hidden there. Thesiger was determined to return for a closer look at Umm as Samim.

Always avid for meat, he suggested they slaughtered Sakhayya, but bin Tafl said there were too many tribesmen about and they would have to give away most of it to others. The country was an endless grey plain now, almost featureless, and the caravan plodded on, seeming to mark time – the horizon always remained the same distance before them and the same distance behind. The passing of time was marked only by the slow circling of the sun. Thesiger could no longer face the sickly dates the others ate at sunrise, and fasted until the evening meal. He found himself longing for the day's end. At last they reached Haushi wells, where they slaughtered the *hazmiyya* whose soles had worn thin, and could not even feed on the local thornscrub. 'We stayed there for two days,' bin Tafl recalled, 'and we cooked some of the meat and dried the rest. When we sat down to eat the meat, the Christian asked, "Is this the meat of the *hazmiyya*?" "Of course," I said. "By God," he said, "you know I'd rather have eaten the meat of a human being than the meat of that she-camel!" "It's meat," I said. "Eat it!" and of course he did.'[77]

From Haushi, it was only a brief ride to Boi in the Yazer, but the going was desperately rough. The camels were exhausted, the men at the last pitch of their energy. For two days they floundered across the *sebkhas*, the camels' hooves breaking through the soft crust to sink into the soft sand beneath. Then, on 31 January 1947, they spotted a tiny nest of figures in the distance. It was Tamtaim, bin Turkia – the Bedouin who had wanted to accompany them – and his small son, bin Anauf. Mabkhaut identified them by their camels from almost a mile away. As they rode near, Thesiger slipped down from his camel and Tamtaim came hobbling forward, his eyes streaming with tears, embracing the Christian with unfamiliar emotion. He said at once that he had been furious when Sultan had deserted them, and had they not appeared on time, had intended personally to come in search of them. 'News had reached them that we had died,' bin Tafl remembered, 'and they were very sad about it. When they saw we were alive they were so happy that they slaughtered a camel.'[78] The party made camp there while Tamtaim sent word to the rest of the tribe, who had scattered widely to graze their camels.

On 4 February, when the original party had reassembled, they set off back to Salalah across the desolate Jiddat al Harasis. 'Sultan was with them,' bin Kabina remembered, 'and Mbarak was still angry with him. He paid him and the others what he owed them, but to those who had come with him across the Sands he gave rifles, extra money and new clothes.' Among the party was young Sa'id, Thesiger's guide as far as Ramlat al Ghafa. 'We were very happy to see Mbarak, and he was happy to be back,' he remembered. 'We rode together from Boi, and we were doing faster marches this time, and everyone was singing and shouting in loud voices, and the camels were full-fed and went well. We came down Jabal Taga, east of Salalah, near Darbat. We slept there the night, and the next day we entered Salalah. The Sultan was there, and the place was full of tribesmen, who fired their rifles over our heads and we put up tents on the beach and the Wali gave us a great feast.'[79] The most welcome news they heard was that the seemingly indestructible Mahsin, his leg still strapped up, had arrived on a camel only a couple of days before. It was 23 February 1947, almost exactly four months after they had first set out from Salalah. Thesiger had ridden 1,500 miles, all but a fraction of it unexplored by Europeans. The following day, accompanied by a surging host of tribesmen, he arrived back at the RAF camp.

Once again the Rawashid had gathered in Salalah, waiting to accompany Thesiger on his second trek to the Hadhramaut. Among them was Salih bin Kalut, an old man with a bald skull and a froth of beard, the father of bin Kabina's half-brother Muhammad, and the architect of Thomas's crossing in 1930. Salih was one of several sons of the celebrated beauty Kalut, and their reputation for courage was known even in the court of Ibn Sa'ud. Heavy in movement, deliberate in speech and ponderous in manner, bin Kalut was the most respected Sheikh of the Rawashid.

On his previous journey through Mahra country, Thesiger had travelled on the northern side of the mountain watershed. This time he wished to travel through the unmapped plateaux and fertile wadis on the southern side. He agreed to take fifteen Rawashid but thirty came along with him, saying that there might be trouble from the Mahra, and that they would divide the pay between them. 'These trips with the Englishman, we considered a chance for the whole tribe to benefit,' bin Kabina explained. 'We chose from among ourselves the people who would go, and the next time someone else would go instead. On this journey Salim bin Ghabaisha, who was my friend and a cousin of mine, was one of those given a bit of money not to go, but he wanted to accompany us, so when the Christian left he followed us. He came to us when we were camping at 'Ayun, and I talked to Mbarak and persuaded him to take bin Ghabaisha, first because he was an excellent hunter – as good as bin Tafl – and second because he had a good camel, and our camels were heavily laden.'[80] Thesiger was immediately attracted to bin Ghabaisha. He was no more than fifteen or sixteen, with an unusually husky voice, and the spare, linear, almost feminine figure which Thesiger admired. He had a grace and quiet dignity that contrasted with the boisterously energetic bin Kabina, altogether a physically stronger, more staid, more ruthless character, with all the courtesy of the Bedu, but without his kinsman's mercurial wit or his penetrating truculence. Thesiger waxed over his appearance in *Arabian Sands*, likening him to 'Antinous' when first seen by Hadrian in the Phrygian woods. Antinous was a young man renowned for his beauty who drowned himself in the Nile to prevent the fulfilment of a prophecy that he would bring about the death of the Emperor Hadrian on his visit to Egypt in 130 AD. 'Bin Ghabaisha was a very beautiful boy,' he commented. 'One can appreciate beauty without doing anything physical – I mean to have slept with bin Kabina or bin Ghabaisha would have been impossible – you'd probably have got knifed at once. Obviously bin Ghabaisha's beauty, or whatever word you like to use, had an effect on me. I liked him because he was so beautiful.'[81] Bin Ghabaisha's reaction to Thesiger was more prosaic: 'I wanted to go with him because he gave the Bedu rifles and camels and money,' he said, 'and those were the things I was interested in. Also a lot of people talked about his journeys, and I wanted to become famous among the tribes like the ones who went with him.'[82]

Mabkhaut, al 'Auf, and a few other Bayt Kathir accompanied Thesiger on this journey, including bin Turkia – who had volunteered to cross the Sands with him, but had been prevented by the weakness of his camel – and his son bin Anauf. Bin Tafl was notably absent. Thesiger wrote that he could not ride with them into Mahra country, since he had two blood-feuds with the Mahra on his hands. However, these blood-feuds had not prevented him riding to the Hadhramaut the previous year. Bin Tafl said that there had been some malicious talk about him to the Wali from people jealous of the money he had made on his previous journeys. 'The Wali didn't order me not to go,' he said, 'but he said if I went the Christian would have to sign a paper taking responsibility if I was killed by the Mahra. I didn't want to be a burden to him on his journey, so I decided to let someone else have a chance. Bin Turkia had wanted to go with the Christian across the Sands and into Duru', so it was better that he went instead of me.'[83] However, he helped Thesiger prepare for the journey and rode out of Salalah with his escort, climbing through the Wadi Garzaz with him, where they parted. 'I was sorry to see him go, when I remembered how he had stood by me when the other Bayt Kathir turned back at Ramlat al Ghafa,' Thesiger admitted. 'I was a bit scathing about him in my book. I regret that now.'[84] According to bin Tafl, Thesiger sent one of the Bayt Kathir trotting after him, with a purse full of Maria Theresa dollars as a parting gift. Bin Tafl's final verdict on Thesiger was: 'He was as tough as we were, and he could ride and shoot as well as a Bedouin, but we always considered him a foreigner and never thought of him as one of us, because he wasn't a Muslim. But this didn't mean we looked down on him. He was a Sheikh: no one has ever done what he did in Arabia, and no one could ever do it in the future.'[85] It was to be almost thirty years before they met again.

A few days later bin Kabina collapsed suddenly while fetching a camel, and lay unconscious for several hours. Thesiger had him moved to the fire, and tried to pour some brandy down his throat, with no success. The other Rawashid began to discuss whether the boy would die, and Thesiger could hardly bear it. 'I remembered with bitter regret how I had sometimes vented my ill-temper on him to ease the strain under which I lived,' he wrote, 'and how he had always been good-tempered and very patient.'[86] One of the Arabs asked where the party would be going tomorrow and Thesiger answered miserably, 'There will be no tomorrow if bin Kabina dies.'[87] Some hours later, though, the lad began to breathe normally, and the next day seemed completely cured. They passed through Mudhay, where Thesiger met bin Ghabaisha's brother, a madman whose wrists were shackled with heavy chain. A few years previously he had, without reason, killed his best friend by smashing his head in with a boulder. Bin Ghabaisha begged Thesiger to use his medicine to cure his brother's madness, but accepted resignedly when Thesiger said, 'Only God can cure him.'[88]

By 15 March they were at Habarut on the borders of Mahra country, where they watched Mahra camel-herds jostling and roaring, raising a fine spume of dust over the watering-place. Bin al Kamam, who had ridden with the caravan from Salalah, parted company with them, riding off by the quicker route through Sanaw, which Thesiger had surveyed the previous year. He was bound for the country of the Daham, in the Yemen, to negotiate for 100 Rawashid camels rustled from Sanaw by a 200-man *gom* of Daham some months earlier. His intention to negotiate with the Daham had been opposed by many of his tribe, who wanted to organize a counter-raid and seize the stolen camels by force. One night when Thesiger had been camping in the Dhofar hills, more than 100 Bedu had gathered around bin al Kamam and bin Kalut to discuss the possibility of such a raid. Among them, Thesiger had been intrigued to have pointed out to him an energetic Bedouin called Mabkhaut bin Duailan, whom he likened to 'an assertive sparrow'. Nicknamed 'the Cat', bin Duailan was the most famous raider among all the Mishqas, and Thesiger regretted that he never got to know him. Although he was travelling with Thesiger as Manahil *rabi'a*, he always ate with another group. He was to die fighting during a raid on the Yam only eight months later, though his name is still revered among the Bedu tribes of the Yemen today.

Leaving the now-familiar palms of Habarut, they scaled the Daru escarpment and found themselves in the dry rocky clefts of Mahra country. They descended into the wide, palm-shaded expanse of the Wadi Kidyat, a branch of the lush Wadi Mahrat – the heartland of the Mahra. Here one travels through tunnels of whiffling palms in shallow, blue water that trickles continually down the wadi after good rains, past ancient block fortresses of mud, and rambling mud tenements raised high on the wadi sides, where even today people will bolt at the sight of strangers. As the Bedu led their camels down the cliffs, some Bayt Khawar – the semi-sedentary palm cultivators of the Kidyat – gathered to prevent them, declaring that the Christian should not pass unless he paid money. Thesiger had never bowed to such demands and had no intention of doing so now. Besides, he had with him a *rabi'a* from the Bayt Khawar, who offered willingly to escort the party along the Kidyat in defiance of his tribe. Thesiger's Bedu were wary of going ahead with the *rabi'a*, though, fearing that someone would be killed by accident, and a blood-feud started between the tribes. The only alternative was to ride along the top of the escarpment – harder going, with no shady palms or green bushes on which to feed their camels – but suitable to Thesiger's purpose since from here he could see the lie of the land, which was essential for his map. They bypassed the Kidyat but descended into the Wadi Mahrat again at the spring of Umm Qarqar, where palms sprouted from beneath the cliffs.

They dawdled along the flat wadi bed at a leisurely pace, moving from palm-grove to palm-grove and settlement to settlement, giving Thesiger ample time to fix the outline of the country. Their plan had been to ride cross-country from here to the next great wadi, the Masila – the southern extension of the Hadhramaut – but the Mahra who inhabited the plateau between refused them entry. This time they had no *rabi'a*, and had no choice but to turn north through the Mahrat. Once again they were halted by the Mahra, who finally agreed to let them pass when Thesiger offered to take five Mahra as paid members of his party. In a charming gesture of hospitality they then declared that they would forgo payment, since they had no animals with which to honour their guests by a feast. Not to be outdone, Thesiger promptly countered that he would give them the equivalent of the sum they would have earned, 'as a present', which meant that everyone saved face. A few days later they crossed the watershed into Manahil country, where they heard rumours of another huge Daham raiding party – 250 strong – which had already murdered seven Manahil and eight Bedu of the 'Awamir. Afraid of being attacked by the Daham while trapped in the gorges of the wadi, Thesiger pushed out scouts and posted sentries after dark. Soon they arrived at the shrine of Nabi Hud in the Wadi Masila, where a white egg-shaped dome stood half-way up the cliff face. The shrine was sacred to the Prophet Hud the Arab Noah who was said to have fled here pursued by enemies and disappeared into the rock. The legend went back to pre-Islamic times, for Hud was the ancestor of both Semites and Hamites, and was believed to have given his name to the Hadhramaut. Since before the days of the Prophet Muhammad, an annual three-day fair had been held beneath the shrine, where Bedu from the deserts to the north rubbed shoulders with Indian, Greek and Arab merchants who had hauled their produce to the port of Mukalla by dhow, and thence up the Hadhramaut by camel. Today, an eerily deserted Hadhrami village stands below the shrine, inhabited only during the annual three days of the fair.

At Nabi Hud there was a gathering of Manahil, who warned Thesiger of the Daham raiders. His party moved cautiously up to the village of Fughama, today the centre of the Hadhramaut's newly established oil industry, knowing that the Daham were rumoured to be in the vicinity of the next large village, Sawm. Here they met a Manahil Sheikh who was desperately trying to rally the tribes against the Daham raiders. Thesiger's Rawashid agreed to join their Manahil allies, despite the fact that they were officially under a truce with the Daham. They camped by a wide stream among tamarisks and palms, leaving their camels saddled in case they should have to move quickly. After dark they heard shots near by, and bin Kalut ordered the Rawashid to extinguish their fires. For several hours they sat in perfect silence, listening to the camels chewing the cud and the hooting of owls. Though he would have enjoyed the excitement of a counter-raid, Thesiger hoped sincerely that he would not be obliged to take part in one. This was British territory, and for an Englishman to have entered the Yemen with a raiding party might have proved very embarrassing for the authorities in Aden. Later al 'Auf and five other tribesmen returned from scouting along the wadi, having seen no sign of the raiders, and though they remained alert till the day dawned, cold and wintry, by morning the threat had dissolved. The Daham had gone.

On 1 May, Thesiger's party saw the pearl-white minarets and houses of Mukalla, set on a promontory above a crystal-clear aquamarine sea. This was journey's end. The Bedu were quartered in the Bedouin Legion camp on the outskirts of the town, while Thesiger was put up at the Residency, where he could enjoy a bath and a shave. He visited his companions shaved and dressed in his European clothes, and claimed that at first they failed to recognize him. Thereafter, when he sat with them in their quarters, he was treated as a visitor. He had, he wrote, 'acquired his inhibitions with his trousers'. He felt estranged from them, having 'abandoned' the life they could not abandon, by returning to a civilization which he claimed to disdain, but could never truly leave. However, in his paper to the Royal Geographical Society in 1948, he wrote: 'Between us was the bond of hardships endured together and the comradeship of desert life ... Often I had been exasperated by their avarice and wearied by their endless discussions, but I had witnessed their courage and self-reliance, their pride of race, and I remembered their patience, generosity and unselfishness. I know that they and their way of life are an anachronism and will tend to disappear, but I also know that amongst them in the desert I have found a freedom of the spirit which may not survive their passing.'[89]

CHAPTER 11

Drawn Along a Road of My Own Choosing
by the Lure of the Unknown

The Hadhramaut was a very different Arabia from the bleak
deserts of Dhofar. The greatest wadi-system in the entire
peninsula, it was a world within a world, shut in by granite walls
1,000 feet high and cut off on each side by barren deserts stretching
to infinity. Here, the Arabs lived in great block-house forts of
mud, designed to impress in peacetime and to defend in war. It
was not unknown for entire families to be besieged in their forts
for years, tunnelling out passages that joined the block-houses
into a great warren, dominated by baroque watchtowers from
which hawk-eyed riflemen looked over palm-groves, orchards,
and patchwork spreads of wheat and golden barley, ready to pick
off interlopers intent on poisoning or burning with kerosene the
precious crops. In contrast with the pocket-sized Bedu tribes of
Dhofar, the great wadi reared a vast population. Three large and
important cities – Tarim, Saiyun and Shibam – were wedged
beneath its sheer red walls. Shibam was the most unusual of these,
a great rambling termitary of a town made up of teetering mud
houses seven or eight storeys high, from which the refuse slopped
down niches in the walls into the narrow alleys beneath. The
buildings seemed to lean unsteadily against one another, forming
an asymmetrical yet crudely oblong mass, pricked with thousands
of slit-windows. Within its warren of tight alleys where goats,
cattle, donkeys and chickens roamed, there were markets and
mosques, yet the town was completely encircled by a wall and
had but one entrance. Thesiger likened walking in its dark streets
to moving around at the bottom of a well.

Shibam was the main market for the notorious Se'ar – the so-
called 'Wolves of Arabia' – who were said to be on good behaviour
only when entering and leaving the town. The Se'ar delighted in

their friendless reputation, being either at war or on terms of temporary truce with all other tribes around them, including the Rawashid, to whom, in normal times, they were deadly enemies. The Se'ar watered in the steppes beyond the Hadhramaut, but their raiding parties thrust right across the Sands into Sa'udi Arabia, savaging the country of the Yam, Dawaasir and Qahtan tribes, in the region of Najran and Sulayil. In days gone by they had scavenged as far east as Mughshin and the Jiddat al Harasis, and many a Bayt Kathiri or Rashidi had cut his reputation defending his tents and herds against their incursions. One section of the Se'ar – the tent-dwelling Bin Ma'aruuf – had even migrated across the Rub' Al Khali and found a place among the Sa'udi tribes on the northern side. If Thesiger was to conquer the western Sands – the last great challenge of the Empty Quarter – he must start from the Hadhramaut. The Rawashid would provide him with a handful of tried and trusted sandsmen, but only among the 'Wolves of Arabia' could the guides he needed be found.

In 1946, Ibn Sa'ud had forbidden him to make this crossing. Yet Thesiger believed that no Sa'udi tribesman would dare murder an Englishman, and resolved to defy the King. After bin Kabina, bin Ghabaisha and the others had ridden back to Dhofar in May, he travelled on to Aden and flew to Jiddah, from where, as a Locust Control officer, he had been down to Najran on the Yemen border with a lad from the Harb tribe. Apart from genuine interest in seeing this famous trading-centre, he intended to gather as much intelligence as he could on the western Sands, and the tribes who grazed on its borders. After two months he returned to Jiddah, where for the first time he met Harry St John Philby. 'I got on well with him,' he recalled. 'There was no sense of rivalry as far as I was concerned, and indeed it was Philby who suggested I should write my journeys up. The fact that he'd become a Muslim was no business of mine – though I thought he'd done it for convenience so he could go on living in Sa'udi Arabia. It wouldn't have been something I'd have done. It didn't matter to me that I couldn't go to Mecca. It's true that Philby was the one who helped open up the oil business, and held the concession for importing cars into the country, but I'm not expecting everybody to follow my ideas – I hate cars and aeroplanes and even the sound of them, but if you're going to damn everyone who has time for motor cars you'll leave the world with myself and perhaps you in it – we'd be the only two people. Philby was a remarkable personality – he gave his whole life to Arabia, and that in itself was remarkable.'[1] Thesiger probably also knew that Philby would be an invaluable ally should he fall into the hands of Ibn Sa'ud – and so indeed it was to prove. He was in London again by July.

Thesiger was aware that the Anti-Locust Unit was unlikely to offer him another assignment in the region of the Empty Quarter. His expeditions had been expensive and provided little positive information. However, O.B. Lean did him the honour of offering him a job on the permanent staff of the Unit, poisoning locusts in the Hejaz. Thesiger declined. He craved only to be back again with bin Kabina and bin Ghabaisha and his other friends from the Rawashid – the thought of Arabia and the Bedu he loved there drove any idea of a regular occupation out of his mind. He had no interest in slaughtering locusts. The war with Germany had rocked the foundations of the Empire, and he doubted that the Sudan Political Service would take him back even if he so desired. He had been, in his own words, 'little more than a nuisance' to them during his six years of service. He had savings and a modest private income. For the rest of his life he would live on that as a 'gentleman of leisure'.

In November 1947, as the cool season began to set in, he arrived back in Mukalla, having already had a message sent to bin Kabina, bin Ghabaisha, and bin al Kamam, to meet him in the Hadhramaut at the time of the new moon. 'When the Christian returned to Mukalla the next year,' bin Kabina recalled, 'he sent a Mahri with a letter from the Hadhramaut, saying he wanted bin Ghabaisha, myself and bin al Kamam to meet him in Tarim. He paid the messenger thirty riyals. I was with 'Amair in the Wadi 'Arba, near Sanaw. The Mahri told us what was in the letter, so we went down to Ghaidat al Mahra to get food for our families, knowing we would be going away. While we were there we visited the house of a Sayyid to have the letter read, just to be sure. The Christian hadn't asked for 'Amair, but bin Ghabaisha was away in Salalah at that time, and bin al Kamam was in the

Yemen again trying to make the Daham and the 'Abida return Rawashid camels, so we decided that 'Amair would go in bin Ghabaisha's place. The thing was that you needed permission to enter the Hadhramaut – not just anyone could go there – so 'Amair pretended his name was bin Ghabaisha, and we travelled to the Hadhramaut together.'[2]

In the meantime, Thesiger had been making his own reconnaissance of Se'ar country. Though the Sc'ar were traditional enemies of the Rawashid, they had now met their nemesis in the more powerful tribes inhabiting the desert rim of the Yemen – the Daham and the 'Abida. The steppes were in turmoil, and the old order was beginning to crumble. The political ripples beneath these new incursions emanated from the court of the Imam of Yemen, to whom all the tribes of this region had once owed allegiance, before the coming of the British. The Mishqas were convinced that the Yemen government was arming the tribes and encouraging them to pillage British Protected territory. Thesiger admired the Se'ar, whom he found 'without the corroding avarice of the Bayt Kathir', and, recruiting two Se'ar tribesmen at Shibam, he visited the well at Manwakh on the edge of the Empty Quarter, knowing that this was probably the place from which he would begin his second great crossing. There had been record rains this summer. A host of tribes were gathered around Manwakh to enjoy the bounty of the harvest, and to discuss truces and blood-money. The land was more disturbed than it had been for years, and the Mishqas of Dhofar were for the first time joining with the Se'ar to fight off raids from their common enemies, who continued to make lightning strikes with large parties, murdering herdsmen and looting camels, and retiring quickly into the Jauf desert, protected by the shield of the Yemen hills. When the eastern Bedu retaliated they would come across the herds of Ibn Sa'ud's tribes – the Yam, Qahtan and Dawaasir, who pastured their herds freely in the desert – and make off with their camels instead. Such errors had occurred frequently throughout Bedu history, for once on the warpath, a *gom* wanted only camels and was not particular about whose they were. One such mistake had happened just before Thesiger's arrival, when a raiding party 140 strong, composed of Manahil, Mahra and Se'ar – all ordinarily at war with each other – under the leadership of the legendary bin Duailan, had lifted a large number of camels from the Yam and shot five tribesmen dead. In the pursuit nine of the raiding party had been killed – including bin Duailan himself. Thesiger was aggrieved at the news of bin Duailan's death, excited by all the talk of raiding, and fearful that the white-hot tensions between the tribes would interfere with his proposed crossing of the western Sands. The tribes into whose territory he must move – the Yam and the Dawaasir – were now officially at war with his Rawashid and any Se'ar guides he might happen to find. Near Manwakh he encountered Muhammad bin Salih, (known as bin Kalut), bin Kabina's half-brother, who gave him the news that bin Kabina had received his letter, and that bin al Kamam was in the Yemen. On learning Thesiger's plan he volunteered to join him across the Sands. Though Muhammad was the scion of one of the most distinguished families among the Rawashid, and had travelled with him previously, Thesiger found him self-important and rather incompetent – indeed, hardly the 'thoroughbred' one would have expected from the 'purest race in the world': he was even going prematurely bald. Thesiger would rather not have had him, but since it looked as if neither bin al Kamam nor bin Ghabaisha would be available, he accepted. He returned to Tarim in the Hadhramaut while Muhammad remained at Manwakh to continue with the discussions.

Bin Kabina and 'Amair – posing as bin Ghabaisha – had managed to pass through Hadhrami bureaucracy, but they missed Thesiger at Manwakh by a few days. 'We found Muhammad, my brother,' bin Kabina remembered, 'and he told us the Englishman had just returned to the Hadhramaut. What we decided was that 'Amair should go down to meet him, saying that I hadn't come because I had foundered my camel. 'Amair said, "If he accepts me, fine, if not I will go straight back to my people."'[3] 'Amair tracked Thesiger and his Se'ar companions to the well at Tamis, coming upon them at night as they sat by a fire, and startling them into grabbing their rifles. Thesiger was delighted to hear that bin Kabina had arrived but disappointed that bin Ghabaisha was beyond reach. He wondered whether he could contact him in Salalah by radio and have the RAF ferry him up from the air-base there. 'Amair tried to persuade him that bin Ghabaisha would never fly in an aeroplane, but not to be convinced, Thesiger whipped off a message to the RAF as soon as he reached the town of Saiyun.

'I was in Salalah selling a camel,' bin Ghabaisha recalled, 'when I met bin Tafl in the market. He said that the Wali wanted to see me about a radio message sent by the Christian. Bin Tafl took me to the Wali's office and left me there. The Wali said, "We received a message asking you to go to the Hadhramaut to meet the Christian Mbarak. Will you go by ship or by plane?" I said I didn't like the sea, so I'd go by plane. The Wali said, "We can give you some medicine to knock you out." I said, "If you do, I won't enter the plane." I didn't know much about aeroplanes, but I knew bin Tafl had been in one, so it would be all right. They thought I'd be afraid of it, but I wasn't. Anyway, we left in the afternoon and we came down in Raidat ash Shahr at night. When I got out of the plane, an Arab who worked for the Christians said, "Tomorrow at three o'clock you'll be going to Aden." I told him I wasn't going to Aden. Then a very tall Christian came who gabbled and gabbled and gabbled and gabbled at the Arab, and then asked me, "Are you going to Mbarak?" I said, "Yes," then I asked him for a letter to enter Mukalla because I remembered we'd had a problem there last time. I spent the night in a tent with one of the soldiers and in the morning the Christian came and gave me the letter. Then we drove by car for two days to the Hadhramaut. We crossed the Jol, and I saw people far below me just like ants. At sunset on the second day we entered Saiyun and later I met Mbarak. 'Amair was with him.'[4]

While he was at Tarim, Thesiger heard alarming news that Ibn Sa'ud, furious at the attacks on his Bedu, had authorized counter-raids by the Yam and Dawaasir into Se'ar territory. The bin Ma'aruuf Se'ar, who lived among the Sa'udis, had promptly fled back into their home country around the wells of al 'Abr, Zamakh and Manwakh. Soon there was further news. A bloodthirsty horde of Yam was pushing into the steppes, lifting camels and killing Arabs, advancing with the precision of a well-oiled fighting machine. The Se'ar were slipping away from their wells like an army in retreat. Thesiger was desperate to get to Manwakh before the Se'ar deserted it. He knew that without them he would have neither camels nor guides. He left Shibam on

17 December with bin Ghabaisha, 'Amair and some guides from the Se'ar, and arrived at Manwakh on 28 December.

Bin Kabina and Muhammad had already been there fifteen days. 'There were raids going on everywhere,' bin Kabina remembered, 'and they said the Yam were coming. At night they would guard their camels with rifles, and in the morning they would send out scouts – five this way, five that way, five the other way. One afternoon a Se'ari arrived and told the Sheikh that the Englishman was coming with about five people. Bin Ghabaisha and 'Amair were with them. The Se'ar had this custom that whenever they saw anybody coming they would fire bullets very close over their heads so that it almost touched your headcloth and you wouldn't know whether they really wanted to kill you or were just playing. That's what they called "welcoming you". We were standing behind the Se'ar as the Christian and the others came and there was this "Kuff! Kuff! Kuff!" and I said, "Muhammad, what shall we do? Perhaps they will kill the Christian and my brother Salim and all of them!" He said, "As soon as you see one of our men fall, shoot one of the Se'ar and then run to another and ask for his protection." By our custom the man couldn't refuse you protection when you asked him. Anyway, the Se'ar Sheikhs were running out in front of their men shouting *yab'ad haykum minkum!* [You are far from your own country!] and we thought this meant they were going to kill the Christian and our brothers. But then they stopped shooting and greeted them properly, saying, "God give you greetings! God give you peace!" [5]

With his small team of four Rawashid, Thesiger now set about obtaining good riding and baggage camels, and plenty of provisions. He desired no repetition of the three starving days at Bir Balagh the previous year. After hours of haggling, his men paid exorbitant prices for five riding camels and four spares for carrying water. The camels were fat after good grazing, but their backs were soft and likely to develop saddle-sores very quickly. While the others chose neat steppe-bred camels, bin Ghabaisha selected a black *hazmiyya* – much to the derision of his kinsmen, who despised the black sand-bred camels as riding beasts. It turned out to be an astute choice, however. Thesiger's main problem was to find a Se'ar guide willing to travel north into the country of deadly enemies, who had just been officially unleashed by Ibn

Sa'ud against his tribe. The Yam were coming, and while the Arabs of the steppes were fleeing, the mad Englishman and his still more crazy Rawashid boys were intending to ride into the eye of the storm. 'Everyone was saying we were mad to do this,' Thesiger recalled. 'You'll all be killed without a shadow of a doubt when you get to the other side. I was thinking more in terms of the difficulties of getting across the Sands, and they kept saying they would send no guide with us. I thought there was no danger, really, from the tribes on the other side, because as soon as I proclaimed I was an Englishman, they probably wouldn't kill me out of fear of trouble with Ibn Sa'ud. I had no idea then that these tribes around Sulayil would have loved to have killed me because I was a Christian. I was completely wrong about this, but the Rashid weren't and yet they were prepared to go with me . . . Such achievement as was mine was to have won their confidence and loyalty so that they would go with me.'[6]

'The Se'ar had been driven out of their wadis by their enemies,' 'Amair recalled, 'and they were afraid of the Yam and the Daham and the 'Abida. They kept telling us that by crossing the Sands we were risking our lives and that we'd all be killed. I thought they were trying to put us off – to make us show we were afraid, because they were old enemies of ours and there were still blood-feuds between us. Then they would take the Christian across themselves and get the reward. They said to us, "You go back home – let the Christian decide for himself!" Mbarak thought that we would be put off by the Se'ar, but we said we would go anyway, because we were Rawashid and didn't want them saying we were afraid, which would always have been remembered.'[7]

'The Se'ar kept saying we were only boys, and had no experience in the Sands,' bin Ghabaisha remembered, 'and that we would be killed if we met the Yam or the Dawaasir. It was a matter of honour. We couldn't give up because they would have laughed at us, then, and all the tribes would have known and laughed at us later on.'[8]

'We were proud of being Rawashid,' bin Kabina commented, 'and though we were afraid, and we knew what the risks were, we didn't want the Se'ar saying we had turned back because of fear.'[9]

*

The western Sands presented a different challenge from Thesiger's eastern crossing in 1946. Here there were no giant dunes such as the 'Urug ash Shiban, but lower ranges of sand flowing in the classic 'frozen sea' formation, interspersed with sand and gravel plains. In the eastern Sands Thesiger's party had covered fourteen days between wells, but then part of the desert had been inhabited. At Ramlat al Ghafa they had met Arabs who had given them camel's milk and allowed them to conserve their water. Moreover, Thesiger had had al 'Auf – a guide who knew every inch of the route. In the western Sands the climbs for the camels would be less difficult, but there were sixteen waterless days between Manwakh and the Hassi – a well on the northern rim of the sand-sea, only a day's march from the Sa'udi town of Sulayil. There would be no hospitable tribes to offer them camel's milk on the way, and once there they would be trapped in the land of men sworn to kill them, with no allies to lend them shelter. In short, the western Sands presented a more perilous prospect than the eastern Sands, and they were without a guide of the calibre of al 'Auf to pilot them across. 'The Se'ar were on the point of leaving,' Thesiger said, 'and this Sheikh absolutely forbade anyone to go with us because he said they'd be going to certain death. It was only my own ignorance that made me reject this fact that as soon as we met any Yam or 'Abida or any Sa'udis they would kill us on sight. Because we wore different clothes they would have known at once we were Mishqas.'[10]

Thesiger wanted to recruit the most experienced Se'ar guide, bin Daisan, who knew the way across the 400 miles of waterless sand that lay before them, and the position of the Hassi. 'The Englishman offered him a rifle and a lot of money,' bin Kabina recalled, 'and fifty rounds of ammunition, saying, "This rifle is for you if you guide us to the Hassi." In the morning he said he would go and then his people said to him no, don't go – maybe you will run into the Daham, the 'Abida, the Yam or the Dawaasir. Then by the evening he changed his mind. Every day it was like that – first agreeing, then changing his mind.'[11] Thesiger increased the promised reward and once again bin Daisan accepted. Then, just when the party was ready to move once again, there came news of skirmishing between the Rawashid and the 'Abida in the Mahra country to the east. Tribesmen on both sides had been killed, and scavengers from the 'Abida were retreating with their booty across Thesiger's line of march. In order to avoid meeting them he delayed his departure, and during the hiatus bin Daisan once more lost his nerve. 'We had to have a *rabi'a* from the Se'ar, even if he didn't know the way,' 'Amair explained, 'otherwise they could have come after us and killed us in the Sands. Anyway, the next day we found two young men and offered them a rifle each to go with us. "What if the Christian doesn't agree?" they asked. I told them we would give them two of our own rifles. They agreed to come: their names were Saalih and Sadr.'[12]

Thesiger remembered, though, that it was a friendly Se'ari called 'Ali who had persuaded the two men to go with him. ''Ali had travelled up with me from the Hadhramaut, and he did everything he could to help us,' he said. 'He told me he knew two men of his section who'd be prepared to go with me. Then bin Kabina and 'Amair went off to collect them and we offered them a rifle and 100 rounds of ammunition each. One of them had been there to the Hassi and knew where it was, and though he hadn't actually crossed the Sands he knew the position of this ridge called the 'Aradh, which stretched for miles across the desert and was a very clear landmark, and all we had to do was to find that. The whole journey we did on a compass bearing really, but the value of this man from the Se'ar was that he'd been there and seen it.'[13]

Before they left the Se'ar, bin Kabina recalled, Thesiger held a shooting contest: 'It was two from the Se'ar against two of our party, bin Ghabaisha and Mbarak, shooting at a rock at 400 paces. The Se'ar both missed the rock, the Christian just hit it on the edge, but bin Ghabaisha broke it in pieces. The day after that we set out into the Sands.'[14] In the morning the wells were crawling with tribesmen filling their skins, muddying the icy water. News had come of the Yam raiders, and the Se'ar were scrambling to move out with their families to the comparative safety of the Wadi Masila. The water was so cold that the camels refused it, and the Bedu had to seize their heads and pour the liquid forcibly down their throats as they roared and spluttered. They then filled up their fourteen skins. Before leaving Thesiger

climbed to the top of a spur with bin Daisan: 'He stood there,'
Thesiger remembered, 'and said we couldn't miss the 'Aradh, and
he pointed with both hands like the Bedu always did and said
that was the direction we should go in. Then I took a compass
bearing on that and he said just keep going in that direction and
you can't miss it.'[15] Thesiger skittered down to where the caravan
was waiting. The Bedu coaxed the bulge-bellied camels to their
feet, knotted up their bridle-ropes, adjusted a load here and there,
and drove them forward, roaring and spluttering in protest,
towards the crusty limestone country that surrounded the Rub' al
Khali. It was 6 January 1948, and Thesiger had begun the most
difficult and dangerous journey of his life.

'After leaving the Se'ar we came across two mountains,' 'Amair
recalled, 'with the Sands on our left and the mountains on our
right. We camped in the Sieh that night and though we had
rabi'as from the Se'ar, we were still on our guard in case some of
them followed us and attacked us in the night. I rode back to see
if any were following, and waited until sunset. The next day we
entered a flat plain.'[16] Here, they came across the tracks of the
'Abida raiders whom they had delayed their departure to avoid,
cutting a wide path across the sand. The 'Abida had passed two
days previously and the tracks were obscured by the great mass of
camels they had driven along with them. Despite the churning,
the Rawashid showed their tracking skills by identifying the
tracks of camels stolen from their fellow tribesmen. As Thesiger
and his party moved on, 'Amair and bin Kabina lingered behind,
scouring the confusing mass to detect the footprints of as many
individual camels as they could. To his dismay, bin Kabina
thought he recognized the tracks of two of his own camels among
the looted stock.

Gravel and sand-steppes metamorphized slowly into the low
dune-country of 'Urug az Zaza, and a bitter north-east wind
rumbled in the earth's throat and slewed across the dunes, driving
needle-sand into their faces. The wind was very welcome, however, since it would cover their tracks from the questing eyes of
pursuers. They took the threat of being followed very seriously.
'When we slept at night, each of us would have his rifle under his
head,' bin Kabina remembered. 'The Christian wanted me on his

right and bin Ghabaisha on his left whenever he slept. Each morning we would say, "Thank God we have woken up alive!" '[17] In the mornings the temperature had slumped to almost freezing, and the icy winds made riding a penance. They had none of the thick knitted socks – the size and shape of boots – the Bedu often wore on the sand, and the skin of their feet began to crack into canyons and gorges in the cold. The muffled figures would walk along in the lee of the camels, creased forward into the wind, using the animals as mobile windbreaks. They swung up into the saddle one by one as the sun simmered the remnants of the night chills. Often they pressed on till sunset without a break, falling into long silences, almost hypnotized by the shuffle and thud of the camels' feet. 'We walked a little but mostly rode, almost from sunrise to sunset,' bin Kabina recalled. 'There was a bit of grazing later on but not much at first, so there was no real reason to stop. The camels were fat, thank God, and in very good condition. But we never travelled at night, because it would have been too cold for them.'[18]

Bin Ghabaisha's memory of the journey was similar. 'We carried on mostly without stopping until an hour before sunset,' he said. 'The camels were strong, but hungry and tired and there was little pasture for them at first – in fact we only found good grazing on one day. We had only one drink of water a day or even once every two days, but we had coffee and tea as well, and we weren't thirsty because it was cold day and night. We never got really tired ourselves because we were used all our lives to this kind of journey. The Christian never got tired either.'[19]

Frequently one of them would halt to try and stop the alarming drip of water from their skins. 'They were new skins,' bin Kabina said, 'and new skins are always likely to leak. The Englishman had bought sheepskins at Shibam or Mukalla, but goatskins would have been much better. Mbarak did know which skins were good and which bad, but the goatskins were only made by the Bedu and you couldn't buy them in the town. The skins made by the Bedu are much better than those made by the town people.'[20] Thesiger wrote that he had bought the sheepskins out of inexperience, though the home-made goatskins they had with them were also new and sweating badly. He reckoned that about half of their water was lost due to these leaky skins, but at least, he commented, the water was fresh and unlike the foul muck that had sustained them in the Sands the previous year.[21]

Scanning the desert surface constantly, the Bedu missed not the slightest detail: the vacant shell of a darkling beetle; the feathered skeleton of a bird; the tracks of an Anderson's gerbil. They were excited when they came across the tracks of oryx and rim antelope stitched this way and that over the heaving sands, indicating that there was grazing at hand. The sand-people customarily followed antelope-spoor to find pasture, and it had been rumoured at Manwakh that rain had fallen in the western Sands in July. Now, however, they could afford no time to trail the animals. As they made camp just before sunset on their second day in the Sands, Thesiger saw a spectral vision. An oryx was coming straight towards them out of the desert. He had seen many oryx before, but always they had been so shy that he had not been able to get within range. The animal seemed to have mistaken them for others of its own kind, for it sauntered up to within 200 yards of the camp. Slowly, bin Ghabaisha felt for his rifle. Thesiger stopped him with a whisper, indicating that he wanted to shoot it: only a handful of Europeans had ever shot an Arabian oryx. The animal was still coming on, brilliant, pristine, noble, its lines picked out perfectly by the sharp sunlight. It was a magnificent white beast with black markings on its head, chest and legs, and long, slightly curved, ferruled black horns. Thesiger gently squeezed the trigger. The crack of his rifle split the sepulchral silence of the desert. The animal spun around and kicked off in a spurt of dust. Perhaps the image of his father shooting an oryx while he was still a child flashed through his mind with a pang of regret. Bin Kabina announced loudly, 'You should have let bin Ghabaisha shoot it!' Thesiger later recounted with some satisfaction that by missing the oryx he had probably saved their lives.

It was not until a year later, when he met bin al Kamam on the Trucial Coast, that the full story of what had happened after their departure was revealed. Bin al Kamam had not been able to travel with Thesiger, since he had been negotiating with the Daham for the return of Rawashid camels. 'Bin al Kamam was in the land of the Daham and the 'Abida with bin Qabla of the Rawashid,' bin Ghabaisha recalled, 'when the news came to them that the Christian was travelling with the Rawashid in their land.

342

They knew that the Christian had asked bin al Kamam to go with him. They sent after us fifteen men in one direction and twenty in another. If they had found us they would have killed us. They prevented bin al Kamam from travelling so he couldn't warn us. The fifteen found our tracks in the Sands and followed them until they found one of our camping places. They said they would follow us and if they found the place we camped the next night before dark they would continue. If they didn't they would go back because that would have meant we were already too far into the Sands. They rode all day but they never came to our camping place, because we were travelling faster than them.'[22] Thesiger maintained that had he not missed the oryx, his party would have halted where they were for a day to dry the meat, and the pursuers would have thus caught up with them. In fact the Daham turned back, and as he watched them riding home later bin al Kamam, who had been waiting to hear of his people's death, realized they were not singing their victory songs. He knew at once that Thesiger's party had outrun them. 'They even told him they'd found our camping site and they said you could see the holes in the ground where we'd put down my bags of gold,' Thesiger recalled. 'Of course there were no bags of gold – we did have some Maria Theresa dollars with us, but these were just food bags, of course, and this is the kind of story that gets put about . . . Like the Bayt Kathir, the Daham weren't at home in the Sands, and they hesistated over following us too far. On the other hand they were ferocious fighters, and though bin al Kamam did tell me they were settled villagers, when I met them years later in the Yemen I found out they were Bedu after all.'[23]

On 12 January they came across a lush carpet of *gassis* sedge, covering the sands for several miles. This was a royal bounty indeed, and they halted for the rest of the day while the camels wandered among the foot-high herbage and snaffled it with hungry satisfaction. The animals had already been showing signs of weakness, and the rich pasture came at an opportune time, for there were taller dunes ahead. While the beasts browsed, Thesiger's men went in search of rim and oryx. Sadr, one of the Se'ar tribesmen, spotted a herd of twenty, but the antelopes were wary as usual and the hunting was unsuccessful. The following day they crossed the gravel plain of Jilida, which bin Daisan had described to them – a hard wedge cutting into the soft sands of the desert, edged with green grasses and supporting yet more dozens of unattainable oryx. North of the Jilida they ran into the dunes of Maradh, mass upon mass of spurling sand-waves like whorls of cloud viewed from the porthole of an aircraft. Maradh was their last great obstacle before reaching the northern edge of the Sands. 'The dunes were not so high as those of the 'Uruq as Shiban,' bin Kabina remembered, 'and they were less steep, because they faced the opposite way, but the camels were already tired and it was an effort to get over them.'[24] Thesiger estimated some of them at 3–400 feet.

They drove the camels on, toiling up the windward slopes and hauling them down the other side, across the rippling giant waves that were sculpted by the winds into crescents and domes, each range taking them an hour to cross. The camels were trembling with exhaustion and thirst, when they came down abruptly into the celebrated *had* pastures where the Yam and the Dawaasir grazed their herds. *Had*, a spiky, calf-high desert bush, is one of the most resistant of all desert species, but Thesiger's camels were so thirsty they were unable to eat it. Had the Yam and Dawaasir been grazing herds on the *had*, they might well have shot Thesiger and his Mishqas on sight. Instead, by an incredible stroke of luck, heavy rains had fallen only ten days earlier on the steppes to the north and the tribes had drifted back out of the Sands, leaving the surface churned up by the tracks of camels, and the remains of camps and fires. Not a soul was to be seen. The signs of Bedu alerted them, however, and from here on Thesiger put two scouts ahead of the main party. They lit their cooking-fires in the late afternoon to avoid fires at night, which would have attracted marauders like moths to a candle-flame. Soon after, the 'Aradh began to take form out of the ocean of sand, a hazy grey line, like a mirage at first, but steadily solidifying into the fortress-wall of granite that Thesiger knew cut die-straight across the Sands and ended near the Hassi wells.

They followed the 'Aradh for two days, and had almost reached the wells when they rode straight into a party of eight men of the Yam on their way to Najran. For a moment there was a stunned silence: 'I could see hatred in their eyes,' Thesiger said, 'and I noticed bin Ghabaisha slipping his safety-catch forward. Luckily they had their rifles hanging from their saddles, whereas we had ours in our hands. I said, "Peace be on you," and one of them replied, and then a boy with them said, "Are they Mishqas?" and a man turned and snarled at him, "Don't you know the Arab? Don't you know the foe?" We said we were the advance party of a large party, so they should be careful because there were others ahead, and this sort of covered our retreat.'[25] A few hours later they arrived at the Hassi wells. Thesiger had become the only Westerner ever to have crossed the Empty Quarter twice.

'When we reached the Hassi there was a Dosri [sing. of Dawaasir] there,' bin Kabina recalled, 'an old man who was working for the Sa'udi government, and had a tent near by. There was a boy with him and they both had camels, but the boy was out hunting when we arrived, and only the old man was at the wells – in fact at the Hassi there are many wells, not just one. The old man drank coffee with us and then went back to his tent. Then the Se'ar who were with us quickly filled their waterskins – they didn't want to meet anyone else from the Dawaasir because there was blood between them. They had two skins of their own and we gave them two more   the best ones we had   and they rode straight back across the Sands the way we had come. When the old Dosri came back, he wanted to know where the other two were. We said they had left two camels in the Sands and they were taking water to them, and we didn't know if they would come back here or go back to their grazing. The way these Dawaasir spoke was heavy-tongued and the Englishman couldn't understand what they said, and we had to tell him. They were dressed like Sa'udis with red headcloths and *'uqals* [headcloth-ropes].'[26] Thesiger stated that the guardian of the well was a Yam, and that, when he learned Thesiger was a Christian, he spat the coffee out and said he would not drink with them further. 'Amair, bin Kabina and bin Ghabaisha, however, all remembered that he was a Dosri, and none recalled any overt hostility until they reached Sulayil.

After resting at the wells for a day, Thesiger's party told the old man they intended to move to Sulayil the following morning. That night the Dosri announced that he and his son would accompany them. 'His hospitality was poor,' bin Kabina commented, 'and he didn't invite us to his tent. In the morning we rode with him to Sulayil, which we reached in the evening. Once we got there he went straight to the 'Amir and betrayed us to him, saying that they had caught us and that two more had escaped into the desert. Luckily the 'Amir was a good man – even though he was a slave – and treated us like guests. He even slaughtered a goat for us.'[27]

It was the 'Amir of Sulayil who first convinced Thesiger that he had been incredibly fortunate to have reached Sulayil alive. 'He said, "You've simply no conception how lucky you've been,"' Thesiger recalled. '"If you'd met a single Arab on your journey the hue and cry would have been out at once and you would certainly have been killed!"'[28] The 'Amir's declaration was emphasized by the attitude of the people in Sulayil, who were hostile and aggressive. The Bedu among them were openly declaring that it was a pity they had not encountered the Christian out in the desert, where they could have murdered him with impunity. This was doubly shocking to Thesiger, because he had been well received previously when travelling in the Hejaz, the Tihama and Assir with Ibn Sa'ud's permission, and in the company of local guards. He now glimpsed the latent hostility to Christians that lay in the Sa'udi character.

'This 'Amir was a good man,' bin Kabina went on, 'but above him there was a more senior 'Amir who wasn't so good; he was the Governor of the Wadi Dawaasir, called bin Madhi, in Hanaw, north-west from Sulayil. Those same scoundrels who had come with us from the Hassi went to report to bin Madhi, and he sent orders to arrest us. Whether these orders came first from bin Sa'ud I don't know. Anyway, we had been at Sulayil for two days, staying in this room. In the mornings bin Ghabaisha and I used to take the camels off to graze, since we were the youngest. When the orders came, they jumped on 'Amair and my brother, Muhammad, and threw them into prison. When we came back with the camels they caught us and they jumped on us before we could do anything. We were only boys and didn't know the ways of the government, and that we shouldn't fight. All we knew was the way to fight on raids – the way of the Bedu – so I cocked my rifle and tried to shoot at them. This Murri who worked for the 'Amir shouted that it was the orders of bin Sa'ud and said,

"Don't fight! Don't fight! You won't be harmed!" Then they threw us into this big room with wooden stocks and they locked us in them. It was just one leg they locked, but it was painful on that one. The other leg wasn't too bad. Our arms were free, but it was just this wood that closed over our legs and there we were all sitting there in a line. We weren't really afraid though, because Muhammad said the Englishman had gone off to send a message to bin Sa'ud, and he wasn't locked up. He said later he had paid thirty riyals to send the message.

'In the morning they took us out and questioned us. It was bin Madhi himself who was asking the questions. He asked each one on his own, but we could hear each other. "Whose are those rifles you've got with you?" he asked. "The Englishman's," I said. "Whose are those camels?" "The Englishman's." "Why do you travel with the Englishman?" "Because he gives us money." The Christian had told us to say that the weapons and camels belonged to us, but my brother, who was the eldest of us, told us to say that they belonged to the Englishman, because if they were ours they would take them, but one government would not take what belonged to another government, and we always thought of the Christian as belonging to the government. Anyway, they were very rough with me because I had cocked my rifle and one of them said, "This is the dog who cocked his rifle when we took him! This is the dog that wanted to kill us! If you don't tell us the truth we will cut out your tongue!" "I am in your hands," I said, "but God knows, I haven't committed any crime." Someone was writing all this down and bin Madhi said, "Let him talk! Let him talk!" '[29]

Actually, the four Bedu must have presented a perplexing picture to their Sa'udi interrogators, since according to 'Amair, they all told different stories. Thesiger had instructed them to say that they were accompanying him on an oryx-shooting trip, and had strayed to the north and watered at the Hassi. 'When they asked me if we were travelling with him for money, I denied it,' 'Amair said, 'and I said he was following the locusts. Then we got confused as to who we should say the camels and rifles belonged to, and some of us said they belonged to us and others that they belonged to him!'[30]

'They threw us back into prison,' bin Kabina explained, 'and a short time later they came and let me out again. They put everything – the baggage, the rifles, everything – into a lorry and they took me and the Christian to bin Madhi's place. I don't know why the Englishman asked for me to go with him, but he said he needed one of us to make the talk clear because he couldn't understand their pronunciation. He preferred me above all my companions, and he might also have been afraid they would harm me because I cocked my rifle. We spent the night in a house in bin Madhi's place at Hanaw. What we heard later was that Philby went to see bin Sa'ud and when he was poured coffee said, "I will not drink your coffee until you free my friend. There is bin Kalut with him and three more of the Rawashid" – bin Sa'ud knew my brother's father, Salih bin Kalut, who was famous – "They are your people" he said, because the Rawashid owed allegiance to bin Sa'ud. Bin Sa'ud said, "Let them stay in prison till the morning!" Then the next morning they let the other three out. The Christian and I weren't in jail, of course, but the next day bin Mahdi said there had been an order for our release, so they put us back on the lorry with our baggage and we returned. We spent the night with an American oil company who gave us some sugar. When we got back, the slave 'Amir said he was sorry we'd been arrested and that he'd been angry with what bin Madhi had done.'[31]

On 29 January the party set out once again for Laila, a town north-east of Sulayil, along a well-defined motor track. 'There were plenty of cars about then,' bin Kabina commented. 'There were American oil companies working in the Wadi Dawaasir, and the people even asked the Englishman why he didn't travel in a car "like the Muslims"! That was very funny!'[32] They rode through monotonous, uninhabited steppe-land and entered Laila one morning. 'In Laila the people gave us a hard time,' 'Amair remembered, 'saying we were not Muslims and it was forbidden to bring a Christian into their territory. We just ignored them, even though we knew they were right. By our custom it would have been shameful to abandon a travelling-companion.'[33] Thesiger recorded that the people of Laila were worse than those of Sulayil, and that the 'Amir had breached Arab hospitality by leaving them for an entire day without food or coffee, even though they were his guests. 'One evening while we were there, the Dawaasir invited us to eat with them,' bin Kabina said, 'and as we sat down to eat they brought in a dog. They said that as we were travelling with a Christian we were used to eating with dogs. The Rawashid don't even keep dogs, and we were really angry about it. We all refused to eat with them. Then the next day Philby came in his car. He gave us sixty riyals each. He had a big tent put up and invited us to eat with him.'[34]

'Philby gave us some money,' 'Amair recalled. 'He was a hospitable man, but I don't think he was a real Muslim, and he became an infidel again later.'[35] Naturally, Thesiger was delighted to see him, and learned for the first time that Philby's intervention with Ibn Sa'ud had saved them. He and Philby talked until three in the morning, while rain beat on the tent overhead. In the morning Philby left to investigate some inscriptions at the ruined city of Qariya.

They were still short of food, and when Thesiger's men tried to buy provisions they were cursed and spat upon, and told that their money would be accepted only if it were publicly washed. They finally obtained provisions through the son of the local 'Amir. The important oasis of Jibrin, a major centre for the Murrah nomads, lay a further 150 miles to the east, but they had no guide, and no one in Laila would consent to go with a Christian. 'I mean, what were we going to do?' Thesiger asked. 'No one would go with us and they were even saying they hoped we would die in the desert. Luckily I had the map Philby had made of the region and I thought it was meticulously accurate. I thought if we followed that on a compass bearing we would probably be all right. To the Bedu the idea of travelling by compass was extraordinary. They were very doubtful indeed. One of them eventually asked me how many days it would take to get to Jibrin and I said eight, and he said, yes, that's what the local people were saying. That was what decided them to do it, and they said, well, we must trust Mbarak. But it was extraordinary because as long as they stayed with me they had to get me to Jibrin. If they'd have abandoned me there and gone off no one would have stopped them, although they might have been a bit hostile.'[36]

'We didn't believe at first that he could do it,' bin Kabina said, 'but we had no choice but to trust him. The greatest of shame for us would have been to return saying we'd left our travelling-companion, and it would have been remembered all our lives, so there was no question at all about abandoning Mbarak or whoever it had been with us, a Muslim or a Christian.'[37] 'It was true that we shouldn't have brought a Christian into Sa'udi territory,' 'Amair commented, 'but he was our travelling-companion and we had agreed to go with him till we reached Abu Dhabi. If we had gone back without him, the tribes would have heard about it and it would have been great disgrace for us, after we had defied the Se'ar. We had no choice, really, but to go on. We hadn't much faith in the idea of a compass and a map then, because we knew nothing about them. But we put our faith in God.'[38]

The trek to Jibrin was a bleak, miserable, monotonous slog. 'It was a severe time,' 'Amair remembered. 'We were hungry and thirsty and the dust was so bad that we could hardly keep our eyes open.'[39] Thesiger was constantly afraid of wandering off his bearing. Jibrin was a pinprick on the vastness of the desert, and an error of a few degrees would take them way past it into unknown sands. 'The camels found it hard going on this stony ground and were inclined to shift off to the south,' he said. 'I realized that if that happened too often I would soon lose my bearing so we had more or less to go straight on the bearing regardless of what the going was like.'[40] They crossed the Dahana, the narrow neck of Sands which joins the Empty Quarter to the Nafud desert like an umbilicus, and here the crescent dunes were in bloom. After seven days they climbed a ridge and saw Jibrin below them, a dark island of life on the endless grey and orange plains. The Bedu exploded into excited chatter, and were soon driving their camels down to a well near by named Umm al Adwa. The well was encircled by desiccated scrub and the camels sniffed unhappily around some unfamiliar plants called *gurdhai*, which Thesiger was himself unable to identify. 'Amair and Muhammad rode off to seek out the Murrah, and just before sunset Thesiger stood up expectantly as they trooped back into camp, the shadows of the camels like great tarantulas on the sand. The news was bad. There were no Murrah here, and no fresh tracks. Jibrin was deserted: there were no provisions to be had. 'They had sold us very little in Laila,' Thesiger said, 'and I thought it was enough to get us to Jibrin where we'd meet the Murrah, but there wasn't a Murri in Jibrin. We thought we might find some dates, but instead they were out of season and we found nothing. They came at me again, what on earth were we going to do? I said there's a well called Dhiby marked on the map – this was Thomas's map, because Thomas had passed through Dhiby on his way to Qatar – and I can get you as far as there. It's the only well marked and whether it's brackish or not I don't know.'[41] What Thesiger did know is that they were now in dire straits, for the camels had found almost nothing to eat since leaving Laila except salt-bushes, which had given them diarrhoea and therefore dehydrated them. The Bedu had had to resort to tying them up to prevent them from grazing. As expected, the baggage camels had developed bad saddle-sores which were infected and evil-smelling, and might themselves prove fatal if the camels continued to be loaded in this condition. 'Amair pared away lumps of infected flesh with his dagger to make them more comfortable, and Thesiger ordered ten waterskins to be filled and loaded. He resigned himself to the fact that some of the camels might be lost.

They moved out the following day, across desolate *sebkhas* where the camels browsed desultorily amid leathery acacias. That night there was an argument over provisions. ''Mbarak said we should reduce the amount of food we were eating,' 'Amair recalled. 'We were only eating one cup of flour each a day, so that was really the limit. I said we can't reduce it more than that. We aren't getting enough as it is. I thought we should slaughter a camel and then we'd have enough to get us to Abu Dhabi. He got very angry about it and in the end I refused to cook. He asked bin Kabina – who was after all only a boy – whether it was just me who didn't want to reduce the food or the others too. Bin Kabina said we were all agreed. The Christian was really furious but in the end he didn't reduce the food.'[42] There is some confusion in the party's memory of what occurred here. Thesiger recalled that the Bedu had asked him to *increase* the amount of food: 'It was Muhammad,' he commented, 'who said we couldn't go on with only one cup of flour a day and a few dates. I said, well, take the lot and eat it all tonight and then we'll know exactly where we are! Obviously, the amount wasn't increased.'[43]

Bin Kabina remembered that the problem revolved around a difference of outlook between Thesiger's caution and Bedu fatalism. 'Mbarak was worried that the food wouldn't last,' he said, 'and we knew it would. We wanted to increase the amount of food, while he wanted to reduce it. We all agreed on increasing it because we were brothers. He said to me, "And what about you? Do you agree with them?" I said, "Yes." The Christian was very angry and said, "Well do what you want, but I'm not taking any responsibility for it." Then, as I was going about making the tea, he threw a heavy bag at me in anger. I was caught by surprise and I seized my dagger and had it half out before I got control of myself. It was Mbarak who had given me that dagger. Anyway, we Bedu stood together and he had to back down. The food was not reduced or increased.'[44]

Cumulus clouds had banked ominously before them since leaving Laila, and now, as they moved out of Jibrin, the expected freezing rain descended, penetrating them to the skin. Almost immune to high temperatures with his lean body, Thesiger suffered terribly from the cold. They had no tent or waterproofs to cover them, and ironically they had almost nothing in which to catch the rainwater. They could not, anyway, have afforded the time to halt. They had ten full skins with them but were unsure when they might reach water again, and were rationing intake to a pint a day. Ironically, therefore, in the midst of pounding showers they remained thirsty. One night as they lay down to sleep, thunder shuddered in the night sky and blue forks of electricity shot in blinding seams down to the desert floor. The cold rain drenched them, cutting like steel through Thesiger's rugs and sleeping-bag, running in streams across the helpless, prone bodies, cocooned in little more than their own clothes. In the morning their sodden wood refused even to yield a warming fire. Hungry and freezing, they toiled on with exhausted, famished, shivering camels, coming through the sheet of rain upon a shallow well. The camels drank, but so foul was the water that they were unable to eat the rice bin Kabina cooked in it, and went hungry again. The next day the weather turned. The sun surged out of its cloak of cloud and warmed them, and the Bedu rode across the damp flats singing, knowing that within days this emptiness would be alive with the blossoms of green plants. On 22 February, Thesiger declared that they were near Dhiby well, and bin Ghabaisha rode off to look for it. He was somewhat surprised to find it precisely where Thesiger had said it would be. Despite the fact that the water was too salty except for the camels to drink, the Bedu were impressed with Thesiger's navigation. The animals remained hungry, however. The sparse strands of *gassis* near the well did little to satisfy them, and every member of the party knew that they might soon collapse from hunger and exhaustion. Abu Dhabi, on the Trucial Coast, still lay 250 miles away. As they loaded the camels with chilled hands the following morning, and set off into the miserable grey shell of the world, Thesiger became convinced the camels would not survive another day. They shambled on in their damp and filthy *dishdashas*, hungry, cold, hardly able to talk, each alone with his silent thoughts. Then suddenly a miracle happened. They walked into rich green grazing – a tiny patch in the vastness of the desert, brought on by one of the mercurial rains on which the Bedu's lives depended. It was enough to bloat their camels' stomachs with fresh food. As the beasts lowered their great necks and swallowed the stuff ravenously, bin Ghabaisha said: 'This grazing has saved our lives.'[45]

The next day they crossed the tail of the Sabkhat Mutti, a great salt-flat which touches the Arabian Gulf. Thesiger was apprehensive of going further north, for al 'Auf had recounted to him tales that camels had become bogged down in the Sabhka's mud. The salt-crystals threw a dazzling glare into their eyes. 'It was like a sea,' 'Amair recalled. 'There were sands and then between them places where the camels sank in. Other parts of it were all right.'[46] When they halted that night, Thesiger and his Bedu held a council. It was still over 200 miles to Abu Dhabi, and water was short. None of them knew if there were wells along the coast, and though there existed a possibility that they might run into friendly Bedu, the fact that they had met no one since leaving Laila, 350 miles away, seemed to render this chance unlikely. If they continued towards Abu Dhabi, and did not find water, they would die. Due east of them lay the oasis of Liwa –

actually a great string of fertile enclaves extending eighty miles through the dunes. 'I said the thing is to find Liwa,' Thesiger recalled, 'and I asked bin Kabina if he would recognize the dunes we had seen the previous year. He said yes, and we decided to head for Liwa. Later he climbed a dune and said, "There they are, I can see them." '47 They arrived at Bir Balagh, where Thesiger had spent his tortured days of starvation in 1947, on 4 March.

It was near here that a strange thing happened. 'We were watering at a place called Khadai, about two days' march from Liwa,' bin Kabina recalled, 'and we dug out the well ourselves. We found grass for the camels and we were making coffee and tea, when the Christian suddenly fell down. "Get up, Mbarak! Get up!" we shouted. "Drink tea!" He didn't answer and we thought he was dying. The Christian has died! No God but God, what shall we do? Now people will say that we killed him! I said we would have to take his body back with us to show that we didn't kill him, but bin Ghabaisha said no, his body would start to smell and spoil the camels. He said we should just leave him here. Then suddenly the Christian stood up and we were very surprised. We expected him to laugh but he didn't, he had just wanted to see what we would do. I told him that he must write us a paper to say that if he died we weren't responsible. We were very serious, but he just said, "Never mind!" '48 Once again, there is some discrepancy in the various memories of this incident. 'Amair recalled that Thesiger fainted after drinking some brackish water: 'We thought he was dead,' he remembered, 'but later he stood up and we saw he had been testing us to see if he could trust us, which he should have known after all we'd been through. Later we asked him to sign a paper saying his companions hadn't murdered him if he died – which would have been a very shameful thing for us.'49

Bin Ghabaisha's account differed slightly. 'It was Muhammad who found the Englishman lying as if he was dead, and he called us. We shook him and shouted, but he didn't wake up, so we thought he was dead. Bin Kabina said we should take him to the Sultan in Liwa to prove we hadn't killed him, but I said that it was the Sultan of Muscat under whose authority we'd been sent to him and we couldn't take him to the Sultan because it was too far. We weren't afraid of what the Sultan would do to us, we were afraid for our reputations, which meant everything to us.'50

Although Thesiger never mentioned this incident in *Arabian Sands*, he later admitted that it had happened. 'Bin Kabina came past me on his camel and caught me with his rifle,' he said, 'and I went over backwards right over the camel's tail and fell on my neck. I thought dammit, I'll pretend I'm dead and see what happens – I'll just make out I've broken my neck. As I lay there, they began to talk about whether they'd bury me or take me, and then I gave a grunt and pretended to come alive again.'[51] It is a curious episode, and the more curious for not having been included in Thesiger's book. Why should he have wished to test his companions in this rather amateurish way, when, he asserted, he had had absolute faith in them from the beginning? One may surmise that there had been new strains on their relationship since arriving in Sa'udi Arabia which had unexpectedly widened the gap between the Christian and his Muslim companions. The most important of these, perhaps, was the onslaught of the puritanical Sa'udi Arabs on the Rawashid, which had made them feel unconsciously like traitors to their own kind. The Rawashid, devout Muslims, who owed allegiance to Ibn Sa'ud himself, had been spat at and cursed because they were helping an infidel for money. Later there had come the conflict over the increased rations, in which Thesiger may have been faced unexpectedly with the reality of Bedu solidarity, expressed by their saying, 'Me and my brother against my cousin: me and my cousin against an outsider.' On his previous journeys there had been the Bayt Kathir–Rawashid jealousy to play on: now it was simply him against them, an inevitable polarization. His feigning death may have been a final attempt to gauge their real feeling of loyalty to him, but it merely evinced a predictable response. Personal emotions do not seem to have entered into it: what mattered to the Bedouin was his reputation, his reputation and his reputation.

Near Bir Balagh they came across an encampment of Bedu from the Manasir, one of whom agreed to guide them through Liwa to Abu Dhabi. For three days they moved slowly through the galaxy of villages that was Liwa, each divided by the sheer walls of great dunes – palm-groves and fields of wheat, inhabited by tribesmen of the Bani Yas who lived in palm-frond cabins on the dunes. Now the struggle to survive was over, the smouldering resentments resurfaced, and the polarization took its fullest form: Thesiger quarrelled with his Arabs over petty trifles.

On 14 March, the five ragged, hungry, desert-scoured men struggled out of the sand and crossed the creek into Abu Dhabi. Knots of townsmen gathered at the well hardly spared them a glance, for the coming and going of Bedu from the deserts was commonplace. The ruler's fort was virtually the only permanent building in the town, an eccentric conglomerate of mud walls, crumbling pillars, Moresco arches and block-house, each portion of which had been added piecemeal. The rusting barrels of ancient cannon lay impotently in the streets – souvenirs of many a set-to with the British fleet when Abu Dhabi was a port on the Pirate Coast. In the harbour *booms* and *sambuks* furled their sails in the sheltered harbour. 'We ended the journey at the fort in Abu Dhabi,' Thesiger remembered. 'The place consisted of the fort and I think two coral houses on the edge of the sea, and a certain number of *burastis* [palm-frond or reed huts], and a well with rather brackish water and a few palm trees. Abu Dhabi did not exist to any sort of extent. There was nothing – you could say there was a fort there, that's all. We ended our journey at the fort, and I remember sitting outside waiting for the door to open so that I could go in and see the Sheikhs. This boy came out and peed, and then we called him over and said tell the Sheikhs there's an Englishman here. Then a bit later a man unbolted the door and came over to us and asked which is the Englishman and they pointed to me, and he took me up to meet Sheikh Shakhbut and his two brothers. They were sitting in quite a small room on mattresses.'[52] Sheikh Shakhbut bin Sultan was then the ruler of Abu Dhabi, and after his dour reception by the Sa'udis it was a relief for Thesiger to find the Sheikh hospitable. However, Shakhbut seemed somewhat surprised to see the Englishman: 'When I appeared in the fort they had no idea I was in the area,' Thesiger said, 'whereas when I'd been near Liwa the previous year they'd heard rumours that an Englishman had been there and they had simply disbelieved that we had come and disappeared without anybody seeing us; they thought this must have been nonsense and just a story from the time Thomas was near there.'[53] Later, Shakhbut gave Thesiger and his men a ramshackle house on the waterfront and told them to stay as long as they liked. Its windows overlooked the shore, and Thesiger spent hours watching the crews of the dhows loading and unloading their cargoes of dates, dried sardines, bales of cloth and mangrove poles. Some of the boats carried barrels of fresh water which were shipped over from the neighbouring islands and sold in the souk. The Sheikh and his brothers, Hiza and Khalid, would frequently drop in to visit them, bringing with them a cluster of armed retainers. Often Thesiger walked with bin Kabina or bin Ghabaisha along the waterfront, watching the boats being caulked or chatting with the Persian merchants in the dappled shade of the bazaars. Here, Bedu from half a dozen different tribes would be striding about, with their wild hair, daggers and rifles, bringing with them the atmosphere of the open desert. Thesiger's companions would hail them in a coffee-shop and exchange the news, which passed by word of mouth in this way, like one billiard ball clipping another, until it had traversed the entire peninsula. Some of these Bedu would join the pearling fleet as divers in the summer months, and Thesiger became fascinated by the pearl trade. Later, he inquired if it would be possible to get a passage on a *boom* returning from Zanzibar to Bahrain. He was told that he would have a better chance in Dubai. He remained in Abu Dhabi for twenty days.

He was in no hurry to leave. The company of two of his Rawashid friends meant more to him than anything, and he sought any excuse to remain with them as long as he could. But he also had his future plans in mind. He decided to head inland again and visit Buraimi. Standing on the border between the authority of the Sheikh of Abu Dhabi and the King of Oman, Buraimi was an oasis divided into nine villages, all but three of which were administrated by the local Sheikh, Zaayid bin Sultan – later to become the world-famous ruler of the United Arab Emirates. He then had his headquarters in the village of Muwaijih. 'The Bedu all said, "Zaayid is a Bedouin and can ride a camel and knows how to fight,"' Thesiger recalled. 'He wasn't really from a Bedouin family, but what they meant was that his people were famous and had the respect of the Bedu. When we arrived there he was sitting on the sand under a tree – an acacia tree – and we couched our camels and walked over to him and they all stood up,

I suppose about twenty people, and we shook hands and he sent for some cushions and rugs and I said no need to do that, but he insisted, and we just sat down and talked. He had known we were coming, of course, because they had sent word from Abu Dhabi.'[54] Zaayid, Shakhbut's younger brother, was then about thirty-two and had been born at al 'Ain, one of the villages in Buraimi. He belonged to the Al bu Falah, a section of the Bani Yas, the settled tribe which also inhabited Liwa, about 15,000 strong. Although governor of Buraimi only since 1946, he was already famous for his wisdom and shrewdness, and his love of camel-racing and falconry: 'He is a forceful personality,' Thesiger wrote, 'and has considerable influence with the Bedu of these parts. He emulates their way of life and spends most of his time hunting and travelling among them.'[55] The Al bu Falah family had until recently been at war with the richer Bin Maktum clan of Dubai, allied with the Bani Qitab Bedouin, and Zaayid had surrounded himself with Bedu retainers from the local tribes. Thesiger's real motive in reaching Buraimi and making a friend of Zaayid was his desire to explore Oman. He had crossed the Sands twice, and no further challenge remained in the Empty Quarter itself, but already he was turning his restless thoughts to the unexplored mountain country of Oman, and the 'undiscovered' quicksand of Umm as Samim. He could not use Dhofar or the Hadhramaut as base-camps again, but Buraimi was the gateway to Oman.

Zaayid agreed to help him in his plans, but advised him to keep them secret, even from his Rawashid. Captain Richard Bird, an ex-Indian Civil Service officer now representing the Iraq Petroleum Company, was also staying in Buraimi. Bird was perhaps the leading authority on the tribes of south Arabia, and had a roving commission from his company to obtain oil concessions and to get oil-explorers into Oman. Thesiger had met Bird earlier in Kuwait and was happy to see this well-known expert, yet he was chary of being associated with the company, and stayed instead with Zaayid. 'I didn't want to get people talking,' he explained, 'because my next object was to get into the interior of Oman which was virtually unexplored at that time. Cox and about two other people had been there. I knew if I was associated with Bird they'd think, Oh yes, he's one of the oil company people. It wasn't that they didn't want the oil, but each tribal

Sheikh wanted to have his own particular agreement with the oil people.'[56] It seems likely that Thesiger's stance was a typical gesture of solidarity with the Arabs rather than a pragmatic one: Ronald Codrai, later the representative of the Iraq Petroleum Company in Dubai, and a close friend of both Bird and Thesiger, commented: 'He didn't want to be tainted with oil company influence which I don't think was a very relevant point – it wouldn't have impinged on his independence at all.'[57] Although Thesiger wrote later that he feared and dreaded the changes the oil companies would bring and were already bringing, this was an intellectual opposition rather than a personal one. It certainly did not prevent his friendship with other civilized Englishmen of the same background, any more than it had affected his partiality for Philby. Thesiger himself belonged to the very class which was helping to bring about the changes that he so detested. Though he later declared that he had 'mistakenly mapped the Empty Quarter', almost as if it were a small oversight, and played down his map-making skills, in fact his maps are astoundingly detailed and professionally produced. He must have been perfectly aware at the time that the oil companies – already operating in Sau'di Arabia for more than a decade – would make use of his map. Nor can he have been too naïve to observe that the formidable amount of geographical data he had amassed on the region, his numerous addresses to learned societies and his geographical papers, made him, whether he liked it or not, one of the pathfinders of the forces of development in southern Arabia. All his life, since his earliest adventure as fireman on the *Sorrento*, Thesiger had had the best of both worlds – the company of the men, and dinner in the officers' mess: all his life he would delight in being able to run with the hare and ride with the hounds.

Thesiger's admiration for Glubb was a typical example of this ambivalence. Glubb was one of the classic British Arabists of the twentieth century – an Englishman who loved and respected the Bedu above any other race. Yet he was essentially a policeman who had been brought to Trans-Jordan in 1930 to raise a force that would control raiding by the Bedu. He recruited his troops from among the Bedu tribesmen themselves, and mounted them in armoured cars. By 1934 – in the short span of four years – he was able to announce that he had achieved what no government had ever succeeded in doing before – the complete subjugation of the Bedouin tribes of north Arabia. Years later even Glubb himself realized that by suppressing the tradition of the raid, he had played a part in destroying the Bedouin society he so admired. As Louise E. Sweet has argued, these raids had equalized wealth between tribes and were an ecological necessity. Without this equalizing tendency, differences between rich and poor became more marked: Bedu society lost the edge that the constant war-footing had supplied. Glubb was not entirely alone in this, of course. Considerably more damage was done by an Arab – Ibn Sa'ud in Sa'udi Arabia – who had politicized and even tried to settle the Bedouin tribes. He was assisted by Thesiger's friend Philby, who believed that 'freed of the curse of tribalism, a united Arabian nation could take its place among the great countries of the earth'.[58] Though Thesiger constantly challenged 'our right' to 'destroy' ancient civilizations, he apparently attached no personal blame to those who had actually 'done the dirty work', so to speak. Men like Dick Bird, St John Philby and John Glubb were members of the Imperial class to which he himself belonged. 'I knew Glubb well and had a great admiration for him,' Thesiger commented. 'Of all the Europeans who have been in touch with the Bedu, he knew more about them than anybody else. He was a Bedouin . . . He said to me that raiding was in a sense an essential part of Bedu life, like playing games at a public school . . . He raised the Arab Legion and they weren't allowed to raid. They stopped the other raids that were going on, but that was inevitable once you got Ibn Sa'ud establishing law and order in the south . . . Of course in the modern world it was impossible . . . [the power of the Bedu] would have been destroyed anyway . . .'[59] Thesiger established his reputation by articulating a generation's sadness at the passing of an era, yet despite his question about our moral rights, he recognized inwardly that the Philbys, the Glubbs and the Birds – and even the Thesigers, perhaps – were pawns in a process over which they had no moral control. Like the upholders of the British Empire, if it had not been them, it would have been somebody else. To Thesiger the true enemy did not consist of individuals, but on the contrary, of mass, populist, egalitarian, mechanized society, which he saw as the bane of individualism. His enemy was the inexorable march of time itself.

*

For a week Thesiger camped at Jabal Hafit, the great blade of granite that dominates the desert in the Buraimi region, where he hunted *tahr* – an endemic species of mountain sheep. He remained as Zaayid's guest for almost a month, during which he sat with the Sheikh in his *majlis*, drinking coffee and imbibing with it the nuances of tribal politics in the Trucial region. 'Anybody could speak in these councils,' he said. 'There was no question of waiting or anything. Some Bedouin would just stand up and say, "Now, Zaayid, what about those camels of mine I told you about yesterday?" And there was no "I'll talk to you later" or anything. Even a boy had a perfect right to say anything, and if there was a discussion some junior boy would stand up and give his views and people would listen.'[60] Like bin Taimur in Oman, Zaayid was already the owner of a car, and offered Thesiger the use of it for his return journey to Sharjah and Dubai on the coast. Wanting to make the most of his last days with bin Kabina and bin Ghabaisha, though, Thesiger gracefully declined. Instead, Zaayid lent him some fine camels. They dawdled north to Sharjah, shooting two feral asses on the way, which Thesiger had skinned and salted for the Natural History Museum. They reached Sharjah on 10 May. There, Thesiger parted with his Bedu companions, but told them he would be back within four months. They would not be returning to Dhofar, but had decided to trek back to Buraimi where they would become retainers of Sheikh Zaayid, and bin Ghabaisha would get his first taste of camel-raiding against Zaayid's enemies, the Bani Qitab. Outside Sharjah, Thesiger shook hands with his travelling-companions, promising to return later that year. They had endured much together: the bond forged from shared hardship could never again be sundered. 'I had been drawn along a road of my own choosing by the lure of the unknown and had been rewarded by our achievements,' Thesiger wrote. 'My companions, by nature realists, might well have hung back at Manwakh or hesistated to continue without a guide from Laila ... I owed everything to their light-hearted gallantry, their constancy and endurance.'[61] Though Thesiger would return to Arabia, he had made his life's two greatest journeys, and the ones upon which his fame would rest. He personally considered his crossing of the western Sands the height of his achievement. There comes a time in every adventurer's life when he knows that nothing he can do will ever be quite the same again: Thesiger had reached the summit of his ambitions. No people would ever be to him as the Bedu were: no land would thrill him like Arabia. The attitude of his Bedu companions was summed up by bin Ghabaisha: 'We were proud of this journey,' he said. 'No one had done it before, and everyone knew it was hard. It made our names famous among the tribes for the rest of our lives.'62

CHAPTER 12

Chapter Closed

After seeing his companions off, Thesiger drove the short distance to Dubai, a large town sited on both sides of a sweeping salt creek. Here he stayed with H.M. Jackson, local representative of the Iraq Petroleum Company, in his spacious, coral-built house near the waterside. Jackson, an excellent Arabic-speaker, was soon to be replaced by Thesiger's old SOE colleague from wartime Syria, Edward Henderson, who would inherit the same house. 'It was right at the corner of the creek,' Henderson remembered, 'the very last house in town with a long verandah, and from there we could watch all the boats going out: their sails were a beautiful sight, as they had to tack out of the creek, passing the boom or spar in front of the mast. There were few solely motor-driven vessels, then: almost everything had a sail.'[1] This house was to become Thesiger's base-camp over the next two seasons, the haven where he could relax, speak English, sit at a table and bathe in a hot bath – in other words reassume the persona of the English gentleman, which he could now slip into and out of like a Savile Row suit.

Two days after his arrival, he was sitting, scrubbed and shaved, on the verandah with Jackson, when a curious little procession appeared at the house: two rather dishevelled and sun-baked Englishmen wearing Arab loincloths, followed by a local sailor carrying the severed head of a monstrous barracuda. One of the Englishmen was Bird, on his way back from Muscat, where he had bumped into the second man, Ronald Codrai, a former RAF officer who was on leave from the Middle East Centre for Arab Studies in Lebanon. They had travelled up the coast from Muscat together in a native *jaulbaut*, and had spent the time fishing: 'I had caught this giant barracuda,' Codrai recalled. 'It was six or seven feet long and Bird said it was the mother and father of all barracudas. He and the crew insisted that I should keep the head. By the time we got to Dubai it was stinking to high heaven, so when we arrived at Jackson's house we didn't get a very good reception from him and Thesiger.'[2] Codrai listened enthralled as Thesiger began to recount his adventures in the Empty Quarter, and engaged Bird on the subject of tribes and personalities. 'The talk was all connected with the tribes that had influence in Buraimi and northern Oman,' he remembered, 'and giving viewpoints on who was really obstructing, because Bird was the most knowledgeable person on the tribes of that part ... Obviously he knew more about them than Wilfred, who was only a seasonal visitor, but they were close friends.'[3] A little later Codrai told Thesiger how he had been with Bertram Thomas – now the director of the Middle East Centre for Arab Studies – when Thomas had read of Thesiger's first crossing of the Empty Quarter in *The Times* in 1947: 'I told him I'd been there when Thomas read the report,' Codrai commented, 'and that Thomas had brushed it aside rather, and said, "Oh well, in these times these modern explorers have radios and all sorts of aids." I told Wilfred this, and of course, nothing could have been further from the truth. I thought for a moment he was going to ignite! Then he smiled and countered it with a rather disparaging remark about Thomas, saying he'd tried to run an officers' mess on his journey, and hadn't always eaten with his men.'[4]

In the 1940s the Trucial Coast (now the United Arab Emirates) was virtually unknown to the outside world – even in other Arab countries. It had not been on the ancient trade-routes, and though a mail-packet plied there regularly from Bombay, Abu Dhabi and Dubai were part of a geographical cul-de-sac, known only to a small number of specialists and to a handful of affluent passengers flying to India by Imperial Airways. There was a refuelling station at Sharjah, and the Imperial Airways flying-boat would ski smoothly across the placid waters of the creek at Dubai, from where the passengers would be taken to the fort and afforded food and protection for the night. From the air, Dubai was a tiny blot on the ragged seam joining desert and sea: an infinite world of sand-bars, dunes and *sebkhas* on one side, translucent turquoise water foaming along the beaches with white flutings of surf on the other. There were the dark stains of palms on the pale ochre screen of the sand, and a cluster of stone-built houses glittering ice-white on the edge of the creek. In 1948 there were about two dozen cars in the region, three of them owned by the Sheikh of Dubai, and five by the oil company.

Thesiger was fascinated by Dubai, the shallow creek, the houses with their unique Persian windtrap towers, the tunnel-like markets roofed with sackcloth or matting, redolent with the heavy scents of cinnamon and ginger, nutmeg and cloves, the mixture of Persians, Baluch, Indians, Arab townsmen, Bedu of the Manasir wearing daggers, tapping camel-sticks, and striding nonchalantly through the colourful bazaars carrying with them the odour of the open sands. He was enthralled by the great variety of sailing-craft in the harbour: the *jaulbauts* with lateen sails and diesel engines, the stumpy sailing-dinghies and the water-taxis. He had hoped to find a passage on one of the big *booms* riding the trade winds back from Mombasa and Zanzibar, but discovered that few of them called in at Dubai. Eventually, a large dhow which had been halted by a naval patrol was towed into the harbour with its auxiliary motor wrecked. The owner was intending to send her to Kuwait under full sail, and agreed to divert her to Bahrain to deliver Thesiger in person: 'The Arabs had been great sailors,' Thesiger said. 'They'd gone right across to India and Indonesia – and this seemed a chance to go on one of their boats and see how one *did* travel in a dhow. It was very hot – we slept on the deck and there was no proper shade on the boat. There were masses of cockroaches, I remember, which I didn't like. We didn't get very far because the wind died almost right away, and there was one bit where it was very rough near the Persian coast. Anyway it was interesting and I got some good photographs. It lasted about seven days and then we put into Bahrain.'⁵ From there he returned to England.

By November he was back, flying into Sharjah with the RAF. He set out from Zaayid's fort at Muwaijih and explored the oasis of Liwa more thoroughly, with bin Kabina, bin Ghabaisha, 'Amair, and bin al Kamam, and in December joined Zaayid for three weeks' hawking with peregrine falcons in the Sands. Thesiger had been interested in falcons since his childhood, though he had never seen them in use among the Bedu of the south. Preparations had been in progress for a fortnight before his arrival, and Zaayid's camels – perhaps the best in Arabia – had been brought up from their pasturages, saddles shaken out, saddle-bags, head-ropes and hobbles purchased from the local market, and heaps of rice, grain and coffee-beans, and jars of butter stockpiled for the expected visitors. The party rode out from Buraimi in the afternoon: Zaayid, his brother Khalid, more than a score of Bedu warriors, bin al Kamam, and Thesiger – mounted on a she-camel lent him by Zaayid. The baggage camels had been sent on ahead, and by sunset they reached their first camp, where the Sheikh's slaves had piled up thorn-bushes into windbreaks against the chill of the winter night. Great cauldrons of rice were simmering on wood fires, and the slaves prepared piles of stones on which to roast the goats they had slaughtered. Some Bedu arrived bringing bowls of foaming camel's milk, and the news that they had spotted *hubara* (McQueen's bustard) – the object of the falcon-hunt – and their tracks near by. There had been heavy rains, and the dunes were alive with the brilliant saffron of *zahra*, and clumps of green sedge and heliotrope. Each day the falconers rode out across them with eight peregrines and three salukis, filling the air with song and loud chatter. If a bustard rose before them one of the falconers would unhood the bird on his wrist and raise his arm, letting it skim above the sand, slowly climbing until it had outflown the turkey-sized bustard. Thesiger would watch the distant specks with the same fascination with which he had observed the peregrines in the Welsh hills as a boy: quickly, the bustard would land in the sands, fighting it out with the small hawk, thrashing it with its powerful wings. As soon as the cry 'It's down!' came, the Arabs would leap into the saddle and dash towards it across the dunes, the salukis rushing in front of them, to find the dead bustard with the falcon tearing at its flesh and the dogs standing guard silently near by.

In January Thesiger set off south into Oman, with five companions including bin Kabina and bin al Kamam, but not bin Ghabaisha or 'Amair, who preferred to tend the camels they had already acquired through Thesiger's munificence or through skirmishes with the Bani Qitab. In this crucible of intrigue, it was inevitable that Thesiger should come under suspicion as a foreigner and a

Christian, and he believed that Zaayid's enemy, Rashid, the energetic son of Sheikh Sa'id of Dubai, had tried to thwart his journey by sending messages to the Duru', to the Al bu Shams – blood-enemies of the Rawashid – and even to the Imam of Inner Oman, warning them that the Christian was about to enter their territory with evil purpose. Codrai, by now a regular member of the Iraq Petroleum Company in Dubai, doubted this, however: 'Wilfred told me he had little regard for Sheikh Rashid, and thought he was a trouble-maker,' Codrai said. 'I had no means of judging at the time, but later I knew Rashid very well and very much doubted that he had interfered and tried to stop him.'[6]

Be this as it may, the Duru' had somehow heard of Thesiger's plans and resolved to prevent his passage. To counter this, Zaayid sent a messenger secretly beyond Duru' country to Salim bin Habarut of the Janaba, a friendly Hinawi tribe inhabiting the desert steppes that lay along the south-eastern coast of Oman. Zaayid requested bin Habarut to meet Thesiger's party at Qusaiwara in the Sands, west of Buraimi. He hoped that bin Habarut would be able to escort the Christian and his men through the country of the Duru' as far as Izz, where stood the tent of Yasir, the paramount Sheikh of the Janaba. 'Zaayid gave me a letter to Yasir,' Thesiger remembered, 'whom I hoped might help me with the Imam. We met bin Habarut and another Arab in the Sands and they said the Duru' wouldn't try to stop us. Anyway it was freezing cold and the camels were staling blood, so we decided to head for the shelter of Wadi al 'Ain, where we lingered for a few days.'[7] When they reached Wadi al 'Ain, however, they were halted by an angry mob of Duru', who declared they would allow no Christian into their land. 'Luckily among the Duru' was bin Staiyun, whom we'd stayed with on our first crossing of the Empty Quarter,' Thesiger said, 'the time we went to Ibri. I had given him a present of money when we left, and he now took my side, saying, "I know this man. He stayed with me and he's a good man. Why are you making trouble when he has a good name? He's been living with the Arabs for the last three years and he's never done us any harm!" Then he walked over to the Duru' Sheikh, bin Kharas, and said, "I'm going to take him through as *rabi'a* in defiance of you!"'[8] Thesiger was unwilling to agree: he had no wish to cause dissension in the tribe, which he knew would be held against him later. He was equally determined not to pay what amounted to blackmail for the right of passage, which he had never done before. Technically his Rawashid and 'Awamir companions were at peace with the Duru', and since it was evident that bin Staiyun would act as a *rabi'a*, there was no reason, by tribal custom, why the party should not proceed. But the presence of a Christian was obviously an anomaly. For two days the tribesmen gathered to discuss the matter: 'All through that day and the next the discussion dragged on,' Thesiger wrote, 'the same old arguments and objections. Each new arrival was given an opportunity and more than an opportunity of expressing his views, which they did even if they had already been expressed a dozen times before by other people, and even the youngest boys were allowed a hearing for as long as they chose to speak.'[9] Finally the Sheikhs drew together in a huddle and came back announcing that Thesiger could continue as long as he skirted their territory along the edge of the Umm as Samim quicksand. This had been his intention all along.

Bin Staiyun guided his party across a featureless gravel plain, across the arid dry-wash of Zuaqti, from where they could see the Umm as Samim. Thesiger was perhaps the first Westerner ever to set eyes on them: as a spectacle, however, they left much to be desired. 'They didn't look like anything,' he commented. 'They looked exactly like the ground all around. You never knew when you were on them and that's why others had gone into them and never come out.'[10] They followed the edge of the quicksands for five days: 'Close at hand it was bordered by a belt of impalpable white gypsum powder,' Thesiger wrote, 'covered over with sand-sprinkled dust through which protruded occasional twigs of drought-stricken salt bush. These sporadic bushes were beacons marking firm land; further out only a slight darkening of the surface indicated the bog below.'[11] The guide proposed to take them across the southern end of the quicksands, and even the hardy Rawashid and 'Awamir, accustomed to travelling almost anywhere, resisted, horrified at the thought of being sucked into this bottomless pit of mud. 'There was one way across the middle,' Thesiger recalled. 'We were all fairly apprehensive, but bin Staiyun said, "No, don't worry, I've been across myself and it's all right." [12] Having traversed the bogs safely, they rode south as far as the coast, near the island of Masirah, exploring the tiny, isolated desert called the Wahiba Sands, and met the friendly Wahiba, the largest and most powerful Bedu tribe in southern Oman, whom he thought 'aristocratic', and almost on a par with his Rawashid. 'We travelled through the Wahiba Sands,' he recalled, 'and finally got to the Batha Badiya with the mountains just behind them. The important thing here was that no one should know I was an Englishman, because the Imam had already been warned that there was an Englishman travelling in forbidden territory and was determined to stop us. There was just myself and bin Kabina and a Wahiba guide, and he told me that if we met anyone I should keep my mouth shut. When people stopped us he said I was a Baluch from Sur. My Arabic would have given me away pretty quickly if I'd had to do any talking. I remember they made me take off my watch so it wouldn't give me away.' [13]

His final task was to get back through the hostile territory of the Imam, and in this his letter from Zaayid to Yasir, the Janaba Sheikh, was crucial. Yasir owed allegiance to the Imam but was under obligation to Zaayid. The Imam had given orders for Thesiger's arrest, and was preparing to have him flung into a deep hole at Nezwa, but Yasir managed to persuade him to let the Englishman go free. 'He came back with the Imam's representative,' Thesiger remembered, 'and instead of being some dour fundamentalist as I'd expected, he was this old man with an obvious sense of humour. We travelled happily back with him to Buraimi, but we met this Sheikh on the road – coming from Ibri to warn the Imam I was in the country – and then he found I had the Imam's representative with me and looked foolish. Bin al Kamam asked him if there was anything he could do for him and the Sheikh said, "If you wanted to do something for me you wouldn't have brought this Christian with you!" And he just hit his camel and went off down the road.' [14] Able to travel openly now, Thesiger rode through the outskirts of Ibri and passed under the vast bulk of Jabal Akhdar, arriving back at Muwaijih on 6 April 1949, having added another 1,000 miles of camel-trekking to his experience.

He flew briefly to Riyadh to meet Ibn Sa'ud at the invitation of

Philby. 'Abdal Aziz looked impressive, as I'd expected,' Thesiger recalled. 'I met him in this big *majlis* and I went over and exchanged compliments. He knew I was the one who had been arrested in Sulayil, but it was all very formal, and I didn't really have a private conversation with him. He gave me a gold watch and a very good cloak.'[15] From there he flew to Kuwait and stayed with the Dicksons. 'Kuwait was still unspoiled,' he said, 'and the Dicksons had this house on the waterfront, and you got wells with Bedu who'd come right across Arabia. There were a few motor cars, but the town itself remained unchanged.'[16] His next port of call was Iraq, where he would later live with the Marsh Arabs over a period of eight years: 'I knew the Marshes were there, but I didn't visit them on that occasion,' he recalled. 'I went to Shiraz on a lorry and then hired a car of my own and went down to Baghdad and then up to Mosul, where I saw the Iraqi Kurds as they'd been in the past, and thought I'd like to visit them. I liked them, and it was magnificent country with very big cliffs and gorges. But then my travel in south Arabia was still my main thing, and I had no idea then it would be curtailed. I thought I would like to come here one day and travel properly on horses with the Kurds.'[17]

In 1950 Thesiger made his last trek through Oman, hoping to climb Jabal Akhdar, its highest mountain. The region was under the Imam's authority, but was governed by Sulayman bin Himyar, a Sheikh who was without the fanaticism of the Imam's other leaders. Greedy for the petrol revenues which he knew might soon be coming his way, though, bin Himyar wished to be established as an independent ruler. Bin Kabina and bin Ghabaisha joined Thesiger for this last journey. When they reached the Wadi al 'Ain, a crowd of Duru' under their truculent Sheikh, bin Kharas, once again held them up. This time there was no moving them, and as Thesiger had been stung twice by a scorpion in the night he was in little mood to argue. However, the acrimony continued for three days, until finally bin Ghabaisha asked Thesiger for his decision. 'What do you think?' Thesiger inquired. 'It's up to you, Mbarak,' bin Ghabaisha answered, 'but if we do remain here you realize that we shall soon be fighting for our lives.' Thesiger decided to pull out, and his party made a detour into the Sands, coming back to within twenty miles of Jabal Akhdar. He managed to send a message to bin Himyar, who relayed back that he would escort Thesiger to the village of Birkat al Mauz at the foot of the mountain. But word had leaked out again, and before bin Himyar could arrive Thesiger's camp was surrounded by 100 murderous Omani townsmen who had been told by their Imam that to kill a Christian was as meritorious in Islam as making the pilgrimage – and much easier. When bin Himyar finally turned up, he made it clear to Thesiger that he could only allow him to visit the mountain if he agreed to intervene with the British government to have him recognized as an independent ruler. Thesiger explained truthfully that he had no political standing, and heard the metaphorical lock tumbling shut, just as it had been opened by the humble locust five years before. His travels in Inner Oman were over.

Back in Dubai he was staying with the local oil company representative – his old friend Edward Henderson – and his assistant, Ronald Codrai. Zaayid had lent Thesiger his car, and he had brought bin Kabina and bin Ghabaisha up with him. On the way they had halted at an oil camp, where the Arabs had been forbidden to stay with Thesiger in the 'European lines', obliging him, out of honour, to sleep with them in the 'native lines'. Henderson and Codrai were, however, perfectly willing to accommodate them, though Henderson found it rather disturbing to have these Bedu in the house. 'We had fun about what sort of food they were going to eat,' he said. 'Sometimes they tried to eat our food, but they didn't like it so we had Arab dishes. They weren't entirely successful using knives and forks – I think they found it strange and very tiresome so we gave that up. We sent for their sort of food and got the cook to do more Arab food when they were with us. They were easy guests except that they did tend to wake us up early in the morning. We had this wind-up gramophone which they learned how to use, but we only had Beethoven, which they weren't very impressed with. I remember once we went out to dinner on a water-taxi, and when we got to the other side of the creek, bin Kabina told the boatman to tie up and come and eat with us. The boatman had already been paid and said he would leave us here as he wanted to continue working. Bin Kabina was very cross because he regarded the boatman as a travelling-companion, and it was a disgrace for him not to eat with us. I think bin Kabina and bin Ghabaisha obviously did admire Thesiger and regarded him as a sort of Sheikh.'[18] Yet Henderson felt little sympathy with Thesiger's view of the destructiveness of progress: 'Thesiger said this development was destructive of the Bedu,' he said, 'but actually the opposite is true – not doing it would have been totally destructive of their society. If they had remained in that traditional state, they would have just faded out or been destroyed by others. It is unnatural to stop progress, and if you don't do it your children will say why the hell didn't you get on with it? When I first came to the Trucial Coast I found life among the Arabs interesting to see and I admired their courage – given the circumstances under which they lived it was admirable, but when you take away the circumstances there's no point in behaving like that any more.'[19] Ronald Codrai added: 'It is futile to wish against change. [Wilfred's attitude] doesn't take into account the wishes of his companions, who often felt underprivileged – especially in terms of medical treatment – and did wish for the benefits of change.'[20]

While Thesiger was with Henderson and Codrai, the local British Political Officer from Sharjah, Stobart, turned up to dinner one evening: 'He said he had an embarrassing duty to perform,' Thesiger recalled. 'The Sultan of Muscat insisted that he removed the Muscat visa from my passport, and I said, well, that's easily done as I haven't got one. I realized then that the net was closing in on me. I'd been warned before, after my second crossing, and I'd been arrested in Sa'udi Arabia. Even after my first crossing I'd received a telegraph from our Resident in Aden saying for my own sake I'd be well advised not to go into Sa'udi territory and that side was closed to me. The only way into the Empty Quarter was now by the Trucial Coast, and here was the Resident there coming along and saying that was closed too. I realized that if I came back they wouldn't allow me in. There was no formality, and we laughed about it, but I could see his position. The British were going to come in and back bin Taimur, in Muscat, who wanted control over Inner Oman where the oil was, and there was this fanatically religious Imam trying to keep the Christians out, and every small Sheikh wanting to make a private arrangement with the oil companies.'[21] Indeed, one of the most amusing aspects of the affair to Thesiger must have been the knowledge that only a year previously bin Taimur had offered him the post of Foreign Affairs adviser in Muscat – a job similar to the one Bertram Thomas had held – which, remembering his frustrating year in Dessie, perhaps, he had turned down.

As they had arrived by car, bin Kabina and bin Ghabaisha had no camels to worry about. 'The following morning I saw them off to Buraimi in a lorry,' Thesiger said. 'There they were, sitting on the back, and the driver was a Palestinian refugee. Bin Ghabaisha was already a wanted man for camel-rustling, and was one of the accepted outlaws in the area. I advised them to get back to Salalah. I said goodbye, and they said, "Go in the safe-keeping of God," and then they drove off. I more or less just went straight to Sharjah airport and got on a plane, and as I flew off, I knew that was it. Chapter closed.'[22]

Thesiger often said in retrospect that, had he not been excluded from Arabia in 1950, he would have stayed on 'for another four or five years': he looked on his 'expulsion' as a kind of exile. He had gone in pursuit of a vision of perfection and discovered in the desert an alternative world where the old skills and heroic notions were still of value. Here, as nowhere else, he had been able to rediscover the connection with nature which had been lost in his own land. While travelling with the Bedu he lived on precisely the same level as his companions, and enjoyed no advantages that they did not have, practising to the full his belief that 'tinned food, mosquito-nets and transistor radios' only serve to exacerbate the already considerable barriers between cultures. He earned their respect, as bin Tafl said, for proving himself as tough and capable as themselves, and indeed 'doing more than he needed to'.

Thesiger was not, however, prepared to abandon a place in his own society to become part of this 'perfect' world: unconsciously, perhaps, he was aware that he could only travel in southern Arabia at all because he belonged to a culture that was more advanced, more powerful and more affluent. His sojourn with the Bedu only had meaning by contrast with his life in his own society, a society he could return to whenever he felt like it. 'I found what I wanted with the Bedu,' he said. 'I went to Arabia, was utterly happy with them and would have stayed on. But this doesn't mean I have to take an oath that I'm going to stay with them for the rest of my life. I wouldn't have wanted to become a Bedu. I wanted to go on being English. Even Philby had never actually become one. It was impossible for me to become an Arab, and I think it's probably impossible for anyone.'[23]

He told author Alexander Maitland that he in no way regretted his Western upbringing and education, nor thought it created a barrier between himself and other people: 'Not in the least,' he commented. 'I live in two different worlds and I'm perfectly happy to do so. Here [in England] I can put on my dark suit and have lunch at the Travellers' [Club]. . . If I was in Arabia in the old days I would step out of these clothes, put on my Arabian shirt and go off with the camels. I like keeping the two worlds utterly distinct.'[24] According to author Jonathan Raban, Thesiger, like Lawrence, was anxious to belabour what he calls 'the decadent life of the London drawing-room', using the Bedu as a stick. They claimed, he wrote, to have found among the Bedouin the simplicity, powers of endurance, and stoic individualism they feared the Englishman was losing in an increasingly technological society: 'They loved him for his spiritual leanness, his ignorance of the "soft" city life from which they themselves were on the run. In the desert they found the perfect theatre for the enactment of a heroic drama of their own – a drama whose secret subject was not the desert at all.'[25]

Although Thesiger found a kind of equality in Arabia – the bond that comes from sharing conditions of hardship – he continued to occupy a position of power in relation to the simple tribesmen, a power given to him largely by the prestige of the British Empire. Even bin Kabina said, 'We always thought of him as belonging to the government.' His affection for the Bedu was genuine, but it was not the reflection of a truly equal relationship. His travelling-companions qualified for respect, even admiration, but it was the same paternalistic respect and admiration the British reserved for the Pathans, the Sikhs, the fighting Sudanese, and certain other martial races of the Empire. He rightly garnered a reputation for upholding the dignity of traditional and 'primitive' peoples, but he himself commented that it was individuals rather than cultures which attracted him. And when he praised 'the Bedu' he did not distribute his praise equally: he admired the Rawashid, but despised the Bayt Kathir; he found the Duru' uncouth but the Wahiba 'aristocratic'; he liked the Se'ar but found the Yam and the Dawaasir fanatically religious. Even among the Rawashid there were individuals he disliked.

A clue to Thesiger's relationship with the wild lands and peoples he travelled among is provided by one of his favourite books, that 'masterwork of Imperialism', Rudyard Kipling's *Kim*. He told one journalist he had read the book forty times, and would gladly read it another forty. In a sense, Thesiger *is* Kim: he is the English boy born in the East, running with the natives in the din and bustle of the bazaar, speaking their tongues, dressing as they dress, travelling with them in a world where the bond between man and man is stronger than that between man and woman. Like Kim, Thesiger might at times dress like a native and talk like a native, but never lost the privileges of the Sahib. Just as Kim is torn between the spiritual quest of his oriental master, the Lama, and his British spymasters in the Great Game, so Thesiger was torn constantly between a deep desire to identify with native peoples, and his inherited loyalty to his class. The discrepancy between his power and that of his companions was fixed in the political and economic realities of his day. But political and economic reality changes. Kim's India threw off the Imperial yoke, just as economic conditions in Arabia altered beyond recognition. Thesiger predicted this in his lecture to the Royal Central Asian Society, presented in 1949: 'The hardy Badu tribesmen, the best stock in Arabia, may become, as a result of circumstances outside their control, a parasitic proletariat, squatting in the fly blown squalor of shanty towns on the outskirts of the oilfields in some of the most barren and inhospitable country in the world . . . Many of the Badu will certainly find employment with these companies . . . but it is uncertain whether as a race they are capable of the sustained effort required on an oilfield. At any rate there will be great numbers who are unadaptable, inept, or physically incapable of finding work, and there will be the women and children . . . they may be unable to adjust themselves almost overnight to these new conditions and so become demoralized. Tribesmen who have never seen a car or an aeroplane or even a European will find themselves suddenly working with Englishmen and Americans who have met their first Arab ten days before. Lads who have never seen an unveiled woman are going to come in contact with European women, not only unveiled, but in their eyes, undressed . . . Bored and disillusioned, they will, I fear, fall an easy prey to the vices and diseases of town life . . .'[26]

Years later, in 1970, Thesiger asked interviewer Timothy Green: 'What right have we to destroy these civilizations which have flourished for generations?'[27] The answer is, obviously, 'None.' But if the question is pertinent, then so is the obverse: what right do we from the affluent West have to tell poverty-stricken men and women they are better off poor, and yet remain rich ourselves? Thesiger lived on a private income: the Bedu did not. Thesiger had the choice of travelling in the desert or returning to a comfortable life at home: the Bedu had no such choice. Though he gave up all material privileges while living among them, it must, in all fairness, be noted that over a five-year period he remained with them only in the relatively pleasant cool months: never in the hard summer – the most difficult season of Bedu life. The Bedu themselves could not flit off to more temperate countries in the hot season. In Thesiger's time a Bedouin could not choose whether his son should go to school or tend camels, whether his children should be taken to hospital or die of some unknown disease for which the only treatment he had was camel's urine or a branding-iron. He could not choose whether to travel by car, camel or aeroplane. Choice is the privilege of the affluent and powerful. Thesiger insisted that the Bedu lived their lives out of choice and could at any time have left the desert and become labourers: 'What they were looking for was this hard life,' he said. 'They weren't doing it because they had to – Bedu were Bedu because they wanted to be Bedu. Their boast was that cold and heat wouldn't hurt them because they were Bedu – the fact that they were Bedu was their answer to every challenge. Bedu life was desperately hard, but it gave them a sense of freedom and they despised people who were leading easier lives. That's why the Rashid looked down on the Bayt Kathir, because their lives were easier. If bin Kabina had thought his life too hard he could have gone and got a job in the Hadhramaut.'[28] Of course, the Bedu were proud of their status: they did look down on settled peoples and less hardy tribes – being Bedu gave them a sense of identity. However, the question of choice is a different one. Their choices, compared with his, were distinctly limited. Here is a paradox that is almost impossible to solve: if we respect, admire and feel genuine affection for these people, should we not also admit that they deserve the same choices that we have? And if they have those choices, as we do, then shall we no longer admire, respect and feel affection for them? On second analysis, Thesiger's paternalistic stance sits uncomfortably on the last decade of the twentieth century.

Thesiger saw the Bedu of south Arabia as an aristocracy being debased by materialism, technology and development: the model had already been provided by the breakdown of traditional society in Europe, where the aristocracy's ancient skills of horsemanship and arms were rendered useless by tanks and aeroplanes. But this was not a true picture of the situation in south Arabia in the 1940s. In fact, the very tribes Thesiger chose to travel with because they were so 'unspoiled' had been economically and politically marginalized for centuries. Dhofar itself was the most underdeveloped region of Arabia because it had been maintained as a sort of private colony by the Sultans of Oman. Thirteen years after Thesiger left, the resentments forged by such restraint exploded in a savage rebellion against Sa'id bin Taimur. The revolt began among the Bayt Kathir, under their leader Musallim bin Nafl, but quickly spread to all sections of the population, as Jorg Janzen has written: 'Since time immemorial the nomads of Dhofar [had] been seriously economically underprivileged . . . this economic and political marginalization eventually led to an armed revolt against the Sultan, and although members of every population group, including the *hadr* [townspeople] participated in the conflict, it was the nomadic element which provided the most determined opposition to the old regime.'[29]

It has been claimed that the Dhofar war was begun by the Communists in neighbouring Yemen: the facts show otherwise. It was ignited because the tribes of Dhofar were unsatisfied with their poverty when all around them their Arab neighbours were growing wealthy. Bin Kabina might have considered labour the work of 'lesser men', but thousands of his kinsmen did not. Many left Dhofar secretly in the 1950s and 1960s to seek jobs in Kuwait, Sa'udi Arabia and the Trucial States. Those workers who returned brought discontentment home in their kitbags: tribesmen from the Bayt Kathir fought on both sides in the war. Musallim bin Tafl was arrested in Muscat on suspicion of aiding rebel forces (an arms shipment arrived addressed to him), and was jailed for life. During his incarceration – which in fact lasted seven years – both his son and his nephew were killed by the rebel side. Later, after Qaboos had overthrown his father, he declared his allegiance to the new Sultan and fought against the rebel forces. Colonel Tony Jeapes, a British SAS officer who encountered him after his prison term, described him as, 'a thin, hard man with a strong, determined jaw covered by a wispy grey beard. He habitually wore rimless steel glasses and his lined face reflected the adventure and hardship that he had endured as a raider of note in his youth.'[30] The Dhofari rebels were not initially seeking a new social order – Marxist elements 'took over' the war in 1966 from Soviet-led south Yemen, long after it was initiated by the Bayt Kathir. Indeed, it was the Communist attempt to reconstruct the traditional order, and above all their ban on Islam, which eventually led to their desertion by many Dhofaris and their ultimate defeat. The original insurgents merely wanted to overthrow the reactionary Sultan who they believed was restricting their access to the wealth which was already pouring into the country from oil revenues. Certainly the Bedu did not want to stop being Bedu, but they did want motor cars, medical treatment, perhaps education for their children. They did not feel, as Thesiger did, that these innovations made them any less Bedu. The situation in Dhofar remained dangerous until, in 1970, Qaboos led a British-incited coup against his father, bin Taimur, in the palace at Salalah. Thereafter the war was won, and Qaboos began quickly to regain the hearts of his subjects by initiating an economic revolution that transformed Dhofar. Bin Ghabaisha bought his first motor car three years later.

From the beginning Thesiger's attitude to the Bedu was one of rivalry: he sought to compete with them and in this believed he had failed: 'The things which they held high were things I admired and couldn't live up to,' he confessed. 'I couldn't compete with them by their standards. I wasn't as generous by nature as they were, I wasn't as hospitable. I mean, on two occasions somebody asked bin Kabina for his loincloth and he gave it to them – well, if someone stopped you somewhere and said, look here, do you mind giving me your coat, what would you say?'[31] Yet his stance remained paternalistic: he seriously underestimated the Bedu's desire for change and their ability to adapt. His axiom that 'all change was for the worse' began from a position of privilege and power. For a man born to the British aristocracy at the very end of the Edwardian era, perhaps, things could only get worse. For the poverty-stricken folk of south Arabia, many aspects of life could only change for the better. For bin Ghabaisha it was not 'worse' to be able to reach Salalah in a day instead of four, nor was it 'worse' to be able to have his children read and write. It was worse for Thesiger, because he was looking at the Bedu in a purely aesthetic light – as one not trapped within their life forever.

Thesiger's view of the history of south Arabia was based on Lawrence's model of successive waves of tribes exploding out of the Yemen hills in response to population pressures. Yet, while there remains some truth in this concept, it is now almost certain that camel-domestication began not in the Yemen, but along the arid coastline of southern Arabia. Five thousand years ago there were no Englishmen, and certainly no Bedu. Some ordinary men and women, of uncertain race, lived around the bays and inlets of south Arabia, with the sea on one side and the great desert on the other. It was to the sea that they looked for sustenance, and archaeologists know from their rubbish dumps that they were primarily fishermen. Often, in the hot months, huge, strange-looking animals with long necks and swollen humps would be found browsing in the wadis that flowed into the sea. At first they hunted these animals for meat, then, slowly, they began to tame them, as Richard Bulliet has written: 'The intermediate steps between hunting and taming can only be guessed at. Probably the scarcity of water facilitated the capture of wild camels at water points, and it is also possible that food was used as a lure since even today dried shark meat and sardines are used in this area as camel-fodder as they are nowhere else in the world.'[32] Soon ingenious souls learned to milk the camels, and eventually to ride them, using the simplest of saddles. At first they would venture only a day's journey from their village, then further and further as they discovered new areas of grazing and new sources of water. They had probably already developed a goatskin bag for carrying water and milk. Soon, a whole new section of society had arisen wholly devoted to pasturing and rearing these animals. They learned to live in caves and under thorn-trees in the wadis themselves – later they spread up into the Sands, developing the woven tent and the litter for women and children. Thus were the Bedu born out of ordinary human ingenuity: that 'terrible technical ingenuity' that Thesiger so despised. For a very long time, these camel-borne nomads were the masters of an innovative technology: they were the 'new men'. They did not colonize and adapt to the desert because it offered 'an unendurable life', but because, on the contrary, it offered rich new possibilities for a relatively comfortable existence. Nomadism in south Arabia may have looked 'inconceivably hard' to outsiders: in fact, to those accustomed to it, it was extremely efficient. It was a rational response to the exigencies of a marginal environment: a technique consciously developed by relatively sophisticated men to make use of that particular terrain. Had this not been so, the Bedu would have died out centuries ago. 'I can never in my whole life remember anyone dying because there was no food due to drought,' bin Ghabaisha said. 'Disease, yes, raids, yes, people dying of thirst when they got lost in the desert, yes, but not because we didn't have enough food to eat. I remember livestock dying in bad years, but not people.'[33] Every single Bayt Kathiri or Rashidi I interviewed confirmed this. If the 'cloud dispersed without rain' as Donald Powell-Cole has said, the nomads would simply move to somewhere it had rained: Thesiger was the first to show that it almost always rained in the Empty Quarter somewhere.[34]

Five millennia later, when the new technology of the internal combustion engine replaced that of the camel, they adapted it to their way of life, grabbing at its new possibilities like the realists they were. It was by no means the first time they had done so. Firearms, money, and imported cloth had each introduced sweeping changes into their way of life centuries before Thesiger knew them. Like every other society on earth, the Bedu were not 'original' but dynamic – changes had continually been going on under the surface. Post-Thesiger Westerners in Arabia, like Donald Powell-Cole, have pointed out that the Bedu are not only happy with the changes in their lifestyle, but have outstripped the imagination of others with respect to development: 'Unlike romantic Westerners who bemoan the passing of this ancient way of life,' Powell-Cole has written, '. . . the [Bedu] praise Allah for the security and peace that today characterize most tribal affairs in Arabia and for the easier life that modern economic development is making possible. Furthermore, they do not agree with either the Westerners or the government officials that nomadic pastoralism is doomed in the modern world. Rather, they are seeking ways – with little outside help or encouragement – to modernize their pastoralism and become actively involved in modern society.'[35]

Thesiger's 'nightmare scenario' did not develop. One might reasonably have expected him to register some kind of pleasure that things had not turned out as he predicted. He did not see any of his former companions again until 1977 when, after an absence of twenty-seven years, he was invited to return by his old friend Zaayid, now ruler of the United Arab Emirates, and Sultan Qaboos of Oman: 'When we landed at Sharjah I didn't feel that it was even the same place,' he said. 'There was nothing when I'd left and then you come back and it's all skyscrapers. I felt disappointment, disillusionment and that this was the final atrocity. I hated what oil had brought to Arabia – the inevitable corruption that wealth brings.'[36] At Salalah, bin Kabina and bin Ghabaisha met him in their cars and the next day arranged to have him flown to bin Kabina's tent by helicopter. 'Their tents were there as they used to be and they'd got as many of the Rashid together as they could,' Thesiger recalled, 'but they'd all come in cars, of course, not a sign of a camel. Bin Kabina still had his camels – they were way out in the desert, but there wasn't a soul there who'd ridden a camel for thirty years. I went down there in a helicopter with a TV crew attached, and the whole thing was meaningless to me because it was all cars and aeroplanes and helicopters.'[37] He finally attained his wish of climbing Jabal Akhdar, with bin Kabina and bin Ghabaisha, now middle-aged men with large families. Thesiger insisted on trekking up on foot, but when his two former companions heard that the air force had offered to take them by helicopter, they protested. 'Well,' Thesiger said to himself, 'already your standards have dropped!'[38] When bin Kabina reported proudly that his son was training as a wireless operator, Thesiger thought: 'Fallen as low as that!'

Despite the fact that, some twenty-eight years after predicting that they would all soon be living in 'fly-blown shanty-towns', he found his former companions still in the desert, still living in tents, but using motor cars instead of camels (he himself owned a Land-Rover by then), and despite confessing himself deeply moved to meet them, the picture he recorded was one of gloom and despondency. 'I realized after all these years, and under these changed conditions, the relationship between us could never be as in the past,' he wrote. 'They had adjusted themselves to this new Arabian world, something I was unable to do.'[39] How completely the tables had turned since his lecture to the Royal Central Asian Society in 1949. Then it had been the Bedu who would be incapable of adapting: now it was Thesiger himself. The wheel of change had finally turned on the Bedu. The illusion had gone.

Jonathan Raban has said: '[Thesiger] is a very traditional British Arabist, romanticizing about the desert. What he cannot stand is that the Arabs made money out of oil and started building cities. He is basically sentimentalist and colonialist.'[40] 'It's true I resent the fact that the Bedu have become affluent,' Thesiger admitted later. 'I can only judge it by personal experience: I admired the Bedu, I lived for five years with them and they were the most memorable years of my life ... but I went back nearly thirty years later and was motored round the place and there were helicopters and iced drinks and I personally rejected the whole thing.'[41] When asked whether this did not indicate that he wished to remain rich while the Arabs remained poor, he replied: 'It's rubbish to say [that]. I just wanted them to remain as they were in the past so that I could go on living with them as they were. But because of the wealth they got and the fact they were travelling about in cars – the Bedu life as I'd known it and valued it was gone. That was what I resented – there was a feeling of loss.'[42] In the 1940s, the Bedu of south Arabia were among the poorest people on earth, and 'wanting them to remain as they were in the past' obviously means wanting them to remain poor. Thesiger elsewhere acknowledged this: 'Everything I admired in the Bedu character was due to their poverty,' he said, 'due to the hardship of their lives, due to the constant struggle for survival. That's what made them what they were. As you ease all that you lower the standards.'[43] Although, on subsequent visits to Oman and the UAE in the 1990s to open photographic exhibitions, he was polite enough to rescind his earlier pronouncements about 'the Arabian Nightmare', which had no doubt embarrassed Sheikh Zaayid, and appeared to have mellowed, his underlying convictions did not seem to have changed: 'I was prepared to try and like it,' he said, 'but it meant nothing compared to the Arabia of the past. I'd find absolutely nothing of interest in travelling round the deserts there, for example. It meant a lot to see bin Kabina and bin Ghabaisha again, but motoring round in Land-Rovers was just meaningless to me.'[44]

Before leaving Sharjah in 1950, Thesiger advised bin Kabina and bin Ghabaisha to return to Dhofar. Bin Kabina followed his advice, but bin Ghabaisha did not. He was to remain in the Trucial States for seven years, establishing a reputation as one of the Gulf's most notorious bandits. Thesiger had always known there was a streak of ruthlessness in the boy which was lacking in the light-hearted bin Kabina. Only months later, he had begun shooting up trucks on the Oman road. In December 1950 he was captured by the Sheikh of Sharjah's men, during a gunfight with the Bani Qitab in which two men were killed and two others wounded. Slammed into Sharjah jail, he had a note sent to Ronald Codrai which ran succinctly: 'I am in prison in Sharjah. Come and get me out.'[45] Codrai passed the request on to Edward Henderson, who dropped in on the Sheikh. 'He readily agreed to let him go,' Henderson recalled, 'provided he stopped fighting or raiding. I had to stand surety for his good behaviour. Bin Ghabaisha himself denied everything, of course, but I made him swear that he would not get into trouble again, and he was let out.'[46] For a while there was an ominous silence from the young raider, which was broken one night when Henderson answered his door to find bin Ghabaisha staggering under the weight of a bleeding Rashidi tribesman. He blurted out that they had been rustling camels near Dubai, and his friend had been shot in the arm. Henderson defied company regulations by having the man sent to Bahrain for medical treatment, though the Rashidi refused to let the doctor amputate his arm. 'He returned with his arm well strapped up, but pretty useless to him,' Henderson remembered, 'and he asked me, "How can I go to Heaven with only one arm?" I said, "It won't matter. You don't have to shoot people in Heaven."'[47] Bin Ghabaisha was in Ibri, in northern Oman, in 1957, when the avaricious Sulayman bin Himyar, backing the forces of the Imam, was finally defeated by a brilliantly executed operation on the part of the British SAS regiment. Johnny Cooper, who had served with Thesiger in Stirling's original SAS as a sergeant and was by now a regular SAS officer, ran into him: 'He was obviously enjoying the fruits of his epic journey with Wilfred Thesiger and was pretty well britched,' Cooper wrote, '. . . but he told me very little about his trek across the Empty Quarter, and seemed more interested in his personal returns than in supporting or acclaiming his old boss as a great explorer . . . He tried a ploy by asking me for two three-ton trucks and a Land-Rover to "do some visits" north into the Trucial States. I declined . . . he stayed around for a few days, then disappeared northwards . . .'[48] Shortly after, he returned to Dhofar, where he was occasionally spotted by British SAS officers during the Dhofar war. Afterwards he settled down at Ghafa', where Thesiger had watered his camels in a rain-pool on his very first journey in the Sieh, to become the overseer of a new well, and to nurse his camel-herd. His eldest son, Sa'id, was brought up in the desert, but asked his father to send him to school. He speaks English and works for a government security department, occupying a fine house on the waterfront at Salalah, next door to the Director of the British Council there.

Salim bin Kabina lives not far away from bin Ghabaisha's cabin, at Bithna, an austere desert-centre where ragged black tents are pitched outside cement bungalows, and where border-guards of the Rawashid squat in an air-conditioned *majlis* in front of a flickering black and white TV. He too has a large herd of camels, and he is frequently to be found across the border in southern Yemen, around his old watering-place at Sanaw. More than anyone, bin Kabina resents Thesiger's twenty-seven-year absence from Dhofar: 'I thought he didn't want to see us,' he commented, 'and in the end he only came because they invited him. He wasn't like before.'[49] His close neighbour is 'Amair, who remains the slightly built, permanently scowling Bedouin Thesiger knew: 'They should have given us some reward for our journey with Mbarak,' he said. 'Once I saw Mbarak's picture of me in a book in Muscat, and they wanted twenty-five riyals for it. Can you imagine paying twenty-five riyals for your own picture!'[50] Musallim bin Tafl now lives in Salalah with his Indian wife and half-Indian sons. For many years, though, he was Vice-Wali of the government centre at Mughshin, built on the Sands above the trickle of water where Thesiger and his party watered their camels in 1945 and 1946. Some years ago, during a border dispute with Sa'udi-Arabia, bin Tafl performed a favour for Sultan Qaboos by taking a troop of his Bayt Kathir up to Mughshin and waving an Omani flag whenever the Sa'udi spotter plane came over. The government centre and his Vice-Waliship was the result. There, he lived in a palatial house with fitted carpets and air-coolers and a shining Land-Cruiser at the door. Often, though, he would patrol his domain in bare feet, still carrying his rifle and dagger at the age of seventy around the palm-groves that were once called 'the Tomb of the Muslims': for despite everything, the habits of a lifetime die hard. In an expansive mood he would usher visitors down to see his fruit-garden near the spring, with its melons and fig-trees, and a little further on would show you the thorn-tree under which they dragged Mahsin's broken body, in a different world, long ago. Bin Tafl has long suffered from poor eyesight and, lured on by the prospect of modern medical aid, he flew off to see a specialist in London. 'The specialist told me that he could not make my bad eye better,' bin Tafl would explain, grinning, 'but that he could make my good eye worse, so that both would be the same, and then I'd be able to wear proper glasses. I thought of the story of the Arab who had five camels and two sons to leave them to, and decided to kill one of them so that his sons would have the same amount!'[51] Bin al Kamam remained a much-respected Sheikh of the Rawashid, and lived in a bungalow in Thumrait, the new town built in the Sieh, beyond the Dhofar hills, until he died of cancer in 1992. Al 'Auf died many years ago, and the silent Mabkhaut, by then Sheikh of the Bayt Jidad section of his tribe, died in 1990. Salih bin Kalut arrived in Dubai in the early 1950s in search of medical help, and encountered Ronald Codrai: 'He inquired quite kindly after Bertram Thomas,' Codrai recalled, 'which reminded me that there was a photograph of him in Thomas's book. He remembered the photograph being taken, and exactly where he had been standing. Then I showed him the photograph, and he immediately turned it upside down.'[52] Muhammad, his son, long ago threw in his lot with the Sa'udis, and became the administrator of a government centre in Murrah country on the edge of the Sands. Saalih and Sadr, the two Se'ar who guided Thesiger across the western Sands, also moved to Sa'udi Arabia, where they live in Sharurah, in the middle of the Sands. Bin Kabina met them some years ago in Abu Dhabi. Nashran bin Sultan grew into a massively powerful individual, and became Sheikh of the Sha'asha section of the Bayt Kathir after his father, Sultan, died. Unlike his father, Nashran has a beard, though he often repeats Sultan's dry rejoinder to those who made fun of his lack of whisker: 'If God considered hair so important, he wouldn't have put it on our private parts!'[53] The astute Sa'id bin Muhammad, ever insisting that he was never possessed by a *zaar*, became the Vice-Wali of Thumrait and still lives there.

*

The world these Bedu grew up in can never come back, and many, like Thesiger, regret its passing. Having myself lived with a Bedouin tribe whose ways had been little changed by the outside world, having trekked by camel more than 15,000 miles in deserts that were still largely wilderness, I find it hard not to sympathize with Thesiger's regret at the passing of 'old Arabia'. Not far from bin Ghabaisha's house, we were welcomed at a black tent in the desert by some Bayt Musann, whose uncles and fathers Thesiger had encountered at Ramlat al Ghafa in 1946. Two Land-Cruisers were parked outside the tent, and many camels were picketed around it, guzzling dried sardines. Baluch servants were busy watering other camels from a tanker, while the Beit Musann sipped coffee in the shade. Inside the tent I noticed a dusty TV set, somewhat hazardously connected to a brace of twelve-volt car batteries. The Bedu were garrulous and friendly and brought us dates, coffee and camel's milk. They talked still about camels and grazing, but having known the life of a truly nomadic tribe, I knew there was something missing – excitement, danger, romance.

And, when all has been said about 'selfish romanticism', even the Bedu themselves agree that something has been lost in the march of progress. During my research, indeed, I found it was the Bedouin rather than the Westerner who was able to provide the most balanced view of development: 'Now everyone's better off,' commented Sa'id bin Muhammad. 'Sultan Qaboos has brought wealth and no one wants to go back to the old times. In those old days every man thought himself clever and brave, and every man thought himself the best. Today all control is in the hands of the state. Then every man was free. We used to kill each other. We used to fight with the Se'ar and the Kurub and everyone used to take each other's camels. Thank God, that has all gone. Now everyone knows that if he takes the property of another it will come back on him. In those days no one knew what was right or wrong. But on the other hand, in those days people were more generous. People are less generous now, because they think more about their own property and wealth. In those times they didn't think about wealth, only that if someone was in need they should give him food and drink to enhance their reputation. No one is bothered about reputation now. Then hospitality and generosity were kings. If a man had two camels, he would ride one and slaughter the other as food for guests. The Bedui in the past was generous and brave. The Bedui in the past was said to be more generous and braver than other people. But today almost everyone is the same: everyone is settled. The old generosity and hospitality is lacking.'[54] Even bin Ghabaisha, while lauding the new prosperity, admitted that he felt the loss of the freedom to move he knew in the old days.[55]

As we left bin Ghabaisha's small cabin, I remembered how in Sa'udi-Arabia I had been saddened to see Bedu of the Murrah –

Powell-Cole's 'Nomads of the Nomads' – freighting camels to market in Hofuf in lorries with cranes to lift and lower them. I had seen Bedu tents pitched on the hard shoulder of motorways, supplied with fridges and generators. I had once travelled down to Jibrin and seen Murrah tribesmen herding camels without even leaving their cars. Now, incredibly, just a little time ago, I had seen Salim bin Ghabaisha doing the same. There was, indeed, something fine and stirring about the old life of fast camels, raids and derring-do. Romantic, perhaps, but there is a piece of romanticism in most of us. After all, the passing of the old ways in the desert was the passing of something valuable for man – something impossible to describe in clear-cut, rational terms. But, as Douglas Newbold told Thesiger in the 1930s, people cannot remain exhibits in a living sideshow for affluent travellers to admire. Bedu pride alone could not have preserved their culture against others equipped with jeeps and aircraft. Change is part of the human process, the motor-engine of life. Given man's technical ability, there was never a chance that any corner of the earth would be spared. Not all change is for the good, but romanticism should not blind us to the fact that the Bedu are not 'noble savages', but men like other men with the same strengths and weaknesses, the same ambitions and desires. Paternalism – that hallmark of the Empire – is untenable in the last decade of the twentieth century. To go forward or back only the Bedu can decide.

Arabian Sands remains for me the supreme account of travels in Arabia, and Thesiger remains my ideal of the desert explorer. Each artist creates his own vision and every traveller in far-flung places reflects his or her own place and time, perceiving in the world the mirror-image of his own soul. Thesiger's romantic, paternalist view is his own truth. There are undoubtedly many more besides.

PART THREE

THE AFTERMATH

CHAPTER 13

A Bit of Duck-shooting

A week before I met Wilfred Thesiger, in Muscat, in 1991, I had a vivid dream. I was sitting in a sort of ante-room with a crowd of Arabs, Kurds, Pathans and other exotic folk, when someone pressed into my hand a letter containing Thesiger's address. My way led up a dark, forbidding tunnel, in which I halted before a Gothic door, carved with eagles, griffons and dragons. I knocked at the door, which creaked open to reveal a dishevelled and unshaven Thesiger. His face was a diaphanous, unfocused image, though I knew at once it was him.

'Can I come in?' I asked.

'No, you can't. Go away!' he replied.

So overpowered was I by this rejection, that when I received a surprise telephone call at my hotel in Muttrah, inviting me to meet him at the British Embassy that evening, I almost turned the invitation down. I had a strong presentiment of conflict. Yet it seemed that Thesiger and I had been on merging paths for years – the meeting seemed ordained by some power greater than either of us. When I had dressed, I descended into the lobby, now suffused with the ethereal half-light of sundown. At first there seemed no one about. Then I saw two Arabs sitting on the floor, drinking tea from an English tea-service. Their camel-sticks lay beside them on the floor – though of course no one rode camels in Muscat in 1991. The Arabs were bin Kabina and bin Ghabaisha, Thesiger's two closest Bedu companions, now greybeards in their sixties. Another strange quirk of fate had brought them here to the same hotel on the day I was to meet their former companion.

'Off to meet Mbarak?' one of them inquired dreamily.

'We met him at the airport this afternoon,' the other said. 'He still looked well and strong. Bin Tafl said to him, "We should have brought the camels to meet you, but we don't use them

391

now." Do you know what Mbarak replied? He said, "You are no longer Bedu. I am the only Bedui left!"'

The dream went on, I thought. The interface of dream and reality seemed strangely out of focus, like Thesiger's features at the great Gothic door. It all seemed inevitable. Inevitable that I should have discovered *Arabian Sands* at such a crucial cusp in my life. Inevitable that I should have become a camel-rider and an Arabic-speaker. Inevitable that I should have got to know bin Kabina and bin Ghabaisha. Inevitable that they should have been sitting here as I left to meet Thesiger for the first time. All my years in the desert had been leading here. All roads led to this.

It was dark when my escort, Ian Bailey, Third Secretary at the Embassy, arrived. Out along the deep curve of Muttrah harbour there were eerie lights and old dhows riding at anchor. I rode hypnotized with concentration, mesmerized by lights and images, as my past opened like a slit stomach and spilled out hidden meanings and concealed symbols. The dream I had had recently about Thesiger was by no means the first. For years I had been dreaming about a man I had never met. Connections and coincidences zipped up together like a game of join-the-dots. The thousands of miles I had ridden by camel; the three years I had spent living with a Bedouin tribe; the many times I had read *Arabian Sands*. I remembered how, in 1984, I had arrived in Wamba, in Kenya, the next town to Thesiger's home base of Maralal. As soon as I had extricated myself from the other passengers in the Land-Rover taxi, and donned my bush-hat, a barefoot Rendille boy had asked with unnerving prescience, 'Have you come to see Mr Wilfred?' When I stuttered, unbelievingly, that I had, he went on, 'Well, you can't, because he's in Kashmir.' Seven years later I had arrived by bus in Maralal itself and wandered down to the wine-shop being run by Thesiger's foster-son, Lawi. Drunken men leaned against a barn-like door. One was being disgustingly sick on the floor inside. Eyes watched me aggressively as I entered. I inquired about Thesiger from the barman and was told, 'He left for England yesterday.'

I watched the lights of Muscat coming up above the harbour. All roads had led to this.

*

53. Thesiger pulling in his *tarada* near a village on the edge of the Marshes, Iraq.

54. Thesiger in his *tarada*.

55. Kathir, one of Thesiger's canoe-boys in the Marshes.

56. Amara, Thesiger's favourite among his canoe-boys, photographed with a wild boar he had just shot.

57. Gavin Maxwell.

58. Thesiger talking to Amara inside a *mudhif*, the traditional guest-house of the marsh people.

59. Applying bitumen to the exterior of a *tarada*.

60. Children gathered around a *tarada* under construction.

61. A floating village in the Marshes, with cows and water buffalo.

62. Constructing a *mudhif* in the Marshes.

63. Amara in 1972.

64. The rocky hills of the Mathews range, which became familiar to Thesiger during his many years in Kenya.

65. Wilfred Thesiger, standing next to a jeep, on the safari in northern Kenya with Lords Airlie and Hambleden in 1972, during which he acted as 'white hunter' with René Babault.

66. Wilfred Thesiger holding a camel while loading, on the 1972 safari.

67. David Ogilvy photographing camels on the 1972 safari.

68. Wilfred Thesiger seated outside his tent, with Samburu *moran* around him. In later life he became the 'Englishman in Africa' whose image he once despised.

69. A Samburu *moran* shooting small birds during the circumcision rites. He wears the traditional ostrich-feather of the circumcision ceremony.

70. Thesiger sharing a joke with a young Samburu during the circumcision rites.

71. Thesiger photographed with a Samburu *moran*.

72. (*Above left*) One of the three portraits of Thesiger completed by artist Derek Hill.

73. (*Above right*) Thesiger on the ketch *Fiona*, with Mac, the skipper.

74. (*Middle*) Thesiger photographed by Eric Newby, after their meeting on the borders of Nuristan, 1956.

75. (*Left*) Thesiger and Princess Sarvath of Jordan at the Pitt-Rivers Museum, Oxford, 1993.

The Embassy stood where it always had, on the edge of the harbour, next door to the Sultan's palace. Our steps rang hollow on the flags of the cool Moorish courtyard with its silent fountain and armorial shields. We climbed a stone staircase to where a huddle of figures were sitting at a low table on the verandah. The first to greet me was Sir Terence Clark, HM Ambassador to Oman. The second was Wilfred Thesiger. The first thing that struck me was a defensive shyness. Thesiger avoided eye-contact: he never looked at me, never spoke to me directly. Even when I asked a question he replied to the Ambassador rather than to me. In appearance, of course, he was awesomely impressive: the massive leonine head with its kedge of nose and satanic shags of eyebrow, the long-boned walker's shanks, the narrowed, suspicious eyes. There was, beneath the shyness, a deep inner strength and an indomitable will which had kept him always on the straight and narrow track of dogged purpose. I explained that I intended to retrace some of his journeys in Oman by camel. 'That's an utter waste of time,' he commented. 'The life of the Bedu ended the moment the first car entered the country.' There was a formidable dogmatism about his statements, I felt. For Thesiger there was little room for debate, but more, there was a defensive line drawn around his experiences, as if the world he had known could only be known by him. I told him I had been staying in Dhofar with bin Kabina and bin Ghabaisha. 'Those people who met me at the airport today?' he commented. 'They're not the same people I knew.' I muttered something about how their appearance had changed. 'No, no, it's not that,' he went on. 'They're not the same *people*.' So fervid was his expression that for a chilling moment I thought he meant that they were impostors. Then I realized that he was telling me that no one else could know the bin Kabina and bin Ghabaisha he had known. They belonged only to him. I asked him a question about Sultan bin Ahmad and he began to answer. Then, without warning, he turned red in the face and fixed me with a menacing glare. 'I think your book is a complete waste of time!' he declared. In the slightly stunned silence which followed, I made my last desperate rally, asking if I could visit him at Maralal. 'You can come up and have a look round,' he said, 'but I'm not going to talk to you. I'm not interested.'

*

I first shared a meal with Wilfred Thesiger almost a year later, at the Safari Lodge in Maralal. We sat at a small table in a room full of golden African light, while a small herd of zebras kicked up scarves of dust at a waterhole only a few yards from the plate-glass windows. The lodge had been built on the very spot where Thesiger had pitched his tent during his first visit to Maralal, almost a third of a century before. Thesiger's vision was failing by then, but he could still make out the curvaceous russet-red forms of the eland which were queuing for their turn at the water and the great wedge of ferocious-looking buffalo which sniffed the dust cautiously with uplifted nostrils as they hesitated in the trees. Beyond them lay the vast verdant sweep of the Maralal valley, ringed by the swelling folds of the hills upon one of which, just out of view, Thesiger's cabin stood. He was dressed as usual in tweed jacket, a good shirt with frayed collar, twill trousers shrunk by injudicious washing to a couple of inches above his shoes – the regal products of Lobb's of St James's, forty years old, reduced to a mass of scars and sutures by less celebrated shoemakers. Thesiger drank Sprite with his food and tasted the thin soup thoughtfully. When the green-trimmed waiters brought the main course of fish stew, he muttered, 'I know it seems ungrateful from one who is being given lunch, but the food here is terrible. It's one of the nicest lodges in Kenya. You'd think they could do something about the food.' Afterwards we retired to an equally sun-lit corner of the deserted lounge and talked over coffee and Kenya Gold – his favourite liqueur.

On that first occasion we were joined, one after the other, by two of Thesiger's foster-sons in Maralal, both of whom surveyed us with baleful eyes and said, 'I have to talk to you, Mzee Juu.' Both spoke remarkably good English, as indeed did most of the Samburu with whom Thesiger had surrounded himself. The first of his 'sons' was Kibiriti, a bulky man – half Turkana, half Samburu – who was handsome until he opened his mouth and revealed the black stumps of teeth. I noticed that he was wearing less expensive versions of Thesiger's clothes – tweed jacket, dark trousers, broad-brimmed hat – and like Thesiger carried a straight walking stick. He kept his own hat on while talking and then, after a time, seemed to remember and apologized. 'That's all right,' Thesiger said. 'You're an African, I'm a European.' Watching them walking outside the lodge together later, after Thesiger had replaced his hat, I noticed with interest that, from the rear, they presented strikingly similar profiles.

The second 'son' was Laputa – the official owner of the house Thesiger lived in – a wan, rather soulful-looking Samburu in his late twenties, with a slightly malevolent stare. Both hustled Thesiger off separately for furtive talks beyond earshot, though I was told later that Kibiriti had come to report that his shop in Baragoi had been burgled and 40,000 shillings' worth of goods taken. Laputa had come to complain that some shysters – whose number included other 'sons' were trying to fiddle him out of his land. Both had come to ask Thesiger for money. These baleful glances, the sentence 'I must talk to you, Mzee Juu' and the furtive private conversations were to become familiar over the following months.

As a conversationalist, Thesiger could be charming, drily humorous and brilliantly entertaining. He could also be aggressive, provocative and occasionally downright rude. At home he would often harangue me on his pet hatreds: mass education, democracy and human rights, thumping the table, belting the floor with his stick and cursing if I dared oppose his views. I was tape recording the conversations, and once when I asked the wrong question he hurled the tape recorder into a chair and turned an apoplectic purple. For the most part, though, he responded with refreshing frankness to even the most intimate questions, speaking in a slow, surprisingly gentle and slightly high-pitched voice. He chose his words carefully some of the time: at other times he would speak with sudden emotional impulse. In general he was outstandingly patient, robust and indefatigable for the age of eighty-two. This corner of the Maralal Safari Lodge became, during the next few months, the site of some of the most fascinating conversations I have ever had – and some of the most fearsome verbal battles. It was here – and at other times in the mud and timber house across the valley – that Thesiger slowly unfolded to me the story of his life.

The years after his exile from Arabia, he told me, were dominated by his sojourns in the Marshes of Iraq. If he had opened a map of the Arab world and stuck in a pin at random, he could not have happened on a region that was less like the Empty Quarter. In the Sands every plant and animal had evolved to the silent music of moisture-conservation. In the Marshes men lived on, in, around or beside water. Here, houses were built on floating islands of vegetation, and a villager had to use his bitumen-caulked canoe merely to visit his next-door neighbour. He lived on fish and the milk of water-buffaloes, supplemented by rice, and used the twenty-foot-tall bamboo-like reeds to build his shelter. If the Bedu of the Sands were the 'most authentic' and noblest of the Arabs, many of the Ma'adan or marshmen were hardly Arabs at all. Looked down on by the Bedu, they were a liberal assortment of races: Turks, Assyrians, Hittites, Medes, Persians and many others, who had acquired Arab culture after the Muslim invasions. They observed Arab customs but were noted more as thieves and looters than for their courage, endurance and patience. Neither was the Marshes a place where men struggled to survive as they did in the deserts: true, it was stiflingly humid there in summer, cold in winter, and inevitably infested with flies, fleas and mosquitoes, riddled with bilharzia and dysentery, yet there were no dragons to be slain here, no great treks to be undertaken. Occupying only 6,000 square miles around the confluence of the Tigris and Euphrates, it was tiny compared with the quarter-million-square-mile Rub' al Khali, and its tribes, compared with those of the Empty Quarter, were vast. The Al bu Muhammad tribe consisted of both cultivators and marsh-dwellers, and numbered a staggering 120,000 people. Nor was there the excitement of raids and skirmishes to liven up the monotony of daily life: nothing more glorious, indeed, than the occasional blood-feud. On the surface, anyway, it seemed odd that Thesiger should have selected this sodden world in which to spend much of the next eight years: the Marshes lay at the other end of the heroic scale, a challenge of a different, distinctly more mundane order. 'I didn't feel the same sense of satisfaction from my time in the Marshes as I did from the Empty Quarter,' Thesiger commented, 'but I liked the people and liked being with them. There was no challenge and no hardship in the sense there had been in the desert, but it was worth getting to know a people about whom hardly anyone knew anything.'[1] Evidently he was looking for somewhere less demanding than the desert and a people less competitive than the Bedu.

*

He was forty years old and his greatest achievements lay behind him. Ineluctably, he began wondering what to do with the rest of his life. Returning to England permanently, or taking up a career again, was now out of the question. The world he had grown up in and been groomed to take part in ruling had almost disappeared. The dreams of returning to Edwardian glory that had haunted the elders of the 1930s had been shattered. In 1947 had occurred an event that would have been unthinkable around the time of Thesiger's birth: India, the keystone of the Empire, had become independent. Soon all other colonies would inevitably follow. Britannia no longer ruled the waves, and as Gavin Maxwell put it, 'the margins of the Atlas were closing in'.[2] Thesiger wanted somewhere he could – if only temporarily – call home: 'I enjoy travelling,' he said, 'but a lot of the time I have been looking for somewhere I can make a base and settle down. I am a traveller all right, but I gave up travelling to some extent to live with the marsh people and did all my travelling in summer when I did go off to various places. What I wanted was country that was unexplored, where there had been no attempt to alter the lives of the people or regulate them and they'd never been administered by an outside force.'[3] The Marshes had the advantage that, though many Westerners had visited them, few had stayed long. The region was still virtually unknown in 1950, an enclave of tradition where the insidious internal combustion engine had not yet arrived.

When Thesiger left Sharjah in March 1950, however, he had scarcely heard of the Marshes. Having seen a little of the Iraqi Kurds the previous year, he resolved to 'see what he could do with them'. After a spell in London he flew out to Kurdistan, where he engaged a young Arabic-speaking Kurd called Nasser as his companion and interpreter. Together they travelled among hamlets of flat-roofed houses stacked around the sides of hills, beneath great mountains capped with silver snow for half the year. They rode across sprawling hillsides forested with maple, terebinth, juniper, oak and wild pear, tagged along with knots of villagers who grazed their flocks of sheep and goats in the high pastures in spring, resting in black tents similar to those of the Bedu. They travelled for a time with the Herki – true Kurdish nomads who wintered in their tents on the plains of Erbil. 'It was a really comprehensive journey,' Thesiger said. 'I don't suppose there was a single village I didn't visit or a single hill I didn't climb. We travelled by horses which didn't belong to me – the Sheikh of one village would take us to his cousins in the next village and I'd stay to lunch with them. They'd provide more horses and a guide and we'd go off again. I was staying with the Kurds the whole time, but I couldn't speak their language. I liked them well enough – they'd got an independent war-like spirit and you couldn't help liking them. But there was this fact of the language and the other thing was that it was so confined. You were always running into a border here and a frontier there. In the end I decided I was more of an Arabist than a Kurdist.'[4]

In October 1950 he travelled with some Kurds as far as Amara on the Tigris, and there encountered a young Old Etonian Vice-Consul named Dugald Stewart. Stewart was an avid wild-fowler and he suggested a spot of duck-shooting in the Marshes near by. Thesiger agreed readily, but without any great expectations. 'We rode across the plain where you got these shepherd tribes,' he recalled, 'who had sheep and goats and used black tents. We halted for one night with the Sheikh of the Bazun, and the next with the al 'Issa. We slept in a reed cabin on the very edge of the Marshes, from where we could hear the water lapping at its banks.'[5]

The following day they entered the secret world of al Hor – the Marshes – in the al 'Issa Sheikh's *tarada* – the high-prowed war-canoe which was by now a status-symbol there and whose pattern had not changed since Sumerian times, 5,000 years ago. As Thesiger was quickly to discover, daily life in the Marshes had itself changed little in those millennia. The blade-prowed canoe cut through jungles of reeds, into glades and lagoons of smooth water, along waterways and across permanent lakes, passing villages of reed houses each on its own floating island – a flotilla of galleons riding at anchor, each with its squad of water-buffaloes mooning around a smoky fire in its open bows. Giant wild pigs haunted the reed-beds and swam in the water; four different species of otters trawled around the floating islands; flights of duck and geese exploded at the canoe's approach in a shimmer of light; coot and heron skimmed away from them with a snap of wings. In the evenings, when the light from the slit-doorways of reed houses fell like pillars of fire across the water, the world was filled with the rhythmic croaking of a billion frogs. Here there were stark naked boys who speared fish with five-pronged spears or poled their canoes through the shallows; men with ancient, wrinkled faces who welcomed the strangers into their houses; male dancers who performed with breathtaking eroticism. Not a heroic world, perhaps, but certainly a strange, almost surreal one. 'It was unexpected and delightful,' Thesiger said, 'and the marsh people seemed completely untouched by Western civilization. Anyway, you could fairly say I went there for a bit of duck-shooting and stayed for much of eight years.'[6]

After a visit to Iran, and another spell in London, he was back on the edge of the Marshes in February 1951, staying with Falih, the son of Majid, Sheikh of the Al bu Muhammad tribe. There is, interestingly, a close parallel between the Marshes and Dhofar in Oman, in that both were enclaves of traditional life, largely preserved by powerful and reactionary overlords. Majid, like many of the marsh Sheikhs, was fantastically rich. In theory all land belonged to the state, but the Sheikhs had leased vast acreages of it and within their domains behaved like feudal landlords. They had no interest in development beyond irrigation pumps, certainly not in schools or hospitals. They were tolerated by the autocratic government of King Feisal because they were bulwarks of his regime. Although the government could step in on occasions to reclaim its land, as it did in one case when an irresponsible Sheikh gambled away his pumps in a card game and left his people destitute, it had little influence within the Marshes themselves. According to Gavin Young, who spent a great deal of time there in the 1950s, many of these Sheikhs treated their people with all the sensitivity of Genghis Khan – one punishment employed by a relation of Majid's, for example, being a nail-filled coffin in which the victim would be shaken around until he became – literally – more pliable. The same Sheikh once had Thesiger's canoe-boy trounced and thrown into the river, merely for mooring the canoe near his house without permission. Gavin Maxwell described how the agent of another Sheikh assaulted a boy suspected of stealing Thesiger's propelling-pencil, before having him thoroughly thrashed on the spot by his men. The Ma'dan lived in fear of these feudal landlords, and were, in fact, little more than serfs. Such were the unpleasant economic facts that had preserved this 'Eden'. Thesiger, whose policy was never to get involved in politics, internal or external, ignored all this because without the backing of the Sheikhs he could not have survived. Dugald Stewart had recommended Falih as the person most able to help him, and Thesiger made use of his support. Anyway, he found the Sheikh's son a man after his own heart: an autocrat who could be savage when thwarted, but who also got on well with his people and could ride, shoot, and handle a canoe. When Thesiger arrived at Falih's base he was welcomed into his *mudhif* or guest-house. Part of the astounding architecture of the Marshes, these *mudhifs* were cathedral-like buildings with ribbed and vaulted roofs made entirely of a certain species of reed, not large, but from inside giving, as Thesiger's many photographs show, the impression of being far more spacious than they actually were. Built always on dry land, their floors were carpeted with reed-matting and a wide coffee-hearth stood near the centre. Often the curved endwalls, supported by upright pillars of plaited reed, would be worked in an intricate latticework which allowed an ethereal play of light. Anyone was entitled to stay in the *mudhif* for a night, and the guest would be given coffee, fed, and brought cushions and blankets to ease his rest on the floor.

Falih, who like all the Sheikhs would never have dreamed of spending even a night in the Marshes, expressed incredulous surprise when Thesiger explained he wanted to stay there. 'He said, well, stay here,' Thesiger recalled. 'I'll look after you and you can go where you want in the Marshes and you can always come back at night to this house. I said no, I wanted to go and live in the Marshes. He said it would be very uncomfortable and this and that, and I said I'm used to hardship and at least I shall have plenty of water, which I didn't in the desert. He said yes, you'll sleep in it and get trodden on by their buffaloes.'' Although Thesiger spent many nights in the marsh villages, Falih's *mudhif* did become his base during his first few trips to the area. Falih sent him on in his canoe to his agent at Qabab – a man called Saddam, who welcomed him with superficial warmth but quickly inquired who paid for Thesiger's journeys, and what he sought among the Ma'dan. Thesiger answered that he sought 'knowledge' – which raised Saddam's eyebrow a quarter-inch higher. He found the marsh people even more suspicious of his motives than the Bedu had been, and felt that they regarded him as a sort of government spy. The Ma'adan were subject to National Service in the army, and many of them would avoid it by resorting to bribery, or by hiring someone else to go in their place. They wanted no one prying into their secrets. Worse than this, though, Thesiger found himself considered 'unclean' as a Christian in a way unthinkable among the Bedu. The Bedouin tribes of Arabia were orthodox or Sunni Muslims and were permitted to eat with Christians or Jews, but like the majority of Iraqis and Iranians, the marshmen were unorthodox Shi'as and held a different view. At first, most of them refused to drink from the same cup as the Christian, and conspicuously washed the vessels he had used afterwards. All this distressed him considerably, for, as always, his object was to be accepted by the local people. Hating to be alone, his normal method of travelling was to obtain as least one Man Friday from the local people to frank him through. But here the people of each village merely fed him and packed him off to another village as soon as was decently possible, evidently pleased to be rid of him and too suspicious to accompany him further. Thesiger was faced with the tedious chore of explaining himself afresh to each new host. However, the key to the hearts and minds of this suspicious folk lay in an unexpected and somewhat bizarre accomplishment: the ability to perform circumcisions. Thesiger had always been fascinated by the practice of circumcision. It was, in Arab society as in many others, the rite of passage from childhood to manhood, the very symbol of the virility in which Thesiger's life was, in a sense, an essay. In Arabia he had watched the operation being performed on several occasions, memorably at Mushaik during his journey in the Hejaz in 1946, where he had seen initiates paraded before a crowd of tribesmen on the backs of slaves. The young men had stood nonchalantly before the audience as their foreskins were sheared off by two more slaves in a singularly cruel manner, scorning any sign of pain. One of them, indeed, had given a wild exhibition of dancing afterwards.

One night, Thesiger's host inquired what was in the two large boxes he was carrying. 'I said it was medicine,' he recalled, 'and he asked me if I was a doctor. I said no, but I knew about medicines. He asked me, "Can you circumcise?" I'd never done one, but I'd seen enough done, so I said, yes, I could do that, why? And he said there's this boy of mine who's about twenty-three and he wants to get married and needs to be circumcised. Could you do it in the morning? I said all right, and in the morning about ten of them turned up to watch. I selected the most intelligent-looking to help me hold the forceps, and as soon as I'd done the first circumcision, the one who was helping immediately dropped the forceps in the manure at his feet and sat down waiting to be done himself. I suddenly realized that all ten of them wanted to be circumcised.'[8] Thesiger quickly saw here a role which, even as a suspect foreigner and an 'unclean' Christian, he could fit into snugly. 'They did have their own circumcisers,' he said, 'who tied the whole thing up with a bootlace and cut the foreskin with a rusty razor and then sprinkled powdered foreskins all over the wound, and the result was septicaemia – not every time, but I saw some appalling cases. Anyway, when news got round that if you were circumcised by me you could go off and cut reeds two days later, they'd be waiting for me at the next village I got to, and after that every village.'[9] Naturally, the professional circumcisers fought back, spreading the rumour that Thesiger's circumcisions rendered his patients sterile. Unfortunately for them, Thesiger had circumcised a large number of adults prior to their marriages, who within a year had produced healthy offspring, thus, in the fullness of time, exposing the professionals as liars.

Thesiger halted at the dilapidated *mudhif* of Jasim, Sheikh of the Fartus, whose young son, Falih, Thesiger and Stewart had met the previous year. Jasim was an Arab-style Sheikh – *a primus inter pares* rather than a great landowner. He was, as Gavin Young recorded, 'a gossamer scrap of a man always puffing at a cigarette-holder, who worked and guided and led his people with a voice not much more emphatic than a whisper'.[10] Jasim accepted Thesiger, and drank out of the same cup from the beginning. He was hospitable, pressing him to stay rather than shunting him off to the next village. 'He also had a queue of boys waiting,'

Thesiger said, 'and I stayed three or four days there. I think the circumcision and the medicine really helped me to gain acceptance. But I think in some cases there was a genuine affection for me. Why not? Anyway, once Jasim of the Fartus accepted me, it was a step forward in being accepted by the entire community.'[11]

His major enemies among the marshmen remained the Sayyids – the holy men who were putative descendants of the Prophet. One of them – a fellow-guest at a *mudhif* where Thesiger was staying – publicly rebuked his host for harbouring an unclean Christian. His hospitality insulted, the host supported Thesiger, saying he was his guest and must be treated as such. The other guests naturally felt it their duty to follow their host's sympathies, which won Thesiger a moral victory. Eventually, he was invited to doctor and circumcise even the Sayyids' children and became tolerated by most.

Thesiger returned to complete his travels in Kurdistan that summer, but in the autumn was again in the Marshes. He bought his own canoe and took on four canoe-boys, Yasin, Hassan, Sabaiti and Amara, three of whom would form his small entourage for the rest of his time there. They were his new gang, and he paid them no regular wage, saying that he did not want servants but companions. He admitted later that when people inquired how much the Christian paid them it gave him a thrill to hear his paddlers reply, 'Nothing, we do it for pleasure.' It was the kind of fiction Thesiger relished, for his boys actually made far more money from him without a regular wage, yet had no claim on him should he decide to drop one of them. In the now-familiar style, they were all adolescent boys of the type Thesiger was attracted to, the most outstanding of them being Amara, 'a handsome, self-possessed youth', as Gavin Maxwell later described him, adding – with the inevitable equine analogy – that he was 'fine-boned, disdainful as an Arab stallion, often moody and withdrawn . . . there could never be anything gauche or awkward in his movements or in his response to an unfamiliar situation'.[12]

Amara was to take a place in Thesiger's affections as his 'beloved companion' over the next several years. Sabaiti, who in contrast had nothing remotely equine about him, but rather the appearance of 'an apologetic crow', was cast in the role of 'family slave'.[13] 'Amara was about fifteen when I met him,' Thesiger said, 'and he was with me for eight years. I had four paddlers, but he was the dominant one, even though he was the youngest. He was an exceptionally good shot, and hunted boar with me.'[14] Only Yasin – a peculiarly argumentative youth – rejected Amara's leadership, and was later replaced by a slightly Mongolian-featured boy called Kathir. One of their duties, apart from paddling, was to subject Thesiger each evening before retiring to a thorough massage – a social custom in whose therapeutic value the marsh people strongly believed. This was a more tolerant milieu than the desert had been. In the Marshes there were professional dancing-boys, male prostitutes, transvestites who donned women's clothes and even women who dressed as men. Thesiger noted approvingly that women who behaved and dressed as men were considered 'a cut above' other women.

Arriving back at the *mudhif* of Falih with his new canoe, Thesiger found that he need not have gone to the expense of acquiring it. The Sheikh's son presented him with a magnificent *tarada* – the thirty-six-foot-long canoe used only by Sheikhs – which cost the then considerable sum of £75. With his *tarada* and his entourage now complete, Thesiger established himself as circumciser and medical-practitioner-extraordinary to the marsh people. 'The area was quite small, though it took you all day to get where you wanted to go in a canoe,' he said. 'We would stop every night in villages, and I went out and stayed sometimes four or five days in one village and then there were the Sheikh's *mudhifs*. We didn't stop at every village, I mean we'd be going and we might pass three or four other villages and we might spend the night in a village or return to Falih's *mudhif* and spend four or five days there. In the villages I'd be doing medicine all day. You try waking up and there are sixty people waiting to be attended to, or being woken up by an old man coughing all over you and saying, "Give me medicine!" Then it would go on until it was dark. A lot of days were spent like that and there was never time to read a book.'[15] Thesiger had made friends with a British doctor in Basra who gave him advice. He was told firmly by the authorities, however, that if anyone died as a result of his ministrations they were entitled to bring a charge against him. 'I still dealt with people I knew were dying anyway,' he commented,

'and in fact I'd say to them, "He's dying and I can't really help."
But no one ever blamed me for the death.'[16] Thesiger's knowledge
of medicine had gradually accrued from experience, and from a
clinical fascination with wounds and diseases. 'If you're travelling
and you're going to be away six months or something and there's
nobody to look after you,' he commented, 'it's just as well if you
know something about medicine. Or if one of your men gets ill.
When I went on my Danakil journey there weren't any injections,
but you had to know what to give them for malaria, or fever or
dysentery, and I used to take quite a bit of medicine. When I was
in the Sudan, there was the native dresser in Kutum, and I used
to watch what he was doing as part of the rounds and I used to
take medicine when travelling in the Sudan. In the desert there
was usually just a small party so there wasn't much occasion to do
doctoring, but in the Marshes I frequently got sixty or seventy
patients in a morning to deal with.'[17] He taught Amara to give
injections and Sabaiti and the others to swab out wounds. 'I took
out an eye once,' he said, 'but it wasn't difficult as the eye was
almost out on its own – a dead eye that was being forced out
under pressure. I treated someone who'd blown most of his hand
off when his gun exploded – I tied it up but there wasn't much I
could do for him. I would never cut open the stomach to find an
appendix or that sort of thing – not proper surgery.'[18] Gavin
Maxwell, who spent some time with him in the Marshes later,
wrote that there was no practitioner in Britain who would have
taken on the variety of complaints that Thesiger tackled in his
surgeries, and one night began compiling a tally of patients:
people with only one eye, people with dog-bites, people with pig-
gores, and others with 'miscellaneous but horrifying ills', also
noting in his diary: 'Four noseless faces tonight.'[19] Maxwell said
that Thesiger had developed a technique of hit-or-miss diagnosis
that had gradually been perfected over the years, but which 'the
profligate use of the latest costly antibiotic drugs . . . rendered the
diagnosis of secondary importance'.[20] Frank Steele, whom
Thesiger first met while he was Vice-Consul in Basra in 1951, and
who was to become one of his closest friends, described how he
would occasionally come across medical cases he could not treat:
'He used to send them down to me in Basra,' Steele recalled, 'and
some poor wretched Arab in the last stages of disease would

appear with a note from Wilfred saying, "Please take this man, my friend so-and-so, and get him cured." And I'd take him to the hospital and the doctor would say there's absolutely nothing we can do. Wilfred became quite famous for sending to Basra Arabs who were beyond cure.'[21]

His attitude to medicine is another classic example of Thesiger's romantic ambivalence. As Jan Morris has pointed out, Thesiger – in the Marshes as a temporary refugee from progress – was himself the very prophet of the world he claimed to disdain: 'He really spent those eight years as a travelling doctor,' Morris wrote, 'armed with needle and antibiotics, performing prodigies of up-to-date mercy . . .'[22] Thesiger believed passionately that the outsider should bring nothing alien into a traditional society, yet medicines were a far more potent intrusion than mosquito nets, canned food, or even transistor radios. Here in the untouched world of the Marshes he introduced an entire institution, which, as Morris suggested, was a harbinger of progress. Thesiger recalled that while he was there someone told him of the greatest medical breakthrough in history: the invention of DDT, which was going to wipe out malaria (in fact the world's greatest killer). 'I thought, well, wipe out malaria,' he commented, 'and what in God's name is going to control the population all over the world? The main problem is population and every time a new disease comes up, they're struggling and struggling to find a cure for it. Well, it's disastrous that people are able to cure others. They were better off before there were these medicines to avail themselves of.'[23]

Author Peter Clark reported Thesiger's solution to the world's population problem: 'The only hope of survival for humankind is if we have some germ that wipes out five million a day and just leaves a few pockets somewhere like the rainforests. It's just like pruning a rose-bush back.'[24] When I suggested to him that if my son were dangerously ill I would be very glad to know there existed the medicines to cure him, Thesiger answered, 'Personally I couldn't care a damn whether your son recovered or didn't. Against that you've got this enormous increase in population which must be attributed largely to medicine and the results of it are infinitely worse than your son dying. If you think in historical terms it has no significance at all.'[25] Yet when the young bin Kabina had collapsed suddenly in the Arabian desert, Thesiger had declared emotionally that 'there would be no tomorrow' if his young friend died.[26] The historical perspective evidently paled to insignificance when the life of someone near and dear to him was involved. Gavin Maxwell suggested, probably rightly, that the Ma'adan had managed to maintain a stable population over the ages because of the high instance of infant mortality due to endemic diseases like bilharzia. Why then was Thesiger going against everything he believed in, to upset the balance of nature in the Marshes?

Frank Steele said that he frequently locked horns with Thesiger over this subject: 'Wilfred deplores the fact that things like antibiotics have been invented,' he commented, 'but he still makes use of them to cure his friends, even though he realizes that by doing so he's adding to the world's population problem. He says, well, these are personal friends of mine. I say, well, Wilfred, that applies to everyone. We are all trying to keep our families and friends alive. If you really believe that medicines are bad you shouldn't be using them but leading a campaign to stop people using drugs.'[27] Was Thesiger's use of expensive modern antibiotics in the Marshes humanitarian or simply the result of a desire to be accepted? The answer is that it was probably both. He had always carried medicines on his journeys, and his marshland 'clinics' were no more than an extension of this. If the practice of medicine on such a scale seems inconsistent with his utterances, then it must be regarded as one of the many contradictions in Thesiger's character. It was the same attempt to divorce the personal from the general which is observable in his hunting and many other aspects of his life – a syndrome which is more common that one might think in the overcrowded world we inhabit today. In real terms, none of us is able to balance perfectly his actions and beliefs.

Thesiger wintered in London again, and was back for a further five months in the Marshes from February to June 1952. By now he was accustomed to the tranquil life in his backwater of the world. 'It was like south Arabia but on a lower note,' he said. 'Basically the whole thing was the same – the hospitality and everything else. If you arrived in a fairly big village, where you hadn't been before, I'd say let's go over to that big house over there and then as we went past another house, they'd shout, "Come here! You're not to go past!" and they'd almost pull you out to make you stay. But the marsh people didn't reach the top like the Bedu did. They hadn't got the quality of nobility, and I don't think you'd have got absolute loyalty from them. I enjoyed being with them. They had the background history and traditions of Arabia – I mean, they could have claimed to be Hittites or this or that – any of the people who'd invaded that part of the world. Alexander the Great had been there, and while he was remembered and revered up in Afghanistan, the marshmen wouldn't have thought about mentioning him. Their heroes were Bedu heroes. To that extent they owed their tradition to the hard life of the Bedu. I didn't find the Marshes as appealing as the Empty Quarter, but there was a charm about them. In another way, of course, it was different from my life in the desert, because in the Marshes I was part of the community and I lived with them – not just a little party travelling in the Sands. There was nowhere to stop but in their houses and one got involved with their families, their brothers and everything else, in a way you didn't in the desert. You met the women and the girls – they weren't segregated, they just sat in a different corner of the house. I hardly ever made a meal and never carried any provisions – I lived exactly as they did.'[28]

When not doctoring, Thesiger passed much of his time slaughtering the thousands of wild boars which infested the marsh regions. 'We just shot boar to kill them,' he commented. 'There were enormous numbers. I don't know what I shot, I mean I shot seventy-four on one day, and seventy-seven on another. I should think I shot about 2,000 while I was there – it made no difference to their numbers. They were dangerous when the marshmen went in and were cutting fodder for their buffaloes. They quite often got attacked and I spent a lot of time stitching people up who'd been gored. It was the same if you had a small patch of rice – then if a pig came and spent the night in it there wasn't much left in the morning.'[29] The marsh boar was perhaps twice the size of the boars found in southern Europe, and would make its nests on islands of reeds. If startled by fodder-cutters it would charge at once, goring them in the face, chest, throat, back or stomach with razor-sharp tushes. The attacks were not often fatal because the boar rarely stayed around to make sure of its handiwork, though it could be aggressive enough to attack full-sized canoes, and Thesiger had once seen the bows of a thirty-six-foot *tarada* completely stoved in during such an attack.

After the war he had made a decision not to hunt again for trophies, but only to shoot for the pot, in defence, or where animals were competing with man. 'It was nothing to do with the war,' he said. 'I had just lost the desire to kill things.'[30] One might remark that if so, the wholesale destruction of 2,000 of these troublesome yet magnificent animals was an odd way of displaying it. There is little doubt that Thesiger was under social pressure here: hunting animals was something he did well, and a skill, like circumcision, which he could put at the disposal of the marsh people to help gain him acceptance. They were themselves excellent shots with their muzzle-loaders, but did not have the resources in ammunition to deal with the vast numbers of pig. Gavin Maxwell wrote that Thesiger 'had earned the gratitude of many villages many times over, for he had killed literally hundreds of pigs . . . and they now felt it to be part of his natural function, like doctoring of their diseases'.[31] In an atmosphere where his total acceptance remained questionable, this must have proved a considerable boon. But though the Ma'adan regarded the boar as their greatest enemy, Thesiger himself would have hated the thought of them being wiped out as the marsh lion had been exterminated within living memory. He frequently found shooting them a mechanical act, devoid of that intense, magical thrill he had felt in his younger days. Bumping off dozens of the animals in a day scarcely required the kind of arduous build-up that was for Thesiger the most important part of the chase: on occasions he could hardly have done more damage had he been hefting a Vickers 'K'. Timothy Green believed that the sheer numbers of wild boar he was obliged to kill contributed unconsciously to his loss of enthusiasm for hunting in the 1960s.[32] Once, however, the pigs almost got their own back. Urged by a local tribesman to shoot a boar in a cornfield, he moved cautiously into the field and came unexpectedly almost nose to snout with a tusker ready to kill. Before he could even get his rifle up the pig was on him, pitching him helplessly on to his back. The animal snorted and dropped saliva, driving its tushes at his chest. Thesiger managed to shield himself with his rifle stock in the nick of time, and the sharp tusks splintered the wood and dealt him a savage wound in the finger. He stood up and saw the pig trotting away, evidently believing it had done its worst. He shouted, and as it swivelled round for another charge, he shot it dead.

When Thesiger arrived at Falih's *mudhif* near the Marshes after visiting Pakistan and England, in February 1953, Falih declared that he was no longer a mere guest and should henceforth sleep in the family fort rather than in the *mudhif*. Falih was entertaining his favourite nephew, Abbas, and invited Thesiger – now referred to by everyone as Sahib, meaning simply 'friend' in Arabic – to accompany them duck-shooting the following day. The next morning they breakfasted on fried eggs, pancakes and buffalo milk, and as they set off in the *tarada*, Thesiger noticed that Abbas was carrying some cartridges in his belt marked 'LG', which the man told him were duck-shot. Opening one up out of curiosity, though, Thesiger discovered they contained the large lead pellets of boar-shot. 'Someone will get killed using these for duck-shooting,' he said. 'They are for boar, not for duck.' Apparently Abbas paid little attention. On the edge of the inner Marshes each of them transferred to a smaller canoe, and while the others went in search of duck, Thesiger began to stalk boar. Finding no trace of them, though, he rejoined the others. Their paddlers kept the small craft gliding parallel, each about seventy yards apart but hidden from each other by veils of reed. They were looking for coot, and as several rose over Thesiger's head, he shot one and stopped to dredge it out of the water. Just then there was a explosion which Thesiger knew instinctively had come from a shotgun fired in his direction. 'For God's sake watch where you're shooting!' he shouted. A little later he heard another shot, followed by the voice of Falih crying, 'You have killed me! You have killed me!' Urging his paddler on, he came to Falih's canoe and found his friend slumped in the stern, with the canoeman trying desperately to hold him up and to keep the craft from capsizing. He had been shot in error by Abbas, who had fired at a heron with the deadly boar-shot, not observing his uncle behind the reeds. Abbas had fled in terror, knowing this would begin a blood-feud, but was later imprisoned by the authorities for three years. Falih was flown to Baghdad by special plane, where he died the following day.

Until then, Thesiger had used Falih's house as a base. Now, invited by his favourite, Amara, he moved to the youth's village of Rufaia outside the Marshes, which became the centre of his activities from then on. It was Sabaiti's village, too, and Amara was later engaged to marry Sabaiti's sister, for whom Thesiger happily furnished the bride price. The doctoring went on as usual, with Thesiger working tirelessly, surrounded by a crowd of clamouring patients, doling out pills, stitching pig-gores and dog-bites, swabbing infections, yelling at his supplicants in Arabic and swearing at Amara when he dropped the hypodermic or passed the wrong bottle: 'You bloody boy! Damn and blast it!' – the only English Amara ever learned.

Thesiger had always liked to punctuate his life among traditional peoples with brief forays back into the civilized world with Western amenities: a hot bath, a good meal, a proper bed, English conversation. His social standing always seems to have provided him with an open door to the highest levels of any British community. Wherever he went he would be put up by the local Consul-General, Consul, High Commissioner, or even the Ambassador – who in some cases turned out to be a relative. In Basra, when his friends Frank and Angela Steele were staying in a hotel during Steele's temporary posting there, he would invariably stay with the Consul, Mark Kerr-Pearse. 'He'd come into Basra from time to time,' Steele remembered. 'We saw a lot of him. The long-suffering Consul used to put him up, but when Wilfred used to turn up at his beautiful house with a tail of four or five scruffy Arabs who'd all doss down in Thesiger's bedroom, there would be great ructions and Mark used to complain to me: "Your friend Thesiger's just arrived with four lice-ridden Marsh Arabs!" We would try to take him off the Consul's hands as much as we could. He used to feed with us, and we took him to the British Club in Basra and he was always relieved to have a change from the food in the Marshes. He was basically a non-drinker rather than a teetotaller, and one night after we'd had a sausages and mash supper I suggested he should try a Drambuie – I thought it would appeal to him because it was sweet. I bought him one and he loved it and ended up having five or six of them, and since then he's always had a fondness for sweet liqueurs.'[33]

*

There was a new mellowness about Thesiger after leaving south Arabia in 1950. Previously his journeys into the heroic world beyond civilization had been jealously guarded as his own private property. In the deserts, especially, he had lived a relatively ascetic life. Now, apart from developing a circle of Western friends in Basra, he began – tentatively at first – to allow other Westerners to glimpse his magic kingdom in the Marshes. Although he would always retain a preference for travelling with the locals, his very first month in the Marshes had been with the eminently civilized Dugald Stewart. Frank Steele was one of the first Englishmen whom Thesiger welcomed to the Marshes for brief visits: 'I'd drive out there and he'd pick me up,' Steele recalled, 'and we'd go off in his *tarada* and do some shooting. He'd have one or two of his Marsh Arabs with him. We'd pole through the Marshes – and they were utterly beautiful stretches of water with these tall reeds; it was tremendously peaceful and a wonderful break from normal life, an absolute haven of peace. The Marsh Arabs had these houses built on floating islands; we'd shoot duck, and even – though it sounds terrible now – coot, which the Arabs ate. I used to bring sandwiches with me from Basra to eat, and he was always happy to share them.'[34] Steele and Thesiger got on so well, in fact, that they were later to travel together in Jordan and Kenya. The Thesiger who had been so pleased to see the back of Haig-Thomas in 1933 was maturing – though still rather crabbily – into a more tolerant individual where his countrymen were concerned. Part of this may have been due to a feeling he had experienced among the Bedu, and which is common to those who spend a long time in other cultures without a support group of their fellow-expatriates – that he was in danger of being forced into a cultural limbo: neither a true Arab nor a true Englishman. The problem was a very real one, and Thesiger maintained that wherever he went afterwards he always had a feeling that there was an Arab looking over his shoulder. This is perhaps why, in later years, Thesiger became increasingly keen to preserve the dress, appearance and attitudes of the tradition from which he arose.

Another young hopeful whom Thesiger invited to the Marshes during this period was Gavin Young, who had wound up in Basra in a shipping company's office. Young's ambition had been to cross Arabia by camel, and hearing of Thesiger's arrival he desperately wangled a lunch date with him at the Consul's house. Thesiger dissuaded him from his camel-journey with the crushing air he frequently employed with such aspirants, and then, obviously having taken a liking to the tall, rugged-looking young man, invited him to the Marshes for a few days. 'He came along for about ten days or so,' Thesiger recalled, 'and he did get on with the marsh people quite well – I suppose he spoke a certain amount of Arabic. He did it once or twice briefly with me and then came back after I'd gone. He was another one who always insisted on wearing Arab dress, though.'[35] Young was entranced by the unspoiled world Thesiger had unveiled to him: 'The natural beauty was hypnotic,' he wrote. 'Black and white pied kingfishers dived for their prey all around us, clusters of storks arced high above, snow-white flotillas of stately pelicans fished in the lagoons; there was always at least one eagle in the sky.'[36] Young managed to adapt rather better than the RAF officer who once joined Thesiger in the Marshes as a survival exercise. The wildness of the region made it a natural sanctuary for runaways, and British Intelligence had put it on an escape and evasion route for crashed aircrew in the event of war with the USSR. Frank Steele, to whom the RAF officer went for advice, suggested that he take every conceivable immunization shot, and stock up with malaria pills and water-filtration kit. 'No,' the officer said. 'I've got to live exactly as if I were a crashed pilot.' Steele then advised him to make his last will and testament. Within a week the human guinea-pig had caught malaria and dysentery, and Thesiger had him carried out by stretcher and rushed to hospital in Basra.

The Westerner who stayed longest in the Marshes with Thesiger was Gavin Maxwell, who spent seven weeks there in 1956 and wrote his descriptive masterpiece, *A Reed Shaken by the Wind*, based on the experience. The book is probably the best intimate portrait that exists of the character of Wilfred Thesiger. Maxwell, an aristocratic Scot, lacked Thesiger's robustness, but had lived a mildly adventurous life in the Outer Hebrides – where he had begun a shark-fishing business – and in Sicily. A sickly physique had disbarred him from active service during the war, and instead he had found a niche training SOE agents in the Scottish

Highlands. Maxwell was on the look-out for a little-known place not 'blocked by the spreading stains of new political empires', and had come across Thesiger's piece on the Marshes in the *Geographical Journal* in 1954. 'I came back once and found a letter in the flat in London,' Thesiger recalled, 'and it said had I any intention of writing a book about the Marshes? I thought this was some publisher's tout trying to get me to write a book, so I wrote back rather curtly and said I had no intention of writing a book about the Marshes or anywhere else. Then I got a telephone call from Gavin Maxwell, who said he'd had my reply and I'd got it wrong. He said he felt the Marshes was a very interesting place and they should have a book written about them and obviously if I was going to write it it would be wrong for anyone else to intrude, but if I wasn't he'd like to go there and try to write a book himself.'[37] They met a few days later at the Guards Club, where over lunch Maxwell explained again. 'I said, well, how would you begin to do this?' Thesiger remembered. 'You don't speak Arabic and if you take an interpreter his very presence will create hostility. You won't get on any sort of terms with them. You know nothing about the Marshes, about Arabs or about anything!'[38] This was standard Thesiger technique – the bludgeon followed by the salve. 'I said I was going back there in a few months,' he continued, 'and I asked him if he'd like to go with me. He said, well, if you're sure I'm not intruding – he was very sort of "right" about this – so we went off together and he stayed with me for seven weeks.'[39] In fact it was not until almost a year after their first meeting that Maxwell was able to accompany Thesiger, and even then it was a last-minute decision. In November 1955, Thesiger returned to London from a motor tour with his mother in Italy. The following January, Maxwell, who had recently been in London undergoing treatment for depression, contacted him again, explaining that he would like to go but would not be free until April. Thesiger countered that he would be leaving shortly for his last trip to the Marshes. Despite his declaration that he had no intention of writing a book, he had already agreed with Longmans to have a go at the work which would become *Arabian Sands*, and knew that the following year he would probably be stuck in Europe. He told Maxwell that he would be spending the early summer with the shepherd tribes of

Iraq rather than in the Marshes themselves. Afterwards, he was planning a long-awaited trek in Afghanistan, which he had already put off in 1955 in order to return to the Atlas Mountains of Morocco. Maxwell was disappointed – the shepherd tribes of Iraq would, he knew, be interesting, but it was the self-contained world of the Marshes on which he had set his heart. He agreed to meet Thesiger in Basra in April, but that night he tossed and turned sleeplessly, telling himself that he had missed a unique opportunity. Not long after sunrise, he phoned Thesiger and asked to go with him the following Monday. Thesiger agreed. On 30 January 1956, they flew to Baghdad.

In Maxwell Thesiger appears as a 'scoutmasterish', yet awe-inspiring man, with rigid beliefs in the right and wrong ways things should be done, and a stern, humourless and perhaps truculent character. As the canoe-boys rose, stretched and yawned in the morning, for instance, their groans would be 'punctuated with dull thuds, as Thesiger, with scoutmasterish jocularity, belaboured their heads with a small pillow, hard and heavy-seeming as a sandbag; a treatment he affected to believe pain-less'.[40]

During Thesiger's surgeries, Maxwell found himself surrounded by a crowd of patients almost as large as the one which besieged Thesiger, and no repetition of the fact that he knew no Arabic seemed to put them off. 'Each displayed his suffering,' Maxwell wrote, 'with a formal and unvarying ritual of pathos; my view became a kaleidoscope of cataracted eyes, suppurating boil-craters, patches of angry rash on brown skins, wounds and swollen genitals.'[41] Thesiger found Maxwell a hindrance rather than a help during these sessions. 'Gavin had said when you're doing some medicine I'd love to help,' he commented. 'I said it wouldn't be much help because I should always have to make the decision and then I'd have to say give him so and so pills. Then he wouldn't be able to tell him how many pills to take, so it would be quicker not to use him at all.'[42] On another occasion, when they had nowhere to stay for the night and were obliged to make camp on an island, Thesiger told him in a rather intimidating tone that they would have to shoot their own dinner. 'And God help you if you miss,' Thesiger said. 'It's food we're after; we can't carry enough cartridges for sport. Your reputation among these people will stand or fall absolutely by what you kill or don't kill and they're all watching you.' 'As an encouraging introduction to shooting while sitting cross-legged in the bottom of a perilously wobbling canoe,' Maxwell commented, 'I felt this could hardly be improved upon.'[43] When Thesiger handed him two cartridges and said that was all he would get, though, Maxwell realized he had been wrong – it could. He was informed that Thesiger expected '200 per cent success' from these two measly rounds, but when Maxwell proceeded to bring down three coots with his first shot, the canoe-boys spoilt the whole bluff by erupting in excitement. Somewhat chagrined, Thesiger said, 'Pity you aren't leaving us now; trouble about reputations won on flukes is that they're so shortlived.' He looked, Maxwell said, 'like a scoutmaster whose oldest and most oafish pupil has tied an accomplished and esoteric knot by accident'.[44] Though Maxwell spoiled the effect by missing a flight of ducks with his next shot, he soon burst the bubble of Thesiger's '200 per cent' myth when he noted that both the Englishman and the 'excellent shot' Amara once took three plugs each at a wild pig before they hit it, and then failed to bring it down. It was not, indeed, until they had followed it up and put another two rounds into it – a total of nine rounds in all – that the beast finally gave out.

For his part, Thesiger soon grew tired of Maxwell, finding him 'querulous and neurotic' at close quarters. He thought Maxwell ineffectual and inept: 'dead baggage', as he told Maxwell's biographer, Douglas Botting. For him, Maxwell's most serious shortcoming was the Scotsman's inability to get on with the marshmen, and what Thesiger saw as an almost total obsession with himself. 'I said to him, now look here, on this trip you've got to be self-sufficient,' he commented, 'and I did say this very strongly. I said for God's sake bring enough books with you to read because I'm not going to be able to look after you the whole time. I know these people and I shall be sitting and talking and talking, but you'll find all this boring. And then again we do a lot of medical work and there are a mass of patients coming in and I can't be interrupted giving injections or doing this and that. "Oh I shall never get bored," he told me. "Just to be there watching is all I want." Well, then later I could see he was a bit sulky in the canoe and I said, "Gavin, for God's sake what's wrong with you now?" "It's not much use telling you because it won't make any difference," he said. "Well," I said, "at least try and it might." "Well," he said, "I can only say if I had somebody staying with me in Scotland I'd have taken more trouble to entertain them than you do." Well, I'd told him this when we came out, that I wasn't going to be able to look after him in that sort of way.'[45]

That Thesiger was not completely accepted in some villages in the Marshes, despite having been doctoring and hunting there already for six years, is clear from Maxwell's writing. At the village of Huwair, for example, Maxwell noticed that the people would not drink from the same cups as them, and washed the vessels immediately afterwards with what seemed to him 'an unnecessary ostentation'. Near another village, Hadam, they met with open hostility when Thesiger began treating a girl of fourteen. The Sheikh's son came rushing out of the local fort, declaring that it was a disgrace for one of their women to be handled by a Christian. Thesiger was furious, and though the situation was quickly defused, it must have been an unpleasant reminder of that day in Laila in 1947, when his men had been cursed for bringing a Christian into the country. On another occasion, while staying with a young villager, their host violated the sacred rights of the guest – not the first time, Maxwell noted, during his seven-week stay – by stealing their valuable bamboo canoe-poles and replacing them with worthless reed ones. When Thesiger discovered the deception and confronted their host, the youth claimed insolently that the reed poles were the ones he had received for safe-keeping the previous day. In fact, Maxwell had himself woken in the night to see the young man engaged in something suspicious, but had thought nothing of it. Seething with rage, Thesiger clapped the man powerfully across the ear with an open hand. It turned out that the poles had been distributed round several houses, and the boy brought them back one by one, claiming each time that this was the last he knew of – only to be sent off again by the cursing Englishman, almost beside himself with fury. The fracas quickly brought an aggressive-looking crowd around Thesiger. Maxwell, who knew nothing of the story until later, returned from a stroll to find him shoving his way perilously through an excited mob 'like a giant among pygmies'. '"Dogs!" he was shouting,' Maxwell wrote, '"dogs, and sons of black dogs! Black dogs and children of pigs!"[46] As they reached the *tarada* and the canoe-boys pushed off, Thesiger continued to stand in the stern, keeping up the torrent of abuse until the craft was fifty yards away, when he sat down, 'presenting to them,' Maxwell recorded, 'the uncompromising back view of righteous indignation.'[47]

One great bone of contention between the two men came over the boar-shooting incident. 'Gavin went off to shoot some duck,' Thesiger recalled. 'He wasn't very far away. I was sitting on the bank and then there was a boar which suddenly charged him. He hadn't got any boar-shot with him, only duck-shot, which would only have maddened the boar. So I thought this was going to be interesting. Well, then the boar got to about three yards away from him and turned off – as I found out later there was a dyke there that it hadn't bothered to jump across. Well, then he promptly fired into its bottom with No.5 bird-shot – the one thing calculated to bring it round on him! When he came back I shouted, "You bloody ass!" and he was very indignant and said, "Why did you call me a bloody ass?" and I said, "Well, in God's name, you go and shoot into that thing's bottom when it was leaving you alone." I told him I was also rather disappointed because I always wanted to see a wild boar kill a man! "Ah!" he said. "That's a nice sort of remark to make!"'[48]

Maxwell wrote that as the boar approached he had expected to be gored, but had decided not to run. Indeed, Thesiger had issued instructions that in case of an unexpected boar attack, he was to wait until the beast was almost upon him, dust him with duck-shot, and then fall flat into the water. This was his intention, and he drew a bead on the charging animal, ready to blast him between the eyes. When the boar reached the 'dyke' – in fact a narrow channel of water between sodden reedbeds – it automatically swerved left, probably mistaking the channel for a deep ditch, and Maxwell pulled the trigger instinctively, not realizing he was already out of danger. When he reached the *tarada*, the canoe-boys insisted on kissing him in relief, but Thesiger – according to Maxwell's version – cursed him for 'A bloody fool!' and added that he was glad Maxwell hadn't panicked: 'We should never have been able to hold our heads up again in the Marshes if you had.'[49]

*

The two Britons also squabbled over the wearing of Arab dress, which Thesiger seemed to believe his exclusive right. In London he had instructed Maxwell to bring two shirts, two pairs of flannel trousers, a pair of shoes, a jacket and a razor. This dress Maxwell found ill-designed for jumping in and out of canoes, sitting cross-legged for hours, wading through mud, not to mention performing natural functions in places where there were no latrines. Thesiger himself wore Arab dress – appropriately, for he disagreed with bringing anything alien into the landscape – yet, with consistent inconsistency, he persuaded Maxwell that it would be wrong for him to wear Arab dress when he neither spoke Arabic nor knew the customs. 'Even I didn't wear their clothes at first,' he protested, 'until Sheikh Falih said to me why don't you wear our clothes as you'll find them more comfortable. Then Gavin arrived and was absolutely determined to wear Arab clothes. I said it was ridiculous as he couldn't speak Arabic and what was the point of dressing up. They were perfectly accustomed to Europeans wearing European dress. Then I came back one day and found he'd got some clothes off the local Sheikh. He hadn't a clue how to wear them and he was wearing the skirt all laced round him as if it was a kilt. Amara took one look at him and remarked that if he dressed like that the canoe-boys wouldn't take him anywhere. Anyway, he got himself photographed like that, but he didn't put it in the book.'[50] He felt that Maxwell wanted to wear Arab dress 'because it was romantic', yet Maxwell pointed out that Arab clothes were simply far better suited to the social environment. In this he was correct. Take urinating, for example: an Arab will not urinate standing up but always squatting down, allowing his flowing skirts to form a screen around him. To urinate in the same position in a pair of trousers, preserving modesty at the same time, requires almost the skills of a contortionist, and looks uncouth beside the Arab method. Arab clothes were simply more practical. Thesiger's protest that he was 'invited to wear Arab dress by Falih', suggesting a reluctance to abandon his native costume, ignores the fact that at other times he changed into his *dishdasha* at the drop of a hat, without any such invitation: in the Sudan, in Arabia, in North Africa during the war, later in the Yemen. As to the question of 'being photographed like that', his album of photographs entitled *The Thesiger*

Collection contains no less than twelve shots of Thesiger decked out like an Arab, and while he appears authentic in some, others display a very curious-looking Bedouin indeed. Maxwell summed up his reaction to this pressure when he wrote, with some forbearance, 'Had I to consider no one but myself I would have exchanged the discomfort for the ridicule.'[51]

Thesiger never quite forgave Maxwell over the business of the otter Mijbil, later to become famous in Maxwell's book *Ring of Bright Water*. The story began with another otter-cub called Chahala, which Maxwell and Thesiger bought from some marshmen. Unfortunately the creature died a few days later, probably because they had fed her meat instead of milk. Maxwell was shattered. 'It died rather a lingering death,' Thesiger said. 'It was sad. Then we went and stopped – luckily it was in a European-style house outside the Marshes, that one of the Sheikhs had – and Gavin suddenly broke down completely and was sobbing, sobbing, sobbing, almost having hysterics. I said, "What's this?" and he said, "Oh well, all my life I longed for something on which I could lavish my heart and I found it in this little otter and then I murdered it!" Well, if you've had a dog that's been with you for a long time and it died you would feel a bit upset, but over a baby otter that had only been with him for a few days that seemed extreme. I was very glad we weren't in a *mudhif* with a whole crowd of Arabs watching us. Then we went down to Basra, and I knew how much he wanted another otter so I hunted round for one and sent it down to him in Basra and he took it home. It turned out to be a new species, and I thought at least he might have named it after me, but he called it *maxwelliae* after himself!'[52]

Ring of Bright Water, based on the story of the otter Mijbil, was published in 1960 and sold over a million copies in English alone. It was made into a popular film, and brought Maxwell a considerable fortune, making his name famous – even more famous, at the time, than that of Wilfred Thesiger. Since Thesiger himself had provided the otter, his annoyance over its name is perhaps justified. Later, they met up in Morocco on a number of occasions, where Maxwell was writing his book *Lords of the Atlas*. It was in Tangier, according to Maxwell's biographer, Douglas Botting, that they met for the last time. Money tended to pour through

Maxwell's hands like liquid. He had left unpaid bills in Iraq, and though he eventually settled them after a certain amount of pressure from Thesiger, it was against the background of this that Maxwell committed the 'final atrocity'. 'Gavin was very odd about money,' Thesiger told Botting. 'In Tangier he hadn't got any – hadn't got a car or anything – so my mother and I would pick him up and take him out to lunch a few times. Just before we left, Gavin said to me, "I do hope you and your mother can come and have lunch with me. I'd like to return your hospitality, and I've invited the Consul-General to join us. You'll find him interesting – he was a prisoner for a long time in China." So we met up at the Rembrandt Hotel for drinks before lunch, and Gavin took me on one side and said, "Can I have a word with you? As you know, I'm absolutely broke and I can't afford to pay for this lunch. Could you pay for it?" So like a bloody fool I said, "Yes, all right, Gavin." I thought the least he would do when the Consul-General came in would be to say, "You owe this lunch to Wilfred – he's insisted on paying for it." But he didn't. He just said, "Well, now, pick yourself a very good lunch." So we had a very expensive lunch at a very expensive restaurant, with wine and liqueurs, and at the end the Consul-General said, "Thank you, Gavin – you've just given me one of the best lunches I've ever had." And then, when no one was looking, Gavin pushed the bill across to me and I said to myself, "Well you've had it, Gavin, I don't really want to see you again." And I didn't.'[53]

Maxwell died of cancer in 1969, and Thesiger later regretted that they had parted on unfriendly terms: 'I didn't dislike Gavin,' he commented. 'He exasperated me a lot, but I found him entertaining and good company . . . He was an excellent ornithologist and a good writer. If he was to walk in here now I'd be happy to see him, but I wouldn't have wanted to go on a journey with him again.'[54]

Maxwell had brought with him a Leica Mk.III camera, and his photographs of the Marshes rival those of Thesiger. While Thesiger was also using a Leica – a Mk.II – he took only black and white photos, whereas Maxwell was already experimenting with new-fangled chromatic film. In February 1959, Maxwell's colour photographs and Thesiger's text were combined in a piece for the *National Geographic Magazine*. Thesiger had taken some excellent shots during his years in Arabia, and by the time he reached the Marshes he had attained the brilliant photographic style for which he was to become famous. On his earliest journeys, using an old Kodak box-camera, his pictures had meant no more than souvenirs and *aides-mémoire* of his journeys, and those taken on his Danakil trek in 1933 had been spoiled by a faulty viewfinder. Though he had acquired his Leica the following year, 1934, the earliest photographs he considered of high enough quality for inclusion in his portfolio-work *Visions of a Nomad* date from the 1940s. 'I bought a Leica before I went to the Sudan,' he commented, 'and I took a certain amount of photos that were just snaps. Then, before I went to Arabia I thought I must certainly try and get some photos. I think a thing I have got is a sense of composition, and I think you either have that or you haven't . . . I consider my photographic skills just a matter of luck.'[55] He continued to use black and white film even after colour film had been introduced, not only because it was in a sense 'traditional', but also because monochrome prints reflected his preference for drawings rather than paintings, for line rather than colour. 'In the old days colour was so very bad, anyway,' he added. 'It's not now, but I'm not going to switch from one to the other. I'm a traditionalist and I've grown up taking black and white photos, and I shall continue to do so.'[56] Thesiger's monochrome photographs produced the same pristine, austere images that he sought so successfully to achieve in his writing. He once wrote, critically, that 'by its very nature [colour photography] aims to reproduce exactly what is seen by the photographer'.[57] Black and white photographs, on the other hand, reproduced the romantic, half-magical world of adventure that he had always sought. By *their* very nature, they gave the impression of looking through a window into an antique, anachronistic world that had long ago vanished. Though he photographed landscapes, architecture, street-scenes, ships and wild animals, Thesiger's photography reflected his passion for people rather than places. 'The thing I like photographing most is portraits,' he explained, 'and to me a portrait is something you don't want colour in. The best of my portraits – and I've done some good ones – would have gained nothing if you'd put them into colour.'[58] He never humped about the mounds of equipment that identify the professional photographer today; indeed, he carried his Leica always in a goatskin bag and, until he left Arabia in 1950, used only a standard lens. He never carried a tripod or a flash, though he did use yellow and polaroid filters. He later acquired a portrait lens and a wide-angle lens, and in Kenya another lens for game photography, though he never used a zoom. There seems an obvious parallel between hunting and photography, but though his interest in the chase declined as his photography matured, Thesiger always denied that one was a substitute for the other. 'In no sense is photography a substitute for hunting,' he said. 'There's no sense of achievement in taking a photograph. Suppose you want to shoot a greater kudu, for instance, you fire a shot and the thing drops. You take a photo and you wait three months to see the result – that in itself [spoils it]. Hunting big-game is dangerous, but you can take a photograph of game without disturbing it very much.'[59] Although the best of Thesiger's work could stand unashamed in any professional exhibition, Ronald Codrai, his friend from the 1940s, and himself an accomplished photographer of the Middle East, commented that Thesiger was never really interested in photography *per se*. 'He's just a very great picture-taker,' Codrai said, 'and he's got a splendid eye for a picture. Due to the circumstances in which he placed himself he had opportunities which others didn't have to place those scenes on film . . . He would go off on his trips, where if he'd bungled it there would have been no second chances . . . He had a good camera and he shot very deliberately with the confidence that what he shot would come out. He didn't do as modern photographers do and take a whole film of the same subject. I think he captured very, very proficiently, and often artistically, the subjects which he had the opportunity to photograph. Usually his portraits of people were taken against the background of their habitat, and he had a nice way of posing people without them feeling self-conscious in front of the camera . . . He is most unpretentious about his photography, though he does make these extreme [but true] claims – like the fact that he's never photographed another European – he loves to put that one over . . .'[60] Indeed, the only Europeans Thesiger regretted not having photographed were Wingate, and his hero, the former Commander in

North Africa, General Auchinleck: 'I regret very much not having photographed Wingate,' he said. 'I could have got some unique pictures of him in the Abyssinian campaign, if only I'd thought of it. Perhaps I should have liked to have photographed Auchinleck, but then I should have regarded it as rather an impertinence to say can I have a photograph. To me it would have been an intrusion. If I met a distinguished person I couldn't go up to him and say can I take your photograph. I'd never have done it . . .'[61]

Towards the end of his time in Iraq, Thesiger would spend longer periods travelling with Amara and Sabaiti on horseback among the shepherd tribes outside the Marshes themselves. Here on the dusty plains beyond the river he recaptured something of the feeling of freedom and space he had known in the desert. They would wander northwards, halting among nomads or cultivators, sleeping in black tents or villages. They hunted wild pig in the tamarisk scrub along the watercourses, Thesiger wielding his .275 rifle as a pistol and firing at the boars from the hip as he rode. Gavin Young later praised this as a prodigy of physical strength, though Thesiger modestly pointed out that the Rigby .275 he was using was not, in fact, a particularly heavy weapon, and in any case, he shot the pigs at almost point-blank range. On their return from one of these treks, he heard the alarming news that Amara's cousin, Badai, had killed the son of a man called Radhawi, apparently in self-defence after a disagreement over a woman. Ma'adan custom decreed that the death of a first cousin was just compensation if the actual killer could not be found, and this put Amara at immediate risk. That night, at Amara's house, Thesiger lay down on the floor with Amara and another lad beside him, their loaded rifles at the ready. Amara's father, Thuqub, sat sentry in the doorway with a rifle across his knees. They lay silent but awake, their ears straining for the movements of a would-be assassin. Each time a dog barked or the wind rustled the vegetation outside, they sat up in alarm. In the morning Thesiger arranged a six-month truce for Amara through the local Sheikh. He left shortly afterwards to begin work on *Arabian Sands*, and when he returned to the Marshes in 1958 the truce had long ago expired. Badai, Amara's cousin, was by then in hiding among the Fartus, and it was rumoured that Radhawi would try to kill Amara. Thesiger sought out Radhawi's house, taking in tow a representative of the powerful Sheikh Majid as well as a Sayyid. With the ponderous weight of this delegation behind him, he confronted Radhawi and demanded a two-year truce for Amara. The marshman, a small, spare figure with hard eyes and a tuft of beard, who had already killed two men, refused even to consider it. Furious, Thesiger leaned forward and said: 'Listen and listen carefully. Either you give me the truce now, or I go in the morning to see the government. You are already wanted on two charges of murder. If you are arrested you will spend the rest of your life in prison . . . I will offer a reward of 100 dinars for your arrest . . . I mean what I say, and what is more if you *had* killed Amara while I was away, I would have made sure you were killed too, whatever it cost me!'[62] After a token protest, Rhadawi granted the truce, and Thesiger walked away unconcerned that he had evoked the name of the government to settle a dispute in this land he so desperately wanted to remain unadministered and untouched by the outside world. Already, though, he had seen that world encroaching upon this lost dimension. Already there were transistor radios in the Marshes. Already Amara's young brother was going to school. 'Hard and primitive,' he wrote of the Ma'adan, 'their way of life has endured for centuries, but in the next few years the marshes will be drained and the marshmen as I have known them will disappear to be merged into the stereotype pattern of the modern world – more comfortable perhaps, but certainly less free and less picturesque. Like many others I regret the forces which are inexorably suburbanizing the untamed places of the world and turning tribesmen into corner-boys.'[63]

As in the Empty Quarter, he had discovered here a redoubt against progress and had remained long enough to watch the beginning of its disintegration. It was a re-run of south Arabia, though, as Thesiger himself admitted, 'on a lower note'. As in Dhofar, the 'forces which were turning tribesmen into corner-boys' were political and economic: they included the ambition of a people to be educated, healthy and affluent – to throw off the shackles that ground them under the heel of their millionaire Sheikhs. Many people, perhaps, regretted the intrusion of schools and hospitals into the pristine world of the Marshes, yet few of the marshmen themselves.

In July 1958, Thesiger said goodbye to Amara and Sabaiti at Basra airport as usual. 'They asked me when I was coming back,' Thesiger recalled, 'and I said I'd be back in a couple of months. I was in Ireland with some relations of mine and somebody came in at teatime and said have you heard the news? I said, "No."' They said there's just been a revolution in Iraq and they've shot the royal family and burnt the British Embassy. So I realized I could never go back. Another chapter in my life was closed.' [64] Unlike his Bedu companions, Thesiger was never to see Amara or Sabeiti again, though Gavin Young, who returned to the Marshes after the revolution to find Majid and the other great Sheikhs gone, brought him news of his former companions. Amara was still living in the same village, though shortly afterwards he disappeared into the warren of Baghdad.

Thesiger was correct in assuming that the Marshes would be drained, but once again his prediction was markedly premature. Part of the Marshes was drained in 1985 to exploit the Qurna oilfield, but during the Iran–Iraq war Saddam Hussain kept the region well flooded as an obstacle to the advance of an Iranian army. The greatest damage, in fact, was done after the Gulf war in 1991, when Saddam began to see the region as a dangerous haven for his Shi'ite opponents and deserters from his armies. The marshland near Amara, where Thesiger had first entered it with Dugald Stewart in 1950, was bombarded by artillery to clear the local population and then occupied by government troops. It was drained using dykes and levees, which were then mined to prevent rebels from destroying them. Saddam Hussain proceeded to embark on a campaign of total genocide of the Marsh Arabs, poisoning the fish and the reedbeds, exposing whole villages to gas attack. A great boom was built across the Tigris–Euphrates watershed, with the object of draining the Marshes entirely. He informed the UN that this was to make way for an 'agricultural scheme'. At the time of writing it is estimated that Saddam's forces have already murdered at least 300,000 people, mostly Shi'ites, in southern Iraq. The remaining Ma'adan have fled to the Iranian borders. While the West cannot remain guiltless in this – the worst negation of human rights since the Second World War – in that Western companies supplied Saddam with his technology, it must be observed that the atrocity has been perpetrated by an Arab leader against his own people.

'In a few years' time,' wrote Gavin Maxwell in *A Reed Shaken by the Wind*, 'that young tribesman whose urgent silhouette I shall carry in my mind's eye as a symbol of the Marshlands will be driving a lorry if he is lucky, pimping on the back streets of Basra for white employees of a Western petroleum company if he is not.'[65] Yet Marsh Arab society was remarkably intact, despite the presence of schools and the departure of the great Sheikhs, when Gavin Young returned there in the 1970s. Much more recently, in the wake of Saddam's genocide against the marsh people, Jim Crumley added of Maxwell's 'young tribesman': 'If he is less lucky still, he will now be a middle-aged corpse, a primary coloured stain beneath the no-fly zone, and where he lies it will not be beautiful.'[66]

CHAPTER 14

An Old Tweed Jacket of the Sort
Worn by Eton Boys

From the early 1950s Thesiger's life assumed a pattern of seasonal migration almost as regular as those of the nomads, but more wide-ranging. In the spring he would be found doctoring in the Marshes or meandering on horseback among the Arab nomads on the banks of the Tigris or the Euphrates. In the summer, though, when the Marshes were unbearably humid, he would turn his thoughts to cooler climes, seeking out the high mountain country of Asia or, in one case, Morocco. The winters would be spent travelling with his mother as a well-heeled tourist in Europe, North Africa or the Middle East. 'I went home to England for three months a year,' he said, 'and I usually took my mother away for a month – we went to Palestine, Syria, Turkey, Greece, Italy, Morocco, Portugal and Spain – if we were going from city to city we'd go by train. For the rest we'd motor it. It was a sort of set thing – I'd come home and we'd go somewhere, and then we'd say, "Where shall we go next year?" We went to all sorts of places, travelling by car, not animals, of course, and we'd stay in reasonable hotels. The idea was actually to give Mollie Emtage – my mother's housekeeper – a break, because she was at it the whole year. I took my mother for a month or six weeks and Mollie would go off and see her family. Anyway it was a pleasure to do it and I saw a lot of Europe that I wouldn't otherwise have seen – Sicily for example. However, I've rarely taken a photograph in Europe – only architecture in Spain and that sort of thing – and I've never photographed another European.'[1] From December to February he would take up his social life in England. 'I'd go off and stay with various people,' he said. 'The Verneys, the ffrench-Blakes, the Rumbolds or three or four other people I used to stay with for a week or two.'[2]

*

High mountains were a new departure for Thesiger: he suffered easily from the cold and had no head for heights. He admired mountaineers like Bill Tilman and Eric Shipton, but had no interest in the kind of expeditions they mounted – teams of Westerners like commando-units in a foreign territory armed with ropes and special equipment. He thought the idea of technical climbing futile, but warmed to Shipton's feeling that it was what lay on the other side of the mountain that counted, rather than the ability required to climb a certain face. He had never been on a rope but was confident that he could go wherever the locals did, knowing that they certainly did not use ropes or carabiners to traverse the high passes. In 1952 he had lunch with Shipton at the Travellers' Club, and the mountaineer told him that the most impressive mountain landscape he knew lay in the Karakoram range in northern Pakistan. Thesiger was intrigued by Shipton's vivid description of the cragged and glaciated ranges of Gilgit and Hunza, and resolved to travel there that summer. Unfortunately he found his way barred. He decided to take second best and instead trekked through Swat and Chitral in the Hindu Kush.

From Peshawar he travelled to Saidu Sharif, capital of Swat, with a Pathan called Jahangir Khan, who spoke some English, and obtained a permit from the local Wali to cross the Kacha Kuni pass into Chitral. The Wali maintained that no other European had ever crossed it, though in fact much of the route had been travelled by an American, Alexander Gardiner, disguised as a Pathan mercenary, in the 1860s. Thesiger had never heard of Gardiner, but regarded the Wali's assertion as nonsense. Yet he felt mildly perturbed as he looked up the Swat valley and saw the light crackling back from the glaciers and the sharp joints and impossible pinnacles of the rock. The landscape was not only moving, it was terrible: 'I'd never seen anything like that in my life,' he commented. 'My home was the desert. Here in the mountains I had to master a completely new way of life – new challenges of height, of snow, of glaciers, of finding food, of standing up to cold. I felt it a formidable undertaking, almost nerve-racking, but it turned out to be easier once I was up there – these things always do.'[3] He had comforted himself with the certain knowledge that the locals did not use special gear to cross into Chitral, indeed he soon saw that they lacked even shoes, merely wrapping their feet in goatskins and their legs in puttees. During the freezing nights they simply rolled themselves up in their cloaks. Beside them Thesiger was well equipped, with his tent, rucksack, sleeping bag, solid fuel, medicines and ice-axe.

He had two mules to carry the gear and provisions and a soldier provided by the Wali, armed with an antique rifle. The tiny party was dwarfed by the overarching buttes and spurs as it crawled steadily up through the sparse forests of chenars, poplars and acacia to the treeline, where Thesiger exchanged his mules for porters. The going now became excruciatingly sheer and they stumbled over rocky screes and slithered across small glaciers. For the last part of the ascent Thesiger wasted a great deal of energy cutting steps with the unfamiliar ice-axe, yet found that the altitude bothered him less than he had anticipated. From the summit of the pass one of the porters led him down to the village of Laspur, where they hired donkeys to carry their baggage through the chasms and scarps to the next settlement, Mastuj. Thesiger now found himself in the Kiplingesque domain through which the Great Game had ebbed and flowed in Victorian times, when British explorers like Younghusband and Moorcroft had been either professional or amateur intelligence agents, seeking to find a natural line of defence in these mountains where the British could dig in against the inexorable advance of the Russian Bear. In the days of the Raj there had been a British post in Mastuj, though Thesiger had to be content with shelter in a rest-house. Later he was introduced to two officers related to the ruler of Chitral, who dragooned him into playing his first game of polo, which he found exhilarating.

His next objective was to reach the lake of Karumbar where the Chitral river rose, and the officers provided him with a man called Malung and his son to escort him there with a horse and a donkey. They trekked through village after village, each isolated from the next like an island in a sea of scorched rock, the air filled with the scent of artemisia and wild roses that bloomed across the track. Thesiger looked up to see, almost due west, beyond ridge upon saw-tooth ridge, the netherland of gossamer cloud and isinglass snow that concealed the raw skin of Tirich Mir, at 25,000 feet, the prince of mountains of the Hindu Kush. The river foamed down the Chitral valley and the track followed a roller-coaster course, zigzagging across it by perilous cantilever bridges which swung nerve-rackingly in the wind. Thesiger and his two men tramped up and down arid bluffs or sometimes trawled through the freezing water. Up here in a cloud-land of screes and glaciers, glowering cumulus in snow-white and grey, they crossed torrent after torrent of gushing water, and on the hillsides Thesiger was thrilled to encounter tribesmen from Afghanistan and western China – Kirghiz, Kazak and Wakih, with their yak-herds scattered among the rocks. A week after leaving Mastuj Thesiger stood on the banks of Karumbar, a limpid blue mirror beneath the skirts of sweeping, snow-capped mountains.

The following day he crossed the Baroghil pass, one of the easier passes in the Hindu Kush. The explorer Biddulph had seen the Baroghil as 'a break in the great mountain barrier', which was open ten months of the year and could be crossed 'without slowing from a gallop'. The acutely sensitive masters of the Great Game had feared the pass as a potential 'gate' through which Russian armies might advance on India. From 12,000 feet Thesiger was delighted to glimpse the mountains of Wakhan and, far below in the Panja valley, the mystical glint of the Oxus river as it wormed a serpentine path around their bights. He trekked back along the foot of Tirich Mir until he reached Chitral, having covered a total of 350 miles since leaving Swat. Thesiger still found the energy to visit a village of the so-called 'Black Kafirs', who preserved the pagan customs and traditions of Kafiristan – the setting for Kipling's adventure yarn *The Man Who Would Be King*. Always in search of the 'unchanging society', he was fascinated by these people who claimed to be 'white men' and who worshipped their ancestors in the form of effigies carved out of solid cedar, groups of which stood in each village. He regretted that the Kafirs across the border in Afghanistan had been forcibly converted to Islam in the previous century, and the region's name changed to 'Nuristan' – 'Land of Light'.

Before returning to London he motored to Waziristan, staying with Pakistani Political Officers at Wana and Miram Shah. He visited Razmak, once a British military base, and compared the rotting barrack-blocks and barbed wire left by the British unfavourably with the majestic forts bequeathed to posterity by the war-like Moghuls. Trapped in a vehicle with an armed escort, he watched colourful Pathan tribesmen leading their camel-caravans out of the passes of Afghanistan, swaggering along freely with their rifles on their shoulders. Tempted, perhaps, by these frustratingly brief glimpses of exotic life, he later paid a reconnaissance visit to Afghanistan. In Kabul he stayed with the British Ambassador, who asked his young Third Secretary, Hugh Carless, to take Thesiger on a short journey in the eastern part of the country. With Carless and an American diplomat called Bob Dreesen, Thesiger travelled by Land-Rover to Ghazni, where there were some remarkable eleventh-century towers: 'We saw these two "Towers of Victory",' Carless remembered, 'and the tomb of the famous Sultan Mahmud who had led twelve armies down into India. Then we went through the town and slept the night in a tea-house in a small village. Wilfred was a great story-teller and enthralled us with his stories of Arabia.'⁴ Thesiger was to encounter Carless under somewhat less comfortable circumstances four years later in Nuristan. For now, however, he was content to gather information and get a feel of the country. He continued his sight-seeing, motoring to Kandahar and Quetta in Baluchistan, before returning to Karachi.

On his journey in the Hindu Kush he had acquired a taste for the remote, adventurous landscapes of Asia, the world of *Kim* that he had dreamed about as a boy at Eton. During the following summer he managed, after a month's haggling, to obtain permission to visit Gilgit, Hunza and Ishkoman in the Karakoram. As usual he was given every assistance by the Foreign Office, in this case the High Commissioner in Karachi. He started from Peshawar, where he engaged an English-speaking Pathan called Faiz Muhammad. They travelled by mule up the Kaghan valley, and Thesiger found himself gazing aghast at the unbelievable majesty of the landscape. Shipton had not exaggerated. Here was Nanga Parbat in all its imperial splendour, a vast conglomeration of peaks set on a massive plinth rising so sheer out of the earth that one had to tilt one's head back to take it in. At 26,500 feet – almost four and a half miles high – it was the great endwall of the Himalaya, and Thesiger sensed instinctively why it had been named 'the Naked Mountain'. Soon they reached Gilgit, the small town that was the key to six of the major mountain passes

that divide India from Central Asia, built on the side of the
rushing torrent of the Gilgit river. Once again Thesiger felt
himself involuntarily stunned by the scenery. He saw the great
guardians of the Gilgit valley, Dobani and Haramosh, and beyond
them, towering like a god over Hunza, the carved claw of
Rakaposhi. 'Physical and overwhelming comes the response,'
wrote John Keay, 'a prickling of the scalp, a shudder of disbelief'
. . . here, quite simply, is 'the most awful and the most magnificent
sight to be met with in the Himalayas'.[5] At Gilgit Thesiger
lingered in the alleys of the market, where men in pancake-pile
caps and embroidered cloaks clutched glasses of piping hot tea
and chapattis. Today, Gilgit is a major tourist centre and in the
summer is packed with visitors. In the market one can obtain
every requisite of the mountaineer, from boots to oxygen cylinders
– the cast-off surplus of 10,000 expeditions. The track along
which Thesiger picked his way painfully with pack-horses is now
the Karakoram highway, and though the valley remains sweep-
ingly beautiful, the landscape is now laced with power-lines and
the towers of pylons. The smallest of villages has its tourist hotel
and TV is to be found in even the remotest household. From
Gilgit, Thesiger trekked on into Hunza. The small caravan made
its way beneath the great glaciers and peaks, along a river that
spurled grey and brown across beaches of polished flat pebbles.
The track wound through hamlets hidden in poplar groves,
where grapevines snaked around the mast-straight trunks and
spilled from the branches in a flutter of green. They passed tiny
squares and terraces of cultivation, through orchards where the
trees were weighed down with ripe mulberries and where the
aroma of apricots filled the air. Everywhere there were golden
apricots drying in the sun, for this fruit was the staple diet of the
Hunza people, yielding a flour that was preserved for the winter
months. Thesiger found the people much to his liking. Traditionally the most war-like of the Karakoram races, they had once
made their living pillaging trade-caravans and selling neighbours
into slavery. Thesiger found them hospitable and dignified. In the
1950s Hunza was already becoming famous as the paradise hidden
in the mountains that made it the setting for John Hilton's
Shangri-La in his novel *Lost Horizon*. It was only fifty-two miles,
but several days' journey, from Gilgit to the mountain village of

Baltit where a fort stood like an eagle's nest on a towering pinnacle, itself rendered insignificant by the sheer wall of ice-coloured, cloud-shrouded granite that stood behind it. Here, Thesiger stayed with the local prince or Mir, and then, with fresh pack-horses, set off north towards the Pamirs. The river dashed on its pebble bed beneath him, filling the air with its roaring, and there was a constant rain of small pebbles from the spurs above. His party crossed the great Batura glacier, where they exchanged the horses for yaks and porters. Thesiger was not impressed by the yaks, which he found impossibly slow compared with donkeys or mules, but he much admired the Hunza porters and regretted he could not communicate with them except through Faiz Muhammad. 'The Hunzas are a magnificent people,' he said. 'They aren't as famous as the Sherpas, but I would rate them as equals.'[6] They reached the shrine at Babaghundi, where Thesiger again met some yak-mounted Kirghiz who seemed to bring with them all the mystery of 'Inner Asia'. The following day his party abandoned their yaks and set off on foot up the Chilinji valley. By one o'clock in the afternoon they had reached the summit and looked down on the interlocking faces of mountains that stretched to infinity around them. The descent was exceedingly steep and covered in soft snow, and as they inched their way down, Thesiger and his porters frequently pitched on to their backs. It took them three days in pelting, freezing snow to descend.

A few days later they entered the small state of Ishkoman, where Thesiger sent home two of his Hunza porters and retained the remaining two, an old man called Mirza and a young one called Latif. The following day, with the addition of some Ishkoman porters, he set off to scale the 14,000-foot Ishkoman pass, which he was warned might be snowbound. They marched for seven hours and spent the night in a disused house. The next morning the porters downed their loads after only two and a half hours' march. They told Thesiger that the pass was still a long way off and that they would not make it before nightfall. Thesiger took a long look at the wall of glaciated rock. To him it seemed no more than a couple of hours away. He was anxious to press on, since he feared that a fresh fall of snow would render the Ishkoman impassable. This might have meant turning back to Chitral, and once he had set his mind on a goal Thesiger was reluctant to give up. He had enough authority to force the porters on, but for once he had underestimated the wisdom of his travelling-companions. He very quickly encountered the first unexpected obstacle: invisible depressions filled with deep snow. Already shattered after battling with this, the porters then had to wrestle with steep, slippery ascents. Thesiger soon realized how much he had miscalculated. He had hoped to reach the summit shortly after noon, but made it only half an hour before sunset. This meant starting the descent in pitch darkness. The heavily-laden porters were already on their last legs and interpreter Faiz Muhammad was in tears. Thesiger decided to take the lead, blazing a trail with Mirza, the old porter from Hunza, close behind. The Ishkoman porters – whom Thesiger now classed as 'rather a poor lot' – tramped on after them. Often Thesiger plunged through the hard crust and fell up to his armpits in snow, yet in spite of such tardy progress the porters had disappeared before he and Mirza had descended 2,000 feet. It was dark, very cold, and there was no fuel here to light a fire. Neither of them had matches, anyway. Mirza urged him to descend as far as the treeline, where they might get help from a village, but Thesiger resolved rigidly to wait for the others or die in the process. Giving up in desperation, Mirza disappeared into the darkness, leaving Thesiger alone, facing possible death from hypothermia and almost certain frostbite if the rest of the party failed to arrive. He bellowed into the night but the darkness swallowed up the noise greedily, and there came back no answer. Thesiger wondered how many of his toes and fingers would be left by morning. Suddenly, without warning, the porters crunched out of the darkness. He was enormously relieved to see them, but concerned to hear that they had been held up by the interpreter, Faiz Muhammad, who had collapsed under a rock overhang. Latif, the younger Hunza porter, had remained with him. Thesiger knew that Latif had bedding with him and that the two could survive the night, so he decided to take the party down to tree-level, where at least they could light a fire. The remaining part of the descent took until after midnight, with the porters dawdling along at snail's pace. Thesiger shivered with cold each time he had to wait for them to catch up. Finally, after negotiating a 500-foot precipice, they found enough wood to make a fire. As they prepared to make camp, Thesiger discovered that the porter carrying his tent was missing. The man had apparently jibbed on the final descent and halted for the night in the shelter of a rock. This meant a very cold, wet night for Thesiger in just his sleeping bag.

At first light, still plagued by the knowledge that he had 'made a mess of things', he started back alone to find Faiz Muhammad and Latif, this time carrying a pack with full equipment. Drained of energy after the nineteen-hour march of the previous day and the cold, almost sleepless night, he found the pack heavy, and wondered if he would make it back up the escarpment. Fortunately he ran into the stragglers after only two and a half hours. Latif was leading the hapless Faiz Muhammad, who staggered down painfully on frostbitten feet. Back at their camp they found the missing Mirza, who had sensibly climbed down to a village in the night and brought some men up to help. On 18 October, Thesiger arrived back at Gilgit. The entire journey had lasted forty days.

The following year Thesiger made his first real trek in Afghanistan. His ambition was still to travel in the little-explored region of Nuristan, whose people were reputedly the descendants of Alexander the Great's army. In Kabul he stayed at the Embassy with his distant relative, Sir Robert Lascelles, then British Ambassador, and was amazed at Lascelles's ability to learn languages: 'Every morning, almost, at breakfast, he'd be studying some new dialect of Afghanistan,' Thesiger said, 'and he mastered them all. I wouldn't have been able to do that.'[7] Nuristan was closed, however, and not even the big guns of the Ambassador could open the way for him. Instead, he contented himself with travelling in the little-known region of the Hazarajat. Furnished with a permit and accompanied by an interpreter called Jan Baz, he travelled for six weeks in the region, crossing back and forwards across the 16,000-foot Koh-i-Baba range which was the spine of the Hazarajat, carrying his baggage on a pony hired in the Maidan region. The land, at first sight rocky and poor, was in fact rich and fertile, the cultivation being concealed by the natural contours of the hillsides. The Hazaras who inhabited the mountains were a people of uncertain origin, ranging in appearance from the Persian to the Mongol, but speaking a Persian dialect. Thesiger believed they were actually Mongols who had been settled in the country in the thirteenth century by either the son or the grandson of Genghis Khan. They had been sent to guard the Khan's borders, Thesiger thought, and had belonged to various different tribes. He found them impeccably honest and industrious, but – an almost cardinal sin to the nomadic Thesiger – they were invariably inhospitable, despite being, like the marsh people, Shi'ite Muslims. At almost every village in which Thesiger's small party halted, someone would approach them and suggest they stop at another village further on. 'They were never unfriendly,' he wrote, 'just mean and inhospitable.'⁸ The Hazaras were a dour bunch, yet despite their lack of hospitality, Thesiger never condemned their culture as he was later to condemn that of the equally inhospitable Persian tribes. He found them physically attractive, and admired the hardship they seemed to endure. Even in summer the nights could be freezing up on the Koh-i-Baba, yet there grew little that could be used as firewood. The Hazaras used dung for cooking, but it would scarcely warm an entire house. Thesiger marvelled that such communities could survive the winter months here at 8 to 12,000 feet. The Hazaras inhabiting the arid northern slopes drove their cattle, sheep and goats up to the high pastures in summer, moving into crude stone shelters roofed with bushes or mats thrown over a frame of poles. Others, in the Surkh-o-Parsa region, moved downwards from their villages after the autumn harvest, pitching tents in the fields and allowing their cattle to manure them for the next planting. Thesiger was fascinated by the variety of customs and even physical types he met with among the Hazaras: he found them 'a tough people, hardy, industrious and honest, but close-fisted, inhospitable and rather dreary'.⁹ He contrasted them, though, with the nomadic Pathans who wandered up into the high country in summer, grazing their great herds of camels and flocks of goats and sheep on the mountain pastures, pitching black tents among the rocks. These Pathans were different in every way from the austere Hazaras, whom they despised as settled farmers and unorthodox Muslims. The Pathans were, 'more welcoming, more amusing and far more colourful', he wrote.¹⁰ They constantly pressed Thesiger's party to drink tea, share a meal or spend the night: they danced and played musical instruments. It was,

Thesiger said, 'the contrast between the farmer and the nomad'.[11] Yet he was quick to point out that these settled people were in no way awed by their Pathan neighbours: indeed, he once saw a Hazara thrash a shrieking Pathan who had allowed his camels to stray into a wheatfield, noting that the nomad did nothing to defend himself. Thesiger had watched Pathan tribesmen leading their caravans out of the mountain passes two years previously, from the window of a car. Now, he was thrilled to be travelling among them. Nevertheless, he retained fond memories of the Hazaras and his uneventful month and a half in their land. In October he returned briefly to the Marshes, then in November met his mother in Amman, for a tour of the Middle East, motoring by hired car to Jerusalem, Beirut, Baalbek, Damascus, the Crak-des-Chevaliers and Tripoli, and returning by boat and train via Istanbul, Athens, Delphi, Rome, Florence and Milan. That summer he returned to Morocco.

Thesiger had last been in Morocco with his mother in 1936, and almost two decades later, in 1955, he decided to walk across the spine of the High Atlas as far as Azrou – a journey of more than 300 miles. He had previously met Tihami al Glawi, the Pasha of Marrakesh, and though they did not meet on this occasion, the Pasha made sure Thesiger was given a letter which would allow him to pass from one Ksar to another throughout his domain. While at the British Consulate in Rabat, Thesiger heard that a multidisciplinary team from the Oxford University Exploration Society – of which he had long ago been a member – were at Taddert in the Atlas, preparing to make a study of a remote Berber village. He caught up with them at the hotel in Taddert as they sat disconsolately in the bar discussing the iniquity of the local Sheikh, who had promised to provide them with twenty mules and then, on the day of their planned departure, had informed them that no mules were available. According to the expedition leader, Bryan Clarke, Thesiger walked in carrying a small suitcase, dressed elegantly in a sports coat and trousers and a pair of peculiarly incongruous cotton shoes. He demanded a drink, Clarke recalled, in excruciatingly bad French, though this was evidently not sufficient proof of his Englishness, for Clarke immediately asserted to the others that he was a Scandinavian, sparking off a heated and somewhat indiscreet debate about the stranger's nationality. Thesiger ended the argument by inquiring, 'Are you the people from Oxford?' to which they nodded embarrassed assent. Clarke, a zoology student at Magdalen College, was not a whit disappointed to learn the newcomer's identity, for on the ferry to Tangier he had bet another member of the team that in some remote part of Morocco they would encounter at least one Oxford man. Now he collected his due with satisfaction. 'Thesiger joined us in our "camp" on the terrace,' he wrote. 'He told us that he had obtained his curious shoes in Kurdistan, and we spent an enjoyable evening listening to hair-raising tales of adventure. We discussed our inability to get mules in Taddert, and he suggested that we should all go to Telouet, where perhaps our letters of introduction might help us to obtain the necessary animals.'[12] They could not depart the next day, which was the Muslim 'Id al Fitr feast, but the day after drove their truck up the 7,000-foot Tizi-n-Tishka pass and across a barren plateau scattered with junipers. The road was already in the process of being asphalted, and Thesiger saw, no doubt to his disgust, gangs of labourers sweating in the wake of a puffing steamroller. Soon, the magnificent kasbah of Telouet — the stronghold of the Pasha of Marrakesh – appeared like a mirage from the centre of a great basin of ochre-coloured dust, its walls flashing a startling white against the scarlet rock. They drove up to the fortress's great gates, and, after a wait, were admitted into the presence of the Pasha's deputy or *khalifa*, who promised them the mules they sought. As the undergraduates prepared for their march to the village of Ait Rbaa, which was to be the object of their study, Thesiger readied himself for his lone trek. 'I had an idea,' Clarke wrote, 'which I put to him with some trepidation. Would it be possible, I asked, for one of us to accompany him on his journey? It would be a magnificent opportunity for us to extend the scope of our work. Very kindly, he agreed.'[13] At Taddert, Thesiger had made particular friends with one of the team, John Newbould, a botany undergraduate at Merton College, who had been an officer in the Commandos. He would gladly have taken Newbould with him, but the previous day the botanist had fallen thirty feet down a cliff while trying to recover a lost ice-axe, and though he had escaped with only lacerations and a cracked elbow, Clarke had packed him off to the hospital in Marrakesh. 'There were five or six of them,' Thesiger recalled, 'and the one I [would have] picked was John Newbould. Then the day before we were to set off he fell off a cliff and damaged his shoulder so he couldn't come. Colin Pennycuick said he would come instead and we would do the journey together.'[14] Pennycuick, a zoologist, later to become a Fellow of the Royal Society and a distinguished professor, appears in the group photograph of the expedition as a rather Bohemian type with unkempt beard and long hair: indeed, Clarke later commented that the locals referred to him as 'the hairy one'. 'He was a nice chap,' Thesiger remembered, 'but he was curious in that he had this sort of cult of looking dirty, with food stains on his clothes and a beard. We got on well, anyway.'[15]

Thesiger and Pennycuick left Telouet with only one mule and a local guide on 2 August, heading for the lake of Tamda. They carried no food with them, and halted almost every night at the fortress-like Ksars of Sheikhs and merchants, where Thesiger's letter from the Pasha ensured a hospitable reception. They trekked along the mustard-coloured escarpments of the southern High Atlas, wheeling around the massif of Ighil Mgoun and tramping along the banks of a stream as far as El Kelaa, where they arrived on 10 August. There they stayed with the local *khalifa*, who took them in his car on an excursion to the market town of Boumalne, set at the base of the great canyons from which the Dades river debouches into the plains. Thesiger's small party then climbed the Dades gorge and followed the river almost to its source. At M'Semrir they met up with Ernest Gellner, later Professor of Anthropology at Cambridge, who was then making his famous study of the mountain Berbers, which would be published as *Saints of the Atlas*. Gellner and his wife Susan had crossed the Atlas watershed from their base at Zaouia Ahansal to the southern side. Gellner recalled that Thesiger was having some difficulties with the guide who had been assigned to him by the Pasha. 'Morocco was in disarray,' he wrote. 'It was the height of the conflict between the nationalists and the French, and the [guide] was terrified. If he went further with Wilfred, far away from his own country, he expected to be murdered. If he went back he'd be punished by his master the Glawi, whose control over that area was still absolute. The man actually kissed Wilfred's feet in his terror. Wilfred gave him a chit in English saying in effect he was honourably dismissed and we recruited another man with a mule called Sidi Hussein who had kin connections in Zaouia Ahansal where we were going and who was willing to come with us.'[16]

Together, the five-strong group crossed the mountains, halting on the Abdi plateau at 9,000 feet, where they were welcomed in the black tents of the nomadic Berber tribes who grazed their cattle there. After several days they descended the cliffs around the plateau and arrived at the Gellners' camp at Zaouia Ahansal. Here, Thesiger and Pennycuick found their progress blocked. For one thing, there had recently been a massacre of Europeans at Oued Zem – about eighty miles away – by the nationalist Smala tribe. The tribe were now subject to ferocious reprisals by the French, who had forbidden all travel. For another, there had been unprecedented floods on the local river, the Asif Ahansal, and all the bridges had been washed away. There was no way to get down to the valley with a mule.

'We stayed with Gellner and his wife,' Thesiger recalled, 'and he suggested we should climb the face of this unclimbed mountain. He asked if I'd climbed and I said never, so he said they would put me in the middle, because Pennycuick had done some climbing. It was rather alarming. Anyway, I had a rope on me and with their assistance I got up, and we were very near the top, but couldn't quite make it. It was getting very late, and Gellner said we'd either have to spend the night on this ledge or abseil down. I told him I'd never abseiled, but he said they'd show me what to do. I was quite alarmed actually, but I did what they told me and dropped over the edge, and by abseiling a couple of times we eventually did get to the bottom before it was dark.'[17]

Gellner recalled that the mountain in question was called Aioui, and a large and imposing cliff face on one side, with a gentle ascent on the other. 'Wilfred, Colin, and I tried to do a new route on the south-facing rock,' he said, 'and after a goodish climb I turned back because I reached a little overhang which I knew I could get over, but if I did so it looked as if I wouldn't have been able to get back. So caution prevailed. Wilfred clearly enjoyed the climb and would have liked to have gone on.'[18]

During their two-week stay with the Gellners, Thesiger and Pennycuick accompanied them on an even more perilous climb, up the gorge of Taria, part of which was said, according to local legend, to be unclimbable. 'The gorge looks ferocious, unbelievably narrow with enormous cliffs either side,' Gellner said, 'but in fact it is not all that difficult ... Whilst climbing this gorge one pitch could only be done by going straight up the middle of a waterfall. As we didn't want to get our clothes wet we all stripped completely naked and put the clothes in a rucksack which we hauled up later. Wilfred had been suffering badly from boils which he discussed at length but could not normally show as they were on his bottom. As Susan climbed after him he was very anxious to know whether she had seen and admired them in their full horror. She told him that the problem of climbing and the natural beauties of the gorge had distracted her attention and prevented her from paying due heed to Wilfred's boils – remarkable and noteworthy though they may have been.'[19] 'We'd just got through this waterfall,' Thesiger remembered, 'and I heard it thundering away in the distance and I said now look here, we must get out of here quick. Gellner and Pennycuick were both saying it doesn't necessarily follow it's going to come here. I said if it did we'd have had it. Mrs Gellner said we could just watch and see if the water was rising. I said there wouldn't be a chance – it would come too quickly – and anyway I said I'd told them what I thought and I was getting out. "If you want to stay here, that's it, I've warned you," I said. Well, we did get out, and it was quite a long way. We were just getting on the plain and water as high as a room came rushing through the gorge. Undoubtedly, I saved their lives.'[20]

'The weather was unstable and it was probably raining higher up,' Gellner recalled, 'and Wilfred constantly warned us that a killer wall of water would eventually come down the gorge. In the end we heeded his warnings and turned back. We spent the night in the village of Taria where the gorge widened. An hour or so after we got there, Wilfred was proved correct and a terrible mass of yellow, muddy water did indeed come down the gorge in a surge. Had we still been in the upper part of the gorge it would no doubt have swept us along with it. Susan says now that Wilfred's anxious warnings – which we derided at the time – saved our lives.'[21]

Back at the Gellners' camp, Susan Gellner struggled to keep

the household fed on what little was obtainable locally: often there was nothing but sardines, and Pennycuick commented that he was unlikely ever again to suffer from sardine-hunger. One day they bought a chicken to vary the diet and Gellner was surprised to find that none of them was willing to dispatch it: 'Colin was a zoologist,' he wrote, 'Thesiger a hardened explorer, but when it came to executing the chicken, we had to ask the local butcher!' When the floods subsided, Pennycuick and Thesiger bade farewell to the Gellners and descended into the valley, where they caught a bus back to Telouet. 'Wilfred was clearly a gentleman of the old style,' Gellner remembered, 'intensely romantic in the sense of having a yearning for societies which had not changed. He struck me as curiously introverted for one famous above all as a man of action.'[22]

Thesiger's delay at Zaouia Ahansal had caused consternation among the members of the Oxford University expedition, now encamped at Idirh, and Clarke was relieved to find them there after their five-week absence on his return from a foray to Marrakesh. For a while, Thesiger was glad to settle into the routine of camp life: 'The villagers were very impressed by Thesiger,' Clarke wrote. 'He was more severe with them than we had ever been, and they concluded that he was an English Pasha.'[23] On 10 September, Thesiger set off by truck from Telouet with John Newbould, now recovered from his fall, to climb Toubkal – at 13,600 feet, Morocco's highest mountain – from a nearby village. The ascent was a hard walk rather than a real climb, and the two men managed to collect a large variety of plant and animal specimens including tree-frogs, snails and a virtually unknown species of carnation. Thesiger and Newbould got on well, and Thesiger looked forward to taking the botanist on his planned trek through Nuristan the following year. After the Oxford expedition's departure, Thesiger spent the rest of September visiting Taroudant, Tiznit, Goulimime, Tafraout, Agadir, Fez, and Taza. In October he accompanied his mother on a tour of Italy from Milan to Venice, Naples, Rome and Sicily, returning to London in November.

When Thesiger left the Marshes in summer 1956 and headed for Kabul, he hoped to find John Newbould there with the barometers and plant-collecting equipment he had requested him to bring for the journey in Nuristan. He arrived in Kabul on 18 July to discover that, for some mysterious reason, the Afghan government had refused his friend a visa. Nuristan – the former Kafiristan – was the section of the Hindu Kush that lay within the borders of Afghanistan along the Chitral border. In 1889, Sir George Robertson, British Agent in Chitral, had spent a year there while the region was pagan and still independent, and in 1896 he had published a fascinating book *The Kafirs of the Hindu Kush*. Two important German expeditions had been there in the 1920s and 1930s and a Danish one in the 1950s: Nuristan was little known, but not unexplored. Since he arrived during the Islamic 'Id al Fitr celebrations it took Thesiger ten days of bureaucracy to obtain the permit he required. However, the University in Kabul kindly loaned him an English-speaking student named Abdul Nawab as interpreter, and Clifford Jupp of the British Embassy motored him up by Land-Rover as far as Kachu, where he had agreed to leave a car for Thesiger's old acquaintance Hugh Carless, who with writer Eric Newby was currently attempting to climb the 20,000-foot peak of Mir Samir. Thesiger hired three Tajiks and two horses to carry his baggage, though he wished later that he had taken Tajik porters from the beginning, and started up the Panjshir valley towards the Chamar pass, which was the gateway to Nuristan. The small caravan passed through scattered farmsteads and small villages, halting at local tea-shops for tea and hookah-pipes. Most of the people here were Tajiks, wearing long striped cloaks and blue or black turbans, but Thesiger's party was soon joined by anyone who happened to be going his way – Tajiks, Pathans or Nuristanis. At a place called Shahnaise, Thesiger suddenly observed two European figures approaching. 'I saw these two people,' he recalled, 'and I had already heard that Carless was in the area, though I'd never heard of Newby. We had stopped, I think, and these figures came down the hillside and they did look in the last stages of exhaustion. Newby had bought some climbing boots in Italy without even trying them on, and they'd tried him on by taking the soles off his feet and there was no skin on their faces. They looked thoroughly desiccated and in what you'd call a bad state.'[24]

'We both already knew that Thesiger was planning a journey in the area,' Carless recalled, 'so we were expecting to see him at some stage. We were quite pleased that we had been into Nuristan before this great explorer, and to meet him as he was going in rather than as he was coming out. There were very few Europeans travelling then, so even when we saw him from a distance I knew it couldn't be anyone else but him. Eric hadn't met him before and didn't know much about him and was therefore delighted to have this subject for the ending of his book. It wouldn't be quite fair to say that we were at the last stages of exhaustion. We were at the end of a very tough journey, that was all.'[25]

Newby described Thesiger as 'a great, long-striding crag of a man, with an outcrop for a nose and bushy eyebrows, forty-five years old and as hard as nails, in an old tweed jacket of the sort worn by Eton boys, a pair of thin grey cotton trousers, rope-soled Persian slippers and a woollen cap-comforter'.[26] Newby's portrait of Thesiger is a caricature of an upper-class Englishman of the Imperial school, bellowing instructions at his non-English-speaking cook: 'Here you! Make some green tea and a lot of chicken and rice!' and producing a massive bunch of keys to unlock the sugar, 'like a housekeeper in some stately home'. All evening, Newby wrote, Thesiger was opening and shutting boxes, giving him tantalizing glimpses of what his baggage contained: a telescope, a string vest, a copy of Stendhal's *Charterhouse of Parma*, and a neatly divided and mounted map of Afghanistan. Much of the evening Thesiger talked to them about the Marsh Arabs and his doctoring, his conversation, according to Newby, punctuated by complaints about the poor quality of British workmanship and declarations that Britain was 'going to pot'. After a dinner of chickens that had looked like pterodactyls alive and tasted like elastic dead, Newby wrote that he and Carless began blowing up their airbeds, an obvious advantage on the hard, rocky ground. Thesiger looked on with evident disapproval at the procedure: 'You must be a couple of pansies,' he said.[27]

'I was sleeping on the ground,' Thesiger recalled, 'and the thing they had which I didn't have was a couple of airbeds and they were puffing them up and I may have said you must be a couple of pansies, but it was only meant as a joke. Actually it was the last thing they looked like, and they'd obviously had a very tough time. Neither of them was an experienced climber, though I should have thought they were both fairly tough characters.'[28] 'As for the airbeds,' Carless commented later, 'Eric still had his, but though I had mine, it was no longer capable of holding any air.'[29]

Some controversy was raised over Thesiger's 'Eton jacket' by Evelyn Waugh, who eventually wrote an introduction to Newby's book *A Short Walk in the Hindu Kush*, for which the encounter with Thesiger provided a fitting climax. In a letter to Newby, Waugh, asked, 'with barely disguised malevolence', how he knew that Thesiger's jacket was the sort worn by Eton boys. Newby, formerly employed in the fashion trade and fairly meticulous on such niceties, had not been at Eton, but had seen Etonians wearing such jackets on the playing fields. He wrote to Thesiger to make doubly certain, though, and Thesiger assured him that it was indeed his old 'change coat' from Billings and Edmonds, the school outfitters, leaving Newby wondering suddenly at 'what a gigantically impressive schoolboy Thesiger must have been at Eton if he was still wearing the same coat at the age of forty-five'.[30] Newby and Carless were up before Thesiger the following morning, and while the explorer lay half-asleep and bleary-eyed in his blankets, Newby took a unique shot of him which he reproduced in his book. 'It wasn't that Eric wanted intentionally to photograph him in bed,' Carless explained. 'It was just that we were leaving and that was the only way he could have photographed him.'[31]

After they had gone Thesiger continued up the pass with his horses, crossing it at 16,500 feet and enjoying the breathtaking view of Mir Samir, which Carless and Newby had recently failed to climb, its great peak glittering with snow. That evening some Nuristanis came to visit them. His Tajiks were apprehensive and feared trouble, but in fact the Nuristanis were friendly, and though Thesiger declined an invitation to spend the night with them in their rock-shelter, they entertained his party with singing and dancing. Thesiger thought them very European-looking, and noted that they went barefoot in this high, cold, rocky country. He said that they were superb mountaineers and would have made excellent porters. He noticed too, however, that they were mercurial in nature, rushing about, flinging themselves down, getting up, asking questions and suddenly losing interest. That they had a streak of unpredictable violence in their character was confirmed later when one of them suddenly hurled a Tajik to the ground, demanding money which he claimed the man owed him. He might perhaps have done him serious injury had Thesiger not pitched his six-foot-three frame into the fray and dragged him off.

A few days later they reached Puchal, the chief village in the Ramgul valley, set in magnificent, soaring mountains whose lower slopes were forested with holly oak. Puchal was an Islamic centre and the Mullahs, now seeing their third Christian within a few days – for Newby and Carless had passed this way – were openly hostile, raging with the red-hot fanaticism of recent converts. Leaving the town on 18 August, Thesiger's caravan was following a narrow track above the river when suddenly one of the horses caught its load on a projecting rock and plunged into the flood. Thesiger's collection of plants, his films, spare lenses, notebooks, passport, money and clothes were in its saddle-bags. One of the Tajik boys promptly splashed into the icy river, rescued the horse and saved Thesiger's precious belongings from being dragged downstream through the nearby rapids.

His plan was to cross the Purdem pass into the Kulam valley, but the going proved too rough for his horses. Spending the night at the rock-shelter of some Nuristanis, they heard a rumour that six bandits had followed them up from Puchal, and had made inquiries about them at the shelter. The bandits apparently intended to kill them on the other side of the valley. Thesiger was sceptical about the story, probably thinking it had been concocted by the Tajik horsemen, who in any case refused to go further. In the morning their Nuristani hosts hurried them on, saying that the bandits might return, and while they were unconcerned whether the Englishman and his party were killed or not, they would rather it had not been in their camp. Thesiger had no choice but to return to Puchal, where he paid off his horsemen and hired Nuristani porters. The Mullahs of the town remained hostile, but the townspeople were not unfriendly and the new porters carried well. However, they soon proved troublesome, dumping their loads and demanding exorbitant wages, knowing that Thesiger had little choice but to accept. The friction was continuous, and this disappointed Thesiger, who had thought the Nuristanis cheerful, humorous and good-tempered. In contrast to the mean but impeccably honest Hazaras, they were 'unreliable, quick tempered, avaricious, and thievish'.[32] However, they crossed the pass and reached Kulam in a single day's haul. From there he trekked down to Jalalabad and crossed the border into Pakistan at Peshawar. 'I had seen a bit of Nuristan,' Thesiger commented, 'but the other part was more exciting, and I wanted to go back and see it.'[33] It was to be almost a decade before he returned.

He stayed for a fortnight with Amara in the Marshes on his way back to Europe, and then flew to Italy, where he joined his mother for a holiday in Naples. In London that winter, Thesiger was approached by a literary agent named Graham Watson of Curtis Brown, who looked at some of his photographs of Arabia and tried to persuade him to write a book about the Empty Quarter. Seven years had passed since leaving south Arabia, and Thesiger had resisted any suggestion that he should compile his experiences into a book. He said later that he knew that to write about the experience would be to detract from it, and Timothy Green recorded that Thesiger believed 'this was his own private experience and he saw no reason to share it with the world'.[34] This impression cannot be perfectly accurate, however, for Thesiger did undoubtedly seek fame as an explorer, and had already contributed seven papers to the *Geographical Journal* on his experiences in Arabia alone. He had had three pieces published in the *Geographical Magazine*, two in the *Illustrated London News*, and given three radio talks to the BBC, which were later published in the *Listener*. The idea that Thesiger was entirely unknown in 1957, or that he had no interest in fame and publicity, is misleading. He had understood the power of publicity well enough at the early age of twenty-three to use his *Times* article as a lever to influence his selection for the Sudan Political Service. However, he thought of fame in terms of the *cognoscenti* rather than in terms of the mass, 'superstar' acclaim which would eventually come his way. He associated the idea of writing a book with the academic efforts he had fared so poorly in at school. He had no pretensions in the literary field, and while his papers were simple geography and his radio talks straightforward travellers' tales, to write a travel book would be to enter the exalted realm of literature. As a man who constantly itched for action and movement, too, he felt himself unable to submit to the long period of 'inactivity' which such a task would entail. 'It's perfectly true that I'd never had any intention of writing a book,' he commented, 'and I'd never do a journey with a view to writing a book because I think that's absolutely futile. When Graham Watson came to look at my photographs with the idea of using some of them, he said, "Look, you've got to write a book." I told him nothing would induce me to write a book and I'd no idea how to do it anyway. It meant sitting down and working hard and probably staying in Europe when I'd rather be off in the Karakoram or something. "Anyway," I told him, "I'm not going to write a book so it's no good going on!" He argued and argued away for three hours, then the next day he came back with Mark Longman of Longmans. They started it all up again and my mother was there and she was backing them up. Finally I said, "To hell with it!" And I said there would be no question of a deadline – "I mean if I get it done or don't get it done we'll see, but I'm not to be told it's got to be done by November week or something." They agreed and the next day Graham Watson told me they'd given me a thousand-pound advance, which was phenomenal at that time, and then the day after that he rang up to say the Americans had offered me another thousand. There had been no question of haggling over the advance, and in fact it wouldn't have made any difference one way or the other.'[35]

1957 turned out to be the only year since coming down from Oxford during which Thesiger never left Europe. Looking around for a suitably tranquil place to write, he hit upon the somewhat surprising destination of Copenhagen. 'I went there because I didn't know anybody there,' he explained. 'It was winter and I felt there wouldn't be much to take me out. I didn't want a more interesting place   I mean I felt that if I'd gone to Venice or somewhere I should have spent my time wandering about the streets and that would have been absolutely fatal. Anyway, in Copenhagen I shut myself up in the Park Hotel in a bed-sitting-room and stayed there four months. I said to myself, now the only way I can do this is to sit down in the morning at 8.30 and not stop till lunchtime. I had to be strict with myself, because if I wasn't in the mood it would have been too easy just to sit down and read another Agatha Christie or something. So I did really do it like that and when I got started I found I was sometimes writing sixteen hours a day. I used to go out just for a quick walk round the park and then come in and work.'[36] Another reason why the bleak Copenhagen appealed to him was because it was so much in contrast to the environment he was writing about. Had he been in Greece or Morocco, he felt, he would have ended up describing the sunsets and landscapes he saw outside the window. There in the small bed-sitting-room, Thesiger relived his experiences with an intensity which was magnified by time. He often felt that bin Kabina and bin Ghabaisha were actually in the room with him. He had no proper diaries, only brief notes, though his photographs were excellent *aides-mémoire*, and he had his *Geographical Journal* papers to fall back on for the outline of his journeys. He sent off the first few pages to his friend from Eton days, Val ffrench-Blake, who read through them and realized that although Thesiger had a great deal to say, much of it was written in clichés. ffrench-Blake devised a code using coloured pencils – red for a cliché, blue for a grammatical mistake, and yellow for an inappropriate choice of words – and sent the sheaf of pages back to the unprotesting Thesiger covered in a rainbow of coloured lines. ffrench-Blake also asked Thesiger why he felt the need to 'always fire with both barrels', meaning that he tended to pile on the adjectives.

Subsequently Thesiger went through the script carefully cutting out superfluities. He always wrote by hand, and sometimes had to rewrite each page ten times to get it perfect. 'After about four months, when I'd to some extent broken the back of it,' he recalled, 'I moved to Halloden in Ireland, where my mother had relations, and I finished it off there. John Verney didn't help me to any great extent, neither did Val ffrench-Blake. I mean, I took the draft to them and they'd say you could have used this word here and that sentence should be changed around, and paragraphing and punctutation – the sort of thing I couldn't do. But they didn't play a major part: it was absolutely my book.'[37] In October Thesiger took his mother to Palermo in Sicily, and he returned to Halloden the following year to add the final touches to *Arabian Sands*. It was published in 1959 and was an immediate success, being hailed by Lord Kinross in the *Daily Telegraph* as 'the book about Arabia to end all books about Arabia'. It was almost immediately granted the status of a classic of travel literature, and has perhaps done more than any other single document to mould the perceptions of a generation of the Arabs and their world. 'The actual writing of the book wasn't a penance,' Thesiger said. 'I relived the whole experience in a way I would never have done otherwise. I produced a book which I think has been a success and that was a memorial to a vanished past and a tribute to a once magnificent people, and that I am proud and pleased to have done. It's one of the very few books that is still being sold in hardback thirty-five years after it was published – that implies success and nobody minds success.'[38]

Mark Cocker has noted that the long gap between the actual journeys portayed in *Arabian Sands* and the written account effected a 'natural editorial process, which left only those elements of deepest personal significance'.[39] Indeed, the tone of *Arabian Sands* is that of high epic. It is written in deeply emotional, highly charged language, in which each act is thrown into relief by the reader's knowledge – right from page one – that the curtain is about to fall on the ancient world of the Bedu: 'If anyone goes there now looking for the life I led, they will not find it' is the crushingly final message on the opening page of the introduction.[40] The reader is immediately aware that he is being given a vision of something which no longer exists – almost the invisible world of *Grimm's Fairy Tales* into which the young man wanders and remains for seven years, emerges not one day older, and searches for in vain during the rest of his life. 'Here in the desert I had found all I asked,' Thesiger wrote. 'I knew I should not find it again. But it was not only this personal sorrow that distressed me. I realized that the Bedu with whom I had lived and travelled . . . were doomed. Some people maintain they will be better off when they have exchanged the hardship and poverty of the desert for the security of the materialistic world. This I do not believe. I shall always remember how often I was humbled by those illiterate herdsmen . . . Among no other people have I felt the same sense of personal inferiority.'[41] This may be regarded as Thesiger's definitive statement about the Bedu and indeed the essence of the Thesiger ethos. 'Only the most jaded reader could fail to share the author's anguish at the thought of these repositories of primitive virtue being destroyed by the lure of easy money in the oilfields,'[42] Kathryn Tidrick has written, correctly, yet we know now, with the advantage of hindsight, that this is not quite what happened. Thesiger claimed that the nomadic tribes of Arabia remained in the desert because that was the life they cherished, yet he confused Bedouin love of their own traditions with a craving for hardship *per se*. It is obviously untrue that the Bedu wanted above all a hard life, since otherwise they would not have exchanged their camels for motor cars. The Bedu were essentially stock-breeders, and they did not see the internal combustion engine as being incompatible with raising goats and camels. As Donald Powell-Cole wrote in 1975: 'Writers such as Thesiger (1959) . . . lament the passing of traditional Arabia and prefer to travel across the desert by camel. The [Bedu] love their camels, talk about them incessantly, and live off them throughout their lives, but they prefer to travel long distances quickly by truck and they all praise the Al Sa'ud and oil for making their life in the desert a bit more comfortable and secure than it was in the other Arabia a few decades ago.'[43] Even Thesiger's close friend, Frank Steele, echoed this view obliquely, noting: 'Some of Wilfred's critics say that he has a tremendously romanticized view of Bedu life, which he self-centredly wants to continue when the Bedu don't want it, and as soon as they had any other choice immediately left this hard life. The Sheikhs in Arabia today will every now and then take off into the desert, but what they are living is a luxurious tented life. None of them want to go back to the old hardships of life. In a sense Wilfred is irrational and I'm sure he'd agree it's self-centred. He likes to think of that kind of life continuing and hates the thought of it being corrupted by Western civilization, whereas the people living that life don't want it to continue and leave it as soon as they can.'[44]

As Steele suggested, Thesiger was almost certainly aware of this ambivalence from the beginning. If his entire *oeuvre* is considered rather than just *Arabian Sands*, it is evident that he was not entirely convinced that the Bedu lived their traditional life out of a preference for hardship. Whereas in *Arabian Sands* he explains that they were 'ascetic by nature', deriving satisfaction from the simplicity of their lives and scorning comforts that others judged essential,[45] in his earlier paper to the Royal Central Asian Society in 1949 – written while he was actually living among them – he took the opposite position: 'The virtues of the desert nomads are,' he wrote, 'enforced by by their circumstances, not by a natural preference for the ascetic way of life. In their own surroundings they are forced to be continent and self-restrained but by nature they are self-indulgent and indolent.'[46]

Looked at with hindsight, *Arabian Sands* succeeds partly by harnessing an explosive emotional force. Our century is obsessed by change – change more rapid and far-reaching than anything which has gone before. Thesiger's parents lived in an age of certainties: Britannia ruled the waves, God was in his Heaven and all was right with the world. Yet Thesiger grew up in an era in which the carpet of assurance was jerked from beneath him day by day, year by year. *Arabian Sands* embodies brilliantly the sense of moral decline which has become the preoccupation of a century. This is certainly what Jonathan Raban meant when he suggested that the real drama of *Arabian Sands* was not events in south Arabia. 'Thesiger's writing has enormous power,' Raban has written. 'His portrait of desert life is so loving, so rich in detail, that one would be a clod not to be moved by it. Yet I felt tricked when I read *Arabian Sands*: Thesiger was making me fall in love with an abstraction – with a version of the Arabs that was impossibly constricting for themselves: a version whose roots were in England and English life, and not truly in Arabia at all.'[47] *Arabian Sands* epitomizes the feeling which, as the anthropologist Claude Lévi-Strauss has said, has gained an increasingly tight chokchold on us as the millennium approaches – that we ourselves may be 'next on the list'.

Thesiger is an intensely emotional writer, and the effect of *Arabian Sands* works partly by positing a situation which never transpired. The Bedu did not succumb to the 'degradation' Thesiger felt they could expect in the new age of oil, as even he himself acknowledged during his later visits to Arabia. The point of *Arabian Sands*, surely, is not really that the Bedu wanted to remain as they were – they were only human after all – but that the quality of their lives, the quality of their social relations, the quality of their strict social code, would be diminished by the interpolation of technological forces. Technology does not necessarily mean a better life, Thesiger is saying; take a good look at the West and judge for yourself. That all this is perfectly valid is self-evident – the decline in the spiritual quality of life in the face of materialism has become the great debate of the end of the millennium. Yet Thesiger overstepped the mark by his insistence that the Bedu had no wish to change. Indeed, his resentment of their apparent willingness to change, and his protectiveness about his own experience – to the extent of telling bin Kabina, 'You are no longer Bedu. I am the only Bedu left' – has occasionally lent him a paradoxical air of satisfaction that the world he knew had disappeared. Since that world had gone forever, no one else could thus share his experiences, which were consequently unique. Thesiger derived his very success – what author Mark Cocker called his 'self-drama' – from the fact that the world had changed. If it had remained the same, he could not have seen himself as 'the last explorer in the tradition of the past'.

It is ironical, perhaps, that when Thesiger finally returned to south Arabia after twenty-seven years' absence, he believed that none of the Bedu had ridden a camel for thirty years. Yet it is clear from a number of travellers who followed Thesiger, notably Jan Morris, who crossed all of Oman in 1955, and the American archaeologist Wendell Phillips, who led a motor expedition in Dhofar in 1956, that Bedouin culture did not change with the abruptness which Thesiger suggested. It is true that both of these travellers used motor vehicles, a fact which, in Thesiger's eyes, disqualified them from the status of true explorers: 'Wilfred Thesiger maintains the day of "real" Arabian exploration ended with the appearance of the wheeled vehicle,' Phillips wrote. 'He has told me personally that he feels, "it is not a question of danger but of atmosphere. With the camels the traveller is in harmony with his surroundings while moving at 3 mph (the proper pace) and in a car he is an intruder, self-sufficent and insulated from the real life of the desert." '[48] Phillips, who was responsible for some of the most important archaeological discoveries ever made in south Arabia, was later to become the Sultan of Oman's financial adviser. He was precisely the kind of fabulously rich, self-confident, pistol-packing cowboy that Thesiger detested. 'He had a penthouse apartment at Claridges,' Thesiger recalled, 'and he invited me to dinner. Well, we sat down and they brought a menu about an inch thick, and he asked me, "What are you going to have?" I said, "Well, what are you having?" He said he was having this little piece of boiled fish on toast, and I said to myself I'll be damned if I'm going to be invited to Claridges by an American millionaire and eat a bit of dry fish on toast, so I ordered the most expensive thing on the menu. Then he asked what I'd like to drink, and told me he was having a glass of mineral water. I thought, well, you don't invite someone to an expensive restaurant like this and expect him to drink a glass of water, so I looked at the wine list and ordered the most expensive bottle. I hadn't a clue what it was, but I told him, "Oh, I've always wanted to try that!" [49]

To Phillips, Thesiger no doubt represented the bitterness and resentment of a dying Empire which he encountered frequently in Arabia, once particularly vociferously in the person of an un-named employee of the Iraq Petroleum Company in Sharjah. This Englishman speaks for Thesiger's generation of Arabists when he says, 'Why don't you trouble-making Americans remain at home where you belong? Isn't your United States big enough for you? Why did you have to encroach where you have no right to be? We British have always ruled the Persian Gulf and if it had not been for you meddlesome Americans we would still manage the affairs of the Middle East as in the past. You dollar-loving Americans know nothing really about Arabia, you learn two or three words of Arabic which you can't pronounce properly, wear an Arab handkerchief on your heads and think you are all Lawrences of Arabia ... Actually, if the truth be told ... England's real enemy in the Arab world is America.'[50]

Arabian Sands must be judged as a superb work of epic literature rather than as a work of philosophy. Like Thesiger's brilliant photographs, it captures a precious instant in the evolution of a society, frames for posterity an image of the Bedu that will forever exist in the 1940s. Like all great art it will be interpreted differently by each successive generation, depending on their perspective and experience. Thesiger's deep regard for his travelling-companions, whether it grew out of neurosis caused by the rejection of his peers, out of a profound egocentrism, out of physical attraction, or out of the paternalistic experience of Empire, is an improvement on the ethnocentric morals of the Victorian–Edwardian era. Whatever spawned it, whatever its hidden motives, Thesiger's stance set a trend which has become a new orthodoxy. If his pride in his background, his élitism, and his enthusing over the quality of British colonialism do not seem to gel with current, 'environmentalist' interpretations of his work, then it should perhaps be remembered that the scientist Isaac Newton, the founder of modern physics, was concurrently an alchemist and mystic. A man may articulate a new trend of thought while still remaining firmly embedded in the old. Literature itself is not definitive or static: my own reaction to *Arabian Sands* has altered profoundly over a decade and a half of re-reading it, while gradually acquiring more knowledge of the desert and its nomads. Yet for me it still remains the single greatest work of travel-writing this century.

CHAPTER 15

A Fairly Hardy and Abstemious Traveller

The margins of the atlas were closing in. In 1950 Thesiger had been excluded from south Arabia. In 1959 he was exiled from Iraq. His thoughts turned once again to Africa, and to the country of his birth – Abyssinia – still ruled by his friend Haile Selassie. He had left Dessie in disillusion in 1945: now he decided to see the Abyssinian plateau, which had always been the object of his interest but which at almost fifty he had never seen except as a soldier with Wingate. He made two long treks by mule in Abyssinia, one north from Addis Ababa along the Blue Nile gorge to Lake Tana, traversing the Simien mountains, the plunging volcanic moonscape that he reckoned the most spectacular scenery in Africa. On this walk he crossed successive almost sheer-sided canyons, thousands of feet deep – one of the most testing trials of stamina he had ever endured. He was thus all the more irritated when the *Illustrated London News* published his photographs from the trek as the product of a 'motor tour', and had them retract the statement the following week. The other safari had taken him south through the country of the nomadic Somali and Boran, covering much of the same ground he *had* motored through by truck in 1944. He wandered as far as the Kenyan border at Moyale, where he met George Webb, then DC on the Kenyan side. Webb, a gifted linguist, increased Thesiger's interest in the Samburu and Turkana tribes south of the border, with whom he was soon to become familar. He gazed down from the edge of the Abyssinian escarpment at Kenya's Northern Frontier District, admiring its austerity and starkness, yet never dreaming that this region would become his second home. Though his 1959–60 treks in Abyssinia had taken him through dramatic scenery, he was looking for more than mere landscapes could offer: a place to settle among a people who appealed to him. While he would always admire Haile Selassie as the noblest of men, his partiality for the Abyssinians – already diminished by his 1944 experience – had waned. In the winter of 1960 he turned up for a third time in Addis Ababa, hoping to make a journey with his friend Frank Steele – now working in Beirut – south to Lake Rudolf (Turkana). This time even Thesiger's connection with the Emperor could not help him obtain permission. As an alternative, Steele, an ex-East Africa ADC, suggested approaching the lake from the Kenyan side through the North East Frontier District. Thesiger was not particularly attracted to Kenya. A resolute supporter of the quickly fading British Empire, for him there were two kinds of empire – the kind he had known in the Sudan where a small aristocratic élite ruled a host of natives, and that of Kenya, with its large contingent of white settlers. Thesiger was perfectly ready to accept British rule and the occasional privileged DC in remote places – as long as he himself was allowed to visit them – but resented the presence of the 'white masses' in Africa, spoiling the sense of adventure with their farms and barbed wire. 'Here in Kenya you did get two rival things,' he said. 'You got the white settlers and the claims to the White Highlands, all that sort of thing which I never felt justified, and I never wanted to go near them . . . When I came up here to the Northern Frontier District it was forbidden territory, and it was run by the local DCs for the benefit of the people. The other side was the White Highlands and the settlers from which I disassociated myself. I've never really known hardly any of them . . . The only people I had any desire to meet were officers of the administration and Game Wardens.'[1]

In November 1960 Thesiger found himself in Nairobi for the first time: 'To get to the Northern Frontier District then you needed a special permit,' he said, 'and I was feeling lost in the New Stanley Hotel wondering how on earth I was going to do it. I went to see someone in the Governor's office and he said I should have a word with George Webb. I told him I couldn't go up to Moyale just to see George Webb, and he told me that George was there in Nairobi as No.2 in Security and Intelligence. I rang him on the spot and he said come down and stay – he'd found a house there. He called for me outside the New Stanley and took me up there, and that became my base in Kenya.

George took me to see the Governor and persuaded him to give me a permit to go anywhere I wanted.'[2]

Thesiger had long since made his name among the *cognoscenti* in exploration circles, and with the publication of *Arabian Sands* was just beginning to gain a reputation with the public that would eventually bring him international fame. His major journeys of exploration were finished: he would make no more contributions to the *Geographical Journal*. Northern Kenya had been explored sixty years earlier, and he himself recalled that cars were everywhere: 'All my journeys in Kenya, starting with the one with Frank Steele, could have been done by car,' he said. 'The DCs were going all over the place by car then. I did it by camel because it was a personal experience I was looking for. It wasn't a necessity to travel by camel, but there again my experience would have lost much if I had done it in a car.'[3] Steele pointed out, however, that the route they eventually took to Lake Turkana could not have been done by vehicle, and that, though DCs did use vehicles extensively, for most of their journey they encountered neither a car nor another white man – something which would be impossible today.

Thesiger had long since lost his purist notions of travelling only with locals: 'My Danakil journey would have been completely wrecked if I'd had other Europeans around,' he said, 'but Frank and I had planned my first journey in Kenya together. He came and joined me specially. He had about two months' leave, of which we spent at least six weeks travelling by camel. We went up through the Mathews and Ndotos to South Horr and then to Lake Rudolf and halted at Loyangalani.'[4] 'We traversed some of the most terrible desert even Wilfred had ever seen,' Steele commented. It was mostly lava-basalt rocks with some sand, and we went over this frightful surface with the sun beating down and reflected back on to us from the ground and the famous Lake Rudolf wind blowing at thirty or forty miles an hour, dry as a bone.'[5] While they were sorting out their kit at George Webb's house in Nairobi, Thesiger scoffed at his friend's spare pair of desert boots: 'Wilfred is a fairly hardy and abstemious traveller,' Steele said, 'and he was rather contemptuous of my spare pair of boots, saying what did I need them for? He said his shoes had been made for him by Lobbs in St James's Street thirty or some extraordinary number of years ago, and they would last through the journey. I said well, we were going through a lot of lava desert, and no thirty-year-old shoes, even made by Lobb, would survive that, but he was very confident and didactic as usual. Anyway they did last three weeks or so, and we were walking along and I suddenly heard this flapping sound. I turned to see what it was, and there was Wilfred indomitably doing a high-stepping action and the sole of his shoe dangling down. I said, "What about your Lobb's shoes then?" He said, "Well, they have lasted me forty-something years!" I happened to have a sailmaker's needle with me and I stitched his shoe up with copper wire. The lava soon wore through it and he had to take my despised spare pair of boots.'[6]

The two Englishmen had six camels and five Africans with them – Somalis, Boran and Turkana – and at night all of them would sleep close together in a group partly for protection, and partly, as Steele put it, 'so as you could poke whoever's turn it was to stoke up the fire, or stop someone snoring'.[7] In the first gristle of pre-dawn light they would make coffee as cloyingly sweet as golden syrup, then saddle the camels and hump on the sacks of food and tanks of water. 'Of course, we had to learn their techniques of loading,' Steele said. 'At first they were very disorganized and at the end of the day would just throw the harness and saddles down in a tangle, but we told them to lay it all out neatly in piles, so that everything would be ready the following day. We carried the water in great metal tanks called *baramils* – which were the most horrible things to handle.'[8] By the time the animals were ready, the day had thickened into the full royal panoply of African light. They would stalk out into the desert for several hours, depending on whether they found water or grazing for the camels; if there was none, they might tramp on for seven or eight hours without a break: 'I was terribly unfit and overweight after office work in Beirut,' Steele commented, 'and by God it just poured off me. On the first few days, Wilfred would be saying, "I don't suppose you'll be able to walk far today," but anyway I soon got fit.'[9]

Normally they would lie up for a couple of hours in the middle of the day, replenishing their moisture with more molasses-thick tea. Afterwards they would continue until they found a suitable camping place – ideally with grazing and water. Often they would buy a sheep or goat from a local *manyatta*, or pot guinea-fowl with their shotguns for the evening stew, served with pyramids of rice and eased down by more gallons of sweet tea. 'The country was full of rhino, lion and elephant,' Steele said, 'and one night I woke up and saw some distance from my bed a damn great grey boulder that hadn't been there the night before. I'm short-sighted and I reached for my glasses with one hand and the rifle with the other, thinking, "That's damned odd!" I suddenly found it was a rhino which had grazed right into our camp. He must have sensed we were there because he gave a snort and took off – fortunately.'[10] Another night they had to make camp in a very narrow valley near to a waterhole, aware from the numerous elephant-droppings of the problems they might face. 'We were lying on our sleeping-bags fully dressed,' Steele recalled, 'knowing that sooner or later something, probably elephant, was going to come down to the waterhole straight over us.' Sure enough, they soon heard the tramp of elephant advancing down the lugga, snapping off branches, snorting and feeding as they came. Steele, who had had a lot to do with elephant during his years in northern Uganda, had no fear that they would be attacked. 'I was just afraid there would be a general mess and confusion,' he said, 'and the elephants would stampede the camels and step on the food bags, mess up everything. We started shying rocks at them and shouting, and building up the fire. They came up to about 100 yards away and there was a stand off for a couple of hours – we felt terrible to be preventing them from getting to the water, but we didn't want them panicking through our camp. Anyway, eventually they just disappeared into the darkness.'[11]

It was after he had been following another herd of elephants that Thesiger returned to the camp limping. He answered Steele's queries with resentful monosyllables, but eventually admitted that something was wrong. Steele discovered that he had torn an Achilles tendon. He bandaged up the heel and they rested for a day, but Thesiger was obliged to hobble on in pain for the next ten days until he could rest it properly. 'Wilfred is simply a marvellous man to do that sort of journey with,' Steele said. 'He's

physically enormously tough, and despite the fact that he'd damaged the tendon he just limped on. He's so determined – if he's
going to get somewhere, he's going to get somewhere. He never
whinges about physical hardship, although he complains like mad
about the Africans wasting the sugar or saddling a camel badly or
something. He never complains about food, and he's got the force
of personality to make even the tough and independent-minded
tribesmen with him go on all day and all night if he wants them
to. We did have some terrible rows – for example, the time he
refused to increase the ration of sugar to the Africans when they'd
run out – saying they'd agreed on one pound of sugar per day. I
pointed out that they'd been given five pounds of sugar on the
basis that it was five days to the next waterhole, and it turned
out to be more, so by rights they should be given more. It wasn't
so much meanness as him refusing to go against what he thought
had been agreed.'[12]

At South Horr they had acquired a Turkana guide called
Leopelele, who they quickly realized had no better notion of their
whereabouts than they themselves did: 'He kept saying the lake
was over there,' Steele recalled, 'and we knew that ourselves. You
could tell from the light in the sky that the lake was getting
nearer. The last days before the lake were really hard, because
we'd been expecting to see it for a day and a half and it didn't
appear and we were crossing this ghastly lava desert. Then
suddenly, the next day we realized that the strip of blue we were
looking at was the lake. We came to the top of an escarpment and
there it was below us – this extraordinary blue with the beautiful
pink Turkana hills across it. It was a marvellous sense of achievement, and you had some sense of what Teleki must have felt like
when he discovered it in the 1880s. You'd never have got that
feeling in a car.'[13]

Thesiger reiterated his friend's feeling: 'You'd have missed so
much if you'd have motored up in a car,' he said. 'It had taken us
a month to get there and suddenly there was the lake below us. If
you go in a car it's, oh – there's the lake – and the next minute
you're away. You don't get the impact Teleki described. In a
minor way we could get it by the very fact that getting there had
been so difficult.'[14]

On that day, despite Thesiger's ailing tendon, they walked for seven hours down to Loyangalani, where they found an airstrip and a small fishing camp already used by a few tourists. The camp was run by an English couple, and consisted of a few straw bungalows and a dining area: 'There was a fridge,' Steele remembered, 'and we drank vast quantities of iced lemon and ate wonderful fresh tilapia and Nile perch which we bought from the El Molo fishing village.'[15] From Loyangalani they tramped on across more execrable lava blocks around Mount Kulal: 'It was really hell,' Steele commented. 'We went round the northern end of Kulal and the country was the worst Wilfred had ever seen and the worst I've ever been through. It was so bad we actually had to place the feet of the camels.'[16] Two weeks later they arrived at the small town of Marsabit in Rendille country, and Steele returned to Nairobi, *en route* to his next posting in London.

Thesiger's Achilles tendon had gradually healed itself despite the bad going, and, shod with a proper pair of boots, he continued to wander around the NFD for another four months with six tribesmen: 'I might spend two or three days in the forests along the Kerio,' he said, 'then up to Lodwar for a couple of days, down to Baringo, where they watered the camels. On the whole I slept in the open, but we did carry a tent in case it rained. On two occasions it did rain really hard and the seven of us crowded into the tent, and I woke up with a Turkana's heels in my mouth.'[17]

In Nairobi, he had applied to the Chief Game Warden for a licence to shoot for the pot. 'The Chief said he'd give me a licence to shoot one animal a week,' Thesiger commented, 'and I said make it two.'[18] When he eventually reached the small District HQ at Maralal, he was confronted by an irate game-warden named Rodney Elliott. 'I got here,' he remembered, 'and I put up my tent almost exactly where the lodge is now. Elliott came over and said, "I understand you've been given permission to shoot two animals a week, non-specified, in my area. Well, I can tell you if I'd had anything to do with it you wouldn't have been given permission." I got everything ready and went over to his office, which was near by, and said, "Six months at two animals a week would entitle me to what?" He said, "I'm not interested in that. I want to know exactly what you did shoot and where." So I wasted quite a lot of time quibbling in his office — sex, date, where and so on – and in the end I wrote it all down and took it to him, and on the thing were two Grant's gazelle, one Thomson's gazelle and a zebra. That was it. I said I didn't come here to shoot a lot of animals, but just took the licence in case we needed to feed ourselves for a time. Then he said, "You'd better come and stay with me – you'll find it more comfortable than your tent." We've been the best of friends ever since.'[19]

Maralal has expanded since colonial times. It now boasts electricity, street-lighting and running water, yet its parched grid of ochre-red streets with their shaded walkways and zinc-roofed stores, kippered over the decades by sun, rain and dust into a spectrum of colours ranging from rust-red to bullet-blue, remains little changed. Today there are telephone boxes, and the frowzy 'Buffalo's Head' hotel where the local whores come out at sundown, and where they serve Tusker beer and bottles of Sprite and release savage dogs in the yard to prevent burglary. When Thesiger first visited the town in 1961, the Samburu still wore almost exclusively their brilliant scarlet *shukas*, and the *morans* or young warriors carried their spears proudly, their hair plastered with red ochre. Surprisingly, despite education and new economic conditions, many of the Samburu today retain their colourful traditional dress. Among those who seem to have rejected the way of the warrior, though, are the teenage street-urchins called the 'Plastic Boys' who make a living accosting the numerous tourists who halt in the town on their way to Lake Turkana, and selling bracelets and bric-à-brac.

By 1960, Sadiq Bhola had already established his famous garage in Maralal, servicing Land-Rovers and selling petrol. His petrol-pumps have now gone, but Sadiq – originally from Pakistan – and his two sons are well-known mechanics and have a hand in virtually everything that goes on in the town. Sadiq even built the famous Maralal Safari Lodge. Ironically, for one who claims to have rejected motor transport, Bhola's garage is Thesiger's second home in Maralal. It is a haven from the parched streets where he can relax on a sofa, drink tea, speak to friends on the telephone, enjoy a meal in tranquillity, or even use the Western-style toilet for which he has his own key. Bhola's sitting-room – where Thesiger is generally to be found – is decorated with suburban taste: pottery ducks in descending order of size on the wall, seashells on the mantelpiece, colour photographs of grandchildren, picture postcards, gaudy oil-paintings, a TV and a shelf of video cassettes. Sadiq, a disarmingly polite man and Thesiger's oldest and most reliable friend in Maralal, displays among his mementoes a black and white photo of a Dodge pick-up. 'I gave Wilfred a lift to Nairobi in that the first time he came here,' he said. 'How proud I was of that car!'

'In those days you could spend almost the entire day in the town and not see a car,' Thesiger added. 'Now they're coming and going all the time. The *Boma* – the administrative area – was where the Safari Lodge stands now and there was a sort of officers' club there. Bhola ran me down to Nairobi on that first occasion, then I did two or three more journeys, and then I thought I'd better buy a car so that at least I could get to the place where I could start my journeys. I bought a new Land-Rover in Nairobi – the first of two that I owned. I felt it was necessary. I couldn't keep scrounging lifts off people. I still did some camel journeys though: I would drive up to Baragoi and leave the car there, then collect it later. Maralal wasn't really my base to start with. My base was with George Webb and later John Seago in Nairobi.'[20] It was only a few years since he had given Ernest Gellner the impression that he could not drive and had hardly been near a motor car, yet here was Thesiger actually buying a car of his own. It was a practical decision, precisely as it would be a decade later for those Bedu whom he had so recently waxed emotional about in *Arabian Sands*. Since technology was there anyway, one had no choice but to use it. It was a perfectly logical development for Thesiger, just as it would be for the Bedu, yet Thesiger would continue inveighing against the internal combustion engine for the next three decades, while teaching his protégés to drive and travelling in a car almost daily. It was irrationality of precisely the same order as his attitude to medical improvements: he wished they did not exist, but since they did he was perfectly happy to make use of them for himself.

After visiting Tanganyika, Lamu and Mombasa, he motored around Portugal with his mother, visited his relatives in Ireland, and shut himself up once again in Copenhagen to work on his second book, *The Marsh Arabs*. Though it had required some persuasion to induce him to write his first book, the second fell into place naturally: 'Having written one I couldn't refuse to do another,' he commented, 'and with *Marsh Arabs* I was quite interested in doing it. *Arabian Sands* seemed to be a success and I didn't see why I shouldn't write another one on the Marshes. Although it wasn't such a success, a lot of people preferred it. It's probably an easier book to read for the ordinary person who knows nothing about Arabs. There are far more people to picture and there's more going on – Falih's death and everything. In the desert there are just four or five people and the immensity of the desert, and the struggle is to write a book and gain this feeling of emptiness without being incredibly boring.'[21] *The Marsh Arabs* is a beautifully written book but, although it was eventually to win the W.H. Heinemann Award, it is, curiously, a less succesful evocation of life in the Marshes than Maxwell's *A Reed Shaken by the Wind*. Maxwell's more superficial picture, with its humour and slight sense of the absurd, is easier for the lay reader to identify with, perhaps, than Thesiger's more involved, more knowing, yet no less affectionate perspective. Critics such as Jan Morris, however, felt that Thesiger had tried unsuccessfully to force the pattern of south Arabia upon the Marshes: 'The thesis rang more convincing when he was writing about the desert Beduin,' Morris wrote, 'and it all seemed absolute as a knife. The civilization of the marsh people, though, really does not sound impressive. They make, by force of habit and physical need, beautiful houses and beautiful boats. They are hospitable to strangers. They are tolerant towards sexual anomalies and very nice to children. For the rest, life among their traditions sounds mostly nasty, frequently brutish and all too often short. Diseases, blood-feuds, crippling superstitions, robberies with violence, bullying Sheikhs, filth, caste-prejudices, graft, and the perpetual risk of being savaged by wild pigs.'[22] Though Morris also added that *The Marsh Arabs* was 'a perplexing, beautiful and haunting book',[23] Thesiger never forgave her for her remarks: 'I have an intense dislike of Jan Morris,' he commented later. '... I've never met him [*sic*] but we've sort of crossed swords mentally ... He's done a review of each of my books and each one more spiteful than the previous one ... all cheap nonsense. I was tempted to write back and say [something disagreeable] but I don't think they'd have published it. I've never read his books and I wouldn't read them because I dislike the man too much.'[24] Ironically, though Thesiger was more involved with the families of his companions in the Marshes than he had been in Arabia, Amara, Sabaiti and the others emerge far less distinctly from the pages than do bin Kabina and bin Ghabaisha – probably because he had less regard for them.

Thesiger spent the following three years travelling by camel in northern Kenya, by donkey in Tanganyika, by car with his mother in Italy, Spain, Morocco and the Canary Islands. On one trip to Morocco, while visiting a friend, the Australian artist Sidney Nolan, Thesiger heard that the former Commander-in-Chief of British Forces in North Africa, General Auchinleck, was in town. 'He said I've got Auchinleck coming to lunch tomorrow,' he recalled, 'and perhaps you'd like to meet him. I'd admired Auchinleck before I ever met him, and I said I'd rather meet him than anyone else I could think of. We had lunch and he had just come to Morocco, where he was going to live for the rest of his life. England had nothing whatever to offer him . . . I said to him after lunch, "Sir, I don't know if I could be of help to you. I've got a car here and I know these mountains. If you'd like me to drive you round the Atlas for a day or so I'd be delighted to do it" . . . So we went off for two days and there were just the two of us in the car together, driving about in the mountains. I had the feeling that two days in the company of this man was something very, very rare. There was only one Auchinleck in my life. I regarded him as being the noblest man I ever met. [He had been] maltreated by Churchill and sniped at by Montgomery and he never tried to justify himself.'[25]

In Florence he continued to work on *The Marsh Arabs* while staying near Sir John Verney. 'I stayed in a *pensione* close to the place the Verneys had taken,' he recalled. 'I'd work most of the day in the *pensione*, and then I'd go up to the Verneys in the evening and we'd discuss what I'd written. I usually wrote six or seven pages a day and I'd ask what he thought of it, and he'd advise me to change this sentence around or that word. He gave me a lot of help.'[26] Another writer whom Thesiger made the acquaintance of at John Verney's was T.H. White, author of the notable Arthurian novel *The Once and Future King*, later turned into the Disney cartoon *The Sword in the Stone*. Thesiger found him a strange man: 'He was never sober unless he'd had six drinks,' he commented, 'and he had this boyfriend whom he tended to dominate. The boy wanted to go off with a friend and do something, and White told him if he did, not to bother coming back, so of course the boy didn't and White was heartbroken, and the whole thing was a minor tragedy. If you got him by himself and he'd had a couple of drinks he'd be entertaining, but otherwise he was out to shock. For instance he started talking about penises with my mother and she said, "I'm sorry Tim, I just don't understand what you're talking about!" '[27] When *The Marsh Arabs* had been published in 1964, Thesiger went back to Iran.

He had seen the country in 1949 and again in 1951, after his first visit to the Marshes with Dugald Stewart, when he had motored as far as Meshed and visited the shrine of Reza Shah, one of the Imams of the Shi'ites. The visit had probably been inspired by Robert Byron's book *The Road to Oxiana*, which he had read previously. Byron may have been the first Westerner to visit the shrine, but in spite of the fact that he was evidently influenced by it, Thesiger considered the book 'a lot of nonsense'. 'There was a picture of Byron in it,' he recalled, 'as this rather down-at-heel person. At that time the Shah had imposed European clothes on everybody, so I suppose if he kept his mouth shut he could have got into the shrine dressed in that down-at-heel way. But there'd have been trouble if they'd found out who he was.'[28] Unlike Byron, Thesiger was able to pull strings with the British Embassy and to get special permission from the Guardian of the Shrine: 'Somehow they got permission,' he commented, 'and I entered the mosque and did the circuit round the shrine.'[29]

In 1964 Thesiger remained in Iran for five months, and made a thorough exploration. In this he was assisted by a Russian émigré, Lew Tamp, who knew a great deal about the country and who motored Thesiger to the starting-point of each journey. Before beginning, however, Tamp took him to see the 200-foot brick tower of Gunbad-i-Qabus – a unique, phallic, Tolkienesque structure with a pointed roof, built in 1006 on the Gorgan Steppes of north-eastern Iran. This visit had also been prompted by Byron's book. 'To him this building was infinitely more beautiful and impressive than the Taj Mahal,' Thesiger said. 'Well, he was talking obvious nonsense. I've seen the Taj Mahal and it's without doubt the most beautiful building in the world. This place was very bizarre, but to say it was more important than the Taj Mahal was sheer rubbish.'[30]

At Bunjurd, Thesiger bought some mules and engaged a muleteer and a Kurdish teacher as interpreter for his journey through the Elburz Mountains, running along the northern border of Iran. The teacher had never before walked further than his own bathroom, and fell far behind on the first day, his feet badly blistered. Exasperated, Thesiger allowed him to ride one of the mules until his feet healed, after which the Kurd insisted on walking. Thesiger found him a humorous and informative companion: 'The three of us travelled through the Elburz Mountains,' he recalled, 'and it was there I acquired a dislike of the Persians. They were very inhospitable, and it wasn't just because I was a Christian. I used to send my Persian mule-man down to the village to see if he could find a house where we could sleep on the roof and time and time again he was turned away by these bloody people!'[31] As as moral judgement such condemnation seems to contradict Thesiger's conviction that traditional peoples should have the right to live as they wish – after all, the Afars were cowardly murderers by most people's standards, yet Thesiger did not condemn them for failing to live up to Western ideals. 'I don't care what ideals they were or weren't living up to,' he commented. 'It's just that it's much more agreeable to travel among people who are hospitable as they would be here [in Kenya]. I don't know if it is a matter of being their culture, but if it is I condemn their culture. I disliked the Persians because they were one of the few traditional peoples I've been with who were inhospitable. And I'm not talking about the townsmen, but the tribal people. They were inhospitable with each other: one night a Persian traveller came to our camp and we asked him why he didn't go to the nearest village, and he said he'd already been and they'd turned him away.'[32] Once, Thesiger's men stopped for lunch by a pleasant, bubbling stream near a small town, when they were approached by a young Persian who advised them not to stay where they were. The children would bother them, he said. He invited them to his house instead, an invitation so rare in this country that Thesiger was delighted. 'So we went in there,' he remembered, 'and he said would we each like a peach and we each had one. Then we asked if we could sleep on the roof and he said we could. I said could he get some oats for our mules and he said he'd undertake to do that. He inquired if I'd like him to kill a sheep for our dinner, and I said don't do that but could he get us a bit of meat? He took us upstairs and brought a lamp and quite a good meal, which he shared with us. Then in the morning I went and asked him how much I owed for the oats he'd bought for the mules, and he said, "I've got it all here," and he'd got a bill for everything we'd had – even the peaches – the oil for the lamp, the use of the roof, the meat and everything. I thought, well, blow me! If you contrast that with the treatment you'd have got in an Arab place. They wouldn't have taken the money even if you tried to give it to them! Anyway, I didn't say anything, I just paid.'[33]

After a few days in the British Embassy camp in the Lar valley, with the Ambassador Sir Denis Wright, Thesiger tramped on again with his two men as far as the Valley of the Assassins, visiting there the ruins of the castle in which the immensely powerful Ishmaeli sect had begun, under Hassan-i-Sabbah, 'the Old Man of the Mountain'. Primed with immense doses of hashish, his fanatical 'Assassins' or 'Hashish Eaters' had been so convinced that they were bound for paradise should they die in his service that they were prepared to leap off the castle battlements, 200 feet above the valley floor, on his command. A few days afterwards Thesiger arrived at Qazvin, having covered more than 400 miles in forty-six days.

His next plan was to travel with the Bakhtiari nomads in the Zagros mountains of south-western Iran. The Bakhtiari were transhumants who moved their sheep, goats, camels and horses in winter along the bleak ridges of the mountains to their low pastures. The entire tribe would move as one, pitching their rectangular black tents along the narrow tracks at night and packing them on their camels the following morning. The Bakhtiari, like the neighbouring Qashgai, were of Turkish origin, and Thesiger found them quite different in temperament from the inhospitable Persians. 'They were friendly,' he recalled, 'and we'd camp near them. They'd come over and offer us tea. I had a plain clothes policeman with me, and we joined them as they were on the move and stayed with them more or less till the end of the migration.'[34]

Thesiger's third and last ambition in Iran was to cross the Dasht-i-Lut or 'Desert of Lot', whose name had long intrigued him. As a desert journey, it presented few of the obstacles he had encountered in the Empty Quarter. He bought two camels, one of which had a jerky stride which he was afraid would reactivate the slipped disc he had suffered a few years earlier. Consequently he walked most of the 200 miles: 'The journey lasted about ten days,' he remembered, 'and they gave me some policemen to go with me. When their officer told them to go they complained, "What crime have we committed that we have to go across the Dasht-i-Lut?" In point of fact I think we more or less camped on water every day and did perhaps six hours a day with the camels. By any other standards it was easy.'[35] The caravan crossed gravel plains salted with tamarisk and punctuated by the low buttes of hills, but Thesiger found the journey devoid of hardship, challenge or even companionship. 'Still, it was quite interesting to see the Dasht-i-Lut,' he said, 'and I saw wild ass there, which the policemen with me promptly tried to shoot until I made enough noise to scare them away. They were quite indignant about that. I thought why try to shoot a wild ass, which is very rare? Not even they would have eaten it. Supposing there were only one or two kudu left in the hills here – I wouldn't want someone to go and to shoot them.'[36] The trek ended at the ancient and unspoiled town of Yazd, where, looking round a mosque, Thesiger spotted another European. Instead of hurrying away, as he once might have done, Thesiger went and spoke to him, and thus met the Irish painter Derek Hill. 'He was studying Islamic architecture,' Thesiger said, 'and it was very interesting to talk to him. His presence enhanced my enjoyment of Yazd, which was quite impressive.'[37] Hill was later to invite Thesiger to his studio in Donegal, where he made three portraits of him, one of which Thesiger's mother bought for £300. 'She thought I liked it,' Thesiger said, 'and I thought she did. Anyway, she hung it over her bed in the flat in Chelsea.'[38] Years later, after Mrs Astley's death, Hill asked to see the portrait again, telling Thesiger that he considered it one of the best half-dozen portraits he had ever done. Thesiger replied that he had no idea where it was, and advised the painter to ask his brother Roddy. Hill wrote to him and was told with brutal frankness that no one in the family had liked the portrait. Wilfred had asked him to dispose of it, and he had promptly given it to a student at the Byam Shaw art school, which happened to be just behind his house. 'It was lost, anyway,' Thesiger said, 'and Derek Hill got very worked up about it and claimed it was the best portrait he'd ever done – which I find difficult to believe. He bothered every one of my friends about it. Roddy gave it to someone at an art college, saying they could use the frame, and no one's seen it since.'[39]

For the time being, Thesiger had no thought of returning to Kenya. He had admired the Samburu and Turkana, but somehow nothing matched his view of the 'noble Arab'. In 1965 he spent three months in Morocco with his mother, and in May returned to Nuristan after a gap of nine years. He had learned his lesson about horses and unreliable Nuristanis: this time he traversed the Chamar pass with a solid squad of Tajik bearers and another student-interpreter. The pass was muffled in an unusual kind of snow called *névés pénitents*, standing in pinnacles two feet high. Now more used to European expeditions, even the Mullahs in Puchal were hospitable and, indeed, Thesiger's only difference with the Nuristanis on this trek was a *faux pas* he made over their hospitality: 'There were seven or eight men with me,' he said, 'and we arrived in a village at lunchtime and the mulberries were in fruit. The village people brought sheets and shook down all the mulberries and gave us a great meal of these, with some fresh bread. Then in the evening I said we couldn't impose on this small village so we went over and cooked our own food. In the morning the people refused to say goodbye to us and when we asked what was wrong, they said we had scorned their hospitality: "We were going to give you dinner and you went and cooked your own!"'[40] After four months in Nuristan Thesiger travelled by car and bus back to Kabul, to Balkh and then into Iran, where he visited Tehran and Meshed once more. On his way home to

London he made a long donkey journey in Trans-Jordan to Petra and Rum with Frank Steele.

The following year he was invited to Addis Ababa for the twenty-fifth anniversary of Haile Selassie's return to Addis Ababa after the victorious campaign by Wingate and Cunningham. Here he was reunited with the likes of Hugh Boustead, Laurens van der Post and Pansy Drew. He watched the mechanized army units trundle past – the tanks and armoured cars, the parachutists and the robot-like display of immaculate drill – without enthusiasm, seeing instead another Abyssinia, one that had gone forever, of dust and flashing spears and warriors crying out their deeds of valour, and horses covered with blood-caked clothing recently looted from the dead: the Abyssinia of fifty years before. His respect and admiration for Haile Selassie were not, however, dented by this modernization: Thesiger 'understood the necessity' for the country's leap into the twentieth century. Since he was fond of asking the question, 'What right have we to destroy ancient civilizations?' it is perhaps worth underlining again that the ancient traditions of Abyssinia were destroyed by the Abyssinian Thesiger admired above all others, indeed above almost all other men – Haile Selassie – just as the power of the Bedu in Arabia was destroyed not principally by Westerners but by an Arab, Ibn Sa'ud, aided and abetted by two Europeans whom Thesiger respected greatly: St John Philby and John Glubb. Yet in the case of Abyssinia Thesiger accepted that the changes were necessary in a way he seemed unable to do among the Bedu – it is constantly as if there are two or more Thesigers at work here.

It was at the anniversary celebration that Thesiger ran into Neil 'Billy' McLean, a former Guards officer who had taken part in Platt's invasion of Abyssinia in 1942. McLean had until recently been MP for Inverness in northern Scotland, but had so much immersed himself in the affairs of the Yemen – now involved in a bloody tussle between Royalists and Republicans – that he had become known as 'our MP for the Yemen'. Eventually he had lost his seat. According to John Cooper, now an SAS major fighting covertly in north Yemen, McLean was 'a very fine soldier and an extremely gentle and kind man'.[41] Thesiger had not known him during the Abyssinian campaign, but had made his acquaintance in the drawing-rooms of Chelsea later. McLean 'invited' Thesiger to join the Royalist forces in Yemen, and put him in touch with the Royalist commanders, who controlled much of the country outside the capital, Sana'a. Thesiger had been nursing a desire to see Yemen – perhaps even to make a base there – since at least 1955, when he had talked about the country to Ernest Gellner. He jumped at this chance and flew to Jiddah, visiting the deposed Imam's secret eyrie in the mountains near Jizan. Here he ran into Cooper, leading a small clandestine squad of SAS men who were officially 'on leave' from their regiment. Cooper recalled that Thesiger was dressed as an Arab just as he had been on their first meeting in North Africa, and informed him that he was going to the Yemen to study 'the many Zeidi and Shaffei dialects of Arabic'. 'When Wilfred arrived in camp, he complained bitterly about the fact that the Imam had sent mules for him,' Cooper has written. 'He said to me: "Gentlemen do not ride on mules, or for that matter, in aircraft and automobiles"' – a typical piece of tongue-in-cheek hauteur from a man who had covered thousands of miles with mules, had motored frequently with his mother during her annual holiday, and had himself arrived by aeroplane.

Thesiger entered the Yemen through Najran, and joined the forces of Prince Hassan, a cousin of Imam Badr, at Shahra. Precisely what his role was remains obscure. Most of the British establishment, naturally, sided with the Royalists against the Republicans, whose supporters, the Nasserite Egyptians, had so humiliated them at Suez – the last flicker of life in the corpse of dead Empire. Although Thesiger told Timothy Green that his sympathy was 'deeply on the side of the Royalists', his commitment to them in retrospect looks at best lukewarm. 'I didn't really feel very strongly about it,' he admitted, 'but with my background and being a traditionalist I was obviously against [republicanism]. Leave the place alone, was my opinion – it was one of the oldest monarchies in the world and it seems a pity to go and destroy it. For what? In order to have a president? I was interested in seeing the Yemen and seeing what was going on in the fighting.'[42] Thesiger's story that he was there to 'study Arabic dialects' is patently phoney to anyone familiar with his distaste for 'linguistic dilettantism', and at times he gave the impression that

474

he had shared the fighting: 'These chaps [the Arabs of Yemen] were my friends,' he told Green in 1970. 'They were pleased that I had come to help them in their fight . . .'[43] Green evidently believed that Thesiger had been in combat in Yemen as a mercenary, though, 'help', of course, may be merely moral or propaganda support. His use of the personal 'we' in later accounts probably suggests only a spiritual commitment to the Royalist side: 'You see we had virtually no modern weapons, and yet the Republicans had Illyushin bombers and Mig fighters – quite a lot of them. As far as I remember we had no aeroplanes. We didn't even have any landing-grounds. And then they had tanks and artillery and we had none – only a few light guns which we fired at intervals, but we kept our end up. If it hadn't been for internal dissension we'd probably have taken Sana'a.'[44] Indeed, Thesiger denied that he played much active part in the fighting: 'You could have called Billy McLean a mercenary – he was helping the Royalists, which I wasn't. When they were shelling Sana'a with mortars I dropped a mortar-bomb down a mortar to say I'd taken some part in the war. I'd like to think it was the one that fell on the Italian Embassy. I didn't like the Italians after what they'd done in Addis Ababa.'[45] The Abyssinian campaign had been over for a quarter of a century and Thesiger claimed elsewhere that he had long ago been 'purged' of his hatred of Italians, yet for a moment he seems to have believed that he was still fighting them. He hinted that his 'true' role was intelligence gathering: 'The Prince gave me odd jobs,' he said, 'to find out what was happening.'[46] That he had been a regular intelligence agent, though, John Cooper thought highly unlikely. 'If Thesiger was there on an intelligence-gathering mission, sitting around with the Princes would not have enhanced it,' Cooper said, 'since their intelligence system was based on how many golden sovereigns would be offered to informers. Prince Hussain had his own intelligence set-up anyway.'[47] In the absence of further evidence, it seems likely that, being the adventurer he was, Thesiger was in north Yemen for no other reason than that it suited him to be there. His lukewarm espousal of the Royalist cause gave him a privileged opportunity to see yet another unspoiled country where few outsiders had been: 'I soon realized I was being accorded semi-official status to which I had no claim,' he wrote honestly, 'but this had its uses.'[48]

In fact, while war was raging sporadically, he managed to trek over most of north and north-eastern Yemen during his six months there in 1966. The constant lurching down steep hillsides and up again for hour after hour, covering only a few miles horizontally in a day, was the most exhausting foot-slogging Thesiger had ever experienced. He was approaching sixty, and his cartilages were worn out after tens of thousands of miles on foot across the most demanding landscapes on earth. There is a sense of 'the return of the exile' in Thesiger's visits to Yemen. The Arabs were, after all, his chosen people, and the race he idealized above all others: his mastery of Arabic and knowledge of Arab culture put him on an immediate footing with his companions. 'The Arabs were the only society I have ever encountered to which, as a whole, you could apply the term "noble",' he said. 'I'm not saying for a moment you don't get noble people among the English, but you couldn't call them noble as a whole. The quality of nobility was a quality associated with the past, a quality which would have earned one a knighthood in the Middle Ages.'[49]

Nowhere is a greater gulf between the ideal and the prosaic observable than in Thesiger's experience in Yemen. He was in the heartland of Arabia, but a world away from the open deserts of the Empty Quarter or even the Marshlands of Iraq. The Yemen is first and foremost a mountain landscape, and the tribes were mountain people who had crafted villages of stone standing at the very peak of the highest hills, on impossible needles of rock, or on the teetering edges of sheer precipices thousands of feet high. They were accessible only by tortuous and narrow tracks which were certainly no pleasure to the vertigo-sufferer. The northern Yemenis – the Zeidi tribesmen – were unorthodox Muslims and, like most mountain dwellers, deeply suspicious of outsiders, especially Christians. They were closed, instrospective, conservative and aggressive. Settled farmers rather than nomads, their surreal landscape of villages built on rock pinnacles and mountainsides converted into stone terraces was partly the result of the generations of feuds that set village against village, clan against clan. Their settlements were fortresses, deliberately constructed as high and as inaccessible as possible, where families could hole up for years if necessary, venturing out armed to the teeth to tend their terraces, and self-sufficient with their own crops and stores of water in mountain cisterns. Physically and culturally many of the tribes had pre-Arab traits, their songs, poetry and architecture showing much in common with the Berbers of North Africa. There was, indeed, little to justify Thesiger's feeling that he was 'returning to friends'. The Royalist–Republican axis was anything but clear-cut. Like the Dhofar war taking place concurrently, the Republican tribes were out not to change the social order but rather to get rid of a tyrannical Imamate and gain access to greater wealth. As in Dhofar, the situation would quickly be exploited by outsiders – the Nasserite Egyptians with an eye on oil-rich Sau'di Arabia, and the Soviets with dreams of a Communist bloc in south Arabia. The war had become the focus of post-Suez Anglo-French concern: David Stirling, a quarter of a century on, was back running tough professionals like Johnny Cooper. There were French mercenaries, dreamers like McLean and other would-be 'Scarlet Pimpernels' such as Mark Lennox-Boyd, Lady Birdwood doling out medical supplies like a latter-day Florence Nightingale, as well as out-and-out oddballs like the self-styled 'Prince' Bruce Bourbon-Condé, a former American paratrooper and philatelic enthusiast with visions of grandeur who intended to become Governor-General of the Yemen's Post Office after the war. However, like the Abyssinian Patriots, the allegiances of the Zeidi tribes were unstable, as Johnny Cooper wrote: 'Many tribes changed their loyalty overnight either before or after battle, thus ensuring that they were always on the winning side and the side which stood the best chance of survival.'[50] No wonder Thesiger would say eventually, 'I didn't like the village Yemenis. I never trusted them, and I felt they would have betrayed me for money.'[51]

His time was spent in constant peregrination between towns and villages, where he would often be fêted as an official visitor with dancing and rifle-firing. He descended into the Tihama, and met again the gay, 'un-Arabian' tribesmen of the coastal plain. Almost everywhere he encountered the results of Egyptian bombing: villages that were ruined husks, mosques reduced to piles of masonry, sick and wounded tribesmen who were the immediate beneficiaries of Thesiger's travelling medicine-chests. Almost everywhere there were the hulks of burned-out tanks and armoured cars, and in the Wadi Badr the bloody remains of an entire Egyptian column wiped out by the Royalists. Driving down to the Royalist lines around Sana'a in a truck crammed with arms and ammunition, Thesiger spent a day in the Jauf desert with his old adversaries, the Daham. He called on them for a couple of days later. It was almost two decades since the Daham had held Musallim bin al Kamam captive and sent out riders into the Sands to intercept Thesiger's party. Oddly – even though the Daham frequently raided Royalist columns – he felt more at home among these Bedu than he ever had among the Yemen highlanders: 'I was glad to get among the Bedu and spend a night with them,' he wrote. 'I felt absolutely at home and absolutely safe, which I never did among the village people. If we'd have met them in the past I'd have been travelling with the Mishqas and consequently have been an enemy, but travelling on my own like that was different.'[52] Nothing is more indicative, perhaps, of Thesiger's ability to jump from role to role – almost from game to game – enemy to ally, Mishqas to Ma'areb, Englishman to Arab, than this brief interlude: Italians, Republicans and Royalists, Hadr and Bedu, marshmen and Fellahin – despite his rhetoric, Thesiger had no real political commitment to these categories. The real enemy – the enemy to the status quo of Thesiger's world – was the Americans. The Americans had sanctioned Suez and the Americans had recognized the Republican government in Sana'a, which the British – largely thanks to Billy McLean – had not.

Thesiger was restless in the Yemen. In December he returned to London, escorted his mother on motor tours in Morocco and Portugal, and endured an operation to have his cartilages removed, recovering on another gentle drive through south Italy, alone. He returned to the Yemen in October for about two and a half months, to join Prince Muhammad bin Hussein in his push on Sana'a. The offensive had been prompted by the pulling out of Egyptian troops after Nasser's trouncing by Israel in the Six Day War. Thesiger had not been with McLean during 1966, but this time they travelled together. While staying in Prince Muhammad's camp, they were bombed with clockwork punctuality by

Russian Illyushins: 'They'd always come after breakfast,' he said, 'so when we'd finished breakfast, we'd say "Isn't it about time we left?" and move out into the nearby lava-field – not all that far – and settle down to watch the castle being bombed. They shot one plane down with small-arms fire and when we went over and looked the corpse was Russian.'[53] On another occasion two Migs came sweeping down the valley and strafed and rocketed the area. 'An explosive bullet burst,' Thesiger remembered, 'and nicked my head. I dropped further into cover, and then I heard McLean, who was with me, exclaim: "Dammit, Wilfred, look what you've done!" I had bled into his cigar box and ruined his cigars!'[54] Thesiger's legs had not fully recovered from his operation, and at times, darting for cover, he would feel as if he were moving in slow motion. Once, as he walked out to select his foxhole, he came under heavy fire from the castle: 'God, I didn't know there were any Republicans here!' Thesiger thought as he hurled himself prostrate. Then he looked up and saw a rather bemused hare skipping across in front of him: 'The whole crowd of soldiers there had immediately opened fire on it,' he said. 'They shot at anything they saw – even the lammergeyers – just for the fun of it!'[55] During another airborne attack he reached cover, clutching his precious mail from home, and opened it while the bombs and rockets rained down, to discover that he had been made an Honorary Doctor of Letters of the University of Leicester. It was a great honour, he felt, for a man who had never dreamed of being a writer, but as the machine-gun bullets burst around him, he wondered grimly if he would live to receive the degree.

As they moved on Sana'a, Prince Muhammad set up his HQ in a large cave. Thesiger, McLean and Lennox-Boyd had no transport, no servant and Thesiger still felt the effects of the operation on his legs. These were miserable times, even for the hardy Thesiger: there was no room to stretch out, often no food, tea or coffee. Thesiger felt constrained and restless, and found the experience of air-raids constantly harrowing. He was convinced, though, that the Royalists would take Sana'a. 'I had to get home because I was going to pick up my mother and take her to Florence,' he said. 'It was fixed, but when I left I felt sure I would miss the victory parade into Sana'a. Of course, they never did take it, because they were squabbling among themselves – like all Arabs. There were negotiations and it was the Republicans who formed the new government.'[56] Motoring back to the Sa'udi Arabian border with McLean, there was one last surprise in store: a personalized attack by a Mig fighter: 'We were in a jeep,' he remembered, 'and the fighter started to come at us. There was a big rock in front of us and we managed to get up against the rock and he missed us. I find it very frightening to have a fighter-plane diving at me.'[57] Thesiger was to visit a more peaceful Yemen almost a decade later, when he saw Sana'a for the first time and made a four-day donkey-trek in the Tihama. But the net result of his seven and a half months in the Yemen was largely negative: it had, perhaps, burst the bubble of his feeling for the Arabs, just as 1944 in Dessie had eroded his feelings for the Abyssinians. Despite his idealization of the Arabs, he had never felt at ease in the Yemen. He had been aware of their aversion to him as a Christian, and had found it impossible, over the religious divide, to form any personal relationships. Reluctantly, after four years, he turned once again to Kenya.

CHAPTER 16

A Mixed-up World

In 1939, Thesiger had been desperate to get away from the 'primitive' Nuer of the Sudan's Equatorial marshes and return to the Arabized peoples of Darfur. Almost thirty years later the wheel had come full circle. In 1968 he left the Arabs of Yemen in some disillusionment to live with the more 'primitive' Samburu and Turkana, who would remain the focus of his interest for the rest of his life. From 1968 he rarely spoke Arabic or mixed with Arabs again. He had felt that he could never live among the Nuer on the same economic level – that he would always be 'the Englishman in Africa' – while with the Arabs he could dress as they did and adopt their customs. Yet by the late 1960s he had reversed his opinion: 'The Turkana are a pastoral tribe, always on the move with their herds of cattle,' he said in 1970. 'They are pagans and at times slightly uncouth, but I much prefer to be with them than a more sophisticated tribe. You can establish a relationship with them that is quite impossible once a group has been exposed to the outside world.'[1]

Yet though Thesiger travelled among the pastoral Turkana and Samburu, he never really lived among them: he never lived in a tribal *manyatta*, speaking the local tongue, carrying spears and wearing a scarlet loincloth. Indeed, he despised the distinguished anthropologist Paul Spencer, who did. 'I thought Spencer going around with ochre hair was idiotic,' he said. 'What on earth was the point of doing that? And then going to see the District Officer to ask help for his Samburu "cousins". They were no more his cousins than the Eskimos are mine!'[2] Thesiger's friend Frank Steele felt this view somewhat unjustified: 'To have lived in a Samburu village wearing European clothes would have been incongruous,' he commented, 'because Spencer had to get himself accepted to a point where he could learn all the facts about

Samburu life that they would not normally divulge. The only way was to wear their clothes.'[3] Thesiger recorded that his object in entering the Marshes was to study the marsh people, and throughout his life he collected a mass of anthropological and ethnological data, yet his interest in traditional peoples was primarily aesthetic. He resented the intrusion of anthropologists like Spencer who were trying to analyse his magical world. 'To hell with anthropologists!' he said. 'Why not leave people alone and not study them! What advantage do they get from being studied? None! And it's the impact of these people – I mean, a woman comes along into man's world, for example, it must have some effect. You get these expeditions and they go off to Nuristan and you get women behaving like that in a society which is rigidly divided between men who look after the animals and women who do things in the houses. It can give the women a whole lot of false ideas and the men too. I don't want this intrusion of alien cultures on top of simpler cultures.'[4]

In Kenya he never quite relinquished the role of 'Englishman in Africa' that he had been so anxious to escape from as a young man, but neither can it be said that he lived like a typical expatriate or white settler, with a fine house and a battalion of servants. 'I don't want servants,' he commented. 'I have no desire to build a house out here and then sit there and sort of shout, "Boy! Bring me a cup of tea!" I like being part of their lives. I accept them in a sense. I mean, Lawi said I was the only Englishman who had ever been here who accepted Africans and English on the same terms. Of course, if I'm being maddened by the children I do shout "Shut up!" and things, but that doesn't convey a superior attitude. I do think I'm accepted by Laputa, Kibiriti and the others.'[5] Thesiger lives in his own style, adopting the economic level of the sedentarized African but separate and distinct from the tribal peoples, and outside the tribal hierarchy. The young men and their families with whom he has surrounded himself are largely detribalized, and most are literate and English-speaking.

Thesiger never mastered Swahili nor learned Samburu or Turkana. His protégés always spoke to him in English: 'My Swahili has never been more than adequate,' he commented, 'and I haven't felt that mattered – in fact it was an advantage.

Now I talk nothing but English to them and you get these children speaking good English because they are talking to me all the time. Here almost everybody you encounter does speak English. You'd have to go up to the mountains to find people who didn't speak it. Some friends of mine have a plane, and flew up country somewhere and landed. When they came back they found this Samburu *moran* with ochred hair and spears lying in the shade of the wing. He read off the number of the plane, and they said, "Oh, you can read!" and he said, "As a matter of fact I can. I'm a pilot!" Well, when you get that ... It would never even have occurred to me to learn Samburu or Turkana   they're probably difficult languages. I can give them some sort of greeting, but actually when they say *suba* [Samburu: good morning] to me, I reply "good morning" in English ... I might have learned Swahili, but in the early days I had no intention of spending the next thirty years of my life in Kenya.'[6]

Thesiger constantly ranged cultures in hierarchies of nobility, and on this scale the Samburu-Turkana evidently rated beneath the Marsh Arabs and the Bedu. 'The Bedu were absolutely honest,' he said. 'Even the marsh people would never have stolen your money or something ... You can't compare the Arabs with the Afars or the Samburu. Undoubtedly you could say that the Arabs were a finer people.'[7] Yet in a sense such comparisons are rendered superfluous by Thesiger's own admission that it was individuals, not societies, that attracted him. It was probably not so much an admiration for the Samburu and Turkana that brought him back to Kenya time after time, but his association with youths such as Erope and Lawi.

Thesiger met Erope on an early march around Lake Turkana when he halted at Lodwar. A game-scout told him that a boy from Loyangalani was stranded there after walking alone round the lake. 'The scout asked me if I'd take him back to Maralal,' Thesiger recalled. 'I agreed, and along came this naked fourteen-year-old called Erope. I gave him some money to buy a *shuka* and he came with me on quite a long journey. He was very helpful and obviously knew a lot about animals, despite being so young. So when I got back to Maralal I gave him some money and got him a lift home. The next year I was at Loyangalani and Erope suddenly turned up and asked if he could come with me. I said yes, certainly, and he was with me for nine years.'[8] Like Idris in the Sudan, Erope was an exceptional tracker and bushman. He had what Thesiger believed to be a sort of sixth sense where animals were about. 'He was very, very good,' he commented, 'and later, when I started doing anti-poaching patrols as a game warden, he'd be about sixteen and you got senior game-scouts deferring to Erope – he got as good as that.'[9]

Thesiger once took Erope and some other Turkana to see a boxing match between Kenya and Russia in Nairobi. Afterwards they urged him to teach them boxing and persuaded him to buy some gloves. Some time later, at Baragoi – north of Maralal – some primary school children asked if they could 'play boxing.' 'One boy, and that was Lawi, was quite outstanding,' Thesiger commented. 'He was only seven years old but he was infinitely the best. Two years later I found him sitting in the car – I'd switched over to a Land-Rover by then. I said, "Hello, Lawi, what are you doing?" He said, "I don't know but I'm coming with you from now on." He joined up with me . . . and he's been with me ever since.'[10]

Thesiger had been made an Honorary Game Warden, thanks to his friendship with Rodney Elliott, and although unpaid, this gave him the right to order scouts to open fire on poachers. Kenya had been independent since 1963, but the Game Department was still run largely by whites. In 1969 he travelled through Tsavo National Park, through part of the Masai Mara and along the Tana river with Denis Zaphiro, the son of Wilfred Gilbert's former oriental secretary in Addis Ababa. They journeyed by car, and though Thesiger was fascinated to see the game he was as usual intensely frustrated to be confined to a vehicle. 'You are completely isolated from your surroundings in a car,' he commented, 'and that's why I get virtually no pleasure at all in motoring about in any vehicle. It's maddening to be somewhere in a National Park and not be able to get out. You're seeing the whole thing under unnatural conditions, because nobody is going to be looking at a lion as close as that unless he's in a car.'[11]

The following year he did some anti-poaching patrols with camels in the Uasso Nero area, taking young Erope with him, and later was invited to spend Christmas with Peter Jenkins, Warden of Meru National Park. When Jenkins proposed that he should do anti-poaching patrols on foot in Meru, Thesiger leapt at the idea. 'He gave me the freedom to go anywhere I liked,' Thesiger said. 'I could sleep anywhere. Nobody else had got such freedom – not even the Adamsons had that.'[12] Though the patrols were uneventful they led on to a further job with Jenkins – laying out a new National Park on the north-eastern side of Lake Turkana. 'It was exciting, because there was raiding going on and a raid did happen while I was there,' Thesiger recalled. 'We found a dead boy on the road – the Merille, an Ethiopian tribe, had been down there – they were always doing raids into Kenya. I wondered what had happened to him because his navel was missing, and then some people told me that the Merille always remove the navel of their victims. I thought the Merille might attack our camp at any moment – we had six or eight scouts with rifles and I thought they might feel it was worth raiding us to get the rifles and ammunition. There must have been thirty or forty of them. It made us very alert, but luckily we weren't attacked. I stayed there and ran the park for several months after Jenkins left. I did tend to go round by car then, but I had the liberty to get out of the car whenever I liked, so in a sense I had the best of both worlds.'[13]

In early 1972 Thesiger travelled with his mother in Portugal. It turned out to be their last trip together. Later that year he went on safari with Lords Airlie and Hambleden and their white hunter, René Babault. 'I wanted to meet Lord Airlie, because his father had been at Haile Selassie's coronation as the equerry of the Duke of Gloucester,' Thesiger said, 'so I went and met them and Airlie's wife and two or three boys. It was a huge safari – they had something like forty camels. I told Airlie I'd known his father, and then René Babault asked me if I'd like to join the safari. He said the man he'd had coming had failed him at the last moment and he badly needed somebody else and if I'd do it he'd take me on full pay. I said I didn't want paying, I'd just enjoy doing it. We started from Wamba and slowly drifted up north: I had Erope with me and he used to go off with Airlie's son, David Ogilvy, and the other boys. He had his own shotgun and used to shoot guinea-fowl with them and they all got on very well. We crossed the Ndotos and went to Ngoronet, and I enjoyed it very much. It was nice to be with them and the only time I've ever travelled under those conditions: beds, good food, wine, smoked salmon – all carried by camel. It was a very good safari free – and then Babault insisted on paying me the money that would have gone to the other man.'[14]

Thesiger returned to London after a number of other journeys in Kenya. This year, however, there was no motor tour with his mother. She was now aged ninety-three and seriously ill. 'Her mind had gone,' he commented. 'In sixty-nine we'd been to Morocco as usual and motored down into the Anti-Atlas in fairly basic conditions. She was already eighty-nine and was ready to sleep out by the car if necessary. The next two years we went to Portugal but her mind had already started to go and she'd reached the stage when she couldn't remember anything. Then in London she couldn't recognize any of us, and was saying, "I wish I could just die quietly." '[15] Thesiger was back in Kenya that July, and came out of the bush to learn from John Seago that his mother had died two nights previously. 'It was something I'd been hoping would happen as soon as possible,' he said. 'You don't feel any remorse under those circumstances. I just said well, thank God for that! It seemed nonsense to go to the funeral and all that – anyway I shouldn't have been there in time. My brother took care of it all.'[16]

After his mother's death Thesiger continued to commute between London and Kenya, spending an average of three months in Europe and nine months abroad each year. 1974 was marred by the death of one of his boys, Kisau. 'He'd been with me a long time and I was teaching him to drive the car,' he remembered, 'and he suddenly got hepatitis. I took him to Wamba and he died the next day. I did feel a sense of loss – he was the only one who's been with me who died like that.'[17] In 1975 he flew to Addis Ababa and paid a nostalgic visit to Danakil country, driving along the new tarmac road to Assab. Maralal was already his base of sorts, though he still had no permanent house there. In 1976 he attended the first part of Lawi's circumcision ceremony. 'It was the traditional way of doing it,' he recalled. 'They built a special circumcision camp and there might have been 200 boys or more being circumcised. They wear black cloaks and get their hair shaved and then they have to go and fetch wood from various places – a special kind of wood which they make into bows and arrows. Then the day before they have to run all the way to Kisima, which is one of the two places in the district they can get the water they require. Then they come back here and they are circumcised the next morning, and they put feathers in their hair and shoot small birds which they hang round their necks. This goes on for about a month. Then they become junior *moran* and they stay in the *moran* for fourteen years. They wanted me to hold Lawi's shoulders while he was being circumcised, which implied a very special relationship. I had that with Lawi anyway, but I told him that as I wasn't always here it was better for him to get one of his own people.'[18] However, during one stage in the ceremony, there was an unwelcome intrusion in the form of a lady journalist, Mary Anne Fitzgerald. 'Thesiger strode across the cow pats and stood before me. Although he had already greeted the men in our party, until then he had treated me as if I was invisible.'[19] 'The circumcision is for men,' Thesiger explained, 'and once you've been circumcised and become a warrior you may never eat in the presence of a woman. Then Mary Anne Fitzgerald intrudes – these women, turning up like that and pushing themselves in. I more or less asked her why she was doing this, and she said she'd got special permission. It made me very angry and I told her to bugger off. These women – they can't take a hint. They can't seem to realize that this is the most important event in a boy's life and the one thing you mustn't have there are women. Then she goes and does that! It was an intolerable intrusion.'[20] Fitzgerald later wrote that Thesiger had himself circumcised some of the boys, 'crouching over [them], shaking antibiotic powder out of a plastic bottle on to their raw penises as if he was salting a stew'.[21] Thesiger commented that he had taken no part in the main ceremony: 'There was one boy who asked me to circumcise him,' he recalled, 'but it wasn't a ceremonial circumcision. He was probably a half-caste Samburu, whose parents wanted him to be circumcised. I have circumcised quite a few Turkana – a lot of them want to be done and they go to the hospital, but if they know they can get it done free by me, they come to me. I haven't done it for years, of course.'[22] There was another case when a car turned up with two Italian couples who wanted to watch the circumcision. 'The chief asked me to deal with it, saying that any man could come and watch but women are not allowed. I told them this and the two very disappointed girls were taken away and the men stood there. Well, as a final sort of climax when they started to circumcise the first boy, one of the men fainted and fell into a thorn-bush! I thought, you know, when the boys are doing this the white man can't even watch it without fainting!'[23]

Thesiger's inherent restlessness continued. He was torn between a desire to settle down and belong, and the traveller's itch to move. In 1977 he returned to Ethiopia, Yemen, the United Arab Emirates and Oman, knowing that he might not go back to Kenya. This meant parting with Erope and Lawi. 'I gave Erope a tent and some money,' he recalled, 'and he said he was going to join the *nuroko* or outlaws, and that he would kill a policeman if necessary and steal his rifle – he was that kind of person. He did go off and joined them and became one of their leaders fighting in the southern Sudan. His brother turned up the other day – sixteen years later – to say he'd been killed. I don't know if that's true or not. But anyway, that was the last I saw of Erope. I got Lawi a job with a safari company – Myles Burton – in Nairobi. It was very good experience for him because he met up with all sorts of Europeans and was in charge of them, even though he was so young himself.'[24]

After his disappointing visit to Dhofar, Thesiger flew to London in April. Here he met up with Gavin Young, by now a distinguished war correspondent and author, who had just published his book *Return to the Marshes*. Young had become attached to the Far East and particularly to Vietnam, having covered the war there, and was now planning a long voyage on the ketch *Fiona* around the South China Sea. It had been a long time since Thesiger had thought of adventure at sea, and he had never seen the Far East. He accepted Young's invitation and, on his way out to join the ketch at Bali, stopped off in India to see the Taj Mahal at Agra and to visit Fatepur-Sikri. He was in Bali on 20 July, to meet the skipper of the *Fiona*, a young Scots-Irishman known simply as 'Mac'. Young and his godson Murray Moncrieff followed a week later, and they weighed anchor on the 31st.

15. Unloading camels in the Empty Quarter today.

16. A fortress in the Hadhramaut, beneath the sheer cliffs of Arabia's greatest wadi system.

17. Wigwam-like tents of the Mahra, a Bedu tribe living in the steppes between Dhofar and the Hadhramaut.

18. Shibam – built entirely of mud. Thesiger considered this the outstanding sight in the Hadhramaut.

19. Mahra tribesmen – these Bedu, speaking a Himyaritic dialect, were occasionally hostile to Thesiger's party.

20. Sheikh Musallim bin Tafl, Thesiger, a Bedouin and Salim bin Kabina at the home of a Sheikh in Izz, northern Oman, October 1991.

21. A Marsh Arab in his *tarada*.

22. An animal shelter among the reeds, Iraq.

23. A girl outside her reed house, Iraq.

24. A *mudhif* or guest house – the huge external pillars are formed by bundles of giant reeds.

25. Baltit Fort at Hunza, where Thesiger stayed with the Mir in 1953.

26. Maralal, where Thesiger made his home in old age.

27. Thesiger outside his house near Maralal, with Lopago on the right.

28. Samburu *moran* at the 'viewpoint', one of Thesiger's favourite spots near Maralal.

29. Samburu *moran* watering their cattle in the hills near Maralal.

For about five months *Fiona* made a leisurely pace around Indonesia, calling at ports in Kalimantan, Sarawak, the Celebes and Brunei. The voyage was part of Young's long-term travels in the footsteps of Conrad, an author with whom, like Thesiger, he had been captivated since his schooldays. The results of his many journeys on this theme would be published in 1991 under the title *In Search of Conrad*, which would be co-winner of the Thomas Cook prize for travel-writing. Young's specific aims on his trip in *Fiona* were first to become acquainted with the waters known to the Bugis, the old pirates of the south Celebes in Conrad's day, and second to see the Berau river, which had been the setting for much of the action in Thesiger's favourite Conrad novel, *Lord Jim*, and the site of Jim's death. It had been Young's offer to 'show him where Jim died' which had persuaded Thesiger to accompany him. *Fiona*, Young noted, was herself a product of Conrad's time (as Thesiger was), having been built in 1912, when Conrad was fifty-six. She was forty-two feet, weighed twenty tons and had a six-foot draught. She belonged to an American millionaire friend of Young's called Jo Menell, who had sailed her twice round the world and then lent her to Mac to pilot Young on his voyage through the South China Sea.

The first part of the passage was not easy. The ketch nosed her way along the coast of Bali and through the Lombok Straits in a raging sea, heading for Kangean Island, marked by a beacon which they missed completely. This obliged Mac to change course for the island of Laut, the setting of another of Conrad's novels – *Victory*. It was, Young wrote, like being at sea in a sieve: 'Water had cascaded into the cabin all night. Every match seemed to be wet, so it was impossible to light the oil lamps which swung, rattling, in their gimbals on *Fiona*'s wooden bulkheads. We pulled on oilskins and lurched clumsily about like drunken men in the sound of creaking wood and the slap and gurgle of the sea against the hull.'[25] The storm passed as quickly as it had come, and the next morning they put into the limpid waters of Laut island under a brilliant cascade of orange and lemon sunlight tumbling through galleries of cloud. There they ran into a *prau* of the modern-day Bugis – the respectable, sea-roving descendants of Conrad's pirates – who challenged them tacitly to a race into harbour. Knowing nothing of 'stays and halliards', as Young put it, Thesiger merely lay back in the stern, 'peering ahead with his deep-set big game-hunter's eyes protected from the sun by an old linen cabbage-leaf hat of the kind old ladies wear to prune rosebushes in'.[26] In August they passed through the Macassar Straits and lay up in Donggala in the Celebes, where they remained for some time, patronizing the local 'Depot 39' coffee-shop on the wharf and rubbing shoulders with the Bugis from their *praus*. When the sailors visited them on *Fiona* and asked permission to come aboard, Thesiger would bellow out, 'Step aboard!' 'It did not seem to matter . . .' Young wrote, 'that he addressed them as if they were members of his London club.'[27]

For Thesiger the voyage was spoiled by the presence of Mac, whose language he found unbearable. '[It] was one long obscen-ity,' Thesiger commented. 'I mean, not just the steady "f-ing" of British troops, which one got used to, like "f-ing-diplo-f-ing-matic" or something, this was really anatomical. It was a pity because he was the only person who could sail the boat. I never knew or really learned which rope to pull unless I was told, and Gavin knew no more.'[28] In Sarawak Thesiger took ten days' leave from the yacht to visit the Royal Geographical Society's expedition at Mullu, led by Robin Hanbury-Tenison and Nigel Winser, explor-ing the incredible cave-system that had been discovered there. Thesiger was impressed by the caves and enjoyed shooting some rapids in an inflatable with Winser, but felt this kind of explora-tion alien to him: 'I mean, they were studying the earthworms and everything else,' he commented, 'and that's fair enough, but it wasn't exploration in the sense of Stanley, Livingstone, Burton, Doughty or myself. I mean, they'd had 100 scientists out there in the course of the year and it was all very comfortable. They lived in these cabins on poles and the plane arrived every Thursday with the letters. There was no question of going without food or water. There was no adventure in it. Well, if you call that exploration . . .'[29] Though this was Thesiger's first experience of tropical jungle, he felt little drawn by its rich greenness: many years previously, in Morocco, he had agreed with the artist Sidney Nolan that green was a colour most attractive when used sparingly. 'I cannot stand the lush green of the English countryside,' he said. 'Green should be a patch of cultivation, perhaps just a fig-tree, in contrast to an expanse of desert; then it becomes valuable.'[30]

Gavin Young had left *Fiona* at Brunei and boarded the *Rajah Brooke*, bound for Singapore, but Thesiger stayed on, alone with Mac. 'The first day out we were on the tail-end of a typhoon,' he said, 'and the sea was running very rough. Mac said you called this "a tall gale". Anyway, there was a rope along the side of the yacht which you could hang on to, but somehow he missed it and was hurled into the bulkhead and lay on the ground making funny noises. I thought at least he'd broken his back ... I thought here I am in the middle of the South China Sea not having a clue how to sail this bloody boat.'[31] Mac was not seriously injured, however, and later, when Thesiger was on watch, he spotted an island ahead and called down to the Skipper, who commented that this meant they were precisely where he had hoped they would be. As *Fiona* drew nearer, they saw the spray going up very high, and Mac told Thesiger to go down and get some rest, saying he would call him when they had rounded the point. 'At about nine o'clock there was a crash,' Thesiger recalled, 'and Mac appeared mouthing every sort of obscenity. I asked what was wrong and he said, "The only thing certain is fucking *death*!" He said there was a big sea and the wind was taking us down on to the reefs. I went up and they were still quite a long way off, and I asked him how long we would last if we got into the reefs, and he said only a few minutes. Somehow, though, we managed to get round the point by four in the afternoon. We should have put straight out to sea as far as we could and then gone round.'[32]

In December they put safely into Singapore harbour and Thesiger left Mac with no regrets. He stayed briefly at Raffles Hotel before catching a train across the straits of Johore into Malaysia. From Kuala Lumpur he paid visits to the Cameron Highlands, where the endemic rhinoceros was still hanging on to existence by a whisker. 'They were chopping down the last place it still lived while I was there,' he recalled, 'and there were protests about it in the papers and things. I wasn't particularly interested in Malaysia, though.'[33] He returned to Singapore and flew back to Delhi, where he met Sir Robert ffolkes, who was employed by Save the Children in Ladakh. Thesiger had already been commissioned to write his third book, *Desert, Marsh and Mountain*, and was looking for a peaceful place to do a month's work. Ffolkes recommended a hotel in Hyderabad, and Thesiger remained there during part of February and March 1978. 'It suited me well,' he said. 'There were quite a few other people staying there, and we used to go off and have dinner in the evening at some Chinese restaurant in the town. I don't much like Indian food – hot curries and things don't appeal to me – I'd much rather have Chinese.'[34] Armed with part of the manuscript of *Desert, Marsh and Mountain*, he returned briefly to London. By June he was back in Nairobi.

Thesiger had had no plans to return to Africa when he had left the country in 1977. Indeed, he had seriously thought about settling in India and would continue to play with the idea over the following years. Two things brought him back to Kenya: first, his aching loneliness and the need for a personal companionship which he had not found in Asia, second, the presence of his friend Frank Steele, who had in 1968 been posted to the High Commission in Nairobi. It was Steele who suggested he should return. 'Anyway, I came back,' he commented, 'and Lawi was working for Myles Burton. I met him in Nairobi, driving a lorry, and he jumped out and told the other driver, "Take it back to Myles Burton, and tell him I'm back with my father!"'[35]

Thereafter, Maralal became his base, and Thesiger, Lawi, and a handful of other Samburu and Turkana constructed a zinc-roofed timber cabin on tribal land. At seventy, Thesiger at last began to put down roots.

He had made his name by railing against technology and the corrupting influence of the West on tribal cultures. Ironically, he was here to become the means by which a small group of Samburu-Turkana tribesmen and their families would become Westernized. Through him they learned good English and acquired a taste for the material goods that Thesiger himself had always despised. It is the ultimate, perhaps inevitable, paradox in the life of the century's greatest traveller that far from adopting their language and traditions, he should have made his protégés more like himself. In this, Thesiger's later years have been a metaphor for and a microcosm of the process of the defunct

British Empire, of which he was a scion. Indeed, he came to see that it was futile for him to try to adapt himself to the lives of a people whose dearest wish was to become like the Westerner they perceived him to be. He and they were pushing, as it were, in opposite directions. The tide of history was too strong for him to breast: 'There's no future for these boys just walking about with their goats and cows in the hills dressed in their *shukas* and carrying their spears,' he told author Alexander Maitland in 1990. 'The future of these people lies in the Kenya of today. I'm proud and glad to have helped Lawi, Laputa and Kibiriti to identify themselves with this changing world. The other day when Julian Pettifer asked Lawi on television about me and cars, Lawi answered: "He hates cars. He's a very bad driver but a good instructor." '[36] In 1959 he had written that the Bedu of Arabia were 'doomed' and denied that their future 'lay in the Arabia of today' ('Some people believe that they will be better off in a more materialistic world. This I will never believe'). This *volte face* was a negation of almost everything Thesiger had made a reputation for. 'It's necessary to change with a changing world and you've got to move with this world,' he declared. 'I don't see any contradiction in what I've written or said – in a place like this you've got to move. I regret the changes that are taking place but they are taking place. I can still enjoy being with Kibiriti, or Laputa or Sungura.'[37]

But Thesiger's statement obviously does contradict his attitude in *Arabian Sands* and indeed in *The Marsh Arabs*: his belief that 'all change is for the worse', a contradiction which cannot be qualified by the words 'in a place like this' or by suggesting that the cases of the Samburu and the Bedu were somehow different, when they stood in precisely the same relation to the modern world. It is tempting to think that by 1980 Thesiger had become trapped in the traditionalist landscape he had enshrined in his books. He was now a very famous man, and his fame rested almost entirely upon *Arabian Sands*. People had begun to expect certain things of him: he had become 'a character'. He knew deep down, perhaps, that the image of traditional peoples he had created in his books was, as Raban said, too constricting for them: it allowed them no space to move and grow. He had, in other words, become imprisoned in a myth of his own creation – a myth he and many others still wanted desperately to believe in.

But since Thesiger himself denied any such contradiction, and in view of the continuing ambivalence of his rhetoric, this explanation does not seem entirely satisfactory. On close analysis, it seems that when Thesiger says 'the future of *these* people' he does not mean the Samburu or the Turkana, or indeed any other traditional peoples, but only those special individuals – Lawi, Kibiriti, Laputa and the others – whom he saw as extensions of himself and objects of his affection. He had no wish to see the individuals he felt affection for end up as 'Plastic Boys', selling trinkets on the streets. Instead, he personally created a tiny élite: a miniature, detribalized, Westernized aristocracy in the town of Maralal. Ineluctably, perhaps even unconsciously, Thesiger systematically and at vast expense went about re-creating a miniature form of the same kind of society which had given him life.

The house he shares today with Laputa, his wife Namitu, and a number of small brothers and children outside Maralal is more spacious than it looks. Designed by Laputa himself as a 'split-level residence', it is set in a fenced-off block of hillside decked out with radiant purple bougainvilleas, poinsettias and geraniums. Laputa originally wired up the house for electricity and bought a generator – the switches and sockets can still be seen – but legend has it that he swapped the generator for a bottle of Johnny Walker whisky – a rare treat in Maralal. Laputa walked into Thesiger's life one day while he was unloading his camels with Lawi near the town. He and a friend begged the *Mzungu* for work, but Thesiger decided he could take only one of them. Lawi plumped for the other boy, but Thesiger chose Laputa. He then asked the youth's name, and, discovering it was 'Tommy Gun', hastily christened him 'Laputa' after his noble childhood hero from *Prester John*. Namitu's ten-year-old brother, whom Thesiger once called 'Bushbaby', has grown into 'Bushboy' and her infant son, Alessandro (named by one of the local Italian Fathers), is condemned unflatteringly by Thesiger to be 'the Little Horror'. Other occupants of the house – mostly small boys – are known as 'Mini-Minor', ironically the name of a famous motor car, 'Mini-Moran' and 'Mini-Uncle'. Kibiriti, whose name means 'Matches', was originally called Awi. Lawi Leboyare – Thesiger's oldest and dearest Samburu companion, who in his early thirties became the local mayor – has retained his real name. So have Thesiger's young favourites, the sixteen-year-old Lopago, his 'bodyguard', and the athletic young Sungura, whom Thesiger is grooming as a potential Olympic boxer (and whose 'professional' name for himself is 'Van Brown', after the Hollywood strongman Van Damme). Laputa, Namitu, Mini-Minor, Mini-Moran, Bushboy, Van Brown: as Thesiger himself put it: 'It's a mixed-up world we're living in, and here in Maralal it's particularly mixed up.'[38]

Though the house is technically Laputa's, Thesiger paid for it as he has paid for everything that his foster-sons own. Laputa, a somewhat inscrutable, intelligent, sensitive-looking young man, has considerable artistic talent, which Thesiger has tried to draw out by ordering a studio built next to the house. He encourages him endlessly to sketch and paint and will proudly display Laputa's fine sketches of lion or baboon to guests. He will even hustle them up to a local tourist lodge, where two of Laputa's pictures of camels – copies from the photographs in *Arabian Sands* – are on display: 'And he'd never even held a brush in his hand before doing those!' Thesiger declares. 'The very fact that Laputa can do these drawings means he can make a name for himself, and he wouldn't be drawing them if I wasn't here.'[39]

The house is roughly E-shaped, with a small, smoky kitchen on the right, and on the left a spare room with steel-grille windows, where scores of distinguished guests have over the years been offered a mattress on the floor. In the centre is Thesiger's sitting-room, from which opens on one side his small bedroom and on the other the bedroom of Laputa and Namitu. The sitting-room is furnished with two huge sofas of dull plastic, a low table and several cupboards. The walls are plastered with postcards and photographs, a map of the world, military uniforms cut from the back of a cereal packet, an over-exposed shot of Shibam in the Yemen, and the portrait of Thesiger from the cover of his autobiography, *The Life of My Choice*. Thesiger erected the world map when he realized that the boys had virtually no conception of geography and wondered how on earth they could ever understand what was going on, and what had gone on, in the world without knowing where the various countries lay. 'I asked Lopago who fought in the war,' he said, 'and he said the English fought the Italians, which is fair enough – that happened near by. Then he said he'd heard of Hitler, and how he'd helped the English fight the Americans. I rather wish he had!'[40] The map has worked fairly well, however, and Thesiger will proudly haul Lepago or one of the other boys in before guests and have him point out England or China – with eighty per cent success.

The bedroom – Thesiger's inner sanctum – holds little but a three-quarter size bed and various cabinets which support or contain copies of *National Geographic*, a few large picture-books, an oblong magnifying glass, an enormous 'ghetto-blaster' radio, a large supply of Bisodol for Thesiger's constant digestive troubles, razor blades, a sack of sugar, and a small hoard of his prized luxuries: Cadbury's Chocolate, Nescafé, Heinz Tomato Ketchup, honey, Marmite and perhaps a bottle of Drambuie or Kenya Gold. He keeps the room well padlocked, for otherwise these items would tend to disappear quickly. Once, having offered a glass of Drambuie to a European guest, he discovered that it had changed miraculously into water: the boys had secretly drunk it and watered it down. If one of the smaller boys has to unlock the room it is with Thesiger's severe admonition: 'If you put your hand into that sugar you will be beaten, boy!' At night the sitting-room-bedroom complex is barricaded, and Thesiger sleeps with his 'bodyguard' Lepago on his bed – more for practical reasons than anything else, since there is no other bed and no room on the floor. On the sitting-room sofas, Bushboy and Mini-Minor curl up. The barricade is an important innovation: not long ago five thugs wearing balaclavas broke in and woke Thesiger roughly from sleep by thrashing him with sticks, demanding, 'Where's your money?' The eighty-two-year-old fought back, yelling, 'Get out!' and kicking one of his assailants so soundly in the stomach that they lost heart and ran off. 'I thought, thank God they didn't have *pangas* [machetes],' he commented. Strangely, 'bodyguard' Lepago was not present that night, neither did the dogs bark. The night-watchman – a septuagenarian Samburu – was locked in the kitchen, and the small boys in the sitting-room just covered their heads with their blankets as the intruders stamped through. When he returned the following morning, Lepago was sorry to have missed it: 'He'd always wanted to kill a man,' Thesiger said.[41]

No one in Maralal had ever been attacked by house-breakers

before, though thereafter several more houses were burgled, and police believed the gang might have come from the south. The absence of Lopago on that particular night, though, and the failure of the dogs to bark, must have looked ominous even to Thesiger. Since then he has barricaded his door every night and carries a long knife and a spear around with him after dark, vowing to kill the intruders if they return. 'I've always wanted to kill someone in that way,' he said. 'I think I'd use the knife rather than the spear – it would be a bit of a bore getting the spear out of a man's body. I'd just chop off his head so that it bounced against the wall. Bushboy could clear up the mess!'[42] While I was staying with him Thesiger advised me to lock my door at night, and asked if he could rely on my help in case of an attack, looking at me appraisingly, I thought, like a general at a new recruit.

Thesiger rises early and the barricades are flung down. He appears in shirt and trousers and washes and shaves in a mugful of water warmed on the charcoal cooker by Namitu and dashed into a plastic bowl. He washes sitting on the sofa, scrubbing his arms and face with a flannel, lathering and scraping his chin with a ordinary Gillette 'Contour' razor. Guests are given the same allowance of water, which is always scarce. The house has no taps and no plumbing. The latrine is a long-drop pit under a canvas awning some yards away towards which Thesiger occasionally disappears at a dignified pace, bearing a mug of water. Water for all purposes is kept in two large open oil-drums on the verandah, where it is constantly scummed with vegetable-matter and dead insects. The drums are filled every day with liquid hauled up from Bhola's garage in Kibiriti's Land-Rover. There is no reason why Thesiger should not have twice the number of water-drums, but this self-imposed frugality is part of the game: if one had four drums, why not electricity, running water and a bathroom? Why be here at all? Sadiq Bhola has for years observed Thesiger's self-imposed austerity, mystified. 'I don't know why he doesn't take more water,' he told Roger Clarke, 'a third barrel. I wouldn't mind. There's no problem.'[43] Inevitably there are recriminations when the water runs out: 'Who's used up all the water?' Thesiger demands, thumping the ground with his stick. 'If I find out there'll be trouble!' He once despised the radio, but since he is now unable to read except with a magnifying glass and for short periods, he has become an avid listener to the BBC World Service, which he tunes into while eating his daily cornflakes, porridge or scrambled eggs. One day he told me: 'The effect of radio on this world has been absolutely disastrous ... just by listening to the news you can cover the world in an hour. It's all been destroyed.'[44] I was staying at the Lodge on that occasion, but the following day I entered his house in the early morning to find him listening intently to his vast portable stereo, which he claimed he did not know how to switch off. After breakfast comes the shopping-list: Thesiger is a habitual list-maker, and calls one of the boys to him to make it up. Each item is carefully priced and the total calculated before Thesiger hands over the money. Unfortunately he is now unable to distinguish between the various denominations, and while the boys are mostly conscientious it is not unknown for a 500 shilling note he has mistaken for a 200 shilling note to be pocketed silently. Though now eighty-three, Thesiger still walks the two miles in to Maralal some days. He remains physically strong, but because of his poor eyesight needs Lopago or one of his other boys to guide him by the hand. Often he has experienced odd hallucinations: stone walls built across the track, huge trees where none ever stood, strange blossoms which take off and float into the air as he watches. Sometimes he accepts a lift into town with Kibiriti, who, in addition to his Land-Rover, owns a large house with a blooming garden, marred only by an idle mini-bus and a disused Toyota Land-Cruiser. The bus was part of Kibiriti's defunct transport business and stands immobile for the lack of a new gearbox. Thesiger constantly nags at his 'son' to get it working, but the gearbox never seems to arrive. The Land-Cruiser is Thesiger's own car, bought for him by Kibiriti (with Thesiger's money), and is perfectly serviceable. It was bought from a man who promised to send the log-book later and never did, and therefore is presumably stolen. Kibiriti, who is the only one of Thesiger's foster-sons unable to read or write, now concentrates mainly on his shop in Baragoi, which has been broken into several times and has had large amounts of goods stolen. Thesiger is ceaselessly expected to foot the bill.

If he is car-borne, Thesiger might drive about the town visiting other members of the 'family' – particularly Sungura, an athletic-looking young Samburu who dresses in fashionably baggy trousers and loud T-shirts, and whom Thesiger sponsored on an Amateur Boxing Association course in Nairobi. Sungura is evidently a fast and powerful boxer, and Thesiger has high hopes that he will make the Olympic team some day. So that he will be able to support himself, Thesiger has set him up in a small shop and a *posho*-mill (*posho* is the local porridge), and financed the construction of several simple houses which he can rent out. Sungura spends much of his time at his boxing club in Nairobi.

Thesiger might look for Laputa, who is frequently absent from the house for a night on the town with his cronies, and may be skulking around some local huts. Thesiger castigates him for abandoning Namitu, though he once nursed him concernedly when he lay in bed feverish for two days. According to Frank Steele, a frequent guest in Maralal, Laputa and Thesiger have a 'love–hate' relationship. Once Thesiger was delighted when Laputa informed him that he had landed a contract to supply the town's army detachment with beef, and shelled out hundreds of thousands of shillings for the purchase of the cattle. Neither the cattle nor the money were ever heard of again.

If he has no guests, which is fairly rare, Thesiger will spend the rest of the day at Bhola's garage, where in the neat sitting-cum-dining-room, opening off a courtyard behind the workshops, he will go through his mail or wait for a phone call. Often he sits outside on the step where Bhola's petrol pump once stood, beneath the only two-storey building in central Maralal, decorated with the logos of Volkswagen, Land-Rover and Michelin, with a great blue and white Total sign that squeaks irritatingly above. Occasionally he will sit in a car watching the world go by, the *morans* in their *shukas* and ochre hair, the women with their shaven heads and checked blankets, red, blue or pink, the old men with their dangling earlobes and pork-pie leather hats. Often there are other Westerners to be seen: Canadian missionaries, Italian Fathers, tourists in Land-Rovers and Suzukis filling up with petrol at the new filling-station further down the street, hitch-hikers, busloads of Western visitors on their way to Lake Turkana. All of these are instantly pounced on by the local 'Plastic Boys', who address them in English and attempt to sell them bracelets, spears and chains manufactured from engine-blocks. Thesiger frequently shoos the boys off with his stick, but feels more pity for them than anger: they are the casualties of the populist system he detests. 'What have the Plastic Boys here gained from going to school?' he demands venomously. 'Nothing! They've had their whole lives disrupted and they've no object in life. They'd have been far better off if their object had been to herd their camels and goats. I don't believe in equal opportunities. I believe the disaster it can have on the majority outweighs the good it does to those who would have made it on their own. [What I believe in] is what went on in the old [British colonial] days when they went on with the lives they were leading and the ones who wanted to get educated could achieve it.'[45] Sometimes tourists will come over and speak to him. 'Are you Wilfred Thesiger?' they inquire, upon which he will beam with pleasure, and as likely as not invite them to dinner. Though happy to be in Africa, Thesiger is by no means the ascetic that people have taken him to be: he craves company and has always done so. 'I love seeing visitors,' he said. 'I like talking and things. The conception that I lead a lonely life on my own [is nonsense]. Even [with the Bedu] in the desert you could have come and watched it and seen that I could never get away from them. I mean, I meet people in the street who say they were hoping they would meet me, and I say why don't you come and spend the night. Quite a lot of people have and I get letters from them quite frequently and of course with my eyes as they are now I can't answer them.'[46]

Thesiger's house in Maralal has often been characterized as a 'retreat' by the press, and occasionally by Thesiger himself. Ironically, it has acted as a magnet for reporters, authors, artists, photographers, journalists and film-makers, and scarcely a week passes when he is not playing host to the *Sunday Times*, the *Independent*, the *Daily Telegraph, Geo*, or some other magazine or newspaper. His picture has even appeared in the fashion magazine *Vogue*. Hundreds of articles have been written on him over the years and he has been the subject of three television documentaries, one of which reached 5 million people. He has been interviewed on television and radio on many occasions, and relishes his role as an international celebrity: 'He likes being famous,' his friend Frank Steele said, 'and who wouldn't? He likes the way people come up to him and the way they are to a degree in awe of him and hero-worship him. At the same time he is very amusing and matter of fact about it, saying, "Oh, another bunch of hero-worshippers!" and he says, "The last time I was in England I hardly got any time to myself because of people wanting to interview me and film me." He likes it and expects it but it hasn't fundamentally changed him.'[47] He is also visited by friends from England such as Frank Steele and Alexander Maitland, by aspiring authors and explorers, acquaintances from Nairobi and other parts of Kenya. Hundreds of well-known writers and travellers have, over the years, made the 'pilgrimage' here, to experience Thesiger's goat stew and a mattress on the floor in his guest-room.

Sitting on Sadiq Bhola's sofa, though, he is constantly bombarded by requests for money from his 'family' and their relations – varying in amounts from a few shillings to thousands of shillings. Frequently Laputa, Kibiriti, Sungura or someone else will turn up with a worried expression and the words, 'I must speak to you, Mzee Juu.' While writing his autobiography he rented Bhola's upper-storey room, where he could work without distraction and at the same time have a view of the street. 'I rent[ed] an office in Bhola's garage, overlooking the main street,' he said. 'That's why everybody here calls me Mzee Juu. It means "the old man, up there".'[48]

Until a few years ago, Thesiger lived with Lawi in the house they built together down in the valley, much nearer the town. Later, when Lawi married, he and his wife Lapipa – a Kikuyu – moved out into a new house next door which is now surrounded by huts for guests and servants and a colourful garden, laid out by Thesiger himself: 'I never had any particular interest [in gardening] until I moved here,' he commented while still at Lawi's. 'If Lawi was living in a *manyatta*, caked over with cowdung and ashes, that would be fine. But since he has a modern house, it seemed a pity not to improve on it and put in some bougainvillea. I know nothing about plants, I just fetch some from the forest, shove them in and hope they'll grow.'[49] The garden's prospect is now somewhat spoiled by the hulks of a rusted Land-Cruiser and a full-size bus perching on bricks, its paneless windows fixing the visitor like blind eye-sockets, and its rotting rump bearing the now faded legend, 'Samburu Express'.

Lawi's house is luxurious compared with Laputa's. It boasts wall-to-wall carpets, plush armchairs, a dining-table and a library of books mostly left by Thesiger. The sitting-room is decorated with framed photographs, expensive china, wall-hangings depicting shire horses, and a TV. Lawi, suave, bright and good-looking, is evidently a person of some note in the town. 'I suppose I am closer to Lawi than anyone, because I've been with him for more than twenty years,' Thesiger said, 'but now his house is always very busy and full of people and I get no personal attention. Here [in Laputa's house] it's a very personal sort of house – more intimate. Lawi's always saying I ought to go back and live there but I don't think I'd want to – too many people about whom I don't know.'[50] The dilapidated Samburu Express was another project which Thesiger sponsored. There is still no asphalt road between Maralal and the nearest town, Rumuruti, and on paper the plan looked a money-spinner. The bus ran for a while and went through eighteen spare tyres before it came mysteriously to a halt. Lawi claimed that the opposition – Kikuyu traders who dominate the town's commercial life – put sand in the petrol tank.

Lawi also opened the town's first wine-shop with Thesiger's reluctant backing, and the contact of one of his friends – an executive of Kenya Breweries. Like the Samburu Express, the shop flourished for a time but later went bust. Indeed, few of the projects Thesiger has sponsored for his sons at great cost have amounted to much, not because of dishonesty, but simply because his protégés do not have the business acumen required to make them work. Thesiger sees no conflict between his lifelong hatred for mechanical transport and supplying vehicles to his foster-sons: 'It's a world where you do have buses,' he said, 'it's practical. This way Lawi can make the money he needs. Kibiriti had a mini-bus and lorries too – all of which I paid for. He had his own transport company. If you're going to move at all and be anybody these are things you've got to do and one has to accept them. They're perfectly prepared to do it. *They* don't dislike buses and things and it's not for me to discourage them.'[51]

While encouraging his own small group of tribesmen to adapt to the modern world and to become educated, he continues to reject universal education for the traditional peoples: 'I think mass education is a disaster,' he said. 'As a result of it you've got a tremendous amount of unemployment. The ordinary boy living on the hill there, why take him away from his parents for nine months of the year . . . until he's lost all association with tribal life? In the old days he was a shepherd and lived a local life. Now none of them want to do this – their ambition is to go off to Nairobi and get a job. I know a man who has graduated from a university and is sweeping out lavatories. It's the only job he can find. When Kenya was British there was no unemployment. You grew up and automatically fitted into your life. If you were a Kikuyu you might manage to get a job as a clerk. The ones who wanted education got it.'[52] The emphasis here is upon the words 'ordinary boy', since Thesiger evidently does not consider his protégés run-of-the-mill. Of bodyguard Lopago, he said, 'It is really going to be to his advantage to stay on another year at school and get his certificates and things . . . I don't say they don't enjoy . . . the association with other boys. You can see that he works desperately hard . . . well, he'll get somewhere, but for every Lopago there are thirty boys who go to school when in the past they'd have been content to dress as a *moran* and take their cows to pasture. I'd like to see it as it was in the old days when the British were here. I think undoubtedly people were a lot happier.'[53]

Thesiger has lunch with one of his 'sons' or with Bhola, and afterwards listens to the news on the BBC. Later Kibiriti gives him a lift home, carrying a newspaper, a cabbage or perhaps a package of goat's meat. Once there, he hauls a decrepit armchair out of the kitchen and sits on the verandah, enjoying the magnificent view and chatting with his current guest as the sun sets in long rose-coloured streaks, and the forest sounds and bush noises slowly take over. Occasionally there is the distant cough of a leopard, or, very rarely now, the panting of elephants moving invisibly through the lugga below. While light remains Thesiger horseplays with the smaller boys, holding up his hand for them to box, or tickling the three-year-old 'Little Horror' until he erupts into peals of delighted laughter. 'The Little Horror is the first child I've ever seen grow up,' he commented, 'and it is interesting to see the way their minds develop. It's a very exceptional little child. I mean, most children of two and a half can't speak three languages. I don't say it's fluent in any of them but it can come in here in the morning and say, "How are you? I'm fine." It's [almost] fluent in Samburu and never stops talking.'[54]

The great objective of the evening is the making of the goat stew, for which Mini-Minor and Bushboy soon begin 'scraping' or dicing carrots and cabbages. They work in silence, and if Thesiger hears any undue giggling an immediate bellow of 'Shut up!' shatters the evening peace like a whipcord. 'Get on with that scraping!' he yells. 'Lepago! Make those boys shut up!' As the light begins to fade a single oil-lamp is lit. Despite the fact that several are available, Thesiger parsimoniously uses only one at a time, with a low wick, so that, as darkness falls, the kitchen becomes a pool of light above table-level with a lake of shadow beneath, in which the small boys and dogs crawl about almost invisible. Namitu prepares the meat. The boys set the stew on the charcoal cooker, and begin to fan. Thesiger, who has by now moved his tattered armchair inside, lays his spear against the wall next to him and grasps his slender stick. If one of the boys slows in his fanning efforts, the stick is raised threateningly: 'Fan, boy, fan! Or you'll be getting a taste of my persuader!' There are two armchairs in the kitchen, pressed close together, and if Thesiger has a guest they sit elbow to elbow in the half-darkness, while he holds forth about his pet subjects. Occasionally he gives the boys lectures on Eton – the fagging and the flogging, which have now, sadly, he says, been abolished. Mini-Minor, Bushboy and the others listen with fascinated attention, until Thesiger suddenly yells: 'Get on with that fanning, bloody boys!' The watchman, a frail-looking Samburu gentleman with silver stubble on his chin and impenetrable glasses, sits on a straight-backed chair, grasping a spear and a knobkerrie: he doesn't speak English, so the entire lecture – indeed the entire conversation – passes over his head. Namitu supervises the cooking and as the pot begins to simmer she sits down on the bed crammed into a corner, where 'Sandi' – 'the Little Horror' – and her baby daughter may be asleep. She reads the newspaper Thesiger has brought up from town, by the light of a torch.

Thesiger tolerates Namitu, a big, soft, bright woman, despite his lack of sympathy with women in general. One of the things that endeared him so greatly to the desert in the 1940s was that there were no women and children intruding: 'You arrived at their camps and you might spend one night there,' he related, 'perhaps once a year. The rest of the time we were on our own . . . On the whole I prefer to be sitting with the men and not have intrusive women. In the Marshes there was one dreadful old woman who was always intruding and taking charge. Her husband was dead and she had taken his place. She was dominant. I don't like dominant women on the whole. I prefer unobtrusive women. I think we are the male sex and we remain the male sex.'[55] He has little sympathy, either, with the Western women who become fascinated by the attractions of the Samburu *moran*: 'If you are a white man and you marry a Samburu woman it is perfectly reasonable,' he said, 'because the father is the dominant person. But if you are an English girl and you marry a Samburu *moran*, you've got no sort of standing. It's an idiotic thing to do.'[56]

The stew begins to simmer, and if the dogs venture too near the savoury-smelling pot, Thesiger's persuader cracks like lightning out of the shadows, sending them off with a yelp. Occasionally a size twelve commando-sole snaps out instead to deliver a crisp kick on a canine buttock. Thesiger's threats are mainly good-natured banter where the boys are concerned, but woe betide the dog or cat that sneaks in unspotted. At least one English guest has been slashed across the body inadvertently as he strove to get at one of his animals in near darkness. When the transistor radio is switched on for the BBC news, he demands absolute silence. If one of the boys so much as whispers there is a shout of 'Shut up!' from Thesiger, and the silence continues until the news is over and everyone can breathe again. The news bulletin may be followed by a pop music programme, which Lopago wants to listen to, only to be instructed: 'Turn that bloody rubbish off and get on with your homework!' by Thesiger. For him, pop music is not only 'noise', but a symbol of the uniformity of populist culture which he feels is destroying the world's diversity: 'One of the things I hate as much as anything is this modern music,' he declares, 'which for some reason seems to have a world-wide appeal. They're all carrying these cassette-players and they play it all the time, to the disappearance of their own traditional music. I have no sense of music – even Bach and Mozart is to me just a jangle of noise – but this pop music is appalling, and Michael Jackson is ghastly. If he came here I'd help to kick him down the street. Talk about the deterioriation of standards: when I was a boy you had people who were worth admiring. Now people flood across the countryside in thousands to go and listen to Michael Jackson or Boy George or the Bongo Man, or someone like that. Michael Jackson landed in Africa – Senegal I think it was – and immediately held his nose because of the stink. Well, if I'd have been there, I'd have kicked his bottom on the spot – he'd have taken his hand down pretty quickly! This represents a fall-off in standards – you base your standards on people you admire – and when it's Boy Jackson or Michael George [sic], I mean the standards have just reached absolute bottom.'

Thesiger claims to be 'tone deaf', though when he lived with Lawi he had a gramophone, and just one record – predictably, perhaps, 'Land of Hope and Glory' – which he played *ad nauseam* until the machine broke. He likes the rousing sound of the Scots bagpipes, and remembers with pleasure a state banquet in London in honour of the Sa'udi King, when ten pipers marched in wearing full Highland regalia. Invited to be the 'castaway' in Roy Plomley's *Desert Island Discs*, he chose as his records Fauré's *Requiem*, which he had heard only a few days previously, some bagpipe music, and a song he had heard while at Eton, 'The Death of Boris Goodenough'. 'The BBC had all these in their library,' he said. 'I wanted to find a good Turkana song; but maddeningly, the Turkana were the one African people whose songs they didn't have.'[57] Showing his preference for the spoken word, he also selected a rendering of T.S. Eliot's *The Waste Land*, which has always been his favourite poem: 'I have no time for Byron, Keats or Shelley,' he said. 'I get no pleasure from reading them. But Eliot, yes. Even when he's completely incomprehensible I can still enjoy his verse.'[58] Frank Steele recalled that on their journey to Turkana, Thesiger would constantly recite great wodges of poetry with many tum-ti-tums filling in the forgotten lines. Thesiger's greatest regret is that he is now unable to read. His favourite books are *Kim* and Conrad's *Lord Jim*, which he has read many times. Tolstoy's *War and Peace* was another favourite, and Susan Gellner recalled that in Morocco he had been reading George Eliot's *Middlemarch*, which, since it concerns the life of an

English village, seems an odd choice. Winston Churchill's *Life of Marlborough* is his favourite non-fiction book, though he admits to having been influenced by Alan Moorehead's *The Fatal Impact* – about the invasion of the Pacific and the destruction of native cultures, Rachel Carson's environmentalist classic *Silent Spring*, and Robert Ardrey's now somewhat discredited picture of human origins, *African Genesis*. He was enthralled by Tolkien's heroic *Lord of the Rings*, and among contemporary travel-books enjoyed Bruce Chatwin's *In Patagonia*, though he found the late Chatwin, with whom he once had dinner at his agent's house, 'the most talkative man I've ever met . . . He never stopped talking all the way through dinner. He was interesting but not fascinating.'[59] Not enamoured of American writers in general, he appreciated Peter Matthiesson's *The Snow Leopard*. In his London flat he has a valuable collection of rare books by African and Arabian hunters and explorers, some of which he has been obliged to sell recently to meet his expenses.

He has collected line drawings but has few paintings, feeling the plain simplicity of line far preferable to splashes of colour. In a world of change he finds literature the one thing that has remained the same: 'But look what's happened to art!' he commented. 'It's absolutely staggering. You go into the Tate Gallery and the first thing you see is a penis. There's a picture of a man standing there cut off at the waist, and there's just this penis. Well, there you are, and in the corner you see an old kettle and some boots and stuff like that laid out there, which you almost kicked out of the way – and that's art. And then you get people making things with bricks that any child could have done. Contrast this with Donatello's David or something – that's the sculpture I'd really have liked to acquire – and you'll see something's gone frightfully wrong with a civilization that can produce this rubbish. And then architecture: the whole appearance of England has been ruined by these high-rise buildings that are all deserted and they go and shove them right down by [Westminster] Abbey. Last time I was there I went to what used to be the docks and there had been some appalling stuff put up.'[60]

During his annual visits to London, Thesiger occasionally visits the cinema with one of his friends, and though by no means a film buff, he enjoyed *Death in Venice* – based on Thomas Mann's classic

– enough to see it twice. He was impressed with *The Kitchen Toto*, a story set in colonial Kenya, mainly because Lawi appeared in it in a walk-on part as a police sergeant. He occasionally watches wildlife films, yet mischievously declares that the best film he has seen is *Gone with the Wind*. He sometimes goes to the theatre while in London, and has watched TV when 'unable to avoid it'. 'Television is largely responsible for this spread of a completely phoney culture,' he commented, 'a sort of synthetic civilization . . . you can go off and make millions of pounds . . . by being a television personality, or by acting in a cowboy film – the "two gun man" who probably wouldn't have a clue what to do with a gun if it came to it. I like listening to the radio, which is not responsible to the same extent as TV, but not when people start telling funny jokes and there's this sort of false laughter, which absolutely maddens me!'[61] Indeed, Thesiger claims not to have any sense of humour at all: 'I always mistrust this thing about humour,' he said. 'Arabs are supposed to have a great sense of humour . . . but I don't think they've got any more sense of humour than I have – and I always think I have none.'[62] The distinguished author Geoffrey Moorhouse described Thesiger as being 'rather blank, with penetrating eyes that look as though they haven't seen much to laugh about'.[63] In his flat in Chelsea there is no TV, though he inherited an old box-shaped wireless from his mother to which he never listens. He was once taken to the opera by friends to celebrate his birthday, but snored most of the way through the performance. Thesiger sometimes appears rather down-at-heel in Maralal, but in London he reverts to Etonian elegance in expensive three-piece dark suits with pocket-handkerchief. Until they went out of fashion, he always sported a bowler hat and rolled umbrella: 'I'd never walk about in a turtle-necked sweater,' he said.

The conversation continues while the stew steams. Namitu reads the papers, the old watchman looks on through his thick lenses, uncomprehending, and the boys fan, hearing the words but without much idea of what Thesiger is talking about. He will sample the stew with a tablespoon, and his standards are exacting. He has been known, in moments of rage, to kick the entire pot over, shouting, 'That's not what I call a stew!' If it meets his approval, however, the pot is removed and the stew left to cool for exactly twenty minutes. Thesiger and his guest eat first, sitting close together, Thesiger in his armchair, the guest on a straight-backed chair at the small table pushed into a corner and bearing the oil-lamp. The others look on disconcertingly. Thesiger is invariably served with a chapatti, though his guest might receive a bowl of rice instead. Tomato ketchup stands on the table, and Thesiger maintains the myth that it is 'very strong' and allows his guest only the merest hint, making a long-drawn-out sucking sound of disapproval if he exceeds the approved amount. Because of his poor eyesight and the flickering of the lamp, soup frequently gets splashed on to the table and drips down on to his cavalry-twill trousers, forming a pool on the floor which a dog or cat immediately homes in to, or is smudged by the frayed cuff of his tweed jacket. After the soup comes the main course – always the same goat stew, served in a large dish and eaten off soup plates.

As dinner proceeds, the discourse continues. Thesiger often insists that he won't be returning to Britain any more, and lists things which he will miss: his friends, the Travellers' Club, dining at Magdalen College. Yet when the time comes around – usually in early summer – he always finds himself persuaded to make the proverbial 'last visit'. In London he is in constant demand for dinners, lunches and presentations, interviews with journalists, sessions with photographers, meetings with writers. Usually, Kibiriti or someone else drives him to Nairobi the day before his flight, and he stays in a small hotel called 'Plum's' or, more recently, with a friend there. These days he generally travels Club Class rather than the less comfortable Economy, and favours the Belgian airline Sabena. In the past his mother's help, Mollie Emtage – a daughter of the former Director of Education in Mauritius – looked after the flat in Tite Street while he was there, and returned to her family in Stratford-upon-Avon while he was away. She had been with Thesiger's family for almost forty years when she died in 1991 – only a day after Thesiger had arrived home – and was regarded as one of them. Shortly after she died he told Mike Griffin that he was wondering how on earth he would manage in London without her: 'I've never boiled an egg or made a cup of tea yet!'[64]

However, in the following years he learned to cope, opening a packet of soup or taking a slice of cheese for lunch, or more often dining at the Travellers' Club. Until his eyes failed he would spend much of the time in London reading. 'I'd sit in the flat and read,' he said, 'a good novel that had just come out or dip into some of my African books -- but as I grew older I lost the power of concentration to read Churchill or something.'[65] Despite Thesiger's remark, the real issue in London was never lack of service. He dreads the loneliness of his large empty flat. 'I've got plenty of English friends,' he said, 'but you know, you go to bed in an empty flat and wake up again in an empty flat and you think well, so-and-so said he'll come at eleven, and you look forward to that, and then perhaps you'll be going out to lunch with somebody else, but it's a different sort of atmosphere. Of course, people find it curious that I live in Maralal with these people. Let them . . . it's not a sexual relationship at all . . . If people want to think I'm sexually attracted to them, let them think it. It isn't true anyway. I mean I think they are attractive – just as bin Kabina and bin Ghabaisha were attractive – but it doesn't mean [anything physical]. I have Lopago sleeping on my bed, but at eighty-three you can't be said to have any sexual feeling anyway, especially when you've had your prostate out . . . It's a personal pull on the part of these people that draws me back. I like being with them. Otherwise what? . . . I mean go back to England and you might see somebody twice a week for lunch . . . you're not living with them . . . I like to have people around me all the time . . . I had it in the desert and I had it in the Marshes . . .'[66] Thesiger admits that when he was with bin Kabina and bin Ghabaisha in south Arabia he was never part of their family and never for a moment imagined that he could be a Bedui. 'But here in Kenya you can get closer to them in a funny way,' he added. 'I don't say they're all that worthwhile getting closer to, but still the life here satisfies me. I mean, if you don't belong to a family in England, you never can belong to it. They may call you Uncle Wilfred, but you're never going to be part of that family. You might be a great friend, but you're not part of the family. You haven't got their traditions, their background, their history. But out here you can be to some extent part of that family, because Africans will accept people into their families quite easily. But by being accepted nominally by Laputa's family or Kibiriti's family doesn't mean I cease to be British.' Thesiger admits that his attitude is patriarchal, but feels that this is in keeping with local culture, in which elders are respected. 'Being patriarchal wouldn't work in England,' he says. 'My attitude to these children is the attitude of the father of the family. I mean if they are told to do something, they damn well do it. In England they wouldn't want to ... I couldn't live the kind of life I live here [in England]. It may be that this is a substitute for having a real family but it is a very satisfactory substitute. Of course some things are irritating − [the dishonesty] − it didn't happen in the desert and it didn't happen in the Marshes. It does happen here, but as against that I enjoy being with them. I like them. I hope some of them will be better for my having been here.'[67]

In 1981 Thesiger took the unprecedented step of inviting Lawi to London, much to the initial disapproval of his housekeeper: 'She started by asking if I meant I was going to have a black staying in the house,' Thesiger recalled, 'and she sort of sniffed. Then when he went after six weeks she gave him a special tie and was very warm and said how much she liked him ... It was the obvious thing to do to invite him there. I thought it would very much expand his experience and it did. I mean all the people here, if you talked about London, they'd imagined a sort of enlarged Nairobi. He saw the Trooping the Colour and Beating the Retreat, and on the last one we had a very good seat with the Queen near by. He saw the ceremonial side of London and I took him to the Tower − all the things he ought to have seen. The knowledge gave him an idea of what Europe was really like and it was an experience that very few people here have had ... I took Lawi because he could pass himself off as someone who had been educated in England ... that wouldn't do for Kibiriti or Laputa. I took him to the Travellers' on almost the first day and I heard somebody say after lunch that he was obviously educated in England ... which school did he go to? Lawi told them he was at Baragoi Primary School ... I mean there he was in a dark suit and he'd settled in and looked absolutely right. We stayed with the Verneys and the Rumbolds and the Oakseys and it was there he met Elspeth Huxley and they got on very well. At the end he said he'd enjoyed it, but he thought it was about time he got back to Kenya − so he obviously hadn't felt he'd rather be there than Kenya.'[68]

Lawi's hectic life as mayor and his chain-smoking brought on a minor stroke at the age of only thirty-two, though having quickly recovered he resigned his mayorship – against Thesiger's advice – in order to put up for election as local MP, representing the President's KANU party in the January 1993 elections. Despite Thesiger's financial backing he failed to be nominated, but quickly fell into the role of local businessman, with plans to start up a casino in the town. More recently he was employed by a South African film company to recruit 100 Samburu *morans* and fly them *en masse* to South Africa for a film: a 'mixed-up world' indeed. When Thesiger first discovered Lawi at Baragoi school, the boy was already working in his spare time to make enough to pay his school-fees, much against the wishes of his parents, who saw no advantage in learning to read or write. 'Lawi today wouldn't be where he is except through the help I've given him,' Thesiger said. 'He would be somewhere, because he's a person of great personal drive and ability.'[69] 'I can't blame myself for anything that's happened in Maralal. The changes were already *en route*. Lawi and all the others are benefiting from my presence because they've got to adapt themselves to this new way of life ... tragically the future lies with towns and development ... I wouldn't accept any responsibility for the changes here. I've assisted a number of people on a path that was absolutely inevitable.'[70]

Thesiger was contented with British colonial rule in Kenya, but his lifelong resentment against the Americans for supplanting the civilization of his father's time with the Coca Cola synthetic culture has sharpened into a rabid opposition to American interference in Kenya's affairs. 'This country benefited enormously from British rule,' he said. 'The British Empire was the greatest empire there has ever been ... I certainly wouldn't say the world was better off without it.'[71] 'The Americans are a complete disaster and what with this constant interference ... how much do they know about Africa? Nothing! ... They've never had the experience. We've had thirty-two years of uninterrupted peace – apart from the Mau Mau near the end, and it would have gone on and evolved, but the moment you insist on multi-party it's a straight return to tribalism ... they've no right at all to say they're not going to give aid unless the country changes its policy. [The British] didn't interfere in this country, we just took it over and established peace and security . . . Here we had the model country in Africa and thirty years of uninterrupted peace except for the abortive air force coup, and then the massacre of the Somalis — they had to be massacred — it was the only way of dealing with them, otherwise they'd have taken over all northern Kenya. Kenyatta got rid of the British and Kenya as a whole accepted it, but it was purely a tribal administration and if you weren't a Kikuyu you hadn't got a hope. Moi then took over and the whole character of the thing changed — he calls himself a Kalenjin, but that's not a tribe in the same way that the Kikuyu is a tribe. He employed Kikuyu in the government, but it was no longer dominated by the Kikuyu. Then the Americans have got to come here and talk about democracy and multi-party and everything and that is idiotic: criminal folly. They say that they're not giving aid to Moi unless he changes his policy and introduces multi-party . . . they've got absolutely no right to cut off aid and make protests . . . The Americans have no tradition or understanding of Africa . . . They say the government is corrupt, but every single African leader, with the one exception of Haile Selassie — who was incorruptible personally but was surrounded by corrupt people — is corrupt. It's part of Africa . . . you have to accept the fact that there is corruption: we had ten years of uninterrupted peace and there was security and no oppression: the odd man got murdered perhaps . . . but again this thing that maddens me is human rights. Who the hell gave them the right to lay down the law?'[72]

I asked Thesiger, by the same token, who gave him the right to lay down the law in the Sudan. His answer revealed his partisanship: 'We were involved in Egypt,' he said, 'and the Egyptian administration was absolutely appalling . . . we introduced an absolutely model administration — the best administration the British have ever had. Better even than India. The Sudan Political Service was probably the finest service that any country has ever had.'[73] Of course, a vital aspect of this 'model administration' was its incorruptibility.

Certainly corruption would not in his day have been accepted as 'part of Africa' but as something unquestionably immoral, to be stamped out.

Thesiger's claim that democracy is unsuited to the African character may be true, but it is clear that his obsession with American interference in Kenya is born of the fear that democracy might well spell the end of his residence in Maralal: 'It infuriates me with the Americans interfering here,' he said. 'They may make all this sort of thing impossible. Things may get chaotic here and I don't know what one does. What does one do if things get bad? Go back to Britain and be bored, lonely and everything else there.'[74] His hatred for the Americans has led him to espouse views surprising for a self-avowed member of the British establishment. 'I was dead against the Gulf war, which was criminal folly,' he said. 'I mean, absolutely idiotic. Bush was pushing us into it and of course trying to turn it into a Falklands victory like Margaret Thatcher . . . Saddam Hussain's next move would have been Israel . . . supposing he'd managed to drag Israel into the war, it would have been the end. Saddam represents to an enormous part of the world somebody who's defied the Americans and got away with it, and I'm merely showing the extent to which the Americans are detested. To someone like Lawi, Saddam is a hero.'[75]

After Thesiger and his guest have eaten their fill – and it is *de rigueur* in the Thesiger household not to finish the stew – the stewpot is handed over to the others, to eat with doughy white spats of *posho* – the local porridge. Thesiger then proceeds to enjoy his own special treat. He lays his chapatti flat on the table, smears honey thickly on it, spreads it carefully with a clasp knife, then cuts it into sections, respreads the honey and eats with great relish. The honey drips incessantly down his chin, on to his jacket and trousers or back on to the table, from which he painstakingly scrapes it off and spreads it on the remaining portion of chapatti once again. The process seems to last for ages, and the guest watches spellbound as Thesiger spreads, cuts, munches, drips, scrapes and cuts again with terrible concentration. Only during this marathon does the conversation break down. When the chapatti is finished, and every available drop of honey scraped off the table, leaving only a sticky surface already under assault by flies, Thesiger puts away his pocket knife and orders tea. The teapot is placed on the table in front of him, and Thesiger, having brought a container of sugar from his locked room, doles it out personally cup by cup. Afterwards the cups are passed round and the talk winds up again against a background of constant banter between Thesiger and the others, sometimes punctuated by the occasional cuff if one of the smaller boys has tried to obtain more than his share of sugar.

Thesiger's life here in Maralal is certainly frugal, far more so than that of his principal 'foster-sons', yet his pride in the distinction it has conferred on him – in a sense a kind of continuing day-to-day adventure – belongs to the same order as that he has enjoyed in being the first Westerner, or one of the few, to visit certain areas. 'I live an unconventional life here,' he commented. 'There is no other Englishman in Kenya who lives like this. When I'm here I'm doing as they do and accepted by them and everything. It gives me pleasure to be accepted ... I have many friends in England, but it would never be possible to become part of their family. I don't think it's possible with English people.' Though Thesiger has frequently stressed his admiration for the British, it is clear that his view of what being British means is fairly restricted: 'Thesiger has been able to perpetuate in his life an old-fashioned secure male-dominated world of public school and Oxbridge, Pall Mall club and comfortable central London flat,' wrote Peter Clark. 'His world is remote from other Englands with their state schools, housing estates, holiday camps, daily commuting and dole queues.'[76]

'I know almost nothing about the working class,' Thesiger commented, 'but when I worked on the trawler and the tramp-steamer I got on with them very well. What I admire about Britain is what it achieved with its Empire, which was absolutely first class. I wouldn't call the British noble as a race, though. It's true that the harder the life the finer the person, but that doesn't apply among the British where things like family background and upbringing come in.'[77]

Thesiger may find acceptance easier among the Africans, but the price has not been cheap: in fact his spartan, parsimonious years in Maralal have been the most expensive project of his life. 'I've needed enough money to keep going, but I've wasted most of it here,' he said. 'What are you to do? I've got a limited time left and I may as well use it. I suppose I have given them hundreds of thousands of pounds. I don't regret it unless I feel it has gone on something that has achieved nothing – not if it has helped them. Of course they are exploiting me – I'm well aware of that. But then if one suffered in consequence it would be worse than being exploited ... On the other hand if money [comes too easily to them] it can in some cases wreck their lives. They obviously have exploited me. I've no idea if there's real affection for me. I think some of them feel it. I mean, it's a thing you never will know even with other English people.'[78]

Frank Steele was alarmed at the rate at which Thesiger was doling out money to his protégés. 'It is part of Samburu culture that if a man is rich it's his duty to give away money,' Steele said, 'and if he doesn't he's something of a social outcast, so they are accustomed to asking rich people for money. Wilfred felt that because they'd all joined him as young lads and he'd brought them up and helped them to become educated and built houses for them, he was more in the relationship of a father than a European to be exploited. I think in some cases it's true and in others, though the Samburu would like it to be true, they can't stop themselves trying to get money out of him.'[79] In the end Thesiger's generosity has not done these families much of a service, since he has merely habituated them to a standard of living which they will not be able to sustain after his death. He has picked up about thirty people from the Samburu-Turkana, Steele said, and given them an affluent way of life far above the rest. 'I went again this year,' he commented, 'and the situation was worse: they were obviously lying to him, saying they'd got a sick aunt in Wamba, please let them have 2,000 shillings and then it turned out there was no sick aunt in Wamba, and they wanted the money just to waste in Maralal. But much bigger sums have been obtained from Wilfred for what was probably a genuine purpose, but they were just not capable of succeeding ... I pointed out to Wilfred that at this rate he would be bankrupt in a few years' time, and when the money ran out I'd be very doubtful if they would look after him. I said, "If you're not careful the 'Last of the Great Explorers' who is lionized in England is going to end up as a poor white in Maralal cadging beds and meals off such people as will help him."'[80]

CHAPTER 17

The Last Explorer

Wilfred Thesiger is the classic adventurer of the twentieth century. From childhood, he set out to define his life by action, and succeeded like few others of this age. 'What has driven me, I suppose, is a desire for adventure,' he said. 'Also the things that have been so much driven out of people's lives in England today. It is this [lack of adventure] which is at the back of all the rowdiness that goes on – boredom with the conventions and the comfortable life, a desire to get some excitement. I've managed to get it with the way I've lived. A lot of people long to do it and never get the opportunity. Or they feel that they can't afford it or can't risk it. I've been prepared to take the risks and go off and do it.'[1]

There are many definitions of adventure. Thesiger's necessarily involved as far as possible unexplored landscapes and the companionship of local, preferably unadministered, peoples. In Thesiger adventure and the preservation of traditional societies were inextricably linked. Without unspoiled peoples in little-known places there would no longer be any scope for him: 'Thank God I'm not eighteen today,' he said. 'I wouldn't know what to do with myself. Nothing would have any interest for me. An Antarctic expedition would have been completely meaningless – penguins wouldn't suffice ... Now they're flying off to Mars, well, what the hell is the point of that? They say it's increasing knowledge. For what purpose? None! Then you have the Americans tramping around on the moon – the whole thing is folly! I heard from a naked fisherman on the shores of Lake Rudolf that men had landed on the moon. Some missionary or other told me it was true and said, "What an achievement!" and I thought it was the ultimate desecration ... I hate the whole damn thing. The essential thing about the Empty Quarter and all these other places was that they were the setting for the people who lived there: the people in that hard, harsh, setting.'[2]

Since his youth Thesiger had cast himself in the role of tragic hero, looking back to the Victorian–Edwardian era as a golden age: 'I craved the past, resented the present and dreaded the future,' he wrote in 1959. He told Mark Cocker that he would like to have been born in 1846, yet it is interesting to note that Richard Burton, who was born roughly when Thesiger claimed he would like to have been, himself wished to have lived in the medieval period. Burton looked back on the Middle Ages as a heroic time of swordsmen, before firearms and gunpowder 'spoiled everything'. Clearly the 'golden age' concept is a facet of the romantic personality. It is part of Thesiger's backward-looking, tragic persona that he should be concerned with 'last' things. The 'last explorer in the tradition of the past' is the role he has, in a sense, groomed himself for from childhood: for to be the last is to be unique.

The evolution of this idea is uncertain: it surfaced in print only in Thesiger's autobiography in 1988, and there is no mention of it in earlier pieces. It may have begun with John Glubb's review of *Arabian Sands* in the *Sunday Times*: 'Wilfred Thesiger is perhaps the last, and certainly one of the greatest, of the British travellers among the Arabs . . .' In his remark Glubb does not mention the word explorer, and though he is equivocal about the word 'last', he is more certain over the epithet 'greatest'. Interestingly, Thesiger shunned the idea of being 'the greatest explorer': 'I always think all the fuss and talk [about being the greatest explorer] is extraordinary,' he said, 'and if they knew me better they wouldn't say it . . . But I do contend that I was the last person with the opportunity to [be an explorer] . . . I was the last one to go off and find an area where the population hadn't been explored – in Danakil country – and one could go and travel as they travelled and live as they lived. Well, now they go off to the Amazon and they're looking at the Indians there and they're justifiably interested in what happens to them, but I feel they should have abolished the Royal Geographical Society's Gold Medal twenty years ago and had a scientific medal instead. I mean, people go off to the South Pole using motor transport and then one of them has to go to a garden party at Buckingham Palace and they come in an aeroplane and fly him out!'[3]

When I asked whether he thought there was any other living explorer or traveller of the same calibre as himself, he said: 'Perhaps Wally Herbert or someone, but I'm really not qualified to say . . .' Probably the greatest living polar explorer, Herbert covered more than 40,000 miles in polar regions with dogs and open boats, much of it previously unsurveyed. His most notable feat was the first crossing of the Arctic Ocean on foot, a distance of 3,800 miles. 'What Herbert did was a great test of endurance, but you couldn't justify it by saying it was the only way one could do it,' Thesiger said. 'Other means were available to him and he rejected them in favour of dogs. It was a personal choice. Where I was so lucky is that there was no question of personal choice. I had to go with the Bedu by camel, and dress like them. I know nothing about the Poles but if I had started with the Eskimos or something it might have been different. There again, their kayaks are fitted with motors now and they have these skidoos and are visited by tourists. You can even go on a package tour to Everest base-camp, where there's a hotel run by the Japanese. That's what the world has come to – that's it, and by the Grace of God I'm on my way out of it!'[4]

Thesiger maintains that he feels no sense of competition with other travellers. 'I don't compete with anybody,' he said, 'but if you take somebody like Sir Ranulph Fiennes, he's not really an explorer in the tradition of the past, with aeroplanes, boats and all this trotting around the globe. I resent being labelled as the same thing. I do stand by the fact that I was the last explorer in the tradition of the past. I was the last one who went with tribes who had had no contact with the West and lived as one of them, the way Livingstone and Thompson did it. If you go off in machines it's not the tradition of the past. Since my time there have been no explorers at all in the tradition of the past. I was the last. Wally Herbert wasn't in the tradition of the past because he could perfectly well have used machines.'[5]

How justified is Thesiger's contention that he is the last explorer? To consider this question I wrote to some prominent contemporary 'explorers', several of whom were themselves winners of the RGS Gold Medal over the past twenty years. I asked them if they believed exploration was finished. Not surprisingly, perhaps, many of the answers I received were haltingly ambivalent. Of those which were not, Sir David Attenborough, wrote: 'There are many kinds of exploration: zoological, geological, botanical – even psychological. But terrestrial exploration itself is, I fear, largely finished.'[6] Dr John Hemming, current Director of the RGS, wrote: 'The past twenty years have been the golden age of exploration in the sense that more information about the planet has been gathered in that time than in any other. But the true explorers of today are scientists, not those individuals who make the newspaper headlines.'[7] A third Gold Medal winner, Tim Severin, wrote: 'In the final analysis I don't think you can speak of anyone being "the last explorer" any more than in most cases you can speak of someone being "the first explorer". Half the time the "first explorer" was only the person who first publicized his achievement.'[8] The distinguished explorer Christina Dodwell opined: 'There are a few idiot modern explorers pretending it's still the time of the Raj. That's inappropriate now. You take what was learned and use it as a springboard to reach a new understanding about our world. ["Exploration"] is always changing to meet [new] requirements. Modern people have a different social conscience and awareness. The world is rapidly changing and I hope that exploration will continue fluidly changing to keep pace.'[9] Perhaps the most clear-cut reply, however, came from the man whose achievements Thesiger acknowledged as being on a par with his own – Wally Herbert: 'The problem for Wilfred in his attitude towards such titles as "last of the great explorers" is that he believes he is *the* one. Any . . . reading of history will show that there is no such person – that in the transition from one period of history to another there are always many "shades" to consider . . . history is a record of human endeavour in which we all play a part, and the last man to ride a camel or drive a dog team is no "better" than the first man to fly a mission to the Moon . . . And what about all those who do *not* seek publicity – the unsung heroes: the true desert travellers, the true polar travellers! You see what I mean?'[10]

The question comes down, in the end, to the proper definition of exploration. According to the *Concise Oxford Dictionary*, to explore is 'to travel extensively through [a country, etc.] in order to learn or discover about it; to inquire into, investigate thoroughly'. By such a definition, Thesiger is not 'the last explorer'. Frank Steele, however, posited a more popular definition: 'Traditionally being an explorer meant going where no one had gone before but the natives,' he said. 'In that sense it could be said that Wilfred was the last of the great explorers in that there is nothing left to explore and we've got satellite photography anyway . . . if you consider exploration to be scientific exploration, then Wilfred is not the last of the great explorers. But in what is popularly and perhaps romantically thought of as exploration, he is.'[11] Thesiger has benefited from the mass media he so despised to achieve almost megastar status in a way his predecessors in Arabia, Philby and Thomas, who both died before the great age of the media, would never have dreamed possible. Although Thesiger himself is always quick to remind others that he was not the first man to cross the Empty Quarter, media hype as well as his superb writing and brilliant photography have ensured that his name has eclipsed those of his predecessors. Who now remembers the name of Bertram Thomas, the first European to cross the Empty Quarter, a decade and a half before Thesiger set out? A children's geography book by a very reputable publisher, pulled at random from a shelf in a public library, reads: 'The desolate Arabian desert [was] first crossed by Wilfred Thesiger in 1946'! 'The last explorer' is a wonderful phrase for blurb-writers and journalists and a satisfyingly unique epitaph for one who has spent much of his life looking back into the past: yet Thesiger can obviously be the last explorer only when the term is qualified and specifically defined. As one of my correspondents suggested, the definition of exploration changes continuously. Thesiger is undoubtedly the last of an era, but it is unlikely, while humans exist, that exploration will cease.

Yet there will never be another Wilfred Thesiger, that is certain. Like Haile Selassie, Thesiger belongs to an epoch which is done: the colonial, Imperial epoch when Europe stood at the crest of world power. That time created a special relationship between Britain, the first industrial power, and the traditional peoples of the pre-industrial lands. To assume that relationship now, as Dodwell suggested, is no longer appropriate. In a single lifetime Thesiger saw an entire world collapse and die. Within our own lifetimes, perhaps, the West itself will cease to be the centre of world civilization, which it has been for the past 500 years. We ourselves may be 'next on the list'.

This sense of decline, is, I believe, the essence of the Thesiger story, intensified in the personality of an extreme romantic. Yet Thesiger was to pay the ultimate price for his romantic idealization of traditional life. He lived by impulse and intuition rather than analytic rationale, and as Horace Walpole said, 'The world is a comedy for those who think and a tragedy for those who feel.' To Thesiger life was never a comedy. The philosopher Babbit wrote: 'No movement has been so prolific of melancholy as emotional romanticism. When the romanticist discovers that his ideal of happiness works out to actual unhappiness, he does not blame his ideal. He simply assumes the world is unworthy of a being so exquisitely organized as himself.'[12]

In old age, despite having become internationally famous, having won almost every available British medal for his journeys, numerous honorary doctorates, and a CBE, Thesiger developed a deep disillusionment with mankind that was perhaps the inevitable outcome of his romantic perspective, and his veneration for the past. 'We were having lunch at Lawi's house,' Frank Steele commented, 'and Wilfred was going on with this great dirge against the modern world, education, technology, medicine and so on, and I said, Wilfred, you must try to stop being so pessimistic. You really must try to cultivate a cheerful mind, as Dr Johnson, or somebody, said. Lawi and Kibiriti joined in and said yes, yes, stop being so miserable all the time. And Wilfred said, "Everything *is* miserable. There's nothing to be cheerful about. Everything is wrong. Everything is going to the dogs." '[13]

As early as 1970, Thesiger said, 'We are dinosaurs – the last of a dying race,' and predicted there would be few humans left in twenty or at the most fifty years. Twenty-odd years later, he was still hammering out the same tune: 'There *can* be no future,' he said. 'It's inconceivable that there could be any human beings on this planet in 100 years' time ... Not only transport but the interference with nature, you've got pollution and the threat to the ozone belt which will mean the heating up of the earth and the melting of the Poles and half the world going under water.'[14] Few will maintain that there is nothing in Thesiger's fears: there is much that is current and pertinent in his view. But after a lifetime of tramping about the earth's most beautiful and inaccessible places, he offers no solution to the world's problems but a return to the past. Thesiger believed that *Arabian Sands* was a tribute to what human beings could do *if they were left alone*. But, of course, no one is ever left alone. There is, I believe, a further lesson to be learned from the lives of the Bedu in *Arabian Sands*: that even under the hardest possible conditions, hunger, thirst, fatigue, heat, cold – even change – the human spirit can survive.

I left Wilfred Thesiger sitting on the verandah of his house on the hill, waiting for the sunset as the last sparklers of light scintillated across the flowing hills. We had been discussing his views on the future: 'A hundred years ago there were no cars,' he had said. 'Well, in a hundred years' time what are we going to have? It won't be long before all the Chinese are demanding cars – you can't put all that pollution into the air and get away with it . . . I don't think development can be checked and that's why I think we're heading for disaster – it's just a matter of guessing whether it's fifty years or 100 years. I see absolutely no hope for the human species.'[15] As we pulled out of the yard I turned for a last glimpse of the great explorer. He had already forgotten me, it seemed, immersed in his thoughts, in the ocean of memories that are more real for him than the present. Despite the despondency of old age, his has been a courageous, heroic life. I suppose I will always remember him like this, the old man with the face carved out of a mountain, forever dreaming and gazing out at the endless sky of Africa – vaster than any sky on earth.

A NOTE ON SOURCES

Much of this text is based on conversations with Wilfred Thesiger which took place in Maralal, Kenya, between September 1992 and February 1993. These conversations varied from informal discussions over lunch, to recorded sessions. A few conversations were taken down in note form either at the time or subsequently: the vast majority were tape recorded. The taped material was transcribed and the quotes edited for style, order, repetition and grammar. Some quotes concerning the same subject have been run together, but great care was taken never to alter the essential content or meaning of the material. Where quotes have been run together, the separate dates have been referred to in the notes. Where quotes were taken from non tape recorded material, the references have been marked 'unrecorded'. The unedited tapes made of these conversations have been deposited in the archives of the Royal Geographical Society and are available for other scholars.

A further block of material derives from conversations with Thesiger's surviving Bedouin companions, mostly made in Oman and the United Arab Emirates between 1991 and 1993. About 70 per cent of these conversations were tape recorded. The rest were taken down in note form. The taped conversations were translated by myself and transcribed. I am deeply grateful to Al Muhandis Muhammad bin Sa'id al Mashali for his help in translating many of these tapes.

Other material derives from conversations with friends and colleagues of Wilfred Thesiger, almost all of which were tape recorded and transcribed. I much appreciate the help of those who agreed to be interviewed, and I have listed their names separately. A number of individuals who were unavailable for interview kindly answered my queries by letter: I am also indebted to them, and again have listed their names separately. The remaining material was taken from documentary sources as outlined in the Notes and Bibliography.

NOTES

ABBREVIATIONS

JRGS: The Geographical Journal (Journal of the Royal Geographical Society)
SNR: Sudan Notes and Records
JRCAS: The Journal of the Royal Central Asian Society

Prologue: The Old Man Up There

1. Wilfred Thesiger, *Arabian Sands*, London, 1959.
2. ibid., p.xiii.
3. ibid., p.154.

Chapter 1: The Immense Cultural Baggage He Carried to Arabia

1. Wilfred Thesiger, *Arabian Sands*, London, 1959, Prologue.
2. ibid.
3. Maxime Rodinson, *Mohammed*, Paris, 1961; trans. Anne Carter, 1971, p.17.
4. James Morris, *Farewell the Trumpets. An Imperial Retreat*, London, 1978.
5. See Kathryn Tidrick, *Heart-Beguiling Araby*, Cambridge, 1981.
6. For the 'Orient' as Western creation, see Edward Sa'id, *Orientalism*, London, 1978
7. Peter Brent, *Far Arabia: Explorers of the Myth*, London, 1977.
8. Salim bin Ghabaisha in conversation with the author, 6 March 1991.

Chapter 2: A Clue to the Perverse Necessity Which Drives Me to the East

1. I am indebted in this description to Richard Pankhurst, *History of Ethiopian Towns from Mid 19th Century to 1935*, Stuttgart, 1985, pp.209ff.
2. Wilfred Thesiger in conversation with the author, 29 November 1992.
3. Thesiger has often, incorrectly, been called an 'Edwardian explorer', though Edward VII died a month before he was born. The classic Edwardian explorers are Shackleton and Scott, who belong to an earlier generation.

4. Wilfred Thesiger in conversation with the author, 28 November 1992.

5. Philip Mason, *The English Gentleman: The Rise and Fall of an Ideal*, London, 1982, p.219.

6. Wilfred Thesiger in conversation with the author, 18/19 February 1993.

7. Philip Mason, *The English Gentleman*, p.226.

8. Philip Mason, *The English Gentleman*, p.219.

9. Wilfred Thesiger in conversation with the author, 28 November 1992.

10. Wilfred Thesiger in conversation with the author, 19 December 1992.

11. Wilfred Thesiger in conversation with the author, 7 November 1992/ 19 February 1993.

12. Mike Griffin, 'A Life in the Day of Wilfred Thesiger', *Sunday Times*, 1985: 'All change is ultimately for the worse. Look what happened in Abyssinia: I wouldn't set foot in it again. I did go back to Arabia eight years ago and it was the most disillusioning thing I've ever done.'

13. Wilfred Thesiger in conversation with the author, 18 February 1993.

14. Wilfred Thesiger in conversation with the author, 19 February 1993.

15. Wilfred Thesiger in conversation with the author, 28 November 1992.

16. Wilfred Thesiger in conversation with the author, 19 February 1993.

17. Wilfred Thesiger in conversation with the author, 6 December 1992.

18. Frank Steele in conversation with the author, 7 January 1993.

19. Wilfred Thesiger in conversation with the author, 28 November 1992.

20. ibid.

21. ibid.

22. Wilfred Thesiger in conversation with the author, 19 February 1993.

23. Reginald Dingwall in conversation with the author, 12 May 1993.

24. Wilfred Thesiger in conversation with the author, 28 January 1993.

25. Alexander Maitland, 'Traveller from an Antique Land', *Blackwood's Magazine*, October 1980, p.245.

26. Wilfred Thesiger in conversation with the author, 28 January 1993.

27. Wilfred Thesiger in conversation with the author, 30 November 1992. This view of Lij Yasu is controversial: Menelik II had extended the Abyssinian Empire far beyond its traditional bounds on the Amhara plateau, to include millions of Muslim and Galla subjects who now virtually outnumbered the Christian Amharas. Menelik had probably chosen Lij Yasu as successor because, as the scion of a powerful provincial family, recently converted from Islam to Christianity, he might exert influence among these new subjects and keep the Empire together. Lij Yasu's power-base thus lay outside the highlands, and most historians conclude that he 'flirted' with Islam as a political move, in order to bring the Muslims and Gallas into line. The Zauditu–Ras Tafari coup is considered a counter-attack by the

traditional Shoan establishment against the parvenu Negus Mikael–Lij Yasu line. See, for example, John Marratis, *Ethiopia: Anatomy of a Traditional Polity*, Oxford, 1974.

28. Leonard Mosley, *Haile Selassie*, London, 1964, p.73.

29. Wilfred Thesiger in conversation with the author, 6 December 1992.

30. Leonard Mosley, *Haile Selassie*, p.52.

31. Wilfred Thesiger in conversation with the author, 6 December 1992.

32. Mark Cocker in conversation with the author, 21 May 1993.

33. Wilfred Thesiger in conversation with the author, 6 December 1992.

34. ibid.

35. Leonard Mosley, *Haile Selassie*, p.90.

36. Wilfred Thesiger in conversation with the author, 6 December 1992.

37. ibid.

38. Actually, many of the Wollo rifles were loaded with dud ammunition: Fituari Habta Giorgis, commander of the Shoan army which had faced Negus Mikael while waiting for Ras Tafari's reinforcements, had pretended friendship to Mikael and Lij Yasu, his treachery being one of the reasons the Emperor's forces had failed to march on Addis Ababa. To cement this 'friendship' he sent the Negus a mule-caravan of ammunition which had been deliberately spiked. This intrigue played a major part in the Shoan victory: see, for example, Leonard Mosley, *Haile Selassie*.

39. Wilfred Thesiger in conversation with the author, 6 December 1992.

40. ibid. Thesiger elsewhere substitutes variously 'lion-skin' and 'sheepskin'.

41. Wilfred Thesiger, *Arabian Sands*, London, 1959, p.19.

42. Wilfred Thesiger in conversation with the author, 6 December 1992.

43. Leonard Mosley, *Haile Selassie*, p.114.

44. Wilfred Thesiger in conversation with the author, 2 December 1992.

45. ibid.

46. ibid.

47. ibid.

48. ibid.

49. ibid.

50. ibid.

51. Kathryn Tidrick, *Heart-Beguiling Araby*, Cambridge, 1981, p.200: 'Wilfred Thesiger was a man who turned his back on civilization in a way which would have been inconceivable to Richard Burton, or Wilfrid Blunt; but then the civilization he was renouncing was rather different from theirs.' It is clear from Thesiger's remarks (see p.374) that he never 'renounced' his place in the establishment: indeed, he maintained that he liked to keep the two worlds distinct.

52. Wilfred Thesiger in conversation with the author, 2 December 1992.

53. Wilfred Thesiger in conversation with the author, 18 February 1993.
54. Wilfred Thesiger in conversation with the author, 3 November 1992.
55. ibid.
56. ibid.
57. ibid.
58. Wilfred Thesiger, *Arabian Sands*, p.18
59. Wilfred Thesiger in conversation with the author, 7 December 1992.

Chapter 3: The Emperor's Guest

1. Wilfred Thesiger in conversation with the author, 6 December 1992.
2. Wilfred Thesiger, *Desert, Marsh and Mountain*, London, 1979, p.21.
3. Wilfred Thesiger in conversation with the author, 6 December 1992.
4. ibid.
5. ibid.
6. Wilfred Thesiger, *Arabian Sands*, London, 1959, p.18.
7. Wilfred Thesiger in conversation with the author, 19 February 1993.
8. Timothy Green, *The Restless Spirit*, London, 1970, p.65.
9. Wilfred Thesiger, *Arabian Sands*, p.142.
10. Mark Cocker in conversation with the author, 21 May 1993.
11. Wilfred Thesiger in conversation with the author, 18 February 1993.
12. Mark Cocker in conversation with the author, 21 May 1993.
13. Wilfred Thesiger, *The Life of My Choice*, London, 1987, p.399.
14. William Manchester, *The Last Lion: Winston Spencer Churchill: Visions of Glory 1874–1932*, London, 1983, p.157.
15. Wilfred Thesiger in conversation with the author, 18 February 1993.
16. ibid.
17. Peter Clark, *Thesiger's Return*, Abu Dhabi, 1992, p.28.
18. Wilfred Thesiger in conversation with the author, 16 December 1992.
19. ibid.
20. ibid.
21. ibid.
22. ibid.
23. Alexander Maitland, 'Traveller from an Antique Land', *Blackwood's Magazine*, October 1982, p.246.
24. Wilfred Thesiger in conversation with the author, 16 December 1992.
25. ibid.
26. Philip Mason, *The English Gentleman: The Rise and Fall of an Ideal*, London, 1984, p.170.
27. Wilfred Thesiger in conversation with the author, 16 December 1992.
28. Wilfred Thesiger, *The Life of My Choice*, p.72.
29. Wilfred Thesiger in conversation with the author, 16 December 1992.

30. ibid.
31. Jeremy Paxman, *Friends in High Places: Who Runs Britain?*, London, 1991, p.125.
32. Wilfred Thesiger in conversation with the author, 16 December 1992.
33. ibid.
34. ibid.
35. Ernest Gellner in a letter to the author, 9 January 1993.
36. ibid.
37. Wilfred Thesiger in conversation with the author, 16 December 1992.
38. Wilfred Thesiger, *The Life of My Choice*, p.79.
39. ibid., p.71.
40. Alexander Maitland, 'Traveller from an Antique Land', p.247.
41. Wilfred Thesiger in conversation with the author, 19 February 1993.
42. Timothy Green, *The Restless Spirit*, p.65.
43. Wilfred Thesiger in conversation with the author, 19 February 1993.
44. Wilfred Thesiger in conversation with the author, 18 February 1993.
45. Wilfred Thesiger in conversation with the author, 7 December 1992.
46. Wilfred Thesiger in conversation with the author, 6 December 1992.
47. ibid.
48. ibid.
49. Ernest Gellner in a letter to the author, 9 January 1993.
50. Alexander Maitland in conversation with the author, undated.
51. Wilfred Thesiger in conversation with the author, 6 December 1992.
52. ibid.
53. ibid.
54. ibid.
55. ibid.
56. Anthony Boyle, *The Climate of Treason*, London, 1979, p.138.
57. Wilfred Thesiger in conversation with the author, 29 November/ 6 December 1992.
58. Wilfred Thesiger in conversation with the author, 29 November 1992.
59. Wilfred Thesiger in conversation with the author, 27 December 1992.
60. ibid.
61. Wilfred Thesiger, *The Life of My Choice*, p.98.
62. Wilfred Thesiger in conversation with the author, 6 December 1992.
63. Wilfred Thesiger in conversation with the author, 9 February 1993.
64. Wilfred Thesiger in conversation with the author, 27 December 1992.
65. ibid.
66. ibid.
67. Wilfred Thesiger in conversation with the author, 30 November 1992.
68. Wilfred Thesiger in conversation with the author, 18 February 1993.
69. Wilfred Thesiger, *The Life of My Choice*, p.91.
70. Evelyn Waugh, *Remote People*, London, 1931, p.43.

71. Evelyn Waugh, *Waugh in Abyssinia*, London, 1936, p.15.
72. Evelyn Waugh, *Remote People*, p.45.
73. ibid., p.41.
74. Wilfred Thesiger, *The Life of My Choice*, p.61.
75. Evelyn Waugh, *Remote People*, p.23.
76. Wilfred Thesiger in conversation with the author, 6 December 1992/ 19 February 1993.
77. Wilfred Thesiger in conversation with the author, 6 December 1992.
78. ibid.
79. Wilfred Thesiger in conversation with the author, 19 February 1993.
80. Wilfred Thesiger in conversation with the author, 6 December 1992.
81. Wilfred Thesiger in conversation with the author, 27 November 1992.
82. ibid.
83. Wilfred Thesiger in conversation with the author, 6 December 1992.
84. Evelyn Waugh, *Waugh in Abyssinia*, p.13.
85. Wilfred Thesiger in conversation with the author, 27 November 1992.
86. Wilfred Thesiger in conversation with the author, 6 December 1992.
87. Timothy Green, *The Restless Spirit*, p.65.
88. Wilfred Thesiger in conversation with the author, 6 December 1992.

Chapter 4: One Merely Assumed One Would Be Successful and As It Turned Out One Was

1. Wilfred Thesiger in conversation with the author, 19 February 1993.
2. ibid.
3. Wilfred Thesiger in conversation with the author, 27 November 1992.
4. Wilfred Thesiger, *Arabian Sands*, London, 1959, p.22.
5. Timothy Green, *The Restless Spirit*, London, 1970, p.65.
6. Wilfred Thesiger in conversation with the author, 27 November 1992.
7. ibid.
8. ibid.
9. ibid.
10. Wilfred Thesiger, *The Life of My Choice*, London, 1987, p.116.
11. ibid.
12. Frank Steele in conversation with the author, 19 May 1993.
13. Wilfred Thesiger in conversation with the author, 27 November 1992.
14. Wilfred Thesiger, *The Times*, 31 July 1934, p.16.
15. Wilfred Thesiger in conversation with the author, 27 November 1992.
16. ibid.
17. Wilfred Thesiger, *The Life of My Choice*, p.135.
18. Wilfred Thesiger, 'The Awash River and the Aussa Sultanate', *JRGS*, January 1935.
19. Wilfred Thesiger, *The Life of My Choice*, p.122.

20. Wilfred Thesiger in conversation with the author, 18 February 1993.
21. ibid.
22. Timothy Green, *The Restless Spirit*, p.75.
23. Byron Farwell, *Burton*, London, 1963, pp.1-2.
24. ibid.
25. Timothy Green, *The Restless Spirit*, p.75.
26. Wilfred Thesiger, *The Times*, 2 August 1934, p.11.
27. ibid.
28. ibid.
29. ibid., pp.11–12
30. ibid., p.12
31. ibid.
32. L.M. Nesbitt, *Desert and Forest*, London, 1934, p.282.
33. Wilfred Thesiger in conversation with the author, 27 November 1992.
34. Things were little changed in Aussa in 1991. When I arrived in Aseita and asked the Chief of Police for permission to travel to Lake Abbé, he first denied there was any such lake, then sent one of his men to show me Lake Adobad (now called Gammarre) in an attempt to convince me that it was Abbé.
35. For 'two lakes' see *The Times*, 2 August 1934. Elsewhere Thesiger refers to 'three lakes'.
36. Wilfred Thesiger, *The Life of My Choice*, p.154.
37. ibid.
38. Wilfred Thesiger, *Arabian Sands*, p.278.
39. Wilfred Thesiger, *The Life of My Choice*, p.164.
40. Wilfred Thesiger in conversation with the author, 7 December/28 November 1992.
41. De Monfreid, Henri, *Secrets of the Red Sea*, trans. H. Buchanan-Bell, London, 1934, p.1.
42. Wilfred Thesiger in conversation with the author, 7 December 1992.
43. ibid.

Chapter 5: Blacks Ruled by Blues

1. Wilfred Thesiger in conversation with the author, 28 November 1992.
2. ibid.
3. ibid.
4. ibid.
5. ibid.
6. Reginald Dingwall in conversation with the author, 12 May 1993.
7. Michael Daly, *Imperial Sudan: The Anglo-Egyptian Condominium*, London, 1991, p.13.
8. Reginald Dingwall in conversation with the author, 12 May 1993.

9. Wilfred Thesiger in conversation with the author, 28 November 1992.
10. ibid.
11. Wilfred Thesiger, 'The Awash River and the Aussa Sultanate', *JRGS*, January 1935.
12. Rosemary Kenrick, *Sudan Tales*, London, 1987, p.172.
13. Wilfred Thesiger, *The Life of My Choice*, London, 1987, p.172.
14. Wilfred Thesiger in conversation with the author, 28 November 1992.
15. Thesiger in *The Life of My Choice* has *Dupuis*. Elsewhere it is invariably *Depuis*.
16. Wilfred Thesiger in conversation with the author, 28 November 1992
17. Reginald Dingwall in conversation with the author, 12 May 1993.
18. Wilfred Thesiger in conversation with the author, 28 November 1992.
19. A.D. Theobald, *Ali Dinar: Last Sultan of Darfur*, London, 1965, p.204.
20. Reginald Dingwall in conversation with the author, 12 May 1993.
21. ibid.
22. Timothy Green, *The Restless Spirit*, London, 1970, p.74.
23. Wilfred Thesiger in conversation with the author, 28 November 1992.
24. ibid.
25. John Baggot Glubb, *War in the Desert*, London, 1960, p.135.
26. Reginald Dingwall in conversation with the author, 12 May 1993.
27. Wilfred Thesiger, *The Life of My Choice*, p.208.
28. Reginald Dingwall in conversation with the author, 12 May 1993.
29. ibid.
30. ibid.
31. ibid.
32. Wilfred Thesiger, *The Life of My Choice*, p.198.
33. Wilfred Thesiger in conversation with the author, 28 November 1992.
34. Wilfred Thesiger in conversation with the author, 7 December 1992.
35. Wilfred Thesiger, *Desert, Marsh and Mountain*, London, 1979, dedication.
36. Timothy Green, *The Restless Spirit*, p.72.
37. ibid.
38. Wilfred Thesiger in conversation with the author, 29 November 1992.
39. ibid.
40. ibid.
41. Mrs Ewen Campbell in a letter to the author, 1987, undated.
42. Wilfred Thesiger in conversation with the author, 19 February 1993.
43. Reginald Dingwall in a letter to the author, 23 December 1993.
44. Wilfred Thesiger in conversation with the author, 7 December 1992.
45. Wilfred Thesiger in conversation with the author, 18 February 1993.
46. Reginald Dingwall in conversation with the author, 12 May 1993.
47. ibid.
48. Wilfred Thesiger, *The Life of My Choice*, p.253.

49. Wilfred Thesiger in conversation with the author, 19 February 1993.
50. Wilfred Thesiger in conversation with the author, 7 December 1992.
51. Wilfred Thesiger in conversation with the author, 19 February 1993.
52. Reginald Dingwall in conversation with the author, 12 May 1993.
53. Wilfred Thesiger in conversation with the author, 28 November 1992.
54. Reginald Dingwall in conversation with the author, 12 May 1993.
55. Wilfred Thesiger in conversation with the author, 19 February 1993.
56. Wilfred Thesiger in conversation with the author, 28 December 1992.
57. ibid.
58. ibid.
59. Frank McLynn, *Burton: Snow upon the Desert*, London, 1990, p.99.
60. ibid.
61. Wilfred Thesiger, *The Life of My Choice*, p.209.
62. Wilfred Thesiger in conversation with the author, 29 November 1992. Though evidently Thesiger had been a firm supporter of the Empire long before taking up his post in the Sudan: he had been a member of the pro-Empire Raleigh Club at Oxford (see Chapter 3).
63. Carl Jung (ed.), *Man and His Symbols*, London, 1964, p.37.
64. Wilfred Thesiger in conversation with the author, 27 November 1992.
65. Reginald Dingwall in conversation with the author, 12 May 1993.
66. Wilfred Thesiger, *The Life of My Choice*, p.214.
67. Wilfred Thesiger in conversation with the author, 27 November 1992.
68. Hugh Boustead, *The Winds of Morning*, London, 1971, p.237.
69. Reginald Dingwall in conversation with the author, 12 May 1993.
70. Wilfred Thesiger in conversation with the author, 18 February 1993.
71. Wilfred Thesiger in conversation with the author, 29 November 1992.
72. Alexander Maitland, 'Traveller from an Antique Land', *Blackwood's Magazine*, October 1980, p.252.
73. For Villas Boas and the Yanomami, see Robin Hanbury-Tenison, *Worlds Apart: An Explorer's Life*, London, 1991, pp.133ff.
74. Wilfred Thesiger in conversation with the author, 7 December 1993.
75. Wilfred Thesiger in conversation with the author, 7 December 1993.

Chapter 6: Lion's Bane

1. Wilfred Thesiger in conversation with the author, 7 December 1992.
2. Wilfred Thesiger in conversation with the author, 27 November 1992.
3. ibid.
4. Wilfred Thesiger, *The Life of My Choice*, London, 1987, p.293.
5. Wilfred Thesiger, 'Galloping Lion', *SNR*, 1939, p.157.
6. Wilfred Thesiger in conversation with the author, 6 December 1992.
7. Reginald Dingwall in conversation with the author, 12 May 1993.

8. Wilfred Thesiger in an unrecorded conversation with the author.

9. Wilfred Thesiger in conversation with the author, 27 November 1992.

10. Wilfred Thesiger, *The Life of My Choice*, p.134.

11. ibid., p.270.

12. Wilfred Thesiger in conversation with the author, 30 November 1992.

13. Frank McLynn in an unrecorded conversation with the author.

14. Wilfred Thesiger in conversation with the author, 27 November 1992.

15. ibid.

16. Wilfred Thesiger in conversation with the author, 6 December 1992.

17. Wilfred Thesiger in conversation with the author, 27 November 1992.

18. Wilfred Thesiger in conversation with the author, 18 February 1993.

19. ibid.

20. ibid.

21. ibid. Though Thesiger once returned to London wearing a lice-ridden Moroccan *galaba* (see Timothy Green, *The Restless Spirit*, London, 1970).

22. Wilfred Thesiger in conversation with the author, 5 December 1992.

23. Wilfred Thesiger in conversation with the author, 18 February 1993.

24. ibid.

25. Thesiger's conviction in this seems to be traceable to a single remark made by Salim bin Kabina in Mukalla; see *Arabian Sands*, 1959, p.201. Conversations with Bedu who travelled with Thesiger, especially Musallim bin Tafl, throw some doubt on this.

26. Wilfred Thesiger in conversation with the author, 29 November 1992.

27. ibid.

28. Wilfred Thesiger, *The Life of My Choice*, p.214.

29. ibid., p.219.

30. Wilfred Thesiger in conversation with the author, 18 February 1993.

31. Wilfred Thesiger in conversation with the author, 28 December 1992.

32. Wilfred Thesiger in conversation with the author, 18 February 1993.

33. ibid.

34. Timothy Green, *The Restless Spirit*, p.75.

35. Wilfred Thesiger in conversation with the author, 29 November 1992.

36. Wilfred Thesiger in conversation with the author, 18 February 1993.

37. Wilfred Thesiger in conversation with the author, 7 December 1992.

38. Wilfred Thesiger in conversation with the author, 5 December 1992.

39. ibid.

40. ibid.

41. Wilfred Thesiger, 'The Mind of the Moor', *The Times*, 21 December 1937, p.15.

42. ibid., p.16.

43. ibid.

44. Wilfred Thesiger in conversation with the author, 18 February 1993.
45. E.E. Evans-Pritchard, quoted in Robin A. Hodgkin, *A Sudan Geography*, London, 1951, p.123.
46. Wilfred Thesiger in conversation with the author, 29 November 1992.
47. ibid.
48. ibid.
49. ibid.
50. ibid.
51. ibid.
52. Wilfred Thesiger in conversation with the author, 19 February 1993.
53. Wilfred Thesiger in conversation with the author, 29 November 1992.
54. Wilfred Thesiger in conversation with the author, 29 November 1992/ 18 February 1993.
55. Wilfred Thesiger in conversation with the author, 29 November 1992.
56. ibid. Actually, Bagnold and his motor teams had come within several hundred miles of Tibesti in the early 1930s.
57. Wilfred Thesiger in conversation with the author, 29 November 1992.
58. ibid.
59. Wilfred Thesiger, 'A Camel-Journey to Tibesti', *JRGS*, December 1939, p.436.
60. Wilfred Thesiger, *The Life of My Choice*, p.288.
61. Wilfred Thesiger, 'A Camel-Journey to Tibesti', p.446.
62. Wilfred Thesiger in conversation with the author, 29 November 1992.
63. ibid.
64. ibid.
65. Wilfred Thesiger in conversation with the author, 18 February 1993.
66. ibid.
67. Wilfred Thesiger, *The Life of My Choice*, p.259.
68. Wilfred Thesiger in conversation with the author, 29 November 1992.
69. ibid.
70. The traditional view was that these men were 'cave dwellers': it has been shown that this idea came from a mistranslation of the word *trogodyte* (= aborigine) for *troglodyte* (= cave-dweller).
71. Lloyd Cabot-Briggs, *Tribes of the Sahara*, London, 1964, p.170.
72. Wilfred Thesiger in conversation with the author, 29 November 1992.
73. ibid.
74. Wilfred Thesiger, 'A Camel-Journey to Tibesti', p.444.
75. Wilfred Thesiger, *The Life of My Choice*, p.318.
76. ibid.
77. Wilfred Thesiger, *Arabian Sands*, London, 1959, p.182.
78. Wilfred Thesiger, 'A Camel-Journey to Tibesti', p.444.
79. Wilfred Thesiger, *Arabian Sands*, p.182.

80. Roger Clark, 'The Noble Savage', *Independent*, 5 June 1993.

Chapter 7: The One Great Emotional Cause of My Life

1. Anthony Mockler, *Haile Selassie's War*, London, 1984, p.198.
2. Wilfred Thesiger in conversation with the author, 29 November 1992.
3. ibid.
4. ibid.
5. ibid.
6. Timothy Green, *The Restless Spirit*, London, 1970, p.77.
7. ibid.
8. ibid.
9. Leonard Mosley, *Haile Selassie*, London, 1964, p.250.
10. ibid.
11. Wilfred Thesiger in conversation with the author, 29 November 1992.
12. ibid.
13. Anthony Mockler, *Haile Selassie's War*, p.217.
14. Wilfred Thesiger in conversation with the author, 29 November 1992.
15. Wilfred Thesiger, *The Life of My Choice*, London, 1987, p.312.
16. Anthony Mockler, *Haile Selassie's War*, p.217.
17. ibid.
18. ibid., p.219
19. ibid., p.227.
20. ibid., p.229
21. ibid., p.231.
22. Wilfred Thesiger, *The Life of My Choice*, p.317.
23. ibid.
24. Wilfred Thesiger in conversation with the author, 29 November 1992.
25. This was the Special Operations Executive's (SOE) first airborne operation: the landing and take-off were considered so difficult that the pilot, Pilot-Officer Collis of 47 Squadron RAF, was awarded the DFC.
26. Anthony Mockler, *Haile Selassie's War*, p.292.
27. ibid.
28. Timothy Green, *The Restless Spirit*, p.77.
29. Leonard Mosley, *Haile Selassie*, p.264.
30. ibid.
31. Hugh Boustead, *The Winds of Morning*, London, 1971, pp.248-9.
32. Anthony Mockler, *Haile Selassie's War*, p.339.
33. Hugh Boustead, *The Winds of Morning*, pp.248-9.
34. Wilfred Thesiger, *The Life of My Choice*, p.332.
35. Hugh Boustead, *The Winds of Morning*, p.167.
36. ibid.
37. Wilfred Thesiger in conversation with the author, 29 November 1992.

38. ibid.
39. ibid. The DSO (Distinguished Service Order) is the highest British award for gallantry after the VC (Victoria Cross). The MC (Military Cross) ranks one degree lower than the DSO.
40. Wilfred Thesiger in conversation with the author, 29 November 1992.
41. Wilfred Thesiger, *The Life of My Choice*, p.353.
42. Wilfred Thesiger in conversation with the author, 29 November 1992.
43. Wilfred Thesiger in conversation with the author, 19 February 1993.

Chapter 8: A Most Peculiar Major

1. Wilfred Thesiger in conversation with the author, 28 December 1992.
2. Gerald de Gaury in a letter to the *Daily Telegraph*, 1955, quoted in *Traces of Travel Brought Home from Abroad*, London, 1983.
3. Wilfred Thesiger in conversation with the author, 19 February 1993.
4. ibid.
5. ibid.
6. ibid.
7. ibid.
8. ibid.
9. ibid.
10. Edward Henderson in conversation with the author, 12 April 1993.
11. Wilfred Thesiger in conversation with the author 19 February 1993.
12. ibid.
13. ibid.
14. Wilfred Thesiger in conversation with the author, 29 November 1992.
15. Edward Henderson in conversation with the author, 12 April 1993.
16. ibid.
17. ibid.
18. Wilfred Thesiger in conversation with the author, 19 February 1993.
19. Wilfred Thesiger, 'Empty Quarter of Arabia', *Listener*, 4 December 1947.
20. Edward Henderson in conversation with the author, 12 April 1993.
21. Wilfred Thesiger in conversation with the author, 29 November 1992.
22. ibid.
23. ibid.
24. Wilfred Thesiger in conversation with the author, 19 February 1993.
25. Wilfred Thesiger in conversation with the author, 29 November 1992.
26. ibid.
27. ibid.
28. Johnny Cooper in a letter to the author, 16 June 1993.
29. Wilfred Thesiger in conversation with the author, 18 February 1993.

30. Johnny Cooper in a letter to the author, 16 June 1993.
31. Wilfred Thesiger in conversation with the author, 29 November 1992.
32. Wilfred Thesiger in conversation with the author, 28 November 1992.
33. ibid.
34. Anthony Kemp, *The SAS at War 1941–45*, London, 1991, p.79.
35. ibid.
36. Wilfred Thesiger in conversation with the author, 19 February 1993.
37. Johnny Cooper in a letter to the author, 16 June 1993.
38. ibid.
39. Johnny Cooper, *One of the Originals: The Story of a Founder Member of the SAS*, London, 1991, p.67.
40. Anthony Kemp, *The SAS at War 1941–45*, p.80.
41. Wilfred Thesiger in conversation with the author, 19 February 1993.
42. Johnny Cooper in a letter to the author, 16 June 1993.
43. Wilfred Thesiger in conversation with the author, 29 November 1992.
44. ibid.
45. Wilfred Thesiger in conversation with the author, 19 February 1993.
46. ibid.
47. ibid.
48. ibid.
49. Wilfred Thesiger in conversation with the author, 29 November 1992.
50. ibid.
51. ibid.
52. ibid.
53. ibid.
54. Wilfred Thesiger in conversation with the author, 5 December 1992.
55. Wilfred Thesiger in conversation with the author, 7 December 1992.
56. ibid.
57. ibid.
58. Timothy Green, *The Restless Spirit*, London, 1970, p.81.
59. Wilfred Thesiger in conversation with the author, 19 February 1993.
60. The Anti-Locust Unit was essentially a colonial body, and was not taken over by the UN Food and Agriculture Organization (FAO) until 1953. Thesiger left the unit in 1947, and thus, contrary to what has sometimes been claimed, never worked for the United Nations.

Chapter 9: The Harder the Life the Finer the Person

1. Wendell Phillips, *Unknown Oman*, London, 1964, p.208.
2. ibid.
3. ibid.
4. See Donald Powell-Cole, *Nomads of the Nomads: The Al Murrah Bedouin of the Empty Quarter*, Illinois, 1975, p.31.

5. Robert Lacey, *The Kingdom*, London, 1981, p.231.
6. Wilfred Thesiger in conversation with the author, 29 November 1992.
7. Nashran bin Sultan in conversation with the author, 13 October 1991.
8. Wilfred Thesiger in conversation with the author, 28 December 1992.
9. T.E. Lawrence (Shaw), in Bertram Thomas, *Arabia Felix: Across the Empty Quarter of Arabia*, London, 1930, Introduction, p.viii.
10. Wilfred Thesiger in conversation with the author, 29 November 1992.
11. ibid.
12. Wilfred Thesiger in conversation with the author, 29 November/ 28 December 1992.
13. ibid.
14. Wilfred Thesiger in conversation with the author, 29 November 1992.
15. ibid.
16. ibid.
17. ibid.
18. Musallim bin Tafl in conversation with the author, 28 September 1991.
19. Wilfred Thesiger in conversation with the author, 29 November 1992.
20. Musallim bin Tafl in conversation with the author, 24 September 1991.
21. Musallim bin Tafl in conversation with the author, 28 September 1991.
22. ibid.
23. ibid.
24. Wilfred Thesiger in conversation with the author, 29 November 1992.
25. Sa'id bin Muhammad in conversation with the author, 2 February 1993.
26. Musallim bin Tafl in conversation with the author, 28 September 1991.
27. Wilfred Thesiger in conversation with the author, 29 November 1992.
28. ibid.
29. Musallim bin Tafl in conversation with the author, 28 September 1991.
30. ibid.
31. ibid.
32. Wilfred Thesiger in conversation with the author, 19 February 1993.
33. ibid.
34. Musallim bin Tafl in conversation with the author, 28 September 1991.
35. Wilfred Thesiger in conversation with the author, 29 November 1992.
36. Timothy Green, *The Restless Spirit*, London, 1970, pp.107–8.
37. Musallim bin Tafl in conversation with the author, 28 September 1991.

38. Salim bin Kabina in conversation with the author, 12 October 1991.
39. Musallim bin Tafl in conversation with the author, 28 September 1991.
40. Wilfred Thesiger in conversation with the author, 29 November 1992.
41. Musallim bin Tafl in conversation with the author, 28 September 1991.
42. ibid.
43. Wilfred Thesiger in conversation with the author, 5 February 1993.
44. Wilfred Thesiger in conversation with the author, 18 February 1993.
45. Musallim bin Tafl in conversation with the author, 28 September 1991.
46. See Louise E. Sweet, 'Camel Raiding of North Arabian Bedouin: A Mechanism of Ecological Adaptation', in *American Anthropologist*, 1965.
47. Bertram Thomas, *Arabia Felix*, p.29.
48. Wilfred Thesiger, 'A New Journey in Southern Arabia', *JRGS*, April 1947.
49. Wilfred Thesiger in conversation with the author, 28/29 November 1992.
50. Musallim bin Tafl in conversation with the author, 28 September 1991.
51. Wilfred Thesiger in conversation with the author, 29 November 1992.
52. ibid.
53. Wilfred Thesiger, 'A New Journey in Southern Arabia'.
54. Wilfred Thesiger, *Desert, Marsh and Mountain*, London, 1979, p.39.
55. Jorg Janzen, *Nomads of the Sultanate of Oman: Tradition and Development in Dhofar*, London, 1980, p.72.
56. ibid., note: p.91.
57. Wilfred Thesiger in conversation with the author, 18 February 1993/ 5 December 1992.
58. Wilfred Thesiger in conversation with the author, 13 November 1992.
59. Donald Powell-Cole in conversation with the author (unrecorded), 26 February 1992.
60. Kathryn Tidrick, *Heart-Beguiling Araby*, Cambridge, 1981, p.30.
61. For 'sardine blockade' see Jorg Janzen, *Nomads of the Sultanate of Oman*.
62. Nashran bin Sultan in conversation with the author, 13 September 1991.
63. ibid.
64. ibid.
65. ibid.
66. Wilfred Thesiger in conversation with the author, 29 November 1992.
67. Salim bin Kabina in conversation with the author, 12 September 1991.
68. Wilfred Thesiger in conversation with the author, 29 November 1992.

69. See Hans Wehr, *A Dictionary of Modern Written Arabic*, Wiesbaden, 1979. *Farrash* is also used with the same meaning in the colloquial Arabic of Oman: see Clive Holes, *Colloquial Arabic of the Gulf*, London, 1984.

70. Nashran bin Sultan in conversation with the author, 13 September 1991.

71. Sa'id bin Muhammad in conversation with the author, 2 February 1993.

72. Musallim bin Tafl in conversation with the author, 28 September 1991.

73. Wilfred Thesiger in conversation with the author, 18 February 1993.

74. Nashran bin Sultan in conversation with the author, 13 September 1991.

75. ibid.

76. ibid.

77. ibid.

78. ibid.

79. ibid.

80. Wilfred Thesiger in conversation with the author, 29 November 1992.

Chapter 10: Conditions Where Only the Best Could Survive

1. George Popov in conversation with the author, March 1991.

2. George Popov in conversation with the author, March 1991.

3. Bertram Thomas, 'A Journey into Rub' Al Khali', *JRGS* 1930.

4. George Popov in conversation with the author, March 1991.

5. ibid.

6. ibid.

7. ibid.

8. Wilfred Thesiger in conversation with the author, 29 November 1992.

9. Timothy Green, *The Restless Spirit*, London, 1970, p.110.

10. Alexander Maitland, 'Traveller from an Antique Land', *Blackwood's Magazine*, 1980, p.247.

11. Wilfred Thesiger in conversation with the author, 5 December 1992.

12. T.E. Lawrence, *Seven Pillars of Wisdom*, London, 1926, p.15.

13. George Popov in conversation with the author, March 1991.

14. Wilfred Thesiger in conversation with the author, 29 November 1992.

15. ibid.

16. Bertram Thomas, 'A Journey into Rub' Al Khali', p.22.

17. Wilfred Thesiger in conversation with the author, 29 November 1992.

18. ibid.

19. 'Amair bin 'Omar in conversation with the author, 8 March 1991.

20. Sa'id bin Muhammad in conversation with the author, 2 February 1993.

21. 'Amair bin 'Omar in conversation with the author, 8 March 1991.
22. Salim bin Kabina in conversation with the author, 12 October 1991.
23. Sa'id bin Muhammad in conversation with the author, 2 February 1993.
24. ibid.
25. Wilfred Thesiger in conversation with the author, 18 February 1993.
26. ibid.
27. Sa'id bin Muhammad in conversation with the author, 2 February 1993. The *zaar* incident is not mentioned specifically in Thesiger's earliest account of this journey, published in *Geographical Journal*, in 1948, though in relation to his description of the Mahra in the same paper, he wrote: 'They [the Mahra] are reputed to be skilled in spells, and the many incantations chanted over the sick by the southern Arabs are always in the Mahra language. I once watched them exorcise an evil spirit (zar) from a demented boy, a curiously biblical scene in the moonlight' (*JRGS*, 1948, p.17). Of Sa'id's denial, Thesiger commented that such amnesia was probably one of the effects of the possession itself.
28. Bertram Thomas, 'A Journey into Rub' Al Khali'.
29. Musallim bin Tafl in conversation with the author, 28 September 1991.
30. Salim bin Kabina in conversation with the author, 12 October 1991.
31. Wilfred Thesiger in conversation with the author, 28 September 1992.
32. ibid.
33. ibid.
34. Salim bin Kabina in conversation with the author, 12 October 1991.
35. Wilfred Thesiger in conversation with the author, 28 September 1992.
36. ibid.
37. Sa'id bin Muhammad in conversation with the author, 2 February 1993.
38. Nashran bin Sultan in conversation with the author, 13 September 1991.
39. Musallim bin Tafl in conversation with the author, 28 September 1991.
40. Salim bin Kabina in conversation with the author, 12 October 1991.
41. Musallim bin Tafl in conversation with the author, 28 September 1991.
42. Salim bin Kabina in conversation with the author, 12 October 1991.
43. Wilfred Thesiger in conversation with the author, 18 February 1993.
44. See Chapter 9.
45. See above.
46. Wilfred Thesiger in conversation with the author, 18 February 1993.
47. ibid.
48. Muhammad bin Salih in conversation with the author, 5 March 1991.

49. Sa'id bin Muhammad in conversation with the author, 2 February 1993.
50. Salim bin Kabina in conversation with the author, 12 October 1993.
51. Raymond O'Shea, in his book *Sand Kings of Oman* (1947), claimed to have visited Liwa in 1944–5 and discovered near by the 'Lost City of 'Ad'. '. . . He must produce more facts to substantiate the account of this journey before it can be accepted,' Thesiger wrote. Apparently no more substantial facts were ever forthcoming. See *JRGS*, January 1949, 'A Further Journey across the Empty Quarter'.
52. Ralph Bagnold, *Libyan Sands*, London, 1935, p.33
53. Wilfred Thesiger in conversation with the author, 21 February 1993.
54. Musallim bin Tafl in conversation with the author, 28 September 1991.
55. Wilfred Thesiger in conversation with the author, 18 February 1993.
56. ibid.
57. ibid.
58. Wilfred Thesiger in conversation with the author, 21 February 1993.
59. Wilfred Thesiger, 'Across the Empty Quarter', *JRGS*, 1948.
60. Wilfred Thesiger in conversation with the author, 30 November 1992.
61. Musallim bin Tafl in conversation with the author, 28 September 1991.
62. Wilfred Thesiger in conversation with the author, 5 December 1992.
63. Salim bin Kabina in conversation with the author, 12 October 1991.
64. Musallim bin Tafl in conversation with the author, 28 September 1991.
65. Wilfred Thesiger in conversation with the author, 30 November 1992.
66. Salim bin Kabina in conversation with the author, 12 October 1991.
67. Musallim bin Tafl in conversation with the author, 28 September 1991.
68. Salim bin Kabina in conversation with the author, 12 October 1991.
69. ibid.
70. ibid.
71. Musallim bin Tafl in conversation with the author, 28 September 1991.
72. Wilfred Thesiger in conversation with the author, 7 December 1992.
73. Salim bin Kabina in conversation with the author, 12 October 1991.
74. Musallim bin Tafl in conversation with the author, 28 September 1991.
75. Salim bin Kabina in conversation with the author, 12 October 1991.
76. Musallim bin Tafl in conversation with the author, 28 September 1991.
77. ibid.
78. ibid.

79. Saʿid bin Muhammad in conversation with the author, 2 February 1993.
80. Salim bin Kabina in conversation with the author, 12 October 1991.
81. Wilfred Thesiger in conversation with the author, 6 December 1992.
82. Salim bin Ghabaisha in conversation with the author, 6 March 1991.
83. Musallim bin Tafl in conversation with the author, 28 September 1991.
84. Wilfred Thesiger in conversation with the author, undated.
85. Musallim bin Tafl in conversation with the author, 28 September 1991.
86. Wilfred Thesiger, *Arabian Sands*, London, 1959, p.189.
87. ibid.
88. ibid.
89. Wilfred Thesiger, 'Across the Empty Quarter', p.18.

Chapter 11: Drawn Along a Road of My Own Choosing by the Lure of the Unknown

1. Wilfred Thesiger in conversation with the author, 29 November 1992.
2. Salim bin Kabina in conversation with the author, 13 October 1991.
3. ibid.
4. Salim bin Ghabaisha in conversation with the author, 7 March 1991.
5. Salim bin Kabina in conversation with the author, 13 October 1991.
6. Wilfred Thesiger in conversation with the author, 7 December 1992.
7. ʿAmair bin ʿOmar in conversation with the author, 8 March 1991.
8. Salim bin Ghabaisha in conversation with the author, 7 March 1991.
9. Salim bin Kabina in conversation with the author, 13 October 1991.
10. Wilfred Thesiger in conversation with the author, 30 November 1992.
11. Salim bin Kabina in conversation with the author, 13 October 1991.
12. ʿAmair bin ʿOmar in conversation with the author, 8 March 1991.
13. Wilfred Thesiger in conversation with the author, 21 February 1993.
14. Salim bin Kabina in conversation with the author, 13 October 1991.
15. Wilfred Thesiger in conversation with the author, 21 February 1993.
16. ʿAmair bin ʿOmar in conversation with the author, 8 March 1991.
17. Salim bin Kabina in conversation with the author, 13 October 1991.
18. ibid.
19. Salim bin Ghabaisha in conversation with the author, 6 March 1991.
20. Salim bin Kabina in conversation with the author, 13 October 1991.
21. Wilfred Thesiger, 'A Further Journey across the Empty Quarter', *JRGS*, 1949.
22. Salim bin Ghabaisha in conversation with the author, 6 March 1991.
23. Wilfred Thesiger in conversation with the author, 19 February 1993.

24. Salim bin Kabina in conversation with the author, 13 October 1991.
25. Wilfred Thesiger in conversation with the author, 30 November 1992.
26. Salim bin Kabina in conversation with the author, 13 October 1991.
27. ibid.
28. Wilfred Thesiger in conversation with the author, 30 November 1992.
29. Salim bin Kabina in conversation with the author, 13 October 1991.
30. 'Amair bin 'Omar in conversation with the author, 8 March 1991.
31. Salim bin Kabina in conversation with the author, 13 October 1991.
32. ibid.
33. 'Amair bin 'Omar in conversation with the author, 8 March 1991.
34. Salim bin Kabina in conversation with the author, 13 October 1991.
35. 'Amair bin 'Omar in conversation with the author, 8 March, 1991.
36. Wilfred Thesiger in conversation with the author, 30 November 1992.
37. Salim bin Kabina in conversation with the author, 13 October 1991.
38. 'Amair bin 'Omar in conversation with the author, 8 March 1991.
39. ibid.
40. Wilfred Thesiger in conversation with the author, 30 November 1992.
41. ibid.
42. 'Amair bin 'Omar in conversation with the author, 8 March 1991.
43. Wilfred Thesiger in conversation with the author, 30 November 1992.
44. Salim bin Kabina in conversation with the author, 13 October 1991.
45. Wilfred Thesiger in conversation with the author, 30 November 1992.
46. 'Amair bin 'Omar in conversation with the author, 8 March 1991.
47. Wilfred Thesiger in conversation with the author, 30 November 1992.
48. Salim bin Kabina in conversation with the author, 13 October 1991.
49. 'Amair bin 'Omar in conversation with the author, 8 March 1991.
50. Salim bin Ghabaisha in conversation with the author, 7 March 1991.
51. Wilfred Thesiger in conversation with the author, 6 December 1992.
52. Wilfred Thesiger in conversation with the author, 30 November 1992.
53. Wilfred Thesiger in conversation with the author, 30 November 1992.
54. Wilfred Thesiger in conversation with the author, 29 November 1992.
55. Wilfred Thesiger, 'A Further Journey across the Empty Quarter'.
56. Wilfred Thesiger in conversation with the author, 30 November 1992.
57. Ronald Codrai in conversation with the author, 19 May 1993.
58. For Glubb's role and Philby's quote see Kathryn Tidrick, *Heart-Beguiling Araby*, Cambridge, 1981, pp.195ff.
59. Wilfred Thesiger in conversation with the author, 5 December 1992.
60. Wilfred Thesiger in conversation with the author, 30 November 1992.
61. Wilfred Thesiger, 'A Further Journey across the Empty Quarter'.
62. Salim bin Ghabaisha in conversation with the author, 7 March 1991.

Chapter 12: Chapter Closed

1. Edward Henderson in conversation with the author, 12 April 1993.
2. Ronald Codrai in conversation with the author, 19 May 1993.
3. ibid.
4. ibid.
5. Wilfred Thesiger in conversation with the author, 7 December 1993.
6. Ronald Codrai in conversation with the author, 19 May 1993.
7. Wilfred Thesiger in conversation with the author, 7 December 1993.
8. ibid.
9. Wilfred Thesiger, 'The Quicksands of Arabia', *Listener*, 15 December 1949.
10. Wilfred Thesiger in conversation with the author, 30 November 1992.
11. Wilfred Thesiger, 'The Quicksands of Arabia'.
12. Wilfred Thesiger in conversation with the author, 30 November 1992.
13. Wilfred Thesiger in conversation with the author, 7 December 1992.
14. ibid.
15. ibid.
16. ibid.
17. ibid.
18. Edward Henderson in conversation with the author, 12 April 1993.
19. ibid.
20. Ronald Codrai in conversation with the author, 19 May 1993.
21. Wilfred Thesiger in conversation with the author, 7 December 1992.
22. ibid.
23. Wilfred Thesiger in conversation with the author, 7 December 1992/ 19 February 1993.
24. Alexander Maitland, 'Traveller from an Antique Land', *Blackwood's Magazine*, October 1980, p.24.
25. Jonathan Raban, *Arabia: Through the Looking Glass*, London, 1979, p.16.
26. Wilfred Thesiger, 'The Badu of Southern Arabia', *JRCAS*, 1950.
27. Timothy Green, *The Restless Spirit*, London, 1970, p.75.
28. Wilfred Thesiger in conversation with the author, 18 February 1993.
29. Jorg Janzen, *Nomads of the Sultanate of Oman*, London, 1980, p.165.
30. Tony Jeapes, *SAS: Operation Oman*, London, 1980, p.55.
31. Wilfred Thesiger in conversation with the author, 28 November 1992.
32. Richard W. Bulliet, *The Camel and the Wheel*, Cambridge, Mass., 1975, p.49. For the domestication of the camel in south Arabia, see pp.48–9.
33. Salim bin Ghabaisha in conversation with the author, 6 March 1991.
34. Donald Powell-Cole, *Nomads of the Nomads*, Illinois, 1975, p.35.
35. ibid., p.24.
36. Wilfred Thesiger in conversation with the author, 5 December 1992.
37. Wilfred Thesiger in conversation with the author, 2 November 1992.

38. ibid.
39. Wilfred Thesiger, *Arabian Sands*, new Preface to Penguin edition, 1984.
40. Jonathan Raban quoted in Suzanne Lowry, 'Have Pen Will Travel', *International Herald-Tribune*, 1987 (undated).
41. Wilfred Thesiger in conversation with the author, 28 November 1992.
42. Wilfred Thesiger in conversation with the author, 5 December 1992.
43. ibid.
44. ibid.
45. Ronald Codrai in conversation with the author, 19 May 1993.
46. Edward Henderson in a letter to the author, 2 September 1991.
47. ibid.
48. Johnny Cooper in a letter to the author, 16 June 1993.
49. Salim bin Kabina in conversation with the author, 23 October 1991.
50. 'Amair bin 'Omar in conversation with the author, 8 March 1991.
51. Musallim bin Tafl in conversation with the author, 28 September 1991.
52. Ronald Codrai in conversation with the author, 19 May 1993.
53. Nashran bin Sultan in conversation with the author, 13 September 1991.
54. Sa'id bin Muhammad in conversation with the author, 2 February 1993.
55. Salim bin Ghabaisha in conversation with the author, 6 March 1991.

Chapter 13: A Bit of Duck-shooting

1. Wilfred Thesiger in conversation with the author, 30 November 1992.
2. Gavin Maxwell, *A Reed Shaken by the Wind*, London, 1957, p.2.
3. Wilfred Thesiger in conversation with the author, 28 November 1992.
4. Wilfred Thesiger in conversation with the author, 7 December 1992.
5. ibid.
6. ibid.
7. ibid.
8. Wilfred Thesiger in conversation with the author, 30 November 1992.
9. ibid.
10. Gavin Young, *Return to the Marshes*, London, 1977, pp.98–9.
11. Wilfred Thesiger in conversation with the author, 30 November 1992.
12. Gavin Maxwell, *A Reed Shaken by the Wind*, p.15.
13. ibid.
14. Wilfred Thesiger in conversation with the author, 30 November 1992.
15. ibid.
16. ibid.
17. ibid.

18. ibid.
19. Gavin Maxwell, *A Reed Shaken by the Wind*, p.80.
20. ibid., p.39.
21. Frank Steele in conversation with the author, 7 January 1993.
22. Jan Morris, review of *The Marsh Arabs, JRGS*, undated.
23. Wilfred Thesiger in conversation with the author, 18 February 1993.
24. Peter Clark, *Thesiger's Return*, Dubai, 1992, p.29.
25. Wilfred Thesiger in conversation with the author, 18 February 1993.
26. Wilfred Thesiger, *Arabian Sands*, London, 1959, p.189.
27. Frank Steele in conversation with the author, 19 May 1993.
28. Wilfred Thesiger in conversation with the author, 30 November 1992.
29. ibid.
30. ibid.
31. Gavin Maxwell, *A Reed Shaken by the Wind*, p.78.
32. Timothy Green, *The Restless Spirit*, London, 1970, p.99.
33. Frank Steele in conversation with the author, 7 January 1993.
34. ibid.
35. Wilfred Thesiger in conversation with the author, 5 December 1992.
36. Gavin Young, *Return to the Marshes*, p.21.
37. Wilfred Thesiger in conversation with the author, 30 November 1992.
38. ibid.
39. ibid.
40. Gavin Maxwell, *A Reed Shaken by the Wind*, p.38.
41. ibid., p.41.
42. Wilfred Thesiger in conversation with the author, 30 November 1992.
43. Gavin Maxwell, *A Reed Shaken by the Wind*, p.53.
44. ibid.
45. Wilfred Thesiger in conversation with the author, 30 November 1992.
46. Gavin Maxwell, *A Reed Shaken by the Wind*, p.218.
47. ibid., p.219.
48. Wilfred Thesiger in conversation with the author, 30 November 1992.
49. Gavin Maxwell, *A Reed Shaken by the Wind*, p.179.
50. Wilfred Thesiger in conversation with the author, 30 November 1992.
51. Gavin Maxwell, *A Reed Shaken by the Wind*, p.131.
52. Douglas Botting, *Gavin Maxwell: A Life*, London, 1993, p.476.
53. Wilfred Thesiger in conversation with the author, 30 November 1992.
54. ibid.
55. Wilfred Thesiger in conversation with the author, 7 December 1993.
56. ibid.
57. Wilfred Thesiger, *Visions of a Nomad*, London, 1987, p.10.
58. ibid.
59. ibid.
60. Ronald Codrai in conversation with the author, 19 May 1993.

61. Wilfred Thesiger in conversation with the author, 30 November 1992.
62. Wilfred Thesiger, *The Marsh Arabs*, London, 1964, p.219.
63. Wilfred Thesiger, 'The Marshmen of Southern Iraq', *JRGS*, September 1954.
64. Wilfred Thesiger in conversation with the author, 30 November 1992.
65. Gavin Maxwell, *A Reed Shaken by the Wind*, p.218.
66. Jim Crumley, 'When Oafs Kick Ass in Eden', *Independent*, 21 January 1993.

Chapter 14: An Old Tweed Jacket of the Sort Worn by Eton Boys

1. Wilfred Thesiger in conversation with the author, 7 December 1992.
2. Wilfred Thesiger in conversation with the author, 5 December 1992.
3. Timothy Green, *The Restless Spirit*, London, 1970, p.101.
4. Hugh Carless in conversation with the author, 25 May 1993.
5. John Keay, *The Gilgit Game*, London, 1979, p.22.
6. Wilfred Thesiger in conversation with the author, 18 February 1993.
7. Wilfred Thesiger in conversation with the author, 28 December 1992.
8. Wilfred Thesiger, 'The Hazaras of Central Afghanistan', *JRGS*, 1955.
9. ibid.
10. ibid.
11. ibid.
12. Bryan Clarke, *Berber Village*, London, 1959, p.58.
13. ibid., p.63.
14. Wilfred Thesiger in conversation with the author, 5 December 1993.
15. Wilfred Thesiger in conversation with the author, 18 February 1993.
16. Ernest Gellner in a letter to the author, 9 January 1993.
17. Wilfred Thesiger in conversation with the author, 7 December 1992.
18. Ernest Gellner in a letter to the author, 9 January 1993.
19. ibid.
20. Wilfred Thesiger in conversation with the author, 18 February 1993.
21. Ernest Gellner in a letter to the author, 9 January 1993.
22. ibid.
23. Bryan Clarke, *Berber Village*, p.118.
24. Wilfred Thesiger in conversation with the author, 5 December 1993.
25. Hugh Carless in conversation with the author, 25 May 1993.
26. Eric Newby, *A Short Walk in the Hindu Kush*, London, 1958, p.247.
27. ibid., pp.247 ff.
28. Wilfred Thesiger in conversation with the author, 5 December 1993.
29. Hugh Carless in conversation with the author, 25 May 1993.
30. Eric Newby, *A Traveller's Life*, London, 1982.
31. Hugh Carless in conversation with the author, 25 May 1993
32. Wilfred Thesiger, 'A Journey in Nuristan', *JRGS*, 1957, p.463.

33. Wilfred Thesiger in conversation with the author, 5 December 1993.
34. Timothy Green, *The Restless Spirit*, p.93.
35. Wilfred Thesiger in conversation with the author, 30 November 1992.
36. ibid.
37. ibid.
38. ibid.
39. Mark Cocker, *Loneliness and Time*, London, 1992, p.68.
40. Wilfred Thesiger, *Arabian Sands*, London, 1959, p.11.
41. ibid, p.329.
42. Kathryn Tidrick, *Heart-Beguiling Araby*, Cambridge, 1981.
43. Donald Powell-Cole, *Nomads of the Nomads*, Illinois, 1975, p.139.
44. Frank Steele in conversation with the author, 7 January 1993.
45. Wilfred Thesiger, *Arabian Sands*, p.329.
46. Wilfred Thesiger, 'The Badu of Southern Arabia', *JRCAS*, 1950.
47. Jonathan Raban, *Arabia: Through The Looking Glass*, London, 1979, p.16.
48. Wendell Phillips, *Unknown Oman*, London, 1964, p.222.
49. Wilfred Thesiger in unrecorded conversation with the author.
50. Wendell Phillips, *Unknown Oman*, p.103.

Chapter 15: A Fairly Hardy and Abstemious Traveller

1. Wilfred Thesiger in conversation with the author, 29 November 1992.
2. Wilfred Thesiger in conversation with the author, 5 December 1992.
3. Wilfred Thesiger in conversation with the author, 7 December 1992.
4. Wilfred Thesiger in conversation with the author, 5 December 1992.
5. Frank Steele in conversation with the author, 7 January 1993.
6. ibid.
7. ibid.
8. ibid.
9. ibid.
10. ibid.
11. ibid.
12. ibid.
13. ibid.
14. Wilfred Thesiger in conversation with the author, 7 December 1992.
15. Frank Steele in conversation with the author, 7 January 1993.
16. ibid.
17. Wilfred Thesiger in conversation with the author, 5 December 1992.
18. ibid.
19. ibid.
20. ibid.
21. Wilfred Thesiger in conversation with the author, 30 November 1992.

22. Jan Morris, review of *The Marsh Arabs*, *JRGS*, undated.
23. ibid.
24. Wilfred Thesiger in conversation with the author, 29 November 1992.
25. Wilfred Thesiger in conversation with the author, 5 December 1992.
26. Wilfred Thesiger in conversation with the author, 30 November 1992.
27. Wilfred Thesiger in conversation with the author, 19 February 1993.
28. Wilfred Thesiger in conversation with the author, 7 December 1992.
29. ibid.
30. ibid.
31. ibid.
32. Wilfred Thesiger in conversation with the author, 18 February 1993.
33. ibid.
34. ibid.
35. ibid.
36. ibid.
37. ibid.
38. ibid.
39. ibid.
40. ibid.
41. Johnny Cooper, *One of the Originals*, 1991, p.41.
42. Wilfred Thesiger in conversation with the author, 19 February 1993.
43. Timothy Green, *The Restless Spirit*, London, 1970, p.108.
44. Wilfred Thesiger in conversation with the author, 19 February 1993.
45. ibid.
46. ibid.
47. Johnny Cooper in an undated letter to the author.
48. Wilfred Thesiger, *Desert, Marsh and Mountain*, London, 1979, p.271.
49. Wilfred Thesiger in conversation with the author, 5 December 1992.
50. Johnny Cooper in an undated letter to the author.
51. Wilfred Thesiger in conversation with the author, 5 December 1992.
52. Wilfred Thesiger in conversation with the author, 19 February 1993.
53. ibid.
54. ibid.
55. ibid.
56. ibid.
57. ibid.

Chapter 16: A Mixed-up World

1. Timothy Green, *The Restless Spirit*, London, 1970, p.108.
2. Wilfred Thesiger in conversation with the author, 28 December 1992.
3. Frank Steele in conversation with the author, 19 May 1993.
4. Wilfred Thesiger in conversation with the author, 28 December 1992.

5. Wilfred Thesiger in conversation with the author, 19 February 1993.

6. Wilfred Thesiger in conversation with the author, 28 December 1992.

7. Wilfred Thesiger in conversation with the author, 5 December 1992.

8. Wilfred Thesiger in conversation with the author, 6 December 1992.

9. ibid.

10. Mike Griffin, 'A Life in the Day of Wilfred Thesiger', *Sunday Times*, 1985.

11. Wilfred Thesiger in conversation with the author, 6 December 1992.

12. ibid.

13. ibid.

14. ibid.

15. ibid.

16. ibid.

17. ibid.

18. ibid.

19. Mary Anne Fitzgerald, *Nomad: One Woman's Journey into the Heart of Africa*, London, 1992, p.317.

20. Wilfred Thesiger in conversation with the author, 6 December 1992.

21. Mary Anne Fitzgerald, *Nomad*, pp.317–18.

22. Wilfred Thesiger in conversation with the author, 16 December 1992.

23. ibid.

24. ibid.

25. Gavin Young, *In Search of Conrad*, London, 1993, p.144.

26. ibid., p.153.

27. ibid., p.160.

28. Wilfred Thesiger in conversation with the author, 29 November 1992.

29. Wilfred Thesiger in conversation with the author, 5 December 1992.

30. Timothy Green, *The Restless Spirit*, p.89.

31. Wilfred Thesiger in conversation with the author, 5 December 1992.

32. Wilfred Thesiger in conversation with the author, 29 November 1992.

33. Wilfred Thesiger in conversation with the author, 5 December 1992.

34. Wilfred Thesiger in conversation with the author, 5 December 1992.

35. Wilfred Thesiger in conversation with the author, 6 December 1992.

36. Alexander Maitland, 'An Explorer's Insight', *Geographical Magazine*, August 1990. A close observation of the actual film, however, reveals that this is not precisely what occurred. Actually, it was Thesiger who suggested to Lawi that he was a 'good instructor' and invited him to agree. See Channel Four Films, *The Last Explorer*, presenter Julian Pettifer, 1989.

37. Wilfred Thesiger in conversation with the author, 7 December 1992.

38. ibid.

39. ibid.

40. Roger Clark, 'The Noble Savage', *Independent on Sunday Magazine*, 5 June 1993.
41. Wilfred Thesiger in conversation with the author, 7 December 1992.
42. ibid.
43. Roger Clark, 'The Noble Savage'.
44. Wilfred Thesiger in conversation with the author, 18 February 1993.
45. Wilfred Thesiger in conversation with the author, 19 February 1993.
46. Wilfred Thesiger in conversation with the author, 28 November 1992.
47. Frank Steele in conversation with the author, 19 May 1993.
48. Mike Griffin, 'A Life in the Day of Wilfred Thesiger'.
49. ibid.
50. Wilfred Thesiger in conversation with the author, 7 December 1992.
51. ibid.
52. ibid.
53. ibid.
54. Wilfred Thesiger in conversation with the author, 28 November 1992.
55. Wilfred Thesiger in conversation with the author, 30 November 1992.
56. Wilfred Thesiger in conversation with the author, 28 November 1992.
57. ibid.
58. Wilfred Thesiger in conversation with the author, 19 February 1993.
59. Wilfred Thesiger in unrecorded conversation with the author.
60. Wilfred Thesiger in conversation with the author, 19 February 1993.
61. Wilfred Thesiger in conversation with the author, 28 November 1992.
62. Alexander Maitland, 'Traveller from an Antique Land', *Blackwood's Magazine*, October 1980.
63. Geoffrey Moorhouse, *The Fearful Void*, London, 1974, p.31.
64. Mike Griffin, 'A Life in the Day of Wilfred Thesiger'.
65. Wilfred Thesiger in conversation with the author, 5 December 1992.
66. Wilfred Thesiger in conversation with the author, 6/7 December 1992.
67. Wilfred Thesiger in conversation with the author, 6 December 1992.
68. ibid.
69. Wilfred Thesiger in conversation with the author, 29 November 1992.
70. Wilfred Thesiger in conversation with the author, 28 November 1992.
71. Wilfred Thesiger in conversation with the author, 19 February 1993.
72. Wilfred Thesiger in conversation with the author, 29 November 1992.
73. Wilfred Thesiger in conversation with the author, 19 February 1993.
74. Wilfred Thesiger in conversation with the author, 28 November 1992.
75. Wilfred Thesiger in conversation with the author, 19 February 1993.
76. Peter Clark, *Thesiger's Return*, Dubai, 1992, p.28.
77. Wilfred Thesiger in conversation with the author, 28 November 1992.
78. ibid.
79. Frank Steele in conversation with the author, 19 May 1993.
80. ibid.

Chapter 17: The Last Explorer

1. Wilfred Thesiger in conversation with the author, 7 December 1992.
2. Wilfred Thesiger in conversation with the author, 28 November/7 December 1992.
3. Wilfred Thesiger in conversation with the author, 28 November 1992.
4. ibid.
5. Wilfred Thesiger in conversation with the author, 29 November 1992.
6. Sir David Attenborough in a letter to the author.
7. Dr John Hemming in a letter to the author.
8. Tim Severin in a letter to the author, 1 October 1991.
9. Christina Dodwell in a letter to the author, 18 September 1990.
10. Wally Herbert in a letter to the author, 6 October 1993.
11. Frank Steele in conversation with the author, 19 May 1993.
12. Babbit quoted in Will Durrant, *The Story of Philosophy*, p.354.
13. Frank Steele in conversation with the author, 7 January 1993.
14. Wilfred Thesiger in unrecorded conversation with the author.
15. ibid.

BIBLIOGRAPHY

ABBREVIATIONS

JRGS: The Geographical Journal (*Journal of the Royal Geographical Society*)
SNR: Sudan Notes and Records
JRCAS: The Journal of the Royal Central Asian Society
NB: Where more than one work by an author is given, titles are arranged chronologically in order of publication.

Newspaper and Magazine Articles

Clark, Roger, 'The Noble Savage', *Independent on Sunday Magazine*, 5 June 1993.

Courtauld, Simon, 'The Last Great Explorer', *Sunday Telegraph Magazine*, 1993.

Crumley, Jim, 'When Oafs Kick Ass in Eden', *Independent*, 23 January 1993.

Griffin, Mike, 'A Life in the Day of Wilfred Thesiger', *Sunday Times Magazine*, 1985 (undated).

Lowry, Suzanne, 'Have Pen Will Travel', *International Herald-Tribune*, 1987 (undated).

Maitland, Alexander, 'Traveller from an Antique Land', *Blackwood's Magazine*, October 1980.

Maitland, Alexander, 'An Explorer's Insight', *Geographical Magazine*, August 1990.

Mbugua, Ngugi, 'The Last British Explorer', *Daily Nation* (Nairobi), 1991.

North, Andrew, 'Saddam's Water War', *Geographical Magazine*, July 1993.

Thesiger, Wilfred, 'An Abyssinian Quest: I Finding a Lost River', *The Times*, 31 July 1934.

Thesiger, Wilfred, 'An Abyssinian Quest: II The Customs of the Dankali', *The Times*, 1 August 1934.

Thesiger, Wilfred, 'An Abyssinian Quest: III Fauna near Aussa', *The Times*, 2 August 1934.

Thesiger, Wilfred, 'An Abyssinian Quest: IV Salt as Currency', *The Times*, 3 August 1934.

Thesiger, Wilfred, 'The Mind of the Moor', *The Times*, 21 December 1937.

Thesiger, Wilfred, 'Sands of the Empty Quarter', *Geographical Magazine*.
Thesiger, Wilfred, 'Travel on the Trucial Coast', *Geographical Magazine*.
Thesiger, Wilfred, 'Empty Quarter of Arabia', *Listener*, 4 December 1947.
Thesiger, Wilfred, 'Hawking in Arabia', *Listener*, 10 November 1949.

Articles Contributed to Learned Societies

Abercrombie, Thomas J., 'Oman: Guardian of the Gulf', *National Geographic Magazine*, September 1981.
Allen, W.E.D., 'Ethiopian Highlands', *JRGS*, January 1943.
Azzi, Robert, 'Oman, Land of Frankincense and Oil', *National Geographic Magazine*, February 1973.
Cheeseman, R.E., 'The Deserts of Jafura and Jabrin', *JRGS*, 1925.
Cox, Percy, 'Some Excursions in Oman', *JRGS*, September 1925.
Glubb, J.B., 'The Bedouins of Northern Iraq', *JRCAS*, 1935.
Glubb, J.B., 'Arab Chivalry', *JRCAS*, 1937.
Ingrams, W.H., 'Hadhramaut: A Journey through Sei'ar Country and through the Wadi Maseila', *JRGS*, 1936.
Sweet, Louise E., 'Camel Raiding of North Arabian Bedouin: A Mechanism of Ecological Adaptation', *American Anthropologist*, 1965.
Thesiger, Wilfred, 'The Awash River and the Aussa Sultanate', *JRGS*, January 1935.
Thesiger, Wilfred, 'Galloping Lion', *SNR*, 1939.
Thesiger, Wilfred, 'A Camel-Journey to Tibesti', *JRGS*, December 1939.
Thesiger, Wilfred, 'A New Journey in Southern Arabia', *JRGS*, April 1947.
Thesiger, Wilfred, 'A Journey through the Tihama, the Assir and the Hejaz Mountains', *JRGS*, October–December 1947.
Thesiger, Wilfred, 'Across the Empty Quarter', *JRGS*, July 1948.
Thesiger, Wilfred, 'A Further Journey across the Empty Quarter', *JRGS*, January 1949.
Thesiger, Wilfred, 'The Badu of Southern Arabia', *JRCAS*, 1950.
Thesiger, Wilfred, 'Desert Borderlands of Oman', *JRGS*, December 1950.
Thesiger, Wilfred, 'The Madan or Marsh Dwellers of Southern Iraq', *JRCAS*, 1954.
Thesiger, Wilfred, 'The Marshmen of Southern Iraq', *JRGS*, September 1954.
Thesiger, Wilfred, 'The Hazaras of Central Afghanistan', *JRGS*, September 1955.
Thesiger, Wilfred, 'A Journey in Nuristan', *JRGS*, December 1957.
Thesiger, Wilfred, 'The Marsh Dwellers of Southern Iraq', *National Geographic Magazine*, February 1959.
Thomas, Bertram, 'The South Eastern Borderlands of Rub' Al Khali', *JRGS*, March 1929.

Thomas, Bertram, 'A Camel Journey across the Rub' Al Khali', *JRGS*, September 1931.

Waloff, N. and Popov, G., 'Sir Boris Uvarov (1889–1970) The Father of Acridology', *Annual Review of Entomology*, 1990.

Books

Bagnold, Ralph, *Libyan Sands – Travel in a Dead World*, London, 1935.

Bence-Jones, Mark, *The Viceroys of India*, London, 1982.

Botting, Douglas, *Gavin Maxwell: A Life*, London, 1993.

Boustead, Hugh, *The Winds of Morning*, London, 1971.

Boyle, Anthony, *The Climate of Treason*, London, 1979.

Brent, Peter, *Far Arabia: Explorers of the Myth*, London, 1977.

Buchan, John, *Prester John*, London, 1910.

Bulliet, Richard W., *The Camel and the Wheel*, Cambridge, Mass., 1975.

Clapham, Christopher, *Haile Selassie's Government*, London, 1969.

Clarke, Bryan, *Berber Village*, London, 1959.

Cocker, Mark, *Loneliness and Time: British Travel Writing in the Twentieth Century*, London, 1992.

Codrai, Ronald, *The Seven Sheikhdoms: Life in the Trucial States before the Federation of the UAE*, London, 1990.

Collomb, Robin G., *Atlas Mountains: Morocco*, Reading, 1980.

Cooper, Johnny, *One of the Originals: The Story of a Founder Member of the SAS*, London 1991.

Cotton, P.H.G. Powell, *A Sporting Trip through Abyssinia*, London, 1902.

Daly, M.W., *Imperial Sudan: 1934–56: The Anglo-Egyptian Condominium*, London, 1991.

De Gaury, Gerald, *Traces of Travel Brought Home from Abroad*, 1983

De Monfreid, Henri (trans. Helen Buchanan-Bell), *Secrets of the Red Sea*, London, 1934.

Dickson, H.R.P., *The Arab of the Desert*, London, 1949.

Farwell, Byron, *Burton*, London, 1963.

Fitzgerald, Mary Anne, *Nomad: One Woman's Journey into the Heart of Africa*, London, 1992.

Foot, M.R.D., *SOE: An Outline History of the Special Operations Executive 1940–46*, London, 1960.

Fulanein, *The Marsh Arab Haji Rikkan*, Philadelphia, 1928.

Geraghty, Tony, *Who Dares Wins: The Story of the SAS 1950–1980*.

Glubb, John Bagot, *War in the Desert*, London, 1960.

Green, Timothy, *The Restless Spirit*, London, 1970.

Halliday, Fred, *Arabia Without Sultans*, London, 1974.

Hanbury-Tenison, Robin, *Worlds Apart: An Explorer's Life*, London, 1991.

Henderson, Edward, *That Strange Eventful History: Memoirs of Earlier Days in the United Arab Emirates and Oman*, London, 1988.

Hitti, Philip K., *History of the Arabs*, London, 1937.

Hodgkin, Robin, *A Sudan Geography*, London, 1951.

Hoe, Alan, *David Stirling*, London, 1992.

Holes, Clive, *Colloquial Arabic of the Gulf*, London, 1984.

Holt, P.M. and Daly, M.W., *The History of the Sudan from the Coming of Islam to the Present Day*, London, 1961.

Hook, Hilary, *Home from the Hill*, London, 1987.

Hyam, Ronald, *Empire and Sexuality*, London, 1980.

Janzen, Jorg, *Nomads of the Sultanate of Oman: Tradition and Development in Dhofar*, London, 1980.

Jeapes, Tony, *SAS: Operation Oman*, London, 1980.

Jung, C.G. (ed.), *Man and His Symbols*, London, 1964.

Kay, Shirley, *The Bedouin*, London, 1978.

Keay, John, *The Gilgit Game*, London, 1979

Kemp, Anthony, *The SAS at War: The Special Air Service Regiment 1941–1945*, London, 1991

Kenrick, Rosemary, *Sudan Tales*, London, 1987.

Lacey, Robert. *The Kingdom*, London, 1981.

Lancaster, William, *The Rwala Bedouin Today*, London, 1981.

Lines, Maureen, *Beyond the North West Frontier*, Oxford, 1988.

Lunt, James, *Glubb Pasha: A Biography*, London, 1984.

McKinnon, Michael, *Arabia: Sand, Sea, Sky*, London, 1990.

McLynn, Frank, *Burton: Snow Upon the Desert*, London, 1990.

Marratis, John, *Ethiopia: Anatomy of a Traditional Polity*, Oxford, 1974.

Mason, Philip, *The English Gentleman: The Rise and Fall of an Ideal*, London, 1984.

Maxwell, Gavin, *A Reed Shaken by the Wind*, London, 1957.

Maxwell, Gavin, *Lords of the Atlas*, London, 1966.

Mockler, Anthony, *Haile Selassie's War*, Oxford, 1984.

Moorhouse, Geoffrey, *The Fearful Void*, London, 1974.

Morris, James, *Sultan in Oman*, London, 1957.

Morris, James, *Pax Britannica: The Climax of an Empire*, London, 1968.

Morris, James, *Farewell The Trumpets: An Imperial Retreat*, London, 1978.

Mosley, Leonard, *Gideon Goes to War*, London, 1955.

Mosley, Leonard, *Haile Selassie*, London, 1964.

Nesbitt, L.M., *Desert and Forest*, London, 1934.

Newby, Eric, *A Short Walk in the Hindu Kush*, London, 1958.

Newby, Eric, *A Traveller's Life*, London, 1982.

Paxman, Jeremy, *Friends in High Places: Who Runs Britain?*, London, 1991.

Philby, St John, *The Empty Quarter*, London, 1932.

Phillips, Wendell, *Unknown Oman*, London, 1964.

Powell-Cole, Donald, *Al Murrah: Bedouin of Arabia's Empty Sands*, from *Nomads of the World*, Washington, 1971.

Powell-Cole, Donald, *Nomads of the Nomads: The Al Murrah Bedouin of the Empty Quarter*, Illinois, 1975.

Pridham, B.R., 'Oman: Change or Continuity?' in Ian R. Netton (ed.), *Arabia and the Gulf: From Traditional Society to Modern States*, London, 1986.

Raban, Jonathan, *Arabia: Through the Looking Glass*, London, 1979.

Sa'id, Edward W., *Orientalism*, London, 1978.

Spencer, Paul, *Samburu: A Study of Gerontocracy in a Nomadic Tribe*, London, 1965.

Sykes, Christopher, *Orde Wingate*, London, 1959.

Theobald, A.D., *Ali Dinar: Last Sultan of Darfur*, London, 1965.

Thesiger, Wilfred, *Arabian Sands*, London, 1959.

Thesiger, Wilfred, *The Marsh Arabs*, London, 1964.

Thesiger, Wilfred, *Desert, Marsh and Mountain*, London, 1979.

Thesiger, Wilfred, *Visions of a Nomad*, London, 1987.

Thesiger, Wilfred, *The Life of My Choice*, London, 1987.

Thesiger, Wilfred, *The Thesiger Collection*, ed. Ian Fairservice, Dubai, 1991.

Thomas, Bertram, *Arabia Felix: Across the Empty Quarter of Arabia*, London, 1930.

Tidrick, Kathryn, *Heart-Beguiling Araby*, Cambridge, 1981.

Verney, John, *A Dinner of Herbs*, London, 1966.

Waugh, Evelyn, *Remote People*, London, 1931.

Waugh, Evelyn, *Waugh in Abyssinia*, London, 1936.

Wehr, Hans, *A Dictionary of Modern Written Arabic*, Wiesbaden, 1979.

Young, Gavin, *Return to the Marshes*, London, 1977.

Young, Gavin, *In Search of Conrad*, London, 1993.

Zweig, Paul, *The Adventurer*, London, 1974.

INDEX

Arabic proper names are indexed alphabetically according to the commonly used element in the names, and where this is prefixed with el, al, or bin these words remain as prefixes but are ignored for purposes of alphabeticization, e.g. El Alamein is indexed under A, Al Murrah tribe is indexed under M, Salim bin Kabina is indexed under K.

Other than in the entry under his name, Wilfred Thesiger is referred to as T.